PENGUIN  CLASSICS

THE PORTABLE TWENTIETH-CENTURY RUSSIAN READER

CLARENCE BROWN was born in Anderson, South Carolina, in 1929. He attended Duke, Michigan, and Harvard universities, and first learned Russian in the Army during the Korean War. A long-time member of the faculty at Princeton University, he is the author of many books of criticism and translation, including Yevgeny Zamyatin's novel *We*, available in Penguin Classics.

The Portable
Twentieth-Century
Russian Reader

Edited with an Introduction and Notes by
CLARENCE BROWN

REVISED AND UPDATED EDITION

PENGUIN BOOKS

PENGUIN BOOKS
Published by the Penguin Group
Penguin Group (USA) Inc., 375 Hudson Street, New York, New York 10014, U.S.A.
Penguin Group (Canada), 90 Eglinton Avenue East, Suite 700, Toronto, Ontario,
Canada M4P 2Y3 (a division of Pearson Penguin Canada Inc.)
Penguin Books Ltd, 80 Strand, London WC2R 0RL, England
Penguin Ireland, 25 St Stephen's Green, Dublin 2, Ireland
(a division of Penguin Books Ltd)
Penguin Group (Australia), 250 Camberwell Road, Camberwell, Victoria 3124,
Australia (a division of Pearson Australia Group Pty Ltd)
Penguin Books India Pvt Ltd, 11 Community Centre, Panchsheel Park,
New Delhi – 110 017, India
Penguin Group (NZ), 67 Apollo Drive, Rosedale, North Shore 0632, New Zealand
(a division of Pearson New Zealand Ltd)
Penguin Books (South Africa) (Pty) Ltd, 24 Sturdee Avenue,
Rosebank, Johannesburg 2196, South Africa

Penguin Books Ltd, Registered Offices: 80 Strand, London WC2R 0RL, England

First published in the United States of America by in simultaneous
hardcover and paperback editions by Viking Penguin Inc. 1985
Published in Penguin Books with a selection from
The Master and Margarita by Mikhail Bulgakov 1993

10

Copyright © Viking Penguin Inc., 1985
All rights reserved

Clarence Brown's review of Andrei Sinyavsky's "A Voice from the Chorus"
appeared originally, in slightly different form, in *The New Republic*.
Copyright © Clarence Brown, 1976

Grateful acknowledgement is made for permission to reprint the following copyrighted work:
Chapter one from *The Master and Margarita* by Mikhail Bulgakov, translated by
Michael Glenny. Copyright © 1967 by The Harvill Press, London, and Harper & Row,
Publishers, Inc., New York. Reprinted by permission of HarperCollins Publishers Inc.
(New York) and HarperCollins Publishers Ltd. (London).

Pages 613–615 constitute an extension of this copyright page.

LIBRARY OF CONGRESS CATALOGING IN PUBLICATION DATA:
Main entry under title: The Portable twentieth-century Russian reader.
1. Russian literature—20th century—Translations into English.   2. English literature—Translations
from Russian.   I. Brown, Clarence, 1929–   II. Title: The Portable 20th-century Russian reader.
[PG3213.P67   1985b]   891.7'008'004   84–19113
ISBN 978-0-14-243757-5

Printed in the United States of America
Set in Janson

ACKNOWLEDGMENTS

In the ocean of gratitude owed by the world of Russian scholarship to my friend the late Carl R. Proffer, my acknowledgment for his kind assistance in the compilation of this book is a small drop. My colleague Herman Ermolaev made numerous suggestions that improved my translation of *Envy*, for which I thank him. Robert Fagles exceeded his duties as my department chairman by his kindly criticism and encouragement. Ms. Carol Szymanski provided essential assistance. For their generous response to inquiries I am grateful also to Carol Avins, Grigory Freidin, and John Glad. Jacqueline Brown's patience with this project has deepened my affection for her. None of the above is to blame for whatever shortcomings remain.

CONTENTS

INTRODUCTION

Where there is personal liking we go.
—Marianne Moore

I

Personal liking guided the choice of literature in this anthology, but there were other criteria as well. Works eligible for inclusion here had to be written originally in Russian and in this century and to be of a literary quality that survived, insofar as possible, translation into English. The first two requirements are purely mechanical; the third makes all the difference. One is occasionally tempted to give greater weight to "importance" than to literary excellence—to choose, that is, works that are in some sense "required" rather than satisfying. I have striven to restrain this pedagogical impulse. Any student of contemporary Russian writing will acknowledge that Ilya Ehrenburg's novel *The Thaw*, which lent its name to a brief episode of heady freedom, is "important." So is Daniil Granin's story "One's Own Opinions." Neither, however, is readable, or perhaps I should say re-readable; their social and political "importance" is the only sort of importance they have. The reader unversed in present-day life in the Soviet Union would require detailed explanation of why Granin's dreary didactic fable, in which some utterly featureless bureaucrat arrives at an uncomfortable self-awareness, is "important"; whatever significance it has is strictly local, temporary, and nonliterary. Over every form of transient meaningfulness I have favored writing that I trust will prove to have literary permanence. If the paper lasts, this book ought to please your grandchildren.

The term *Soviet literature*, which is often misunderstood and deserves a brief comment, is absent from the title and rarely found in this book. Outside the USSR "Soviet literature" is roughly understood to mean Russian literature written in Russia after 1917. It is not so understood on its home territory, where the term applies to the prodigious output of belles lettres in the more than 120 distinct languages of the Soviet Union. What is more, any aspirant to inclusion in the ranks of Soviet literature has also to pass an unstated but clearly understood ideological test. Osip Mandelstam's passport contained the word *Jew* in the blank after "Nationality," but he was a citizen of the Soviet Union who wrote, in Russia and in Russian, the greater part of his works after 1917. He was perennially in trouble with the literary police and perished along with millions of other victims of Stalin's terror in some Siberian camp in 1938. His recent move from almost total oblivion to literary ascendancy was accomplished entirely in the West. He is therefore not a Soviet writer. Andrei Sinyavsky's passport carried the word *Russian* as the indication of his nationality, and up to the mid-1960s he was, to all outward appearances, a member of the Soviet literary Establishment. He was also writing, in Russia and in Russian, works of great literary merit, but this he did secretly, as the infamous "Abram Tertz," and when he was exposed in 1966 he was sent to a labor camp—where he wrote three more extraordinary books!—and then was forcibly exiled and stripped of his citizenship. Whatever the distinction of his former services to Soviet literature, he is emphatically no longer a Soviet writer.

The term *Soviet*, therefore, is an award conferred, withheld, or revoked by those who have appointed themselves to be its custodians. I am content that this should be so, for it vastly simplifies the task of the anthologist of Russian literature in this century. I have not to worry whether Akhmatova or Pasternak or Solzhenitsyn or Voinovich are or are not Soviet writers: They are all, inalienably and forever, members of the grand enterprise known as Russian literature for the most unarguable of reasons—they have molded their common birthright, the Russian language, into works of permanent value.

While we are speaking of terms, it might be worth noting that the term *émigré literature* is becoming more and more dispensable with every passing year; it now denotes practically the same thing as Russian literature, since the Soviet authorities increasingly resort to forced foreign exile as the solution of their problems with dissident writers. Even though such a central masterpiece as Gogol's *Dead Souls* was largely written in Rome, it was formerly an exception for great Russian writing to spring from foreign soil. Today, however, now that the vast diaspora of Russian excellence has reached what is called the "Third Wave," it is almost the rule that anything worth reading in Russian will have been written in Paris or London, Tel Aviv or Hollywood, Vermont or New York (especially Brooklyn).

Is nothing of value now being written in Russia? The example of Bulgakov's *The Master and Margarita* should serve as a caution against too assured an answer. It was written in the Soviet Union in the 1930s, but since no one knew that fact (it lay hidden in a drawer for decades) it forms no part of the literature of that time. This is a great pity, as Konstantin Paustovsky observed in 1967: "How could it have happened that books whose artistic merit was negligible and which at most revealed the sharpness and cunning of their authors were presented as masterpieces of our literature, whereas excellent works ... lay hidden and only saw the light of day a quarter of a century after they were written ... ? The damage done is irreparable. Had for instance the works of Andrei Platonov and Mikhail Bulgakov appeared when they were written, our contemporaries would have been immeasurably richer in spirit."*

Who knows what novels like Pasternak's *Dr. Zhivago*

* Quoted by Joseph Barnes in his translation of Andrei Platonov, *The Fierce and Beautiful World* (New York: E. P. Dutton, 1970), p. 19.

or memoirs like Nadezhda Mandelstam's *Hope against Hope* are quietly ripening in some place of concealment in the motherland? I do not. It is therefore better to content oneself with saying that among what is *visible* there are no works of genius to compare with the stories of Varlam Shalamov or the novels of Sasha Sokolov. There are no literary journals that contain anything like the aesthetic and intellectual excitement to be found in *Kontinent* and *Sintaksis* and the plethora of others published in France, Germany, England, Israel, Canada, and the United States.

II

Personal liking depends in some measure, of course, upon understanding, and it is probably impossible thoroughly to understand any work in this book without some grasp of the unique role that literature has historically played in Russia, both that of the czars and that of the Politburo. It is, in a word, political.

A Russian writer, living in Russia, is in many ways unfree, but in one particular he has literally no choice at all. Let us conceive a scale of 0 to 10, with 10 denoting literature that is officially sanctioned and blatantly propagandistic, and 0 denoting the complete absence of these qualities—not antagonism to the radiant future of Communism, simply silence. There is no point on this scale, including 0, that is not political. One's *oeuvre* may consist of stories encouraging abstinence from alcohol, promptness of arrival at the workplace, the reporting of economic crime, and general hopefulness about the future; or it may consist of difficult, private poems about being tired of living and scared of dying, written as though the world had never heard of powers and principalities. The second, by conspicuously ignoring the demands made by the Party and the State upon literature, is thoroughly political. If anything, it is even more political than the first, for it involves deliberate choice, deliberate flouting of the social command, whereas the first is largely automatic and requires no more than the "sharpness and cunning" of which Paustovsky spoke.

One of the results of this state of affairs is that when Western scholars come to write of modern Russian literature they employ a unique, politically saturated diction, which, if it were employed in writing of French or Spanish or German literature, would look very strange indeed. The normal person, confronted with the following brief lexicon, would never dream that the subject under discussion was imaginative writing:

admonish	death	glossed over	Realism (So-
attack	decisions	guide	cialist)
backward	(key)	harshness	recalcitrant
(socially)	declaration	imprisonment	recantation
censored	denunciation	intimidation	revisionism
clandestine	didacticism	liberalization	screws (polit-
coddling	(wooden)	meeting	ical)
coercion	discipline	(closed)	standoff (ner-
conformity	embattled	pillory	vous)
controls	excluded	problems	upsurge
correct	exile	proclamation	valve (safety)
crackdown	formulas	prohibition	

While most people can imagine how tiresome it is to participate in a public literary life marked by the general stressfulness implied by this vocabulary, only a few have experienced one other, exhilarating result of the attention accorded to belles lettres. In Russia, literature *matters*. It matters to everyone, from the pinnacle of power down. Imagine its being discussed in the White House whether a book by, say, Norman Mailer might or might not be published. And yet literature is routinely on the agenda of the Politburo. It was Nikita Khrushchev who personally determined that a new era in Soviet letters was to be inaugurated by the publication of Solzhenitsyn's *One Day in the Life of Ivan Denisovich*.

Interesting as this is, it is perhaps more important that literature matters—and in what way it matters—to writers themselves. Every visitor to the Soviet Union who has enough Russian and enough entrée into private society has been intrigued to hear writers converse on a level of seriousness, even urgency, almost unknown to literary gatherings in the West. When Daniel Halpern, the poet and editor of *Antaeus*, was interviewing Cyril Connolly, the late English man of letters, he asked him what writers talked about when they got together. Connolly truthfully replied that they talked about "the misfortunes of other writers and their own income-tax troubles."*

No doubt Russian writers might enjoy the liberty of wasting their time in this way. Nadezhda Mandelstam told me that she yearned for a world in which one might discuss the relative merits of butchers and the marriage plans of one's niece, and no one would commit the solecism of bringing up poetry as a topic (her idea of a "nice" bourgeois world). But in fact her kitchen was a true salon, where writers regularly forgathered to read their works in progress and to discuss literature from every point of view, from certain technical aspects of prosody to the ethical component in "village prose." Some of these writers had resounding names (and are practically all now in the West), and some would never be published. But they were all engaged in a common enterprise of the utmost seriousness. They by no means approved of one another without reserve, but there existed between them something like a covenant—call it the Russian Word—into which they had entered by the irretrievably ethical and moral (and political) act of shaping language into replicas of human thought and feeling.

But, useful though it might be, the knowledge of how a Russian might respond to these works in their original form need not constrain your own response to them in English. How should you respond? By searching purely and simply for what Nabokov has called "aesthetic bliss"—enjoyment enriched by comprehension and love. *Faithful Ruslan* (see p. 525), Vladimov's harrowing

---

* *Antaeus*, No. 4 (Winter, 1971), p. 122.

novel about a ferocious guard dog at a concentration camp, poses for Russians profound philosophical and ethical questions, which have been lengthily debated in the émigré press (it cannot be published in the USSR). But the Western reader will find it thoroughly satisfying on the narrative level alone, for it is one of the greatest animal stories in the world, superior even to Tolstoy's *Strider*.

III

Any anthology of more or less contemporary writing shares the helplessness of any dictionary that aspires to freeze the contemporary vocabulary of a language at some ideal synchronic moment: Both are out of date before the manuscript even goes to the printer. Words continue to be born regardless of the lexicographer's deadline, and material for Supplement One begins to accumulate before the parent volume goes on sale. The anthologist, to be sure, cannot pretend to the dictionary maker's catholic ambition, to say nothing of his scientific objectivity. The anthologist assembles his volume in a sort of despairing loneliness, aware that his altogether unscientific predilections took shape long before those of most of his readers. He is necessarily surer of his earlier selections, with which he has lived longer, but is increasingly anxious about works of later date and is assailed with misgivings concerning all that he has not read and considered of the most recent writings. Though one might point to the span of years separating Tolstoy's prose (1905) from that of Sasha Sokolov (1977) as a respectable enough portion of this century (which has, after all, a few years to run), even the most well-disposed critic might feel obligated to observe that the book as a whole lists noticeably toward the early and middle years of its period. The centerpiece, Olesha's 1927 novel *Envy*, accounts for over a quarter of the whole and thus contributes heavily to this effect, but what really accounts for it is all that is implied by the epigraph to this introduction. There being no excuse, it would seem pointless to offer one.

Drudgery though it certainly was at times to compare translations, to plead for permissions, and prospectively to dread the outrage occasioned by the omission of X for the sake of Y (of all people!), I now look back on this banquet of words with much pleasure, which I hope nothing will prevent your sharing. These writers, after all, continue in our time the tradition that has made Russian, along with English and classical Greek, one of the three supreme literatures of the world.

Note to the Revised Edition

In 1984, when I completed the manuscript that became this book, the world had scarcely heard the name Gorbachev. The cataclysmic years that ensued utterly changed the material and spiritual conditions in which the writing gathered here came into being. So far as I am aware, everything that was banned as unpublishable in the Soviet Union when I wrote the above introduction and headnotes to each selection has now been copiously published in Russia, some of it in several editions. Where possible, I have altered the notes to reflect the new circumstances, corrected other minor imperfections, and added a new selection from the work of Mikhail Bulgakov.

January 1993   —C.B.
                                        Princeton, N.J.

THE PORTABLE
TWENTIETH-CENTURY
RUSSIAN READER

Leo Tolstoy

(1828–1910)

No anthology of Russian writing in this century can safely
ignore the presence in its first decade of the world's greatest
novelist. By the time Leo Tolstoy died in the stationmaster's
room at Astapovo in 1910 at the age of eighty-two, he was far
more than the author of *War and Peace* and *Anna Karenina*:
He was a world figure whose moral authority was felt in
every corner of the globe and could only be compared with
that of the Pope. The International Tolstoy Society had been
founded in 1900. The object of this universal attention (if not
always adulation) was, however, no more at peace with himself than he had ever been. His increasing revulsion against
his literary manner, his own sinful nature, and the heroine
herself of his crowning literary achievement made the completion of *Anna Karenina* all but impossible. At least he
could have Anna smoke cigarettes and practice contraception,
two of the numerous sins against which he was to thunder
denunciations in pamphlets and articles. An ethical mentor
for millions throughout the world, he was within the Russian
Empire a kind of third force beside the Czar and the Church.
Some of his teachings seem all but demented. He advocated
total abstinence from sexual intercourse even within marriage
and, reminding himself that this must lead to the extinction
of mankind, said that moral actions must be taken with no
view to their consequences. (His thirteenth child was born in
1888, when Tolstoy was sixty.) In the last scrap of writing
from Tolstoy's hand as he lay dying we read: *Fais ce que*

dois, adv ... This favorite proverb would have continued: ...
advienne que pourra, that is, Do what you must, happen
what may.

Fortunately, Tolstoy had other imperatives than lecturing
the czar on the evils of autocracy; encouraging vegetarianism,
resistance to military conscription, and religious and racial
tolerance; and promoting a kind of unchurched piety. He had
to write fiction, and even such fiction as "Alyosha the Pot"
(1905), which conforms to his new demand for unadorned
simplicity though it all but ignores another requirement—
that art must transmit a clearly discernible moral lesson.
Alyosha's pathetic fate moves our hearts to pity, but most
readers will wonder what exactly we are to do or refrain from
doing as a consequence of reading about it. Nor could Tolstoy deny himself the psychological portraiture that he had
renounced, though it occurs here with a thoroughly modern
indirection. When Alyosha first awakens to the notion of dis-
interested sympathy, of plain human fondness, the thought is
so astonishing that Tolstoy's syntax collapses into a kind of
hash: this is an image of Alyosha's almost languageless men-
tality groping happily toward a new idea. (Most translators
thwart Tolstoy by rendering this story in a style suitable for
the drawing rooms of *War and Peace;* I have tried to be as
low, simple, and even ungrammatical as the original.)

Tolstoy thrust this story from him with his usual repug-
nance for his own work, and thought it a failure. A better
guide to its worth is the great Symbolist poet Alexander Blok
(see p. 74), who, on reading it when it was first published in
1911, jotted down in his diary for 13 November: "One of the
greatest works of genius I've read—Tolstoy's 'Alyosha the
Pot.'"

ALYOSHA THE POT

Alyosha was the younger brother. He was called "Pot" because one time his mother sent him to take a pot of milk to the deacon's wife and he tripped and broke the pot. His mother gave him a beating and the boys began to tease him with the name "Pot." Alyosha the Pot—that was his nickname from then on.

Alyosha was a skinny, lop-eared boy (his ears stuck out like wings) with a big nose. The boys used to tease him: "Alyosha has a nose like a dog on a hill!" There was a school in the village, but writing didn't come easy for Alyosha and, besides, there wasn't that much time for study. The older brother worked for a merchant in town, so Alyosha had to help his father from the time he could walk. Six years old and he was already watching after the sheep and the cow in the pasture with his baby sister, and a little older he was looking after the horses day and night. By the time he was twelve he was plowing and driving the wagon. He wasn't strong but he knew how to do things. He was always in a good mood. The boys would laugh at him and either he would keep quiet or he would laugh, too. When his father yelled at him he kept quiet and listened. And the minute the yelling stopped he smiled and went on with whatever it was he had to do.

Alyosha was nineteen when his brother got drafted. So his father fixed it for Alyosha to get his brother's old job as hired man with the merchant. They gave Alyosha his brother's old boots and his father's cap and jacket and took him to town. Alyosha was tickled pink with his new clothes, but the merchant didn't like the way Alyosha looked.

"I thought I was going to get a man to take Simon's place," said the merchant, looking Alyosha up and down, "and what's this snot-nose supposed to be? What good is he to me?"

"He can do anything—he can hitch up a team and go get stuff and he works like crazy. He just looks puny but you can't wear him out."

"Well, looks like I'll have to find out."

"And the main thing is, he'll never give you any back talk. He'd rather work than eat."

"Oh, what the hell. Leave him here."

So Alyosha began to live at the merchant's.

The merchant didn't have a big family. There was his wife, his old mother, and his oldest son, married, who didn't finish school, was in the business with his father; and the other boy had a good education, finished school and went to college before they threw him out, and he lived at home; and then there was a daughter, a high-school girl.

At first they didn't like Alyosha. He was just too much of a peasant. His clothes were terrible and he didn't know how to behave and didn't even know what Russian to use for people above his level. But before long they got used to him. He was an even better worker than his brother. It was the truth that he never talked back, because they sent him to do everything, and he did everything right that minute, very willingly, never even rested between one job and the next. And at the merchant's it was just like at home—they piled everything on Alyosha. The more he did the more they all piled things on him. The merchant's wife, and his mother, and his daughter, and his son, and the steward, and the cook, all sent him here, there, and yonder; do this and do that. All you could hear was, "Run, get this," or "Alyosha, take care of this," or "Alyosha, don't tell me you forgot!" or "Alyosha, make sure you don't forget!" And Alyosha was forever running and taking care of things and looking after things and he never forgot and managed it all and kept on smiling.

It wasn't long before he wore out his brother's boots

and the boss let him have it for walking around with his boots falling apart and his toes sticking out, and he ordered some new boots for him in the market. The boots were new and Alyosha was thrilled to have them, but he had the same old feet, and toward evening they were killing him and he was mad at the boots. Alyosha was afraid that when his father came to collect his week's pay he'd be mad about the merchant taking the boots out of the pay.

In the wintertime Alyosha would get up before dawn, chop the firewood, sweep the yard, and feed and water the cow and the horse. Then he would light the stoves, shine the shoes, brush the boss's clothes, set the samovars going after he'd cleaned them, and then the steward would call him to move some merchandise or else the cook would set him to kneading dough and cleaning pans. Then they'd send him to town with a note for somebody, or to fetch the daughter at her school, or to get some lamp oil for the old lady. And there'd always be somebody to say "Where the hell have you been so long?!" Or, "Why should you bother? Alyosha will run get it. Alyosha! Oh, Alyosha!" And Alyosha ran to get it.

He would grab a bite to eat when he could, and it was a rare thing for him to be back in time to eat with the rest of them at night. The cook would yell at him for not being on time, but she still felt sorry for him and put aside something hot for him to have at dinner and supper. There was really a lot of work to get ready for the holidays and during the holidays. And Alyosha really loved the holidays, because during the holidays he would get tips—not a whole lot, about sixty kopecks, but still it was his own money. He could spend it however he wanted to. As for his week's pay, he never laid eyes on that. His father would come in and pick that up and all Alyosha heard from him was complaining about how fast he was wearing out boots.

When he'd saved up two rubles from his tips, he took the cook's advice and bought himself a red knitted jacket, which when he put on he couldn't keep a straight face he was so happy.

Alyosha never said much and when he did say something it always came out in short, broken pieces. And if ever they told him to do something or asked him *could* he do so and so, why, he'd say "Sure" before they were hardly finished and he'd start doing it and do it.

He didn't know a single prayer. His mother had taught him some but he'd forgotten them all, but he still prayed, mornings and evenings, prayed with his hands, and crossed himself.

That's how Alyosha lived for a year and a half, and then suddenly, in the second half of the second year, something happened to him that had never happened before in his life. This something was that he found out, to his amazement, that besides those connections between people based on someone needing something from somebody else, there are also very special connections: not a person having to clean boots or take a parcel somewhere or harness up a horse, but a person who was in no real way necessary to another person could still be needed by that person, and caressed, and that he, Alyosha, was just such a person. This he learned from the cook, Ustinya. Ustinya was an orphan, young, who worked just like Alyosha. She started feeling sorry for Alyosha and Alyosha felt for the first time that he—he himself, not his work—but he himself was needed by another person. When his mother felt sorry for him he didn't even notice because it seemed to him that was the way it was supposed to be—it was just the same as him feeling sorry for himself. But here all of a sudden he saw that this Ustinya, no kin to him at all, felt sorry for him anyway, and would leave him some buttered cereal in the pot and then prop her chin on her bare arm and watch him while he was eating it. And he would glance at her and she would start laughing and then he would start laughing.

This was so new and strange that at first Alyosha was afraid. He felt like this might stop him working the way he used to work. But he was happy anyway, and when he looked at his pants that Ustinya had mended he'd shake his head and smile. Often when he was working or on the way somewhere he'd remember Ustinya and say, "Oh, yes, Ustinya!" Ustinya helped him out whenever she could and he helped her. She told him about herself, how she'd lost both her parents, how an aunt had taken her in, how she'd got this job in town, how the boss's son had tried to talk her into doing something stupid and how she'd cut him dead. She loved to talk and he liked listening to her. He heard that in cities it often happened that peasants who'd been hired as workers got married to cooks. And one time she asked him if they were going to marry him any time soon. He said he didn't know but that he didn't feel like being married to a country girl.

"Oh? You have your eye on somebody?" said she.

"Well, I'd marry you. Would you?"

"Well, listen to Pot! Pot comes right out with the question," said Ustinya, and gave him a little poke in the back with her hand. "Why wouldn't I?"

At Shrovetide his old man came to town to pick up his wages. The merchant's wife had learned that Alyosha had taken it into his head to marry Ustinya, and she didn't like it. "She'll get pregnant and what good will she be with a kid?" she told her husband.

The boss turned over Alyosha's money to his father.

"How's my boy doing? All right?" said the peasant. "I told you he wouldn't talk back."

"Well as far as back talk goes I don't get any back talk, but he's up to some foolishness. Got the idea he's going to marry the cook. But I won't have the help marrying. That doesn't suit us."

"Why that fool ..." said his father. "Don't you give it another thought. I'll tell him to forget the whole thing."

His father went into the kitchen and sat down at the table to wait for his son. Alyosha was out running errands and came back all out of breath.

"I thought you had some sense, and now what are you thinking of?" said his father.

"Nothing ... I ..."

"What, nothing? You were thinking of getting married. I'll marry you off when the time comes, and I'll marry you to a fit woman, not one of these town sluts."

His father talked for a long time and Alyosha stood there and sighed. When his father was finished Alyosha smiled.

"Well, we can just forget it."

"That's right."

When his father had gone and left Alyosha alone with Ustinya (who had been standing behind the door and heard everything the father said to the son), he told her:

"Looks like our plan won't work. You hear? He got mad, won't let me."

She began to weep quietly into her apron.

Alyosha said, "Tch. Tch."

"Have to mind him. Looks like we have to forget about it."

That night when the boss's wife called him to close the shutters, she said, "Well, you going to obey your father and forget that nonsense?"

"Looks like I have to," said Alyosha with a laugh, and then he began to cry.

From that time on Alyosha never mentioned marriage to Ustinya again and went on living the way he had before.

One day during Lent the steward sent him to clean the snow off the roof. He climbed up on the roof, cleaned it all off, and had started clearing the frozen snow out of the gutters when his foot slipped and he fell with his shovel. Unfortunately he did not fall in the snow but onto an iron roof over a door. Ustinya and the boss's daughter ran up to him.

"Alyosha, are you hurt?"

"A little. It's all right."

He tried to stand up but he couldn't and began to smile. They carried him into the yardkeeper's lodge. The doctor's orderly came. He examined him and asked him where it hurt.

"It hurts all over, but it's all right. Just so the boss don't get mad. Better send tell Daddy about it."

Alyosha lay in bed for two days and on the third day they sent for the priest.

"You aren't going to die, are you?" Ustinya asked.

"What do you think—we live forever? Have to die sometime . . ." said Alyosha, speaking quickly as always. "Thanks, Ustinya, for being nice to me. See—it's better they wouldn't let us get married, it'd all be for nothing. Now everything's fine."

He prayed with the priest but only with his hands and his heart. In his heart was the thought that if it's good down here when you do what they tell you and don't hurt anybody, then it'll be good up there too.

He didn't talk much. He just kept asking for water and looked like he was amazed at something.

Then something seemed to startle him and he stretched his legs and died.

(1905)

Anton Chekhov

(1860–1904)

Several things distinguish Chekhov from all the other writers of classical Russian literature. He had no trace of nobility in his veins (his grandfather had been a serf and his father was a storekeeper). His unique knowledge of human physiology and psychology resulted from scientific observation and not from aesthetic or mystical theory (he was a medical doctor). He completely transformed two distinct genres of literature, the short story and the drama—and he did so on an international plane, not merely within Russia. His character was untouched by the slightest tinge of anti-Semitism or contempt for the female sex. And finally (one might go on but there must be an end) his Russian style, the finest flower of the Russian nineteenth century, was so completely devoid of sentimentality and rhetoric, so delicately nuanced and modulated, that even a critic of Prince Mirsky's normal acuteness could find it lacking in "raciness and nerve."

Mirsky held other preposterous opinions about Chekhov as well. He wrote that his characters had no individuality, that his plays were invertebrate creations of pure atmosphere, and that his flat style made him the easiest of all Russian writers to translate. All this is the opposite of the truth. Some exoneration might be found in the fact that when Mirsky was writing his great history of Russian literature in England (and in English) in the 1920s, Chekhov was the darling of the literary world around him, eclipsing even Dostoevsky.

Perhaps Mirsky felt that the adulation had gone too far and had to be checked.

Today, however, the many thousands of English-speakers who are able to approach Chekhov in his own language must read such opinions with astonishment, for there is hardly another Russian writer who offers such a variety of human types, settings, and situations; such a diapason of emotions from helpless laughter to genuine sadness; such a sane, healthy, and understanding relationship between author and characters; or a style of such exquisite balance and unpretentious beauty that even foreigners can glimpse its perfections.

Chekhov is probably best known in the West for four plays that made the fortunes of the Moscow Art Theater and revolutionized the drama—*The Seagull, Uncle Vanya, The Three Sisters,* and *The Cherry Orchard.* Russians, however, tend to think of him first as the author of short stories. He never wrote a novel, though such long works as "The Duel" or "My Life," had they been written in French, would surely not be denied that title. His stories range from the hilarious slapstick pieces with which he supported himself and his relatives while studying medicine to the unsurpassed masterpieces written at the very end of his life. Chekhov's renovations in the short story form have become so familiar from the practice of his multitudinous imitators that one does not readily perceive them in his own work. It is like the case of the student who, on reading Shakespeare for the first time, found him excessively full of quotations.

"The Bishop" was written in 1902 and is the last but one of Chekhov's stories. It is a challenge to the good reader. The autobiographical elements are immediately apparent: Chekhov knew he was dying, and it is scarcely going too far to suppose that the reflections and emotions of the dying Bishop Pyotr mirror those of his creator. But by what dispensation may this brief account of a clergyman's last days and hours be called a story? Utterly clear and simple, unmarked by any hint of the author's emotions, it appears to be little more than a report, and glides into the understanding without a hitch and without the least surprise. One leaves a first reading with the conviction of having understood everything (except, perhaps, why it is so highly esteemed). A letter that Chekhov

wrote to his editor in February 1902, when he was reading
the proof, is suggestive: He said that if the censor cut so much
as a single word, the story was not to be printed. With that
authoritative direction in mind, one who rereads "The
Bishop," weighing the smallest details, will discover a story
of unsuspected subtlety and significance.

THE BISHOP*

I

It was on the eve of Palm Sunday; vespers were being
sung in the Staro-Petrovski Convent. The hour was nearly
ten when the palm leaves were distributed, and the little
icon-lamps were growing dim; their wicks had burnt low,
and a soft haze hung in the chapel. As the worshippers
surged forward in the twilight like the waves of the sea, it
seemed to His Reverence Pyotr, who had been feeling ill
for three days, that the people who came to him for palm
leaves all looked alike, and, men or women, old or young,
all had the same expression in their eyes. He could not see
the doors through the haze; the endless procession rolled
toward him, and seemed as if it must go on rolling for
ever. A choir of women's voices was singing and a nun
was reading the canon.

How hot and close the air was, and how long the
prayers! His Reverence was tired. His dry, parching
breath was coming quickly and painfully, his shoulders
were aching, and his legs were trembling. The occasional
cries of an idiot in the gallery annoyed him. And now, as a
climax, His Reverence saw, as in a delirium, his own
mother whom he had not seen for nine years coming to-

* [This translation by Marian Fell has been slightly revised by the
editor.]

ward him in the crowd. She, or an old woman exactly like her, took a palm leaf from his hands, and moved away looking at him all the while with a glad, sweet smile, until she was lost in the crowd. And for some reason the tears began to course down his cheeks. His heart was happy and peaceful, but his eyes were fixed on a distant part of the chapel where the prayers were being read, and where no human being could be distinguished among the shadows. The tears glistened on his cheeks and beard. Then someone who was standing near him began to weep, too, and then another, and then another, until little by little the chapel was filled with a low sound of weeping. Then the convent choir began to sing, the weeping stopped, and everything went on as before.

Soon afterward the service ended. The fine, jubilant notes of the heavy chapel-bells were throbbing through the moonlit garden as the bishop stepped into his coach and drove away. The white walls, the crosses on the graves, the silvery birches, and the faraway moon hanging directly over the monastery, all seemed to be living a life of their own, incomprehensible, but very near to mankind. It was early in April, and a chilly night had succeeded a warm spring day. A light frost was falling, but the breath of spring could be felt in the soft, cool air. The road from the monastery was sandy, the horses were obliged to proceed at a walk and, bathed in the bright, tranquil moonlight, a stream of pilgrims was crawling along on either side of the coach. All were thoughtful, no one spoke. Everything around them, the trees, the sky, and even the moon, looked so young and intimate and friendly that they were reluctant to break the spell, which they hoped might last forever.

Finally the coach entered the city, and rode down the main street. All the stores were closed but that of Erakin, the millionaire merchant. He was trying his electric lights for the first time, and they were flashing so violently that a crowd had collected in front of the store. Then came wide, dark streets in endless succession, and then the highway, and fields, and the smell of pines. Suddenly a white crenellated wall loomed before him, and beyond it rose a tall belfry flanked by five flashing golden cupolas, all bathed in moonlight. This was the Pankratievski Monastery, where His Reverence Pyotr lived. Here, too, the calm, brooding moon was floating directly above. The coach drove through the gate, its wheels crunching on the sand. Here and there the dark forms of monks started out into the moonlight and footsteps rang along the flagstone paths.

"Your mother has been here while you were away, Your Reverence," a lay brother told the bishop as he entered his room.

"My mother? When did she come?"

"Before vespers. She first found out where you were, and then drove to the convent."

"Then it was she whom I saw just now in the chapel! Oh, Father in heaven!"

And His Reverence laughed for joy.

"She told me to tell you, Your Reverence," the lay brother continued, "that she would come back tomorrow. She had a little girl with her, a grandchild, I think. She is stopping at Ovsianikov's inn."

"What time is it now?"

"It is after eleven."

"What a nuisance!"

His Reverence sat down irresolutely in his sitting-room, unwilling to believe that it was already so late. His arms and legs were racked with pain, the back of his neck was aching, and he felt uncomfortable and hot. When he had rested a few moments he went into his bedroom and there, too, he sat down, and dreamed of his mother. He heard the lay brother walking away and Father Sisoi the priest coughing in the next room. The monastery clock struck the quarter.

His Reverence undressed and began his prayers. He spoke the old, familiar words with scrupulous attention, and at the same time he thought of his mother. She had nine children, and about forty grandchildren. She had lived from the age of seventeen to the age of sixty with her husband the deacon in a little village. His Reverence remembered her from the days of his earliest childhood, and, ah, how he had loved her! Oh, that dear, precious, unforgettable childhood of his! Why did those years that had vanished forever seem so much brighter and richer and gayer than they really had been? How tender and kind his mother had been when he was ill in his childhood and youth! His prayers mingled with the memories that burned ever brighter and brighter in his heart like a flame, but they did not hinder his thoughts of his mother.

When he had prayed he lay down, and as soon as he found himself in the dark there rose before his eyes the vision of his dead father, his mother, and Lyesopolye, his native village. The creaking of wagon-wheels, the bleating of sheep, the sound of church-bells on a clear summer morning, ah, how pleasant it was to think of these things! He remembered Father Semyon, the old priest at Lyesopolye, a kind, gentle, good-natured old man. He himself had been small, and the priest's son had been a huge strapping novice with a terrible bass voice. He remembered how this young priest had scolded the cook once, and had shouted: "Ah, you she-ass of Jehovah!" And Father Semyon had said nothing, and had only been mortified because he could not for the life of him remember reading of an ass of that name in the Bible!

Father Semyon had been succeeded by Father Demyan, a hard drinker who sometimes even went so far as to see green snakes. He had actually borne the nickname of "Demian the Snake-Seer" in the village. Matvey Nikolaich had been the schoolmaster, a kind, intelligent man, but a hard drinker, too. He never thrashed his scholars, but for some reason he kept a little bundle of birch twigs hanging on his wall, under which was a tablet bearing the absolutely unintelligible inscription: "Betula Kinderbalsamica Secuta."* He had had a woolly black dog whom he called "Syntax."

The bishop laughed. Eight miles from Lyesopolye lay

* Fractured Latin and German: "Twigs children-healing flogger."

the village of Obnino, possessing a miraculous icon. A procession started from Obnino every summer bearing the wonder-working icon and making the rounds of all the neighboring villages. The church-bells would ring all day long first in one village, then in another, and to little Pavel (His Reverence was called little Pavel then) the air itself seemed tremulous with rapture. Barefoot, hatless, and infinitely happy, he followed the icon with a naïve smile on his lips and naïve faith in his heart.

Until the age of fifteen little Pavel had been so slow at his lessons that his parents had even thought of taking him out of the ecclesiastical school and putting him to work in the village store.

The bishop turned over so as to break the train of his thoughts, and tried to go to sleep.

"My mother has come!" he remembered, and laughed.

The moon was shining in through the window, and the floor was lit by its rays while he lay in shadow. A cricket was chirping. Father Sisoi was snoring in the next room, and there was a forlorn, friendless, even a vagrant note in the old man's cadences.

Sisoi had once been the steward of a diocesan bishop and was known as "Father Former Steward." He was seventy years old, and lived sometimes in a monastery sixteen miles away, sometimes in the city, sometimes wherever he happened to be. Three days ago he had turned up at the Pankratievski Monastery, and the bishop had kept him here in order to discuss with him at his leisure the affairs of the monastery.

The bell for matins rang at half-past one. Father Sisoi coughed, growled something, and got up.

"Father Sisoi!" called the bishop.

Sisoi came in dressed in a white cassock, carrying a candle in his hand.

"I can't go to sleep," His Reverence said. "I must be ill. I don't know what the matter is; I have fever."

"You have caught cold, your Lordship. I must rub you with tallow."

Father Sisoi stood looking at him for a while and yawned: "Ah-h—the Lord have mercy on us!"

"Erakin has electricity in his store now—I hate it!" he continued.

Father Sisoi was aged, and round-shouldered, and gaunt. He was always displeased with something or other, and his eyes, which protruded like those of a crab, always wore an angry expression.

"I don't like it at all," he repeated—"I hate it."

II

Next day, on Palm Sunday, His Reverence officiated at the cathedral in the city. Then he went to the diocesan bishop's, then to see a general's wife who was very ill, and at last he drove home. At two o'clock two beloved guests were having dinner with him, his aged mother, and his little niece Katya, a child of eight. The spring sun was peeping cheerily in through the windows as they sat at their meal, and was shining merrily on the white table-cloth, and on Katya's red hair. Through the double panes they heard the rooks cawing, and the magpies chattering in the garden.

"It is nine years since I saw you last," said the old mother, "and yet when I caught sight of you in the convent chapel yesterday I thought to myself: God bless me, he has not changed a bit! Only perhaps you are a little thinner than you were, and your beard has grown longer. Oh, holy Mother, Queen of Heaven! Everybody was crying yesterday. As soon as I saw you, I began to cry myself, I don't know why. His holy will be done!"

In spite of the tenderness with which she said this, it was clear that she was not at her ease. It was as if she did not know whether to address the bishop by the familiar "thee" or the formal "you," and whether she ought to laugh or not. She seemed to feel herself more of a poor deacon's wife than a mother in his presence. Meanwhile Katya was sitting with her eyes glued to the

face of her uncle the bishop as if she were trying to
make out what manner of man this was. Her hair had
escaped from her comb and her bow of velvet ribbon,
and was standing straight up around her head like a
halo. Her eyes were foxy and bright. She had broken
a glass before sitting down, and now, as she talked, her
grandmother kept moving first a glass, and then a wine-
glass, out of her reach. As the bishop sat listening to his
mother, he remembered how, many, many years ago, she
had sometimes taken him and his brothers and sisters to
visit relatives whom they considered rich. She had been
busy with her own children in those days, and now she
was busy with her grandchildren, and had come to visit
him with Katya here.

"Your sister Varenka has four children"—she was telling him—"Katya is the oldest. God knows why, her father
fell ill and died three days before Assumption. So my
Varenka has been thrown out into the cold world."

"And how is my brother Nikanor?" the bishop asked.

"He is well, thank the Lord. He is pretty well, praise be
to God. But his son Nikolasha wouldn't go into the
church, and is at college instead learning to be a doctor.
He thinks it is best, but who knows? However, God's will
be done!"

"Nikolasha cuts up dead people?" said Katya, spilling
some water into her lap.

"Sit still, child!" her grandmother said, quietly taking
the glass out of her hands.

"How long it is since we have seen one another!" exclaimed His Reverence, tenderly stroking his mother's
shoulder and hand. "I missed you when I was abroad, I
missed you dreadfully."

"Thank you very much!"

"I used to sit by my window in the evening listening to
the band playing, and feeling lonely and forlorn. Sometimes I would suddenly grow so homesick that I used to
think I would gladly give everything I had in the world
for a glimpse of you and home."

His mother smiled and beamed, and then immediately drew a long face and said stiffly:

"Thank you very much!"

The bishop's mood changed. He looked at his mother, and could not understand where she had acquired that deferential, humble expression of face and voice, and what the meaning of it might be. He hardly recognized her, and felt sorrowful and vexed. Besides, his head was still aching, and his legs were racked with pain. The fish he was eating tasted insipid and he was very thirsty.

After dinner two wealthy lady landowners visited him, and sat for an hour and a half with faces a mile long, never uttering a word. Then an archimandrite, a gloomy, taciturn man, came on business. Then the bells rang for vespers, the sun set behind the woods, and the day was done. As soon as he got back from church the bishop said his prayers, and went to bed, drawing the covers up closely about his ears. The moonlight troubled him, and soon the sound of voices came to his ears. Father Sisoi was talking politics with his mother in the next room.

"There is a war in Japan now," he was saying. "The Japanese belong to the same race as the Montenegrins. They fell under the Turkish yoke at the same time."

And then the bishop heard his mother's voice say:

"And so you see, when we had said our prayers, and had our tea, we went to Father Yegor——"

She kept saying over and over again that they "had tea," as if all she knew of life was tea-drinking.

The memory of his seminary and college life slowly and mistily took shape in the bishop's mind. He had been a teacher of Greek for three years, until he could no longer read without glasses, and then he had taken the vows, and had been made an inspector. When he was thirty-two he had been made the rector of a seminary, and then an archimandrite. At that time his life had been so easy and pleasant, and had seemed to stretch so far, far into the future that he could see absolutely no end to it. But his health had failed, and he had nearly lost his eyesight. His doctors had advised him to give up his work and go abroad.

"And what did you do next?" asked Father Sisoi in the adjoining room.

"And then we had tea," answered his mother.

"Why, Father, your beard is green?" exclaimed Katya suddenly. And she burst out laughing.

The bishop remembered that the color of Father Sisoi's beard really did verge on green, and he, too, laughed.

"My goodness! What a plague that child is!" cried Father Sisoi in a loud voice, for he was growing angry. "You're a spoiled baby, you are! Sit still!"

The bishop recalled the new white church in which he had officiated when he was abroad, and the sound of a warm sea. Eight years had slipped by while he was there; then he had been recalled to Russia, and now he was already a bishop, and the past had faded away into mist as if it had been but a dream.

Father Sisoi came into his room with a candle in his hand.

"Well, well!" he exclaimed, surprised. "Asleep already, Your Reverence?"

"Why not?"

"It's early yet, only ten o'clock! I bought a candle this evening and wanted to rub you with tallow."

"I have a fever," the bishop said, sitting up. "I suppose something ought to be done. My head feels so queer."

Sisoi began to rub the bishop's chest and back with tallow.

"There—there—" he said. "Oh, Lord God Almighty! There! I went to town today, and saw that—what do you call him?—that archpresbyter Sidonski. I had tea with him. I hate him! Oh, Lord God Almighty! There! I hate him!"

III

The diocesan bishop was very old and very fat, and had been ill in bed with gout for a month. So His Reverence

Pyotr had been visiting him almost every day, and had received his suppliants for him. And now that he was ill he was appalled to think of the futilities and trifles they asked for and wept over. He felt annoyed at their ignorance and cowardice. The very number of all those useless trivialities oppressed him, and he felt as if he could understand the diocesan bishop who had written "Lessons in Free Will" when he was young, and now seemed so absorbed in details that the memory of everything else, even of God, had forsaken him. Pyotr must have grown out of touch with Russian life while he was abroad, for it was hard for him to grow used to it now. The people seemed rough, the women stupid and tiresome, the novices and their teachers uneducated and often disorderly. And then the documents that passed through his hands by the hundreds of thousands! The provosts gave all the priests in the diocese, young and old, and their wives and children* marks for good behavior, and he was obliged to talk about all this, and read about it, and write serious articles on it. His Reverence never had a moment which he could call his own; all day his nerves were on edge, and he grew calm only when he found himself in church.

He could not grow accustomed to the terror which he involuntarily inspired in every breast in spite of his quiet and modest ways. Everyone in the district seemed to shrivel and quake and apologize as soon as he looked at them. Everyone trembled in his presence; even the old archpresbyters fell down at his feet, and not long ago one suppliant, the old wife of a village priest, had been prevented by terror from uttering a word, and had gone away without asking for anything. And he, who had never been able to say a harsh word in his sermons, and who never blamed people because he pitied them so, would grow exasperated with these suppliants, and hurl their petitions to the ground. Not a soul had spoken sincerely and naturally to him since he had been here; even his old mother had changed, yes, she had changed very much! Why did she

* Lower Russian Orthodox clergy are permitted to marry.

talk so freely to Sisoi when all the while she was so serious and ill at ease with him, her own son? It was not like her at all! The only person who behaved naturally in his presence, and who said whatever came into his head, was old man Sisoi, who had lived with bishops all his life, and had outlasted eleven of them. And therefore His Reverence felt at ease with Sisoi, even though he was, without a doubt, a rough and quarrelsome person.

After morning prayers on Tuesday the bishop received his suppliants, and lost his temper with them. He felt ill, as usual, and longed to go to bed, but he had hardly entered his room before he was told that the young merchant Erakin, a benefactor of the monastery, had called on very important business. The bishop was obliged to receive him. Erakin stayed about an hour talking in a very loud voice, and it was hard to understand what he was trying to say.

After he had gone there came an abbess from a distant convent, and by the time she had gone the bells were tolling for vespers; it was time for the bishop to go to church.

The monks sang melodiously and rapturously that evening; a young, black-bearded priest officiated. His Reverence listened as they sang of the Bridegroom and of the chamber swept and garnished, and felt neither repentance nor sorrow, but only a deep peace of mind. He sat by the altar where the shadows were deepest, and was swept in imagination back into the days of his childhood and youth, when he had first heard these words sung. The tears trickled down his cheeks, and he meditated on how he had attained everything in life that it was possible for a man in his position to attain; his faith was unsullied, and yet all was not clear to him; something was lacking, and he did not want to die. It still seemed to him that he was leaving unfound the most important thing of all. Something of which he had dimly dreamed in the past, hopes that had thrilled his heart as a child, a schoolboy, and a traveler in foreign lands, troubled him still.

"How beautifully they are singing today!" he thought. "Oh, how beautifully!"

IV

On Thursday he held a service in the cathedral. It was the festival of the Washing of Feet. When the service was over, and the people had gone to their several homes, the sun was shining brightly and cheerily, and the air was warm. The gutters were streaming with bubbling water, and the tender songs of larks came floating in from the fields beyond the city, bringing peace to his heart. The trees were already awake, and over them brooded the blue, unfathomable sky.

His Reverence went to bed as soon as he reached home, and told the lay brother to close his shutters. The room grew dark. Oh, how tired he was!

As on the day before, the sound of voices and the tinkling of glasses came to him from the next room. His mother was gaily recounting some tale to Father Sisoi, with many a quaint word and saying, and the old man was listening gloomily, and answering in a gruff voice:

"Well, I never! Did they, indeed? What do you think of that!"

And once more the bishop felt annoyed, and then hurt that the old lady should be so natural and simple with strangers, and so silent and awkward with her own son. It even seemed to him that she always tried to find some pretext for standing in his presence, as if she felt uneasy sitting down. And his father? If he had been alive, he would probably not have been able to utter a word when the bishop was there.

Something in the next room fell to the floor with a crash. Katya had evidently broken a cup or a saucer, for Father Sisoi suddenly snorted, and cried angrily:

"What a terrible plague this child is! Merciful heavens! No one could keep her supplied with china!"

Then silence fell. When he opened his eyes again, the bishop saw Katya standing by his bedside staring at him, her red hair standing up around her head like a halo, as usual.

"Is that you, Katya?" he asked. "Who is that opening and shutting doors down there?"

"I don't hear anything."

He stroked her head.

"So your cousin Nikolasha cuts up dead people, does he?" he asked, after a pause.

"Yes, he is learning to."

"Is he nice?"

"Yes, very, only he drinks a lot."

"What did your father die of?"

"Papa grew weaker and weaker, and thinner and thinner, and then came his sore throat. And I was ill, too, and so was my brother Fedia. We all had sore throats. Papa died, Uncle, but we got well."

Her chin quivered, her eyes filled with tears.

"Oh, Your Reverence!" she cried in a shrill voice, beginning to weep bitterly. "Dear Uncle, Mother and all of us are so unhappy! Do give us a little money! Help us, Uncle darling!"

He also shed tears, and for a moment could not speak for emotion. He stroked her hair, and touched her shoulder, and said:

"All right, all right, little child. Wait until Easter comes, then we will talk about it. I'll help you."

His mother came quietly and timidly into the room, and said a prayer before the icon. When she saw that he was awake, she asked:

"Would you like a little soup?"

"No, thanks," he answered. "I'm not hungry."

"I don't believe you are well—I can see that you are not well. You really mustn't fall ill! You have to be on your feet all day long. My goodness, it makes one tired to see you! Never mind. Easter is no longer over the hills and far away. When Easter comes you will rest. God will give us time for a little talk then, but now I'm not going to worry you any more with my silly chatter. Come, Katya, let His Lordship have another forty winks——"

And the bishop remembered that, when he was a boy, she had used exactly the same half-playful, half-respectful tone to all high dignitaries of the church. Only by her strangely tender eyes, and by the anxious look which she gave him as she left the room could anyone have guessed that she was his mother. He shut his eyes, and seemed to be asleep, but he heard the clock strike twice, and Father Sisoi coughing next door. His mother came in again, and looked shyly at him. Suddenly there came a bang, and a door slammed; a vehicle of some kind drove up to the front steps. The lay brother came into the bishop's room, and called:

"Your Reverence!"

"What is it?"

"Here is the coach! It is time to go to our Lord's Passion——"

"What time is it?"

"Quarter to eight."

The bishop dressed, and drove to the cathedral. He had to stand motionless in the center of the church while the twelve Gospels were being read, and the first and longest and most beautiful of them all he read himself. A strong, valiant mood took hold of him. He knew this gospel, beginning "The Son of Man is risen today—," by heart, and as he repeated it, he raised his eyes, and saw a sea of little lights about him. He heard the sputtering of candles, but the people had disappeared. He felt surrounded by those whom he had known in his youth; he felt that they would always be here until—God knows when!

His father had been a deacon, his grandfather had been a priest, and his great-grandfather a deacon. He sprang from a race that had belonged to the church since Christianity first came to Russia, and his love for the ritual of the church, the clergy, and the sound of church-bells was inborn in him, deeply, ineradicably implanted in his heart. When he was in church, especially when he was taking part in the service himself, he felt active and valorous and happy. And so it was with him now. Only, after the eighth Gospel had been read, he felt that his voice was becoming so feeble that even his cough was inaudible; his head was aching, and he began to fear that he might collapse. His legs were growing numb; in a little while he ceased to have any sensation in them at all, and could not imagine what he was standing on, and why he did not fall down.

It was quarter to twelve when the service ended. The bishop went to bed as soon as he reached home, without even saying his prayers. As he pulled his blanket up over him, he suddenly wished that he were abroad; he passionately wished it. He would give his life, he thought, to cease from seeing these cheap, wooden walls and that low ceiling, to cease from smelling the stale scent of the monastery.

If there were only someone with whom he could talk, someone to whom he could unburden his heart!

He heard steps in the adjoining room, and tried to recall who it might be At last the door opened, and Father Sisoi came in with a candle in one hand, and a teacup in the other.

"In bed already, Your Reverence?" he asked. "I have come to rub your chest with vinegar and vodka. It is a fine thing, if rubbed in good and hard. Oh, Lord God Almighty! There—there—I have just come from our monastery. I hate it. I am going away from here tomorrow, my Lord. Oh, Lord, God Almighty—there——"

Sisoi never could stay long in one place, and he now felt as if he had been in this monastery for a year. It was hard to tell from what he said where his home was, whether there was anyone or anything in the world that he loved, and whether he believed in God or not. He himself never could make out why he had become a monk, but then, he never gave it any thought, and the time when he had taken the vows had long since faded from his memory. He thought he must have been born a monk.

"Yes, I am going away tomorrow. Bother this place!"

"I want to have a talk with you—I never seem to have the time—" whispered the bishop, making a great effort to speak. "You see, I don't know anyone—or anything—here——"

"Very well then, I shall stay until Sunday, but no longer! Bother this place!"

"What sort of a bishop am I?" His Reverence went on, in a faint voice. "I ought to have been a village priest, or a deacon, or a plain monk. All this is choking me—it is choking me——"

"What's that? Oh, Lord God Almighty! There—go to sleep now, Your Reverence. What do you mean? What's all this you are saying? Good-night!"

All night long the bishop lay awake, and in the morning he grew very ill. The lay brother took fright and ran first to the archimandrite, and then for the monastery doctor who lived in the city. The doctor, a stout, elderly man, with a long, gray beard, looked intently at His Reverence, shook his head, knit his brows, and finally said:

"I'll tell you what, Your Reverence; you have typhoid."

The bishop grew very thin and pale in the next hour, his eyes grew larger, his face became covered with wrinkles, and he looked quite small and old. He felt as if he were the thinnest, weakest, puniest man in the whole world, and as if everything that had occurred before this had been left far, far behind, and would never happen again.

"How glad I am of that!" he thought. "Oh, how glad!"

His aged mother came into the room. When she saw his wrinkled face and his great eyes, she was seized with fear, and, falling down on her knees by his bedside, she began kissing his face, his shoulders, and his hands. He seemed to her to be the thinnest, weakest, puniest man in the world, and she forgot that he was a bishop, and kissed him as if he had been a little child whom she dearly, dearly loved.

"Little Pavel, my precious!" she cried. "My little son, why do you look like this? Little Pavel, oh, answer me!"

Katya, pale and severe, stood near them, and could not understand what was the matter with her uncle, and why Granny wore such a look of suffering on her face, and spoke such heart-rending words. And he, he was speechless, and knew nothing of what was going on around him. He was dreaming that he was an ordinary man once more, striding swiftly and merrily through the open country, a staff in his hand, bathed in sunshine, with the wide sky above him, as free as a bird to go wherever his fancy led him.

"My little son! My little Pavel! Answer me!" begged his mother.

"Don't bother His Lordship," said Sisoi angrily, crossing the room. "Let him sleep. Nothing to do there ... what for! ..."

Three doctors came, consulted together, and drove away. The day seemed long, incredibly long, and then came the long, long night. Just before dawn on Saturday morning the lay brother went to the old mother who was lying on a sofa in the sitting-room, and asked her to come into the bedroom; His Reverence had gone to eternal peace.

Next day was Easter. There were forty-two churches in the city, and two monasteries, and the deep, joyous notes of their bells pealed out over the town from morning until night. The birds were caroling, the bright sun was shining. The big marketplace was full of noise; barrel organs were droning, concertinas were squealing, and drunken voices were ringing through the air. Trotting-races were held in the main street that afternoon; in a word, all was merry and gay, as it had been the year before and as, doubtless, it would be the year to come.

A month later a new bishop was appointed, and everyone forgot His Reverence Pyotr. Only the dead man's mother, who is living now in a little country town with her son the deacon, when she goes out at sunset to meet her cow, and joins the other women on the way, tells them about her children and grandchildren, and her boy who became a bishop.

And when she mentions him she looks at them shyly, for she is afraid they will not believe her.

And, as a matter of fact, not all of them do.

(*1902*)

Maxim Gorky

(1868–1936)

Gorky, the most unassailable icon in the official account of
Soviet literature and its central mystery, Socialist Realism, is
an irritating bafflement to men of good will. Chekhov, as
usual, is some comfort. In a letter written near the end of his
life (February 1903) Chekhov said: "I agree . . . that it's hard
to form an opinion of Gorky." And: "In my opinion there
will come a time when Gorky's works will be forgotten, but
he himself is not likely to be forgotten even a thousand years
from now."* Chekhov was friendly toward Gorky. In 1902,
when the younger writer was expelled from the Academy of
Sciences for inciting factory workers to disobey the authorities, Chekhov resigned in protest. He did not, of course, live
to witness Gorky's post-Revolutionary activities—his prodigious aid to starving writers and scholars, his much publi-
cized association with Stalin, and his elevation to sainthood
in the pantheon of Soviet literature. But with his usual pre-
science, Chekhov knew that persons of his own general temperament would never overcome an essential ambivalence
toward Gorky or the feeling that the man, for better or worse,
would ultimately prove more significant than anything he
had written.

Gorky's real name was Alexei Maximovich Peshkov (the

* *Anton Chekhov's Life and Thought: Selected Letters and Commentary,* edited by Michael Henry Heim and Simon Karlinsky
(Berkeley: University of California Press, 1975), p. 447.

name *Gorky* means "bitter"), and his social origin was many
rungs below that of Chekhov. He spent his early childhood in
conditions so squalid that cattle seemed fortunate by comparison. He was on his own from an early age and drifted
through an extraordinary variety of jobs in the Russian hin-
terland (in one of them he was apprenticed to an icon
painter). Reading his autobiographical trilogy (probably his
best-sustained work), one concludes that the pseudonym was
ill-chosen, for Gorky seems entitled to a great deal more bit-
terness than he actually displayed. His principal talent as a
writer was for the sharpest possible observation of the people
and events he had actually witnessed and, at least in his role
as narrator, for a sustained sympathy toward men and
women of all kinds. He had a gigantic gusto for life and—autodidact that he was—an almost excessive reverence for
learning, the latter being coupled, by the usual paradox
of his nature, with a kind of redneck suspicion of intellectuals.

He naturally welcomed the Revolution, but not the Bolshevik usurpers of it, concerning whom he wrote things so
devastating that they could be published only after the collapse of Soviet power. He left Russia in 1921 for reasons of
health, living first in Germany and then in his villa in Sor-
rento, but he continued to participate in the literary life at
home. When he returned in 1928, his sixtieth birthday was
the occasion for an enormous celebration. His death in
1936 is one of the more spectacular of the millions of enigmatic demises during the Stalinist terror. At one time the
official version was that Trotskyite enemies of the people
had arranged for Gorky to fall ill with influenza and then
be killed by suborned doctors. The rumor that Gorky's
murder had been ordered by Stalin is of course also alive.
No one knows.

What is known is that Gorky could protect Isaac Babel
(see p. 187), on the one hand, from the most powerful de-
tractors, and, on the other, deny Osip Mandelstam (see p.
169) a pair of trousers from the emergency relief stores under
his control. Gorky's pacifist soul responded to the Odessa
Jew's depiction of the horrors of cavalry combat; but the Petersburg Jew's incomprehensible verbal magic was deeply
suspect.

We can at least be grateful for the unlikely conjunction of a writer from the lowest depths, Gorky, with a writer from the pinnacle of the ancient nobility, Tolstoy. They were evidently fascinated with each other. No other picture of the sage of Yasnaya Polyana is quite so convincing as that glimpsed through the shrewd peasant eyes of Gorky, who was impressed but unafraid and, on the elemental level of man to man, loving.

RECOLLECTIONS OF LEO TOLSTOY

I

You can't help noticing that one thought more than any other gnaws at his heart—the thought of God. At times it seems that it isn't even a thought but a sort of effort to resist something that he senses above him. He would like to talk about this more often than he does, but he thinks about it constantly. I doubt that this is a sign of old age, some presentiment of death—no, I think it comes from his splendid human pride. Wounded pride, maybe. After all, if you're Leo Tolstoy, it's insulting to have to submit to something called a streptococcus. If he were a scientist he would certainly make the most brilliant hypotheses, enormous discoveries.

II

He has astonishing hands. They are ugly and knotted with swollen veins, but they are still uncommonly ex-

pressive and filled with creative power. Leonardo da
Vinci probably had such hands. You could do anything
with hands like those. Sometimes when he is talking he
keeps moving his fingers, gradually clenching them into
a fist, and then suddenly spreads them out at the very
moment when he utters some wonderful, weighty word.
He looks like a god—not the Lord of Hosts or some
Olympian deity, but that old Russian god that "sits
on a maple throne under a golden linden tree." Not terribly majestic, but probably shrewder than all the other
gods.

III

He treats Sulerzhitsky* with all the tenderness of a
woman. Chekhov he loves like a father, in that love you
can sense the pride of a creator; but what Suler inspires in
him is simply tenderness, an unflagging interest and delight that seem never to tire the sorcerer. Maybe there's
something slightly comical in this feeling, like an old
man's love for a parrot or a pug-dog or a cat. Suler is a sort
of fascinating wild bird from some strange unknown
country. A hundred men like Suler could change the face
and the soul of some provincial town. They would beat its
face in and fill its soul with a passion for inspired and
stormy mischief. It's easy and amusing to love Suler, and I
am surprised and angry at how casually women treat him.
Of course it could be that their casualness is a skillful disguise for caution. There's no relying upon Suler. What
will he do tomorrow? He might toss a bomb at someone or
he might run off with some group that sings in taverns.

* Leopold Antonovich Sulerzhitsky (1872–1916) was trained as an
artist and stage designer, though he was expelled from school for
making revolutionary speeches. A devoted disciple of Tolstoy, he
was entrusted by the master with organizing the emigration of the
Dukhobors to Canada in 1898 and 1899. The proceeds from Tolstoy's last novel, *Resurrection*, enabled the religious sect to make the
journey and escape persecution at home. At the time of his death,
Sulerzhitsky was a director of the Moscow Art Theater.

The man's energy wouldn't run out for several hundred years. There's so much of the fire of life in him that he seems to throw off sparks like white-hot iron.

But once he really was furious at Suler. Leopold had a penchant for anarchism, and he would talk ardently and often on the subject of individual freedom, a subject that inevitably led Tolstoy to make fun of him.

I remember one time when Sulerzhitsky got hold of one of Prince Kropotkin's* little pamphlets and was set on fire by it and went about the whole day telling everyone about the wisdom of anarchism and driving everyone crazy with his philosophizing.

"Oh, Lyovushka, do stop, you're becoming tiresome," said Tolstoy in a vexed tone. "You're like a parrot forever repeating one word—freedom, freedom. But what does it mean? If you achieve freedom of the sort that you have in mind, how do you imagine the future will be? In the philosophical sense—bottomless emptiness, and in life, in actual practice—you'll be an idler, a beggar. If you're free in your sense of the word, what will bind you to life, to other people? Look at the birds—they're free, and yet they build nests. But you won't build a nest. You'll satisfy your sexual needs wherever the opportunity presents itself, like a dog. Think about it seriously and you'll see, you'll feel, that freedom in the ultimate sense is emptiness, boundlessness."

Frowning angrily, he was silent for a moment and then added, in a quieter tone: "Christ was free, and so was the Buddha, and both took upon themselves the sins of the world, they willingly entered into the prison of life on earth. And further than that no one has gone, no one. But you, but we—what of us? We're all looking for freedom from our obligations to our fellow man, but that is precisely what makes us human beings, that sense of our obligations, and if it weren't for that, we would live like animals . . ."

---

* Prince Pyotr Alekseevich Kropotkin (1842–1921) was a leading theorist of anarchism.

He smiled and said, "Still, what we're arguing about now is how we must live better. There's not too much sense in it, but not too little, either. Here you are arguing with me and you get so angry that your nose turns blue, but you don't hit me, you don't even swear at me. If you really felt yourself to be free you'd finish me off—it's as simple as that."

And after another pause he added, "Freedom—that is when everything and everybody agree with me, but in that case I wouldn't exist, because none of us has any sense of himself except in conflicts, contradictions."

IV

Goldenweiser* was playing Chopin, which inspired the following thoughts in Tolstoy:

"A certain minor German prince once said, 'If you want to have slaves you must compose as much music as possible.' That's true, a true observation. Music does blunt the mind. The Catholics understand this better than anyone. Our priests, of course, will never stand for Mendelssohn being played in church. There was a priest in Tula who assured me that Christ himself was no Jew, though he was the son of the Jewish God and a Jewish mother. This much he admitted, but he still said, 'He couldn't have been a Jew.' I asked him, 'But then how...?' He shrugged his shoulders and said, 'That mystery passeth my understanding!' "

V

"The Galician prince Vladimirko was the very model of an intellectual. As early as the twelfth century he said 'with exceeding boldness': 'There are no miracles in our time.' Six hundred years later all the intellectuals are rehearsing the same refrain: There are no miracles, there are

---

* A. B. Goldenweiser (1875–1961) was a composer and pianist.

no miracles. And the people, down to the last man, believe in miracles exactly as they did in the twelfth century."

VI

Tolstoy said, "The minority need God because they have everything else, and the majority because they have nothing."

But I would put it this way: The majority believe in God out of faintheartedness; only a few believe out of the greatness of their spirit.*

In a reflective mood he once asked, "Do you like Andersen's fairy tales?" "I didn't understand them when they appeared in Marko Vovchok's translation, but about ten years later I got hold of his book, read them through, and it suddenly dawned upon me with such clarity that Andersen was terribly lonely. Terribly. I don't know his biography. He seems to have been dissolute, traveled about a lot, but that only confirms my feeling—he was lonely. Especially because he addressed himself to children, though it's a fallacy to suppose that children have more pity on a person than grown-ups. Children feel no pity for anything, they don't know how to pity."

VII

He advised me to read the Buddhist catechism. He always talks sentimentally on the subject of Buddhism or Jesus Christ. About Christ his talk is unusually bad—his words are devoid of enthusiasm, emotion, any spark of real, heartfelt fire. I think he regards Christ as naive and pathetic and although (at times) he admires him, he scarcely feels any love for him. It's as though he feared that if

* In the margin of the printed text Gorky wrote: "In order to avoid misunderstanding, I should add that I regard religious writing the same way I do artistic writing—the lives of Buddha, Christ, and Mohammed I see as novels in the mode of fantasy."

Christ walked into a Russian village he would be laughed at by the girls.

IX*

He reminds one of those pilgrims who spend their lives trudging over the earth, leaning on their staff, covering thousands of versts from one monastery to the next, one pile of relics to the next, horribly homeless and strangers to everyone and everything. The world is not for them, nor God either. They pray to Him out of habit, but in their heart of hearts they detest Him: Why does He drive them from one end of the earth to the other, why? People are nothing but stumps, roots, stones in your path—you run up against them and at times they hurt you. People would never be missed. Yet, you sometimes enjoy the startled look on a man's face when he realizes how unlike him you are, how little you agree with him.

X

"Frederick the Great put it very well: 'Everyone must save himself *à sa façon*.' He also said: 'Debate as much as you like, so long as you obey.' But when he was dying he confessed: 'I'm tired of ruling slaves.' So-called great men are always terribly contradictory. This is forgiven them along with every other sort of stupidity. Not that being contradictory is stupid; a stupid man is stubborn but he doesn't know how to be contradictory. Yes—Frederick was a strange man. He merited his fame as the greatest emperor the Germans ever had, and yet he couldn't stand them. He even disliked Goethe and Wieland."

XI

Speaking yesterday evening about the poems of Balmont, he said, "Romanticism is nothing but the fear of looking

* Sections VIII and XVII have been omitted.

truth in the eye." Suler didn't agree with him and, lisping with agitation, read some more of the poems in a very emotional way.

"Lyovushka, that isn't poetry—it's chicanery, nonsense, it's pointless 'word-weaving,' as they called it in the Dark Ages. Poetry is not artificial. When Fet wrote

> I know not yet what I shall sing;
> I only know the song is there.

he expressed the genuine, the people's feeling for poetry. The peasant doesn't know either what he's going to sing—O, the river-o—and so on; but it turns out to be a real song, straight from his heart, like a bird's song. These new poets of yours make everything up. These stupid French things called *'articles de Paris'*—that's exactly what your word-weavers are up to. Nekrasov's trashy verse is also made up."

"And Béranger?" Suler asked.

"Béranger is altogether different! What do we have in common with the French? They are sensualists. The life of the spirit is not so important for them as the life of the flesh. The first thing in every Frenchman's mind is woman. They're a worn-out, decayed people. Doctors say that consumptives are all sensualists."

Suler began to argue with the forthrightness that was so characteristic of him, spluttering a multitude of thoughtless words. Tolstoy looked at him, and said with a broad smile, "You're as capricious today as a young woman who needs to get married and has no suitor."

XII

The illness has made him even drier, it has burnt out something that was in him, with the result that he has become inwardly somehow lighter, more transparent, more receptive to life. His eyes are still sharper, his glance—penetrating. He listens attentively, just as though he were calling to mind some forgotten thing or as though he were

confidently waiting to learn something new, hitherto unheard-of. At his estate, Yasnaya Polyana, he had struck me
as a man to whom everything was known and who had
nothing further to learn—a man for whom all questions
had been settled.

XIII

If he were a fish he would of course swim only in the
ocean, never visiting the inland seas, especially not the
fresh water of rivers. Here he is surrounded by schools of
freshwater fish who find what he says neither interesting
nor useful, but his silence doesn't frighten or touch them.
And he is a master of the impressive silence, like a real
hermit who shuns the things of this world. Though he
talks a good deal on the topics which he feels obliged to
discuss, one still senses that there are many more topics on
which he keeps silent. There are things one tells to no one.
He no doubt has thoughts that frighten him.

XIV

Someone sent him an excellent version of the tale of the
boy baptized by Christ. He took pleasure in reading it
aloud to Suler and Chekhov—he's an astonishing reader!
The part where the devils torture the landowners struck
him as highly amusing, and this somehow annoyed me.
He is incapable of feigning, but if that wasn't feigning—
it's all the worse.

Then he said, "Look how wonderfully the peasants tell
a story. Everything is simple. Few words, but much feeling. True wisdom needs few words—like 'God have
mercy.' "

But it is a savage story.

XV

His interest in me is ethnographical. In his eyes I am a
person from a little-known tribe—that's all.

XVI

I read him my story "The Bull." He laughed a great deal and praised me for knowing "the sleight of hand of language."

"But you arrange words clumsily. All your peasants speak with great intelligence. In real life their talk is stupid and awkward—you can't understand right away what it is a peasant is trying to say. They do this on purpose. Underneath the stupidity of their words they hide their wish for the other man to express himself first. A good peasant will never let you know right away what he's got on his mind. He doesn't gain anything by that. He knows that people treat a stupid man simply, without any tricks—and that's just his aim. But you—you stand there revealed in front of him and he immediately sees all your weak points. He doesn't confide in people: A peasant is afraid of telling his own wife his innermost thoughts. But the peasant you write about wears his heart on his sleeve. In every story there's some sort of solemn assembly of wise men. And they all speak in aphorisms, which is also false. Aphorisms are alien to Russian."

"But what of the proverbs and sayings?"

"Those are different. They aren't freshly coined every day."

"But you yourself often speak in aphorisms."

"Never! . . . And then you prettify everything, people and nature, but especially people! Leskov did the same—a foolish writer, full of mannerisms, and no one reads him today. Don't submit to anyone, don't be afraid of anyone, and everything will be fine."

In one of the notebooks of his diary, which he gave me to read, I was struck by a strange aphorism: "God is my desire."

Today when I was returning the notebook to him I asked him what that meant.

"An unfinished thought," he said, squinting at the page. "I must have meant to say, 'God is my desire to know him.' No, that isn't it ..." He laughed, rolled the note-book into a tube, and thrust it into the wide pocket of his blouse. His relations with God are very vague. Their relationship sometimes seems to me like that of "two bears in one den."

XVIII

About science.

"Science is gold bullion turned out by some fradulent alchemist. You try to simplify it and make it accessible to all the people and all you're doing is minting a heap of counterfeit coins. When the people understand what this money is really worth they aren't going to thank us."

XIX

We were strolling in the park of the Yusupov estate* and he was telling me the most wonderful stories of how the Moscow aristocracy lived. A big old Russian peasant woman was working on a flower bed, bent double, exposing her elephantine legs and shaking her ponderous breasts. She held his attention for a while.

"All that magnificence and wild living was supported upon exactly this sort of caryatid—supported not only by the work of the peasants, not only by the quitrent they had to pay, but, in the plainest sense of the word, by the people's blood. If the nobility had not from time to time mated with such mares as this, it would have died out long ago. You can't squander your strength the way the young men of my day squandered theirs without having to pay for it. But many of them, after they'd had their fling, married some girl from among the house serfs and produced good litters. So that, here too, it was peasant strength that saved them. You can see it everywhere. Half the stock of the aristocracy had to spend its strength upon itself, and

* The estate of the Yusupovs bordered on Gaspra, the estate of Countess Panina, near Yalta on the southern coast of the Crimea, where Tolstoy was staying in 1901–2.

the other half had to dilute itself with thick blood from the peasant village, and that blood itself also got diluted. That helped."

XX

He is fond of talking about women and does so often, like a French novelist, but always with that Russian peasant crudeness which (at first) made such a disagreeable impression upon me. Today in Almond Grove he asked Chekhov, "Did you chase ass a lot when you were young?"

Chekhov, with an embarrassed grin, stroked his little beard and mumbled some indistinct answer. Tolstoy, gazing out to sea, said, "I was a tireless f——."

This he uttered in a sorrowful tone, though the last word in his sentence was a pungent peasant expression. That was the first time I noticed how simply he used such a word, as though he knew of no word that might replace it. And all similar words issued forth from his bearded lips with such simplicity and naturalness that they seemed to have lost somewhere their soldierly coarseness and dirt. I recall my first meeting with him, when he discussed my stories "Varenka Olesova" and "Twenty-Six Men and a Girl." Judged by ordinary standards, what he said was one "indecent" word after another. I was embarrassed by this and even offended—I thought he regarded me as incapable of understanding any other form of speech. I understand now that it was stupid to be offended.

XXI

He was sitting on a stone bench under some cypresses. A small, gray, dried-up old man, he still looked like the Lord of Hosts, though a little tired, and was having a good time trying to whistle in time with a finch. The bird was singing deep in the dark green foliage, and he was peering into it, his eyes screwed up and his lips pursed in a childish way as he whistled clumsily.

"What a fierce little bird! Listen to him bash out that tune! What sort is it?"

I told him about the finch and its jealous nature.

"One song his whole life long . . . and jealous! Man has hundreds of songs in his heart, but he's criticized for being jealous . . . is that fair?" He said this in an abstracted way, as though talking to himself. "There are moments when a man tells a woman more than she ought to know about him. He tells her and forgets it, but she remembers. Perhaps jealousy comes from some fear of abasing one's soul, the fear of humiliation and ridicule. The dangerous woman is not the one who holds you by the p—— but the one who holds you by the soul."

When I remarked that this seemed to contradict his own story "The Kreutzer Sonata," a wide beaming smile spread across his whole beard and he said, "I'm no finch."

On our walk that evening he suddenly said:

"Man endures earthquakes, epidemics, the horrors of disease and every sort of spiritual affliction, but throughout the ages his most tormenting tragedy has been, is today, and forever will be—the tragedy of the bedroom."

He smiled triumphantly as he said this. He sometimes smiles in the broad, tranquil manner of a man who has overcome some terribly difficult thing, or who has suddenly been relieved of a long, gnawing pain. Every thought fastens itself upon his soul like a tick; either he pulls it off at once or else he allows it to suck its fill of his blood and fall off of its own weight, unnoticed.

Once he was talking very entertainingly about the Stoics when he suddenly stopped, shook his head, and, frowning sternly, said, "*Knitted*, not *knitten!* The adjective from *weave* is *woven*, but there's no such word as *knitten* . . ."

That sentence clearly had nothing to do with the Stoics or their philosophy. Noticing my perplexity, he nodded his head in the direction of the door to the next room and hastened to explain: "Someone in there said '*knitten* blanket.'" Then he went on, "But Renan just spreads out some sort of sickly sweet gossip . . ."

He often said to me, "You tell a story well, in your own words in a strong, not a bookish manner."

But he almost never failed to notice some lapse of style, and then he would say in an undertone, as though speaking to himself: "Here you've used the native Russian word *podobno* [like] but right next to it you've used the borrowed word *absolyutno* [absolutely] where you could have used the native *sovershenno* for the same meaning . . . !'

At times he would reproach me: "You describe someone as a *rickety subject.* Surely you don't think one can put side by side two words from such different stylistic levels? That's no good . . ."

His sensitivity to the formal aspects of language struck me at times as almost painfully intense. Once he said, "In a book by X, I came across the words *koshka* [cat] and *kishka* [gut] in a single sentence . . . revolting! I nearly vomited!"

Sometimes he would speculate: "What's the connection between *podozhdyom* and *pod dozhdyom?*"*

He would talk about Dostoevsky's language more often than any other: "His style is inelegant and even deliberately ugly—I'm convinced it was deliberate, just showing off. He would flaunt it. In *The Idiot* one of his phrases runs 'In the impudent pestering and *prading* of his acquaintance' where he deliberately distorts the word *parading* simply because it's a foreign, Western word. But you can also find unforgivable blunders in Dostoevsky. His idiot says, 'The donkey is a kind and helpful *person*,' but no one laughs, even though such language must provoke laughter or at least some sort of remark. He says that in the presence of three sisters who were fond of making fun of him—especially Aglaya. This is regarded as a bad book, but the worst thing in it is that Prince Myshkin is an

---

* "We shall wait" and "in the rain." Except for near homophony, there is no connection. The following paragraph, containing some complex speculations about Russian words, has been omitted.

epileptic. If he were in good health, his warmhearted naïveté and his purity would touch us deeply. But Dostoevsky lacked the courage to make him a healthy man. And he didn't like healthy people, anyway. He was sure that if he himself was sick, the entire world was sick . . ."

He was reading Suler and me a version of the scene in *Father Sergius* where the hero succumbs to temptation—a pitiless scene. Suler puffed out his cheeks and began to squirm uneasily.

"What's the matter with you? Don't you like it?" Tolstoy asked.

"Well it's terribly cruel, like something out of Dostoevsky. That rotten girl, with breasts like pancakes, and everything. Why couldn't he have committed the sin with a beautiful, healthy woman?"

"That would have been sin without any justification. But this way you can justify the sin by his pity for the girl—who would want her the way she is?"

"I don't understand that."

"There's a great deal you don't understand, Lyovushka—you aren't very sharp."

The wife of Andrei Lvovich came in and the conversation was broken off. When Suler and she had left for another part of the house, Tolstoy said to me, "Leopold is the purest man I know. He's the same way: If he were to do something bad, he'd do it out of pity for someone."

XXII

Most of all he talks about God, the peasants, and women. About literature he rarely speaks, and then skimpily, as though literature had nothing to do with him. He feels toward women, in my opinion, an irreconcilable enmity and loves to punish them—all, that is, except those of rather limited character like his own Kitty or Natasha Rostova. Is this the hostility of a man who has failed to experience all the happiness that he might have done, or the hostility felt by the soul against the "degrading passions of the flesh"? But it is hostility, cold hostility, like that in *Anna Karenina*.

On Sunday he spoke very well about the "degrading passions of the flesh" when he was talking with Chekhov and Yelpatevsky* about Rousseau's *Confessions*. Suler wrote down what he said, but then when he was making coffee he burned his notes in the fire. Another time he burned Tolstoy's opinions on Ibsen and mislaid his notes on the symbolism of the marriage ceremony, about which Tolstoy had said some very pagan things, agreeing in part with V. V. Rozanov.†

XXIII

This morning some peasants of the Evangelical Baptist sect came from Theodosia to see Tolstoy, and he spent the whole day talking rapturously about peasants.

"They came in—both such strong, solid fellows—and one says, 'Well, here we are, unbidden' and the other says, 'And God grant we leave unbeaten.' " And he laughed like a child, shaking all over.

After lunch on the terrace he said: "We'll soon cease to understand the people's language altogether. Where we say 'the theory of progress,' 'the role of personality in history,' 'the evolution of science,' 'dysentery,' and so on, the peasant says, 'Murder will out'—and all the theories, histories, and evolutions become pitiful and ridiculous, because the people don't understand or need them. But the peasant is stronger than us, he's got more vitality, and the

* S. Y. Yelpatevsky (1854–1933), a Populist writer, revolutionary, and medical doctor, left literary portraits of Tolstoy, Chekhov, Gorky, and others.

† Rozanov (1856–1919), a leading philosopher and critic, theorized about the central role of the sexual instinct in the nature of man. He is the author of a notable study of Dostoevsky, to whose former mistress he was married.

same thing might happen to us that happened to the Attsur tribe. Someone told a scholar, 'The Attsurs have all died out, but there's a parrot here that knows a few words of their language.' "

XXIV

"With her body a woman is more honest than a man, but her mind is full of lies. Still, she doesn't believe herself when she lies—Rousseau lied and believed it."

XXV

"Dostoevsky wrote about one of his insane characters that the man lived in order to wreak vengeance on himself and others for the fact that he had spent his life in the service of something he didn't believe in. He was writing about himself: That is, he could have been writing about himself."

XXVI

"Some of the expressions in Holy Scripture are amazingly obscure. What, for instance, is the meaning of the words: 'The earth is the Lord's and the fulness thereof'? That isn't from the Bible—that's some sort of popular-science materialism."

"You've explained these words somewhere," said Suler.

"And much good came of it ... 'A ton of talk for an ounce of sense ...' "

And he smiled cunningly.

XXVII

He loves to ask difficult, tricky questions:

"What do you think of yourself?"

"Do you love your wife?"

"What do you think of my son Lev—does he have any talent?"

"Do you like my wife?"

It's not possible to lie to him. Once he asked me, "Do you like me, Alexei Maximovich?"

This is the sort of mischief that one expects from one of the heroes of Russian folklore; Vaska Buslaev, that mischief maker from Novgorod, played such tricks in his youth. He keeps "probing" and testing, just as though he were getting ready for a fight. It's interesting, but I don't much like it. He's a devil, and I'm only an infant, and he ought to leave me alone.

XXVIII

Perhaps a peasant is nothing more to him than—a bad smell. He always notices it and can't help talking about it.

Last night I told him about my battle with General Cornet's widow, and he laughed until the tears came and his chest began to ache and he kept on peeping in a thin little voice: "With a shovel! On her ————! A shovel right across her a——! Was it a wide shovel?"

Later, when he'd recovered, he said in a serious tone, "Still, you were generous with your blow—another man would have struck her on the head for that. Very generous. But you understood that she desired you?"

"I don't remember . . . I don't think I did . . ."

"What! It's obvious! Of course she did."

"I wasn't living for that at the time . . ."

"It doesn't matter what you were living for! You aren't much of an asshound, that's clear. Another man would have made his fortune from that incident, become a man of property, and died a drunkard along with her."

After a pause he said, "You're funny. No offense, but you're funny. And it's very strange that, with all your right to be bitter, you're still a kind man. Yes, you might be bitter. You're strong—that's good."

And after another pause, he added thoughtfully, "I don't understand your mind—it's a very complicated mind; but your heart is intelligent . . . yes, an intelligent heart."

NOTE: When I was living in Kazan I entered the service of General Cornet's widow as yardman and gardener. She was a young Frenchwoman, plump, with the tiny feet of a girl. She had amazingly beautiful eyes, which were restless and always wide with greed. Before her marriage I think she worked in a shop or as a cook or perhaps even as a "woman of pleasure." She would be drunk from early morning and would come into the garden dressed in nothing but a chemise with an orange-colored robe thrown over it and a pair of red morocco slippers of Tartar design and with a thick mane of hair, which hung in careless strands about her rosy cheeks and shoulders. A young witch. She would stroll about the garden singing French songs and watching me work and from time to time would go up to the kitchen window and call out:

"Pauline, bring me something."

This "something" never varied—a glass of wine with ice in it.

On the ground floor of her house three young women, the Princesses D.-G., were living like orphans. Their father, a general, had gone off somewhere and their mother was dead. Mme. Cornet conceived a dislike for these girls and tried to oust them from their apartment by all sorts of mean tricks. She spoke Russian poorly but she swore magnificently, like a seasoned wagon driver. I hated the way she treated these harmless girls—they were so sad, frightened, and helpless. One day around noon two of them were strolling in the garden when suddenly the mistress, drunk as ever, came out and began to scream at them to chase them from the garden. They began to leave quietly, but Mme. Cornet stationed herself in the gateway and, plugging it up with her person like a cork, she addressed them with some of those grim Russian words that make even horses shudder. When I asked her to stop swearing and allow the young ladies to pass, she screamed:

"I know you! You are climbing to zeir weendow when is night!"

I got angry and grabbed her by the shoulders and

pulled her away from the gate, but she broke away and, turning to face me, threw open her robe, lifted her gown, and screamed:

"I am bettair zan zeez mouses!"

At that I became really furious. I spun her around and hit her bottom with the shovel so hard that she leapt through the gate and ran about the yard in the utmost astonishment, screaming, "O! O! O!"

After that I got my passport from her confidante Pauline—also a drunk but a very shrewd old woman—took the bundle of my belongings under my arm, and had started out of the courtyard, when Mme. Cornet, standing in the window and waving a red kerchief, called to me: "I no call police—is all right! Leesten! Come back—don' be afraid!"

XXIX

I once asked him, "Do you agree with Poznyshev* when he says that doctors have killed, and are still killing, hundreds of thousands of people?"

"And is that something that interests you very much?"

"Very."

"Then I won't tell you!"

And he grinned and twiddled his thumbs.

I remember in one of his stories a comparison between a country horse doctor and a medical doctor.† The horse doctor says, "But words like 'glanders' and 'staggers' and 'blood-letting'—are they really any different from 'nerves' and 'rheumatisms' and 'organisms' and so on?"

And this he could write after the discoveries of Jenner, Behring, and Pasteur! There's a mischief maker for you!

XXX

How strange that he should love to play cards. He plays seriously, excitedly. And his hands become so nervous

* The principal character in Tolstoy's "The Kreutzer Sonata."

† "Polikushka" (1863).

when he takes cards in them that you would think he was holding live birds, not dead bits of cardboard.

XXXI

"Dickens said a wise thing: 'We are granted life under the absolute condition that we defend it with all our courage up to the last moment.' In general, however, he was a sentimental, wordy writer and not awfully clever. But he did know how to construct a novel better than anyone else, and of course better than Balzac. Someone said, 'Many are smitten with a passion for writing books, but few are ashamed of them afterwards.' Balzac wasn't ashamed, and neither was Dickens, though they both wrote their share of bad books. Still, Balzac is a genius—there's no other name for him than genius . . ."

Someone brought him Lev Tikhomirov's pamphlet "Why I Ceased Being a Revolutionary."* Tolstoy picked it up from the table and waved it in the air as he said:

"Everything he writes about political assassination is good—that there's no clear idea behind this form of struggle. The only idea behind it, says this reformed murderer, is the anarchic absolutism of one individual, and contempt for society, for humanity. That's right. Except that 'anarchic' is a misprint—he meant 'monarchic.' It's a good, true idea, one that all terrorists stumble over—I'm speaking of the honest ones. The born murderer won't stumble. There isn't anything that would trip him. But he's nothing but a murderer who got in with the terrorists by accident."

XXXII

He can sometimes be as self-satisfied and unbearable as some fundamentalist preacher from the other side of the

* Tikhomirov was a member of the People's Will Party, which was responsible for the assassination of Alexander II in 1881. He was later pardoned by Alexander III and became a reactionary and monarchist.

Volga, and that is terrible in a man who is one of the great spiritual forces of this world. Yesterday he said to me: "I'm more of a muzhik than you are—I feel more like a muzhik."

Good God! He shouldn't boast of that, he really shouldn't!

XXXIII

I read him some scenes from my play *The Lower Depths*. He listened carefully and then asked:

"Why do you write this?"

I explained as best I could.

"You're forever attacking everything like some game-cock. And another thing—you always want to cover up all the chips and cracks with your own paint. Remember where Hans Christian Andersen says: 'The gold leaf will wear off but the pigskin remains.' And our peasants say: 'Everything passes, truth alone lasts.' Better not paint things over, or it'll be worse for you in the end. And then too, your language is so bouncy, so tricky—that's no good. You should write more simply. Ordinary people speak very simply; sometimes it even seems incoherent, but it's still good. You'll never hear a peasant ask, the way some learned young lady once asked, 'Why is a third larger than a fourth when three is always less than four?' Don't use tricks."

The way he spoke, you could see he was very unhappy, that he didn't like what I'd read him at all. He was silent for a while, then, looking past me, he said in a gloomy tone of voice:

"Your Old Man is not a sympathetic character—his goodness is not believable. As for the Actor, he's all right, he's good. Do you know my *Fruits of Enlightenment*? I've got a cook in that play who is like your Actor. It's hard to write plays. The Prostitute is also good. There must be some like her—have you seen them?"

"Yes, I have."

"One can tell that. The truth can't be faked. But you

say an awful lot in your own voice as author. That's because you don't have any characters—all your people have one face. It must be that you don't understand women—they don't come off at all, not one. No one remembers them ..."

Andrei Lvovich's wife came in to call us to tea. He got up and left so quickly that you could see he was glad to come to the end of that conversation.

XXXIV

"What's the most frightening dream you ever had?"

I rarely dream and hardly ever remember them, but there were two dreams that stuck in my memory, probably forever.

I dreamed once of a scrofulous, putrid sky, greenish-yellow in color, with flat, round stars giving off no rays, no light, like sores on the skin of someone with a wasting disease. A kind of slow, reddish lightning slid around amongst them like some sort of snake, and when it touched a star, the star would swell up like a balloon and burst without making a sound. It would leave behind a dark spot like a puff of smoke, which would quickly sink into the rotten, watery sky. So, one after the other, all the stars burst and vanished and the sky became darker and more terrifying; then it seemed to boil up and explode into lumps that began to fall on my head like some runny gelatin, and between the lumps I could see shiny black roofing iron.

Tolstoy said, "Well, you got that from some learned book, you were reading something about astronomy, so you had a nightmare. How about the other dream?"

The other dream: a snowy plain, smooth as a sheet of paper, not a hill nor a tree nor a bush anywhere, just here and there a birch rod or two sticking up out of the snow. Across the snow of this dead wasteland, from one horizon to the other, there was a road that you could hardly see, like a yellow stripe, and along this road went a pair of gray felt boots, walking very slowly, with no one in them.

He raised his shaggy, wood-demon brows and stared fixedly at me, thinking.

"That's . . . horrible! Did you really dream that or make it up? There's something literary about this one, too."

And he suddenly seemed to get angry and began to talk in a stern tone of voice, tapping his finger on his knee:

"But you're not a drinker, are you? You don't look as if you ever drank much. But there's something drunk about these dreams. There was a German writer named Hoffmann, and he'd have card tables running down the street—that sort of thing. Well, he was a drunk—or an 'alaholic' as our literate cabbies would say. Empty boots walking—that really is horrible! Even if you did make it up—it's good! Horrible!"

A smile suddenly spread across his whole beard so that even his cheekbones gleamed.

"Wait, just imagine this: Suddenly on Tverskaya Street there's a card table running along with curved legs and its leaves flapping up and down and puffs of chalk dust coming out of it, and you can even see the figures on the green felt. That's because some tax collectors have been playing vint on it for three days hand running and the table can't take it and has run away."

He laughed and I suppose he must have noticed that I was a little put out by his not believing me.

"You're insulted because I found your dreams literary? Don't be offended. I know that people sometimes think up things unconsciously, completely unacceptable things, and then it seems they dreamed them and didn't make them up. One old landowner told of how he dreamed he was walking through a forest, came out onto the steppe and saw before him two hills, and they suddenly turned into a woman's tits. And a dark face rose up between them that had two moons like walleyes on it in the place of eyes, and he was standing between the woman's legs and right in front of him was a deep, dark ravine sucking him in. His hair began to turn gray after that and his hands started to shake and he went abroad to take the water cure with Dr.

Kneiper. That was just the sort of dream he deserved to have—he was a real hell-raiser."

He clapped me on the shoulder.

"But you're not drunk or a hell-raiser—so what are you doing with such dreams?"

"I don't know."

"We don't know anything about ourselves!"

He sighed, narrowed his eyes, and added in a quieter voice:

"We don't know anything!"

When we were strolling this evening he took me by the arm and said, "Boots walking along—eerie, right? Nobody in them and they march along—hup, two, three, four—the snow crunching underneath them. Oh, that's good! Still, you're very literary, very literary! Don't be angry, it's just that it's bad and you'll have trouble with it."

I doubt that I'm more literary than he is, but he seemed to me a cruel rationalist today, no matter how he tried to soften the blows.

XXXV

He sometimes strikes me as a person who has just arrived from some distant place where people have different ways of thinking and feeling and treating one another—and they even move differently and speak a different language. He sits over in the corner, tired and gray, as though he had the dust of some other earth sprinkled over him, and stares fixedly at everyone with the eyes of some mute alien.

Yesterday just before dinner he appeared in the parlor in exactly this state, just arrived from somewhere far away, sat down on the sofa, and, after a moment's silence, rocking back and forth and massaging his knees with his hands, suddenly said:

"There's much more to come—oh yes, much more to come."

Someone (I forget who), about as tranquil and stupid

as a flatiron, asked him, "Your remark—what was it about?"

He fixed him with a piercing gaze, bent still lower, and, glancing toward the terrace where Dr. Nikitin,* Yelpatevsky, and I were sitting, asked:

"What are you talking about?"

"About Plehve."†

"About Plehve ... Plehve," he repeated the name slowly and meditatively as though he had never heard it before, and then he gave himself a shake like a bird fluffing its feathers, laughed quietly, and said:

"Something silly has been going through my head all day. Someone told me he'd read this on a tombstone:

> Beneath this stone Ivan Egoriev sleeps;
> A leather merchant he, who many skins of sheeps
> Tanned well, was kind, but died,
> And left his wife with nary a single hide.
> He was but young, and might of done much more,
> Yet God him took, and shut the Heavenly door
> Early Saturday morning of Easter week.

and so on— there was more."

He was silent for a moment and then, smiling and shaking his head, added:

"There's something about human stupidity—if it isn't wicked—that is very touching, even sweet. There always is ..."

They called us in to dinner.

XXXVI

"I don't like drunkards, but I know people who, when they drink, become interesting and acquire a sort of wit, subtlety, and richness of thought and speech that they

* D. V. Nikitin (1874–1960) was the Tolstoys' house physician from 1902 to 1904.

† V. K. Plehve (1846–1904) was one of the most notorious reactionaries in the government of Nicholas II.

would never have when sober. At such moments I bless the existence of wine."

Suler used to tell the story of how he and Tolstoy were walking down Tverskaya Street when they noticed in the distance two cuirassiers headed toward them. Their brass armor glinting in the sun, their spurs jangling, they walked along in step as though they were two parts of one creature, and their faces shone with the self-satisfaction of strength and youth.

Tolstoy began to rail against them:

"What magnificent idiocy! They're nothing but circus animals trained with a stick . . ."

But as the cuirassiers passed them he stopped and followed them with an admiring gaze. Enraptured, he said:

"How beautiful they are! Ancient Romans, eh, Lyovushka? Strength, beauty—oh, my God! How wonderful that is, a handsome man—how wonderful!"

XXXVII

One hot day he overtook me on the lower road. He was headed toward Livadia, riding on a quiet little Tatar horse. Gray, shaggy, wearing a white, mushroom-shaped hat of light felt, he looked like a gnome.

He reined in his horse and struck up a conversation with me. I walked along at his stirrup and said, among other things, that I'd had a letter from Korolenko.[*] Tolstoy shook his beard angrily:

"Does he believe in God?"

"I don't know."

"You don't know the most important thing. He believes, but he's ashamed to admit it in front of atheists."

He spoke in a grumbling, capricious way, and screwed up his eyes in vexation. It was clear that I was holding him back, but when I was about to take my leave he stopped me:

"Where are you off to? I'm riding slowly."

---

[*] V. G. Korolenko (1853–1921) was a novelist, journalist, and editor.

He resumed talking:

"Your Andreev*—he's also afraid of the atheists, but he believes in God, too. God terrifies him."

At the edge of the estate of Grand Duke A. M. Romanov three of the Romanovs were standing in the road in a tight little group and talking: the master of the Ai-Todor estate, Georgi, and, if I'm not mistaken, Pyotr Nikolaevich from Dyulber—all of them big, fine men. A one-horse carriage blocked the road, and a saddle horse stood across it, so that Leo Nikolaevich couldn't pass. He fixed a stern, expectant glare on the Romanovs. But they had already turned their backs on him. The saddle horse pawed the earth and shifted somewhat to one side, allowing Tolstoy to pass.

When he'd ridden for about two minutes in silence, he said:

"They recognized me, the idiots."

And a minute later:

"The horse knew that one makes way for Tolstoy."

(1919)

* L. N. Andreev (1871–1919), short story writer and novelist, was the author of *The Seven That Were Hanged* (1908).

Ivan Bunin

(1870–1953)

When Bunin died in Paris in 1953, the end of the classical period in Russian literature of the nineteenth century had finally arrived. Though his early volumes of poetry appeared in the 1890s, at a time when the Russian Symbolists were thoroughly ventilating and renewing the art of verse, Bunin serenely continued in the tradition of Fet and Polonsky, and was never tempted by modernism. Symbolism was an urban phenomenon. Bunin, born into a family of impoverished noblemen in the district of Orel, was agrarian to the core of his being. His best works deal with themes familiar to the Southern school of American literature: the decay of the gentry and the degradation of the village. He also wrote stories set in the exotic Mediterranean and Oriental scenes of which he had firsthand knowledge through his extensive traveling.

Though he collaborated with Gorky on the magazine *Znanie* (Knowledge), Bunin was emphatically opposed to the Bolshevik regime and left Russia in 1920 to spend the rest of his life in exile. He wrote bitterly of what was taking place in his homeland. In 1933 he became the first Russian writer to receive the Nobel Prize, which predictably irked the Soviet Establishment. When Varlam Shalamov (see p. 402) was so incautious as to utter the opinion that Bunin was a great classic of Russian literature—the year was 1937—his crime earned him seventeen years of hard labor in Siberia. But in 1955, after Stalin's death and Shalamov's release, it was possible to read in one of Gorky's letters: "It is no exaggeration to say that Bunin is the best prose stylist of the present day." Bunin is today published and praised in the USSR.

Bunin's prose is indeed a remarkable instrument, greatly superior to his rather conventional verse and, in the best sense of the word, more poetic. It bears comparison to the style of Chekhov; no praise could be higher.

LIGHT BREATHING

In the cemetery, on a fresh mound of earth, there is a new cross made of oak—strong, heavy, and smooth.

It's April, the days are gray; one can see the monuments stretching into the distance through the still-barren trees of the cemetery—which is of the sprawling, provincial type—and the cold wind clatters and clatters the porcelain wreath at the foot of the cross.

A rather large, convex medallion made of porcelain has been let into the cross itself, and on the medallion is the photograph of a schoolgirl with joyous, wonderfully vivacious eyes.

It is Olya Meshcherskaya.

Nothing would have made one single out this girl from the crowd of her brown-uniformed classmates. What was there to say of her except that she belonged to the number of pretty, rich, and happy girls; that she was intelligent; but that she was rather wild and awfully deaf to the scolding of her teacher? Then she began to blossom and develop so rapidly that one could all but measure the changes by the hour. At fourteen she had a slender waist and shapely legs and clearly defined breasts and all of those bodily forms whose charm has never yet been cap-

tured by ordinary human language. At fifteen her beauty
was already famous. How meticulously her school friends
arranged their hair, how careful they were about their
persons, how they calculated their least movements! But
she—she was afraid of nothing—not of ink stains on her
fingers, nor of a suddenly flushed face, nor of her hair
coming undone, nor even of a knee exposed to full view if
she fell while running. Without the least effort or strain,
and almost, it seemed, without her noticing it, she acquired all those traits that set her apart from the entire
school during the two final years—grace, elegance, clever-
ness, and the brilliant light in her eyes. At parties no one
danced so well as Olya Meshcherskaya, no one skated so
well as she, no one had a larger retinue of admirers at
balls, and she was for some reason more popular with the
younger girls than anyone else. Gradually she grew into a
young lady, and gradually her schoolgirl fame became a
permanent thing, and then the talk started: that she was
flighty, that she lived for nothing but boys, that a student
named Shenshin had fallen madly in love with her, and
that she loved him, too, but treated him so capriciously
that he tried to kill himself . . .

During the last winter of her life the word around the
school was that Olya Meshcherskaya had simply gone out
of her mind from the wild gaiety of her life. The winter
was clear, cold, and snowy. The bright sun would set
early and with unfailing serenity behind the tall grove of
firs in the school park, promising more frost and sunshine
on the morrow, more strolling along Cathedral Street,
more skating in the city park, another rosy evening sky,
music, and the swarm of skaters, among whom Olya
Meshcherskaya seemed the freest and happiest of all.
Then one day, during the noon recess, when she was flying like a whirlwind through the assembly hall to escape
some blissfully squealing little girls, she was suddenly
summoned to the office of the school principal. She
stopped in midflight, sighed deeply (though only once),
smoothed her hair with a quick, already womanly gesture,
settled her pinafore properly upon her shoulders, and ran

off upstairs, her eyes shining brightly. The principal, a young-looking woman though with hair already gray, sat placidly knitting at her desk beneath the portrait of the Tsar.

"Good morning, Mlle. Meshcherskaya," she said in French, without lifting her eyes from her knitting. "This is unfortunately not the first time that I have been obliged to summon you here for the purpose of speaking to you with reference to your deportment."

"Yes, Madame?" answered Meshcherskaya, as she approached the desk with bright and lively eyes, though without the trace of an expression on her face, and curtsied with the easy grace of which she alone was capable.

"... to speak to you with little hope of making any impression, as I have unfortunately had occasion to learn," said the principal as she jerked on the yarn, causing the ball of wool on the polished floor to spin and attract Meshcherskaya's attention. Raising her eyes, she went on: "I shall not repeat myself, nor shall I speak at great length."

Meshcherskaya was very fond of this unusually clean and large study, which was so wonderfully fragrant on frosty days with the smell of the gleaming tile stove and the fresh lily of the valley on the desk. She glanced at the young Tsar, whose full-length figure stood against the background of some brilliant hall, and at the straight part in the principal's neatly coiffed gray hair, and was expectantly silent.

"You are no longer a little girl," said the principal with much solemnity. She was becoming secretly annoyed.

"Yes, Madame," Meshcherskaya answered simply and almost gaily.

"But you are not yet a woman," said the principal with even more solemnity, her dull face turning slightly pinker. "First of all, what sort of hairdo is that? That's a woman's hairdo!"

"It isn't my fault, Madame, that I have nice hair," said Meshcherskaya, and slightly touched her beautifully done hair with both hands.

"Ah, that's it! Not your fault!" said the principal. "Not your fault how your hair is done, not your fault that you're wearing those expensive combs, not your fault that you are beggaring your parents by going about in slippers worth twenty rubles the pair! But I tell you again, you have completely lost sight of the fact that you are still nothing but a schoolgirl . . ."

At which point Meshcherskaya, no whit less simply and calmly than before, politely interrupted her:

"Forgive me, Madame, but you are making a mistake: I am a woman. And the person responsible for that is . . . do you know who? My father's friend and neighbor, and your own brother, Alexei Mikhailovich Malyutin. It happened last summer in the country . . ."

And it was a month after this conversation that a Cossack officer, ugly and commonplace in appearance, who had absolutely no connection with the level of society to which Olya Meshcherskaya belonged, shot her dead on the platform of a railroad station in the midst of a large crowd of people who had just arrived on the train. And Olya Meshcherskaya's unthinkable confession, which had so staggered the school principal, was proven correct in every detail: The officer stated to the interrogators that Meshcherskaya had led him on, that they had had intimate relations, that she had promised to marry him, and then, on the day of the murder, when she was at the station seeing him off to Novocherkassk, she had suddenly told him that it had never entered her head to love him, that she had only been making fun of him with all that talk about marriage, and then she let him read the page in her diary where she described the encounter with Malyutin.

"I read that page right there on the platform—she was walking around waiting for me to finish—and then I shot her," said the officer. "I've still got it with me—just look at what she wrote there under July 10th last year."

This is what was written in the diary:

"It's after one o'clock in the morning now. I fell fast asleep and then woke up again almost at once . . . I'm a woman now! Papa, Mama, and Tolya all went to town and

I stayed here by myself. I was so glad to be all alone! This morning I walked in the garden, then across the field and in the woods, and I felt like I was the only person in the whole world, and I had the most beautiful thoughts I ever had in my life. And I had lunch all alone, too, and then played the piano for an hour, and the music made me feel like I was going to live forever and be the happiest person that ever was. Then I took a nap in Papa's study, but Katya woke me up at four o'clock to tell me Alexei Mikhailovich had come. I was very glad to see him and invite him in and talk to him and all. He was driving a pair of his beautiful horses and they stood hitched near the veranda the whole time, and he stayed on because it had been raining and he wanted to wait till the road dried out a little later. He said he was sorry he hadn't caught Papa at home, and he was very funny and pretended to be my sweetheart and joked about how he'd been in love with me for ages. When we took a walk in the garden before tea the day had cleared up again, but the garden was dripping wet, but it looked nice in the sun even though it had gotten quite cool, and he took me by the arm and said he was Faust with his Margarete. He's fifty-six but he's still very good looking and he always dresses so well—except I didn't like that cape he came in—and he uses an English cologne, and his eyes are very young and dark, but his beard—which is very nice, in two long parts—is completely silver. We had tea on the glassed-in veranda, and afterwards I felt sort of tired and lay down on the sofa and he smoked. Then he moved over and sat beside me and started saying all sorts of nice things to me again, and then he took my hand and started looking at it and kissing it. I covered my face with a silk handkerchief and he kissed me on the lips several times right through the handkerchief ... I don't know how it could have happened, I must have gone out of my mind—never did I think I was that kind! There's only one way out for me now ... He makes me so disgusted, I'll never get over this!"

These April days the town seems so clean and dry and the cobbles so white that it's easy and pleasant to walk over them. Every Sunday, after the service, a small woman dressed in mourning, in black kid gloves and carrying an umbrella with an ebony handle, walks along Cathedral Street toward the edge of town. She takes the paved road around the dirty square where there are a lot of smoke-blackened smithies and a fresh wind blows in from the fields, and she goes on between the monastery and the jail, where you can see the cloudy sky and the fields gray in the early spring, and then to where you pick your way through the puddles standing near the monastery wall and turn left and see what looks like a big, low garden with a white wall around it and over the gate a painting of the Assumption of the Blessed Virgin. The small woman crosses herself quickly and continues on her usual way along the main path. When she reaches the bench opposite the oaken cross she sits there in the cold spring wind for an hour, sometimes two hours, until her feet in their light shoes and her hands in the thin leather gloves are completely numb. Listening to the spring birds singing sweetly even in the cold, listening to the porcelain wreath clattering in the wind, she sometimes thinks she would give half her life if only her eyes had never beheld this dead wreath. This wreath, this mound of earth, the oaken cross! Is it possible that beneath them lies the girl whose eyes shine so deathlessly from the porcelain medallion on the cross, and how can one thought encompass both this pure gaze and the horror now linked to the name of Olya Meshcherskaya?—But in the depths of her soul this small woman, like all who are passionately devoted to some dream, is happy.

This woman is Olya Meshcherskaya's teacher, middle-aged and unmarried, who has for long dwelt in the fantasy world that replaces, for her, real life. The first to fill this fantasy was her brother, a junior naval officer who was poor and completely ordinary; she bound her very soul to him and to his future, which for some reason she expected to be brilliant. After he was killed at Mukden, she strove to convince herself that her daily toil was in the service of some lofty ideal. The death of Olya Meshcherskaya captivated her and she began to live a new dream. Now it was Olya Meshcherskaya who obsessed all her thoughts and feelings. She comes on every holiday to visit the grave, fixes her eyes by the hour on the oaken cross, and recalls Olya Meshcherskaya's pale little face among the flowers in her coffin—and recalls something else, something she once overheard. Once, during the noon recess, Olya Meshcherskaya was strolling about in the school park with her best friend, a tall, stout girl named Subbotina, and telling her something very, very, hurriedly:

"I read in one of Papa's books—he's got all these funny old books—I read about what it takes for a woman to be beautiful. . . . There was so much, I've forgotten half of it, of course, but anyway, there was dark eyes like boiling pitch. Honestly! It said 'boiling pitch'! And then eyelashes black as night, a gentle glow to the cheeks, a slender figure, arms longer than usual—how's that? 'longer than usual'!—small feet, a moderately large bosom, shapely legs, shell-pink knees, sloping shoulders—I practically learned a lot of it by heart it's so true!—but the main thing, do you know what that is? . . . Light breathing! And I've got it! Listen how I breathe . . . isn't that it?"

And now this light breathing has been wafted anew through the world, in this cloudy sky, in this cold spring wind.

(1916)

Nadezhda Teffi

(1872–1952)

"Teffi" is the pen name of Nadezhda Buchinskaya (née Lokhvitskaya). She started her career as a poet, but quickly found her true métier in the comic story, the form with which her name is inseparably associated. She was already wildly popular in pre-Revolutionary Russia—Nicholas II was one of her fans—and there were even brands of perfume and candy bearing her name. Like many another Petersburg writer, she welcomed the February Revolution but could not stomach the Bolsheviks. She emigrated in 1919 and found her place in literary history as *the* chronicler of Russian Paris, which practically belongs to her, as the Drones Club belongs to Wodehouse or the guys and dolls of Broadway to Damon Runyon.

Her popularity grew, if anything, in spite of the fact that her droll portrayal of the empty pretensions, fabricated pedigrees, and eternal gossiping of the émigré community had a distinctly sharp edge. Her emphasis on the sterility of exile existence was naturally very welcome to those in charge of Soviet propaganda, so she continued to be published (selectively) in Russia. In one of her feuilletons, a former general surveys the Place de la Concorde, admits that it is, of course, very nice—"but *ke-fer? fer-to ke?*" This subtly Russianized sigh—"*Que faire?*"—became something like the bleak, self-deprecating slogan of the Paris in which noblemen drove taxis and ladies of the manor got themselves up in gypsy garb to serve tea in restaurants and everyone wrote memoirs (which differed, said Teffi, in that some were written by hand, others on the typewriter).

Practically everything she wrote was published in newspapers. The necessity of having something ready every Sunday did not always allow for the fine-tuning of her effects, but even the pressure of the deadline and the limitations of space did not prevent Teffi from producing many of the classics of the Russian comic story. "Time" is such a bittersweet masterpiece.

TIME

It was an excellent restaurant, with shashlik, pelmeni, suckling pig, sturgeon, and an artistic program of entertainment. The artistic program was not limited to Russian numbers alone—to "Bast Shoes" and "Bublichki" and "Black Eyes." Among the performers were Negresses and Mexicans and Spaniards and gentlemen of the indeterminate jazz tribe who sing incomprehensible nasal words in all languages while rolling their hips. Even avowedly Russian artists, after crossing themselves backstage, sang encores in French and English.

The dance numbers, which permitted the artists not to reveal their nationality, were performed by ladies with the most supernatural names: Takuza Iuka. Rutuf Yay-Yay. Hékama Yuya.

There were among them dusky, almost black, exotic women with elongated green eyes. There were rosy-golden blondes and fiery redheads with brown skin. Almost all of them, right down to the mulattoes, were Russian, of course. With our talents, even that isn't hard to achieve. "Our sister poverty" has taught us worse things.

The decor of the restaurant was chic. It is precisely this word that defined it best of all. Not luxurious, not magnificent, not elegant, but—chic.

Little colored lampshades, little fountains, green aquaria with goldfish set into the walls, carpets, the ceiling painted with incomprehensible things, among which one discerned now a bulging eye, now a lifted leg, now a pineapple, now a piece of nose with a monocle glued to it, now a lobster tail. It seemed to those sitting at the tables that all these things were falling on their heads, but apparently this was just what the artist had intended.

The help was courteous. They never said to latecomers: "Hold on. What are you shoving for when there ain't no seats? This ain't no streetcar."

The restaurant was frequented as much by foreigners as by Russians. One could often see some Frenchman or Englishman, who apparently had already been at this establishment, bring in some friends with him and, with the expression of a magician swallowing a piece of burning cotton, empty a glass of straight vodka into his mouth and then, his eyes bulging, stop it in his throat with a *pirozhok*. His friends would regard him as a courageous crank and, smiling suspiciously, would sniff at their glasses.

The French love to order *pirozhki*. For some reason they are amused by this word, which they always pronounce with the stress on the *o*. This is very strange and inexplicable. With all Russian words the French use the stress characteristic of their own language, on the last syllable. With all words except *pirozhki*, which of course requires that last-syllable stress.

Vava von Mersen, Musya Riewen, and Gogosya Livensky were sitting at a table. Gogosya moved in the highest circles, although only in their outer periphery; therefore, in spite of his sixty-five years, he still answered to the infantile nickname Gogosya.

Vava von Mersen, who had also long ago grown up to an elderly Varvara, had a head of tightly wound dry curls the color of tobacco, so thoroughly cured that, were one to cut them off and chop them up fine, they could be used to fill the pipe of some undemanding skipper of the merchant fleet.

Musya Riewen was youngish, a mere child who had just been divorced for the first time, melancholy, sentimental, and delicate—which didn't prevent her from gulping down glass after glass of vodka, with no effect perceptible either to herself or to others.

Gogosya was an enchanting *raconteur*. He knew everyone and talked about everyone loudly and at length. Occasionally, at risqué moments, he switched, in the Russian manner, to French, partly so that "the servants wouldn't understand," partly because a French indecency is piquant while a Russian one offends the ear.

Gogosya knew just what to order in which restaurant, greeted all *maîtres d'hôtel* with a handshake, knew the names of the chefs, and remembered what he ate, when, and where.

He loudly applauded the successful numbers on the program, and shouted in a lordly bass:

"Atta boy! Good show!"

Or:

"Good for you, sweetheart!"

He knew many of the customers, gestured to them cordially, and sometimes hooted so the whole room could hear, "*Comment ça va?* Is Anna Petrovna *en bonne santé?*"

In a word, he was a marvelous customer, who filled three-quarters of the premises all by himself.

Opposite, by the other wall, a table was occupied by an interesting group. Three ladies. All three more than middle-aged. To put it bluntly—they were old.

The one in charge of the whole affair was small, compact, her head screwed directly into her bust, without the slightest hint of a neck. A large diamond brooch rested against her double chin. Her grey, excellently styled hair was covered with a flirtatious black hat, her cheeks were powdered with pinkish powder, her very modestly rouged mouth revealed bluish porcelain teeth. A splendid silver fox fluffed above her ears. The old lady was very elegant.

The other two were uninteresting and had evidently been invited by the smartly dressed old lady.

She chose both the wine and the courses very carefully, while her guests, obviously knowing a thing or two, also expressed their opinions sharply and defended their positions. They all attacked their food convivially, with the fire of genuine temperament. They drank sensibly and with concentration. They quickly became flushed. The main old lady filled out all over, even turned slightly bluish, and her eyes bulged and became glassy. But all three were in a happily aroused state, like Africans who have just skinned an elephant, when their joy demands that they continue dancing but their full stomachs fling them to the ground.

"What amusing old ladies," said Vava von Mersen, directing her lorgnette toward the merry company.

"Yes," Gogosya ecstatically joined in. "That's a happy age. They don't have to watch their figures, they don't have to conquer anyone or please anyone. If you have money and a good stomach, it's the happiest age. And the most carefree. You don't have to plan your life any more. Everything's been accomplished."

"Look at that one, the main one," said Musya Riewen, contemptuously lowering the corners of her mouth. "A bouncy cow, that's all she is. And I can just see that's the way she's been all her life."

"Life's probably been very good to her," Gogosya said approvingly. "Live and let live. She's merry, healthy, rich. Maybe she wasn't even bad looking once. Now, of course, it's hard to tell. A lump of pink fat."

"I think she must have been stingy, greedy, and stupid," Vava von Mersen put in. "See how she eats and drinks. A sensual animal."

"But still, someone probably loved her, and even married her," Musya Riewen drawled pensively.

"Someone simply married her for her money. You're always imagining something romantic which just doesn't occur in real life."

Tyulya Rovtsyn interrupted the conversation. He was from the periphery of the same circles as Gogosya, and therefore to the age of sixty-three preserved the pet name of Tyulya. Tyulya was also sweet and pleasant, but poorer than Gogosya, and everything about him was played in a more minor key. After chatting for a few minutes, he got up, looked around, and approached the merry old ladies. They greeted him happily, like an old acquaintance, and made him sit down at their table.

Meanwhile the entertainment program was following its normal course.

A young man came out on the stage, licked his lips like a cat who's eaten some chicken meat, and, to the howling and syncopated tinkling of the jazz band, performed an English song with a sort of pleadingly feminine cooing. The words of the song were sentimental and even melancholy, the tune monotonously doleful. But the jazz did its job without going into these details. And it sounded as if a sad gentleman were tearfully recounting his failures in love, while some madman was wildly jumping, roaring, and whistling and beating the tearful gentleman on the head with a brass tray.

Then two Spanish ladies danced to the same music. One of them uttered a shriek while running off, which considerably raised the spirits of the audience.

Then a Russian singer with a French name came out. At first he sang a French song and then, as an encore, an old Russian song:

> Your humble slave, I'll go down on my knees,
> I do not struggle, ruinous fate, with thee.
> I'll bear disgrace, bitter indignities
> All for the joy of having you with me.

"Listen! Listen." Gogosya suddenly pricked up his ears. "Oh, how many memories it brings back! There's such a terrible tragedy connected with that song. Poor

Kolya Izubov ... Maria Nikolaevna von Rutte ... the count ..."

> Whene'er my gaze encounters your dear eyes
> I'm in the grip of tortured ecstasy ...

the singer uttered languidly.

"I knew all of them," Gogosya recalled. "The song was written by Kolya Izubov. Charming music. He was very talented. A sailor ..."

> And so are mirrored the e'er blessèd stars
> In the turbulent, unfathomable sea ...

the singer continued.

"How enchanting she was! Both Kolya and the count fell madly in love with her. And Kolya challenged the count to a duel. The count killed him. Maria Nikolaevna's husband was in the Caucasus at the time. He returned, and there was this scandal, and Maria Nikolaevna was nursing the dying Kolya. The count, seeing that Maria Nikolaevna was with Kolya all the time, put a bullet through his brain and left a death note for her, saying that he knew of her love for Kolya. The letter, of course, fell into her husband's hands, and he demanded a divorce. Maria Nikolaevna loved him passionately and was literally not to blame in any way. But von Rutte didn't believe her; he took an assignment in the Far East and left her. She was in despair, suffered madly, wanted to enter a convent. After six years her husband sent for her to come to him in Shanghai. She flew there, reborn. She found him near death. They lived together for only two months. He understood everything, he had loved only her all that time, and had been in torment. All in all, it's such a tragedy that it's simply amazing how that little woman could live through it all. At this point I lost sight of her. I heard only that she got married, and her husband was killed in the war. It seems that she perished also. Killed during the

Revolution. Tyulya over there also knew her well, even languished over her in his time."

In the tu-u-urbulent, unfathomable sea.

"A remarkable woman. There are none like her nowadays."

Vava von Mersen and Musya Riewen maintained an injured silence.

"There are interesting women in any period," Vava von Mersen finally said through clenched teeth.

But Gogosya only patted her on the hand mockingly and good-naturedly.

"Look," said Musya, "your friend is talking about you with his old ladies."

Indeed, both Tyulya and his ladies were looking directly at Gogosya. Tyulya got up and approached his friend, and the main old lady nodded her head.

"Gogosya!" said Tyulya. "It turns out that Maria Nikolaevna remembers you very well. I told her your name, and she recalled you right away and is very glad to see you."

Gogosya was taken aback. "What Maria Nikolaevna?"

"Madame Nelogina. Well—the former von Rutte. Have you really forgotten?"

"Good Lord!" Gogosya grew agitated. "You know, we were just talking about her. Why, where is she?"

"Let's go over to her for a minute," Tyulya hurried him. "Your dear ladies will excuse you."

Gogosya jumped up, looking around in amazement.

"Why, where is she?"

"Why, over there. I was sitting with her just now.... We're coming, we're coming!" he shouted.

And the main old lady nodded her head and, merrily parting her strong fat cheeks with her painted mouth, gleamed affably with her even row of blue porcelain teeth.

(*1947?*)

Alexander Blok

(1880-1921)

There are numerous Russians for whom Blok is the greatest poet after Pushkin. He mesmerized his contemporaries not only by his art but also by his very appearance: no one since Byron had been endowed with a more "poetical" exterior. He was anything but an intellectual (in our sense), and in this respect was the antithesis of his sometime friend Andrei Bely (see p. 79). An intuitive poet, attentive to the least velleities of his inner nature, Blok considered the cerebral analysis of poetry to be a species of philistinism. He was a master of technique, and controlled every tonality of which Russian is capable—from the soiled street language of popular ditties to the ultimate asepsis of classical form—but he did not want to talk about it.

Blok might well have become a thoroughgoing intellectual from his biological inheritance and his surroundings. His father, estranged from the family, was a professor of law in Warsaw. His maternal grandfather was a famous scientist and rector of the University of Saint Petersburg. The household in which he grew up was a gathering place for scientific and artistic genius, and the poet's wife was the daughter of a family friend, the great chemist Mendeleyev.

Whatever his status in Russian literature as a whole, Blok is unarguably the greatest of those who called themselves Symbolists. And among that group he is perhaps one of the easiest to understand on a superficial level, for he had but one *idée maîtresse*—that of a female figure who underwent several metamorphoses, none of them terribly difficult to decipher in our psychologically overprivileged age. The first is named in the title of the book that made Blok's fame, *Verses about the Beautiful Lady* (1904). In typically Symbolist fashion, the beautiful lady in question was both a flesh-and-blood woman and also "Sophia," the female emblem of divine wisdom. His fetching good looks notwithstanding, Blok had scant success with the living prototype (or with any other woman), so the second feminine image to dominate his poetry was that of the whore—depicted in the poem "The Stranger," reprinted here. It is a very ladylike whore, to be sure, and she is, like her respectable sister, a conduit to other worlds. The antithesis of lady versus whore was resolved by the synthesis of the third and final female image, that of Mother Russia herself. For Blok, she combined all the elements of the first two. The ambivalent relationship with his native land, adoring and loathing, produced poems based for the most part on her medieval past; and the poems, such as "On the Field of Kulikovo," are mystically evocative and powerful beyond anything not actually a part of that past.

The work that many deem to be Blok's masterpiece is, however, resolutely contemporary. "The Twelve" is a long narrative mélange of gutter language and ethereal beauty depicting the progress through Revolutionary Petrograd of twelve Bolshevik soldiers—a drunken, lustful, and homicidal rabble—whipped by the wind and snow of the new era and sweeping aside the fat priests and capitalist exploiters of the old regime. As if their number alone were not sufficiently indicative of the apostles, Blok provides in the last lines of the poem the actual figure of Jesus, in his guise as the Man of Sorrows, who is ambiguously either leader or target.

Needless to say, this pleased almost no one. Opponents of the Revolution were outraged at the mere suggestion that Christ might be, however mistily, its instigator, and the atheists of the new reality wanted no truck with the hated deism that they saw as one of the instruments of the old tyranny. Few episodes in Blok's biography reveal his essential nature more clearly than his reaction to this nearly universal disapprobation of "The Twelve." He undertook a second look at the end of his poem only to report, helplessly, that the figure in the crown of thorns was indeed Christ. Nothing to be done: It simply *was* Christ. This faith that the poem was the external notation of immanent fact characterized all the Symbolists, though none so strongly as Blok.

"The Twelve" is a great poem that complacently furnishes any political meaning enthusiasts demand of it. As for Blok himself, it is clear that he welcomed what he supposed the Revolution to portend. He was soon disabused. His death in August 1921 was no less "mystical" than his life, and inanition is probably the suitably vague and suggestive name for the disease that killed him. Blok complained that he no longer heard the music from which his poems had always arisen, that harmony was gone. In the great oration he delivered in February of that year, on the eighty-fourth anniversary of Pushkin's death, Blok declared that it was not the bullet of D'Anthes that had killed Russia's greatest writer, but the lack of air. He was speaking, as poets generally do, of himself.

A GIRL WAS SINGING

A girl was singing in the choir with fervour
of all who have known exile and distress,
of all the vessels that have left the harbour,
of all who have forgotten happiness.

Her voice soared up to the dome. Glistening,
a sunbeam brushed her shoulder in its flight,
and from the darkness all were listening
to the white dress singing in the beam of light.

It seemed to everyone that happiness
would come back, that the vessels all were safe,
that those who had known exile and distress
had rediscovered a radiant life.

The voice was beautiful, the sunbeam slender,
but up by the holy gates, under the dome,
a boy at communion wept to remember
that none of them would ever come home.

(1905)

THE STRANGER

These evenings over the restaurants
the air is hot and strangely cloying,
and shouts drift from the drunkards' haunts
on the putrid breath of spring.

Far off, over dusty side-streets can be seen—
over snug villas mile on mile—
the golden glint of a baker's sign,
and one can hear the children wail.

And every evening, past the level-
crossing, the jocular swells,
bowlers tilted at a rakish angle,
stroll between ditches with their girls.

Over the lake the rowlocks scraping
and women screeching can be heard,
and in a sky inured to everything
the moon leers down like a drunkard.

Each evening my one and only friend,
reflected at my glass's brink,
like me is fuddled and constrained
by the thick, mysterious drink.

And next to us, at the tables beside
our table, somnolent waiters pass
and drunks to one another, rabbit-eyed,
call out '*In vino veritas.*'

Each evening, at the appointed moment
(or is this only in a dream?)
a girl's shape in a silken garment
shows dark against the window's steam.

And slowly between the drunkards weaving,
as always unescorted, there
she sits down by the window, leaving
a mist of perfume in the air.

And a breath of ancient legends gathers
about her silk dress as it swings,
about her hat with its mourning feathers,
and her slender hand with its rings.

And rooted there by this curious presence,
I search the shadowy veil once more
and through it see an enchanted distance
beyond an enchanted shore.

Vague confidences in my ear are loosed,
and the sun is suddenly mine,
and every crevice of my soul is sluiced
and flooded by the sticky wine.

And now the nodding ostrich-feather plume
begins to hypnotize my brain,
and eyes that are unfathomable bloom
blue on a distant shore again.

Deep in my soul there lies a treasure;
the only key to it is mine!
And you are right, you drunken monster!
I know now: there is truth in wine.

(*1906*)

Andrei Bely

(1880–1934)

Born Boris Nikolaevich Bugaev into a family of distinguished intellectuals, Bely took his pseudonym (which means "Andrew White") in 1902 when he began to publish in the milieu of the Symbolists, who were still notorious for the attention-getting outrageousness of their earliest publications. Bely was one of the most prodigiously gifted, fecund, and innovative writers in all of Russian literature. As a poet he was merely excellent; as a literary theoretician he completely renovated the perception of Gogol and elaborated a scheme of Russian versification that is still a source of fruitful dispute; as a novelist he all but reinvented Russian prose and wrote what is incomparably the most significant single work of modern Russian fiction, *Petersburg*. It appeared in English in 1959, in a deeply flawed and misleading translation (which is, alas, still available). In 1978 an excellent, fully annotated translation by Robert A. Maguire and John E. Malmstad was published. Allowing for the usual delay in such matters, the student of modern letters must now add *Petersburg* to the works by Flaubert, Kafka, Proust, and Joyce that it is essential to know.

Bely's masterpiece began to appear in 1913, came out as a book in 1916, and was so completely revised by the author in 1922 that the result was practically a new book. One delights in the reliable factualness of such a statement, for almost every other utterance that one can make about *Petersburg*, especially in so brief a note as this, is wholly inadequate when it is not downright false (in the sense that a contradictory statement might be made with equal assurance).

For example: The basic plot of *Petersburg* is quite simple—a revolutionary organization targets a reactionary government minister for assassination and entrusts his son with planting the bomb. That is "true," but in so limited a sense as to be almost useless. It assumes, for instance, that *plot* has the same meaning as it has in speaking of, say, *Anna Karenina*. By separating "government minister" from "son," one leads the reader to believe that they are entirely distinct characters, but they are not. And it is, of course, my statement of the plot that is simple, for nothing at all in this multidimensional prose labyrinth is simple.

Two excerpts from this most unexcerptable of novels follow in the Maguire-Malmstad translation. They convey a sense of Bely's constantly shifting manner, if only some of the suspenseful excitement in the bizarre tale. In the first excerpt, one encounters a passage of self-consciously lyrical nature writing, which is, however, dense with reference to the real Petersburg, the actual events of the times (Russia's defeat in Manchuria at the hands of Japan, the peasants' burning of manor houses), and precise meteorological reports, which Bely carefully researched. The central figure is that of the government minister who is to be blown up—a condign fate (being scattered into space) for a little monster who, in the immensity of Russia, suffers from an emblematic agoraphobia. Recalling snatches of Pushkin is one of the ways by which he anchors himself within reliable psychic limits.

In the second excerpt we find the same figure receding or trying to recede into one of his interior spaces, a dream, which includes another dream. Visual and phonic notations from the perimeter of consciousness are punctuated by the ossified language of bureaucratic documents. The angular geometry of his room, the angular folding of his clothes, and the angular motions of calisthenics form his safe and comfortable routine, which dissolves in the phantasmagoria of his flickering awareness. The narrative voice talks to itself, there are voices off, there are unassigned sounds, and the son, the assassin, comes home.

From PETERSBURG

I
Arguments in the Streets Became More Frequent

Those were foggy days, strange days. Noxious October marched on with frozen gait. It hung out dank mists in the south. October blew off the golden woodland whisper, and that whisper fell to earth, and there fell the rustling aspen crimson, to wind and chase at the feet, and whish, plaiting yellow-red scatterings of leaves. And that sweet chirruping, which in September swims in a leafy wave, had not swum for a long time. And now the tomtit hopped forlorn in branches black, which all autumn long send forth their whistling from woods, gardens, and parks.

Now an icy tree-felling wind was coming upon us in clouds of tin. But all believed in spring: a popular cabinet minister had indicated that spring was coming.

Now the ploughmen had ceased to scratch at their lands, and abandoning their harrows and wooden ploughs, they assembled in small clusters by their huts. They talked and argued, and then suddenly, all of one mind, moved on the master's colonnaded house. Through all the long nights the sky shone bloody with the glow of conflagrations in the countryside.

Yes! Thus it was in the villages.

Thus it was in the towns as well. In workshops, in print shops, in hairdressers', in dairies, in squalid little taverns, the same prating shady type was always hanging around. With a shaggy fur hat from the fields of bloodstained Manchuria pulled down over his eyes, and with a Browning from somewhere or other stuck in his side pocket, he thrust badly printed leaflets into people's hands.

Everyone feared something, hoped for something, poured into the streets, gathered in crowds, and again dispersed. In Archangelsk, in Nizhne-Kolymsk, in Saratov, in Petersburg, in Moscow everyone acted the same way: everyone feared something, hoped for something, poured into the streets, gathered in crowds and again dispersed.

Petersburg is surrounded by a ring of many-chimneyed factories.

A many-thousand swarm plods towards them in the morning, and the suburbs are all aswarm. All the factories were then in a state of terrible unrest. The workers had turned into prating shady types. Amidst them circulated Brownings. And something else again.

The agitation that ringed Petersburg then began penetrating even to the very centers of Petersburg. It first seized the islands, then crossed the Liteiny and Nikolaevsky Bridges. On Nevsky Prospect circulated a human myriapod. However, the composition of the myriapod kept changing; and an observer could now note the appearance of a shaggy black fur hat from the fields of bloodstained Manchuria. There was a sharp drop in the percentage of passing top hats. Now were heard the disturbing antigovernment cries of street urchins running at full tilt from the railway station to the Admiralty waving gutter rags.

Those were foggy days, strange days. Noxious October marched on. Dust whirled through the city in dun brown vortexes, and the rustling crimson fell submissively at the feet to wind and chase at the feet, and whish, plaiting yellow-red scatterings of words from leaves.

Such were the days. Have you ever slipped off at night into the vacant plots of city outskirts to hear the same importunate note "oo?" Oooo-oooo-ooo: such was the sound in that space. But was it a sound? It was the sound of some other world. And it attained a rare strength and clarity, "Oooo-oooo-ooo" sounded softly in the suburban fields of

Moscow, Petersburg, Saratov. But no factory whistle blew; there was no wind; and the dogs remained silent.

Have you heard this October song: of the year nineteen hundred and five?

Beloved Delvig Calls for Me

His hand resting on the marble banister, Apollon Apollonovich caught his toe in the carpeting, and—stumbled. His step slowed involuntarily. Quite naturally, his eyes lingered on an enormous portrait of the Minister.

A shiver ran down Apollon Apollonovich's spine: the place was badly heated.

He had a fear of space.

The landscape of the countryside actually frightened him. Beyond the snows, beyond the ice, and beyond the jagged line of the forest the blizzard would come up. Out there, by a stupid accident, he had nearly frozen to death.

That had happened some fifty years ago.

While he had been freezing to death, someone's cold fingers, forcing their way into his breast, had harshly stroked his heart, and an icy hand had led him along. He had climbed the rungs of his career with that same incredible expanse always before his eyes. There, from there an icy hand beckoned. Measureless immensity flew on: the Empire of Russia.

Apollon Apollonovich Ableukhov ensconced himself behind city walls for many years, hating the orphaned distances of the provinces, the wisps of smoke from tiny villages, and the jackdaw. Only once had he risked transecting these distances by express train: on an official mission from Petersburg to Tokyo.

Apollon Apollonovich did not discuss his stay in Japan with anyone. He used to say to the Minister:

"Russia is an icy plain. It is roamed by wolves!"

And the Minister would look at him, stroking his well-groomed gray mustache with a white hand. And he said nothing, and sighed. On the completion of his official duties he had been intending to ...

But he died.

And Apollon Apollonovich was utterly alone. Behind him the ages stretched into immeasurable expanses. Ahead of him an icy hand revealed immeasurable expanses.

Immeasurable expanses flew to meet him.

Oh Rus, Rus!

Is it you who have set the winds, storms, and snows howling across the steppe? It seemed to the senator that from a mound a voice was calling him. Only hungry wolves gather in packs out there.

Undoubtedly the senator had been developing a fear of space.

The illness had been aggravated since the time of that tragic death, and the image of his friend visited him night after night, and through all the long nights kept looking at him with a velvety gaze and kept stroking the well-groomed gray mustache with his hand:

> He's gone, and Rus he has deserted,
> The land he raised aloft. . . .

That fragment of verse arose whenever he, Apollon Apollonovich, traversed that hall.

And still another fragment arose:

> My turn has come, in very truth . . .
> Beloved Delvig calls for me,
> The comrade of my lively youth,
> The comrade of my youth despondent.
> The comrade of my youthful song,
> Of feasts, and purest dedication.
> To where familiar shades now throng
> His spirit's gone for all the ages.

Recalling these fragments, he ran out, with particular preciseness, to extend his fingers to the petitioners.

II
The Senator's Second Space

Apollon Apollonovich's bedroom: four perpendicular walls and the single gash of a window with a lace curtain. The sheets, towels, and pillowcases were distinguished by their whiteness. The valet sprayed the sheets with an atomizer.

Instead of perfume, Apollon Apollonovich recognized only triple-strength eau de cologne.

Apollon Apollonovich always undressed without help.

He would throw off his dressing gown briskly. In a most precise manner he would fold and place on a chair his little jacket and his miniature trousers. And in his underwear, just before going to bed, he would firm up his body with calisthenics.

He would fling his arms and legs apart, and twist his torso, squatting up to twelve and more times. Lying on his back, Apollon Apollonovich would set about working his legs.

He resorted to exercises especially on the days when he suffered from hemorrhoids.

Afterwards he would pull up the blanket in order to embark upon a journey, for sleep is a journey.

Apollon Apollonovich did the same today.

Completely covered up (except for the tip of his nose), he hung suspended over a timeless void.

"What do you mean a void? What about the walls, the floor? And so forth?"

Apollon Apollonovich always saw *two* spaces: one, material (the walls of the rooms, of the carriage), the other, not exactly spiritual (it was also material). Now, how should I put it: over Ableukhov's head, Ableukhov's eyes saw bright patches and dots of light, and iridescent dancing spots with spinning centers. They obscured the boundaries of the spaces. Thus one space swarmed in the other space; you know, the kind that seems to be made of Christmas tree tinsel, of little stars and of little sparks.

He would close his eyes and open them. And the misty

spots and stars, like foam on bubbling blackness, would unexpectedly and suddenly form into a distinct picture: of a cross, a polyhedron, a swan, a light-filled pyramid. And all would fly apart.

Apollon Apollonovich had his very own secret: a world of contours, tremors, sensations—a *universe* of strange phenomena just before sleep. Apollon Apollonovich, while falling asleep, would remember all the inapprehensibilities of the past, rustlings, little crystallographic figures, stars racing through the gloom (one such star kept drenching the senator with golden boiling water, and shivers ran over his skull). He would remember everything he had seen the day before so as not to remember it again.

Just before the last instant of diurnal consciousness Apollon Apollonovich, while falling asleep, would notice that the bubbling vortex suddenly formed into a corridor stretching off into an immeasurable expanse. What was most surprising was that the corridor began from his head, i.e., it was an endless continuation of his head, the sinciput of which suddenly opened up into an immeasurable expanse. Thus the old senator, just before falling asleep, would get the impression that he was looking not with his eyes but with the center of his very head, i.e., he, Apollon Apollonovich, was not Apollon Apollonovich, but *something* lodged in the brain, looking out from there, from the brain. With the opening up of the sinciput, something could run along the corridor *until it plunged into the abyss*.

That is what the senator's *second space* was.

His head under the blanket, he now hung suspended from the bed. Now the lacquered floor fell away from the legs of the bed into the unknown, but a distant clatter reached the senator's ears, like the clatter of small pounding hooves.

And the clatter was drawing near.

A strange, very strange, extremely strange circumstance: he cocked an ear at the moon, and yes: very likely someone was knocking.

He stuck out his head.

A star moved toward the sinciput and promptly disappeared. The panels of the parquet floor instantly rose up from the abyss to meet the legs of the iron bed. And Apollon Apollonovich, tiny and white, resembling a plucked chicken, suddenly rested his yellow heel on the rug.

And he ran out into the corridor.

The moon illuminated the rooms.

In his undershirt, a lighted candle in his hands, he journeyed forth into the rooms. Trailing after his troubled master was the bulldog with his little docked tail, jangling his collar and breathing heavily through his pug nose.

Like a flat lid, the hairy chest heaved in deep wheezes. And a pale green ear hearkened. And a pier glass gave back a strange reflection of the senator: his arms and chest were swathed in blue satin. The satin gave off a metallic glint. Apollon Apollonovich found himself in armor, like a little knight. From his hands protruded not a candle but a luminous phenomenon.

Apollon Apollonovich plucked up his courage and rushed into the hall. The clatter came from there.

"Tk-tk . . . tk-tk-tk. . . ."

"According to just what article of the Code of Laws?"

As he shouted this out, he saw that the phlegmatic bulldog was breathing heavily and peaceably beside him; but—what effrontery!—from the hall came a shout:

"According to an emergency regulation!"

Indignant at this reply, he rushed into the hall.

The luminous phenomenon was melting away in his little fist. It flowed between his fingers like air; it came to rest at his feet in a little ray. The clatter was the clicking of the tongue of some worthless Mongol with a face he had already seen during his stay in Tokyo. Nonetheless, it was Nikolai Apollonovich: seen in Tokyo. Apollon Apollonovich did not want to understand this. He rubbed his eyes with his little fists (two points rubbed one against the other—the space of the hand and the space of the face). And the Mongol (Nikolai Apollonovich) was approaching with a mercenary motive.

The senator shouted a second time:
"According to just what regulation?
"And what paragraph?"
Space replied:
"There are neither paragraphs nor regulations!"

And unknowing, unfeeling, suddenly bereft of weight, of the very sensation of his body, he lifted the space of his pupils upward (tactile sensation could not tell him definitely that his eyes had been lifted upward by him, for the sense of corporeality had been thrown off by him)—in the direction of where the sinciput was located. And he saw there was no sinciput. There, where heavy bones compress the brain, where sight no longer exists, there Apollon Apollonovich saw in Apollon Apollonovich only a gaping circular breach (in place of the sinciput). The breach was a blue circle. At the fateful moment when according to his calculations the Mongol (imprinted on his consciousness but no longer visible) was stealing toward him, something, with a roar like the wind in a chimney, began rapidly pulling his consciousness out through the blue sincipital breach: into that which lies beyond.

Something scandalous had taken place (and his consciousness noted that there had already been something similar but he could not recollect when). Something scandalous had taken place; a wind had blown Apollon Apollonovich out of Apollon Apollonovich.

Apollon Apollonovich flew out through the circular breach, into darkness, above his own head (which looked like the planet *earth*), and—he flew apart into sparks.

There was pretemporal gloom; and consciousness swarmed—not, for example, a universal consciousnes, but consciousness, pure and simple.

Putting forth two sensations, consciousness now turned back. They descended like arms, and sensed: a form of some kind (reminiscent of the bottom of a bathtub), filled with stinking abomination. The sensations began splashing about in the bathtub with the dungy water. The sensations now stuck to the vessel. Consciousness struggled to break away, but the sensations were pulling a heavy something.

And consciousness saw that very thing it inhabited: a little old yellow man. He was resting his yellow heels on a rug.

Consciousness proved to be the little old man himself. From his bed the little old man was listening closely to the distant clatter.

And Apollon Apollonovich understood: his journey through the corridor, through the hall, through his head had been only a dream.

And hardly had this thought occurred to him when he woke up: a double dream!

And he was not sitting but lying down, his head under the blanket. The clatter turning out to be a slamming door.

Nikolai Apollonovich had returned home.

"I see. . .

"I see. . .

"Fine."

Except something was wrong with his back: a fear of being touched on the spine. Was this the beginning of: tabes dorsalis?

(1916)

Evgeni Zamyatin

(1884-1937)

The fact that Zamyatin was not fully rehabilitated in Russia until after the demise of the USSR is testimony to the pain that he must cause tyrants and bureaucrats of any persuasion, left or right. In his theoretical as well as in his imaginative works, Zamyatin promulgated with monomaniacal passion his *idée maîtresse:* life, energy, heresy versus death, entropy, dogma. The notion of never-ending revolution, the duty to dissent, the primacy of messy, awkward, natural human inclinations over the neatness of sanitary government regulations—these are the positions not of an economic, military, or political enemy, but of an ideological enemy, the most dangerous of all.

Zamyatin was that rarest of creatures, a practical man of the world, a qualified engineer and scientist, and at the same time one of Russia's most gifted theoreticians and practitioners of the art of writing. The comparison with Vladimir Nabokov (see p. 363) is irresistible. Zamyatin's original passion for the opposition at the base of much of his thought (energy versus entropy) seems to have grown out of his biography of Julius Robert von Mayer, the father of thermodynamic theory. His ideas appear with his customary succinct force in the most famous of his essays, "On Literature, Revolution, Entropy, and So On." *We*, his masterpiece and a forerunner of Orwell's *1984* and Huxley's *Brave New World*, depicts a facet of the antiutopia where entropy (in social if not in physical terms) has reached perfection.

The short story "The Cave" reveals Zamyatin's human sympathy for two helpless and decent old people whose lack of that form of thermal energy supplied by a small iron stove drives them to crime and suicide. As in much of his work, two historical eras are depicted with meaningful simultaneity: The desolate capital of Russia in the starved aftermath of revolution and civil war is painted as though it were the Ice Age habitat of prehuman troglodytes.

THE CAVE

Glaciers, mammoths, wastes. Black, nocturnal cliffs, vaguely like houses; in the cliffs—caves. And there is no telling what creature trumpets at night on the rocky path among the cliffs and, sniffing the path, raises clouds of powdered snow. It may be a gray-trunked mammoth, it may be the wind, and it may be the wind is nothing but the glacial roar of some supermammoth. One thing is clear: it is winter. And you must clench your teeth tightly to keep them from chattering, and you must split wood with a stone ax, and each night carry your fire from cave to cave, deeper and deeper, and huddle closer in more of those shaggy hides.

At night among the cliffs where ages ago stood Petersburg, a gray-trunked mammoth was roaming. And muffled up in hides and coats and blankets and rags, the cave dwellers were constantly retreating from cave to cave. On the feast of the Intercession of the Holy Virgin Martin Martinych and Masha shut up the study; three weeks later they moved out of the dining room and entrenched themselves in the bedroom. They could retreat no farther: there they must withstand the siege or die.

In the troglodytic Petersburg bedroom all was as it had been in Noah's ark not long ago—the clean and the unclean in diluvial promiscuity: Martin Martinych's desk, books, stone-age cakes of ceramic appearance, Scriabin opus 74, a flatiron, five potatoes lovingly scrubbed white, nickel-plated bedsprings, an ax, a chiffonier, firewood. And in the center of this universe was its god, a short-legged, rusty-red, squat, greedy cave god: the iron stove.

The god roared mightily. In the dark cave the great miracle of fire was wrought. The humans, Martin Martinych and Masha, silently, gratefully, piously stretched out their arms to him. For one hour it was spring in the cave; for one hour hides, claws, tusks were shed, and through the frozen brain-crust sprang green shoots—thoughts:

"Mart, you have forgotten that tomorrow . . . Yes, I see you *have* forgotten."

In October, when the leaves are already yellowed, withered, wilted, blue-eyed days may occur. If you tilt your head on such a day so as not to see the earth, you may believe that there is still joy, it is still summer. And it was the same with Masha: if you shut your eyes and only listened to her, you could believe that she was the same, that in a moment she was going to laugh, get up from her bed, hug you; and only an hour ago her voice had sounded like a knife on glass—not her voice at all, not she. . . .

"Oh, Mart, Mart! How everything . . . You didn't used to forget. The twenty-ninth: St. Mary's Day . . ."*

The iron god was still roaring. There was no light: it wouldn't come until ten. The shaggy dark reaches of the cave were swaying. Martin Martinych, squatting (tie yourself in a knot, tightly—still more tightly!), his head tilted, kept looking at the October sky, so as not to see the withered, wilted lips. And Masha——

"You see, Mart, if we could start the stove in the morning tomorrow, so that all day it would be the way it is

* Masha is a familiar form of Maria. Russians were usually named for saints, and the name day was celebrated, rather than the birthday.

now! What do you say? How much is left? About a cord in the study?"

It was ages since Masha had been strong enough to make her way to the Polar study, and she did not know that . . . Tighten the knot, tighter!

"A cord? I think . . ."

Suddenly it was light: it was exactly ten o'clock. And without saying any more, Martin Martinych screwed up his eyes and turned away: when it was light it was more difficult. You could see now that his face was crumpled and earthy. Many people have earthy faces now: reverting to Adam.

But Masha went on:

"And you know, Mart, perhaps I'll try and get up . . . if you start the stove early."

"Of course, Masha, of course. . . . On a day like that . . . Of course, I'll start it early."

The cave god was quieting down, shrinking into himself. And now he was quite still, just crackling faintly. One could hear that downstairs at the Obertyshevs' someone was using a stone ax to split knotty logs, the remains of a barge—hewing Martin Martinych into pieces with a stone ax. One piece of Martin Martinych was smiling in a clayey way and grinding dried potato peelings in a coffee mill to make cakes with. Another piece of Martin Martinych was stupidly, blindly knocking against the ceiling, the windowpanes, the walls, like a bird that had flown into a room from outdoors: "Where find wood— where find wood—where find wood?"

Martin Martinych put on his coat and fastened it with a leather belt (the cave dwellers have a myth that this keeps you warmer). In the corner by the chiffonier he lifted the pail noisily.

"Where are you going, Mart?"

"I'll be back directly. To get water downstairs."

On the dark stairway, crusted with ice because of the water splashed on it, Martin Martinych stood awhile, swaying, sighed, and clanking the pail as if it were a prisoner's chain, went downstairs to the Obertyshevs': the water in their flat was still running. The door was opened by Obertyshev himself; he wore a coat belted with a rope and was unshaven. His face was a waste overgrown with reddish dusty weeds. Through the weeds were visible yellow stone teeth and among the stones a lizard's instantaneous tail: a smile.

"Ah, Martin Martinych! Come to fetch water? Please, please, please."

The tiny cubicle between the outer and inner door was so narrow that one could scarcely turn around in it with a pail. Here Obertyshev kept his stack of wood. Clayey Martin Martinych knocked against the logs, and this made a deep dent in the clay. And there was even a deeper dent when he knocked against the corner of the chest of drawers in the dark passage. He made his way through the dining room; here were the Obertyshev dam and her three cubs. The dam hurriedly hid a dish under a napkin: a human had come from another cave, and—who knows?— he might fly at her and seize it.

In the kitchen, as he turned on the faucet, Obertyshev smiled a stone-toothed smile:

"Well, how's your wife? How's your wife? How's your wife?"

"What's there to say, Alexey Ivanych? Just the same. It's a bad business. Tomorrow is her name day, and I haven't . . ."

"No one has, Martin Martinych, no one has, no one . . ."

The bird that had flown into the kitchen was rustling its wings and fluttering right, left, and suddenly dashed its breast in despair against the wall:

"Alexey Ivanych, I wanted . . . . Alexey Ivanych, couldn't I borrow at least five or six pieces of wood from you?"

Yellow stone teeth showed through the weeds, the eyes grew yellow teeth, all of Obertyshev sprouted teeth which grew longer and longer.

"Good heavens, Martin Martinych! Good heavens! Good heavens! We ourselves are . . . You know very well how it is nowadays, you know very well, you know very well . . ."

Tighten the knot, tighter, still tighter! Martin Martinych gave himself a final twist, lifted the pail and made his way through the kitchen, the dark passage, the dining room. In the doorway of the dining room Obertyshev stuck out his lizard-nimble instantaneous hand:

"Well, so long . . . Only don't forget to slam the door, Martin Martinych, don't forget. Both doors, both, both—there is no keeping warm."

On the dark, ice-crusted landing Martin Martinych set down the pail, turned around, and shut the inner door tight. He listened, but heard only his own dry bony shivering and his jerking breaths forming a dotted line. In the narrow cubicle between the two doors he put out a hand and touched one log, and another, and another . . . No! Quickly he shoved himself back onto the landing and closed the outer door, but not tightly. He only needed to slam it so that the lock would click.

But he could not bring himself to do it. He could not slam the door on Masha's tomorrow. And upon the dotted line made by Martin Martinych breathing two Martin Martinyches engaged in a duel to the death: the old one, the Scriabin one, who knew "I may not," and the new one, the caveman, who knew "I must." The caveman, gnashing his teeth, knocked the other Martin Martinych down and throttled him, and Martin Martinych, breaking his nails, opened the door, plunged his hand into the stack of wood—one billet, another, the fourth, the fifth, thrust under his coat, stuck into his belt, dropped into the pail. Then he slammed the door and rushed upstairs with huge animal leaps. Halfway up the staircase, on one of the ice-coated steps, he suddenly stiffened and squeezed himself into the wall: downstairs the door clicked again and he heard Obertyshev's dust-clogged voice:

"Who's there? Who's there? Who's there?"

"It's me, Alexey Ivanych. I forgot to slam the door. . . . I wanted . . . I went back—to slam it hard. . . ."

"You? Hm . . . How could you? One must be more

careful, more careful. Everything gets stolen now, you know yourself, you know yourself. How could you?"

The twenty-ninth. All day long a low, cotton-batting sky, with holes which let icy air through. But the cave god, his belly stuffed since morning, roared benevolently—and suppose there are holes, suppose Obertyshev, bristling with teeth all over, counts his billets—let him, it doesn't matter: only today matters; "tomorrow" makes no sense in a cave; centuries will pass before the words "tomorrow," "the day after tomorrow," will again assume meaning.

Masha got up, and swaying in an impalpable wind, did her hair in the old way: over the ears and parted in the middle. It was like a last dry leaf fluttering on a naked tree. From the middle drawer of his desk Martin Martinych took out papers, letters, a thermometer, a small blue medicine bottle (this he hurriedly thrust back, so that Masha should not see it); and finally from the furthest corner he drew a little black lacquered box. At the very bottom of it there was still some real—yes, yes, quite real—tea! They had real tea. Martin Martinych, his head tilted, listened to a voice which was almost as it used to be:

"Mart, do you remember, my blue room, and the piano with a cover on it, and on the piano an ash tray in the shape of a wooden horse, and I was playing, and you came up to me from behind . . ."

Yes, that evening the universe was created, and the moon with its wonderful wise snout, and the nightingale trill of the bells in the hall.

"And do you remember, Mart: the window was open, a green sky—and below, from another world, an organ-grinder?"

Organ-grinder, wonderful organ-grinder, where are you?

"And on the embankment . . . the branches still bare, the water pink, and the last blue block of ice floating past, and looking like a coffin. And it was only funny, the coffin; because of course, we would never die. Remember?"

Downstairs they had started chopping wood. Suddenly, this stopped and there was the sound of running and shouting. Split in two, one half of Martin Martinych saw the immortal organ-grinder, the immortal wooden horse, the immortal block of ice, while the other half, breathing in a dotted line, counted the chunks of wood with Obertyshev. And now Obertyshev has finished counting: he is putting on his coat and, bristling with teeth, slams the door ferociously, and——

"Wait, Masha, I think, I think someone is knocking at the door."

No. No one. No one yet. One can still breathe; with head tilted one can still listen to that voice so like what it used to be.

Twilight. The twenty-ninth had grown old. Staring, dim, old woman's eyes, and everything shrinking, hunching under that fixed stare. The ceiling is caving in, the armchair, the desk, the beds, Martin Martinych himself— are all flattening out, and on the bed—Masha, perfectly flat, like paper.

It was evening when Selikhov came, the chairman of the house committee. He used to weigh some 250 pounds, but now half of him was gone and he rattled in his jacket like a nut in a gourd. But he had kept his rumbling laugh.

"Well, Martin Martinych, in the first place, in the second place, allow me to congratulate your spouse on her name day. Of course, of course! Obertyshev told me . . ."

Martin Martinych was shot out of the armchair, and he jerked about, hurrying to speak, to say something, anything.

"Tea . . . right away, this very minute. We have real tea today. Real! Let me just . . ."

"Tea? I'd prefer champagne, you know. You haven't any? You don't say. Haw-haw-haw! And the other day my friends and I made home-brew out of Hoffmann drops.* It was a circus! Didn't we get soused. 'I am Zino-

* A sedative.

viev,'* one fellow said; 'on your knees!' A circus! And when I was crossing the Field of Mars on my way home I met a man in nothing but a vest, I swear! 'What's wrong?' I asked. 'It's all right,' says he. 'I've just been robbed, I'm walking home, to Vasilyevsky Island.' A circus!"

Masha, a flattened, papery Masha, laughed in her bed. Tying himself in a tight knot, Martin Martinych laughed more and more loudly, in order to refuel Selikhov so that he might go on talking, only go on, and when he was finished with this, talk of something else. . . .

But Selikhov was petering out, and at last he was silent except for gentle snorts. He rolled to right and to left in the shell of his jacket and then got up.

"Well, let me kiss your little hand, birthday girl! AFF! What, you don't get it? A fond farewell—AFF as *they* say.† A circus!"

He was rumbling away in the passage, in the foyer. In a moment he would be gone, or . . .

The floor was gently swaying and tossing under Martin Martinych. With a clayey smile he held onto the doorpost. Selikhov was panting with the effort of getting his feet into huge overshoes.

Mammothlike in overshoes and overcoat, he straightened out and recovered his breath. Then he silently took Martin Martinych's arm, silently opened the door leading into the Polar study, and silently sat down on the sofa.

The floor of the study was an ice floe, the ice floe cracked gently, broke off from the shore and floated Martin Martinych, spinning him around so that Selikhov's voice, coming from the farther shore, where the sofa stood, was scarcely audible.

"In the first place, in the second place, my dear sir, I must tell you: I would gladly squash this Obertyshev like

* Grigory Zinoviev, a leading Bolshevik, who was head of the Petrograd Soviet. In 1936 he was executed for "confessedly" plotting against Stalin and the Soviet regime.

† Poking fun at the Bolsheviks' weakness for abbreviations, which were a novelty at the time.

a louse, by God. ... But you understand, since he has made a formal declaration, since he says he'll go to the police ... What a louse! I can only give you this advice: go to him this very minute and stop his mouth with that wood."

The ice floe was spinning faster and faster. Tiny, flattened, hardly visible, a mere splinter, Martin Martinych replied—replied to himself, speaking not of the wood, but of something quite different:

"All right. Today. This very minute ..."

"Excellent, excellent. He is such a louse, such a louse, I tell you ..."

It was still dark in the cave. Clayey, cold, blind, Martin Martinych awkwardly stumbled against all the things that lay about there promiscuously. He started: a voice like Masha's, like what it used to be:

"What are you and Selikhov talking about? What? Ration books? And I was lying and thinking, Mart: if we could only pull ourselves together and go somewhere, South perhaps. ... How noisy you are! Are you doing it on purpose? You know I can't stand it, I can't, I can't!"

A knife scratching glass. But now it didn't matter any more. His arms and legs were mechanical contrivances. To lift and lower them chains were required, a crane, a windlass, and to work the windlass one man was not enough: three were needed.

Working the windlass with an effort, Martin Martinych placed the teakettle and the pan on the stove and threw in the last of Obertyshev's billets.

"Do you hear me? Why don't you answer? Don't you hear?"

Of course, this wasn't Masha, no, it wasn't her voice. Martin Martinych moved more and more slowly, his feet stuck in the sand, it was getting increasingly difficult to work the crane. Suddenly a chain slid off a pulley, his arm dropped and stupidly knocked against the teakettle and the pan so that they went crashing down on the floor, while the cave god hissed like a snake.

And from over yonder, from the distant shore, from the bed, came a stranger's shrill voice:

"You are doing it on purpose! Go away! This minute! I don't want anyone, I want nothing, nothing! Go away!"

The twenty-ninth was dead, and dead the immortal organ-grinder and the block of ice in the water, pink with sunset, and Masha. And this was well. And there must be no incredible tomorrow, no Obertyshev, no Selikhov, no Martin Martinych; everything should die.

Mechanical, remote, Martin Martinych was still going through the motions of handling things. Perhaps he started that stove again and picked up the pan from the floor and set the teakettle to boil, and perhaps Masha was speaking. He did not hear: there were only the dully aching dents in the clay made by words and by the corners of the chiffonier, the chairs, the desk.

Martin Martinych was slowly extracting from the desk bundles of letters, a thermometer, sealing wax, the box of tea, more letters. And at last from the furthest recess came the little blue medicine bottle.

Ten o'clock: the light was on. Electric light, naked, hard, simple, cold, like cave life and death. And next to the flatiron, opus 74, the cakes—quite simply, the little blue medicine bottle.

The iron god roared benevolently, devouring the parchment-yellow, the bluish, the white paper of the letters. The teakettle gently called attention to itself—making a noise with its lid. Masha turned around:

"Is the tea boiling? Mart, darling, give me ..."

She saw. A moment shot through and through with clear, naked, cruel electric light; Martin Martinych squatting before the stove, a pink reflection, as on water at sunset, on the letters, and over yonder the little blue medicine bottle.

"Mart ... should we already ...?"

Silence. Indifferently devouring the immortal words, bitter, tender, yellow, white, blue, the iron god was purring gently. And Masha, as simply as if she were asking for tea:

"Mart, darling! Give it to me!"

Martin Martinych smiled distantly.

"But you know, Masha, there's only enough for one."

"Mart, but as it is, I'm not living any more. This isn't me any more, anyhow, I'm going to ... Mart, you understand, don't you? Mart, have pity on me! Mart!"

Oh, that voice, the old voice ... And if you tilted your head ...

"Masha, I have deceived you: there isn't a single piece of wood in the study. And I went to the Obertyshevs' and there in the entry ... I stole, and Selikhov came to ... I must take it back at once, and I have burnt it all, every bit. ..."

The iron god was unconcernedly dozing off. Dying down, the walls of the cave flickered gently and so did the houses, the cliffs, the mammoths. Masha.

"Mart, if you still love me ... Please, Mart, just remember."

The immortal wooden horse, the organ-grinder, the block of ice ... Martin Martinych slowly rose from a kneeling position. Slowly working the crane with an effort, he took the blue little bottle from the desk and handed it to Masha.

She threw off the blanket, sat up in bed, pink, swift, immortal—like the water at sunset, then seized the little bottle, laughed:

"There, you see: not for nothing did I lie here and think of going away somewhere. Light another lamp—right here, on the table. So. Now throw something more into the stove."

Without looking, Martin Martinych fished some papers out of the drawer and tossed them into the stove.

"Now ... Go and take a little walk. I think the moon is out, *my* moon: remember? Don't forget to take the key. You'll slam the door to, and without a key ... Who will let you in ... ?"

No, there was no moon. Low, dark, thick clouds, like a vaulted ceiling, and the world one enormous silent cave. Narrow, endless passages between walls; and dark ice-coated cliffs resembling houses; in the cliffs—deep purple hollows; in the hollows, around the fire, humans, crouching. A light icy draught blows the powdery snow from under your feet, and over the white powder, the massive cliffs, the caves, the crouching humans, moves with inaudible, measured steps, some supermammoth.

(*1922*)

Velimir Khlebnikov

(1885–1922)

One wonders at times whether Khlebnikov actually existed or was merely the subject of a legend that has now become frozen by many retellings. His origins and early life belong to the remote Asiatic periphery of Russia, and though he was later to be a familiar figure on the streets of the capital, his inspiration, as in "Nikolai," appears always to have derived from the circumference. Mayakovsky and others lovingly acknowledged Khlebnikov as a master whose tireless experiments with the verbal material of poetry pointed the way for their own discoveries. To his fellow Futurists (and not only Futurists) he was a saint who sacrificed literally everything in life to poetry; to others he was certifiably mad; and to still others he was a fraud. This conjunction of opinions is scarcely novel: It is the fate of all who, like Khlebnikov, disassemble the foundations of an art—in this case, the very words of which poetry consists—and put them back together in unheard-of combinations. Labels never fit any great creative artist, of course, but *Futurist* seems perversely inappropriate to Khlebnikov, whose life was spent burrowing in the past among the root systems in the subsoil of ancient Slavic culture.

The one work of his that must be quoted is a short tour de force entitled "Incantation by Laughter," which consists for the most part of the root *smekh* (laugh) extended by every conceivable affix. Translators love to test their ingenuity and the resources of their own language against it:

You who laugh it up and down, laugh along so laughily;
    Laugh it off belaughingly!
Laughters of the laughing laughniks, overlaugh the laugh-
    athons!
Laughiness of the laughish laughers, counterlaugh the
    Laughdom's laughs!*

And so on. But you get the point. By saying "and so on" I am
not being facetious; I am alluding to Mayakovsky's account of
how Khlebnikov would read one of his verbal contraptions to
an audience. Having recited enough to acquaint his listeners
with the basic process at work, he would break off with "et
cetera, et cetera," since the poem itself was subordinate to the
linguistic invention that had produced it. Wallace Stevens
wrote: "Every poem is a poem within a poem: the poem of
the idea within the poem of the words." Khlebnikov was evidently content with the poem of the idea.

    Khlebnikov's remarkable prose has only lately begun to be
appreciated. Some of it is no less inspissated than the most
experimental poems, but, just as he occasionally wrote poems
of a Pushkinian clarity, much of the prose is accessible to the
mind of an intelligent child. "Nikolai" is logical and sequen-
tial in the telling. There are, to be sure, little intrusions of
Khlebnikovian strangeness, which I have striven to represent
in the translation. But if the story is untypical—not of
Khlebnikov but of what critics choose to emphasize in his
work—it is a perfect paradigm of his fascination with a kind
of unhoused, feral sinking back into some primal condition. If
labels meant anything, one might call this as much Acmeist
as Futurist in inspiration; and it anticipates the later concerns
of writers as different as Yuri Kazakov (see p. 491) and Andrei Platonov (see p. 116). One thing is certain: Nikolai, the
near-mute, the fugitive hunter, is one of the masks of his inspired creator.

* *Modern Russian Poetry*, translated by Vladimir Markov and Mer-
rill Sparks (New York: Bobbs-Merrill, 1967).

NIKOLAI

Strange peculiarity of an event, it leads you indifferent past what has been awarded the name terrible and, on the contrary, you look for depths and secrets behind a trivial event. I was walking down the street and stopped when I saw a crowd assembling around some carts. "What is going on here?" I asked a man who happened to be walking by. "Look," answered he, laughing. Indeed, in the gravelike silence an old black horse was stomping his hoof with a measured beat against the pavement. Other horses were listening, their heads inclined in a deep bow, taciturn and immobile. In the pounding of the hoof one heard thought, fate descried, a command, and the other horses, miserably hanging their heads, gave ear. The crowd was collecting quickly until the driver arrived from somewhere, yanked the reins of the horse, and drove off.

But the old black horse with its vague reading of fortune and its dreary comrades remained in my memory.

The vicissitudes of a vagrant life are redeemed by magical events. Among these I number my meetings with Nikolai. If you met him you would probably pay no attention. Only his slightly swarthy forehead and chin would betray him. And his eyes, which, with an excess of honesty, expressed nothing at all, might have told you that you had to do with an apathetic hunter who found people tiresome.

But this was a solitary volition, having its own path and its own end of life.

He was not with people. He was like those estates that are cordoned off from the highway by a fence and turned by the fence in the direction of a dirt track.

He seemed taciturn and simple, cautious and miserable.

His disposition seemed even poor. Drunk, he would become rude and insolent with his acquaintances, would insistently demand money of them but—strange thing—would feel a flood of tenderness toward children: Wasn't it because they had not yet turned into people? I've known this same trait in other people, too. He would gather round him a crowd of children and spend all the money in his pocket on the wretched candies, cookies, and cakes adorning the shelves of the shopkeepers. Whether or not he meant to say, "Look, people, treat others as I am treating them," still, since such tenderness was hardly his normal occupation, his silent sermon had a greater impact on me than the sermon of some teacher with a loud and universal fame.

But who in any case is going to decipher the soul of a solitary gray hunter, a stern chaser of wild boars and wild geese? I recall in this connection the harsh sentence passed on the whole of life by a certain defunct Tatar, who left behind a deathbed note with the brief but arresting message: "I spit on the entire world."

To the Tatars he seemed an apostate and traitor, and to the Russian authorities a dangerous firebrand. I confess that I have more than once wished to add my signature to that note dictated by apathy and despair. But this silent exhibition of freedom from the iron laws of life and its stern truth, this hazel tree gathering wild flowers at its feet, these are nevertheless symptoms of a profound trait; they conceal a simple and stern thought preserved by his, in the face of all odds, honest eyes.

In a certain old album, many years old, amongst the faded old men bending with age, with a decoration on their chest, amongst the finicky old women with a gold chain in their hand and eternally reading an open book, you might also happen upon the modest yellow likeness of a man with hardly remarkable facial features, with a straight beard, and with a double-barreled shotgun on his lap; his hair was divided by a simple part.

If you ask who this faded photograph is, you will be

briefly informed that it is Nikolai. But detailed explanations will most probably be avoided. A slight cloud passing over the face of your informant will indicate that he was not treated as a complete outsider.

I knew this hunter. One might treat people in general as varying interpretations of one and the same white head with white curls. Then the contemplation of forehead and eye in various interpretations will present you with an endless variety, as a struggle of light and shadow on one and the same stone head, replicated in old men and children, in businessmen and dreamers, an infinite number of times.

And he, of course, was merely one of the interpretations of this white stone with eyes and curls. But can anyone not be that?

Much has been told of his feats as a hunter. When he was asked to bring in some game he would ask, with his distinguished taciturnity, "How many?" And disappear. God knows by what stratagems, but he would reappear carrying what had been ordered. Wild boars knew him as a silent and terrible enemy.

Cherni—that place where rushes grow at the edges of the shallow sea—he had learnt by heart. Who knows, if only it were possible to penetrate into the soul of the winged tribe peopling the mouth of the Volga, how the image of that terrible hunter had been imprinted upon it? When they filled with their moan those desert shores, could one not hear in their sobbing the news that the bark of Avian Death had come ashore? Did he not seem to them, with the shotgun over his shoulder and the gray cap on his head, a terrifying creature with otherworldly powers?

The terrible merciless deity would also appear among the desolate sands: The white or black flock would bruit abroad with lengthy shrieks the death of their comrades. One small corner of this soul, however, knew pity: He always spared nests and the young, who knew only the sound of his retreating steps.

He was secretive and taciturn, more frequently reticent;

and those only to whom he had disclosed the bare periphery of his soul might have surmised that he condemned life and harbored "the contempt of a savage" for the whole of human fate. One might, however, understand this state of the soul best of all by saying that the soul of "nature" was obliged thus to condemn innovation, if that soul had to pass via this hunter's life from the world of the "perishing" to the world of those coming to replace it, gleaming with valedictory eye at the snowstorms of ducks, at unpeopled wastelands, at the world of blood spilt by red geese across the surface of the sea, if it had to pass over to the land of white stone piles driven into the streambed, the fine lacework of iron bridges, of anthill cities, a strong but ungracious twilight world!

He was simple, straightforward, even crudely stern. He was a good nurse, tending his sick comrades; and this tenderness toward the weak and readiness to be their shield might have been the envy of a medieval cuirassier in a plumed helmet.

He set off for the hunt as follows: He would get into his skiff, where two dogs that he had raised from puppies awaited him, fasten the sail to the grommet, and set off downriver, using sometimes the towrope and sometimes the oars. I should add that on the Volga there is a tricky wind that will fly offshore in moments of utter quietness and capsize any careless fisherman who can't manage to strike his sail.

At the campsite the boat was turned over to make a shelter, iron rods were driven into the ground, and by the fire the hunter began his twenty-four-hour days before leaving for the feast. The intelligent, taciturn dogs were fed in the boat, which had absorbed the smells of all the game known to the Volga region; black cormorants and the big leg of a boar lay here beside partridges and bustards.

The wolves howl softly: "There they come," "There they go."

His wish was to die far from the company of men, concerning whom his disenchantment was immense. He wandered about among men while denying them. Cruel by profession, he settled among the hunted nonpeople, to whom he appeared as a cruel prince, the bearer of death; but he was on their side in the fight between people and nonpeople. Thus Melnikov, the scourge of the Old Believers, could still write *In Mountains and Forests*.

No, he could not be imagined as anything other than a sort of Perun of the Birds—cruel, but faithful to his subjects, in whom he perceived a kind of beauty.

There were people whom he might call his friends; but the more his soul emerged from its "shell," the more powerfully he upset the balance between himself and them to his own advantage; he would become arrogant, and the friendship a temporary ceasefire between two belligerents. The rupture might arise from the most trivial of causes, and his gaze would say, "No, you are not one of us," and he would become dour and distant.

Only to a few was it clear that this man did not in fact belong to humankind at all. With his meditative eyes, his taciturn mouth, he had already been, for two or three decades, the chief priest in the temple of Murder and Death. Between the city and the wilderness there exist the same axes, the same difference, as between devil and demon. Intelligence takes its origin at that point where one is capable of choosing between evil and good. The hunter had made this choice on the side of the demon, the great unpeopled void. He stated emphatically that he did not wish to be buried in a cemetery; why did he not want a quiet cross? was he a stubborn heathen? and what did he learn from that book which he alone had read and the ashes of which no one now would ever read?

But death did not go against his wishes.

Once the local newspaper printed a report that the boat and body of an unknown man had been found in the region known to the local inhabitants as "Horses Gate." The report added that a double-barreled shotgun lay beside the body. Since this was the year of the Black Death and the ground squirrels, those pretty denizens of the steppe, were dying by the thousands, forcing the nomads to strike their tents and flee in terror, and since the hunter was already a week overdue and nowhere to be seen, people who knew him sent out a search party full of alarmed expectation and grim foreboding. When the party returned, they confirmed that the hunter was dead. Their story, heard from some fishermen, ran as follows.

When they'd already passed several nights in a fishing camp that they had set up on a deserted island, a strange black dog would appear every evening, station herself near the hut, and set up a forlorn howl. Beating and shouting had no effect on her. They drove her off, though not without a presentiment as to what these visits from a strange black dog on a uninhabited island might portend. But she never failed to reappear the following night, howling gruesomely and poisoning the fishermen's sleep.

Finally a kindhearted watchman went out to her: She gave a yelp of pleasure and led him to the overturned boat: Nearby, his gun in his hand, lay the remains of a man totally picked clean by the birds, there being flesh left only in his boots. A cloud of birds were wheeling above him. A second dog, half dead, lay at his feet.

Whether he died of fever or the plague was not known. Waves lapped the shores in measured rhythm.

Thus he died having achieved his strange dream—to come to his last end far away from people.

But friends nevertheless placed a modest cross over his grave. Thus died the wolfslayer.

(*1913*)

Anna Akhmatova

(1889–1966)

Akhmatova was her pseudonym. She was born Anna An-
dreyevna Gorenko in Odessa, where her father was a naval
officer, but she is associated in everyone's mind with the elegant village near Petersburg, Tsarskoye Selo, where she grew
up, and with the metropolis. She was married for a brief,
stormy time to Nikolai Gumilyov, leader of the Acmeists,
and was the closest friend of Osip Mandelstam (see p. 169).
These three were the greatest of the poets who identified
themselves with the school, though for many Akhmatova's
work remained the most consistently "Acmeist" of all—a delicious paradox in view of the exaggerated emphasis on masculine hardness in the early manifestos of the group. Her
great theme during the first part of her career was the depiction of love from the woman's point of view, which in her
case was dry-eyed, unsentimental, and completely unde-
ceived. In brief lyrics that had a strongly narrative and dra-
matic element, she chiefly portrayed not so much love as
nonlove where love might have been, not the meeting but the
nonmeeting of lovers (such coinages with the negative particle were frequent in her diction).

Though Akhmatova's five volumes of poetry published
between 1912 and 1922 established her name among poets of
the first rank, the execution in 1921 of her former husband
Gumilyov (for alleged counterrevolutionary plotting) was
sufficient to exclude her from publication for some twenty
years. During this time she continued to write—and even to

be written about by admiring critics—but she could not print her work.

One of the strongest traits in her nature was her love of and her almost mystical identification with Russia. Although she understood those who fled the airless tyranny of Stalin to live and write abroad, she deplored their forsaking her people in their misery; emigration was, for her, unthinkable. Hitler's invasion spurred Akhmatova to some of the greatest patriotic poetry in any language. There are passages of Miltonic fury and, finally, of a "masculine hardness" that no other Acmeist ever surpassed. Feeling herself a citizen of world culture, she also wrote a poem of outrage at the blitz of Shakespeare's London. Known by heart to millions of her countrymen, these works made her continued suppression seem less advisable to the literary authorities, and for a while she enjoyed a limited access to the printing press. In 1946, however, when the war and its expedient fraternization with the West were over, Akhmatova was singled out (along with Zoshchenko [see p. 215] and the already-dead Mandelstam) as the first to be denounced. With the delicacy of feeling that marked the literary utterances of Stalin's accomplices, she was called "a mixture of nun and whore."

Immensely intelligent and learned, Akhmatova had recourse to translating and scholarship. She knew Pushkin's life and works as though they had been intimate contemporaries in Tsarskoye Selo; several of her articles remain part of the indispensable scholarship on Pushkin's work. The regal manner of Anna Akhmatova was not an empty pose: While in official disgrace she was privately acknowleged not only by ordinary people and fellow artists, but even by the literary bureaucrats in charge of her repression, as the queen of Russian culture.

Selections of her poetry were published once again in 1958 and in 1961, but two masterpieces in the long form —*Requiem*, about the visitations of the Terror upon her own family, and *Poem without a Hero*, an all but encrypted meditation on persons and events in her life—could be published only after the fall of Soviet power. In the mid-1960s Akhmatova was allowed abroad twice: to Italy to receive an international award, and to Oxford to receive an honorary degree. Her travel across Europe by train—poor health prevented her flying—was treated by admirers as something like a royal progress.

Three things in this world he loved;
the choir at vespers, white peacocks,
and worn maps of America.
He didn't like crying children,
or tea with raspberry jam,
or hysterical women.
    . . . and I was his wife.

                                        (*1911*)

We're no good at saying good-bye.
We wander around, shoulders touching.
It's begun to get dark already.
You look vacant, I say nothing.

We'll stop in this church and see
someone buried, or christened, or married.
We'll leave, avoiding each other's eyes.
Why does nothing work out for us?

Or we'll go in this graveyard and sit
where someone has already sat on the snow
and you'll draw with the end of your stick
dream-chambers where we'll live forever.

                                        (*1917*)

DANTE

Even dead he wouldn't come back
to his old city, his Florence.
He didn't look back when he left, not this one.
It's to him that I sing this song.
Night. A torch. One last embrace.
His savage fate howling just outside the door.
He cursed this city from Hell,
and in Heaven itself could not forget her.
But he was not the one to walk about barefoot,
in sackcloth, with a lighted candle
through the Florence that he yearned for—
faithless Florence, mean, for whom he waited long ...

(*1936*)

When a man dies
the portraits of him change.
The eyes have a different look
and the lips smile a different smile.
I noticed this first on coming home
from a certain poet's funeral.
There've been many occasions to check it since.
And I was right.

(*1940*)

COURAGE

We know what now lies in the balance,
What now is coming to pass we know.
The hour of courage has struck on our clock.
And courage will never abandon us.
We're not afraid to be shot dead,

Not bitter to be bereft of home.
We will defend you, Russian speech,
Guard you, great Russian tongue.
Free and unsullied we will carry you through,
Save you from bondage, for our children's children,
Forever!

(*1942*)

Andrei Platonov

(1899–1951)

Platonov—he officially changed his name from Klimentov—
was forever falling out of official favor and finding his way
back into it. When he made one of his periodic (posthumous)
comebacks in 1966 with the publication of a collection of
stories, Ernest Hemingway happened to be enjoying an enormous vogue in Russia, and someone discovered that Hemingway had once chanced upon a translation of one of
Platonov's stories and had praised it in an interview with Soviet journalists. None of the Soviet journalists had ever heard
of Platonov. It is *nekulturny* (uncultured) to be flagrantly
unaware of a native author praised by a world-famous foreign
writer. Thus Hemingway is no doubt in part responsible for
his Russian colleague's return to print—not that Platonov
lacked influential admirers among his own countrymen.
(Kafka, proscribed for years, also first began to appear in the
USSR after a leading Soviet writer—perhaps deliberately—
disgraced himself at an international conference by declaring
that he had never heard of him.)

True or not, the Hemingway story ought to be true, for
there is a natural affinity between the two writers. Each
found his central theme in the prosaic heroism of enduring at
the furthest edge of physical and emotional existence, at the
place where the line between life and death seems to fade and
even to lose all interest. Each was fascinated by death. Platonov appears to have thought it the natural condition of
man, life being an evanescent and transient arrangement.

He reminds one also of Beckett in certain turns of phrase that reverse our normal perception of living and dying. "I was on my way to my mother," says Molloy, "whose charity kept me dying." To live, in Beckett, is to "finish dying." In "The Potudan River," Nikita inquires about his wife, "And she's alive now?" His father answers, "So far, she hasn't died."

But, superficial resemblances aside, Platonov is unlike Hemingway or Beckett. More surprisingly, his mature work is unlike that of any Russian writer who preceded him (younger writers have plentifully learned from him). His language is somehow ragged and crude, the transitions almost haphazard, and the stories shaped by chance and the weather. But these elements of his style are so perfectly reflective of his subject matter that they have the effect of the most consummate artifice.

He was born into the large family of a poor railroad worker in the small provincial town of Voronezh, or rather in a drab workers' settlement—part town and part country—nearby. The distinction in Russia between townsman and countryman is rather more extreme than elsewhere, and Platonov was a bit of each. His education was technical (he was a qualified electrical engineer) and his fondness for machinery of all kinds was as practical and down to earth as that of the Futurists was aesthetical and mad. He fought on the side of the Reds in the Civil War and even joined the Party, at least for a while. Part peasant and part worker, Platonov derived from his education a passion for management, for the logical ordering of existence (he was at one time in charge of extensive land-reclamation and electrification schemes). Odd therefore that his earliest fall from grace should have resulted from works satirizing the excessive management imposed from above by the Soviet bureaucracy, excessive scientism, and the excessively material interests of the new managerial class.

Platonov was certainly an intractable writer; still, one wonders at the harshness of his treatment. In 1946, the same year when Zhdanov read Akhmatova (see p. 111) and Zoshchenko (see p. 215) out of literature, Platonov published an innocuous and sentimental little story entitled "Homecoming" about the difficulties experienced by a Soviet veteran in returning to his wife and children (which he laudably man-

aged to do). V. Ermilov, the powerful editor of the principal
literary newspaper, used it as the basis for a denunciation
that might well, in those times, have been a death warrant.
But if Platonov had formidable enemies such as Ermilov and
Fadeev, he also had a staunch protector in Mikhail Sholo-
khov. He was, in any case, a born survivor and repeatedly redeemed himself, as he did during the Second World War, for
instance, by filing newspaper accounts of Soviet heroism
from the front lines. Whether able to publish or not, he appears never to have ceased writing. Much of his work has
only recently appeared in his native land.

THE POTUDAN RIVER

Grass was growing again on the packed dirt roads of the
civil war, for the fighting had stopped. With peace the
countryside grew quiet again, and almost empty of people: some had died in the fighting, many were getting over
their wounds, resting with their families, forgetting the
heavy work of war in long sleep, while a few of the demobilized soldiers had not yet managed to get home and were
still walking in their old overcoats, with packs on their
backs and field helmets or sheepskin hats on their heads—
walking through the thick, unfamiliar grass which they
had not earlier had time to see, or maybe it had been
trampled down before by their marching, and not growing. They walked with stunned, astonished hearts, seeing
again the fields and villages spread out along the roads;
their spirit had changed in the torment of war, in its sick-
nesses, and in the joy of victory. They were walking now
as if to some new life, only vaguely remembering what
they had been like three or four years before, for they had

been transformed into different people. They had grown out of their age, and become wiser, they had grown more patient, and they felt inside themselves the great worldwide hope which had now become the central idea of their still-small lives which had no clear goal or purpose before the civil war.

The last of the demobilized Red Army soldiers returned to their homes late in the summer. They had been retained in labor armies where they were used at various unfamiliar jobs, and they were sad, and only now were they told to go home to their own lives and to living in general.

A former Red Army soldier, Nikita Firsov, had been walking for two days along the hills which stretch out above the Potudan River toward his home in a little-known district town. He was a man of twenty-five, with a modest face which seemed always sorrowing but perhaps this expression came not from grief but from some controlled goodness of character or from the usual concentration of youth. Light-colored hair, uncut for a long time, stuck out around his ears from under his cap, and his big gray eyes looked with a kind of sullen tension at the quiet, ordinary, monotonous countryside, as if he were not a local man.

About noon Nikita Firsov lay down next to a little stream which ran from a spring along the bottom of a gorge down to the Potudan. He dozed on the ground under the sun, in the September grass which had stopped growing here since spring. It was as if the warmth of life had grown dark in him, and Firsov fell asleep in the quiet of this deserted place. Insects flew over him, a spider web floated above him, a wandering beggar stepped across him and, without touching the sleeper, uninterested in him, went on about his business. The dust of summer and of the long drought stood high in the air, making the light in the sky weaker and more diffuse, but still the time of peace, as usual, moved far behind the sun. Suddenly Firsov awoke and sat up, heavily, panting in fright as if he had lost his wind in some invisible running and fighting.

He had had a strange dream of being smothered by the hot fur of a small, well-fed beast, a kind of little animal of the fields fed on pure wheat. This animal, soaked in sweat from its efforts and from its greed, had squirmed through the sleeper's mouth into his throat, trying to burrow with his paws into the center of his soul, trying to stop his breathing. Choking in his sleep, Firsov wanted to scream and to run away, but the little animal pulled itself out of him by its own effort and disappeared—blind, wretched, frightened, and trembling itself—into the darkness of its night.

Firsov washed his face in the stream, and rinsed out his mouth, and then he went on quickly; his father's house was not far away, and he could get there by evening.

As soon as it started to get dark, Firsov saw his birthplace in the dim onset of night. It was a gradual sloping ridge which rose from the bank of the Potudan up to the high-lying fields of rye. On this ridge was the small town, almost invisible now in the darkness. Not a single light was burning.

Nikita Firsov's father was asleep: he went to bed as soon as he came home from work, before the sun had gone down. He lived alone, his wife had died a long time ago, two sons had been killed in the imperialist war and his last son, Nikita, was off at the civil war. Perhaps he would come back, the father thought, for the civil war was going on closer to where people lived and there was less shooting than in the imperialist war. The father slept a lot, from sunset right through until dawn; otherwise, if he didn't sleep, he'd start to think, imagining what had been long forgotten, and his heart would be torn with sorrow over his wasted sons, and with regret for the lonely life behind him. In the mornings he would go off quickly to the workshop making peasant furniture where he worked; he could endure this, and forget about himself. But by evening, his spirits would be low again and he would go back to the room where he lived, and sleep almost in terror until morning came: he had no need for kerosene. At dawn the flies would begin to bite him on his bald spot, and the old man would wake up and take a long time dressing, putting on his shoes, washing, sighing, stamping around, fixing up his room, muttering to himself, stepping outside to look at the weather, then going back in—all this just to waste the time that had to be filled before his work began in the furniture workshop.

On this particular night, Firsov's father was sleeping as he always did, out of both habit and fatigue. A cricket had lived in the wall of the house for nobody knew how many summers—this might have been the same cricket as the summer before last, or its grandson. Nikita walked up to the wall and knocked on his father's window; the cricket was silent for a little, as if he were listening—who was this strange man who came so late? The father got up from the old wooden bed on which he had slept with the mother of all his sons; Nikita himself had been born on this same bed. The old man was in his underwear, which had shrunk from long wearing and from laundering so that now it came only to his knees. The father leaned close to the windowpane and looked through it at his son. He had already seen and recognized him but he went on looking, wanting to look his fill. Then little and skinny, like a boy, he darted around through the hall and the courtyard to open the gate which had been locked for the night.

Nikita walked into the old room with its stove that could be slept on, its low ceiling, its one window onto the street. It had the same smell as in his childhood and as three years before when he had gone off to war; he could catch even the smell of his mother's skirt there—the only place in the world where that smell was left. Nikita took off his pack and his cap, slowly slipped off his coat, and sat down on the bed. His father was standing in front of him all this time, barefoot and in his underwear, not daring yet to greet him properly, or to start talking.

"Well, how is it with the bourgeois and the Cadets?" he asked after a minute. "Did you kill them all, or are there some left?"

"We killed almost all of them, I guess," his son said.

"They're a flabby sort!" the old man said, talking about

the bourgeois. "Whatever they might have done, they'd just got used to living free of charge."

Nikita stood up in front of his father, and now he was the taller, by a head and a half. The old man stood quietly next to his son in the humble bewilderment of his love for him. Nikita put his hand on the father's head and drew it to his chest. The old man leaned against his son and started to breathe deeply and fast, as if he had just reached his resting place.

On another street in this town, running straight out into the fields, stood a wooden house with green shutters. An elderly widow had once lived here, a teacher in the town school, with her two children, a boy of ten and a daughter of fifteen, a fair-haired girl named Lyuba.

Some years before, Nikita Firsov's father had wanted to marry the widow teacher, but he soon gave up the idea. He took Nikita, twice, when he was still a little boy, to call on the teacher, and Nikita saw the thoughtful girl Lyuba there, sitting, reading a book, paying no attention to the strange guests.

The old teacher served tea with crackers to the cabinet-maker and made some remarks about enlightening the people's minds and about repairing the stoves in the school. Nikita's father sat there silently, he was embarrassed, he quacked and coughed and smoked his little cigar, and then shyly drank his tea out of the saucer, not touching the little crackers because—he explained—he was already full.

There were chairs in the teacher's apartment, in both of its two rooms and in the kitchen, with curtains hung at the windows, and in the first room there were a little piano and a wardrobe, while the second, farther, room had beds, two armchairs upholstered in red velvet, and a great many books on shelves along the wall—probably a whole collected edition of some kind. This furniture seemed too luxurious to both the father and the son, and after having visited the widow twice, the father stopped going there. He never even managed to tell her that he had wanted to marry her. But Nikita would have liked to see the little piano again, and the pensive girl who had been reading, and he asked his father to marry the mother so they could call on her again.

"I can't, Nikita," the father told him then. "I've had too little education, so what would I talk to her about? And I'd be ashamed to invite them here; we haven't any china, and our food's not much good. . . . Did you see what armchairs they had? Antiques, from Moscow! And that wardrobe? With fretwork all over the front—I know what that is! And the daughter! She's probably going to go to the university."

And the father had not seen his old flame for several years, and had only occasionally missed her, perhaps, or thought about her at all.

The day after he came back from the civil war Nikita walked over to the military commissariat to register in the reserve. Then he walked around the whole familiar town where he had been born, and his heart ached at the sight of the rundown little houses, the broken walls and wattle fences, and the occasional apple trees in the courtyards, some of which had died and dried up for good. In his childhood these apple trees had still been green, and the one-storied houses had seemed big and rich, lived in by mysterious, intelligent people, and the streets then had been long, the burdocks high, and even the weeds growing in the empty lots and in the abandoned kitchen gardens had looked in the old times like sinister, dense forests. But now Nikita saw that the houses of the townspeople were miserable and tiny, they needed paint and repairs, even the weeds in the bare spots were poor things, lived on only by ancient, patient ants, and all the streets petered out in empty land or in the light-filled distance of the sky—the town had become a little one. Nikita realized this meant he had already lived a lot of his life, once large and mysterious objects had become small and boring to him.

He walked slowly by the house with green shutters where he had once gone to call with his father. He knew the paint on the shutters was green only from memory, for only traces of it were left now, it had been faded by the sun, and washed by storms and showers, right down to the wood itself, and the metal roof of the house had rusted badly, so that rain probably ran right through it now, and soaked the ceiling above the little piano. Nikita looked carefully into the window of this house; there were no curtains any longer, and a strange darkness could be seen on the other side of the window glass. Nikita sat down on a bench near the gate of this dilapidated but still familiar little house. He thought maybe someone would play the piano, and he would listen to the music. But everything inside was quiet, telling him nothing. After he had listened for a little, Nikita looked into the courtyard through a crack in the wall; old nettles were growing there, a little path wound through some bushes toward the shed, and three wooden steps led into the building. It must be that the old teacher and her daughter Lyuba had both died a long time ago, and the boy had probably gone off to the war as a volunteer . . .

Nikita walked back to his home. The day was moving toward its evening, his father would soon be coming back for the night, he would have to talk over with him how he was going to live from now on and where he would go to work.

There were a few persons walking along the main street in town, because people were beginning to perk up after the war. Now there were office workers and students on the street, demobilized soldiers and those convalescing from wounds, young people, men who worked at home or in handicraft trades, and others like them; factory workers would come out to walk later, after it had grown quite dark. People were dressed in old clothes, poorly, or else in outworn military uniforms dating from imperialist times.

Practically all the walkers, even those going arm in arm and about to be married, were carrying some kind of household goods. Women were carrying potatoes in kitchen bags, or sometimes fish, men held their bread rations under their arms, or a half a cow's head, or they held tripe fixed for the kettle carefully in their hands. Almost no one seemed dejected except for an occasional tired old man. The younger ones were usually laughing, and looking closely at each other, in high spirits and confident, as if they were on the eve of eternal happiness.

"Hello!" a woman said shyly to Nikita from one side.

The voice both touched and warmed him at the same time, as if someone dear to him and in some trouble had called on him for help. But then it seemed to Nikita that it had been an error and that it was not he who was being greeted. Afraid of making a mistake, he looked slowly around at the people who were walking past him. There were only two of them, and both of these had gone by him. Nikita looked behind him—a big, grown-up Lyuba had stopped and was looking at him. She gave him a sad, embarrassed smile.

Nikita walked up to her and looked her over carefully, as if to see if she had kept herself in good shape, for even in his memory she was precious to him. Her Austrian boots, tied up with a string, were clearly worn-out, her pale muslin dress came only to her knees, probably because that was all the cloth there was; the dress filled Nikita with compassion for Lyuba right away, he had seen dresses like that on women in their coffins, while here the muslin was covering a living, grown-up, even if impoverished body. She was wearing an old woman's jacket on top of the dress—probably Lyuba's mother had worn it when she was a girl, and there was nothing on Lyuba's head—just her hair twisted below her neck into a light-colored, firm braid.

"You don't remember me?" Lyuba asked him.

"No, I haven't forgotten you," Nikita answered.

"One should never forget," Lyuba said with a smile.

Her clear eyes, filled with some secret emotion, were looking tenderly at Nikita as if they were feasting on him. Nikita was looking at her face, too, and his heart was both glad and sorry at the sight of her eyes, which were sunk deep from hardships she had lived through and lighted up with confidence and hope.

Nikita walked back with Lyuba to her home—she still

lived in the same house. Her mother had died not long before, and her young brother had been fed during the famine by a Red Army field kitchen and had grown used to it and gone off to the south with the Red Army to fight the enemy.

"He got used to eating porridge, and there wasn't any at home," Lyuba said.

Lyuba was living now in just one room—she didn't need any more. Nikita looked with a sinking feeling at this room where he had first seen Lyuba, the little piano, and the expensive furniture. Now there was no piano, and no wardrobe with fretwork on its front, there were just the two upholstered chairs, a table and a bed, and the whole room was no longer as interesting and as mysterious to him as it had been when he was younger—the paper on the walls was faded and torn, the floor was worn down, next to the big tiled stove stood a small iron one in which a handful of chips could be burned to make a little heat.

Lyuba pulled a notebook out of the top of her dress and took off her shoes, so that she was barefoot. She was studying medicine at the district academy; in those days there were universities and academies in all the districts because the people wanted to advance their knowledge as quickly as they could; like hunger and want, the senselessness of life had tormented the human heart too long, and it was high time to find out what the existence of men was all about, was it something serious, or a joke?

"They hurt my feet," Lyuba said, pointing to her shoes. "You sit down for a while, and I'll get into bed, because I'm terribly hungry, and I don't want to think about it . . ."

Without undressing, Lyuba climbed under the blanket on the bed and placed her braid on top of her eyes.

Nikita sat there silently for two or three hours, waiting for Lyuba to go to sleep. Then night fell, and Lyuba stood up in the darkness.

"My friend, probably, won't be coming today," Lyuba said sadly.

"What of it? Do you need her?" Nikita asked.

"Very badly," Lyuba said. "They have a big family, and the father is in the army, she brings me supper when there's something left over . . . I eat, and then we study together . . ."

"But do you have any kerosene?" Nikita asked.

"No, they gave me firewood. . . . We light the little stove, and then we sit on the floor and we can see by the flame."

Lyuba smiled helplessly, and ashamed, as if some cruel, unhappy thought had occurred to her.

"Probably her older brother didn't fall asleep," she said. "He doesn't like to have his sister feed me, he begrudges it . . . But I'm not to blame! I'm not so fond of eating: it isn't me, but my head starts to ache, it starts to think about a piece of bread and keeps me from living and thinking about anything else . . ."

"Lyuba!" a young voice said outside the window.

"Zhenya!" Lyuba called out.

Lyuba's friend walked in. She took four big baked potatoes out of the pocket of her jacket and put them on the iron stove.

"Did you get the histology book?" Lyuba asked her.

"And where would I get it?" Zhenya answered. "I signed up for it at the library . . ."

"Never mind, we'll get along without it," Lyuba declared. "I memorized the first two chapters in the department. I'll recite it, and you take notes. Won't that work?"

"Even better!" Zhenya answered, laughing.

Nikita stoked up the little stove so its flames would light the notebook, and then got ready to go back to his father's for the night.

"You won't forget me now?" Lyuba asked as she said good-bye to him.

"No," Nikita said. "I have nobody else to remember."

Firsov lay around the house for a couple of days and then went to work in the same furniture workshop where his father was employed. They listed him as a carpenter and assigned him to getting materials ready, and his pay was lower than his father's, hardly more than half as much. But Nikita knew this was temporary, while he got used to the trade, and then they would give him a rating as a cabinetmaker, and his pay would be better.

Nikita had never lost his habits of work. In the Red Army people were busy not just making war—in their long halts and when they were being held in reserve Red Army soldiers dug wells, repaired the huts of poor peasants in the villages, and planted bushes on the tops of ravines to keep the earth from washing away. For the war would be over and life would go on, and it was necessary to think about this in advance.

After a week Nikita went to call on Lyuba again; he took her some boiled fish and some bread as a present—it was the second course of his dinner at the workers' restaurant.

Lyuba was hurrying to finish a book by the window, profiting from the light still in the sky, so Nikita sat quietly for a while in her room, waiting for the darkness. But soon the twilight caught up with the quiet on the street outside, and Lyuba rubbed her eyes and closed her textbook.

"How are you?" Lyuba asked him in a low voice.

"My father and I get along, we're all right," Nikita said. "I brought you something to eat there, go on and eat it, please."

"I'll eat it, thank you," Lyuba said.

"Then you won't go to sleep?" Nikita asked.

"No, I won't," Lyuba answered. "I'll eat my supper now, and I'll be full!"

Nikita brought some kindling from the shed, and lit the iron stove to make some light. He sat down on the floor, opened the door of the stove and fed chips and little twigs to the flames, trying to keep the heat at a minimum with as much light as possible. Lyuba sat down on the floor, too, when she had eaten the fish and the bread, facing Nikita and next to the light from the stove, and began to study her medical book.

She read silently, sometimes whispering something,

smiling, and writing down some words on a pad in a small, quick handwriting, probably the more important points she read. Nikita just took care that the fire burned properly, and only from time to time—not often—looked at Lyuba's face, and then stared at the fire again for a long time because he was afraid of bothering Lyuba with his looking at her. So the time went, and Nikita thought sadly that it would soon go by completely and it would be time for him to go home.

At midnight, when the clock struck the tower, Nikita asked Lyuba why her friend Zhenya had not come.

"She's got typhus, for the second time, she'll probably die of it," Lyuba answered, and she went back to reading her medicine.

"That's really too bad!" Nikita said, but Lyuba did not answer him.

Nikita pictured to himself a sick and fevered Zhenya, and it seemed to him he could have fallen really in love with her, if he had known her earlier and if she had encouraged him a little. For she was also pretty, it seemed: it was a shame he had not seen her clearly in the dark and could hardly remember what she looked like.

"Now I want to sleep," Lyuba said, sighing.

"Did you understand everything you read?" Nikita asked her.

"Absolutely all! Do you want me to tell it to you?" Lyuba offered.

"You don't have to," Nikita said. "You'd better keep it for yourself, because I'd forget it anyway."

He swept the floor around the stove with a broom, and went home to his father.

After that he called on Lyuba almost every day, except that sometimes he let a day or two go by so that Lyuba would miss him. Whether she missed him or not he didn't know, but on these empty evenings Nikita had to walk for eight or ten miles, around and around the whole town, trying to control himself in his solitude, to endure his longing for Lyuba and to keep himself from going to her.

When he did call on her, he was usually busy stoking

the little stove and waiting for her to say something to him in the moments when she wasn't reading in her book. Every time Nikita brought her some supper from the restaurant at the furniture workshop; she ate her dinners at the academy, but they served too little there and Lyuba was thinking a lot, studying, and still growing, too, so she didn't get enough nourishment. The first time he was paid Nikita bought a cow's horns in a neighboring village and boiled meat jelly on the little stove all night while Lyuba was busy at her books and her notebooks until midnight, when she mended her clothes, darned her stockings and washed the floor until the dawn came, and then took a bath in the courtyard in a tub filled with rainwater before people who might see her had even wakened from their sleep.

Nikita's father was lonely every evening all alone, without his son, but Nikita never said where he was going. "He's a man now, in his own right," the old man thought. "He might have been killed or wounded in the war, so since he's still alive, let him go!"

One day the old man noticed that his son had brought home two white rolls. But he wrapped them up right away in a piece of paper, and didn't offer either of them to his father. Then Nikita put on his army cap, as was his habit, and walked out into the night, taking the two rolls with him.

"Nikita, take me along with you," the father begged him. "I won't say a thing, I'll just look . . . It must be interesting there, with something happening!"

"Another time, father," Nikita said, embarrassed. "Besides, it's time for you to sleep, you've got to go to work tomorrow."

Nikita didn't find Lyuba that night, she wasn't home. He sat down on the bench by the gate, and began to wait for her. He put the white rolls inside his shirt so that they would keep warm until Lyuba arrived. He sat there patiently until late in the night, watching the stars in the sky and the few people passing by who were hurrying home to their children, listening to the sounds of the town clock striking in the tower, the barking of dogs in the court-yards, and various other quiet, unclear sounds which are not made in the daytime. He could probably have sat there, waiting, until he died.

Lyuba appeared, unheard, out of the darkness in front of Nikita. He stood up, but she told him: "You'd better go home," and she was crying. She walked into her room, and Nikita waited a little longer outside, not understand-ing, and then walked after her.

"Zhenya's dead," Lyuba said to him in the room. "What will I do now?"

Nikita was silent. The warm rolls were lying against his chest—he didn't have to take them out right then, right then there was nothing that had to be done. Lyuba was lying on the bed in her clothes, her face turned to the wall, and she was crying to herself, soundlessly and almost without stirring.

Nikita stood alone for a long time in the night-filled room, ashamed to disturb someone else's deep sorrow. Lyuba paid him no attention, because the sadness of one's own grief makes people indifferent to all other suffering. Nikita sat down without being asked on the bed at Lyuba's feet, and took the rolls out of his shirt to put them down somewhere, but for the moment he couldn't find anywhere to put them.

"Let me stay with you now!" Nikita said.

"But what will you do?" Lyuba asked, in tears.

Nikita pondered, afraid of making a mistake or of acci-dentally offending Lyuba.

"I won't do anything," he answered. "We'll just live as usual, so you won't be so worried."

"Let's wait, we've no reason to hurry," Lyuba declared pensively and prudently. "But we've got to think what we can bury Zhenya in—they haven't any coffin . . ."

"I'll bring it tomorrow," Nikita promised, and he put the rolls down on the bed.

The next day Nikita asked the foreman's permission and started to make a coffin; they were always allowed to make coffins freely, without paying for the lumber. From lack of experience he took a long time making it but then he fashioned the place for the dead girl to lie inside it with special care and neatness; Nikita himself was upset just by thinking about the dead Zhenya and some of his tears fell among the shavings. His father, who was walking by, walked up to Nikita and noticed his trouble.

"What are you so sad about: has your girl died?" the father asked.

"No, her girl friend," he answered.

"Her girl friend?" the father said. "Well, plague take her! . . . Here, let me even up the side of that coffin, you've made it look bad, it's not right."

When he finished work, Nikita carried the coffin to Lyuba; he didn't know where her dead friend was.

A warm autumn lasted for a long time that year, and people were glad of it. "It's been a bad harvest, so we'll save on firewood," thrifty persons said. Nikita Firsov had ordered ahead of time a woman's coat to be made for Lyuba out of his Red Army overcoat, and it had been ready for quite a while without any need to wear it, thanks to the warm weather. Nikita kept right on going to Lyuba's as he had before, to help her live and in return to get what he needed for the enjoyment of his own heart.

He asked her once how they should go on living—together or apart. And she answered that she would have no chance to feel happy before the spring, because she had to finish her medical academy as quickly as she could, and then they would see. Nikita listened to this long-term promise, he wasn't asking for any greater happiness than what he already had, thanks to Lyuba, and he did not even know if there was anything better, but his heart was shivering from its long endurance and from uncertainty— what did Lyuba need of a poor, unschooled, demobilized man like him? Lyuba sometimes smiled when she looked at him with her bright eyes, which had large, incomprehensible spots in them, and the face around her eyes was filled with goodness.

Once Nikita started to cry, while he was covering Lyuba with a blanket for the night before he went home, but Lyuba only stroked his head and said: "Well, you'll be all right, you mustn't worry so while I'm still alive."

Nikita hurried home to his father, to take refuge there, to come to his senses, and to stay away from Lyuba for several days in a row. "I'll read," he decided, "and I'll start to live the way I ought to, and I'll forget Lyuba, I won't remember her or even know her. What has she got that's so special? There are millions of persons on this earth, and better than she is, too! She's not good-looking!"

In the morning he couldn't stand up from the bedding where he slept on the floor. His father, going out to work, felt his head, and said:

"You're burning up. Lie down in bed! You'll be sick for a while, and then you'll be better.... You weren't wounded anywhere in the war?"

"Nowhere," Nikita answered.

Toward evening he drifted into unconsciousness; at first he saw the ceiling all the time, with two late flies on it about to die, sheltering themselves there for warmth with which to go on living, and then these same things began to fill him with melancholy and revulsion—it was as if the ceiling and the flies had penetrated into his brain, he couldn't drive them out or stop thinking about them in one steadily swelling thought which had already eaten up all the bones in his head. Nikita closed his eyes, but the flies were seething in his brain, and he jumped up from the bed, to drive the flies from the ceiling, but fell back on the pillow; it seemed to him the pillow still smelled of his mother's breath—his mother had slept right here next to his father—Nikita remembered her, and then he lost consciousness.

After four days, Lyuba found out where Nikita Firsov lived and showed up there for the first time. It was in the middle of the day, all the houses where workers lived were empty, the women had gone out to get food, and the children not yet old enough for school were scattered through the courtyards and the clearings. Lyuba sat on Nikita's bed, stroked his forehead, wiped his eyes with the end of her handkerchief, and asked him:

"Well, how about it, where do you hurt?"

"Nowhere," Nikita said.

His high fever had taken him far away from people and from things around him, and he barely saw and recognized Lyuba; afraid to lose her in the darkness of his flickering consciousness, he held on with his hand to the pocket of her coat, made over from his Red Army greatcoat, and he clung to it as an exhausted swimmer, between drowning and being saved, clutches at the shore. His illness was trying all the time to sweep him over the shining, empty horizon—into the open sea where he could rest at last on its slow, heavy waves.

"You have the grippe, probably, and I'll cure you," Lyuba said. "Or maybe it's typhus. But never mind—it's nothing to be frightened of."

She lifted Nikita by the shoulders and leaned his back against the wall. Then quickly and insistently she dressed him in her coat, she found his father's muffler and tied it around the sick man's head, and she stuck his feet into a pair of felt boots which were waiting under the bed for winter to come. With her arms around Nikita, Lyuba told him to move his legs and she led him, shivering, out into the street. A horse cab was waiting there, Lyuba pushed the sick man into it, and they drove off.

"He's not long for this world," the driver said and he turned to his horses, urging them with his reins into a gentle trot.

In her own room Lyuba undressed Nikita, put him to bed, and covered him with the blanket, an old strip of carpet, a decrepit shawl of her mother's—with everything she had that could keep him warm.

"Why stay there at your house?" Lyuba asked with satisfaction, tucking the blanket around Nikita's burning body. "Just why? Your father's off at work, you lie there all day alone, you get no care of any kind, and you just pine for me ..."

For a long time Nikita thought and wondered where Lyuba had got the money for the cab. Maybe she had sold her Austrian boots, or her textbook (she would have learned it by heart first, so she wouldn't need it) or else she had given the cabdriver her entire monthly stipend.

At night Nikita lay there in deep trouble: sometimes he understood where he was, and could see Lyuba who had lit the stove and was cooking food on it, and then he could see only the unknown phantoms of his mind, operating independently of his will in the compressed, feverish tightness of his head.

His fever chills grew steadily worse. From time to time Lyuba felt Nikita's forehead with the palm of her hand, and counted the pulse in his wrist. Late in the night she poured out some warm water for him and then, taking off her outer clothing, lay down under the blanket with the sick man because he was shaking with chills and had to be warmed. Lyuba put her arms round Nikita and drew him to her while he rolled himself into a ball, away from the cold, and pushed his face against her breast in order to sense more closely this other, higher, better life and to forget his own torment, and his own shuddering, empty body. But now Nikita did not want to die—not because of himself, but in order to keep on touching Lyuba, this other life—and so he asked her in a whisper if he would get well or if he would die: for she had studied and must know the answer.

Lyuba hugged Nikita's head in her arms, and answered: "You'll be well soon. . . . People die because they get sick all alone, and have nobody to love them, but you're with me now . . ."

Nikita grew warm, and fell asleep.

After three weeks Nikita was well again. Snow had already fallen outside, everything had suddenly grown quiet, and Nikita went home to spend the winter with his father. He did not want to bother Lyuba until she had finished the academy. Let her mind grow to its full size, for she came from poor people, too. The father was glad at his son's return, even though he had visited him at Lyuba's two days out of three, each time taking some food for his son while for Lyuba he took no present of any kind.

In the daytime Nikita started to work again at the workshop, in the evenings he visited Lyuba, and the winter went well; he knew that she would be his wife in the spring and that a long and happy life would start then. Sometimes Lyuba would poke him, push at him, run away from him around the room, and then—after the playing—Nikita would kiss her carefully on the cheek. Usually Lyuba would not let him touch her without some reason.

"Or else you'll get tired of me, and we've still got a whole life ahead of us!" she said. "I'm not that attractive, it just seems so to you."

On their day off Lyuba and Nikita took walks along the winter roads outside the town, or they walked, half-frozen, along the ice of the sleeping Potudan River—far downstream as it ran in summertime. Nikita would lie on his stomach and look down through the ice to where the quiet flowing of the water could be seen. Lyuba too would settle down next to him and, touching each other, they would watch the flowing of the water and they would talk about how happy the Potudan River was because it was running out to the sea and because this water under the ice would flow past the shores of faraway lands where flowers were now blooming and birds singing. When she had thought a little about this, Lyuba made Nikita stand up from the ice at once; he was now going around in an old quilted coat of his father's, it was too short for him and didn't keep him very warm, so he might catch cold.

They patiently were friends with each other almost all winter long, tormented by anticipation of their imminent future happiness. The Potudan River was also hidden under the ice all winter long, and the winter grain was sleeping under the snow—these natural phenomena calmed Nikita Firsov and even comforted him: his heart was not the only thing lying buried until spring. In February, waking up in the mornings, he would listen—were there new flies buzzing yet? Outdoors he would look at the sky and at the trees in the garden next door: maybe the first birds were already flying in from faraway countries.

But the trees, the grass and the eggs of the flies were all still asleep in the depth of their strength, in embryo.

In the middle of February, Lyuba told Nikita that final examinations would begin on the twentieth, because doctors were so badly needed and people could not wait long for them. And by March the examinations would be over, and then the snow could stay and the river could go on running under its ice until July if they wanted to! Happiness would start in their hearts before warmth began in nature around them.

During this time—just before March—Nikita wanted to get out of the town, to make the time go more quickly until he and Lyuba could live together. He volunteered at the furniture workshop to go out with a brigade of carpenters to repair furniture in village Soviets and village schools.

At the same time his father finished making, at his own pace, a big wardrobe as a present for the young people. It was like the one which had been in Lyuba's room when her mother was about to become the bride of Nikita's father. In the old carpenter's eyes life was repeating itself for a second or third time. You could understand this but you couldn't change it, and Nikita's father, sighing deeply, loaded the wardrobe on to a sledge and hauled it to the home of his son's intended bride. The snow was getting warm and melting under the sun, but the old man was still strong and he pulled the sledge with some effort even across the black stretches of bare earth. He was secretly thinking that he himself could easily marry this girl, Lyuba, although he had once been too shy for her mother, but he was somehow still ashamed, and he didn't have enough at home to attract and pamper a young girl like her. And Nikita's father concluded from this that life was far from normal. His son had only just come back from war, and here he was leaving home again, this time for good and all. The old man would have to pick up a beggar off the streets, not for the sake of family life but so that there might be some kind of second being in the house, if only a domesticated hedgehog or a rabbit: it might upset life and dirty everything up, but without it he'd cease to be a man.

When he gave Lyuba the wardrobe, Nikita's father asked her when he would be coming to her wedding.

"Whenever Nikita comes back. I'm ready now," Lyuba said.

That night the father walked fourteen miles to the village where Nikita was fixing desks in a school. Nikita was asleep on the floor in an empty classroom, but the father woke him and told him it was time to go back to the town—he could get married.

"You get going, and I'll finish the desks for you," the father told him.

Nikita put on his cap and right away, without waiting for the dawn, set out on foot for the town. He walked alone through the whole second half of the night through empty country: the wind off the fields was blowing fitfully around him, sometimes in his face, sometimes against his back, and sometimes disappearing entirely into the silence of the ravine next to the road. The ground lay dark along the slopes and in the high fields, the snow had run down into the bottom lands, there was the smell of young water and of rotting grass dead since the autumn. But the autumn was already a forgotten, long-past time— the earth was now poor and free, it would give birth to everything from scratch and only to new things which had never lived before. Nikita wasn't even in a hurry to get to Lyuba; he liked being in that dim light of night on that unthinking, early ground which had forgotten all that had already died on it and knew nothing of what it would give birth to in the warmth of the new summer.

Toward morning Nikita got to Lyuba's house. A light hoar frost covered the familiar roof and the brick foundations—Lyuba was probably sleeping sweetly now in her warm bed, and Nikita walked past her house so as not to wake his bride, not to let her body cool just because of him.

By evening of that day Nikita Firsov and Lyuba Kuznetsova had been registered in the district Soviet as married, and they went back to Lyuba's room, and didn't know what to do. Nikita now felt it on his conscience that complete happiness had arrived for him, that the person he needed most in all the world wanted to live together with him, as if there were some great and priceless goodness hidden inside him. He took Lyuba's hand and held it for a long time; he delighted in the warm feeling of her palm, through it he could feel the distant beating of the heart he loved, and he thought about the mystery he could not understand: why Lyuba was smiling at him, and loved him for reasons he could not guess. He knew precisely, for himself, just why Lyuba was dear to him.

"First of all, let's eat," Lyuba said, and she took her hand away from Nikita.

She had already got something ready: on completing the academy she had been given a bigger stipend both in provisions and in cash.

Nikita shyly started to eat the different tasty dishes his wife had prepared. He could not remember that anyone had ever given him something for nothing, he had never visited people in his whole life just for his own satisfaction, and then been fed by them too.

When they had eaten, Lyuba got up from the table first. She opened her arms to Nikita, and said:

"Well!"

Nikita stood up and embraced her shyly, afraid of hurting something in this special, tender body. Lyuba herself squeezed him hard to help him, but Nikita asked her: "Wait a minute, my heart is hurting badly," and Lyuba released her husband.

Dusk had fallen outside, and Nikita wanted to start the stove, to get some light, but Lyuba said: "We don't have to, I've finished studying, and today's our wedding day." Then Nikita turned down the bed while Lyuba undressed in front of him, feeling no shame before her husband. Nikita walked over to his father's wardrobe and took off his own clothing quickly and then lay down next to Lyuba for the night.

Nikita got up very early the next morning. He cleaned

up the room, lit the stove to boil the teakettle, brought in water in a pail from the shed for washing, and ended up not knowing what else to do, while Lyuba went on sleeping. He sat down on a chair, and grieved: now Lyuba would probably tell him to go back to his father for good because, it appeared, one had to know how to take pleasure, and Nikita couldn't torment Lyuba just for the sake of his own happiness, but all his strength was pounding inside his heart, rushing up into his throat, leaving nothing anywhere else.

Lyuba woke up and looked at her husband.

"Don't be downhearted, it's not worth it," she said smiling. "You and I'll fix everything together."

"Let me wash the floor," Nikita asked her, "else it will be dirty here."

"Well, go on and wash it," Lyuba agreed.

"How pitiful and weak he is from his love for me!" Lyuba thought in bed. "How good and dear he is to me! May I always be a girl to him! I can stand it. And maybe some time he'll start loving me less, and then he'll be a strong man."

Nikita was fidgeting with a wet mop on the floor, scrubbing the dirt from the boards, and Lyuba laughed at him from the bed.

"Here I am a married woman!" she told herself with delight, and she stretched out in her nightgown on top of the blanket.

When he had scrubbed the room, Nikita wiped all the furniture with a wet cloth, then he added cold water to the pail of hot water and pulled a washbasin out from under the bed so that Lyuba could wash in it.

After they had drunk tea, Lyuba kissed her husband on the forehead and went off to work at the hospital, telling him that she would be back at three o'clock. Nikita touched the place on his forehead where his wife had kissed him, and stayed by himself. He didn't know why he wasn't going to work today—it seemed to him it was shameful now for him to be alive, and maybe he did not have to. Why did he need to earn money now? He decided somehow to live out the rest of his life, until he wasted away from shame and grief.

Having looked over all the family property in their new home, Nikita found the food he needed to fix a one-dish dinner—a thick beef soup. After this work, he lay face down on the bed and began to count how much time would have to go by before the rivers started to flow again, when he could drown himself in the Potudan.

"I'll wait until the ice breaks up; it won't be long now," he said out loud, to calm himself, and he dozed off.

Lyuba brought a present back with her from work—two earthenware bowls with winter flowers in them: the doctors and the nurses had celebrated her wedding. And she had held herself important and mysterious in front of them, like a real married woman. The younger girls among the nurses and nurses' aides were envious of her, one earnest worker from the hospital pharmacy asked Lyuba confidentially: was it true or not that love was something fascinating but that getting married for love was truly an entrancing happiness? Lyuba answered her that this was the honest truth, and that this was why people go on living in this world.

The husband and wife talked with each other in the evening. Lyuba said that they might have children, and that they should think about this ahead of time. Nikita promised to begin making some children's furniture in overtime at the workshop: a little table, a chair, and a cradle-bed.

"The revolution is here for good, now it's all right to have children," Nikita said. "There'll never be unhappy children ever again."

"It's all right for you to talk, but I'm the one who'll have to bear them," Lyuba said, pouting.

"Will it hurt?" Nikita asked. "In that case, better not to have children, not to suffer . . ."

"No, I'll survive it, thanks just the same," Lyuba agreed.

At twilight she fixed the bed, and then, so it wouldn't be too crowded for sleep she extended it with the two

chairs for their feet and had them sleep across it. Nikita
lay down as he was instructed, was silent, and late in the
night he cried in his sleep. But Lyuba didn't fall asleep for
a long time, she was listening to his crying, and she carefully wiped Nikita's sleeping face with the end of the
sheet, and in the morning, when he woke up, he had no
memory of his sadness in the night.

After that their life together went on at its own pace.
Lyuba took care of people in the hospital, and Nikita
made his furniture. In his free time and on Sundays he
worked in the yard and in the house, although Lyuba
didn't ask him to do this—she herself no longer knew exactly whose house it was. Once it had belonged to her
mother, then it had been taken over as government property but the government had forgotten about the house—
no one had ever come to check on its condition or to ask
any money as rent. It made no difference to Nikita. He
managed to get some green paint, through acquaintances
of his father, and he painted the roof and the shutters as
soon as spring weather had set in. With the same diligence
he gradually fixed up the decrepit old shed in the yard
outside the house, repaired the gate and the fence, and
prepared to dig a new cellar since the old one had caved in.

The ice was already breaking up in the Potudan River.
Nikita walked down to the bank twice, looked at the flowing water, and made up his mind not to die as long as
Lyuba could stand him, and whenever she couldn't stand
him any longer, he'd manage to end it all. The river
wouldn't freeze over quickly. Nikita usually did his work
around the house slowly so as not to be sitting in the
room, making Lyuba tired of him. And whenever he finished it completely, he would fill the hem of his shirt with
clay from the old cellar and walk back into the room.
There he would sit on the floor and shape little human figures and other objects out of the clay, with no meaning or
likeness to anything—things like hills with animal heads
growing out of them, or the root system of a tree in which
the root seemed an ordinary root but so tangled and im-

passable, with each of its branches pierced by another, gnawing at and torturing itself, that looking long at this root made you want to go to sleep. Nikita smiled carelessly and blissfully while he worked with his clay, and Lyuba would sit there on the floor next to him, sewing linen or singing little songs that she had heard at some time, and along with what she was doing she would caress Nikita with one hand, sometimes stroking his head, sometimes tickling him under his arm. Nikita lived through these hours with his heart beating gently, and he did not know if he needed something higher and mightier, or if life in actual fact was nothing very big—just about what he already had. But Lyuba would look at him with her tired eyes full of patient goodness, just as if what was good and happy had become heavy work for her. Then Nikita would knead his clay toys back into the clay from which he had made them, and he would ask his wife if she didn't want him to stoke up the stove, to heat water for tea, or to go out somewhere on an errand . . .

"You don't have to," Lyuba would say, smiling at him. "I'll do it all myself. . . ."

And Nikita understood that life was indeed something very big, and maybe beyond his strength, that it was not all concentrated in his pounding heart—it was still stronger, more interesting and dearer in another person he could not reach. He picked up the pail and went to get water at the town well where the water was cleaner than in the tanks on the street. Nikita could not drown his grief with anything, with any kind of work, and he was afraid of the approaching night as he had been in childhood. When he had got the water, Nikita went along with the full pail to call on his father.

"What's the matter, didn't you have a wedding?" his father asked. "Did you do it in the Soviet way, secretly. . . ?"

"We'll have it yet," his son promised. "Come on, help me make a little table, with a chair and a cradle-bed. You talk to the foreman tomorrow, so he'll give me the material. . . . Because we'll be having children, probably."

"Well, why not? That's possible," the father agreed. "But you shouldn't be having children soon: it's not time yet . . ."

In a week Nikita had made for himself all the children's furniture he needed; he stayed late every evening, and worked hard at it. His father sanded each piece neatly, and painted it.

Lyuba set up the child's furniture in a special corner, decorated her unborn child's table with two earthenware bowls of flowers, and hung a newly embroidered towel over the back of the chair. Lyuba hugged Nikita in thanks for his devotion to her and to her unknown children, she kissed his throat, pressed herself against his chest, and warmed herself next to her beloved, knowing that there was nothing else that could be done. And Nikita dropped the hands with which he had covered his heart and stood there silent in front of her because he did not want to look strong when he was really helpless.

Nikita went to sleep early that night and woke up a little after midnight. He lay there in the quiet for a long time and listened to the sounds of the clock striking in the town—half past twelve, one, half past one, a single peal for each of the three times. In the sky outside the window a vague kind of growing started—it was not yet dawn but only a movement in the darkness, a slow stripping away of empty space, and all the things in the room and the child's furniture, too, began to be visible, but after the dark night they had lived through they looked miserable and exhausted, as if they were calling out for help. Lyuba stirred under the blanket, and she sighed; perhaps she too was not asleep. In any case Nikita kept quiet, and began to listen hard. But Lyuba didn't stir any more, she was breathing evenly again, and it pleased Nikita that Lyuba was lying there next to him, alive, essential to his soul, and not even realizing in her sleep that he, her husband, even existed. As long as she was whole and happy, Nikita needed for his own life only his consciousness of her. He dozed off in peace, comforted by the sleep of someone close and dear to him, and then he opened his eyes again.

Lyuba was crying, carefully, almost inaudibly. She had covered over her head, and was tormenting herself there alone, squeezing her grief to keep it down without a sound. Nikita turned his face to Lyuba and saw how quickly she was breathing and how dispirited she was as she sadly hid under the covers. Nikita was silent. It's not possible to comfort every grief, there is some grief that ends only after the exhaustion of the heart, in long oblivion or in the distraction of the cares of daily living.

By dawn Lyuba had grown quiet. Nikita waited for a while and then lifted the corner of the blanket and looked at his wife's face. She was sleeping quietly, warm, at peace, with dry eyes . . .

Nikita got up, dressed quietly, and went outside. A pale morning was starting across the world, and a wandering beggar was walking down the street, carrying a full bag. Nikita started to follow this man, so as to have a feeling of going somewhere. The beggar walked out of the town and set off along the high road to the settlement of Kantemirovka where from time immemorial there had been a big bazaar and many prosperous people. It's true, they gave little away to a poor man there, and the beggar could really feed himself only in the faraway villages where poor peasants lived, but still it was fun in Kantemirovka, interesting, one could live at the bazaar just by watching the crowds of people, distracting the spirit for a little while.

The beggar and Nikita got to Kantemirovka about noon. In the outskirts of the town the beggar sat down in a ditch, opened his bag, and he and Nikita ate together, and then inside the town they went off in different directions because the beggar had his own plans and Nikita had none. He came to the bazaar, sat down in the shade next to a merchant's bin with a hinged cover, and stopped thinking about Lyuba, about the cares of life, and about himself.

The watchman at the bazaar had already lived there for twenty-five years and all this time he had lived a rich life with his fat, childless old lady. The merchants and the cooperative stores were always giving him leftovers of meat, they sold him sewing materials at cost and even household necessities like thread, soap, and such products. For a long time he had been a small trader himself, selling broken-up packing cases and hoarding the money in a savings account. His responsibility was to sweep up the trash all through the fair grounds, to wash the blood from the counters in the butchers' row, to clean the public latrines, and at night to patrol the trading sheds and the stores. But he only strolled up and down the bazaar at night in a warm sheepskin coat while he turned the hard work over to beggars and vagabonds who passed the night at the bazaar; his wife almost always emptied the remains of yesterday's meat and cabbage soup into a garbage pail, so the watchman could feed some poor wretch for cleaning the latrines for him.

His wife used to order him not to do the dirty work himself, seeing how gray his beard had grown—he was no longer to be a watchman, but a supervisor. But it was hard to get a beggar or a tramp to work forever in exchange for grub like that; he'd work for a day, eat what was given him, ask for more, then disappear back into the countryside.

Recently the watchman had driven the same man out of the bazaar for several nights in a row. When the watchman shoved him, as he slept, this man would get up and walk away, saying nothing, and then he would sit down or lie down somewhere else behind a bin which was farther away. Once the watchman hunted this homeless man all night long, his blood fairly sparkling with his passionate desire to torment and to subdue this strange, exhausted creature. Twice the watchman threw his stick at him and hit him in the head, but by dawn the vagabond was still hiding from him—probably he had quit the fair grounds completely. In the morning the watchman found him again—he was sleeping on the roof of a cesspool at the latrines, out in the open. The watchman called to the sleeping man, who opened his eyes but did not answer, looked at him and then dozed off again with complete indifference. The watchman thought—this must be a dumb man.

He prodded the sleeper's stomach with the end of his stick and gestured with his arm that he should follow him.

In his neat, official apartment—kitchen and one room—the watchman fed the dumb man from an earthenware pot of cold soup, and after he had eaten ordered him to take a broom, a shovel, a scraper and a pail of lime from the shed and to clean the latrines thoroughly. The dumb man looked at the watchman with dull eyes: probably he was deaf, too. . . . But no, he couldn't be, because the dumb man picked up in the shed all the tools and things he needed, just as the watchman had told him. This proved that he could hear.

Nikita did the job accurately, and the watchman came back later to see how it looked; for a start, it was tolerable, so the watchman took Nikita to the place where horses were hitched and told him to pick up all the manure and take it away in a wheelbarrow.

At home the watchman-supervisor instructed his wife that now she was no longer to scrape the leavings from their supper and dinner into the garbage pail but to keep them in a separate crock: let the dumb man have his fill to eat.

"And I suppose you're going to have him sleep in the room, too," the wife asked him.

"That's not the point!" the man declared. "He'll spend the nights outside: for he's not deaf, let him lie there and listen for robbers, and when he hears one, he'll run and tell me. Give him a piece of sacking, he'll find a place and make himself a bed."

Nikita lived for a long time at the bazaar. Having first become unused to talking, he thought, remembered, and worried less and less. It was ony rarely that a weight lay on his heart, and he endured this without reflecting about it, and the feeling of grief inside him gradually weakened and disappeared. He was already used to living at the bazaar, and the crowds of people, the noise of voices, all the daily happenings, kept him from remembering about himself and from his own concerns—food, rest, and the desire to see his father. Nikita worked all the time; even at

night when he would fall asleep in an empty box somewhere in the empty bazaar, the watchman-supervisor
would come up to him and order him just to nap and to
listen, not to sleep like the dead. "You've got to," the
watchman told him, "only the other day the crooks ripped
two boards off a shop and ate fifteen pounds of honey
without any bread." And by dawn Nikita was already
working, hurrying to get the bazaar clean before the people came; in the daytime he couldn't eat, there was the manure to be shoveled into the communal cart, a new pit to
be dug for slops and sewage, or old boxes to be broken up
which the watchman got free from the traders and then
sold, board by board, to peasants from the country, and
then there was still more work to do.

In the middle of the summer they took Nikita to jail on
suspicion of having stolen some chandler's goods from the
government store at the bazaar, but the investigation
cleared him because this dumb, desperately tired man was
too indifferent about the charge against him. The investigator could find no evidence of any desire for life or enjoyment or satisfactions of any kind in Nikita's character or in his modest work at the bazaar as the watchman's helper. In jail he didn't even eat up the food that
was given to him. The investigator realized that this was
a man who did not know the value of either personal or
public property, and there was not even any circum-
stantial evidence against him in the case. "There's no reason to dirty up a prison with a man like that!" the investigator decided.

Nikita stayed in jail for five days, and then went back to
the bazaar. The watchman-supervisor was already tired
out from having to work without him, so he was overjoyed
when the dumb man showed up again. The old man summoned him to his apartment and gave him hot, fresh cabbage soup to eat, breaking all the rules of thrift in his own
household. "Let him eat for once—it won't ruin him!" the
old watchman-supervisor reassured himself. "And then
back to yesterday's cold leftovers, when there are any."

"Go over and clean up the rubbish along the grocers'

row," the watchman instructed Nikita when he had eaten up the soup.

Nikita went back to his usual place. By now he was only dimly aware of himself at all, and he thought very little about anything that happened to come into his mind. By autumn, probably, he would have forgotten entirely what he was. Looking around at the activity of the world he would have ceased to have any understanding of it. Other people might think this man was living but actually he would be there and exist only in forgetfulness, in the poverty of his mind, in his loss of consciousness, as if in some warmth of his own, taking shelter from mortal grief....

Soon after his stay in jail, at the end of summer when the nights were growing longer, Nikita started once to lock the door to the latrines, as required by the rules, when he heard a voice from inside:

"Wait a little, before you lock up! Are you afraid someone's going to steal something out of here?"

Nikita waited for the man. His father walked out of the building, holding an empty sack under his arm.

"Hello, Nikita!" the father said, and he suddenly began to cry, sadly, ashamed of his tears and not wiping them away so as not to admit that he was crying. "We thought you were a dead man long ago. This means you're all right?"

Nikita embraced his thin drooping father; his heart, which had grown unused to feeling, had now been touched.

Then they walked through the empty bazaar and settled down in the passageway between two big merchants' bins.

"I just came for some barley, it's cheaper here," his father explained. "But I was late, you see, the bazaar is closed. Well, I'll spend the night now, and tomorrow I'll buy it and go back home. And what are you doing here?"

Nikita wanted to answer his father, but his throat dried up and he had forgotten how to talk. He coughed, and whispered:

"I'm all right. Is Lyuba alive?"

"She threw herself in the river," his father said. "But some fishermen saw her right away and pulled her out— she was in the hospital for a while, she got better."

"And she's alive now?" Nikita asked in a low voice.

"So far she hasn't died," his father declared. "Blood runs often from her throat; she probably caught cold when she tried to drown herself. She picked a bad time —the weather had just turned bad and the water was cold . . ."

The father pulled some bread out of his pocket, gave half of it to his son, and they sat there for a little, chewing their supper. Nikita was silent, and the father spread his sack out on the ground, and got ready to lie down on it.

"Have you got any place to sleep?" the father asked. "If not, you lie on the sack, and I'll lie on the ground. I won't catch cold, I'm too old. . . ."

"But why did Lyuba drown herself?" Nikita whispered.

"What's the matter? Does your throat hurt you?" the father asked. "You'll get over it. . . . She missed you badly, and just wasted away from grief, that's why . . . For a whole month she just walked up and down the Potudan River, back and forth, along the bank for sixty miles. She thought you'd drowned and would come to the surface, and she wanted to see you. While, it turns out, you were right here all the time. That's bad . . ."

Nikita thought about Lyuba, and once more his heart filled with grief and with strength.

"You spend the night here alone, father," Nikita said. "I'm going to have a look at Lyuba."

"Go on then," the father agreed. "It's good going now, cooler. And I'll come back tomorrow, then we'll talk things over . . ."

Going out of the settlement Nikita started to run along the deserted high road. When he got tired, he walked again for a while, then he ran again in the free, light air spread over the dark fields.

It was late at night when Nikita knocked at Lyuba's

window and touched the shutters he had painted once with green paint. Now the dark night made them look blue. He pressed his face against the window glass. A pale light was filtered through the room, from the white sheets dropping off the bed, and Nikita could see the child's furniture he had made with his father—it was all there. Then Nikita knocked loudly on the window frame. But Lyuba still did not answer, and she didn't come to the window to see who he was.

Nikita climbed over the gate, went through the shed and then into the room—the doors were not locked; whoever lived here was not worried about protecting his property from thieves.

Lyuba was lying under the blanket on the bed, her head covered.

"Lyuba!" Nikita called to her in a low voice.

"What?" Lyuba asked from under the blanket.

She wasn't asleep. Maybe she was lying there all alone in terror, or sick, or thought the knock on the window and Nikita's voice were a dream.

Nikita sat on the edge of the bed.

"Lyuba, I've come, it's me," Nikita said.

Lyuba lifted the blanket away from her face.

"Come here to me, quickly," she begged in her old, tender voice, and she held out her arms to Nikita.

Lyuba was afraid this would all go away; she grabbed Nikita by the arms and pulled him to her.

Nikita hugged Lyuba with the force that tries to pull another, beloved person right inside a hungering soul; but he quickly recovered his senses, and felt ashamed.

"I didn't hurt you?" Nikita asked.

"No, I don't feel anything," Lyuba answered.

He wanted her badly, so she might be comforted, and a savage, miserable strength came to him. But Nikita did not find from loving Lyuba intimately any higher happiness than he had usually known—he felt only that his heart was now in charge of his whole body and could divide his blood with his poor but necessary pleasure.

Lyuba asked Nikita—maybe he could light the little

stove for it would still be dark outside for a long time. Let there be a fire inside the room, she wouldn't be sleeping anyway, she wanted to wait for the dawn and look at Nikita.

But there was no more firewood in the shed. So Nikita ripped two boards off the side of the shed, split them into pieces and some kindling, and stoked up the little stove. When the fire was burning well, Nikita opened the little door so the light could shine outside the stove. Lyuba climbed out of bed and sat on the floor, facing Nikita, where there was some light.

"Is it all right with you now, you won't be sorry to live with me?" she asked.

"No, I'm all right," Nikita answered. "I'm already used to being happy with you."

"Build up the fire, I'm chilled to the bone," Lyuba asked him.

She was wearing only her worn-out nightgown, and her thin body was freezing in the cool half-light of early morning at the end of summer.

(1937)

Boris Pasternak

(*1890–1960*)

All but unknown in the West before 1957—the year of the "Zhivago affair"—Pasternak is today probably the best known of all modern Russian writers, though "Lara's Theme" from the soundtrack of the successful film version of *Dr. Zhivago* may have as much to do with his celebrity as any considered literary judgment. While he is inevitably thought of in the West as a novelist, the view in Russia, where *Dr. Zhivago* has only recently appeared, is predictably different. Though he did write some remarkable prose (much of it later incorporated into *Dr. Zhivago*), Pasternak's reputation in his native land rests almost exclusively on his poetry, and in part on his poetic translations.

The book that established his fame, *My Sister, Life* (1922), was written in a concentrated wave of inspiration in the summer of 1917. It brims with the exalted sense of liberation that the first of the two revolutions of that year brought with it. Though there had been two earlier books, *A Twin in the Clouds* (1914) and *Above the Barriers* (1917), *My Sister, Life* marks the beginning of the *great* Pasternak, and it is worth noting that the name *Zhivago* in his last work also derives from the Russian word for "life." It has been remarked that the word springs all too readily to Russian lips, but Pasternak's achievement was to infuse it with a fresh and altogether personal content. No other writer, with the possible exception of Rilke (a friend of the Pasternaks), evinces such a feeling of kinship with natural phenomena (note the telling words *twin* and *sister* in his titles); and Pasternak's kinship at times amounts to a virtual oneness. The "life" to which he was a brother was a democratic continuum in which the humble articles furnishing a room stood on an equal footing with nature's grand occasions and with the human consciousness uniting them. Pasternak enlarged the capacities of Russian speech to accommodate teacups, lightning bolts, and the perceiving intelligence in a syntax that almost defied interpretation. One did not so much read the early poetry of Pasternak as *earn* it by the hard work of prolonged attention. His course, like that of his beloved Tolstoy, was from complexity to simplicity, from the cerebral contortions of his early hermetic verse to the almost peasant plainness of the poems attributed to Dr. Zhivago. There is nothing shallow or insipid about the later style. The poems yield their richness only to the truly sophisticated reader who is not deceived by their apparent lack of complication.

Those familiar only with the ordeal of Pasternak's last years—the vicious persecution of him for having allowed *Zhivago* to be published abroad, the coerced rejection of the Nobel Prize for Literature in 1958—will be surprised to learn that, in fact, he led something of a charmed existence. He was born into a well-to-do family of Jewish artists and intellectuals of international fame and brilliant connections. His father, Leonid, was a celebrated painter and a friend of Leo Tolstoy (see p. 1), whose work he illustrated, and his mother was a talented pianist. Rilke and Scriabin were among the intellectual elite who frequented the world in which Pasternak grew up. Undecided on how best to exercise his talents, he tried both philosophy and music before arriving at the decision to be a poet. His name is usually linked with the Futurists, but this is misleading, for Pasternak was the most radically unclubbable of Russian writers. A loner by temperament, he was ideally unsuited for an age when individualism was regarded initially as a sort of social disease and ultimately as a crime. And yet Pasternak appears to have been untouchable, for he moved unscathed through the years of Stalin's genocidal fury. This mystery has naturally given rise to various conjectures about the relationship between the tyrant and the poet. According to one account, Pasternak, having characteristically refused to sign a collective letter of condolence to Stalin on the death of his wife, Alliluyeva, sent an opaque message of his own that inspired in the dictator the notion that he was clairvoyant—though why this should have ensured Pasternak's safety rather than his immediate elimination escapes me.

VARYKINO

(from *Dr. Zhivago*)

1

In the winter, when Yurii Andreievich had more time, he began a notebook. He wrote: "How often, last summer, I felt like saying with Tiutchev:

> 'What a summer, what a summer!
> This is magic indeed.
> And how, I ask you, did it come
> Just like that, out of the blue?'

What happiness, to work from dawn to dusk for your family and for yourself, to build a roof over their heads, to till the soil to feed them, to create your own world, like Robinson Crusoe, in imitation of the Creator of the universe, and, as your own mother did, to give birth to yourself, time and again.

"So many new thoughts come into your head when your hands are busy with hard physical work, when your mind has set you a task that can be achieved by physical effort and that brings its reward in joy and success, when for six hours on end you dig or hammer, scorched by the life-giving breath of the sky. And it isn't a loss but a gain that these transient thoughts, intuitions, analogies are not put down on paper but forgotten. The town recluse whipping up his nerves and his imagination with strong black coffee and tobacco doesn't know the strongest drug of all—good health and real necessity.

"I am not going further than this. I am not preaching Tolstoyan austerity and the return to the land, I am not trying to improve on socialism and its solution to the agrarian problem. I am merely stating a fact, I am not building a system on the basis of our own accidental experience. Our example is debatable and unsuitable for deductions. Our economy is too mixed. What we produce ourselves—potatoes and vegetables—is only a small part of what we need; the rest comes from other sources.

"Our use of the land is illegal. We have taken the law into our own hands, and we conceal what we are doing from the state. The wood we cut is stolen, and it is no excuse that we steal from the state or that the property once belonged to Krueger. We can do all this thanks to Mikulitsyn's tolerant attitude (he lives in much the same way as we do), and we can do it safely because we are far from the town, where, fortunately, nothing is known, for the time being, about our illegal activities.

"I have given up practicing medicine, and I don't tell anyone that I am a physician, because I don't want to restrict my freedom. But there are always some good souls who get wind of the fact that there is a doctor in Varykino. So they trudge twenty miles to consult me, and bring a chicken or eggs, or butter, or something. And there is no way to persuade them that I don't want to be paid, because people don't believe in the effectiveness of free medical advice. So my practice brings in a little. But our chief mainstay, Mikulitsyn's and ours, is Samdeviatov.

"He is a fantastically complicated character. I can't make him out. He is a genuine supporter of the revolution and he fully deserves the confidence that the Yuriatin Soviet has in him. With all the powers they have given him he could requisition the Varykino timber without so much as telling Mikulitsyn or us, and he knows that we wouldn't protest. On the other hand, if he felt like robbing the state, he could fill his pocket and again no one would say a word. He has no need to bribe or share with anybody. What, then, is it that makes him take care of us; help the Mikulitsyns, and everyone in the district, for instance, the stationmaster at Torfianaia? All the time he is on the road, getting hold of something to bring us. He is just as familiar with Dostoievsky's *Possessed* as with the Communist Manifesto, and he talks about them equally well. I have the impression that if he didn't complicate his life so needlessly, he would die of boredom."

II

A little later the doctor wrote:

"We are living in two rooms in a wooden annex at the back of the old house. When Anna Ivanovna was a child Krueger used it for special events—the dressmaker, the housekeeper, and the retired nurse.

"It was pretty dilapidated when we came, but we repaired it fairly quickly. With the help of experts we rebuilt the stove, which serves both rooms. We have rearranged the flues and it gives more heat.

"In this part of the grounds the old garden has vanished, obliterated by new growth. But now, in winter, when everything is inanimate, living nature no longer covers the dead; in snowy outline the past can be read more clearly.

"We have been lucky. The autumn was dry and warm. It gave us time to dig up the potatoes before the rains and the cold weather. Not counting those we gave back to Mikulitsyn, we had twenty sacks. We put them in the biggest bin in the cellar and covered them with old blankets and hay. We also put down two barrels of salted cucumbers and two of sauerkraut prepared by Tonia. Fresh cabbages hang in pairs from the beams. There are carrots buried in dry sand, and radishes and beets and turnips, and plenty of peas and beans are stored in the loft. There is enough firewood in the shed to last us till spring.

"I love the warm, dry winter breath of the cellar, the smell of earth, roots, and snow that hits you the moment you raise the trap door as you go down in the early hours before the winter dawn, a weak, flickering light in your hand.

"You come out; it is still dark. The door creaks or perhaps you sneeze or the snow crunches under your foot, and hares start up from the far cabbage patch and hop away, leaving the snow crisscrossed with tracks. In the distance dogs begin to bark and it is a long time before they quiet down. The cocks have finished their crowing and have nothing left to say. Then dawn breaks.

"Besides the tracks of hares, the endless snowy plain is patterned by those of lynxes, stretching across it neatly, like strings of beads. The lynx walks like a cat, putting one paw down in front of the other, and they say it travels many miles in a night.

"Traps are set for them, but instead of the lynxes the wretched hares get caught, half buried in the snow, and are taken out, frozen stiff.

"At the beginning, during spring and summer, we had a very hard time. We drove ourselves to the utmost. But now we can relax in the winter evenings. Thanks to Samdeviatov, who supplies us with kerosene, we sit around a lamp. The women sew or knit, Alexander Alexandrovich or I read aloud. The stove is hot, and I, as the appointed stoker, watch it for the right moment to close the damper so as not to waste any heat. If a charred log prevents the fire from drawing properly, I remove it and run out with it smoking and fling it as far as possible into the snow. It flies through the air like a torch, throwing off sparks and lighting up the white rectangular lawns of the sleeping park and then buries itself, hissing, in a snowdrift.

"We read and reread *War and Peace*, *Evgenii Onegin* and Pushkin's other poems, and Russian translations of

Stendhal's *The Red and the Black*, Dickens's *Tale of Two Cities*, and Kleist's short stories."

III

As spring approached, the doctor wrote:

"I believe Tonia is pregnant. I told her and she doesn't believe it, but I feel sure of it. The early symptoms are unmistakable to me, I don't have to wait for the later, more certain ones.

"A woman's face changes at such a time. It isn't that she becomes less attractive, but her appearance is no longer quite under her control. She is now ruled by the future which she carries within her, she is no longer alone. Her loss of control over her appearance makes her seem physically at a loss; her face dims, her skin coarsens, her eyes shine in a different way, not as she wants them to, it is as if she couldn't quite cope with all these things and has neglected herself.

"Tonia and I have never drifted apart, but this year of work has brought us even closer together. I have noticed how efficient, strong, and tireless she is, how cleverly she plans her work, so as to waste as little time as possible between one job and another.

"It has always seemed to me that every conception is immaculate and that this dogma, concerning the Mother of God, expresses the idea of all motherhood.

"At childbirth, every woman has the same aura of isolation, as though she were abandoned, alone. At this vital moment the man's part is as irrelevant as if he had never had anything to do with it, as though the whole thing had dropped from heaven.

"It is the woman, by herself, who brings forth her progeny, and carries it off to some remote corner of existence, a quiet, safe place for a crib. Alone, in silence and humility, she feeds and rears the child.

"The Mother of God is asked to 'pray zealously to her Son and her God,' and the words of the psalm are put into her mouth: 'My soul doth magnify the Lord, and my spirit hath rejoiced in God my Saviour. For He hath regarded the low estate of his handmaiden: for, behold, from henceforth all generations shall call me blessed.' It is because of her child that she says this, He will magnify her ('For He that is mighty hath done to me great things'): He is her glory. Any woman could say it. For every one of them, God is in her child. Mothers of great men must have been familiar with this feeling, but then, all women are mothers of great men—it isn't their fault if life disappoints them later."

IV

"We go on endlessly rereading *Evgenii Onegin* and the poems. Samdeviatov came yesterday and brought presents—nice things to eat and kerosene for the lamps. We have endless discussions about art.

"I have always thought that art is not a category, not a realm covering innumerable concepts and derivative phenomena, but that, on the contrary, it is something concentrated, strictly limited. It is a principle that is present in every work of art, a force applied to it and a truth worked out in it. And I have never seen art as form but rather as a hidden, secret part of content. All this is as clear to me as daylight. I feel it in every bone of my body, but it's terribly difficult to express or to define this idea.

"A literary creation can appeal to us in all sorts of ways—by its theme, subject, situations, characters. But above all it appeals to us by the presence in it of art. It is the presence of art in *Crime and Punishment* that moves us deeply rather than the story of Raskolnikov's crime.

"Primitive art, the art of Egypt, Greece, our own—it is all, I think, one and the same art through thousands of years. You can call it an idea, a statement about life, so all-embracing that it can't be split up into separate words; and if there is so much as a particle of it in any work that includes other things as well, it outweighs all the other ingredients in significance and turns out to be the essence, the heart and soul of the work."

V

"A slight chill, a cough, probably a bit of temperature. Gasping all day long, the feeling of a lump in my throat. I am in a bad way. It is my heart. The first symptoms that I have inherited my poor mother's heart—she suffered from it all her life. Can it really be that? So soon? If so, my tenure in this world is short.

"A faint smell of charcoal in the room. A smell of ironing. Tonia is ironing, every now and then she gets a coal out of the stove and puts it in the iron, and the lid of the iron snaps over it like a set of teeth. It reminds me of something, but I can't think of what. Must be my condition.

"To celebrate Samdeviatov's gift of soap we have had two washing days and Sashenka has been running wild. As I write he sits astride the crosspiece under the table and, imitating Samdeviatov, who takes him out in his sleigh whenever he comes, pretends that he is giving me a ride.

"As soon as I feel better I must go to the town library and read up on the ethnography and history of the region. They say the library has had several important donations and is exceptionally good. I have an urge to write. But I'll have to hurry. It will be spring before we know where we are—and then there'll be no time for reading or writing.

"My headache gets worse and worse. I slept badly. Had a muddled dream of the kind you forget as you wake up. All that remained in my memory was the part that woke me up. It was a woman's voice, I heard it in my dream, sounding in the air. I remembered it and kept hearing it in my mind and going through the list of our women friends—I tried to think of someone who spoke in that deep, soft, husky voice. It didn't belong to any of them. I thought it might be Tonia's, and that I had become so used to her that I no longer heard the tone of her voice. I tried to forget that she was my wife and to become sufficiently detached to find out. But it wasn't her voice either. It remains a mystery.

"About dreams. It is usually taken for granted that you dream of something that has made a particularly strong impression on you during the day, but it seems to me it's just the contrary.

"Often it's something you paid no attention to at the time—a vague thought that you didn't bother to think out to the end, words spoken without feeling and which passed unnoticed—these are the things that return at night, clothed in flesh and blood, and they become the subjects of dreams, as if to make up for having been ignored during waking hours."

VI

"A clear, frosty night. Unusual brilliance and perfection of everything visible. Earth, sky, moon, and stars, all seem cemented, riveted together by the frost. Shadows of trees lie across the paths, so sharp that they seem carved in relief. You keep thinking you see dark figures endlessly cross the road at various places. Big stars hang in the woods between branches like blue lanterns. Small ones are strewn all over the sky like daisies in a summer field.

"We go on discussing Pushkin. The other night we talked about the early poems he wrote as a schoolboy. How much depended on his choice of meter!

"In the poems with long lines, his ambition did not extend beyond the town of Arzamas; he wanted to keep up with the grownups, impress his uncle with mythologism, bombast, faked epicureanism and sophistication, and affected a precocious worldly wisdom.

"But as soon as he stopped imitating Ossian and Parny and changed from 'Recollections of Tsarskoie Selo' to 'A Small Town' or 'Letter to My Sister' or 'To My Inkwell' (written later in Kishinev), or 'To Yudin,' the future Pushkin was already there.

"Air, light, the noise of life, reality burst into his poetry from the street as through an open window. The outside world, everyday things, nouns, crowded in and took possession of his lines, driving out the vaguer parts of speech.

Things and more things lined up in rhymed columns on the page.

"As if this, Pushkin's tetrameter, which later became so famous, were a measuring unit of Russian life, a yardstick, as if it had been patterned after the whole of Russia's existence, as you draw the outline of a foot or give the size of a hand to make sure that the glove or the shoe will fit.

"Later in much the same way, the rhythm of spoken Russian, the intonations of ordinary speech were expressed in Nekrassov's trimeters and dactyls."

VII

"I should like to be of use as a doctor or a farmer and at the same time to be gestating something lasting, something fundamental, to be writing some scientific paper or a literary work.

"Every man is born a Faust, with a longing to grasp and experience and express everything in the world. Faust became a scientist thanks to the mistakes of his predecessors and contemporaries. Progress in science is governed by the laws of repulsion, every step forward is made by refutation of prevalent errors and false theories. Faust was an artist thanks to the inspiring example of his teachers. Forward steps in art are governed by the law of attraction, are the result of the imitation of and admiration for beloved predecessors.

"What is it that prevents me from being a doctor and a writer? I think it is not our privations or our wanderings or our unsettled lives, but the prevalent spirit of high-flown rhetoric, which has spread everywhere—phrases such as 'the dawn of the future,' 'the building of a new world,' 'the torch-bearers of mankind.' The first time you hear such talk you think 'What breadth of imagination, what richness!' But in fact it's so pompous just because it is so unimaginative and second-rate.

"Only the familiar transformed by genius is truly great. The best object lesson in this is Pushkin. His works are one great hymn to honest labor, duty, everyday life!

Today, 'bourgeois' and 'petty bourgeois' have become terms of abuse, but Pushkin forestalled the implied criticism in his 'Family Tree,' where he says proudly that he belongs to the middle class, and in 'Onegin's Travels' we read:

> 'Now my ideal is the housewife,
> My greatest wish, a quiet life
> And a big bowl of cabbage soup.'

"What I have come to like best in the whole of Russian literature is the childlike Russian quality of Pushkin and Chekhov, their modest reticence in such high-sounding matters as the ultimate purpose of mankind or their own salvation. It isn't that they didn't think about these things, and to good effect, but to talk about such things seemed to them pretentious, presumptuous. Gogol, Tolstoy, Dostoievsky looked restlessly for the meaning of life, and prepared for death and drew conclusions. Pushkin and Chekhov, right up to the end of their lives, were absorbed in the current, specific tasks imposed on them by their vocation as writers, and in the course of fulfilling these tasks they lived their lives, quietly, treating both their lives and their work as private, individual matters, of no concern to anyone else. And these individual things have since become of concern to all, and their works, like apples picked while they are green, have ripened of themselves, mellowing gradually and growing richer in meaning."

VIII

"First signs of spring. Thaw. The air smells of buttered pancakes and vodka, as at Shrovetide. A sleepy, oily sun blinking in the forest, sleepy pines blinking their needles like eyelashes, oily puddles glistening at noon. The countryside yawns, stretches, turns over, and goes back to sleep.

"Chapter Seven of *Evgenii Onegin* describes the spring, Onegin's house deserted in his absence, Lensky's grave by the stream at the foot of the hill.

'The nightingale, spring's lover,
Sings all night. The wild rose blooms.'

Why 'lover'? The fact is, the epithet is natural, apt: the
nightingale *is* spring's lover. Moreover, he needed it for
the rhyme. I wonder whether the nickname Nightingale,
for the brigand son of Odikmantii, in the well-known
Russian folk epic, is not a metaphor based on similarity of
sound. How well the song characterizes him!

'At his nightingale whistle,
At his wild forest call,
The grass is all a-tremble,
The flowers shed their petals,
The dark forest bows down to the ground,
And all good people fall down dead.'

We came to Varykino in early spring. Soon the trees grew
green—alder and nut trees and wild cherry—especially in
the Shutma, the ravine below Mikulitsyn's house. And
soon after that the nightingales began to sing.

"Once again, as though hearing them for the first time, I
wondered at the difference between their song and that of
all other birds, at the sudden jump, without transitions,
that nature makes to the richness and uniqueness of their
trills. Such variety and power and resonance! Turgenev
somewhere describes these whistling, fluting modulations.
There were two phrases that stood out particularly. One
was a luxurious, greedily repetitive tiokh-tiokh-tiokh, in
response to which the vegetation, all covered with dew,
trembled with delight. The other was in two syllables,
grave, imploring, an appeal or a warning: 'Wake up! Wake
up!'"

IX

"Spring. We are preparing for the spring sowing. No time
for a diary. It was pleasant to write. I'll have to stop until
next winter.

"The other day—and now it really was Shrovetide—right in the middle of the spring floods, a sick peasant drove his sleigh into the yard through the mud and slush. I refused to examine him. 'I've given up practicing,' I said. 'I have neither medicines nor equipment.' But he persisted. 'Help me. My skin is bad. Have pity on me. I am sick.' What could I do? I don't have a heart of stone. I told him to undress. He had lupus. As I was examining him I glanced at the bottle of carbolic acid on the window sill (don't ask me where it comes from—that and a few other things I couldn't do without—everything comes from Samdeviatov). Then I saw there was another sleigh in the yard. I thought at first it was another patient. But it was my brother, Evgraf, who had dropped in on us out of the blue. The family took charge of him—Tonia, Sashenka, Alexander Alexandrovich. Later I went out and joined them. We showered him with questions. Where had he come from? How had he come? As usual, he was evasive, he smiled, shrugged, spoke in riddles.

"He stayed about two weeks, went often to Yuriatin, and then vanished suddenly as if the earth had swallowed him. I realized while he was staying with us that he had even more influence than Samdeviatov and that his work and his connections were even more mysterious. What is he? What does he do? Why is he so powerful? He promised to make things easier for us so that Tonia should have more time for Sashenka and I for practicing medicine and writing. We asked him how he proposed to do this. He merely smiled. But he has been as good as his word. There are signs that our living conditions are really going to change.

"It is truly extraordinary. He is my half brother. We bear the same name. And yet I know virtually nothing about him.

"For the second time he has burst into my life as my good genius, my rescuer, resolving all my difficulties. Perhaps in every life there has to be, in addition to the other protagonists, a secret, unknown force, an almost symbolic figure who comes unsummoned to the rescue, and perhaps in mine Evgraf, my brother, plays the part of this hidden benefactor?"

At this point Yurii Andreievich's diary breaks off. He never went on with it.

(*1957*)

HAMLET
(from *Dr. Zhivago*)

The tumult stills. I stand upon the stage
Against a door-post, dimly reckoning
From traces of a distantly-heard echo
What my unfinished lifetime may yet bring.

The black of night pours from these opera glasses
That in their thousands train their sights on me:
But Abba, Father, if it be your will,
Remove this chalice in your clemency.

Unswervingly your purpose holds my love,
This rôle you've set I am content to play;
But now a different drama takes the scene:
Spare me this once the treading of your way.

And yet the order of the acts is planned,
The way's end destinate and unconcealed.
Alone. Now is the time of Pharisees.
To live is not like walking through a field.

(*1957*)

MARCH
(from *Dr. Zhivago*)

The sun burns on perspiring earth,
The vale is live and blustering,
And work seethes in the able hands
Of that stout dairymaid, the spring.

Anaemic, wasting fast away,
The snow runs off in veins of blue,
But still the cowshed steams with life,
The pitchfork's teeth breathe health anew.

These nights, these passing days and nights!
At noon the thaw-beat on the pane,
The icicles' drip on the roof,
The constant stream's sleepless refrain!

The stables, cowshed, everything
Flung open wide! Birds pecking snow!
And freshness over all from dung
From which all life and causes flow!

(1957)

Osip Mandelstam

(1891–1938)

Though Mandelstam was born in Warsaw and wrote some of his greatest works in Moscow and in remote places of banishment, his name continues to be associated with Saint Petersburg (Leningrad), where he grew up and first came to fame. His father was a Jewish leather merchant, an eccentric autodidact with a taste for German philosophy, and his mother a cultivated music teacher, proud of the intellectual distinction of her family. Mandelstam was educated at home and then at the Tenishev School, a new and emphatically modern and egalitarian establishment to which, a decade later, the liberal Nabokovs sent their son Vladimir (see p. 363). Mandelstam was enrolled for a while at the Sorbonne, at Heidelberg, and at the university in Saint Petersburg, where he studied eclectically and nonchalantly, and without receiving a degree. But like most of the Symbolist poets, who were his earliest models, and like his great friend Anna Akhmatova (see p. 111), he was thoroughly versed in the languages—ancient as well as modern—of European culture, and was broadly and deeply erudite. Some of the difficulty in his writing arises from his generous assumption that his readers would also be at home in the great "museum without walls" of Western (and Russian) culture.

By the time his first book of poems (*Stone*) appeared in 1913, Mandelstam was an Acmeist, a school label to which he loyally professed allegiance long after it had ceased to be current or pertinent to what was actually being written. But for this greatest of the Acmeists, as for Akhmatova, the name had come to stand not so much for certain literary standards as for a complex of ethical, religious, political, and aesthetic motivations. At one point Mandelstam called it simply a question of taste. At a dangerous later time, provoked by a hostile audience, Mandelstam riskily defined Acmeism as "a longing for world culture."

The word *revolution* inspired in Mandelstam, as it did in most Russian intellectuals, a kind of sacred optimism—they saw in it the promise of social justice and the rationalization of life. But Mandelstam was among the first to intuit—if not actually to know—that something had gone terribly wrong: Childlike peasants at one end of the social scale and artists and scientists at the other were soon to be equally in thrall to the philistine usurpers of the Revolution, who were contemptuous of both folk and cosmopolitan elite culture.

He was suspect from the beginning. Nikolai Gumilyov, organizer of the Acmeists, had been executed by firing squad for counterrevolutionary sedition in 1921. The new etiquette of those days demanded that one denounce any friend who had been truant in his enthusiasm for collectivism, but Mandelstam blatantly violated this rule. Nor would he write suitable poems or prose. And being a Jew in the country that has enriched the international lexicon of savagery with the word *pogrom* did not help.

No one could consider it altogether politic to have composed in 1934—to compose orally, not to write, for such a thing could never be written—a witty lampoon on Stalin, picturing the dictator with his cockroach mustaches tormenting the human filth that adoringly surrounded him. Mandelstam was arrested, tortured, and sent to a remote spot in the Urals, where he attempted suicide by leaping from a hospital window. He was finally confined to a comparatively mild exile in the town of Voronezh.

The miracle was that he was alive at all. Not entirely well in his mind and completely unwell in his body, Mandelstam nevertheless wrote poems that have become canonical among certain of his countrymen and, in translation, rather well known abroad. He tried in this exile to save not himself but his presumptive widow by writing the standard "Ode to Stalin." This stuck in his throat for a while, and resulted in many adjacent (and occasionally superb) poems. But it eventually came, as it did to every writer whose choice was either to praise Stalin or to condemn a loved one to death. He praised Stalin. Among the thousands of extorted eulogies Mandelstam's is not the worst.

THEODOSIA

I

The Harbor Master*

The starched white tunic inherited from the old regime made him look miraculously younger and reconciled him with himself: the freshness of a gymnasium student and the brisk cheerfulness of an executive—a combination of qualities which he prized in himself and feared to lose. He conceived of the entire Crimea as one blinding, stiffly starched geographical tunic. On the other side of Perekop was night. There beyond the salt marshes there was no longer any starch, there were no washerwomen, no glad subordination, and it would be impossible there to have that springy step, as after a swim, that permanent excitement: the blended sense of well-bought currency, of clear government service and, at the age of forty, the feeling of having passed one's exams.

Conditions were only too favorable. The businesslike briefcase was arranged with the easy domestic elegance of a travelling case, with little recesses for razor, soap dish, and brushes of various kinds. Without him, that is without the harbor master, there passed not one single ton for the

* This translation, first published in 1965, has been slightly revised.

barley men and the wheat men, not one ton for the grain shippers, not even for Rosh himself, the commissioner of yesterday, today an upstart, nor for the legendary Kanitfershtan, lazy and languid in the Italian manner, who shipped barley to Marseilles, nor for the wheaty Lifschitz, a scrawny turkey, the minister of the public garden of Ajvazovskij, nor to the Tsentrosoiuz,* nor to the Reisners, whose affairs were going so well that instead of their silver they celebrated their golden wedding anniversary, and the father, out of happiness, fraternized with the son.

Each of the filthy steamers, smelling of the kitchen and soya, with a crew of mulattoes, and with a captain's cabin that was thoroughly heated, like the international sleeper, but more like the garret of a well-to-do doorman, carried away his tons, too, indistinguishably mixed with the others.

People knew perfectly well that they were selling, along with the grain, the land on which they walked, but they went on selling that land, observing how it crumbled into the sea, and counting on leaving when they should feel under their feet the last slip of the sinking earth.

Whenever the harbor master walked along the densely shaded Italian Street, beloved by its old residents, he was stopped every minute, taken by the arm, and led aside—which was, by the way, one of the customs of the city, where all matters were decided on the street and no one knew on leaving home when he would reach or even whether he would reach the place he had set out for. And he had developed the habit of talking with everyone just about as he would have talked with the wife of a superior—inclining his ovoid head to one side, keeping always to the left—so that the person to whom he was talking was left from the outset grateful and embarrassed.

He would greet certain of the elect as if they were old friends returning from a long voyage, and would award them juicy kisses. He carried these kisses about with him like a box of fresh peppermints.

* Central Union of Consumers' Cooperatives.

At nightfall, since I did not belong to the respected citizenry of Theodosia, I would knock at various doors in search of a place to bed down. The northeast wind was raging in the toy streets. The Ginsbergs, the Landsbergs, et al. drank their tea with white Jewish *chale* bread. The Tartar nightwatchmen walked about under the windows of money-changing shops and secondhand stores, where chibouks and guitars were draped in the silk dressing-gown of a colonel. Occasionally, too, there would pass by a belated company of cadets thundering with the soles of their English boots and rending the air with a certain paean containing several indecent expressions, which were omitted during the day at the insistence of the local rabbi.

It was then that I would rush about, in the fever familiar to every vagrant, searching for a place to sleep. And Aleksandr Aleksandrovich would open to me as a nightly asylum the harbor administration office.

I think there never was a stranger lodging for the night. At the sound of the electric bell the door was opened by a drowsy, secretly hostile servant, made of canvas. The bright light bulbs, white as sugar, flashed on, lighting up vast maps of the Crimea, tables of ocean depths and currents, diagrams and chronometric clocks. I would carefully remove the bronze inkstand from the maritime conference table, covered with a green cloth. Here it was warm and clean, as in a surgical ward. All the English and Italian ships that had ever awakened Aleksandr Aleksandrovich were registered in journals and lay sleeping like bibles on the shelves.

In order to understand what Theodosia was like under Denikin and Wrangel, one must know what it was like before. It was the particular quirk of this city to pretend that nothing had changed, that everything remained just exactly as it had always been. And in old times the city resembled not Genoa, that nest of military and mercantile predators, but gentle Florence. In the observatory at Harbor Master Sarandinaki's, the recording of the weather and plotting of isotherms were not the only activities:

there were also weekly gatherings to hear plays and poetry, both by Sarandinaki himself and by other inhabitants of the city. The Chief of Police himself once wrote a play. Mabo,* the director of the Azov Bank, was better known as a poet. And when Voloshin would appear in the pock-marked roadways of Theodosia in his town outfit—woolen stockings, velveteen trousers, and velvet jacket—the city was seized by a sort of classical melting mood and merchants ran out of their shops.

There's no disputing it: we should be grateful to Wrangel for letting us breathe the pure air of a lawless sixteenth-century Mediterranean republic. But it was not easy for Attic Theodosia to adjust herself to the severe rule of the Crimean pirates.

That is why she cherished her kindly patron, Aleksandr Aleksandrovich, that sea-kitten in a tropical cork helmet, a man who, blinking sweetly, looked history in the face and answered its insolent tricks with a gentle meow. He was, however, the sea-god of the city—in his own way, Neptune. The more powerful the man, the more significant his manner of getting up. The French kings did not even get up, but *rose*, like the sun, and that not once but twice: the "small" and "great" rising. Aleksandr Aleksandrovich awoke together with the sea. But how did he keep in touch with the sea? He kept in touch with the sea by telephone. In the half light of his office there was a gleam of English razors and the smell of fresh linen and strong eau de Co-

---

* Mixail Vasil'evič Mabo (1879–1961) left the Soviet Union in 1921. I had the pleasure of an interview with him in Freehold, New Jersey, where he was living in retirement, a few weeks before his death. Mabo (or Mabo-Azovskij, to use his nom de plume) recorded some of his recollections of Mandelstam in an article in the *Novoe Russkoe Slovo* (New York) for 14 January 1949. Perhaps it should be noted that Mabo remembers Aleksandr Sarandinaki to have been Harbor Master in Kerč, not Theodosia, where the post was filled by a certain A. Novinskij. And, to fulfill a pledge made to Mabo, I should like to record that he did not write poems, as Mandelstam says, but plays, and he was still writing them at the time of his death.

logne and of a sweetish imported tobacco. These splendid masculine sleeping quarters, which would have been the envy of any American, were nevertheless a captain's deckhouse and the hub of maritime communications.

Aleksandr Aleksandrovich would awake with the first steamer. Two aides, orderlies in white sailcloth, as schooled in their work as hospital attendants, would burst into headlong action at the first telephone bell and whisper to the chief, who at that moment resembled a drowsy kitten, that there had arrived and was anchored in the roads some English, Turkish, or even Serbian steamer. Aleksandr Aleksandrovich opened tiny little eyes and, though he was powerless to change anything about the arrival of the ship, said, "Ah! Good! Very good!" Then the ship became a citizen of the roads, the civic day of the sea got under way, and the harbor master changed from a sleeping kitten into the protector of merchants, into the inspirer of the customs house and of the fountain of the stock exchange, into the cognac god, the thread god, the currency god—in short, into the civic god of the sea. There was in him something of the swallow, fretting with housewifely concern over her nest—for the time being. And you would not notice that she was training with her little ones for a flight over the Atlantic. For him evacuation was not a catastrophe nor a chance occurrence, but a joyous flight across the Atlantic (according to his instinct as a father and family man); it was, so to speak, the triumph of his lifelong resiliency. He never said anything about it, but he prepared for it, perhaps unconsciously, from the first moment.

II
The Old Woman's Bird

At the farther end of Italian Street, beyond the last secondhand store, past the abandoned gallery of the Gostin-nyj Dvor, where there was formerly a carpet auction, behind the little French house, ivy covered and with jalousies, where the theosophist Anna Mikhailovna starved to death in the upholstered parlor, the road takes an upward turn toward the quarantine quarter.

From January on, the winter became extraordinarily harsh. Heavy artillery was transported along the ice at frozen Perekop. In the coffeehouse next door to the Astoria, English soldiers—"bobbies"*—set up a warming station. They sat in a circle around the brazier, warmed their large red hands, sang Scottish songs, and so crowded the delicate proprietors that they were prevented from cooking coffee and frying eggs. Warm and gentle, the sheep-spirited city was turned into hell. The honorary village idiot, a merry, black-bearded Karaite, no longer ran about the streets with his retinue of urchins.

The quarantine quarter: a labyrinth of little low-lying clay-walled houses with tiny windows, zigzag lanes with clay fences as tall as a man, where one stumbled over ice-covered rope or into cornel bushes. A pitiful clay Herculaneum just dug out of the earth and guarded by ill-tempered dogs. During the day you walked through this little city as though following some extinct Roman urban plan, and at night, in the impenetrable gloom, you were ready to knock at the door of any *petite bourgeoise* if only she would shelter you from the vicious dogs and let you in where the samovar was. The life of the quarantine district was centered about the concern for water. It guarded as the apple of its eye its ice-covered pumphouse. The noise of a clamorous female assembly never subsided on the steep hillock where the jets of pumped water had no time to freeze, and where, to keep the buckets from overflowing when they were raised, filled to the brim, the old women sealed their icy burden with floats of fagots.

The idyl of quarantine lasted several days. In one of the clay huts I rented a room from an old woman for the price of a hen's egg. Like all the housewives of the quarantine quarter, the old woman lived in the festive cleanliness of

* Mandelstam's error for "tommies."

one about to die. She did not simply tidy her little house, she purified it. In the hallway there was a tiny washbowl, but so miserly was the flow of water that there was not the faintest possibility of milking it to the end. There was the smell of bread, of the burnt kerosene in a dull nursery lamp, and the pure breath of old people. The clock ticked ponderously. Like large grains of salt, the winter stars were sprinkled about the court. And I was glad that the room was warm with breath, that someone was pottering about behind the wall, preparing a meal of potatoes, onions, and a handful of rice. The old woman kept her tenant like a bird: she thought it necessary to change his water, clean out his cage, and scatter some grain. At that time it was better to be a bird than a man, and the temptation to become the old woman's bird was enormous.

When Denikin was retreating from Kursk, the military authorities herded the railroad workers and their families together, put them into heated cars, and before they realized what was going on they were rolling off to the Black Sea. Now these railroad birds from Kursk, taken from their comfortable roost, had settled in the quarantine, made themselves at home, cleaned their pots with bricks, but had still not recovered from their astonishment. The old women could not talk without a superstitious horror of how they had been "taken down from Kursk," but as for talk about being taken back, there was none, since it was irreversibly supposed that they had been brought here to die.

If one went outside on one of those icy Crimean nights and listened to the noise of footsteps on the snowless clayey earth, frozen solid like our northern wheel tracks in October, if in the darkness one groped with the eyes among the city's hills—populated sepulchres, but with extinguished lights—if one swallowed that gruel of smothered life, thickened with dense barking of dogs and salted with stars, one began to sense with physical clarity the plague that had descended upon the world, a Thirty

Years' War, with pestilence, darkened lamps, barking of dogs, and, in the houses of little people, appalling silence.

III
The Royal Mantle of the Law

Breath, condensed in droplets, settled on the yellow walls of the bathhouse. Tiny black cups, guarded by sweating glasses of ferriferous Crimean water, were arranged as bait for the red snout-like lips of Karaites and Greeks. There where two were sitting a third immediately planted himself, and behind the third, suspiciously and as if for no reason at all, there stood two more. The little groups scattered and resolved like tumors, governed by the peculiar law of the gravitation of flies: people clung round the unseen center, buzzing and hanging above a piece of invisible sugar, and dashed away with malicious whining from some deal that had fallen through.

The dirty little newspaper of the OSVAG,* printed on gray pulp that always looked like proof sheets, called up impressions of Russian autumn in the shop of a petty merchant.

Meanwhile, above the fly-weddings and braziers, the life of the city proceeded along large, clean lines. From the Mithradates—the ancient Persian fortress on a stone mountain resembling cardboard stage-setting—to the long arrow of the breakwater and the strictly genuine backdrop of highway, prison, and bazaar, the city described the aerial flanks of a triangle formation of cranes and offered to negotiate peace between the earth, sky, and sea. As in most of the amphitheatrical cities of the southern coast, its light blue and gray flocks of gleefully stupid houses ran down from the mountain like a consignment of sheep.

The city was older, better, and cleaner than anything that was going on in it. No dirt stuck to it. Into its splendid body bit the pincers of prison and barracks, along its

* The information and propaganda section of the White Army.

street walked cyclopes in black felt cloaks, *sotniks*,*
smelling of dog and wolf, guardsmen of the defeated
army, wearing service caps and charged to the soles of
their shoes with the foxy electricity of health and youth.
On some people the possibility of committing murder
with impunity acts like a fresh mineral bath, and for such
people, with their childishly impudent and dangerously
empty brown eyes, the Crimea was simply a spa where
they were following a course of treatment, keeping to a
stimulating and salutary regime, suited to the requirements of their nature.

Colonel Tsygalsky played nursemaid to his sister, fee-
bleminded and lachrymose, and to the eagle—the sick,
pitiful, blind, broken-clawed eagle of the Volunteer
Army. In one corner of his quarters the emblematic eagle,
as it were, pottered about invisibly to the tune of the hissing primus stove, and in the other, wrapped in an overcoat
or a down shawl, huddled his sister, looking like a mad
clairvoyant. His extra pair of patent leather boots cried
out to go—not, like seven-league boots, to Moscow—but
to be sold at the bazaar. Tsygalsky was born to nurse
someone and especially to guard someone's sleep. Both he
and his sister looked like blind people, but in the colonel's
eyes, bright with agate blackness and feminine kind-
ness, there stagnated the dark resolve of a leader, while
his sister's contained only bovine terror. He gave his
sister grapes and rice to eat and would sometimes bring
home from the cadet academy certain modest ration
packets, which reminded one of the food rations given
out to intellectuals and those who lived in the House of
Scholars.

It is difficult to imagine why such people are necessary
in any army at all. Such a man would be capable, I think,
of throwing his arms around a general at some critical
moment and saying, "Forget it, my dear fellow—let's
rather go to my place and have a talk." Tsygalsky used to

* A Cossack military rank (equivalent to lieutenant in the Russian
army); originally, a commander of a unit of one hundred men.

go to the cadets to lecture on gunnery like a student going to his lesson.

Once—embarrassed by his voice, the primus stove, his sister, the unsold patent leather boots and the bad to-bacco—he read some verses aloud. There was the awk-ward expression, "I care not: without the throne or with the czar . . ." and some further wishes about the kind of Russia he needed—"crowned with the royal mantle of the Law"—and so on, all reminding one of the rain-blackened Themis on the Senate in Petersburg.

"Whose poem is that?"

"Mine."

Then he revealed to me that somnambulistic landscape in which he lived. The chief feature of this landscape was the abyss that had opened up where Russia had been. The Black Sea extended all the way to the Neva: its waves, thick as pitch, licked at the slabs of the Isaac Cathedral and broke with mournful foam against the steps of the Senate. In this wild expanse, somewhere between Kursk and Sevastopol, swam the royal mantle of the Law, as if it were a lifebuoy, and it was not volunteers but some sort of fishermen in canoes who salvaged this queer appurtenance of the governmental toilet, about which the colonel him-self could scarcely have known or guessed before the revo-lution.

The colonel: a nursemaid decked in the royal mantle of the Law!

IV
Mazesa da Vinci

When a phaeton with empty seats like plush medallions or a one-horse break with a wedding-pink canopy made its way into the scorching backwater of the upper town, the clopping hooves could be heard four blocks away. The horse, sweeping sparks with its legs, belabored the hot stones with such force that it seemed as if a staircase must be formed of them.

It was so dry that a lizard would have died of thirst. A

man in sandals and green socks, overcome by the appearance of the thundering carriage, stood looking after it for a long time. His face showed such astonishment one would have thought they were carting uphill the hitherto unused lever of Archimedes. Then he walked up to a woman who was sitting in her apartment and bartering goods right out of the window, which she had turned into a counter. After tapping a melon with his silver gypsy ring, he asked that it be cut in half for him. But when he had gone as far as the corner, he came back, exchanged the melon for two home-made cigarettes, and quickly made off.

In the upper town the houses have to a certain extent the character of barracks or bastions; they give the pleasant impression of stability and also of natural age, equal to that of human life. Leaving aside archeology and not very remote antiquity, they were the first to turn this rough land into a city.

The house of the parents of Mazesa da Vinci, the artist, shamefully turned its domestic and lively rear toward the stone quarry. Soiled biblical featherbeds sprawled in the hot sun. Rabbits melted like sterilized down, running this way and that, spreading over the ground like spilled milk. And not too far, not too near, but right where it had to be, stood the hospitable booth with its door flung wide open. On the slanting yardarms of twine there flapped an enormous wash. The virtuous armada progressed under martial, maternal sail, but the wing belonging to Mazesa was overwhelming in the brilliance and wealth of its rigging: black and raspberry blouses, silk ankle-length night shirts, such as are worn by newlyweds and angels, one of zephyr cloth, one à la Beethoven—I am of course speaking only of the shirts—and one resembling evening dress with long ape-like arms to which had been added some homemade cuffs.

Laundry dries quickly in the south: Mazesa walked straight into the yard, and ordered all that to be taken down and ironed at once.

He chose his name himself, and to those who inquired about it he would reply only reluctantly with the explanation that he liked the name da Vinci. In the first half of his sobriquet—Mazesa—he retained a blood link with his family: his father, a small, very decent man, having no fear of seasickness, transported drapery goods to Kerch in a powered sailboat, and he was called simply Mr. Mazes. And thus Mazesa, with the addition of the feminine ending, turned the family name into his first name.

Who does not know of the shipboard chaos of the renowned Leonardo's studio? Objects swirled in a whirlwind in the three dimensions of his ingenious workshop; pigeons got in through the dormer window and soiled with their droppings precious brocade, and in his prophetic blindness the master stumbled against the humble articles of everyday life of the Renaissance. Mazesa inherited from his involuntary godfather this fruitful uproar of the three dimensions, and his bedroom resembled a Renaissance vessel under sail.

From the ceiling there hung a large cradle basket in which Mazesa liked to rest during the day. Light flocks of down luxuriated in the dense, noble blackness. A ladder, brought into the room by the stubborn whim of Mazesa, was placed against the entresol, where there stood out among an assorted inventory the framework of some heavy bronze lamps that had hung in the days of Mazesa's grandfather in a Karaite prayer house. From the crater of a porcelain inkstand with sad synagogical lions there protruded several bearded, splintered pens, which had long been unacquainted with ink. On the shelf, under a velvet drape, was his library: a Spanish bible, Makarov's dictionary, Leskov's *Cathedral Folk*, the entomology of Fabre and Baedeker's guide to Paris. On the night table, next to the envelope of an old letter from Argentina, there was a microscope, which gave the false impression that Mazesa would peer into it on waking up in the morning.

In the little city seized by Wrangel's condottieri, Mazesa was completely unnoticed and happy. He took walks, ate fruit, and swam in the free pool, dreamed of buying the white rubber-soled shoes which had been received at the Tsentrosoiuz. His relationship with people and the entire world was built on vagueness and sweet reticence.

He would go down the hill, select in the city some victim, cling to him for two, three, sometimes six hours and, sooner or later, bring him through the scorching zigzag streets back home. In doing this he was, like a tarantula, performing some dark instinctive act peculiar to him alone. He said the same thing to everyone: "Let's go to my place—we have a stone house!" But in the stone house it was the same as in the others: featherbeds, carnelian stones, photographs, and woven napkins.

Mazesa drew only self portraits, and specialized in studies of the Adam's apple.

When the things had been ironed, Mazesa began to get ready for his evening's outing. He didn't wash but passionately immersed himself in the silver girlish mirror. His eyes darkened. His round feminine shoulders trembled.

The white tennis pants, Beethoven shirt, and sport belt did not satisfy him. He took out of the wardrobe his morning coat and in full evening ensemble—unimpeachable from sandals to embroidered skull cap—with black cheviot fins on his white thighs, he went out into the street, already washed in the goat milk of the Theodosia moon.

(1925)

THE ADMIRALTY

In the northern capital a dusty poplar languishes.
The translucent clockface is lost in the leaves,
and through the dark green a frigate or acropolis
gleams far away, brother of water and sky.

An aerial ship and a touch-me-not mast,
a yardstick for Peter's successors, teaching
that beauty is no demi-god's whim,
it's the plain carpenter's fierce rule-of-eye.

The four sovereign elements smile on us,
but man in his freedom has made a fifth.
Do not chaste lines of this ark
deny the dominion of space?

The capricious jellyfish clutch in anger,
anchors are rusting like abandoned plows—
and behold the locks of the three dimensions are sprung
and all the seas of the world lie open.

                                              (*1913*)

The thread of gold cordial flowed from the bottle
with such languor that the hostess found time to say
here in mournful Tauris where our fates have cast us
we are never bored—with a glance over her shoulder.

On all hands the rites of Bacchus, as though the whole
          world
held only guards and dogs. As you go you see no one.
And the placid days roll past like heavy barrels. Far off
in the ancient rooms there are voices. Can't make them
          out. Can't answer.

After tea we went out into the great brown garden.
Dark blinds are dropped like eyelashes on the windows.
We move along the white columns looking at grapes.
          Beyond them
airy glass has been poured over the drowsing mountains.

I said the grape vines live on like an antique battle,
with gnarled cavalry tangling in curving waves.
Here in stone-starred Tauris is an art of Hellas: here,
          rusted,
are the noble ranks of the golden acres.

Meanwhile silence stands in the white room like a
      spinning wheel,
smelling of vinegar, paint, wine cool from the cellar.
Do you remember in the Greek house the wife they
      all loved?
Not Helen. The other. And how long she embroidered?

Golden fleece, where are you then, golden fleece?
All the way the heaved weight of the sea rumbled.
Leaving his boat and its sea-wearied sails,
Odysseus returned, filled with space and time.

(*1917*)

LENINGRAD

I've come back to my city. These are my own old tears,
my own little veins, the swollen glands of my childhood.

So you're back. Open wide. Swallow
the fish-oil from the river lamps of Leningrad.

Open your eyes. Do you know this December day,
the egg-yolk with the deadly tar beaten into it?

Petersburg! I don't want to die yet!
You know my telephone numbers.

Petersburg! I've still got the addresses:
I can look up dead voices.

I live on back stairs, and the bell,
torn out nerves and all, jangles in my temples.

And I wait till morning for guests that I love,
and rattle the door in its chains.

(*1930*)

O Lord, help me to live through this night—
I'm in terror for my life, your slave:
to live in Petersburg is to sleep in a grave.

(1931)

THE LAST SUPPER

The heaven of the supper fell in love with the wall.
It filled it with cracks. It fills them with light.
It fell into the wall. It shines out there
in the form of thirteen heads.

And that's my night sky, before me,
and I'm the child standing under it,
my back getting cold, an ache in my eyes,
and the wall-battering heaven battering me.

At every blow of the battering ram
stars without eyes rain down,
new wounds in the last supper,
the unfinished mist on the wall.

(1937)

Mikhail Bulgakov

(1891–1940)

In several ways, Bulgakov resembles Anton Chekhov. He was a physician, having finished the Medical School in his native Kiev in 1916. He was a playwright, and during his most fruitful years in the theater he was associated with Chekhov's old house, the Moscow Art Theater. He could provoke laughter as handily as Chekhov, though his humor had far more satirical bite to it, and he wrote a quantity of short stories. And like Chekhov, he eventually gave up medical practice for the life of a writer.

His great difference from Chekhov is that he wrote novels. *The Master and Margarita*, the first chapter of which follows, belongs next to Bely's *Petersburg* (see p. 79) and Pasternak's *Dr. Zhivago* (see p. 153) as one of the supreme masterpieces in modern Russian letters.

Asked to identify Bulgakov, a contemporary would have answered that he was a playwright, author of *The Days of the Turbins* (1926) and a perennially popular stage adaptation of Gogol's *Dead Souls* (1932). Audiences knew him also for such satirical comedies as *Zoika's Apartment* and *The Crimson Island*. After 1927, none of his works were printed during his lifetime. Not even the standard western histories of Soviet literature were aware of Bulgakov as being someone other than the interesting literary craftsman of certain plays and short fiction.

Then, in 1966–67*, there appeared *The Master and Margarita*, the germ of which had first occupied Bulgakov in the 1920s. It accompanied him through his creative life and absorbed the supreme effort of his imagination in its many evolving forms. When he diagnosed his own progressive illness and calculated with icy accuracy the exact amount of time remaining in his life, he put aside all else and completed the manuscript. He had the pages bound, knowing that no Soviet publisher would ever do so. Blind toward the end, he dictated the epilogue to his wife and had it pasted into the bound manuscript. For over a quarter of a century after his death, this summit of his artistic achievement lay in total obscurity.

Like the novels of Bely and Pasternak, *The Master and Margarita* is a work of philosophical and ethical rumination, but it exceeds both of them in scope (they seem almost local beside its cosmic range) and in metaphysical and religious depth. For headlong somersaults of fantastic illusion and breathtaking dislocations of narrative it simply has no competitors. To summarize it is impossible. To exemplify it in a brief passage is extremely difficult. But I am happy to follow the lead of Ellendea Proffer, author of numerous studies of Bulgakov, who observes that the opening chapter contains most of the fundamental themes of the book.

All of the three broad categories into which the narrative falls are present in the personalities and events of chapter one: the satirical picture of official Moscow literary life (Berlioz); Pontius Pilate's encounter with Jesus Christ (the hack poet Ivan Bezdomny has written a poem about Jesus); and the fantastic story of the nameless writer known as the Master (Bezdomny will be a disciple) and his love Margarita.

It is the Devil himself who holds everything together, and did so from the start: among the working titles in the 1920s were *The Black Magician* and *The Consultant with a Hoof*. He is the mysterious "foreigner" of the first chapter. Only the

---

* The first (censored) version of the novel appeared in two issues of the journal *Moskva*. The full text was published in Moscow in 1973.

initial of his name, Woland, appears here, and we get only a glimpse of his power: he provides precise hints as to the manner of the untidy death that Berlioz will meet in a few pages, he settles the question being disputed by declaring that the historical existence of Jesus is not to be doubted, and the last words of the chapter, spoken by the Devil, are precisely those that open the second chapter, which is the beginning of the story of Pilate's encounter with Christ.

From THE MASTER AND MARGARITA

I
Never Talk to Strangers

At the sunset hour of one warm spring day two men were to be seen at Patriarch's Ponds. The first of them—aged about forty, dressed in a grayish summer suit—was short, dark-haired, well-fed and bald. He carried his decorous hat by the brim as though it were a cake, and his neatly shaven face was embellished by black horn-rimmed spectacles of preternatural dimensions. The other, a broad-shouldered young man with curly reddish hair and a check cap pushed back to the nape of his neck, was wearing a tartan shirt, wrinkled white trousers and black sneakers.

The first was none other than Mikhail Alexandrovich Berlioz, editor of a highbrow literary magazine and chairman of the management committee of one of the biggest Moscow literary clubs, known by its abbreviation as MASSOLIT; his young companion was the poet Ivan Nikolayich Poniryov, who wrote under the pseudonym of Bezdomny.

Reaching the shade of the budding lime trees, the two

writers went straight to a gaily painted kiosk labeled "Beer and Soft Drinks."

There was an oddness about that terrible day in May which is worth recording: not only at the kiosk but along the whole avenue parallel to Malaya Bronnaya Street there was not a person to be seen. It was the hour of the day when people feel too exhausted to breathe, when Moscow glows in a dry haze as the sun disappears behind Sadovaya Street —yet no one had come out for a walk under the limes, no one was sitting on a bench, the avenue was empty.

"A glass of lemonade, please," said Berlioz.

"There isn't any," replied the woman in the kiosk. For some reason the request seemed to offend her.

"Got any beer?" inquired Bezdomny in a hoarse voice.

"Beer's being delivered later this evening," said the woman.

"Well what have you got?" asked Berlioz.

"Apricot juice, only it's warm," was the answer.

"All right, let's have some."

The apricot juice produced a rich yellow froth, making the air smell like a hairdresser's. After drinking it the two writers immediately began to hiccup. They paid and sat down on a bench facing the pond, their backs to Bronnaya Street.

Then occurred the second oddness, which affected Berlioz alone. He suddenly stopped hiccuping, his heart thumped and for a moment ceased, then started beating again but with a blunt needle sticking into it. In addition Berlioz was seized by a fear that was groundless but so powerful that he had an immediate impulse to run away from Patriarch's Ponds without looking back.

Berlioz gazed miserably about him, unable to say what had frightened him. He went pale, wiped his forehead with his handkerchief and thought, "What's the matter with me? This has never happened before. Heart playing tricks . . . I'm overstrained . . . I think it's time to chuck everything up and go and take the waters at Kislovodsk."

Just then the sultry air coagulated and wove itself into the shape of a man—a transparent man of the strangest appearance. On his small head was a jockey cap, and he wore a short check jacket fabricated of air. The man was seven feet tall but narrow in the shoulders, incredibly thin and with a face made for derision.

Berlioz' life was so arranged that he was not accustomed to seeing unusual phenomena. Paling even more, he stared and thought in consternation, "It can't be!"

But alas it was, and the tall, transparent gentleman was swaying from left to right in front of him without touching the ground.

Berlioz was so overcome with horror that he shut his eyes. When he opened them he saw it was all over, the mirage had dissolved, the checkered figure had vanished and the blunt needle had simultaneously removed itself from his heart.

"The devil!" exclaimed the editor. "D'you know, Ivan, the heat nearly gave me a stroke just then! I even saw something like a hallucination. . . ." He tried to smile, but his eyes were still blinking with fear and his hands trembled. However, he gradually calmed down, flapped his handkerchief and with a brave enough "Well, now . . ." picked up the conversation that had been interrupted by their drink of apricot juice.

They had been talking, it seemed, about Jesus Christ. The fact was that the editor had commissioned the poet to write a long antireligious poem for one of the regular issues of his magazine. Ivan Nikolayich had written this poem in record time, but unfortunately the editor did not care for it at all. Bezdomny had drawn the chief figure in his poem, Jesus, in very somber colors, and in the editor's opinion the whole poem had to be written again. And now he was reading Bezdomny a lecture on Jesus in order to stress the poet's fundamental error.

It was hard to say exactly what had made Bezdomny write as he had—whether it was his great talent for graphic description or complete ignorance of his subject, but his Jesus had come out . . . well, completely alive, a Jesus who had really existed, although admittedly a Jesus who had every possible fault.

Berlioz, however, wanted to prove to the poet that the main object was not who Jesus was, whether he was bad or good, but that as a person Jesus had never existed at all and that all the stories about him were mere invention, pure myth.

The editor was a well-read man and able to make skillful reference to the ancient historians, such as the renowned Philo of Alexandria and the brilliantly educated Josephus Flavius, neither of whom mentioned a word of Jesus' existence. With a display of solid erudition, Mikhail Alexandrovich informed the poet that, incidentally, the passage in Chapter 44 of the fifteenth book of Tacitus' *Annales*, in which he describes the execution of Jesus, was nothing but a later forgery.

The poet, for whom everything the editor was saying was a novelty, listened attentively, fixing Mikhail Alexandrovich with his bold green eyes, occasionally hiccuping and cursing the apricot juice under his breath.

"There is not one oriental religion," said Berlioz, "in which an immaculate virgin does not bring a god into the world. And the Christians, lacking any originality, invented their Jesus in exactly the same way. In fact, he never lived at all. That's where the emphasis has got to be placed."

Berlioz' high tenor resounded along the empty avenue, and as Mikhail Alexandrovich picked his way around the sort of historical pitfalls that can only be negotiated safely by a highly educated man, the poet learned more and more useful and instructive facts about the Egyptian god Osiris, son of Earth and Heaven, about the Phoenician god Tammuz, about Marduk and even about the fierce little-known god Vitzli-Putzli, who had once been held in great veneration by the Aztecs of Mexico. At the very moment when Mikhail Alexandrovich was telling the poet how the Aztecs used to model figurines of Vitzli-Putzli out of dough, the first man appeared in the avenue.

Afterward, when it was frankly too late, various persons collected their data and issued descriptions of this man. As to his teeth, he had platinum crowns on the left side and gold ones on the right. He wore an expensive gray suit and foreign shoes of the same color as his suit. His gray beret was stuck jauntily over one ear and under his arm he carried a walking stick with a knob in the shape of a poodle's head. He looked slightly over forty. Crooked sort of mouth. Clean-shaven. Dark hair. Right eye black, left eye for some reason green. Eyebrows black, but one higher than the other. In short—a foreigner.

As he passed the bench occupied by the editor and the poet, the foreigner gave them a sidelong glance, stopped and suddenly sat down on the next bench a couple of paces away from the two friends.

"A German," thought Berlioz. "An Englishman," thought Bezdomny. "Phew, he must be hot in those gloves!"

The stranger glanced over the tall houses that formed a square around the pond, from which it was obvious that he was seeing this locality for the first time and that it interested him. His gaze halted on the upper stories, whose panes threw back a blinding, fragmented reflection of the sun which was setting on Mikhail Alexandrovich forever; he then looked downward to where the windows were turning darker in the early-evening twilight, smiled patronizingly at something, frowned, placed his hands on the knob of his cane and laid his chin on his hands.

"You see, Ivan," said Berlioz, "you have written a marvelously satirical description of the birth of Jesus, the Son of God, but the whole joke lies in the fact that there had already been a whole series of sons of God before Jesus, such as the Phoenician Adonis, the Phrygian Attis, the Persian Mithras. Of course not one of these ever existed, including Jesus, and instead of the nativity or the arrival of the Magi you should have described the absurd rumors about their arrival. But according to your story the nativity really took place!"

Here Bezdomny made an effort to stop his torturing hiccups and held his breath, but it only made him hiccup more loudly and painfully. At that moment Berlioz interrupted his speech because the foreigner suddenly rose and approached the two writers. They stared at him in astonishment.

"Excuse me, please," said the stranger with a foreign accent, although in correct Russian, "for permitting myself, without an introduction . . . but the subject of your learned conversation was so interesting that . . ."

Here he politely took off his beret and the two friends had no alternative but to rise and bow.

"No, probably a Frenchman," thought Berlioz.

"A Pole," thought Bezdomny.

I should add that the poet had found the stranger repulsive from first sight, although Berlioz had liked the look of him, or rather not exactly liked him but . . . well, been interested by him.

"May I join you?" inquired the foreigner, politely and as the two friends moved somewhat unwillingly apart he adroitly placed himself between them and at once joined the conversation. "If I'm not mistaken, you were saying that Jesus never existed, were you not?" he asked, turning his green left eye on Berlioz.

"No, you were not mistaken," replied Berlioz courteously. "I did indeed say that."

"Ah, how interesting!" exclaimed the foreigner.

"What the hell does he want?" though Bezdomny and frowned.

"And do you agree with your friend?" inquired the unknown man, turning to Bezdomny on his right.

"A hundred percent!" affirmed the poet, who loved to use pretentious numerical expressions.

"Astounding!" cried their unbidden companion. Glancing furtively around and lowering his voice, he said, "Forgive me for being so rude, but am I right in thinking that you do not believe in God either?" He gave a horrified look and said, "I swear not to tell anyone!"

"Yes, neither of us believes in God," answered Berlioz with a faint smile at this foreign tourist's apprehension. "But we can talk about it with absolute freedom."

The foreigner leaned against the back rest of the bench and asked, in a voice positively squeaking with curiosity, "Are you . . . atheists?"

"Yes, we're atheists," replied Berlioz, smiling, and Bezdomny thought angrily, "Trying to pick an argument, damn foreigner!"

"Oh, how delightful!" exclaimed the astonishing foreigner

and swiveled his head from side to side, staring at each of them in turn.

"In our country there's nothing surprising about atheism," said Berlioz with diplomatic politeness. "Most of us have long ago and quite consciously given up believing in all those fairy tales about God."

At this the foreigner did an extraordinary thing—he stood up and shook the astonished editor by the hand, saying as he did so, "Allow me to thank you with all my heart!"

"What are you thanking him for?" asked Bezdomny, blinking.

"For some very valuable information, which as a traveler I find extremely interesting," said the eccentric foreigner, raising his forefinger meaningfully.

This valuable piece of information had obviously made a powerful impression on the traveler, as he gave a frightened glance at the houses as though afraid of seeing an atheist at every window.

"No, he's not an Englishman," thought Berlioz. Bezdomny thought, "What I'd like to know is, where did he manage to pick up such good Russian?" and frowned again.

"But might I inquire," began the visitor from abroad after some worried reflection, "how you account for the proofs of the existence of God, of which there are, as you know, five?"

"Alas!" replied Berlioz regretfully. "Not one of these proofs is valid, and mankind has long since relegated them to the archives. You must agree that rationally there can be no proof of the existence of God."

"Bravo!" exclaimed the stranger. "Bravo! You have exactly repeated the views of the immortal Immanuel on that subject. But here's the oddity of it: he completely demolished all five proofs and then, as though to deride his own efforts, he formulated a sixth proof of his own."

"Kant's proof," objected the learned editor with a thin smile, "is also unconvincing. Not for nothing did Schiller say that Kant's reasoning on this question would only satisfy slaves, and Strauss simply laughed at his proof."

As Berlioz spoke he thought to himself, "But who on earth *is* he? And how does he speak such good Russian?"

"Kant ought to have been arrested and given three years in Solovki asylum for that 'proof' of his!" Ivan Nikolayich burst out completely unexpectedly.

"Ivan!" whispered Berlioz, embarrassed.

But the suggestion to pack Kant off to an asylum not only did not surprise the stranger but actually delighted him. "Exactly, exactly!" he cried, and his green left eye, turned on Berlioz, glittered. "That's exactly the place for him! I said to him myself that morning at breakfast, 'If you'll forgive me, Professor, your theory is no good. It may be clever but it's dreadfully incomprehensible. People will think you're mad.'"

Berlioz' eyes bulged. "At breakfast . . . to Kant? What is he rambling on about?" he thought.

"But," went on the foreigner, unperturbed by Berlioz' amazement and turning to the poet, "sending him to Solovki is out of the question because for over a hundred years now he has been somewhere far away from Solovki, and I assure you that it is totally impossible to bring him back."

"What a pity!" said the impetuous poet.

"It is a pity," agreed the unknown man with a glint in his eye, and went on: "But this is the question that disturbs me—if there is no God, then who, one wonders, rules the life of man and keeps the world in order?"

"Man rules himself," said Bezdomny angrily in answer to such an obviously absurd question.

"I beg your pardon," retorted the stranger quietly, "but to rule, one must have a precise plan worked out for some reasonable period in the future. Allow me to inquire how man can control his own affairs when he is not only incapable of compiling a plan for some laughably short term, such as, say, a thousand years, but cannot even predict what will happen to him tomorrow?

"In fact—" here the stranger turned to Berlioz—"imagine what would happen if you, for instance, were to start organizing others and yourself, and you developed a taste for it—then suddenly you got . . . he, he . . . a slight heart attack." At this the foreigner smiled sweetly, as though the thought of a heart attack gave him pleasure. "Yes, a heart attack," he repeated the word sonorously, grinning like a cat, "and that's the end of you as an organizer! No one's fate except your own interests you any longer. Your relations start lying to you. Sensing that something is amiss, you rush to a specialist, then to a charlatan, and even perhaps to a fortuneteller. Each of them is as useless as the other, as you know perfectly well. And it all ends in tragedy: the man who thought he was in charge is suddenly reduced to lying supine and motionless in a wooden box, and his fellow men, realizing that there is no more sense to be had of him, incinerate him.

"Sometimes it can be even worse: a man decides to go to Kislovodsk—" here the stranger stared at Berlioz—"a trivial matter you may think, but he cannot because for no good reason he suddenly jumps up and falls under a streetcar. You're not going to tell me that he arranged to do that himself? Wouldn't it be nearer the truth to say that someone quite different was directing his fate?" The stranger gave an eerie peal of laughter.

Berlioz had been following the unpleasant story about the heart attack and the streetcar with great attention, and some uncomfortable thoughts had begun to worry him. "He's not a foreigner . . . he's not a foreigner," he thought. "He's a very peculiar character . . . but I ask you, *who* is he?"

"I see you'd like to smoke," said the stranger unexpectedly, turning to Bezdomny. "What kind do you prefer?"

"Do you mean you've got different kinds?" glumly asked the poet, who had run out of cigarettes.

"Which do you prefer?" repeated the mysterious stranger.

"Well, then, Our Brand," replied Bezdomny, irritated.

The unknown man immediately pulled a cigarette case out of his pocket and offered it to Bezdomny.

"Our Brand."

The editor and the poet were not so much surprised by the fact that the cigarette case actually contained Our Brand as by the cigarette case itself. It was of enormous dimensions, made of solid gold, and on the inside of the cover a triangle of diamonds flashed with blue and white fire.

Their reactions were different. Berlioz thought, "No, he's a foreigner." Bezdomny thought, "What the hell is he?"

The poet and the owner of the case lit their cigarettes, and Berlioz, who did not smoke, refused.

"I shall refute his argument by saying," Berlioz decided to himself, "that of course man is mortal, no one will argue with that. But the fact is that—"

However, he was not able to pronounce the words before the stranger spoke: "Of course man is mortal, but that's only half the problem. The trouble is that mortality sometimes comes to him so suddenly! And he cannot even say what he will be doing this evening."

"What a stupid way of putting the question," thought Berlioz and objected: "Now there you exaggerate. I know more or less exactly what I'm going to be doing this evening. Provided, of course, that a brick doesn't fall on my head in the street."

"A brick is neither here nor there," the stranger interrupted persuasively. "A brick never falls on anyone's head. You in particular, I assure you, are in no danger from that. Your death will be different."

"Perhaps you know exactly how I am going to die?" inquired Berlioz with understandable sarcasm at the ridiculous turn that the conversation seemed to be taking. "Would you like to tell me?"

"Certainly," rejoined the stranger. He looked Berlioz up and down as though he were measuring him for a suit and muttered through his teeth something that sounded like: "One, two . . . Mercury in the second house . . . the moon waning . . . six—accident . . . evening—seven," then announced loudly and cheerfully, "Your head will be cut off!"

Bezdomny turned to the stranger with a wild, furious stare, and Berlioz asked with a sardonic grin, "By whom? Enemies? Foreign spies?"

"No," replied their companion, "by a Russian woman, a member of the Komsomol."

"H'm," grunted Berlioz, upset by the foreigner's little

joke. "That, if you don't mind my saying so, is most improbable."

"I beg your pardon," replied the foreigner, "but it is so. Oh, yes, I was going to ask you—what are you doing this evening, if it's not a secret?"

"It's no secret. From here I'm going home, and then at ten o'clock this evening there's a meeting at the MASSOLIT and I shall be in the chair."

"No, that is absolutely impossible," said the stranger firmly.

"Why?"

"Because," replied the foreigner and frowned up at the sky where, sensing the oncoming cool of the evening, the birds were flying to roost, "Anna has already bought the sunflower oil; in fact, she has not only bought it but has already spilled it. So that meeting will not take place."

With this, as one might imagine, there was silence beneath the lime trees.

"Excuse me," said Berlioz after a pause, with a glance at the stranger's jaunty beret, "but what on earth has sunflower-seed oil got to do with it . . . and who is Anna?"

"I'll tell you what sunflower oil's got to do with it," said Bezdomny suddenly, having obviously decided to declare war on their uninvited companion. "Have you, comrade, ever had to spend any time in a mental hospital?"

"Ivan!" hissed Mikhail Alexandrovich.

But the stranger was not in the least offended and gave a cheerful laugh. "Yes, I have, I have, and more than once!" he exclaimed laughing, though the stare that he gave the poet was mirthless. "Where haven't I been! My only regret is that I didn't stay long enough to ask the professor what schizophrenia was. But you are going to find out from him yourself, Ivan Nikolayich!"

"How do you know my name?"

"My dear fellow, who doesn't know you?" With this the foreigner pulled the previous day's issue of *The Literary Gazette* out of his pocket, and Ivan Nikolayich saw his own picture on the front page above some of his own verse. Suddenly what had delighted him yesterday as proof of his fame and popularity no longer gave the poet any pleasure at all.

"I beg your pardon," he said, his face darkening. "Would you excuse us for a minute? I should like a word or two with my friend."

"Oh, with pleasure!" exclaimed the stranger. "It's so delightful sitting here under the trees and I'm not in a hurry to go anywhere, as it happens."

"Look here, Misha," whispered the poet when he had drawn Berlioz aside. "He's not just a foreign tourist, he's a spy. He's a Russian *émigré*, and he's trying to trip us up. Ask him for his papers and then he'll go away."

"Do you think we should?" whispered Berlioz anxiously, thinking to himself, "He's right, of course."

"Mark my words," the poet whispered to him. "He's pretending to be an idiot so that he can trap us with some compromising question. You can hear how he speaks Russian," said the poet, glancing sideways to see that the stranger was not eavesdropping. "Come on, let's arrest him and then we'll get rid of him."

The poet led Berlioz by the arm back to the bench.

The unknown man was no longer sitting on it but standing beside it, holding a booklet in a dark gray binding, a fat envelope made of good paper and a visiting card.

"Forgive me, but in the heat of our argument I forgot to introduce myself. Here is my card, my passport and a letter inviting me to come to Moscow for consultations," said the stranger gravely, giving both writers a piercing stare.

The two men were embarrassed. "Hell, he overheard us," thought Berlioz, indicating with a polite gesture that there was no need for this show of documents. While the stranger was offering them to the editor, the poet managed to catch a glimpse of the visiting card. On it in foreign lettering was the word "Professor" and the initial letter of a surname which began with a "W."

"Delighted," muttered the editor awkwardly as the foreigner put his papers back into his pocket.

Good relations having been re-established, all three sat down again on the bench.

"So you've been invited here as a consultant, have you, Professor?" asked Berlioz.

"Yes, I have."

"Are you German?" inquired Bezdomny.

"I?" rejoined the professor and thought for a moment. "Yes, I suppose I am German," he said.

"You speak excellent Russian," remarked Bezdomny.

"Oh, I'm something of a polyglot. I know a great number of languages," replied the professor.

"And what is your particular field of work?" asked Berlioz.

"I specialize in black magic."

"Like hell you do!" thought Mikhail Alexandrovich. "And . . . and you've been invited here to give advice on *that?*" he asked with a gulp.

"Yes," the professor assured him, and went on: "Apparently your National Library has unearthed some original manuscripts of the ninth-century necromancer Herbert Aurilachs. I have been asked to decipher them. I am the only specialist in the world."

"Aha! So you're a historian?" asked Berlioz in a tone of considerable relief and respect.

"Yes, I am a historian," adding with apparently complete inconsequence, "this evening a historic event is going to take place here at Patriarch's Ponds."

Again the editor and the poet showed signs of utter amazement, but the professor beckoned to them and when both had bent their heads toward him he whispered, "Jesus did exist, you know."

"Look, Professor," said Berlioz, with a forced smile, "with all respect to you as a scholar, we take a different attitude on that point."

"It's not a question of having an attitude," replied the strange professor. "He existed, that's all there is to it."

"But one must have some proof . . ." began Berlioz.

"There's no need for any proof," answered the professor. In a low voice, his foreign accent vanishing altogether, he began: "It's very simple: early in the morning on the fourteenth of the spring month of Nisan the Procurator of Judea, Pontius Pilate, in a white cloak lined with blood red . . ."

Isaac Babel

(1894–1941?)

Babel was born in the perennially threatened and infinitely fecund Jewish community of Odessa, a small but wonderfully cosmopolitan port on the Black Sea that has provided the world with more musical and artistic genius than might reasonably be expected. He was asthmatic, nearsighted, short, and ugly. To the first of these endowments he himself attributed his fondness for brief sentences; to the rest might be attributed some of the self-deprecating melancholy of his nature—he depicts himself as a person with "spectacles on [his] nose and autumn in [his] heart"—and also his continual struggle against the obstacles placed in his way by tall, healthy, blond persons. Why he should have matured with a remarkably sweet temper and a gay and generous character is a mystery.

Indeed, much about Babel is mysterious. Some of the mystery derives from the familiar veil over the violence of those days: No one knows why, how, or even exactly when Babel died after he was suddenly arrested in May 1939. But he himself is responsible for much of the confusion. In a brief autobiographical note he attributes to Gorky (see p. 29) his first success in getting published in 1916, but researchers have now found work published three years earlier. He states also that on Gorky's advice he went "into the world" to learn about life, and wrote nothing for some seven years; but work published in those years has now come to light. Did he serve in the Cheka, the secret police? He writes that he did. His wife calls this one of the preposterous inventions with which he sensationalized his past.

But about one of the central episodes in Babel's life there is more than mystery. There is a kind of absurd black comedy. In 1920, during the Civil War, the Jew Babel enlisted on the Bolshevik side with Budyonny's First Cavalry, a regiment of Cossacks! This is something like a lone cat's voluntarily cultivating the society of a pack of hounds; for the image of the Cossack horseman, saber in hand, is the quintessential horror in the collective Jewish nightmare of the pogroms that swept through Central and Eastern Europe, to say nothing of Southern Russia. But Babel admired the Cossacks, sometimes with the eye of a dispassionate observer and sometimes with a kind of helpless envy. He admired their physical power and masculine beauty, their devotion to one another, their almost surreal courage in combat—even their inhuman ferocity.

The experience of the Polish campaign resulted in the stories that eventually composed his masterpiece, *Red Cavalry* (1926). As the central character and narrative voice Babel created a puny, bespectacled intellectual, despised by his comrades until he demonstrates his capacity, though slight, for being cruel like them. Obviously autobiographical, this fictional personage has even less claim upon our credibility than Babel's utterances about his historical self. Indeed, it is one of the writer's greatest achievements to maintain a certain distance between this Babel-like narrator and the true creative consciousness behind the stories.

Another achievement is the lyrical intensity with which Babel describes the beautiful natural backdrop to the horse army's bloody marauding, on the one hand, and, on the other, the Apollonian coolness with which he records scenes of Cossack savagery (such as that of an old woman compelled to ingest the severed genitals of her husband). Babel's laconism, his sifting of the Russian lexicon for the single right word— Flaubert and Maupassant had been his models when he wrote his schoolboy stories in French—made his fame, for his style and his sensibility were absolutely new to Russian fiction.

The other locale in which his work is set is treated differently. This is his native Odessa, specifically the Jewish quarter, Moldavanka, and within that quarter a sort of Jew all but unknown to the world of polite letters: the big-time crook. Benya Krik is in his occasionally bumbling way as ruthless as any Cossack, but his adventures are not horrible, only hilarious. Babel's Odessa is full of color and amusement and the joie de vivre that makes the city's placement on Slavic soil seem a puzzling lapse of geography. There is the usual phony autobiography. But the stories are accomplished with consummate narrative skill and with the inimitable rightness of Babel's prose rhythms, and are therefore anything but trivial. "My First Fee," written in this manner though set in Tiflis, has beneath its comic exterior a profoundly original statement concerning the role of the artist.

MY FIRST GOOSE

Savitsky, the commander of the Sixth Division, stood up when he saw me. I was struck by the beauty of his gigantic body. He stood up and his purple riding breeches, the crimson cap on the side of his head, and the ribbons pinned to his chest seemed to cut the hut in half, as a banner cleaves the sky. The smell of unobtainable perfumes and the cloying coolness of soap emanated from him. His long legs looked like girls sheathed to the neck in shining riding boots.

He smiled at me, struck his riding whip against the table, and pulled toward him an order that had just been dictated by the Chief of Staff. It was an order to Ivan Chesnokov to march the regiment entrusted to him in the direction of Chugunov-Dobryvodka and, on making contact with the enemy, to destroy same. . . .

". . . for which same destruction," the division commander wrote, smudging the whole sheet, "I make this same Chesnokov responsible up to and including the supreme penalty; and I'll finish him on the spot—which you, Comrade Chesnokov, since you've been working with me for some months at the front, can be sure of. . . ."

The commander of the Sixth signed the order with a flourish, tossed it to the messengers, and turned his gray eyes, dancing with merriment, on me.

"Say your piece!" he cried, cleaving the air with his whip. Then he read the order that assigned me to the staff of the division.

"Put it down in the Orders of the Day," the division commander said, "put it down and put him down for every entertainment except the front line. Can you read and write?"

"I can," I answered, full of envy of his steely strength and youthful complexion, "I hold a law degree from Petersburg University——"

"You're one of those mama's boys," he roared, laughing. "Glasses on his nose, too, uh. A lousy little squirt! They send you without consulting us. They're liable to carve you to pieces here because of those glasses. Think you'll make it with us, do you?"

"I'll make it," I answered and went with the quartermaster to the village to find a billet for the night. The quartermaster carried my trunk on his shoulder. The village street lay before us. The dying sun, round and yellow as a pumpkin, was expiring, lending a rosy tinge to the sky.

We walked as far as a cottage with garlands painted on it, where the quartermaster stopped and said suddenly with a guilty little smile:

"Glasses bring trouble around here and nothing can be done about it. They make it a dog's life for an educated man. But if you mess up a lady—a real clean little lady— then you'll see how popular you'll be with the boys."

He shifted his feet around, with my little trunk on his back, came right up close to me, then turned away as if in despair and trotted into the nearest yard. Cossacks were sitting around there on a pile of hay, shaving each other.

"Here, men," the quartermaster said, putting my little trunk down on the ground. "In accordance with Comrade Savitsky's orders, you are to give this man a billet and no nonsense about it, because this man's suffered plenty in the learning line."

The quartermaster, who had turned purple in the face, went off without looking back. I raised my hand to my cap, saluting the Cossacks. A young fellow with lank, flaxen hair and a handsome face walked up to my little trunk, picked it up, and tossed it out through the gate. Then he turned his behind toward me and very expertly started emitting obscene sounds.

"Gun number double zero," an older Cossack shouted to him and burst out laughing, "open running fire. . . ."

The fellow exhausted his uncomplicated talent and walked off. Then, crawling around on the ground, I began to collect the manuscripts and my rags and tatters of clothes that had spilled out of the trunk. I picked them up and carried them to the other end of the yard. Near the cottage, on a brick stove, stood a kettle. Pork was cooking in it. The steam poured from it like smoke pouring out of the chimney of a village house; it aroused in me a feeling of hunger mixed with infinite loneliness. I covered my broken trunk with hay, making a pillow out of it, and lay down on the ground to read Lenin's speech at the Second Congress of the Comintern, in *Pravda*. The sunlight fell on me from behind the jagged hills, the Cossacks stepped on my feet, the young fellow made fun of me untiringly, and my favorite lines failed to reach me along this path of thorns. Then I put the paper aside and went over to the landlady, who was spinning yarn on the porch.

"Landlady," I said, "I need some food."

The old woman raised her half-blind eyes the whites of which had overflowed into the irises, looked at me, and looked away again.

"Comrade," she said after a pause, "with all this business, I feel like hanging myself."

"God damn your soul," I muttered, annoyed, and I pushed the old woman in the chest with my fist. "I'm not here to converse with you."

Turning away, I saw a saber someone had left nearby. A stern-looking goose was roaming about the yard, placidly preening its feathers. I caught up with it and pinned it to the ground. The goose's head burst under my boot and its brains spilled out. The white neck was stretched out in the dung and the wings twitched above the slaughtered bird.

"God damn your soul," I said, digging the sword into the goose. "Cook it for me, landlady."

The old woman, her cataracts and her glasses gleaming, lifted the bird, wrapped it in her apron, and carried it off to the kitchen.

"Comrade," she said after a pause, "I could hang myself," and she closed the door behind her.

In the meantime, in the yard, the Cossacks had settled down around their kettle. They sat immobile and stiff like heathen priests, without looking at the goose.

"That fellow'll fit in with us," one of them said of me. He winked and ladled out some cabbage soup with his spoon.

The Cossacks started to eat their supper with the restrained elegance of peasants who respect one another. I cleaned the saber with sand, went out by the gate, and came back in again, feeling depressed. The moon was already hanging over the yard, like a cheap earring.

"Hey, lad," Surovkov, the oldest of the Cossacks, called out to me suddenly, "come and sit with us and have something to eat, until your goose is ready."

He took a spoon out of his boot and gave it to me. We sat there, spooning up their homemade cabbage soup, and then we ate the pork.

"Is there anything in the paper?" asked the flaxen-haired youth, making a place for me.

"In the paper, Lenin writes ..." I said, fishing out *Pravda*, "Lenin writes that we are short of everything. . . ."

And loudly, like a triumphant deaf man, I read Lenin's speech to the Cossacks.

The evening wrapped me in its dusky sheets of revivifying moisture and laid a maternal palm on my burning forehead. I read, savored the words, and observed, as I savored them, the concealed curve in Lenin's straight approach.

"The truth tickles everyone's nostrils," said Surovkov when I had finished, "but how can you pull it out from the tangled heap ... and yet he hits on it in one go, like a chicken pecking grain. ..."

Surovkov, the platoon leader of the Staff Troop, said this about Lenin, and then went off to sleep in the hayloft. Six of us slept there. We kept each other warm, our legs entangled, under the holed roof that let in the starlight. I dreamed and saw women in my dreams, and only my heart, bloodstained from the killing, whined and dripped misery.

(1926)

HOW IT WAS DONE
IN ODESSA

I spoke first.

"Reb Arie-Leib," I said to the old man, "let's talk about Benya Krik. Let's talk about his meteoric rise and his ghastly end. Three silhouettes block my imagination. There's Froim Grach. Can't the steel of his deeds bear comparison with the strength of the 'King'? There's Kolia Pakovsky. That man's rage had in it all that is needed to wield power. And how is it possible that Haim Drong failed to recognize the blaze of the new star? Well, why was it, then, that Benya Krik alone climbed to the top of the rope ladder while all the others were left hanging below on its shaky rungs?"

Reb Arie-Leib, who was sitting on the cemetery wall, remained silent. The green peace of the graves stretched before us. A man seeking an answer must be patient. And dignity befits a man who possesses knowledge. That's why Reb Arie-Leib remained silent as he sat on the cemetery wall. Then he told me this story.

Why him? You want to know why him and not them? All right. Just forget for a minute that you have spectacles on your nose and autumn in your heart. Stop being tough at your desk and stammering with timidity in the presence of people. Imagine for one second that you raise hell in public places and stammer on paper. You're a tiger, a lion, a cat. You can spend a night with a Russian woman and leave her satisfied. You're twenty-five. If rings had been fastened to earth and sky, you'd have seized those rings and pulled the sky down to the earth. And your papa is Mendel Krik, the carter. What's such a papa got to think about? He thinks about gulping down a big glass of vodka, about bashing in somebody's face, about his cart horses—and that's all. You want to live and he forces you to die maybe twenty times a day. So what would you do if you were in Benya Krik's place? You—you would do nothing. But he did something. And that's why he's the King while the hand in your pocket has nothing in it but thin air.

So Benya went to Froim Grach, who even then had only one eye to look at the world with and was what he is today. He said to Froim:

"Take me on, Froim. Take me aboard your boat. The boat I'm on will go places."

And Grach said to him:

"Who are you? Where do you come from? And, in general, how do you keep breathing?"

"Just try me, Froim," Benya said, "and let's stop messing up a clean tablecloth."

"Okay, let's stop messing up the tablecloth," Grach said. "I'll try you."

And the holdup men held a council to decide about Benya Krik. I wasn't present, but I heard that a council did take place. The big boss at that time was the late Leon the Bull.

"What's going on under this Benya boy's hat?" the late Bull asked.

And one-eyed Grach expressed his opinion thus:

"Benya don't say much," Grach said, "but what he says is to the point. It makes you wish he'd say a bit more."

"If that's so," the late Bull decided, "let's try him out on Tartakovsky."

"Let's try him on Tartakovsky," the council decided, and those of them who still had some conscience squatting in their hearts blushed on hearing that decision.

Why did they blush? You'll find out if you listen.

We used to call that Tartakovsky "Jew-and-a-Half" or "Nine Holdups." "Jew-and-a-Half" because no single Jew could possibly store in his person as much arrogance and money as Tartakovsky had. He was taller than the tallest Odessa cop and weighed more than the fattest Jewish woman. And he was called "Nine Holdups" because Leon the Bull and company had held up his business not eight times and not ten but exactly nine times. Benya, who wasn't the king then, was given the honor of holding up Tartakovsky's office for the tenth time. When Froim informed him of this, Benya said "Yes" and walked out, slamming the door behind him. Why did he slam the door? You'll find out if you keep listening.

Although he is one of us, that Tartakovsky has the heart of a murderer. He came from among us, he is our flesh and blood, as if we'd been brought into this world by the same Jewish mama. Half Odessa worked for him in his stores. And yet it was people from his own Moldavanka district who caused him all his troubles. Twice they snatched him for ransom and once, during a pogrom, they organized his funeral and even had a choir singing at it. That was when the Sloboda hoodlums were beating up Jews on Bolshaya Arnautskaya Street. Tartakovsky, getting away from them, ran into a funeral procession, choir and all, on Sophia Street.

"Who's this being buried with a choir?" Tartakovsky inquired.

Passers-by told him it was Tartakovsky's funeral. The procession reached the Sloboda cemetery. Then our men took a machine gun out of the coffin and started spraying the Sloboda hoods with it. But Jew-and-a-Half hadn't foreseen that. Jew-and-a-Half was scared to death. And how could a man in his important position not be scared to death under such circumstances?

A tenth holdup for a man who'd already been buried once was very tactless. And Benya, who wasn't yet the king, appreciated that better than anyone. But he had said "yes" to Grach and so, that very same day, he wrote Tartakovsky a letter very much like all letters written on such occasions:

Dear Mr. Tartakovsky:

I would appreciate it if, by next Saturday, you'd place under the rainwater barrel, etc., etc. Now, should you fail to do so, as you have failed on various similar occasions, you may expect a great disappointment in your family life.

Most respectfully, your acquaintance,
Benzion Krik

Tartakovsky took the trouble to answer quite promptly:

Benya!

If you were an idiot, I'd have written to you as one writes to idiots. But I am not aware that you are one, and I hope I am not wrong—God forbid. It looks to me as if you're trying to pass for a naïve boy. As if you hadn't heard about that bumper crop in Argentina last year that is forcing us to sit here without a single customer for our wheat. And let me tell you frankly: I am sick of eating such bitter bread in my old days and going through all this unpleasantness after working like a cart horse all my life. And what do you think I got from all that endless slaving? Ulcers, aches, worries, and sleepless nights! Quit fooling, Benya. Take this advice from one who is much more your friend than you realize.

Reuben Tartakovsky

Jew-and-a-Half did his best. He wrote the letter. But somehow it got lost in the mail. So, getting no answer, Benya was very hurt. The next day he was in Tartakovsky's office with four friends. These four masked fellows, each holding a gun in his hand, came rolling into the room.

"Stick 'em up," they suggested, waving their guns around.

"Work a bit more calmly, Solomon," Benya remarked to one of his men who was shouting louder than the others. "You must get out of this habit of being nervous when you're on the job." Then Benya turned to the clerk, who was pale as death and yellow as clay, and asked him:

"Jew-and-a-Half come around today?"

"The boss hasn't been in," the clerk answered.

This clerk's name was Joseph Muginstein and he was

the bachelor son of Aunt Pesia who sold chickens on Seredinsky Square.

"So who's in charge here now?" they pressed poor Muginstein.

"Well, I am," Muginstein said, now green as green grass.

"Then let's get that safe opened up, with God's help," Benya told him, and an opera in three acts began.

Nervous Solomon stowed money, securities, watches, and jewelry into a suitcase and the late Joseph Muginstein stood by with his hands sticking up in the air, while Benya told stories from the life of the Jewish people.

"Now since he fancies himself a Rothschild," Benya was saying of Tartakovsky, "let him light himself up like a torch. Tell me, Muginstein, as a friend, what do you think of this: I send him a business letter—so why doesn't he take a five-kopeck fare on a streetcar to my place to drink a glass of vodka and have a little snack with the family? What was there to stop him from opening his heart to me? Why didn't he say to me something like, 'Look here, Benya, here's my financial situation: wait, give me a couple of days, give me time to draw breath, to throw up my hands in surprise.' What d'you think I could've said to him? Now, pigs, Muginstein, don't get together and discuss things; but people do. Do you understand what I mean, Muginstein?"

"I do," Muginstein said. He was lying because he couldn't see at all why a wealthy and respected citizen like Jew-and-a-Half, maybe the most important man in Odessa, would want to take a streetcar to drink a glass of vodka with the family of a carter like Mendel Krik.

Meantime, misfortune lurked under the windows like a beggar at dawn. Then misfortune burst noisily into the office. And although this time it came in the shape of a Jew by the name of Sava Butsis, it was drunk as a water carrier.

"Ho-hoo-ho!" Sava shouted. "Please forgive me, Benya dear, I know I'm terribly late!" And he started stamping his feet and waving his hands. Then he fired a shot and the bullet hit Muginstein in the belly.

Do I have to tell you? There was a man and now he's no more. An innocent bachelor lives his life without harming anyone, like a bird in a tree, and then he suddenly gets himself killed for no good reason. In comes a Jew looking like a sailor or something; he takes a shot—not at some bottle to get a little prize, but into a human belly. What more is there to say?

"Let's get the hell out of here," Benya said. He was the last to leave, but as he left, he said to Butsis:

"I swear by my mother's tomb, you'll lie next to him, Sava."

Now tell me, young man, you who clip coupons from other people's bonds, what would you have done in Benya Krik's place? You wouldn't have known what to do, but Benya did. And that's why he's the king, while the two of us are sitting here on the wall of the Second Jewish Cemetery, shading our eyes with our hands.

Aunt Pesia's unfortunate son didn't die at once. One hour after they had brought him to the hospital, Benya arrived there. He demanded to see the head nurse and the doctor in charge and, without removing his hands from the pockets of his cream-colored trousers, he said to them:

"I have a special reason for wanting patient Joseph Muginstein to recover. If it's any help to you, let me introduce myself: I'm Benzion Krik. Spare no expense: camphor, air cushions, private room—you'd better not stint him anything, for if you do, every doctor in this hospital, even if he's a doctor of philosophy, can expect nothing but six feet of earth in the near future."

But despite all that, Muginstein died that very night. And only then did Jew-and-a-Half raise a stink all over Odessa.

"Where do the police end and where does Benya begin?" he shouted.

"The police end wherever Benya begins," sensible people tried to make him see, but Tartakovsky wouldn't sim-

mer down. Finally, a red automobile appeared on Seredinsky Square with a musical horn that played the first
measures of the march from *Pagliacci.* In broad daylight,
the car stopped by the little house where Aunt Pesia
lived.

The car's engine roared, its tailpipe spat smoke, its
chromium shone, its fumes stank, and its horn blared
music. Someone jumped out of the car and walked
straight into the kitchen where little Aunt Pesia was keen-
ing and rolling on the earthen floor in mourning. Jew-
and-a-Half was there too, sitting on a chair, waving his
arms about.

"You filthy rat-face, you murderer!" he screamed, at the
sight of the visitor. "May the earth vomit your corpse! A
nice fashion you're trying to start around here—killing
live people!"

"Monsieur Tartakovsky," Benya said to him quietly,
"for more than twenty-four hours, I'm crying about the
dear departed like he's my own brother. But I know you
sneeze at my youthful tears. You ought to be ashamed of
yourself, Monsieur Tartakovsky. Tell me—which of your
safes have you hidden your shame in? I hear you had the
nerve to send the mother of our dear departed a measly
hundred rubles! My brains stood on end along with my
hair when I heard that, Monsieur Tartakovsky!"

At this point Benya paused. He was wearing a brown
jacket, cream-colored pants, and raspberry-red shoes.

"Ten thousand rubles in a lump sum!" Benya roared
suddenly. "And a pension until she dies—and may she go
on living for a hundred and twenty years. And if you say
no, Monsieur Tartakovsky, just step out of here and we'll
go for a little ride in my car."

After that, they exchanged words. Jew-and-a-Half
called Benya names. I wasn't present during the argument, but those who were remember it. They finally
agreed on five thousand down and a pension of fifty rubles
a month for life. Then Benya spoke to the disheveled little
woman who was still rolling on the floor.

"Aunt Pesia," he said, "if you want my life, you can

have it, but even God makes mistakes. It was a huge mistake, Auntie Pesia, but wasn't it a mistake on God's part to settle Jews in Russia where they live like in hell? Why couldn't He have settled Jews in Switzerland where they'd be surrounded by first-class lakes, where they'd breathe mountain air and be surrounded by nothing but the French? So, you see, everyone goes wrong sometimes, even God. Listen to me, Auntie Pesia: you're getting five thousand in a lump sum and fifty a month as long as you live, so go ahead and live, please, until you're a hundred and twenty. And Joseph will get a first-class funeral—there'll be six horses like six lions, and two carriages for the wreaths, and the choir from the Brodsky synagogue, and Minkovsky in person will sing over your late son."

And the next morning the funeral took place. You can ask the cemetery beggars about that funeral. Ask the *shammeses* of the synagogue about it, the kosher poultrymen, the old women from the Second Almshouse. Never before had there been such a funeral in Odessa and never will the world see another like it. The traffic cops put on white cotton gloves that day. In the synagogues, decorated with greenery, their doors and windows flung wide open, electric lights burned. Black plumes swayed on the white horses drawing the hearse. Sixty choirboys headed the procession, singing in women's voices. The elders of the synagogue of kosher poultrymen supported Aunt Pesia by the arms. Behind the elders walked representatives of the Association of Jewish Office Employees and behind them, the Jewish lawyers, doctors, midwives, and medical nurses. The poultrywomen of the Old Market marched on one side of Aunt Pesia and on the other, draped in orange shawls, the statuesque milkmaids of Bugayevka. They stamped their feet like troopers on a parade ground. A smell of milk and the sea came from their wide, swaying hips. And behind them all plodded Reuben Tartakovsky's employees. There were a hundred of them, or maybe two hundred—or, it could be, two thousand. They wore black jackets with silk lapels, and their new shoes squeaked like suckling pigs tied in a bag.

And now I'll speak like the Lord spoke out of that burning bush on Mount Sinai. Let my words enter your ears. All this I saw, saw it with my own eyes as I sat on this cemetery wall next to Lisping Mosia and Shimshon who works in the undertaker's office. Yes, I, Arie-Leib, a proud Jew who lives near the dead, saw it with my own eyes.

The hearse drove up to the cemetery chapel, and the coffin was placed on the steps. Aunt Pesia was trembling like a sparrow. The cantor got out of his carriage and intoned the funeral dirge; sixty choirboys sang the responses. At that second, the red car shot around the corner, its horn sounding the first measures of the *Pagliacci* march as it came to a halt. The people were as quiet as the dead. The trees, the choirboys, the beggars, all were silent. Four men got out from under the car's red roof. They were carrying a wreath of roses such as no one had ever seen before. And when the funeral service was over, the four men placed the coffin on their steel shoulders and, their eyes burning and chests bulging, marched along amid the Association of Jewish Clerks.

Benya Krik, whom no one called the "King" yet, walked in front and was the first at the grave. He stepped onto the mound of upturned earth and stretched out his hand.

"What are you doing, young fellow?" Kaufman of the Undertakers' Brotherhood asked, rushing up to him.

"I wish to make a speech," Benya said.

And he did make a speech. Everyone who wanted to hear it heard it. I, Arie-Leib, heard it, and Lisping Mosia who was sitting next to me on the cemetery wall.

"Gentlemen and ladies," Benya Krik said, and as he spoke the sun stood over his head like a sentry with a rifle, "you have come here to pay your last respects to a poor man who worked by the sweat of his brow for a brass kopeck. In my name and in the name of all those who are not present here, I thank you. Gentlemen and ladies, what did our beloved Joseph see in his life? Well, perhaps he only saw a few things that are not even worth mentioning.

What was his occupation? Well, he counted money that wasn't even his. In the name of what did he die? Well, he died for the entire working class. There are people doomed to die before they've even begun to live. Here there was a bullet flying around that pierced Joseph's doomed breast, although he had seen nothing in his life but two or three things that are not even worthy of mention. There are people who know how to drink vodka and there are those who don't know how to drink vodka but still drink it. And those who know how to drink get a kick out of both misfortune and joy, while the others suffer for all those who drink vodka without knowing how to drink. Therefore, gentlemen and ladies, after we have finished praying for our poor Joseph, I request that you see off to his grave one Sava Butsis, whom you don't know yet, but who is already deceased."

When he had finished this speech, Benya stepped down from the mound. Everything was silent, men, trees, and cemetery beggars. Two gravediggers brought an unpainted coffin to the grave next to Joseph's. Stammeringly, the cantor completed his prayer. Benya threw the first shovelful of earth into Joseph's grave and moved over to Sava's. Like a flock of sheep, all the lawyers and the ladies with brooches followed him. He forced the cantor to sing the full service over Sava and the sixty choirboys had to sing the responses again. Sava Butsis never dreamed of such a funeral service, and you can take the word of Arie-Leib, a very ancient old man, for that.

They say that on that day Jew-and-a-Half decided to close his business. I wasn't there when it happened. But what I did see with the eyes of Arie-Leib was that neither the cantor nor the choir nor the Undertakers' Brotherhood presented bills for their services at that funeral. And that's all I was able to see, because after they had moved slowly a few steps from Butsis' grave, people suddenly began sprinting as if running from a house on fire. They scattered in carriages, on carts, on foot. And the four men who had arrived in the red automobile left in it. The musical claxon played its bars, the engine roared, and the car drove off. And Lisping Mosia, who tries to beat me to the best spots on the cemetery wall, looked after the red automobile and said, "He's the King."

Now you know all there is to know. You know who was the first to say the word "King." It was Mosia. You know, too, why he didn't call either One-eyed Grach or Mad Dog Kolia Pakovsky that. You know everything. But what good can it do you if you still have spectacles on your nose and autumn in your heart?

(1923)

MY FIRST FEE

To live in Tiflis in the springtime, to be twenty years old and not to be loved is a terrible thing. It happened to me. I had a job as a proof-reader in the printing plant of the Caucasus Military District. The river Kura seethed under the windows of my garret. As it rose behind the mountains, the sun lit up its muddy whirlpools in the mornings. I rented the garret from a Georgian couple who had just been married. The man had a butcher's shop in the Eastern Market. On the other side of the wall he and his wife, crazed with love, turned and twisted like two large fish in a small tank. The tails of these two frantic fish thrashed against the wall. They made the whole attic shake—it was burnt black by the sun—tore it from its foundations and bore it off into infinity. Their teeth were clenched tight in the relentless fury of their passion. In the mornings the wife, Miliet, went downstairs for bread. She was so weak she had to hold on to the banister in order not to fall. Groping for the steps with her small feet, she had the faint, vacant smile of someone recovering from an illness. With her hand on her small breasts, she bowed to everybody she met on the way—to the old Assyrian, who was green with age, to the man who came round selling kerosene, and to the old hags, deeply seared with wrinkles, who sold skeins of wool. At nighttime the heaving and moaning of my neighbors was followed by a silence as penetrating as the whine of a cannon ball.

To live in Tiflis, to be twenty years old, and to listen at night to the storms of other people's silence is a terrible thing. To get away from it, I raced out of the house down to the Kura, where I was overwhelmed by the steam-bath heat of the Tiflis spring. It hit you for all it was worth and knocked you out. I wandered along the hump-backed streets with a parched throat. The haze of spring heat drove me back to my attic, to that forest of blackened stumps lit by the moon. There was nothing to do but to look for love. Of course, I found it. For better or worse, the woman I chose was a prostitute. Her name was Vera. I prowled after her every night along Golovin Avenue, not daring to speak to her. I had neither the money for her, nor the words—those tireless, trite and nagging words of love. From childhood all the strength of my being had been devoted to the invention of tales, plays and stories— thousands of them. They lay on my heart like toads on a stone. I was possessed by devilish pride and did not want to write them down prematurely. I thought it was a waste of time not to write as well as Leo Tolstoi. My stories were intended to survive oblivion. Fearless thoughts and consuming passions are worth the effort spent on them only when they are dressed in beautiful clothes. How can you make these clothes?

It is difficult for a man who has been captured by an idea and tamed by its snake-like gaze to expend himself in the froth of meaningless and nagging words of love. A man like that is ashamed to cry in sorrow; he hasn't got the sense to laugh in joy. Being a dreamer, I hadn't mastered the absurd art of happiness. I would be forced, therefore, to give Vera ten rubles out of my meagre earnings.

When I had made up my mind, I started to wait one evening outside the "Sympathy" restaurant. Tartars in blue Circassian tunics and soft leather boots sauntered past me. Picking their teeth with silver tooth-picks, they eyed the crimson-painted women—Georgians, with large feet and slender thighs. There was a touch of turquoise in the fading light. The flowering acacias along the streets began to moan in a low, faltering voice. A crowd of officials in white coats surged along the boulevard, and wafts of balmy air from Mount Kazbek came down towards them.

Vera came later, when it was dark. Tall and white-faced, she sailed ahead of the ape-like throng as the Virgin Mary rides the prow of a fishing boat. She drew level with the door of the "Sympathy" restaurant. I lurched after her:

"Going somewhere?"

Her broad, pink back moved in front of me. She turned around:

"What's that you say?" She frowned, but her eyes were laughing.

"Where are you going?"

The words cracked in my mouth like dried sticks. Vera changed her step and walked by my side.

"Ten rubles, is that all right?"

I agreed so quickly she got suspicious.

"But do you have ten rubles?"

We went into a doorway and I handed her my purse. She counted the twenty-one rubles in it; her grey eyes were screwed up and her lips moved. She sorted out the gold coins from the silver.

"Give me ten," she said, handing back the purse, "we'll spend another five and you keep the rest to live on. When do you get your next pay?"

I said: in four days' time. We came out of the doorway. Vera took me by the hand and pressed her shoulder against me. We went up the street, which was growing cooler. The pavement was littered with withered vegetables.

"It'd be nice to go to Borzhom and get away from the heat," she said.

Vera's hair was held by a ribbon which caught and re-fracted flashes of light from the street-lamps.

"Well, clear off to Borzhom."

That's what I said: clear off. That's the expression I used, for some reason.

"I haven't got the dough," Vera said with a yawn and

forgot all about me. She forgot all about me because her day was made and because I was easy money. She knew I wouldn't turn her in to the police, or rob her of her money and her earrings during the night.

We reached the foot of St. David's Mount. There, in a bar, I ordered *kebab* for us. Without waiting for it to come, Vera went over and sat with some old Persians who were discussing business. Leaning on their polished sticks and nodding their olive-coloured skulls, they were telling the owner it was time he expanded his trade. Vera butted into their conversation. She took the side of the old men. She was for transferring the business to Mikhailovsky Boulevard. The owner, blinded by flabbiness and caution, just wheezed. I ate my *kebab* alone. Vera's bare arms flowed from the silk of her sleeves; she banged her fist on the table, her earrings flitted to and fro among the long, faded backs, yellow beards and painted finger-nails. The *kebab* was cold by the time she came back to the table. She had become so worked up that her face was flushed.

"You can't shift him, the mule ... You can really do business, you know, on Mikhailovsky with Eastern cooking."

One after another, Vera's acquaintances came past the table—Tartars in Circassian tunics, middle-aged officers, shopkeepers in alpaca jackets and potbellied old men with tanned faces and greenish blackheads on their cheeks. It was midnight by the time we got to the hotel, but Vera had a hundred and one things to do here as well. There was an old woman who was getting ready to go and see her son in Armavir. Vera left me and went to help her pack—knelt on her suitcase, strapped pillows together, and wrapped pies in grease-proof paper. The broad-shouldered old woman in a gauze hat with a handbag at her side went around to all the rooms saying goodbye. She shuffled along the corridor in her elastic shoes, sobbing and smiling with all her wrinkles. It took a whole hour to see her off. I waited for Vera in a musty room with three-legged chairs, an earthenware stove and patches of damp in the corners.

I had been tormented and dragged round the town for so long, that this love I wanted now seemed like an enemy, an inescapable enemy.

Outside there was another, alien life shuffling in the corridor or suddenly bursting into laughter. Flies were dying in a phial filled with a milky liquid. Each died in its own way. The death throes of some were violent and lasted a long time. Others died quietly, with a slight quiver. Next to the phial on the worn table-cloth was a book: a novel by Golovin about the life of the boyars. I opened it at random. The letters lined up in a single row and then got all jumbled together. In front of me, in the square frame of the window was a steep, stony hill-side with a winding Turkish street going up it. Vera came into the room.

"We've just said goodbye to Feodosya Mavrikeyevna," she said. "She was just like a mother to us, you know. She's traveling all alone, the old woman, she's got nobody to go with her."

Vera sat down on the bed with her knees apart. Her eyes were far away, roaming in the pure realms of her care and friendship for the old woman. Then she saw me in my double-breasted jacket. She clasped her hands and stretched herself.

"You're tired of waiting, I bet. . . . Never mind, we'll get down to it in a moment."

But I just couldn't make out what Vera was going to do. Her preparations were like those of a surgeon getting ready for an operation. She lit a kerosene stove and put a saucepan with water on it. She threw a clean towel over the headboard of the bed, and above it hung an enema bag with a douche; the white tube dangled down from the wall. When the water got hot, she poured it into the bag, threw a red crystal into it and started taking off her dress, pulling it over her head. A large woman with drooping shoulders and crumpled stomach stood before me. Her flabby nipples pointed blindly sideways.

"Come over here, boy," my loved one said, "—while the water's getting ready."

I didn't move. I was numb with despair. Why had I exchanged my loneliness for the misery of this sordid den, for these dying flies and three-legged chairs?

O Gods of my youth! How different it was, this dreary business, from the love of my neighbors on the other side of the wall, their long, drawn-out squeals.

Vera put her hands under her breasts and wobbled them.

"What are you so miserable about? Come here." I didn't move. She pulled her petticoat up to her belly and sat down on the bed again.

"Are you sorry about your money?"

"I don't worry about my money," I said in a cracked voice.

"How come you don't worry about your money? Are you a thief or something?"

"I'm not a thief."

"Do you work for thieves?"

"I'm a boy."

"I can see you're not a cow," Vera muttered. She could hardly keep her eyes open. She lay down, pulled me towards her and started running her hands over me.

"I'm a boy," I shouted, "a boy with the Armenians, don't you understand?"

O God of my youth!—Five of my twenty years had been spent in making up stories, thousands of stories which gorged themselves on my brain. They lay on my mind like toads on a stone. Dislodged by the force of loneliness, one of them fell to the ground. It was evidently a matter of fate that a Tiflis prostitute was to be my first "reader." I went cold all over at the suddenness of my invention and I told her my story as a "boy with the Armenians." If I had given less time and thought to my craft, I should have made up a hackneyed tale about being the son of a rich official who had driven me from home, a tale about a domineering father and a downtrodden mother. But I didn't make this mistake. A well-devised story needn't try to be like real life. Real life is only too eager to resemble a well-devised story. For this reason—and because this was how my listener liked it—I was born in the small town of Alyoshki in Kherson province. My father worked as a draftsman with a steam-boat company. He sweated over his drawing board day and night to give us, his children, a good education, but we all took after our mother who was interested only in having a good time. At the age of ten I started stealing from my father. When I was grown up I ran away to Baku, to some relatives of my mother's. They introduced me to an Armenian called Stepan Ivanovich. I moved in with him and we lived together for four years.

"But how old were you then?"

"Fifteen."

Vera was expecting me to tell her about the misdeeds of the Armenian who had corrupted me, but I went on:

"We lived together for four years. Stepan Ivanovich was the most decent and trusting person I've ever met. He believed every word his friends said to him. I ought to have learned a trade during those four years, but I didn't do a thing. All I cared about was playing billiards. Stepan Ivanovich's friends ruined him. He gave them bogus bills of change, and his friends presented them for payments."

"Bogus bills of change"—I don't know how they came into my mind, but I did right to bring them in. Vera believed everything after that. She wrapped herself in a shawl which quivered on her shoulders.

"Stepan Ivanovich was ruined. He was thrown out of his apartment and his furniture was sold by auction. He became a traveling salesman. I wasn't going to live with him now that he had no money, so I moved in with a rich old church warden."

The "church warden" was filched from some writer: he was the invention of a lazy mind which can't be bothered to produce a real live character.

I said "a church warden," and Vera's eyes flickered and went out of my control. Then, in order to restore the situation, I installed asthma in the old man's yellow chest. Attacks of asthma made him wheeze hoarsely. He jumped out of bed at night and panted into the kerosene-laden air of Baku. He soon died. The asthma finished him off. My relatives wouldn't have anything to do with me. So here I was in Triflis with twenty rubles in my pocket—the very same rubles which Vera had counted in the doorway on Golovin Avenue. A waiter in the hotel were I was staying had promised to get me rich customers, but so far he had sent me only Armenian inn-keepers with great fat bellies. These people liked their own country, their songs and their wine, but they trampled on other people, men or women, as a thief tramples on his neighbor's garden.

And I started talking a lot of rubbish I had picked up about innkeepers. My heart was breaking from self-pity. It looked as though I was utterly doomed. I was trembling with sorrow and inspiration. Trickles of ice-cold sweat started down my face like snakes moving over grass warmed by the sun. I stopped talking, began to cry and turned away. The kerosene stove had gone out a long time ago. The water had boiled and gone cold again. The rubber tube was hanging from the wall. Vera went silently up to the window. Her back, dazzling white and sad, heaved before me. In the window, it was getting light around the mountain tops.

"The things people do," Vera whispered, without turning around. "God, the things people do."

She stretched out her bare arms and threw the shutters wide open. The paving stones on the street hissed slightly as they grew cooler. There was a smell of dust and water. Vera's head was shaking.

"So you're a whore—like us bitches."

I bowed my head.

"A whore like you."

Vera turned round to me. Her petticoat hung sideways on her body like a rag.

"The things people do," she said again, in a louder voice. "God, the things people do. Have you ever been with a woman?"

I pressed my cold lips to her hand.

"No, how could I? They wouldn't let me."

My head shook against her breasts which welled freely

above me. The taut nipples thrust against my cheeks. They were moist and wide-eyed like baby calves. Vera looked down at me from above.

"Sister," she whispered and sat down on the floor at my side. "My little sister."

Now tell me, I should like to ask you: have you ever seen a village carpenter helping his mate to build a house? Have you seen how thick and fast and gaily the shavings fly as they plane a beam together? That night this thirty-year-old woman taught me all the tricks of her trade. That night I learned secrets you will never learn, I experienced a love which you will never experience, I heard the words that one woman says to another. I have forgotten them: we are not supposed to remember them.

We fell asleep at dawn. We were awakened by the heat of our bodies, a heat which lay in the bed like a dead weight. When we woke up, we laughed to each other. I didn't go to the printing plant that day. We drank tea in the bazaar of the Old Town. A placid Turk poured us tea from a samovar wrapped in a towel. It was brick red and steamed like newly shed blood. The hazy fire of the sun blazed on the sides of our glasses. The long-drawn-out braying of donkeys blended with the hammering of tinsmiths.

Copper jugs were set up in rows on faded carpets under tents. Dogs nuzzled at the entrails of oxen. A caravan of dust was flying towards Tiflis, the town of roses and mutton fat. The dust was blotting out the crimson fire of the sun. The Turk poured out more tea for us and kept count of the rolls we ate on an abacus. The world was beautiful just to give us pleasure. When I was covered all over with fine beads of sweat, I turned my glass upside down. After I'd paid the Turk, I pushed two five-ruble pieces over to Vera. Her plump leg was lying across mine. She pushed the money away and removed her leg.

"Do you want us to quarrel, sister?"

No, I didn't want to quarrel. We agreed to meet in the evening and I put the two gold pieces, my first literary fee, back into my purse.

All this was a long time ago, and since then I have often received money from publishers, from learned men and from Jews trading in books. For victories that were defeats, for defeats that turned into victories, for life and for death they paid me trifling sums—much smaller than the one I received in my youth from my first "reader." But I am not bitter. I am not bitter because I know I shall not die until I have snatched one more gold piece—and this will be my last—from the hands of love.

(1922–1928)

Mikhail Zoshchenko

(1895–1958)

Like Ring Lardner, S. J. Perelman, Flann O'Brien, and many another master of literary comedy, Zoshchenko was a writer whose professional merriment masked an obscure but tormenting wound. His pain was, in part, purely physical and obvious: he had been gassed as a soldier in the First World War and suffered for the rest of his life from the damage to his liver and heart. But he himself realized that his essential melancholy antedated this bodily trauma.

He avenged himself on the world, and assisted millions of readers in doing so, by laughing at it. Even dictatorships—or especially dictatorships—require jesters who have a limited license to make fun of otherwise protected people and institutions. Zoshchenko occasionally had his license revoked, but by and large he managed to be safely hilarious. In the story "Bees and People," one scarcely notices that the reason Panfilich is able to find many hives of honeybees for sale is that the populations of *three villages* in which their former owners lived had been forcibly relocated to the Far East. In this aptly named story, there is a certain unstated connection between the bees and the people. Ostensibly an account of how good old Russian ingenuity wins out in the end, it does not fail to suggest that bees whose lives are disrupted can at least have the satisfaction of a vengeance denied their former keepers.

Zoshchenko's style is at once unique and restlessly mutable. Like that of Gogol, it changes so much from story to story, and even within one story, that no single persona can be identified with it. It is called *skaz*, a Russian term that has been pointlessly imported into English, since no Russian or foreign theorist has ever been able to assign to it a meaning that might justify its encumbering the lexicon of criticism. It means roughly a style that conveys an impression of oral (usually subliterary) speech. "Impression" is the key word. To seek in Zoshchenko's invented language some ethnographically authentic reflection of how Soviet bureaucrats and philistines actually spoke would be like looking for the language of cockroaches in Don Marquis's *archy and mehitabel.*

Before Sunrise appeared, of all inopportune moments, in 1943, at the height of the Second World War. The censor must have been looking the other way; in any case, publication was stopped after two installments, and the work remains unfinished. Distinguished historians of Soviet literature have found it baffling; E. J. Brown calls it a novel and an elaborate exercise in humor; G. P. Struve opines that it might, after all, be a hoax. Like many Russian masterpieces, it is completely unclassifiable and deeply flawed. The least inadequate description of it is perhaps "the history of a self-analysis."

Zoshchenko set out to discover the cause of his lifelong melancholy by painstakingly reviewing his whole existence, even that which preceded consciousness itself (hence, "before sunrise"). He felt that healing might begin by uncovering some forgotten psychic wound and correctly interpreting it. If this sounds like one of the tenets of classical psychoanalysis, it is, though Zoshchenko mentions Freud (officially proscribed by the authorities) only to reject his method in favor of the condoned theories of Pavlov. If *Before Sunrise* were limited to its superficial exposition of psychological theory, it would have little value. But its artistic merit rests upon numerous "snapshots" (as he called them)—vivid and telegraphically terse little vignettes drawn from a period that extended from Zoshchenko's earliest memories to his young manhood.

BEES AND PEOPLE

A Red Army soldier came to a certain collective farm for a visit. And as a present for his relatives he brought a jar of flower honey.

And everyone liked that honey so much that the farm decided to set up a beekeeping operation of its own.

But no one around there kept bees, so the members of the collective had to do everything from the ground up— build the hives and then get the bees out of the forest and into their new apartments.

When they saw what a long time all this would take, they lost their enthusiasm. "There's no end to it," they said. "We'll be running here and there and first thing you know it'll be winter and we won't see that honey till next year. And now's when we need it."

But one of the collective farmers was a certain Ivan Panfilich, a fine man, no longer in his first youth, aged seventy-two. As a young man he had kept bees.

So he says, "If we're going to have our tea with honey this year, then somebody has got to go somewhere where there's bees being kept and buy what we're thinking about."

The farmers say, "This farm is loaded. Money is no object. Let's buy bees in full production, already perched in the hives. Because if we went and got bees out of the woods they might turn out to be no good. They might start turning out some kind of horrible honey like linden or something. But we want flower honey."

And so they gave Ivan Panfilich some money and sent him off to the city of Tambov.

He arrives in Tambov and the people there tell him, "You did the right thing coming to us. We've just had three villages relocated to the Far East and there's one extra beekeeping setup left behind. We can let you have it for next to nothing. But the thing is—how are you going to transport these bees? That's what we don't know. This is what you might call loose goods. In fact it has wings on. The least little thing and it'll fly every which way. We're afraid you'll get to the addressee with nothing but hives and eggs."

Panfilich says, "One way or another I'll get them there. I know bees. Been associated with bees my whole life."

And so he took sixteen hives to the station on two carts. At the station he managed to get hold of a flatcar and he put his hives on that flatcar and covered them up with a tarpaulin. And it wasn't long before the freight train took off and our flatcar rolling along with it.

Panfilich struck a pose on the flatcar and addressed the bees: "It's okay, boys," said he, "we'll make it! Just hang on in there in the dark a little while and when we get there I'll put you out in the flowers. And I think you'll find what you want there. But whatever you do, don't get upset about me carrying you in the dark. I covered you all with that tarpaulin on purpose so nobody would be crazy enough to fly out while the train's running. Something might happen and you wouldn't be able to hop back on board."

And so the train traveled on for a day. And another day.

By the third day Panfilich was getting a little worried. The train was going slowly. Stopping at every station. Standing there for hours. And he couldn't tell when they were going to get to where he was going.

At Polya Station Panfilich got down off his flatcar and looked up at the stationmaster. "Tell me, sir," he asked, "are we going to be stopping long at your station?"

"I really couldn't tell you," the stationmaster answered. "You could be here till evening."

"If we'll be here till evening," Panfilich said, "then I'm taking off the tarpaulin to let my bees out into your fields.

Otherwise they'll be worn out from this trip. This makes three days they've been sitting under the tarpaulin. They're perishing. They haven't had anything to eat or drink and they can't feed the little ones."

"Do whatever you like! What do I care about your flying passengers! I've got my hands full without them. And I should get excited about your little ones—that's the limit! Of all the stupid . . . !"

Panfilich went back to his flatcar and took off the tarpaulin.

And the weather was magnificent. Blue sky. Good old July sun. Fields all around. Flowers. A grove of chestnuts in bloom.

So Panfilich took the tarpaulin off the flatcar and all at once a whole army of bees took off into the blue.

The bees circled, looked around, and headed straight for the fields and forests.

A crowd of passengers surrounded the flatcar, and Panfilich used it as a platform to lecture them on the usefulness of bees. But while the lecture was going on, the stationmaster came out of the station and began signaling the engineer to start the train.

Panfilich gasped "Ach!" when he saw these signals, got terribly upset, and said to the stationmaster, "But my dear sir, don't send the train on, all my bees are out!"

The stationmaster said, "Well, you just whistle them back into their seats! I can't hold the train longer than three minutes."

Panfilich said, "*Please!* Just hold the train till sundown. At sundown the bees will be back in their seats. Or at least unhook my flatcar. I can't go without the bees. I only have a thousand left here; there are fifteen thousand in the fields. Try to understand the fix I'm in! Don't harden your heart to this tragedy!"

The stationmaster said, "I'm not running a health farm for bees! I'm running a railroad! The bees flew away! Beautiful! And on the next train they'll tell me the flies have flown away! Or the fleas have jumped out of the sleeping car! What am I supposed to do—hold up the train

for that? Don't make me laugh!" And with that he sig-
naled the engineer again.

And the train started off.

Panfilich, white as a sheet, stood on his flatcar, his arms
spread wide, his gaze sweeping from side to side, his body
trembling with indignation.

But the train goes on.

Well, a certain number of bees did manage to jump on
while the train was moving. But most of them stayed behind in the fields and groves of trees. Soon the train was
out of sight.

The stationmaster returned to the station and settled
down to work. He was writing something in the log and
drinking tea with lemon. Suddenly he heard a kind of
racket on the station platform.

He opened the window to see what had happened and
he saw that the passengers waiting there were in a frenzy,
hopping and lurching around. The stationmaster asked,
"What happened?"

"Bees have stung three passengers here," they answered, "and now they're attacking the rest. The sky is
black with them!"

Then the stationmaster saw that a whole dark cloud of
bees were circling around his station. They were looking
for their flatcar, naturally. But there wasn't any flatcar. It
had left. So they were attacking people and whatever else
got in the way.

No sooner had the stationmaster left the window to go
out on the platform than in through the window flew a
swarm of bees, mad as hell. He grabbed a towel and began
waving it about to drive the bees out of the room.

But evidently that was his great mistake.

Two bees got him on the neck, a third on the ear, and a
fourth stung him on the forehead.

The stationmaster wrapped himself up in a towel and
laid down on the sofa and commenced to give out these
pitiful groans. Soon his assistant ran in and said, "The
bees have stung other people besides you. The telegraph
operator got stung on the cheek and now won't work."

The stationmaster, lying on his couch, said, "Oy! What are we going to do?"

At this point another employee ran up and said, "The ticket seller—I mean to say, your wife, Klavdia Ivanovna—just got stung on the nose. Now her appearance has been ruined for good."

The stationmaster let out even louder groans and said, "We've got to get that flatcar with that crazy beekeeper back here at once." He jumped off his sofa and grabbed the telephone. From the next station down the line he heard: "Okay. We'll uncouple the flatcar right away. Only we don't have an engine to pull it to you."

The stationmaster screamed, "We'll send you the engine! Uncouple that flat at once! The bees have already stung my wife! My station Polya is deserted! All the passengers are hiding in the shed! There's nothing but bees flying around in the air! And I absolutely refuse to go outside—let there *be* train wrecks!"

And it wasn't long before the flatcar was delivered. Everyone gave a sigh of relief when they saw the flatcar, with Panfilich standing on it.

Panfilich ordered the flatcar to be placed precisely where it had been before, and the bees, when they saw their car, instantly flew up to it. But there were so many bees, and they were in such a hurry to take their seats, that there was a crush. And they raised such a buzzing and humming that a dog started howling and the pigeons scattered into the sky.

Panfilich, standing on the platform, spoke to them: "Easy, boys, don't rush. Plenty of time! Everybody sit where their boarding pass says!" In ten minutes all was quiet. When he'd made sure everything was in order, Panfilich stepped down off his platform. And the people standing around the station began to clap. And Panfilich, like an actor, bowed to thank them and said: "Turn your collars down! Show your faces! And stop trembling—the stinging is over!"

When he'd said this, Panfilich went to the stationmaster. The stationmaster, wrapped in his towel, was still lying on his sofa gasping and groaning. When Panfilich entered he groaned even louder.

"My dear sir," said Panfilich, "I'm very sorry that my bees stung you. But it was your own fault. You can't be so indifferent to things, whether they're big or little. Bees can't stand that. Bees sting people for that without giving it a second thought."

The stationmaster groaned even louder, and Panfilich went on: "Bees absolutely will not stand for being pushed around by indifferent bureaucrats. You probably treated them the way you treat people—and you see what you get."

Panfilich glanced out the window and added, "The sun's gone down. My fellow travelers have taken their seats. I have the honor to bid you good day! We're off!"

The stationmaster feebly nodded his head as though saying, "Be off quickly!" And in a low whisper he added, "Sure you've got all the bees? See you don't leave any!"

Panfilich said, "If two or three bees get left they can be of help to you. Their buzzing will remind you of what has happened." With this, he left the room.

The next day toward evening our splendid Panfilich reached his destination with his live merchandise. They greeted him with a band.

(*1941*)

From BEFORE SUNRISE

Easter Eve

I'm hurrying to matins. I stand in front of the mirror tightly buttoned into the dress uniform of my school. In my left hand I hold white kid gloves. With my right I straighten the astonishing part in my hair.

I'm not particularly satisfied with the way I look. Very youngish.

I could have looked a bit older at sixteen.

Nonchalantly throwing my overcoat round my shoulders, I go out onto the landing.

Tata T. is coming upstairs.

She's amazingly pretty today in her short fur jacket, with her muff in her hands.

"Aren't you going to church?" I ask.

"No, we are celebrating at home," she says, smiling. And coming closer to me, adds, "Happy Easter ... Mishenka ..."

"It isn't midnight yet," I mumble.

Twining her arms round my neck. Tata gives me a kiss.

This is not the three traditional Easter kisses. This is one kiss, which lasts a full minute. It slowly dawns upon me that this is not a Christian kiss.

My first reaction is happiness, then surprise, then ... I laugh.

"Why are you laughing?" she asks.

"I didn't know people kissed that way."

"Not *people*," she says. "Men and women, silly!"

She caresses my face with her hand and kisses my eyes. Then, hearing a door slam on her landing, she hurries up the stairs, beautiful and mysterious—just the sort of girl I'd want to love forever.

I'm Not Coming Home

We're headed to New Village. There are about ten of us. We're very excited. Our comrade Vas'ka T. has quit school, left home, and is now living on his own somewhere near Black River.

He left the eighth class of our Gymnasium. Didn't even wait for the final exams. In other words, to hell with everything.

Secretly, we are delighted by what Vas'ka has done.

The house is wooden. Decayed, shaky stairs.

We go all the way up to the attic floor and enter Vas'ka's room.

Vas'ka is sitting on an iron cot. His shirt collar is unbuttoned. On the table are a bottle of vodka, bread, and sausage. A thin girl, about nineteen, is at Vas'ka's side.

"She's the one he left home for," someone whispers to me.

I look at this slender girl. Her eyes are red from weeping. She glances at us fearfully.

Vas'ka jauntily fills our glasses with vodka.

I go downstairs into the yard. There's an old woman in the yard. This is Vas'ka's mama.

"It's all her fault, the slut!" cries Mama. "If it weren't for her, Vas'ka would never have left home."

Vas'ka appears at the window.

"Oh, go away, Mama," he says. "You've been hanging around here for days. You're just causing a racket, that's all. Go on, go away. I've told you, I'm not coming home."

Pursing her lips in grief, Mama sits down on the stairs.

Was It Worth Hanging Yourself?

A student named Mishka F. hanged himself. He left a note: "Don't blame anyone—the reason was unsuccessful love."

I knew Mishka slightly. Awkward. Shabby. Unshaven. Not very bright.

But the students got along well with him—he was an easygoing, sociable person.

As a mark of respect for his tragic end we decided to drink to his eternal rest.

We gathered at a tavern on Maly Prospect.

First we sang "Fast As the Waves Flow Away All Our Days." Then we began to reminisce about our friend. No one, however, was able to remember anything special.

Then someone recalled that Mishka had once eaten three or four dinners, one after the other, in the university dining hall. Everyone laughed. We started recalling all sorts of trivia and nonsense from Mishka's life. You wouldn't believe how we laughed.

Choking with laughter, one student said. "Once we had planned to go to a dance. I stopped by to get Mishka. He didn't want to wash his hands, he was in such a hurry, so he stuck his fingers into some face powder to mask the dirt under his nails."

There was an explosion of laughter.

Someone said, "Now we understand why his love was unsuccessful."

When we'd done laughing we began to sing "Fast As the Waves" again. And one student would stand up and conduct with an emphatic flourish of his hand every time the song reached the words: "They'll bury you when you die as though you'd never lived."

After that we sang "Gaudeamus," "Evening Bells," and "Dir-lim-bom-bom."

At the Name-Day Party

Evening. I'm walking home. Feeling very glum.

"Hi, honey," someone says.

There's a woman in front of me. She is rouged and powdered. Under a hat with a plume I see a common face with high cheekbones and thick lips.

Frowning, I start to walk away, but the woman says

with an embarrassed smile: "Today is my name day . . . come to visit me . . . for a cup of tea."

I mumble, "Sorry. I don't have the time . . ."

"I go with anyone who invites me," says the woman. "But today I decided to celebrate my name day. I decided to invite someone myself. Please, don't say no . . ."

We go up some dark stairs, threading our way among cats. We go into a small room.

On the table are a samovar, some nuts, preserves, and pretzels.

We drink our tea in silence. I don't know what to say, and my silence embarrasses her.

"Are you really all alone—no friends, no relatives?"

"No," she says. "I haven't been here long. From Rostov."

When I'd finished my tea I put on my coat to leave.

"Do you really like me so little that you won't even stay with me?" she says.

This seems to me funny and lifts my mood. I'm not disgusted by her. I kiss her good-bye on her thick lips. And she asks:

"Drop by again sometime?"

I go out on the stairs. Maybe I should remember her apartment? In the dark I count the number of steps to her door. But I lose count. Maybe I should strike a match and look at the number of her apartment? No—not worth it. I'll never come to her again.

Hell

We're sitting in a sort of barn. Seven hundred paces from the trenches. Bullets whistle by. And shells explode quite close to us. But the regimental commander, Balo Makaev, is happy, he's practically merry. We have a regiment again—a battalion hastily brought up to strength.

For seventy-two hours we've held off the German attack and haven't retreated.

The commander is dictating to me. "Write," he says,

A notebook rests on my field bag. I write a report to Division HQ.

A heavy shell hits ten paces from the barn. Garbage, dirt, and straw shower down on us.

Through this smoke and dust I see the commander's smiling face.

"Never mind," says he. "Write."

I settle down to writing again. My pencil is literally bouncing around from the explosions nearby. Across the courtyard from us a building is on fire. Another heavy shell explodes with a terrific roar. This one was right next door. Fragments shriek and groan past us. For some reason or other I hide a hot little bomb splinter in my pocket.

There's no reason to remain in this barn, which doesn't even have a roof over it now.

"Does the commander not think it would make more sense to move toward the forward line?" say I.

"We stay here," says the commander stiffly.

The enemy artillery hits the village with hurricane fire. The air is filled with groans, howls, screams, and gnashing of teeth. It seems to me I've wound up in Hell.

I thought I was in Hell! Hell is where I was twenty-five years later when a half-ton German bomb hit the house two doors down from me.

My Fiancée Vava

I arrived in Arkhangelsk gloomy and terribly depressed. Nevertheless, or perhaps because of this, they immediately undertook to find a bride for me.

My intended turned out to be Vava M., the daughter of a very wealthy seafood dealer.

I had not seen this girl, and she had not seen me. But such matchmaking was the custom there. It provided some occupation for ladies who had nothing to do.

My first meeting with my fiancée was arranged with

much ceremony—in the winter garden of some luxurious house.

Before me there stood a very young, very quiet girl.

They left us alone so that we might have a conversation.

I was always taciturn. But what happened that evening was simply a catastrophe. I literally did not know what I was expected to talk about. I extracted words from myself as though with pliers in order to fill the horrifying pauses.

The girl looked at me in alarm and also kept silent.

I had no hope of being rescued. Everyone had withdrawn into distant rooms and firmly shut the door to the winter garden.

Then I began to recite poetry.

I started by reciting poems from Vera Inber's fashionable little book *Sad Wine*. Then I began to recite Blok and Mayakovsky.

Vava listened to me intently, never breathing a word.

When the people came back I was almost enjoying myself. I asked Vava whether she liked what I had recited for her. She said quietly:

"I don't like poetry."

"Then why on earth did you listen to a whole hour of it?!" I exclaimed, adding in an undertone, "You idiot."

"It would have been impolite of me not to listen to what you were saying."

Infuriated, I practically did a military about-face and left the girl.

An Old Man Dies

I am standing in a peasant hut. On the table lies an old man dying.

He's been there for three days and hasn't died.

Today there is a small wax candle in his hand. It falls over and goes out, but they light it again.

His relatives stand at the head of the table. Their gaze never wanders from the old man. All around there is the most unbelievable poverty, filth, rags, misery.

The old man is lying with his feet toward the window. His face is dark, tense. His breathing is irregular. At times it seems that he is already dead.

Leaning toward the old woman, his wife, I say softly:

"I'll go get the doctor. He shouldn't be left lying there on the table for three days."

The old woman shakes her head.

"Don't upset him," she says.

The old man opens his eyes and looks with his bleary gaze at those standing around him. His lips whisper something.

One of the women, young and dark-complexioned, bends over the old man and listens silently to his mumbling.

"What's he want?" asks the old woman.

"He wants titty," answers the woman. And, quickly unbuttoning her blouse, she takes the old man's hand and places it on her naked breast.

I see the old man's face brighten up. Something like a smile spreads across his lips. His breathing becomes more regular and peaceful.

Everyone stands silently, stock-still.

Suddenly the old man's body is shaken by a violent spasm. His hand falls helplessly. His face becomes stern and absolutely still. He stops breathing. He's dead.

Immediately the old woman begins to wail. And after she starts they all wail.

I leave the hut.

(*1943*)

Yuri Olesha

(1899–1960)

Timeo hominem unius libri (I fear the man of one book), wrote St. Thomas Aquinas. His words are generally quoted today in disparagement of the man whose mental horizons are limited to a single book. Aquinas, however, meant that a man who has thoroughly mastered only one good book can be dangerous as an opponent. The Greek poet Archilochus meant something like this when he said that the fox knows many things but the hedgehog knows one big thing. It is the man of one book, the hedgehog, who gains the victory.

Yuri Karlovich Olesha is, for all practical purposes, a *homo unius libri*, but that one book, *Envy*, is indeed dangerous. It is also a masterpiece that leaves one in a state of pleasant bewilderment. It baffles and charms, for it appears to mean what you wish it to mean. When it appeared in 1927—a decade after the Revolution and half a decade before the imposition of Socialist Realism—it astonished and pleased practically everyone, regardless of factional allegiance. It astonished because Olesha had been a writer of topical doggerel for a railwaymen's newspaper whom no one suspected of possessing such literary power, and it pleased because zealots of all persuasions (like you and me) thought that they discerned in Olesha's fable a vindication of their own views. Had he gone on to become a thoroughly reliable Soviet writer—and there is depressing evidence that he strove to do so—his book, fitted with an introduction telling the reader how to understand it correctly, might still be around in Soviet bookstores. But by the time Olesha finally drank himself into the grave in 1960, *Envy*, the darling of his young imagination, had long been forgotten, and he himself was little more than an amiable wraith at a certain restaurant table. Toward the end, he began composing a book of autobiographical fragments and other aperçus. Though he left it in a chaotic state, *No Day Without a Line*—his second-best book—was compiled and published after his death. Today, Olesha is esteemed primarily by those who read him in translation; he is known in Russia chiefly to literary specialists.

Is he better understood today? I am not sure, for *Envy* deserves, even more than Melville's *Pierre*, to be subtitled "The Ambiguities." The theme of the book is scarcely novel for its time: the conflict of the old world with the new, the painful abandonment of traditional values for a baffling new reality. There are only six important characters neatly divided into two sets of three, and we are never in the slightest doubt as to which of the conflicting worlds they represent. The radiant future of Communism clearly belongs to three of them: Andrei Babichev, the fabulously energetic and efficient servant of the State; his adopted son, Volodia Makarov, a golden boy, soccer hero, and model New Man; and Valia—the ideal consort for Volodia—who is beautiful, healthy, virtuous, and sexier than one has any right to expect of a Russian fictional heroine. The rotten old world lives on in Nikolai Kavalerov, our antihero, a drunken failure whose envy of the foregoing trio provides the theme of the book; Ivan Babichev (brother to Andrei and father to Valia), a disreputable old windbag and liar; and Anichka Prokopovich, a widow whose physical repulsiveness is equaled only by her certifiable nymphomania.

Described in this way, the book hardly seems ambiguous. But something, as we detect almost at once, is clearly wrong. The author's sympathy (and therefore ours) appears to be helplessly invested on the side of the old era that is dying. We recognize in it our real home, or perhaps the home that we should like to have had—a place where, whatever its faults, one feels comfortable, respected, free, and somehow authentic. Nothing could be more rebarbative than the gleaming new stainless-steel dystopia with its standardized sausages that Andrei Babichev is planning for us. This being so, why must the representatives of our preferred realm be lazy, hallucinating drunks, while the advocates of the new are paragons of energy, health, and sanity?

But are they? The characters are in fact a good deal more complicated than I have suggested. Volodia, for instance, is a splendid physical specimen, full of courage, enthusiasm, and athletic prowess made more attractive by modesty. But in his long letter to his benefactor, Andrei—the one passage where we have the most unmediated glimpse into his soul—he strikes us not only as disgustingly fawning and devious, but also as more than a little sissified; the strange wrist-slapping tone of poor-little-me against big-strong-you induces considerable dubiety about their real relationship. Are they adoptive father and son, or old pederast and young catamite?

Or take that volcano of controlled energy, Andrei Babichev. There is certainly something odious about his fat physicality—his jouncing breasts and fleshy excrescences—to say nothing of his crass philistinism. But is he not sacrificing himself for a brighter, safer, cleaner, and healthier world? And who can blame him for being outraged when his fundamental generosity is abused by Kavalerov and his sanity endangered by the dottiness of his brother?

That brother, Ivan, is under no circumstances to be trusted by you—he even dupes his own creator, as I shall show—but you will find it hard to resist the appeal of his insane courage, his humor, the surreal flights of his imagination, and his eloquent defense of home, motherhood, and the most absolute freedom for the individual—including the freedom to be idle, sloppy, and crazy. The framers of the Bill of Rights might have found Ivan trying but not altogether uncongenial.

And we cannot help but sympathize with Nikolai Kavalerov, the foreground consciousness of the book and nearest surrogate for the author (Olesha gave him his own age, twenty-seven). But it is a rare reader who will not feel impatience with his general spinelessness and immaturity, to say nothing of the envy that corrodes what little character he has. We somehow love him without liking him.

But if the book poses, and declines to resolve, questions of a moral and ethical nature, it also poses a question that is even more fundamental to the reader of fiction: What are we to take as "really" happening in this novel? Where is the boundary between dream and reality?

Does Ophelia, the mechanical monster created by Ivan, really exist? We might take her grand moment in the crowd scene near the end—when our imaginations, unimpeded by a description of her, make her infinitely more terrifying than the quaint contraptions in "horror" films—as arising from the narcotized brain of Kavalerov. But outside the dream, does Ophelia exist? The book will not unequivocally answer.

Ivan is arrested at one point. How? We first read that he beards his powerful brother in a crowded street, makes a scandal, and is flung into the arms of a policeman by Commissar Babichev, who shouts, "To the GPU!" (the dreaded secret police, forerunners of the KGB). Released after ten days and one hilarious interrogation, he rejoins his drinking pals. They ask whether it is true that he was arrested in this disgraceful way. Ivan, lying as usual, we suppose, laughs and denies it all. A policeman merely came up to his table in a restaurant and detained him for questioning—a far more dignified arrest. Some pages later we find Ivan having a beer with Kavalerov. A policeman comes up to his table and takes him away. "He was arrested," the author coolly informs us, "as we have already mentioned in the previous chapter." But has Olesha forgotten his own story? Or is *he* now lying? Is he, if not deliberately lying, duped by his own character? Could it be that we were not meant to take seriously that vividly depicted arrest on the street, which is, after all, said to be a rumor? Don't ask. The book will not tell you.

But we can't help asking. One might hazard an answer by suggesting that one of the purposes of the book is to suggest the elusiveness of certainty and "truth," the routine delirium of ordinary life at a time when the familiar scale of human values has been scrapped in favor of some purely notional future.

One does not, however, read—or re-read—*Envy* for the questions that it raises. One returns to it to experience the exhilaration of Olesha's skill as a writer. Like Beckett, whom he resembles at times, Olesha knew that the bleakest conceivable statements on the human condition can—and perhaps should—be couched in a style that rejoices in the possibilities of language.

Envy is simply great fun to read. It is dated, of course, but it is delightfully dated. It is redolent of the 1920s and the silent films, above all the comedies of Chaplin, to whom Olesha must have been referring when he wrote: "Like the penniless drunk in the comedy who is picked up by a rich man and taken to his castle." In the occasional ornamental excess of its prose, in its self-consciously Cubist cityscapes, in the almost surrealistically theatrical depiction of crowd scenes (reminiscent of the Nature Theater of Oklahoma in Kafka's *Amerika*), *Envy* has a distinctly period charm.

But Olesha's comic genius, his skill as a storyteller, his slyly ironical and gamin slant on life (the birthright, apparently, of Odessa writers) will always appeal to readers who enjoy the gleeful hatred, silly zestfulness, and sheer creative bliss of a young man writing the book he was born to write.

ENVY

Part One

I

He sings in the mornings in the toilet. You can imagine what pleasure he takes in life, how healthy he is. His desire to sing is pure reflex. These songs of his—devoid of melody or words and consisting entirely of "ta-ra-ra," belted out in numerous variations—might mean something like this:

"How I like to live—ta-ra! ta-ra!—my bowels are supple—ra-ta-ta-ta-ra-ri—my juices run the right way—ra-ti-ta-du-da-ta—go to it, peristalsis! good gut!—tram-ba-ba-bum!"

In the morning when he passes me (I pretending to be asleep) on his way from the bedroom to the door leading into the depths of the apartment, the bathroom, my imagination is wafted after him. I hear the racket in the narrow closet, too tight for his big body. His back rubs against the inside of the door he's just slammed, his elbows collide with the walls, and he shuffles his feet. An oval piece of translucent glass has been set into the toilet door. He turns the switch, and the oval, lit from within, becomes a splendid opal-colored egg. With my mind's eye I see that egg, hanging in the darkness of the hallway.

He weighs around 220 pounds. He was going down some stairs not long ago when he suddenly realized that his breasts were jouncing up and down in rhythm with his steps. That's why he resolved to add another set to his calisthenics.

This man is a model of what the masculine person should be.

He usually does his exercises not in his own bedroom but in the room of uncertain function where I live. There's more space and air here, more light, more sunshine. Coolness pours in through the open door of the balcony. Besides, there's a washbasin here. The bath mat is brought in from his bedroom. He arrives naked to the waist, in his homespun drawers, which are fastened by one button in the middle of his stomach. The rose and blue world of the room whirls in the mother-of-pearl lens of this button. When he lies on his back on the bath mat and starts raising his legs one after the other, the button gives up. His groin lies bare. His magnificent groin. His tender macule. His private nook. The groin of a progenitor. I once saw the same sort of groin, suede and matte, on a male antelope. One glance from him must be enough to spark the amorous currents flowing through the girls who work for him, his secretaries and shop girls.

* * *

He washes himself like a little boy: whistles, dances about, snorts, howls. He scoops up water by the handful and, failing to get so far as his armpits with it, splashes it over the mat. The water sprinkles on the straw in large, clean drops. Foam falling back into the basin bubbles like a pancake. Sometimes the soap blinds him, whereupon he grinds his fists into his eyes with savage curses. There's an enormous racket when he gargles. People stop in the street under the balcony and look up.

The morning is as rosy and quiet as might be. Spring is at its height. Every windowsill has its flower box, through the chinks of which one glimpses the warm red color of yet another flowering season.

(Things don't like me. Furniture does its best to trip me. Once, the corner of some lacquered piece or other literally bit me. The blanket and I always have the most complicated relationship. Soup, when it is served to me, never cools. If some trifle or other—a coin or a cuff link—falls off the table, it generally rolls under some practically immovable piece of furniture. I creep about on the floor and, if I raise my head, see the buffet laughing.)

The blue straps of his suspenders hang at his sides. He goes into his bedroom, locates his pince-nez on the chair, puts it on in front of the mirror, and returns to my room. Here, standing in the middle of the room, he lifts both straps of his suspenders onto his shoulders at one time as though they were some sort of burden. Not a word does he address to me. I pretend to be sleeping. Two burning clusters of sun rays are concentrated in the metallic clips of his suspenders. (Things like him.)

He doesn't need to comb his hair or smooth his beard and mustache. His hair is cut short and his trim little mustache nestles right under his nose. He looks like a large, fat boy.

He has seized a flask. The glass stopper thereof has squeaked slightly. He has poured the cologne into his palm and passed that palm over the globe of his head from the forehead to the nape of the neck and back again.

He drinks two glasses of cold milk in the morning. He takes the little pitcher out of the buffet, pours out the milk, and drinks it standing up.

My first impression of him overwhelmed me. My mind could not have admitted, could not have conceded the existence of such a person. He stood in front of me, redolent of cologne, in his elegant gray suit. His slightly puckered lips looked fresh. He was, it turned out, a fop.

I am often waked up at night by his snoring. Half asleep, I don't understand what is going on. Some menacing voice seems to be repeating over and over: "Krakatoh-oo . . . krra . . . ka . . . toh-uuuu . . ."

They've given him a splendid apartment. What a vase there is on a lacquered stand near the door to the balcony! A vase of the most delicate porcelain, rounded and tall, the translucency of which reveals a tender, blood-red venation. It reminds one of a flamingo. The apartment is on the fourth floor. The balcony is suspended in insubstantial space. The wide suburban street resembles a highway. Across the street is a park, a heavy, tree-crowded park, typical of the outskirts of Moscow—an unkempt assemblage of vegetation that has grown up, as though in an oven, in the vacant lot between three walls.

He is a glutton. He usually eats out. Yesterday evening he came back hungry and wanted something to eat. There was nothing in the buffet. He went out (there's a shop on the corner) and returned with a whole market basket: 250 grams of ham, a can of sprats, a can of mackerel, a large loaf of French bread, a good half-moon of Dutch cheese, four apples, a dozen eggs, and a jar of "Persian Pea" marmalade. He ordered an omelette and tea (the house has a communal kitchen where two cooks take turns on duty).

"Dig in, Kavalerov," he invited me, as he himself fell upon the food. He ate the eggs straight from the pan, removing bits of white as if he were chipping off enamel. His eyes became bloodshot, he took off and put on his pince-nez, smacked his lips, snorted, and his ears moved.

I enjoy observing things. Did you ever notice that salt will fall off the tip of a knife without leaving a trace—the knife shines as though it had never been touched; that a pince-nez straddles the bridge of the nose like a bicycle; that man is surrounded by little inscriptions, a squirming ant swarm of little inscriptions: on forks, spoons, plates, the frame of a pince-nez, buttons, pencils? No one notices them. They have to struggle for existence. They change from one form to another, all the way up to the immense letters on billboards. They rebel, class against class: The letters on street signs wage war against the letters on posters.

He ate his fill. He reached for the apples with his knife, but he'd no more than pared the yellow cheek of one when he threw it down.

A certain People's Commissar once praised him highly in a speech: "Andrei Babichev is one of the most remarkable men in this country."

He, Andrei Petrovich Babichev, occupies the post of Director of the Food Industry Trust. He is a great sausage maker, pastry man, and cook.

And I, Nikolai Kavalerov, am his fool.

II

He runs everything that has to do with victuals.

He's greedy and jealous. He'd like to cook all the omelettes, all the pies, all the cutlets, and bake all the bread himself. He'd like to engender the food himself. He gave birth to "The Quarter."

And his child is growing. The Quarter is going to be a gigantic establishment: the largest dining room, the largest kitchen in existence. A two-course dinner will cost a quarter.

War has been declared on ordinary kitchens.

A thousand kitchens can already be considered captured.

He's going to put an end to do-it-yourself cooking, "small-family" sizes, half-bottles, and so on. He will combine all the meat grinders, camp stoves, frying pans, faucets ... It is going to be what you might call the industrialization of the kitchen.

He's organized a number of commissions. His vegetable peelers, produced in a Soviet factory, turned out to be excellent. A German engineer is building the kitchen. Numerous plants are filling Babichev's orders.

I've learned the following about him:

One morning he, the Director of a Trust, with his briefcase under his arm, a very solid citizen, an obviously official personage, mounted an unfamiliar staircase amidst all the charms of a rear entrance and knocked on the first door he came to. In this Harun al-Rashid manner he descended upon a kitchen in a workers' tenement somewhere on the edge of town. He saw soot, dirt, demented furies tearing about in the smoke, and weeping children. He was immediately set upon. He was in everyone's way, this enormous man, taking up their space, light, and air. Besides that, he had a briefcase, a pince-nez, and an elegant and cleanly air about him. The furies decided that he must be a member of some commission. Arms akimbo, they lit into him. He left. Thanks to him (they screamed after him) the kerosene stove had gone out, a glass had been broken, and the soup had been oversalted. He left without having said what he'd meant to say. He has no imagination. What he meant to say was:

"Women! We shall blow the soot off you, cleanse your nostrils of smoke, and your ears of this infernal racket—we shall force the potato to discard its own peel by magic, instantaneously, we shall restore to you all those hours that the kitchen has stolen from you—you'll get half your life back. You, young wife, you make soup for your husband. And half your day goes into that miserable puddle of soup! We are going to transform those miserable puddles of soup of yours into glistening seas, borscht into oceans of borscht, heap up kasha in mounds, unleash glaciers of fruit jelly. Listen to me, housewives, just wait. We promise you: The sunshine will flood across your tile floors, copper kettles will glow like fire, your plates will be as clean as lilies, your milk as thick as mercury, and your soup so fragrant that the very flowers upon the table will be envious."

Like some fakir, he manages to be in ten places at once.

In his memoranda he has frequent resort to parentheses and underlining—he's afraid that they will misunderstand or mix things up.

Here are some samples of his memos:

To Comrade Prokudin:

The candy wrappers (enclosed find 12 samples) have to be designed with the consumer in mind (chocolate, fillings and so on), but in a new way. But no "Rosa Luxemburg" (found out this already in use—for pastilles!!), best of all wd. be something scientific (or poetic—geography? astronomy?) with a serious name but still with an appealing sound—"Eskimo"? "Telescope"? Phone me tomorrow, Wednesday, in the office, between 1–2 P.M. Without fail.

To Comrade Fominsky:

See to it that the first course of every (50- and especially 75-kopeck) dinner has a piece of meat on it (cut as it should be, as in a *private restaurant*). Insist on this. Is it true that: (1) the beer snacks are served without trays? (2) the peas are small and tough?

He is petty, suspicious, and tedious as a concierge.

At ten this morning he arrived from the cardboard factory. Eight people were waiting to see him. He received: (1) The Director of the Smoke Curing Plant. (2) A representative of the Far-Eastern Canning Trust (he grabbed a can of crabs and ran out to show it to someone. When he returned he set it down next to his elbow and was a long time in regaining his composure, glancing constantly at the sky-blue can, laughing and scratching his nose.) (3) An engineer working on the construction of a new warehouse. (4) A German—something to do with trucks (they spoke German; he must have ended the conversation with a proverb, since it came out in a rhyme and they both laughed). (5) An artist who had brought along a sketch for an advertisement (he didn't like it—said the color should be dull blue—chemical, not romantic). (6) Some restaurant manager, who wore cuff links in the shape of milky white sleigh bells. (7) A stringy man with a wavy beard who spoke about heads of cattle. (8) A charming country dweller. This last meeting was something special. Babichev rose and went forward almost as though he meant to embrace his visitor. This latter filled the entire office with his fetchingly clumsy, shy, smiling, suntanned, bright-eyed presence—a perfect Levin out of Tolstoy. He smelled of wild flowers and dairy dishes. The conversation concerned state farms. A dreamy expression appeared on the faces of both participants.

At four-twenty Babichev left for a meeting at the Supreme Soviet for the National Economy.

III

At home in the evening he sits in the palm-green glow of his lampshade. Before him there lie sheets of paper, notebooks, small slips filled with columns of figures. He flips through the pages of his desk calendar, jumps up, looks for something in the bookcase, takes out files, kneels on the chair, and, his belly resting on the table and his fat face in his hands, reads. The green platform of the table is covered by a sheet of glass. What, in the final analysis, is so special about this scene? A man is working, a man is at home, in the evening, working. A man, his eyes fixed on a sheet of paper, is picking his ear with a pencil. Nothing special about that. And yet his every act amounts to say-

ing: You, Kavalerov, are a nobody. Of course he doesn't
come right out and say this. I daresay the thought never
entered his head. But the thought is clear without words.
Some third person conveys it to me. Some third person
drives me into a frenzy as I sit watching him.

"The Quarter!" he shouts. "Yes sirree, The Quarter!"

All of a sudden he starts laughing. He's come across
something killingly funny in his papers or his figures.
Choking with laughter, he summons me. He brays as he
pokes a piece of paper with his finger. I look and see nothing. What is so funny? In the same place where I can't
even discern the basis for a comment he has found some
departure from the rules so outrageous that he is breaking
up with laughter. I listen to him in horror. This is the
laughter of an evil genius. I listen to him the way a blind
man listens to a rocket exploding.

"You are a nobody, Kavalerov. You don't understand
anything."

He doesn't actually say this, but it doesn't require
words.

Sometimes he doesn't get home until very late at night.
Then I get my orders by telephone:

"Is this Kavalerov? Listen, Kavalerov. I'm expecting a
call from the Bread Trust. Tell them to call 2-73-05, extension 62. Write that down. Have you written it down?
Extension 62, Chief of Concessions. Bye-bye."

He really does get a call from the Bread Trust.

"Bread Trust?" I repeat. "Comrade Babichev is with
the Chief of Concessions . . . What? The Chief of Concessions. You can get him at 2-73-05, extension 62. Have you
got that? Extension 62, Chief of Concessions. Bye-bye."

Bread Trust calling for Trust Director Babichev. Babichev is with the Chief of Concessions. What has any of
this to do with me? And yet I derive a certain pleasure
from participating obliquely in the fate of the Bread Trust
and Babichev. I experience administrative elation. Of
course the role I play is trifling. The role of a toady.
What's the matter? Do I respect him? Fear him? No. I

consider myself just as good as he is. I am not a nobody. I'll prove it.

I'd like to catch him at something, discover his weak side, some position that he's left unguarded. The first time I happened to see him getting dressed in the morning I was sure that I'd caught him, that he was through being impenetrable.

Drying himself off, he walked out of his room to the threshold of the balcony and stood there a few feet away from me, still drying himself and twisting the towel in his ears, and finally turned his back to me. When I saw that back, that plump torso from behind, bathed in sunlight, I nearly screamed. His back gave everything away. The fat on his body was a tender yellow color. The scroll of another man's destiny was unrolling in front of me. Babichev's forebears had taken good care of their skin. The rolls of fat had been gently arranged on their bodies. They had bequeathed to the Commissar that fineness of skin, that noble color and pure pigmentation. And the main thing, that which filled me with a sense of triumph, was that I saw a birthmark on the small of his back—a special, inherited, aristocratic birthmark, a tender little thing, translucent, filled with blood, attached to the body by a little stem—the sort of thing by which mothers recognize their kidnapped children decades later.

"You're a nobleman, Andrei Petrovich! You're only pretending!" I almost uttered these words aloud.

But then he turned to face me.

On his chest, under his right collarbone, there was a scar. Round, slightly in relief, like the imprint of a coin on wax. It was as though a branch had grown in that place and been chopped off. Babichev had done time at hard labor. He tried to escape and they shot him.

"Who is Jocasta?" he once asked me out of the blue. The most extraordinary questions pop out of him at times, especially in the evening. He's busy all day. But his eyes

glide over posters, window displays, and his ears pick up
words from conversations near him. This raw material
collects in him. I'm the only person he ever talks to who
has nothing to do with business. He senses that he ought
to strike up a conversation. For serious conversation I am
regarded as unsuited, but he is aware of the fact that people, when they are at leisure, do have chats. He decides to
make a certain contribution to this universal human custom. So he directs idle questions at me. I answer them. I
am His Majesty's fool. He thinks I am a fool.

"Do you like olives?" he asks.

"Yes, I know who Jocasta is! Yes, I like olives, but I
don't want to answer idiotic questions. I'm no more stupid
than you are." That is how I should answer him. But I
lack the courage. He smothers me.

IV

I've been living under his roof for two weeks. One night
two weeks ago he picked me up, drunk, near the door of
a bar.

They'd thrown me out of the bar.

The argument in the bar had developed gradually. At
first nothing indicated that a scandal was brewing. On the
contrary, friendship between the two tables might well
have developed: Drunks are sociable people. A large group
at the other table, which included a woman, invited me to
join them, and I was on the point of accepting their invitation, but the woman, who was very beautiful, slender,
and wearing a blue silk blouse that hung loosely on her
collarbones, made a joke at my expense. I took offense,
turned in my tracks, and proceeded back to my own table,
carrying my beer stein in front of me like a lantern.

At this a veritable storm of jokes came my way. And I
may in fact have seemed rather comical—some sort of
mop-headed clown. A man's deep bass laughter followed
me. Someone threw a pea at me. I went round my table
and stood facing them. Beer spilled on the marble tabletop
and I couldn't free my thumb, which had got stuck in the

handle of the stein. Completely drunk, I burst into a torrent of confessions, a bitter stream about equally composed of self-abasement and arrogance:

"You ... troupe of monsters ... wandering troupe of freaks ... you've kidnapped a girl" (others in the bar turned to listen: The mop-headed clown had a strange way of expressing himself, his speech stood out against the general hubbub in the background). "You on the right under the palm—you are freak number one. Stand up and let everyone see you ... Pay attention, comrades, respected public ... Quiet! Orchestra, a waltz if you please! A melodious, neutral waltz! Your face is a harness. The cheeks are held tight by wrinkles ... and they aren't wrinkles, but reins. Your chin is the ox. Your nose the driver, dying of leprosy. And all the rest is the load of manure. Be seated. And now for monster number two. The man with cheeks that look like knees ... very pretty! Look your fill, citizens: A troupe of freaks is passing through ... And you! How did you ever get in that door? Didn't your ears get stuck? And you, rubbing yourself against that kidnapped girl, ask her what she thinks of your blackheads. Comrades!" (I turned in all directions.) "These people ... these here ... they dared laugh at *me?!* That one laughed ... Do you know how you laugh? You emit the sounds of an enema ... Young lady ... 'in gardens embellished by springtime, Empress, there is no rose that might compare with the beauty of your eighteen summers!' ... Young lady! Cry out! Call for help! We will save you. What is the world coming to? He's feeling you up and you sit there? You like it?" (I paused and then said in a ceremonious tone:) "I summon you. Come, sit here with me. Why did you laugh at me? I stand before you, unknown young lady, and beg of you: Do not lose this chance to be with me. Simply arise, push them away, and come hither. What can you expect from him, from any of them? ... What? Tenderness? Intelligence? Caresses? Loyalty? Come to me. It is absurd even to compare me with them. I can give you infinitely more ..."

Even as I spoke I was horrified at what I was saying. I

vividly recalled those special dreams in which you know: This is a dream—I can do anything I please since I know I'll wake up. But this time there was clearly not going to be any waking up. My irreparable words were snowballing madly.

They threw me out.

I lay unconscious. When I came to I said: "I call them but they don't come. I call the bitches but they don't come." (My words applied equally to all women at once.)

I was lying in the gutter on the opening to a storm sewer, my face against the grating. The air inside the sewer, which I was inhaling, was musty, thick with mustiness; something was moving inside the black cube of the sewer, the garbage was alive. I saw the sewer at the moment of falling and the memory of it determined the form of my dream. The memory was a concentrate of the alarm and fright I had experienced in the bar, the humiliation and fear of being punished, and in the dream it emerged transformed as a scene in which I was being pursued—I was running, trying to get away, exerting all my strength—and the dream suddenly came to an end.

I opened my eyes, trembling with the joy of escape. But I was still half-unconscious and took this new state as the transition from one vision to another, and in this new vision the main role belonged to my rescuer, the one who had saved me from the pursuers, the unknown one whose hands and sleeves I was now covering with kisses, thinking that I was still in a dream, the one around whose neck I had thrown myself, weeping bitterly.

"Why am I so miserable? What a hard life I have!" I babbled.

"Place him so his head will be higher," said my rescuer.

I was being taken somewhere in a car. Regaining consciousness, I saw the sky—a pale, bright sky that was rushing from the direction of my feet and past my head. This vision was thunderously loud and dizzying and ended each time with an onset of nausea. When I awoke in the morning I fearfully reached for my legs with my hands. Still unsure where I was or what had happened to me, I remembered being pushed and shaken about. The thought jabbed through my brain that I had been in an ambulance, that they had amputated my legs while I was drunk. I put out my hands, certain that I would encounter the thick round barrel of a bandage. But it turned out that I was simply lying on a sofa in a large clean bright room with two windows and a balcony. It was early morning. The stone balcony, pink in the light of dawn, was peacefully warming itself.

When we became acquainted that morning I told him about myself.

"You were a sorry sight," he said. "I felt terribly sorry for you. You could of course take offense—who does this man think he is, messing about in someone else's life? In that case, please forgive me. But, if you don't mind, why not live here for a while, have a normal life? I'd be very glad. There's plenty of room. Light and air. And there's work you can do—some proofreading, going over certain material. How about it?"

What were the reasons that impelled this famous personage to condescend in such a manner to an unknown young man of suspicious appearance?

V

One evening two secrets were revealed.

"Andrei Petrovich," I asked, "who is that in the picture?"

There's a photograph of a dark-complexioned young man on his writing table.

"What's that?" He always forces one to repeat a question. His thoughts cling to the paper and he can't tear them away all at once. "What say?" He is still absent.

"Who is that young man?"

"Oh. That's a fellow named Volodia Makarov. A remarkable young man." (He never speaks to me in a normal way. As though there were nothing serious about which I might ask a question. It always seems to me that the answer I get from him is a proverb or a couplet or simply some kind of mumbling. Now, for instance, instead of answering in a normal conversational tone—"a remarkable young man"—he scans the phrase, almost sings it.)

"In what way is he remarkable?" I ask, taking revenge by the spitefulness of my tone. But no degree of spitefulness would attract his notice.

"Oh, no. He's simply a young man. A student. You're sleeping on his sofa," said he. "The fact is that he's more or less my son. He's been living with me for ten years. Volodia Makarov. He's away at the moment. Gone to see his father. In Murom."

"Oh, that's who . . ."

"Yes, that's who."

He got up from his table and walked about.

"He's eighteen. A famous soccer star."

("Ah—a soccer star," thought I to myself.)

"Well, then," said I. "That is indeed remarkable! To be a famous soccer star—that is indeed a considerable achievement." (What am I saying?)

He didn't hear me. He was overpowered by his blissful thoughts. From the doorway to the balcony he was gazing into the distance, the sky. He was thinking of Volodia Makarov.

"He is a youth absolutely unlike any other," he said suddenly, turning to me. (I see that my presence here when his thoughts are on this Volodia Makarov strikes him as offensive.) "I owe him my life, to begin with. Ten years ago he saved me from being killed. They were about to put my head on an anvil and smash my face in with a sledgehammer. He saved me." (He likes talking about the boy's heroism. It's clear that he often thinks about it.) "But that's not the important thing. The important thing is that he is the completely new man. Well—so much for that." (And he returned to his table.)

"Why did you pick me up and bring me here?"

"Eh? What say?" he mumbled. It would take him a moment to hear my question. "Why I brought you here?

What a pitiful sight you were. It was impossible not to be touched. You were sobbing. I suddenly felt terribly sorry for you."

"And the sofa?"

"What about the sofa?"

"When your young man comes back . . . ?"

Without a moment's thought, very simply and merrily he said:

"Then you'll have to give up the sofa . . ."

I ought to get up and bust him one in the face. He felt pity, you see, this celebrated personage, he took pity on a miserable young man who had strayed from the path of virtue. But only temporarily. Until the return of his number one boy. He merely feels bored in the evening. But later he'll throw me out. He talks about this with perfect cynicism.

"Andrei Petrovich," I say. "Do you understand what you just said? You're a bastard!"

"What's that you say?" His thoughts are coming unstuck from the paper. In a second his hearing will repeat my sentence for him, and I pray to the Fates that his hearing gets it wrong. Could he really have heard me? Well, what the hell. Get it over with.

But at this point an external circumstance intervened. I was not yet destined to fly out of the house.

On the street beneath the balcony someone shouts:

"Andrei!"

He turns his head.

"Andrei!"

He abruptly stands up, pushing himself away from his table with his palms.

"Andryusha! Dear boy!"

He goes out on the balcony. I go up to the window. We both look down at the street. It is dark. What light there is on the sidewalk comes from the windows. In the middle of the street stands a short, wide man.

"Good evening, Andryusha. How've you been? How's The Quarter?"

(I look through the window at the huge Andryusha. I can hear his heavy breathing.)

The man in the street keeps up his shouting, but somewhat less loudly.

"Why don't you say something? I've come to give you a piece of news. I've invented a machine. A machine called 'Ophelia.' "

Babichev turns around quickly. His shadow falls sideways across the street and nearly causes a storm in the foliage of the park on the other side. He sits down at his table and drums his fingers on the glass surface.

We hear a shout: "Watch yourself, Andrei! Don't put on airs with me! I'll ruin you, Andrei . . ."

At this Babichev again leaps up and runs out onto the balcony, his fists clenched. The trees now toss about in good earnest. His shadow throws itself like some Buddha athwart the city.

"Who do you think you're fighting, you no-good bum?" says he. The railing of the balcony quivers. He pounds it with his fist. "Who do you think you're fighting, you bum? Get away from here! I'll have you arrested!"

"Good-bye!" comes from below. The fat little man doffs his hat, stretches forth his arm, waves his hat (can that be a bowler? a bowler, forsooth!); his politeness is affected. Andrei is no longer on the balcony; the little man, sowing his footprints like a row of corn, makes off in the middle of the street.

"There you are!" Babichev screams at me. "There you are! Fine thing, isn't it? My brother Ivan. What a bastard!"

He paces around the room, stewing. And again he screams at me:

"Who is he—Ivan? Who? He's a loafer, a harmful person, a carrier of disease! He ought to be shot!"

(The dark-complexioned youth in the photograph smiles. He has a plebeian face. He shows his unusually gleaming, masculine teeth. A whole glistening cage of teeth he exhibits—like a Japanese.)

VI

Evening. He's working. I'm sitting on the sofa. There is a lamp between us. The lampshade, from where I sit, eliminates the upper part of his face; it ceases to exist. Beneath the lampshade hangs the lower hemisphere of his head. On the whole, it resembles a painted terra-cotta piggy bank.

"My youth coincided with the youth of the century," I say.

He's not listening. His indifference offends me.

"I often think about this century. We live in a brilliant age. And it's a splendid fate, isn't it? I mean when the youth of the century and the youth of a man coincide."

His hearing picks up the repetition. For a serious man, repetition is something funny.

"Youth . . . youth!" he repeats. (Tell him that he'd just heard and repeated two words and he wouldn't believe it.)

"In Europe the way is wide open for a gifted man to win fame. People love it there when someone else becomes famous. Just do any sort of remarkable thing there and they'll take you under the arms and set you on the highroad to glory. But with us there's no way for an individual to achieve success. Isn't that right?"

I might as well have been talking to myself. I make a noise, words come out, and that's what they amount to: noise. And my noise doesn't bother him.

"In our country the roads to fame are blocked by barriers. A gifted man must either fade away or else make up his mind to raise all sorts of hell and lift the barriers. Take me, for instance—I feel like arguing. I want to demonstrate the force of my personality. I want my own glory. People here are afraid to pay any attention to a man. I want a lot of attention. I'd like to be born in a little French town, grow up daydreaming, set myself some sort of lofty goal, and, one fine day, leave the little town and go on foot to the capital and there, working like a maniac, achieve my goal. But I wasn't born in the West. And now I'm told:

Not even the most remarkable personality, let alone yours, is worth anything. And I'm gradually getting used to this truth, though objections could be raised to it. I even think, look, you can become famous as a musician, a writer, a general, a person who walks across Niagara Falls on a tightrope . . . Those are legitimate means of becoming famous—that is the personality striving to show itself . . . But just imagine how it would be here, where people talk so much about purposefulness, about usefulness, where a man is expected to be sober, to have a realistic approach to things and events, if someone were suddenly to up and do something manifestly absurd, to bring off some ingenious piece of nonsense, and then to say, 'You do it your way, I'll do it my way!' To go out into the public square, do something all alone, then make your bow to the spectators: I have lived and I have done what I wished to do."

He doesn't hear a thing.

"Even if what you do is—kill yourself. Suicide with no motive whatsoever. As a prank. To show that everyone has the right to be the arbiter of his own fate. Even now. To hang myself in your doorway."

"You'd do better to hang yourself at the entrance to the Supreme Soviet for the National Economy on Visigoth Place, or Nogin, as it's now called. There's a huge arch there—have you seen it? That would make a great impression."

In the room where I lived before I moved here there was a terrifying bed. I feared it as though it were an apparition. It was hard as a barrelhead. My bones would creak on it. It had a blue blanket on it, which I had bought in Kharkov at a Lady Day fair during one of the famine years. An old peasant woman was selling pies. They were covered with a blanket. As they cooled off they still had enough of the warmth of life to sizzle and squirm like a litter of puppies. I was living poorly at the time, like everybody else, and that whole picture exuded such an air of well-being, coziness, and warmth that I firmly resolved to buy myself just such a blanket. My dream came true.

One fine evening I slid beneath a blue blanket. I writhed and squirmed under it, its warmth made me shake as though I were made of jelly. It was rapturous falling asleep. But as time passed the patterns on the blanket swelled out and turned into pretzels.

Now I sleep on an excellent sofa.

I deliberately move about so as to evoke the sound of its new, tight, virginal springs. Little separate droplets of sound come running out of its depths. It creates the impression of air bubbles streaming up to the surface of the water. I fall asleep like a child. On the sofa I fly back into childhood. I know bliss. Once again, like a child, I can control the little interval of time separating the first heaviness of the eyelids, the first blurring of vision, from the onset of real sleep. Once again I am able to prolong that interval, to savor it, to fill it with agreeable thoughts, and—before being completely engulfed in sleep, while still in command of conscious awareness—to watch these thoughts already take on dream-flesh, as when bubbles of sound from watery deeps are transformed into quickly rolling grapes, and then a plump cluster of grapes appears, and a whole vineyard, thick with clusters, and the path along the vineyard, a sunlit road, summer heat . . .

I'm twenty-seven.

Once when I was changing my shirt I caught sight of myself in the mirror and was suddenly struck by my amazing resemblance to my father. There is in reality no such resemblance. A memory came back to me: I was a boy in my parents' bedroom watching my father as he changed his shirt. I felt sorry for him. He no longer had the possibility of being handsome or famous, he was already done, completed, there was no longer any chance that he might be anything other than what he was. Such were my thoughts as I pitied him and quietly prided myself on my own advantage. And now I had recognized my father in myself. It was not a resemblance in outward form, no, it was something else, a sort of sexual resemblance I would call it: It was as though I had suddenly sensed my father's seed in me, in my very substance. And as if someone had said to me: You're done. Complete. There won't be any more. Sire a son.

The time has already passed when I might have been handsome or famous. I'm not going to make my way from any little town to the capital. I'm not going to be either a general, or a People's Commissar, or a scholar, or a marathoner, or an adventurer. I dreamt all my life about some extraordinary love. Soon now I shall return to my old apartment, to the room with the terrifying bed. The neighbors are vile. There's the widow Prokopovich. She's all of forty-five, but the people in the building still call her "Anichka." She cooks dinner for the hairdressers' cooperative. She's arranged a kitchen out in the hall. The hotplate is in a dark little niche. She feeds cats. The quiet, skinny cats fly up to her hands as though galvanically impelled. She throws them some sort of organ meat and innards. The floor, as a result, looks as though it had been embellished with mother-of-pearl spittle. I once slipped on something's heart—a small, tight object, something like a chestnut. She walks about entangled in animal guts and veins. A knife glistens in her hand. She moves the guts aside with her elbows, the way a princess would deal with cobwebs.

The widow Prokopovich is old, fat, and decrepit. You could squeeze her out of her casing like liverwurst. In the mornings I used to come upon her at the lavatory in the hall. She wouldn't be fully dressed and would smile at me with a *womanly* smile. On a stool beside her door would be a basin of water with hairs combed out of her head floating on the surface.

The widow Prokopovich is the symbol of my disgrace as a man. She seems to be inviting me: Please, I'm all yours, blunder into my room at night, I leave the door unlocked on purpose, I'll be glad to see you. We'll live together, have fun. But forget those dreams of yours about some extraordinary love. That's all over. Besides, neighbor, take a good look at yourself: overweight, wearing pants that need letting out. What more do you want? That one? The one with the delicate hands? The one you dream about? The one with the oval face? Forget it. You could be their daddy. Come on—what do you say? I've got a terrific bed. My late husband won it in a lottery. There's a quilt on it. I'll look after you. I'll comfort you. What do you say?

At times the expression on her face was downright indecent. Sometimes when she ran into me a little sound would roll up out of her throat, a round little vocal droplet ejected by some spasm of ecstasy.

I'm not a daddy, you slumgullion! You won't snare me, you bitch!

I am falling asleep on Babichev's sofa.

I dream that a beautiful girl, laughing softly, slips between the sheets with me. My fondest wishes are coming true. But how, how will I pay her back? I get scared. No one has ever loved me without being paid for it. As for whores, even they would try to take me for all they could. What will this one ask for? As always in dreams, she reads my mind and says:

"Oh, don't worry. It'll only be a quarter!"

A memory from the distant past: When I was a schoolboy I was taken to the wax museum. There in a glass cubicle was a handsome man in evening clothes, a still-smoking wound in his chest, dying in someone's arms.

My father explained: "That's the French President, Carnot. He was shot by an anarchist."

The President was dying. He was still breathing, his eyes rolled back. As slow as the hands of a clock the President's life was going. I stared as though in a trance. A splendid man, his beard thrust upward, was lying in a greenish cubicle. It was all splendid. That was the first time I heard the rumbling of time. Years sped past above me. I choked back ecstatic tears. I resolved to become famous, so that one day my own wax double, filled with the rumble of centuries, which few men are permitted to hear, would be just as elegantly poised inside a greenish cubicle.

I'm now writing some routines for entertainers: monologues and comic verse about tax collectors, Soviet debutantes, men who made a killing during Lenin's New Economic Policy, alimony, and so on.

> Our office is so filled with racket and noise
> That no one can tell the girls from the boys,
> So someone gave Lily, the boss's new friend,
> A key to the room with the sign reading MEN.

Still, it may be that one day in some enormous waxworks exhibition there will stand the wax figure of a strange man with a potato nose, a pale, kindly face, disheveled hair, boyishly plump, wearing a jacket bereft of all but the middle button, and on the glass cube will be a sign:

NIKOLAI KAVALEROV

And nothing else. Just that. And everyone who sees it will say: "Ah!" and remember some sort of stories or maybe legends. "Ah yes—that's the one who lived back in that remarkable era, who despised everyone and envied everyone, boasted, gave himself airs, wore himself out with great plans, wanted to accomplish much and never did anything—and wound up committing some vile, disgusting crime . . ."

VII

I turned from Tverskaya Street into a side street. I was headed for Nikitskaya Street. Early morning. The street is articulated, like an arm or leg. I move through it from joint to joint like painful rheumatism. Things don't like me. The side street is sick of me.

A small man in a bowler hat was walking ahead of me.

At first I thought he was in a hurry, but it soon became clear that his hasty gait and the agitation of his whole upper body were simply the little man's way of walking.

He was carrying a pillow. He was holding a large pillow in a yellow pillowcase by one corner. His knee kept hitting it. As a result, shallow depressions in its surface came and went.

Sometimes in the center of a town, along some side street, you will find a romantic, flowering hedge. We were at the moment walking past such a hedge.

A bird on a twig flashed, flicked its tail, and made a sound that somehow reminded me of a hair clipper. The man ahead of me turned around to look at the bird. Walking behind him, I managed to see no more than the first phase, the half-moon of his face. He was smiling.

"It is like a hair clipper, isn't it?" I almost shouted, certain that the same resemblance must have struck him.

Bowler hat.

He takes it off and carries it, his arm around it, as though it were a cake. His other hand carries the pillow.

The windows are open. On the ledge of one, on the third floor, there is a blue bud vase with a flower in it. The bud vase attracts the little man. He steps off the sidewalk, goes to the middle of the street, stops under the window, and raises his head. The bowler now tilts at a rakish angle on his head. His grasp on the pillow is firm. One of his knees has already sprouted some down.

I observe what is going on from behind the corner of a building.

He calls to the bud vase:

"Valia!"

A girl dressed in something pink instantly makes her stormy appearance in the window, upsetting the vase.

"Valia," says he, "I've come for you."

Silence. Water from the bud vase dribbles down the surface of the wall.

"Look what I've brought you. Can you see it?" (He holds up the pillow with both hands.) "Recognize it? You slept on it." (He laughs.) "Valia, come back to me. Won't you? I'll show you Ophelia. Will you?"

There was another silence. The girl lay pressed to the windowsill, her tousled head hanging over it. The vase next to her tottered. I remembered that the girl, a second after appearing in the window and almost before having seen the man in the street, had leaned forward on her elbows, which had now given way.

Clouds were moving across the sky, and across the windowpanes, and in the windowpanes their paths melded.

"I beg of you, Valia, come back. It's so simple—just run down the stairs."

He waited.

People stopped to gape at the scene.

"You don't want to? Okay, good-bye."

He turned, adjusted his bowler, and set off down the middle of the street in my direction.

"Wait! Wait, Daddy! Daddy! Daddy!"

He quickened his pace and broke into a run. He passed me. I saw that he was not young. He had turned pale and was breathing hard from the running. A funny, stout little man was running with a pillow pressed to his chest. But there was nothing insane in that.

The window became vacant.

She raced in pursuit of him. She ran as far as the corner, but there the emptiness of the side street merged into the multitude. She did not find him. I was standing beside the hedge. As the girl came back I walked toward her. She thought that I might help her, that I might know something, and stopped. A tear, following the curve of her cheek, flowed down as though on the side of a vase. She suddenly straightened up, ready to ask me some urgent question, when I interrupted her by saying:

"You rustled past me like a bough full of blossoms and leaves."

In the evening I read proof.

. . . So the blood collected at the time of slaughtering can either be processed into food, for the preparation of sausage, or used in producing light and dark albumin, glue, buttons, paints, fertilizers, and food for cattle, poultry, and fish. The suet from cattle of every sort and the organic offal with a high fat content can be processed into edible fats such as lard, margarine, and imitation butter as well as industrial products such as stearine, glycerine, and lubricating oils. The heads and feet of sheep can be processed by means of spiral electric drills, automatic cleaners, gas lathes, cutting machines, and blanching tubs into food products, industrial bone oil, cleaned hair, and bones for a variety of products . . .

He is talking on the telephone. He gets about ten calls per evening. Who couldn't he be talking to? But suddenly I hear him saying:

"That is not cruelty."

I prick up my ears.

"That is not cruelty. You asked me, so I'm telling you. That is not cruelty. No, no! You can be absolutely sure of that. Do you hear me?—He humbles himself? What? Walks about under your windows? Don't you believe it. Those are his little tricks. He hangs around under my own windows. He likes hanging around under windows. I know him. What? Did what? You cried? All night long? You're wasting your time crying all night. Go mad? We'll send him off to the funny house— Ophelia? Which Ophelia? Oh, the hell with it. He's been raving about some Ophelia—Whatever you like, but I'm telling you you're doing the right thing—Yes, yes—What? A pillow? Really? [Laughter.] I can imagine. What? What? The one you slept on? Think of that—What? But how is that pillow better than the one you're sleeping on now? Every pillow has its own story. In other words, don't let it bother you—What?—Yes? [At this point he was quiet and listened for a long time. I was on the edge of my chair. He finally burst out laughing.]—A bough? What? What sort of bough? Full of flowers? Flowers and leaves? What? That was probably one of the alcoholics he hangs around with."

VIII

Imagine to yourself an ordinary sausage, a cooked salami: a thick, evenly rounded log of meat, lopped off what started out as a big, heavy piece. At its blind end the skin is tied into a wrinkled knot from which a bit of string hangs like a tail. In short, a salami. Weighing maybe a little more than a kilo. The surface has beads of sweat on it and there are little yellow bubbles of fat under the skin. On the cut end the same fat looks like white dots.

Babichev was holding this sausage in the palm of his hand. He was talking. The doors swung open and shut. People came in. It got crowded. The sausage, like some live thing, hung suspended from Babichev's pink, municipal hand.

"Is that a sausage or is that a sausage?" asked he, addressing himself to the company at large. "No, just look at it. It's a pity Shapiro isn't here. We must have Shapiro. Ho-ho! Terrific! You called Shapiro? Busy? Keep trying."

Then the sausage was on the table. Babichev lovingly arranged a sort of pallet for it. He backed away from it, never losing sight of it, located a chair with his rear end, sat down, seized his thighs with his fists, and dissolved in laughter. He raised one fist, saw fat on it, and licked it off.

"Kavalerov! [More laughter.] You free at the moment? Please go to Shapiro. At the warehouse. You know which? Go straight to him and take this [indicating the sausage with his eyes]—have him take a look at it and call me."

I took the sausage to Shapiro at the warehouse. Babichev was telephoning in all directions.

"Yes, yes!" he roared, "yes! Absolutely first-rate! We'll send it to the exhibition. We'll send it to Milan! Of course to Milan! Yes! Yes! Seventy percent veal. A tremendous victory. No, not 50 kopecks, wise guy—thirty-five. Isn't that terrific? It's beautiful!"

He drove away.

The ruddy pot of his laughing face hung suspended in the window of the car. Still on the run, he thrust his Tyrolean hat into the doorman's hands and, his eyes bulging, ran up the stairs, heavy, noisy, and abrupt as a wild boar. The word "sausage!" rang out in office after office. "The very one . . . what did I tell you? . . . Fabulous!"

While I was wandering through the sunlit streets he was telephoning Shapiro from each office.

"They're bringing it to you, Solomon, you'll see! You'll explode . . ."

"You don't have it yet? Ho-ho, Solomon . . ."

He was wiping the sweat from his neck, digging the handkerchief deep into his collar, practically tearing it, grimacing and suffering.

I arrived at Shapiro's. Everyone saw that I was carrying the sausage and everyone made way for me. A path opened before me as though by magic. Everyone knew that the emissary with Babichev's sausage approached. Shapiro, a melancholy old Jew with a nose that looked, in profile, like the numeral 6, was standing in the warehouse yard under a wooden porch. The door, which, like all warehouse doors, framed a wavy summer darkness (you can see the same tenderly chaotic darkness by closing your eyes and pressing the lids with your fingers), led into a vast barn. A telephone was on the outside wall next to the door. Some sort of yellow documents hung on a nail in the wall beside it.

Shapiro took my salami, hefted it, rocked it back and forth in his hands (rocking his head at the same time), lifted it to his nose and smelled it. Then he walked out from under the porch, laid the sausage on a box and, with his pocketknife, carefully cut off a soft little slice. In total silence the slice was chewed, pressed to the roof of his mouth, sucked, and slowly swallowed. The hand holding the pocketknife was removed to one side, where it slightly shuddered: The owner of the hand was wholly absorbed in his sensations.

"Ach!" having swallowed, he sighed. "That Babichev is a hero. Has he made a sausage. No, really, he's done it. For such a sausage, thirty-five kopecks! Who would believe it?"

The telephone rang. Shapiro slowly rose and went to the door.

"Yes, Comrade Babichev. I congratulate you and I wish to kiss you."

Wherever he was, Babichev was shouting with such force that I could hear, even at my considerable distance from the telephone, his voice and the cracking and rattling sounds in the instrument. The receiver was so shaken by these mighty shocks that it almost leapt from the feeble fingers of Shapiro. His face contorted, he even waved at it with his other hand, the way one waves at some idiot who's preventing you from hearing something you want to hear.

"What am I to do?" I asked. "Does the sausage stay with you?"

"He asks that you bring it home to him, to the apartment. He has invited me to come partake of it this evening."

That did it.

"You mean he wants me to schlepp this thing home? Can't he buy another one?"

"You can't buy such a sausage as this," said Shapiro in a reverent tone. "It has not yet gone on sale. This is a prototype."

"It'll go off."

Shapiro folded up his knife and slid it along the seam of his trousers into his pocket. All the while he was smiling slightly, looking at me from what had become the slits of his eyes, and slowly, in the manner of an old Jew, read me a lesson:

"I have just congratulated Comrade Babichev on a sausage that does not go off in the space of one day. Were it otherwise, I should not have congratulated Comrade Babichev. Today, we are to consume it. Place it in the sun, have no fear, in the direct sun. It will smell like a rose."

He disappeared into the darkness of the barn, returned with a waxed parchment paper, and seconds later I held in my hands a masterfully done-up package.

From the very beginning of my acquaintance with Babichev I had heard talk of this famous sausage. Somewhere or other they were experimenting, trying to produce some special sort that would be nourishing, clean, and cheap. Babichev was forever checking on the progress in various places; little overtones of concern would creep into his voice as he asked questions and gave advice; his expression as he hung up the phone would be at times grave, at others sweetly excited. The desired species was finally produced. There came sliding out of the mysterious incubators, swinging like the heavy trunk of an elephant, a thick, firmly packed length of gut.

The first time Babichev held a piece of this gut in his hand, he turned crimson with embarrassment, like the groom who has just seen how beautiful his young bride is and what a charming impression she is making on the guests. In happy confusion he looked round at everyone and immediately laid down the piece of sausage and moved it farther away from him, the gesture of his upraised hands seeming to say: "No, no. Don't let me go on. I stop where I am—better that than suffer torment later. It is not possible that success of this kind should occur within the space of one simple human life. Fate is up to some trick. Take it away. I am not worthy."

Carrying a kilo of this astonishing sausage in my hands, I trudged along aimlessly.

I am standing on a bridge.

To my left is the Palace of Labor, behind me—the Kremlin. There are boats and swimmers in the river. A launch quickly slips past beneath my bird's-eye point of vantage. From this height what should be a launch looks like a gigantic almond sliced lengthwise. The almond vanishes beneath the bridge. Only now do I recall the smokestack of the launch and the fact that near the stack there were two people eating borscht from a kettle. A cloud of white smoke, transparent and already disappearing, flies in my direction. But it doesn't fly all the way, crosses over into other dimensions, and reaches me only with its last trace, now rolled into an all but invisible astral hoop.

I felt like throwing the sausage in the river.

A remarkable man, this Andrei Babichev. A member of the society of political prisoners, one of our rulers, he regards this day as his day, a personal celebration. For the sole reason that he was shown a sausage of a new sort . . .

Is it possible to celebrate that? Can this really be glory?

He was radiant today. Yes, the imprint of glory was visibly upon him. But why do I feel no love, no elation, no reverence at the sight of this glory? I'm torn apart by hatred. He, the ruler, the Communist, he is building a new world. And in that new world glory bursts forth from the hands of a sausage maker who has produced a new kind of sausage. I don't understand this glory—what does it mean? History, monuments, the lives of famous men—these never spoke to me of such glory as this . . . Has the nature of glory changed, then? And everywhere, or only here where the new world is under construction? I feel, of course, that this new world being built is the main, the triumphant thing . . . I'm not blind, I've got a head on my shoulders. You needn't teach me, explain things to me . . . I can read and write. This world right here is the one in which I long for glory! I want to beam just as Babichev was beaming today. But no new kind of sausage is going to make me beam.

I trudge along through the streets with my package. A lousy piece of sausage is in control of my movements, my will. I don't want that!

Several times I was ready to chuck the package over the railing. But all I had to do was imagine the damned piece of sausage coming out of its wrappings on the way down and slipping with all the accuracy of a torpedo into the waves, when another vision instantly threw me into a cold sweat. I saw Babichev moving in on me—a terrifying, implacable idol with bulging eyes. I'm afraid of him. He smothers me. Without even looking at me, he sees right through me. He doesn't look at me. I see his eyes only from the side, but when his face is turned toward me, they aren't visible: Nothing glistens there but his pince-nez—two round, blind plaques. He isn't interested in looking at me. He has no time and no wish to do so, but I know that he sees through me.

That evening Solomon Shapiro and two others came over and Babichev took care of the refreshments. The old Jew had brought a bottle of vodka, and they ate bits of the famous sausage as they drank. I declined to partake of this meal. I watched.

The art of painting has immortalized many a feast. The generals of armies, the doges of Venice, and simple, fat trenchermen are shown feasting. Whole epochs have been captured. Plumes wave about, the drapery falls in attractive folds, cheeks glisten.

This scene demands a new Tiepolo! Here at a feast are personages worthy of such an artist ... They are sitting under a bright hundred-watt bulb, around a table, and are talking animatedly. Paint them, new Tiepolo, paint "The Feast at the Industrial Executive's"!

I can already see your painting in a museum. I see the museum goers standing before your picture. They cannot for the life of them understand what your fat giant in blue suspenders is talking about with such enthusiasm ... He is holding on his fork a slice of sausage. It is long since time for the slice to have vanished into the mouth of the speaker, but there is no way for it to vanish in there, for the speaker is far too taken with what he is saying. What is he talking about?

"They don't know how to make sausage links in this country!" the giant in blue suspenders was saying. "You call those things we make sausages? Shut up, Solomon. You're a Jew, you don't know anything about sausages—what you like is that dried-up kosher meat ... We don't have any sausages. What we have are sclerotic fingers, not sausages. Real link sausages squirt out juice when you prick them. I'll do it, just you watch, I'll make sausages like that."

IX

We had gathered at the airport.

"We," I say! I, of course, was an afterthought, a little man someone had chanced to take along. No one spoke to me, no one was interested in my impressions. It wouldn't have mattered in the least if I had stayed home.

A Soviet airplane of some new design was scheduled to

take off. Babichev had been invited. The invited guests were allowed beyond the barrier. Even in this select company Babichev was the center of things. He had only to enter into a conversation with someone for a circle to gather round him. Everyone listened to him with respectful attention. He was an imposing sight in his gray suit, a grandiose man, the arc of his shoulders higher than all the others'. A pair of black binoculars hung by a strap on his stomach. While listening to his partner in conversation he would put his hands in his pockets and rock gently back and forth on his widely spread feet, heel to toe and toe to heel. He has a habit of scratching his nose, and when he has scratched it, he bunches together the ends of his fingers and inspects them closely. Like schoolboys, his listeners mechanically imitate his gestures and expressions. They also, to their own surprise, scratch their noses.

I walked away from them in a fury. I sat at the snack bar and, caressed by a fresh breeze, drank a beer. I took my time with the beer, watching the breeze fashion tender ornaments out of the ends of the cloth on my table.

At the airport many miracles were taking place all at once: Daisies were blooming right on the field, very close to the barrier—ordinary daisies scattering their yellow dust; low along the line of the horizon round clouds were rolling as though they had been puffed from a cannon; wooden signs painted a blinding red pointed in various directions; high in the air a silken proboscis, the wind sock, swung back and forth, alternately inflating and deflating; and along the grass—the green grass of ancient battles, grazing deer, and romanticism—flying machines were creeping. I savored this taste, these enchanting juxtapositions and combinations. The rhythmic contractions of the silken proboscis conduced to reflection.

From earliest childhood the name Lilienthal—transparent and fluttering as the anterior wings of an insect—has had, to my ear, a miraculous sound. This name is linked in my memory with the beginnings of aviation and seems itself capable of flight, as though it were stretched over light bamboo struts. Otto Lilienthal, that soaring man, was killed. Flying machines lost their resemblance to birds. The light-yellow translucent wings have given way to fins, which seem to beat against the ground on takeoff. In any case, they raise clouds of dust. A flying machine now looks like a ponderous fish. How quickly aviation turned into an industry!

A military march suddenly thundered. The People's Commissar for War had arrived. The People's Commissar hastened along the path, outstripping his entourage. So fast and powerful a walk makes wind—the foliage was set in motion as he passed. The orchestra played elegantly, and elegant was the step of the People's Commissar for War in time with the orchestra.

I rushed to the gate leading to the field. But I was stopped. "Keep back," said a soldier, and put his hand on top of the gate.

"How come?" I asked.

He turned away. His eyes were fixed on the interesting events that were unfolding. The designer of the plane, a pilot in a ruddy leather jacket, was standing at attention before the People's Commissar for War. A belt ran tightly round the Commissar's stocky back. Both were saluting. Everything was motionless. The orchestra alone was entirely in motion. Babichev was rigid, his stomach protruding.

"Let me through, Comrade!" I repeated, tugging the soldier's sleeve.

"I'll throw you off the airport," said he.

"But I was already there. I only left for a moment. I'm with Babichev!"

One had to show an invitation. I had none. Babichev had simply dragged me along with him. Of course I didn't care whether I got on the field or not. I had a fine view of everything here behind the barrier. But I insisted. It was something more important than merely seeing things up close that was driving me up the wall. I had a sudden vivid realization that I had nothing whatsoever to do with the people who had been convened for this great and important event, that my presence among them was absolutely

useless, that I had no connection at all with any of their
great affairs, whether here on the airfield or anywhere
else.

"But, Comrade," I blurted out, "I'm not just an ordinary citizen!" (I could not have hit on a better phrase to
put some order into the chaos of my thoughts.) "Who do
you think I am? A nobody? Kindly let me through. I'm
supposed to be out there." (I waved my hand toward the
group of people around the People's Commissar for War.)

"You are not supposed to be out there," smiled the soldier.

"You ask Comrade Babichev!"

Standing on my toes, I cupped my hands and shouted:
"Andrei Petrovich!"

At that instant the orchestra fell silent. The last beat of
the drum rumbled off underground.

"Comrade Babichev!"

He heard me. The People's Commissar for War also
turned round. Everyone turned round. The pilot raised
his hand to his helmet, picturesquely warding off the sun.

I felt a stab of terror. There was I, a little man with a
potbelly, in a pair of secondhand trousers, dancing around
somewhere behind the barrier—how dare I distract them?
And when it became quiet, when they, even without
knowing who had called one of them, had frozen in their
expectant poses—I couldn't find the strength to call again.

But he knew, he saw, he heard that it was I who had
called him. One second more and it was all over. The
members of the group resumed their previous poses. I was
on the point of tears.

Then I got on my toes again, cupped my hands, and,
deafening the soldier, bellowed into the forbidden distance:

"Sausage maker!"

And again:

"Sausage maker!"

And again and again and again:

"Sausage maker! Sausage maker! Sausage maker!"

I saw only him, Babichev, who with his Tyrolean hat

was taller than the others. I remember wanting to close my eyes and sit down behind the barrier. I don't remember whether I did close my eyes or not, but if I did, then I managed in any case to see the main thing that happened. Babichev turned his face toward me. For one-tenth part of a second it remained turned toward me. There were no eyes. There were the two plaques of his pince-nez, shining like dull mercury. The fear of some instantaneous retribution threw me into a state resembling sleep. I had a dream. I was so certain of being asleep that I had a dream. And the most terrifying thing in the dream was that Babichev's head turned toward me on its own axis, as though it were on a pivot, while his torso remained stationary. His back was still turned to me.

X

I left the airport.

But the noisy festivities still held my attention. I stopped on a green bank and stood there, covered in dust, propped against a tree. The bushes surrounded me as though I were the central figure in a shrine. I picked the tender, sour little berries off some plant, sucked them, and spat them out. I stood with my pale, good-natured face lifted up and gazed at the sky.

Over at the airfield a plane took off. Bright yellow in the sun and hanging at an angle like a shop sign, it zoomed over me with a terrible purring sound and all but stripped the leaves from my tree. Higher and higher it went. I followed it with my eyes as I danced about over the bank: Away it flew, now flashing in the light, now turning black in shadow. As the distance changed, so did it. It assumed the form of various objects—a rifle bolt, a penknife, a trampled lilac blossom . . .

The triumphant maiden flight of a new Soviet aircraft had taken place without me. The war was on. I had insulted Babichev.

At any moment now they will come barreling out of the gates of the airfield. The drivers have already sprung into action. There is Babichev's blue automobile. Alpers, his chauffeur, sees me and motions me to get a move on. I turn my back to him. My shoes are entwined in the green pasta of the grass.

I must have a talk with him. He must understand. I must explain to him that he is the one to blame. He, not I! But he will be with others when he leaves. I have to see him privately. He'll go from here straight to the office. I'll beat him there.

At the office I was told that he was at the construction site.

At The Quarter? To The Quarter then!

Some ill wind drove me forward. It was as though the speech that I had to say to him had already torn itself out of my mouth and I was now chasing it, speeding after it lest it leave me behind and I lose it and forget it.

The building under construction appeared to me a yellow mirage hanging in the air. So there it was, The Quarter! It was far off, behind some other buildings. The various details of the scaffolding merged into one, and it hovered in the distance, a gossamer beehive . . .

I approach. Racket and dust. I develop deafness and cataracts. I passed along the wooden walkways. A sparrow took flight from a stump, the boards gave slightly, reminding me funnily of childhood games on seesaws, and I walked along, smiling at the sawdust settling on me and turning my shoulders gray.

Where should I look for him?

A truck is blocking my way. It can't get in. It struggles, goes up, and falls back, like a beetle trying to crawl from a flat surface up a slope.

The route I must follow is so complicated I might as well be inside the whorls of an ear.

"Comrade Babichev?"

They point: over there. Nearby someone is knocking the bottoms out of barrels.

"Where?"

"Over there."

I walk along a girder over an abyss. I keep my balance. Something like the hold of a ship gapes beneath me.

Boundless, dark, and cool. The whole thing resembles a shipyard. I'm in everyone's way.

"Where?"

"Over there."

He can't be caught.

One time he flashed into view: The upper part of his body passed by above some sort of wooden deck. Gone. And there he was again, up above, far away—we were separated by an immense empty space that would soon be one of the inner courts of the building.

He's been detained. There are several others with him: caps, aprons. Never mind—I'll call him aside so as to say the thing I must say to him: Forgive me.

Someone showed me a shortcut to the other side.

Only one flight of steps left to go. I can already hear voices. A few steps more and I'm there . . .

But this is what happened. I have to stoop over so as not to be swept away. I bend over, grabbing at the wooden step with my hands. He flies past over me. Yes—he flew through the air.

In the wild perspective at which I saw him his figure seemed motionless, and it wasn't his face I saw at all, only the nostrils. Two holes. I could have been under a monument looking up.

What was going on?

I tumbled down the steps.

He vanished. He flew away. He flew off somewhere else on an iron waffle. A latticework shadow followed his flight. He was standing on some sort of iron contraption that swung in a semicircle, howling and clanging. God knows what it was—some kind of technical equipment, a crane maybe. It was a platform made of lengths of rail, laid crosswise. It was through the spaces in between that I had seen his nostrils.

I sat down on the step.

"Where is he?" I asked.

The workers around me were laughing, and I looked round in all directions, smiling like a clown who had just topped off his number with a hilarious pratfall.

"I'm not the one to blame," I said. "He's to blame."

XI

I resolved not to go back to him.

My old room already belonged to someone else. There was a lock on the door. The new tenant was not at home. I remembered that the face of the widow Prokopovich looked like a padlock. Surely she was not going to enter my life again?

That night was spent on the street. The most charming of mornings spread itself above me. Several other unhoused wretches were sleeping on benches in my vicinity. They were lying knotted up, their arms plunged into their sleeves and pressed against their bellies, looking like bound, beheaded Chinamen. Aurora laid her cool fingers upon them. They coughed, groaned, shook themselves, and sat up, their eyes still shut and their arms still folded.

The birds awoke. Small sounds could be detected, talking to themselves, the voices of the birds, the voices of the grass. In the niche of a brick wall pigeons began to fuss about.

I got up trembling. Yawning, I shook like a dog.

(Windows were opened. A glass was filled with milk. Judges pronounced sentences. A man who had worked through the night came to the window and was surprised, not recognizing the street in this unaccustomed light. A patient asked for a drink of water. A little boy ran into the kitchen to see whether a mouse had been caught in the trap. The morning had begun.)

That day I wrote a letter to Andrei Babichev.

I sat down to eat at the Palace of Labor on the Solyanka—meat pies à la Nelson and beer—and wrote as follows:

Andrei Petrovich:

You've sheltered me. You've taken me under your

wing. I've been sleeping on your astonishing sofa. You know what a lousy life I used to lead. On that night of blessed memory you felt sorry for me, you took in a drunk.

You surrounded me with linen sheets. The smoothness and chill of the fabric seemed made on purpose to calm my stormy nature, to ease my anxiety.

My life even came to include the ivory buttons on the quilt cover, in which, if you only turned them the right way, swam a circle of color, the whole rainbow of the spectrum. I recognized them at once. They had come back from some long-forgotten, some ultimate corner of my childhood memories.

I had a bed.

For me, that word itself was as distant and poetic as the word "somersault."

You gave me a bed.

From the pinnacle of well-being you bestowed upon me a cloud-bed, a nimbus that clung to me by a kind of magical warmth, swaddling me in memories, in sweet regrets and hopes. I began to hope that much could yet be salvaged out of what had been my youthful destiny.

You were my salvation, Andrei Petrovich!

Only think: A famous man made me his intimate companion, a remarkable civic leader took me into his home. I want to tell you what my feelings are.

To tell you the truth, they all come down to one single feeling: hatred.

I hate you, Comrade Babichev.

The purpose of this letter is to take you down a peg or two.

I began to feel afraid the first day I came to live with you. You crushed me. You sat on me.

You stand in your shorts. The beery smell of your sweat spreads through the air. I look at you and your face starts to grow strangely larger, your body grows larger—it's as though some clay figure, some idol, had begun to swell and expand. I'm about to scream.

Who gave him the right to crush me?

How am I worse than he is?

Is he more intelligent?

Richer in spirit?

More subtle in temperament?

Stronger? More important?

Is he greater not only by virtue of his position but also in actual fact?

Why must I acknowledge his superiority?

Such were the questions I put to myself. Every day that I spent in observation has given me another particle of the answer. A month has gone by. I now know the answer. And no longer fear you. You're nothing but a dumb functionary. That's all. It wasn't by any personal significance of your own that you crushed me. Oh no! By this time I know you through and through—I see you as though you were in the palm of my hand. My fear of you has passed away like other childish things. I'm rid of you. You're a phony.

I was bothered by doubts at one time. I thought, maybe I *am* nothing compared with him? Maybe I'm just a climber and he's showing me what it means to be a really big man?

But it turned out you're just a functionary, ignorant and stupid like all the functionaries who went before you and will follow after you. And like all functionaries, you're a petty tyrant. Nothing but petty tyranny can explain the storm you raised over a piece of mediocre sausage, or the fact that you picked up an unknown young man off the street and took him home with you. And it may be the same petty tyranny that led you to make a companion of Volodia Makarov, about whom I know nothing except that he's a soccer player. You're a squire. You need clowns and hangers-on. I have no doubt that Volodia Makarov himself ran away from you because he couldn't take being made fun of. You must have systematically turned him into a fool, the same as you did me.

You said that he lived in your house like a son, that he saved your life, and you even got a very dreamy look on your face as you talked about him. I remember. But it was all a lie. You feel uncomfortable about admitting that you're a squire at heart. But I've seen the birthmark on the small of your back.

At first, when you said that the sofa belonged to so-and-so and that when he returned I would have to get the hell out, I was insulted. But it took me only a minute to realize that you were cold and indifferent to him and to me. You're the squire—we're the hangers-on.

But allow me to assure you that neither he nor I—neither of us will ever come back to you again. You have no respect for people. If he comes back to you, it'll only be because he's stupider than I am.

The way my life has turned out, I don't have any record as a revolutionary or as a political prisoner. No one is going to trust me with any such weighty business as manufacturing seltzer water or organizing the keeping of bees.

But does that mean that I'm a bad child of our century, and you're a good one? Does that mean that I'm a nothing and you're a big something?

You found me on the street . . .

How idiotically you behaved!

"On the street" you decided—"fine—let him do some work—read proof, edit copy, check stuff, all fine." You didn't show mercy to a young man on the street. This was more of your own infatuation with yourself. You're a functionary, Comrade Babichev.

Who did you take me for? Some ruined member of the lumpenproletariat? You decided to help me on my feet? I thank you. I'm strong—are you listening?—I'm strong enough to be ruined and pick myself up and be ruined again.

I'd like to know what you're going to do when you've read this letter. Maybe you'll try to have me sent away, or maybe shut up in an asylum. You can do anything— you're a big man, a member of the government. After all, you said your own brother ought to be shot. You said: We'll lock him up in Kanatchikova.

Your brother, who made such an odd impression, is a mystery to me; I don't understand him. There's some secret here, something I know nothing about. The name "Ophelia" holds a strange excitement for me. And as for you, I think you're afraid of that name.

Still, I can put two and two together. I see something coming. But I'll be in your way. Yes, I'm almost sure that's the way it is. But I won't let you. You want to get your hands on your brother's daughter. I only saw her once. Yes, I'm the one who spoke to her about the bough full of blossoms and leaves. You have no imagination. You made fun of me. I heard what you said over the phone. You tried to slander me in the girl's eyes just as you slandered him, her father. You can't bring yourself to admit that the girl whom you want to take over and turn into one of your fools, the way you tried to make us into fools, that this girl has a tender, tormented spirit. You want to utilize her just as you utilize (I'm deliberately using your own word here) "the heads and feet of sheep with the aid of wittily applied spiral electric drills" (from your brochure).

But no, I won't let you do it. I can hear you now: Oh, what a tasty little piece! You glutton, you worship your own gut. Is there anything that would stop you where your physiology is concerned? What would stop you from ruining the girl? The fact that she's your niece? But you laugh at the very notion of family, of genealogy. You want to tame her.

And that's why you thunder against your brother like such a madman. No one needs more than a glance to see that he's a remarkable man. I don't even know him yet and I think he's a genius. In what, I don't know. You persecute him. I heard how you beat your fist on the railing. You forced his daughter to leave her own father.

But you aren't going to hound me to death.

I'm going to defend your brother and his daughter. Listen to me, you idiot who laughed at the bough full of blossoms and leaves. Just listen: Yes, that was the only way, the only expression for the rapture I felt when I saw her. And just what words are you preparing for her? You called me an alcoholic for the simple reason that I spoke to the girl in the sort of figurative language that is beyond you? What people don't understand they find either laughable or terrifying. Right now you're laughing, but I'll soon make you feel terrified. Don't make the mistake of thinking that all my thoughts are figurative—I'm able to think quite realistically. What the hell—I can also talk about her, about Valia, in ordinary language, and, please, I can describe her right now in words even you can understand, just to get you excited, to dangle in front of your nose the things you are not going to get, my dear sausage maker.

Yes, she stood before me—but wait, first I'll tell you in my own style: She was lighter than a shadow, the lightest of shadows might have envied her—the shadow of the falling snow; yes, first let's have it in my style: It was not with her ear that she listened to me, but with her temple, her head slightly bent; yes, her face is like an almond in its sun-warmed color, in its high cheekbones, its roundness, tapering toward the chin. Can you understand this? No? Let's try again. Her blouse had come slightly undone from the running and I saw that she was not tan all over, and I saw on her bosom the light-blue turnpike of a vein . . .

And now—your style. Description of individual desired for purposes of entertaining palate. Before me stood a young girl aged about 16 years, almost a child, wide in the shoulders, eyes gray, hair short & unkempt, a charming young person, elegant as a figure on a chess board (sorry, my style!), medium height.

You won't get her!

She's going to be my wife. All my life she's the one I dreamt of

Let's go to it! Let's have it out! You're thirteen years older than I am. Those years are behind you and ahead of me. One or two more achievements in the area of sausage manufacture, one or two more fast-food establishments—those are the limits within which you might accomplish something.

My God, do I have different dreams!

You're not going to get Valia—I will. We'll go to Europe and make a great noise—to Europe, where they love glory.

I'll get Valia as a prize—for everything: for all the insults, for the youth I never managed to see, for my dog's life.

I used to tell you about the filthy old cook. Remember—about how she washed up in the hallway? Okay, but now I'm going to see something different: A room somewhere is going to be full of sunshine one of these days, and there'll be a blue basin near the window, and the window will shimmer in the basin, and Valia will be washing at the basin, the sun sparkling on her arms as on the scales of a golden fish, and splashing, and playing trills on the keyboard of the water . . .

I'll do anything to make this dream come true. You are not going to utilize Valia.

So long, Comrade Babichev.

How could I have spent a whole month playing this humiliating role? I'm never coming back to you. Just wait— maybe your first fool will come back. Give him my best. How glad I am that I'm never coming back!

Every time my feelings get hurt by something I know that right away, by the association of ideas, I'm going to recall one of those evenings spent near your desk. What wretched memories!

Evening. You're at your desk. Your rapturous self-love radiates from you. "I'm working," these rays crackle like static, "do you hear me, Kavalerov, I'm working, don't bother me . . . sh-h-h! . . . you nobody."

And in the morning the praises fly out of numerous mouths:

"A great man! A remarkable man! A man of personal perfection—Andrei Petrovich Babichev!"

But at the same time that these toadies were singing their hosannas to you, at the same time when you were bursting with self-satisfaction, there was a man living right next to you whom no one ever noticed, whose opinions were never asked; a man who was following your least movement, studying you, observing you, and not from below, like a slave, but calmly, like a man among men, and this man concluded that you are a big shot in the civil service and nothing else, a commonplace person who got swept up into an enviable position by external circumstances, period.

Well, enough fooling around: That's all I wanted to say to you.

You tried to make me your clown—an enemy is what you got. "Who do you think you're fighting, you no-good bum?"—that's what you yelled at your brother. I don't know who you had in mind—yourself, your party, your factories, stores, bee farms—I don't know. But it's you I'm fighting against: against the world's commonest squire, egotist, sensualist, idiot, who is certain that everything will end well for him. I'm fighting for your brother, for the girl you've deceived, for tenderness, for inspiration, for personality, for names that make the blood race, like "Ophelia," for all the things you're trying to quash, you "remarkable man." Give my best to Solomon Shapiro . . .

XII

The cleaning woman let me in. Babichev had already left. The traditional milk had been drunk. The chalky glass stood on the table. Beside it was a plateful of pastries that looked like Hebrew letters.

Man's life is a trifle. The movement of worlds is menacing. When I moved in here the sunshine would sit like a rabbit on the doorsill at two o'clock in the afternoon. Thirty-six days have passed. The rabbit has jumped into another room. The earth has moved through the ordained portion of its path. The sunny little rabbit, a child's plaything, reminds us of eternity.

I went out onto the balcony.

On the corner a group of people were listening to the pealing of some bells. They were ringing in a church that couldn't be seen from the balcony. This church is famous for its bell ringer. The idlers were craning their necks. They could see the celebrated bell ringer at his work.

I myself once spent a good hour standing on the corner. The arches disclosed the interior of the bell tower. There in the sort of sooty darkness that one finds in attics, among beams wrapped in cobwebs, was the bell ringer, in a frenzy. Twenty bells were pulling at him. He was leaning back, his head bent, like a coachman, and he might have been yelling something. He was twirling on one central point in the midst of a gloomy spiderweb of ropes and would now go limp, hanging by his extended arms, now throw himself into a corner, ruining the overall design of the web—a mysterious musician, barely discernible, black, and perhaps as ugly as Quasimodo.

(It was of course the distance that made him appear so terrible. You could, if you wanted, say that he was a little man dealing with platters and plates. And you could call the pealing of the famous bell tower a mixture of the racket from a restaurant and a train station.)

Listening from the balcony, I heard the bells go: "Tom-vir-lir-li! Tom-vir-lir-li! Tom-vir-lir-li!"

Some fellow named Tom Virlili was swarming around in the air.

> Here's Tom Virlili,
> Tom with his tom-tom,
> O, young Tom!

The tousled bell ringer set to music many of my mornings. Tom—that is the sound of the big bell, the big caldron; Virlili—the little dinner bells.

Tom Virlili entered into my life on one of the splendid mornings to which I awoke under this roof. The musical phrase was transformed into a verbal phrase. In my imagination this Tom stood vividly before me.

A youth, come to have a look round the city. An absolutely unknown youth, he has already arrived, is here, already sees the city, which is asleep, which suspects nothing. The morning fog has only begun to lift. The city drifts in its valley like a brilliant green cloud. Tom Virlili smiles and presses his hand to his breast as he looks at the city, searching out those lineaments known to him since childhood from books of pictures.

The youth has a rucksack on his back.

There is nothing he won't accomplish.

He incarnates the very arrogance of youth itself, all the proud, hidden dreams.

Days will go by and soon (the little rabbit of the sun will not have managed to leap many times from the doorsill to the next room) soon boys who themselves dream of roaming about with a rucksack on their back in the outskirts of the city, in the outskirts of glory, will be singing the little song about the man who did whatever he wished:

> Here's Tom Virlili
> Tom with his tom-tom,
> O, young Tom!

And that is how the ringing bells of an ordinary little Moscow church got transformed in my brain into a romantic daydream (blatantly West European in origin).

I'll leave my letter on the table, gather up my personal effects (into a rucksack?), and leave. I placed the letter, folded in four, on the glass covering of his desk, right next to the portrait of the one whom I regarded as my companion in misery.

There came a knock at the door. Could it be he?

I opened the door.

At the door, rucksack in hand and smiling his merry Japanese smile, as though he had discerned through the closed door his dear, dream-caressed friend, stood, looking rather like Valia, the shy Tom Virlili.

It was the dark-complexioned youth, Volodia Makarov. He glanced at me in surprise and then took in the room with his eyes. Several times his gaze returned to the sofa, to beneath the sofa, where my shoes protruded.

"Greetings!" I said.

He walked over to the sofa, sat down, stayed there awhile, then went into the bedroom, remained awhile, came back, stopped near the flamingo vase, and asked me:

"Where is Andrei Petrovich? At the office?"

"I can't say for sure. Andrei Petrovich will be back this evening. There's a chance that he'll bring a new fool with him. You're the first, I'm the second, he'll be the third. Or perhaps there were fools even before you? And it may be that he'll bring a girl home with him."

"Who?" said Tom Virlili. "What did you say?" he asked, his face twisted in puzzlement. His ears lay back.

He sat down on the sofa again. The shoes under the sofa worried him. It was plain that he wanted to touch them with the heel of his boot.

"Why did you come back?" I asked. "Why in hell did you come back? We've played our role—you and I. He's busy with something else now. He's in the process of corrupting a girl. His own niece, Valia. You understand? Get out of here! Listen to me!"

(I rushed toward him. He sat absolutely still.)

"Listen to me! Do what I did! Tell him everything, the whole truth! Look! (I grabbed my letter from the desk.) Here's the letter I wrote him . . ."

He pushed me aside. His rucksack lay down in its accustomed corner near the sofa. He picked up the telephone and called the office.

That's how my effects got left behind.

I beat it out of there.

XIII

The letter went with me. I decided to destroy it. The soccer player was indeed living with him as his son. The way the rucksack made itself comfortable in its corner, the way his eyes checked out the room, the way he lifted the receiver and gave the number—all this made it clear that he was an old hand around there, that he was at home. The place belonged to him. I'd had a bad night and it showed. I didn't write what I'd meant to write. Babichev would not have understood my outrage. He would have blamed it all on envy. He would have thought that I envied Volodia Makarov.

It's a good thing the letter went with me.

Otherwise, I might have fired a blank.

I was mistaken in thinking that Volodia was his fool and entertainer. Consequently, my going to his defense in my letter was a blunder. On the contrary. Now that I'd met him I could see how arrogant he was. Babichev was nurturing and grooming his own likeness. The result would be the same bombastic, blind sort of human being.

The way he looked at me said: "Sorry, but you're mistaken. *You're* the hanger-on. *I* am fully entitled. I am the heir apparent."

I was sitting on a bench when I suddenly made a dreadful discovery.

The paper folded in four was the wrong one—mine was larger, this was not my letter. Mine was still there. In my haste I had grabbed something else. This is what I read:

My dear sweet Andrei Petrovich, greetings, greetings! How on earth are you? Has your new lodger not strangled you yet? Hasn't Ivan Petrovich hounded you with his "Ophelia"? Watch out: They'll be in cahoots, those two—your Kavalerov and Ivan Petrovich—and wipe you out. Watch out and take care of yourself, because, remember, with your weakness anyone can take advantage of you . . .

Whatever possessed you to become so trusting? You take any riffraff off the street into the house? Kick him the hell out! The very next day you should have told him: Okay, young man, you've slept it off, now good-bye! What an old softy you are! When I read your letter where you said you'd thought about me and felt sorry for that drunk in the street and picked him up and brought him back all for my sake, because you said you thought that I too might have an accident and be lying somewhere just like that—when I read that I laughed and then wondered what it meant. It didn't sound like you at all, it sounded like Ivan Petrovich.

It turned out just the way I thought it would: You brought that con artist home and then of course you were lost, you didn't know what to do with him. You thought: To ask him to clear out is just too embarrassing and God only knows what to do! Isn't that right? All right, so I *am* preaching. It's the sort of work you do that makes you so sensitive: all those fruits and herbs and little bees and calves and all that sort of thing. But I'm an industrial man. Go ahead and laugh, Andrei Petrovich! You're forever laughing at me. But you see, I'm already the new generation.

So now what's going to happen? Say I come back—then what's going to happen to your oddball? Suppose he starts crying and won't leave the sofa? And you'll feel sorry for him. Yes, I am jealous. I'll kick him out of there—I'll break his face. You're so kindhearted. All you do is shout and bang your fist and swagger about, but when it's time to act—you feel sorry. If it weren't for me, Valia would still be suffering at Ivan Petrovich's. How are you holding her back there? Hasn't she gone back to him? You know yourself what a sly one that Ivan Petrovich is, how he can pretend. He even says himself that he's a cheap crook. Right? So don't feel sorry for him.

Why don't you try and arrange something for him in some dispensary? He'll run away. Or your Kavalerov—offer him something in a dispensary. He'll be insulted.

Okay, that's enough. Don't be angry. Remember what you yourself said: You teach me, Volodia, and I'll teach you. So we're teaching each other.

I'll be there soon. In a day or so. Hello from Daddy. Farewell, dear old Murom! What a town. At night when I'm out walking I understand that there really isn't a town here at all, strictly speaking. Nothing but shops. Is that a town? A collection of shops, that's all. And everything is for them, for the sake of the shops. The shops are supreme. At night an Egyptian gloom settles on the town, you know what I mean, utter blackness—spooky! But out on the edge of town, where the workshops are, the lights are shining—they're having a ball!

Here's what I saw in this town. A calf chased after a district inspector, after his briefcase (which he was carrying under his arm). It was running, smacking its lips, wanted to chew the briefcase I suppose. Nice picture. A hedge, a puddle, the inspector walking along in his red cap pretty as you please, and this calf has ideas about his briefcase. If that isn't a contradiction ... !

I can't stand these calves. I am a man-machine. You won't know me. I've turned into a machine. Or if I haven't yet turned into one, I want to. The machines here are animals—thoroughbred animals! Wonderfully indifferent, proud machines Not like those things in your sausage factories. You're doing things on the level of cottage industry. All you do is slaughter calves. I want to be a machine. I want to get your advice. I want to be proud of my work—proud of the fact that I'm working. You know, to be indifferent to everything but work. I've begun to envy machines—that's what it is! Am I not as good as a machine? After all it was we who thought it up and built it and it turned out to be twice as ferocious as we are. Set it going and it takes off! Works right through a job without a shiver of waste motion. I want to be like that, too. You see what I mean, Andrei Petrovich—without a single wasted motion. Oh how I want to talk to you!

I copy everything you do. I even smack my lips when I eat, the way you do.

How often I think of my good luck. You raised me up, Andrei Petrovich! It isn't every Komsomol member who lives the way I do. And I live with you, with the wisest, the most remarkable personality. People would pay anything for such a life. Of course I know that many people envy me. Thank you, Andrei Petrovich. Now don't laugh and say I'm writing you a love letter. He talks about being a machine and then writes love letters, right? No, it's the truth—I'm going to be a machine.

How are things? Is The Quarter being built? Nothing collapsed? How about "Warmth and Strength"? That all settled? And Kampfer?

And what's going on at home? I understand some unknown citizen is sleeping on my sofa? He'll leave his lice in it. Remember how they lugged me back from the soccer match? People talk about it to this day. Remember how frightened you were when they carried me in? It's true, isn't it—you were frightened? You were blubbering over me, Andrei Petrovich! I was lying on the sofa, my leg as heavy as a rail. I was watching you—you were at your desk, behind the green shade, writing. I'm looking at you, and suddenly you look at me, and I immediately close my eyes—just as I used to do with Mama!

By the way, speaking of soccer. I'm going to play on the Moscow team against the Germans. And maybe—if Shukhov doesn't beat me out—on the USSR team! Nice, huh?

How's Valia? Of course, we'll get married! In four years. You laugh and say we won't make it. But I hereby declare to you that it'll happen four years from now. Yes, I am going to be the Edison of the new age. She and I will kiss for the first time when your Quarter opens. Yes. You don't believe me? She and I have an agreement. You don't know anything. On the day when The Quarter opens we'll be on the grandstand and kiss to the sound of the music.

Don't forget me, Andrei Petrovich. Suppose I came home and it turned out that your Kavalerov is now your best friend, that I'm forgotten, that he's replaced me. He's doing calisthenics with you, driving to the construction site, and what all not? But maybe he turned out to be a remarkable fellow, much nicer than me. Maybe you and he are good friends and I, the Edison of the new age, will have to clear the hell out? Maybe you're sitting with him right now, and with Ivan Petrovich, and with Valia, and laughing at me? And your Kavalerov has already married Valia? Tell the truth. Then I'll kill you, Andrei Petrovich. Word of honor. For betraying all our talks, our plans. Is that clear?

Well, I've carried on much too long. I'm keeping a busy man from his work. I talk about no wasted motion and then get carried away myself. That's because I miss you so—right? Well, good-bye my dear and respected friend, good-bye. See you soon.

XIV

An immense cloud with the outlines of South America was hanging over the city. It was brilliant, but the shadow it cast was menacing. The shadow was moving with astronomical slowness across Babichev's street.

All those who had already entered the estuary of that street and were proceeding against the current saw the movements of the shadow. Their eyes darkened. The shadow took the ground from beneath their feet. They seemed to be walking on a revolving sphere.

I was fighting my way down the street with them.

The balcony was still hanging there. A jacket lay across the railing. The church bells were silent. I had now replaced the idler on the corner. A youth appeared on the balcony. The sudden overcast surprised him. He raised his head, looked out, and leaned over the railing.

The stairway. The door. I knock. My lapel twitches from the beating of my heart. I've come for a fight.

I'm let in. Whoever opened the door for me steps back, holding the door against himself. The first thing I see is Andrei Babichev. Andrei Babichev is standing in the middle of the room, his legs spread so as to accommodate an army of Lilliputians. His hands are plunged into his trousers pockets. His jacket is unbuttoned and pulled back, the hems of it on both sides forming festoons behind his pocketed hands. His pose is eloquent: "We-e-lll?"

I see only him. Volodia Makarov I can only hear.

I walk toward Babichev. It begins to rain.

I shall fall on my knees before him at once:

"Don't drive me away, Andrei Petrovich! Don't drive me away! I understand everything now. Believe me, as you believe Volodia! Believe me: I'm also young, I'm also going to be the Edison of the new age, I'll also adore you!

How could I have been so asleep, so blind, as not to do
everything to make you love me! Forgive me, let me stay,
give me four years, too . . ."

But, without falling on my knees, all I do is ask in a sardonic tone:

"What on earth keeps you home from work?"

"Get out of here!" is his reply.

His answer came as promptly as though I were playing
straight man to him, but it was some little time before my
own consciousness picked up my cue.

Something unusual had happened.

It was raining. Perhaps there was lightning.

I don't want to speak figuratively. I want to speak simply. I once read the book *The Atmosphere*, by Camille
Flammarion. (What a celestial name! Flammarion—that is
itself a star!) He describes ball lightning and the astonishing effect of it: A large, smooth sphere rolls without a
sound into a room and fills it with blinding light . . . Oh,
the furthest thing from my mind is to make some vulgar
comparison. But the cloud was suspicious. And the
shadow did move forward as though in a dream. And it
was raining. And the bedroom window was open. You
mustn't leave windows open in a storm! The draft . . . !

Along with the rain, along with the raindrops bitter as
tears, and the gusts of wind, which set the flamingo vase to
running like a flame, inflaming the drapes and chasing
them up under the ceiling, there appeared from the bedroom . . . Valia.

But I alone was flabbergasted by her entry. Actually,
everything was quite normal: A friend had arrived and his
friends had hastily gathered to greet him.

Babichev might in fact have gone to fetch Valia, who
might very well have been looking forward to this day.
Everything was normal. And as for me—I ought to be
packed off to the dispensary and treated by hypnosis so
that I would cease thinking in images, so that I would not
ascribe to a girl the effects of ball lightning.

But I'll ruin your "normal" for you!

"Get out of here!" my hearing finally repeated.

"Everything is not so normal as you think . . ." I began.

There came a draft of air. The door had remained open. The wind caused me to sprout a large wing. It flapped madly above my shoulder, blowing into my eyes. Half my face was anesthetized by the draft.

"Everything is not so normal as you think," say I, pressing myself against the doorjamb so as to break the horrible wing. "You went away, Volodia, and in the meantime Comrade Babichev lived with Valia. And while you are waiting out your four years, Andrei Petrovich will manage to have all the fun he likes with Valia . . ."

I found myself behind the door. Half my face had been anesthetized. I may not have felt the blow.

The lock clicked above me as though a branch had snapped off and I tumbled down from a splendid tree—an overripe, lazy fruit, popped by the fall.

"That's done it," said I placidly as I picked myself up. "Now I shall kill you, Comrade Babichev."

XV

It is raining.

The rain walks along Tsvetnoi Boulevard, strides past the circus, turns right into the avenues, and, when it reaches the summit of Petrovsky, suddenly goes blind and loses its assurance.

As I cross Trubnaya Square I think about the fabulous fencer who walked through the rain warding off the drops with his foil. His foil glistened, his cape fluttered, the fencer twirled, he was everywhere at once, like a flute, and . . . he stayed dry. He got his paternal inheritance. I got soaked to the skin and also, I think, got slapped in the face.

I find that a landscape looked at through the wrong end of a pair of binoculars gains in brilliancy, shine, and three-dimensionality. The colors and the contours are somehow more defined. A thing, without ceasing to be the same familiar thing, can suddenly become ridiculously small and unusual. The observer's sensations are like those of a child. Exactly as though he were dreaming. Watch and you'll see how a man looking through the wrong end of his binoculars develops a radiant smile.

When the rain was over, the city glistened in all of its three dimensions. Everyone saw it: The streetcar was painted carmine; the cobblestones of the pavement were anything but monotone—some of them were even green; a painter high up on a building emerged from the niche where he had taken refuge from the rain like a pigeon and walked along against his brick background; a boy at a window was catching the sun in his mirror . . .

I bought an egg and a French roll from an old woman. I cracked the egg against a streetcar post right in front of the passengers who were hurrying away from the Petrovsky Gate.

I set off uphill. Benches passed by at the level of my knees. The middle of the avenue here was slightly higher than the sides. Splendid mothers had spread their kerchiefs on the benches and were sitting upon them. Their eyes were the color of fish scales and glistened in their sunburnt faces. The sun had also tanned their necks and shoulders. But the ample young breasts visible in the blouses were white. Lonely and rejected, I sadly drank in this whiteness, whose name was: milk, motherhood, marriage, pride, and purity.

A nurse was holding an infant who seemed to have been dressed in imitation of the Pope.

A girl in a red ribbon had a sunflower seed hanging on her lower lip. The girl was listening to a band and hadn't noticed that she'd strolled into a puddle. The mouths of the tubas reminded one of elephants' ears.

For all of them together—the mothers, the nurses, the girls, the musicians wrapped up in their instruments—I was only one thing: a figure of fun. The trumpet players looked at me askance and puffed out their cheeks even more. The girl giggled, which caused the seed finally to fall. She discovered the puddle at the same moment. She blamed her own clumsiness on me and turned her face angrily aside.

I'll prove that I'm no clown. No one understands me. What people don't understand seems to them funny or terrifying. They are all going to be terrified.

I walked toward a street mirror.

I love street mirrors. They suddenly spring up across your path. You're following an ordinary, peaceful route—an ordinary route through the city, promising neither miracles nor visions. You walk along with nothing in particular in view, you raise your eyes, and suddenly, in an instant, it becomes clear to you that something unheard-of has befallen the world and its laws.

Gone now are the laws of optics and geometry; gone, too, the very nature of what had been your means of progress, your movement, your desire to go in no other direction than the one in which you were, in fact, going. You begin to think that you are seeing with the back of your head—you even smile abstractedly at passersby, it is so embarrassing to have such an advantage.

"Ah," you sigh softly.

The streetcar that just vanished from your gaze now rushes past you again, cutting along the edge of the avenue like a knife through a tart. The straw hat hanging by its blue ribbon from someone's arm (you'd seen it only a moment ago, it had caught your attention, but you'd had no time to look back at it) now returns and glides past before your eyes.

The distance unfolds before you. Everyone is certain that this is a house, that is a wall, but with your special advantage you know: It is not a house! You've discovered the secret: There is no wall here, there is a secret world in which everything that you've just seen repeats itself, and what is more, repeats itself with all the three-dimensionality and brilliancy conveyed only via the wrong end of binoculars.

You have in fact walked yourself silly. So sudden was the violation of all the rules, so implausible the change of all proportions. But you're glad that your head is in a whirl ... When you finally see what has happened you rush up to the glass quadrangle reflecting the blue sky. Your face hangs immobile in the mirror; it alone has kept its natural form, it alone remains as a particle of the true world while all else has fallen, changed, and acquired a new truth to which you could not by any means accommodate yourself though you stood for a whole hour in front of the mirror, where your face seems to be part of a tropical park. The green of the foliage is too green, the blue of the sky too blue.

There's no way you can say for sure (unless you turn away from the mirror) which way the pedestrian you see in the mirror is headed ... only by turning aside ...

I was looking in the mirror chewing on the remnant of my French roll.

I turned my head.

The pedestrian had turned up from somewhere to the side and was headed toward the mirror. I prevented his being reflected in the glass. The smile that he had prepared for himself fell to my lot. He was a head shorter than me and lifted up his face.

He had hurried up to the mirror to find and flick off a caterpillar that had fallen on the edge of his shoulder. Lifting his shoulder like a violinist, he flicked the creature away with a snap of his fingers.

I was still thinking of the optical illusions and sleight of hand of the mirror and therefore, still not having recognized the man, asked him:

"What direction did you come from? How did you get here?"

"How?" he replied. "How did I get here?" (He fixed his clear eyes on me.) "I myself thought myself up."

He doffed his bowler, revealing the bald patch on his head, and bowed to me with extravagant courtesy. He bowed the way panhandlers bow to the dispensers of handouts. The bags under his eyes were also like those of a bum—the color of lilac stockings. He was sucking on a piece of candy.

Instantly I realized what had happened: This was my friend, my teacher, my consoler.

I grasped him by the hand and almost fell at his feet as I said:

"Tell me, answer me . . ."

He raised his eyebrows.

"What . . . is Ophelia?"

He made ready to reply. But the sweet juice of his lozenge appeared at the corners of his lips. Melting with excitement and emotion, I waited for his answer.

Part Two
I

The approach of old age did not alarm Ivan Babichev.

True, he could from time to time be heard to utter complaints anent the swift passage of life, the lost years, and the stomach cancer that he supposed himself to have . . . But these complaints were too lighthearted and were in all probability not even sincere: complaints of a purely rhetorical nature.

He would, for instance, press his hand to the left side of his chest and ask with a smile:

"What sort of sound do you suppose a ruptured heart makes?"

He once showed some friends of his the back of his hand, where the veins made the pattern of a tree, and launched forth into the following improvisations:

"Here," quoth he, "is the tree of life. Here is the tree that tells me more about life and death than the flowering and fading trees of the parks. I don't recall exactly when I discovered that there was a tree growing on the back of my hand . . . But it must have been at that wonderful period when the flowering and fading of the trees had not yet begun to speak to me about life and death but only about the end and beginning of the school year! It was light blue then, this tree, it was light blue and graceful, and the blood—which at the time I thought to be a light, not a liquid—rose above it like the dawn and imparted to the whole landscape of my fist the look of a Japanese watercolor . . .

"The years have gone by. I have changed. And the tree has changed.

"I remember a splendid time when it branched in all directions. There were moments when I took pride in watching its irresistible flowering. It became rough and brown as a bear—a sign of its hidden power! I was able to call it the powerful rigging of my hand. But now, my friends! How feeble it is, how rotten!

"It seems to me that twigs have snapped off, that hollows have appeared in the trunk . . . Sclerosis, my friends! And the fact that the skin has become glazed, and the tissue beneath it watery—is that not the fog settling over the tree of my life, the same fog that will soon envelop all of me?"

There were three brothers Babichev. Ivan was the second. The oldest was named Roman. He had belonged to a revolutionary squad and been executed for taking part in a terrorist act.

The youngest brother, Andrei, had emigrated and was living in Paris. "How do you like that?" Ivan wrote to him. "We've got a martyr in the family! Wouldn't Grandma have loved that!" To which his brother Andrei, with his usual rudeness, answered curtly: "You are simply a bastard." Thus was established the discord between the brothers.

Ever since childhood, Ivan had regularly astonished his family and acquaintances.

As a twelve-year-old boy he had demonstrated to the members of his family a strange-looking apparatus, something like a lampshade with a fringe of sleigh bells, and assured them that by using his apparatus he could, on command, produce in any person any desired dream.

"All right," said his father, who was a Latinist and the Director of the Gymnasium. "I believe you. I wish to see a dream out of Roman history." ("What precisely?" the boy had asked in a businesslike manner.) "It doesn't matter. The Battle of Pharsalus. But if this doesn't work I'll tan your hide."

Late that evening a marvelous sound could be heard here and there through the house. The Director of the Gymnasium was lying down in his study, as flat and stiff from anger as though he were in his coffin. The mother was hovering about near the spitefully closed doors to the study. Little Ivan, an amiable smile on his face, was walking around the sofa, shaking his lampshade the way a tightrope walker shakes his Chinese parasol. Next morning the father, still in his nightshirt, sprang in three bounds from his study to the bedroom of the plump, kind, sleepy, lazy little Ivan, whom he jerked out of the bed. It was scarcely light, something might still have been dreamt, perhaps, but the Director tore open the curtains, thus falsely greeting the break of day. Mother tried to prevent the beating, she interposed her hands, screaming:

"Don't hit him, Peter, don't hit him . . . He made a mistake . . . Honestly, he did . . . So what if you didn't have the dream? The sound was carried in a different direction . . . you know this apartment—it's damp. It was I, I who saw the Battle of Pharsalus. I dreamed of the battle, Peter!"

"Don't lie for him," said the Director. "Or tell me the details: What distinguished the armor of the Balearic archers from the armor of the Numidian slingsmen? Well, madam?"

He waited a moment, the mother began to sob, and the little experimenter got his whipping. He conducted himself like Galileo. The evening of that same day the maid announced to her mistress that she would not accept the proposal of marriage made to her by a certain Dobrodeev. "He's forever lying, you can't believe him," the maid explained. "All night long I dreamt of horses. They were all galloping, such terrible horses, wearing something like masks. And to see a horse in a dream signifies lying."

Losing all control over her nether jaw, the mother proceeded like a sleepwalker to the doors of the study. The cook turned rigid at her stove, feeling that she too was losing control of her nether jaw.

The wife's hand touched the husband's shoulder. He was sitting at his desk, reattaching to his cigarette case a monogram that had fallen off.

"Peter," said the mother softly, "I'd like you to have a talk with Frosia . . . It seems Frosia dreamt of the Battle of Pharsalus . . ."

There is no record of how the Director reacted to the housemaid's dream. As for Ivan, it is known that a month or two after the episode of artificial dreams he was already spreading stories about a new invention of his.

The story ran that he had invented a special sort of soapy mixture and a special sort of little pipe, by means of which one could produce an astonishing soap bubble. In flight, this bubble would expand to the following proportions: Christmas tree bauble, beach ball, then country-house-flower-bed-sized balloon, and so on and on up to the size of a dirigible—and then it would burst and shower upon the city in a brief golden rain.

His father was in the kitchen. (He belonged to that gloomy species of fathers who pride themselves on knowing this or that culinary secret, and who regard as their exclusive privilege, say, to determine the number of bay leaves needed for some renowned, inherited soup recipe, or perhaps to specify the exact number of seconds that an egg must remain in a pot of boiling water in order to attain that ideal condition known as "mi-dur."

Outside, in a small courtyard and just underneath the kitchen window, little Ivan was carrying on about his inventions. This reached the jaundiced ear of the father, who stuck his head out the window. Some little boys were clustered around Ivan, who was filling them with nonsense about his soap bubble. It was to be as big as a hot-air balloon.

The Director's choler rose anew. The eldest son, Roman, had left the family a year ago, and the father was now venting his spite on the younger sons.

God must have scraped the bottom of the barrel for these sons, thought he.

He sprang away from the window so angry that he was even grinning. At dinner he waited to hear what Ivan would have to say, but Ivan kept mum. "He seems to feel contempt for me, seems to think me a fool," the Director fumed to himself. Toward the end of the day, when Babichev's father was drinking tea on his balcony, suddenly somewhere very far away above the farthest background of his field of vision—deliquescent and glassy, gleaming in the fine yellow rays of the setting sun—there appeared a large orange sphere. It was floating slowly, describing a diagonal line across the background . . .

The Director flung himself into the room and, peering through an open door into the next room, immediately saw Ivan on the window ledge. The schoolboy was leaning far out the window and loudly clapping his hands.

"My satisfaction on that day," recalled Ivan Petrovich, "was perfect. My father got a fright. For a long time afterwards I tried to read the expression on his face, but he hid his eyes. And I began to feel sorry for him. He turned quite black—I thought he was about to die. And so I magnanimously disclosed my ruse. He was a dry, petty man, my father, but he took little notice of what was going on round him. He didn't know that the balloonist Ernest Vitollo was to fly over the city that day. There had been splendid posters announcing the fact. I confessed that I had tricked him, though without meaning to. I must tell you that my experiments with soap bubbles did not produce the results I had dreamt of."

(The facts argue that at the time when Ivan Babichev was twelve years old ballooning was still in its infancy, and it is most unlikely that any flights were made then over provincial cities.

But if this was all fantasy—so what? Fantasy is reason's sweetheart.)

His friends listened to Ivan Babichev's improvisations with great pleasure.

"And if I'm not mistaken, the night after that dis-

tressing day Papa *did* dream of the Battle of Pharsalus. He
didn't go to school the next morning. Mama took some
mineral water to him in his study. In all probability he
was shaken by the details of the battle. It may be that he
couldn't reconcile himself to the way the dream made fun
of history . . . Maybe he dreamed that the outcome of the
battle was decided by Balearic slingsmen who arrived in
hot-air balloons . . ."

Such was the conclusion of Ivan Babichev's novella
about soap bubbles.

On another occasion he shared with his friends the following incident from the period of his adolescence:

"A student named Shemiot was courting a young lady
named . . . but now I can't remember her name . . . wait
. . . wait . . . no, let's call her Lilia Kapitanaki. Anyway,
her heels made a little goatlike sound. We boys knew
everything that went on in the courtyard of our building.
The student used to languish underneath Lilia's balcony,
though he was both eager and afraid at the same time to
call her forth from the golden depths beyond the balcony
door—and this was a girl who must have been all of sixteen, which is to say, in the eyes of us boys, an old woman.

"His student's cap was blue, his student's cheeks red,
when he rode up on his student's bicycle. And his student's melancholy was indescribable one Sunday in
May—one of those Sundays of which no more than a
dozen are stored in the records of meteorological science, a
Sunday when the breeze was so sweet and caressing that
one wanted to tie a sky-blue ribbon round its brow—
when the student, racing up to the balcony, descried upon
it, her elbows propped upon the railing, Lilia's aunt. This
lady was dressed in as many colors and flowery patterns as
the slipcover of an armchair in a provincial sitting room;
her person was composed of knots, crescents, and frills,
the whole surmounted by a coiffure resembling a snail . . .
And the aunt was clearly delighted to see the student. She
flung open to him an embrace, as it were, from her emi-
nence, and announced to him in a voice that was pure po-

tato, and so dampened by saliva, so full of tongue, that she seemed to be speaking while chewing something hot:

" 'Lilia is leaving for Kherson. She's leaving today. At seven-forty. She's going for a long time. She's going for the whole summer. She asked me to give you her greetings, Sergei Sergeevich. Greetings!'

"But the student, with a lover's intuition, understood everything. He knew that Liliechka was sobbing in the golden depths of the room, that her heart tugged her to the balcony, that even without seeing him she saw him in his tunic, which, since it was white, attracted by the laws of physics the maximum number of light rays and shone with a blinding alpine whiteness ... But there was no escape, the aunt was all-powerful.

" 'In exchange for your bicycle,' I said to the student, 'I'll get even for you. I know that Lilia doesn't want to go anywhere. There's been a terrible uproar about sending her away. Give me your bicycle.'

" 'How will you get even for me?' asked the student in alarm. But a few days later, looking like a perfect angel, I took a cure for warts to Lilia's aunt, saying that my mother had sent it over. The aunt had a large wart in a cleft beneath her lower lip. The aging lady smothered me with kisses, which gave me the feeling of being shot at point-blank with a new slingshot ... My friends, the student had his revenge. The aunt's wart sprouted a flower, a shy little wild bluebell. It swayed gently in the breeze of the aunt's breathing. Her disgrace was complete. She tore about in the courtyard, her arms flung to the heavens, throwing everyone into a panic ...

"My happiness was twofold. In the first place, my attempt to grow flowers out of warts had succeeded brilliantly. And in the second place, the student had given me his bicycle. And, my friends, in those days a bicycle was a rarity. Cyclists were still the butt of caricatures ..."

"And what became of the aunt?"

"Oh, my friend—she lived with the little flower till the autumn. She could scarcely wait for the days of strong wind, and when they finally arrived, she set out through the back alleys, avoiding the populous parts of the city, to somewhere or other in one of the garden suburbs ... Moral torments gnawed at her. She hid her face with a scarf, the little flower amiably tickled her lips, and that tickling sounded like the whisper of her melancholy younger days, like the specter of that one kiss that she'd driven away practically stamping her feet ... She stopped on the top of a hill and dropped the scarf.

"She prayed to the wind: 'Come, wind, disperse it, blow it to the four corners of the earth! Come strip away these accursed petals!'

"Out of pure meanness, the wind stopped. However, to compensate for this, a bee whose mind had snapped flew up from a neighboring dacha and took aim at the little flower. He began to weave buzzing figure eights around the poor woman. The aunt took to her heels, made it home, ordered the servants to admit no one, and sat down before her mirror to survey her face, which, already mythically enhanced by a flower, had now been stung by a bee, and was changing before her very eyes into some sort of subequatorial yam. What a horror! And simply to snip off the flower—that was too risky! It was after all a wart! One could get blood poisoning!"

Young Ivan Babichev was a jack-of-all-trades. He composed verses and little musical dramas, was very good at sketching, and knew how to do a multitude of things. He even devised a sort of dance in order to display at their best the salient features of his own person: obesity and sloth. (Like numerous remarkable people in their youth, he was a fat lout.) The name of the dance was "Little Mug." He used to sell kites, whistles, Chinese lanterns, and the boys all envied him his skill and fame. He was known in his neighborhood as "The Mechanic."

Later on Ivan Babichev did indeed graduate from the Polytechnic Institute in Petersburg as a mechanical engineer (the very same year his brother Roman was executed). Until just before the outbreak of the European

war, Ivan worked as an engineer in a shipyard in Niko-
layev, a town near Odessa.

Then . . .

II

But, was he ever really an engineer?

At the time when The Quarter was under construction,
Ivan occupied himself with an enterprise that was barely
respectable—one that for an engineer was simply disgraceful.

Picture this: In a bar he draws the portraits of all
comers, he composes extemporaneous verses on any assigned topic, reads the future in the palms of customers,
and exhibits the power of his memory by repeating any
fifty words given to him at random.

There were times when he would whip a deck of cards
out of his vest, instantly transforming his appearance into
that of a sharper, and do tricks.

People would invite him to sit down for a drink. He
would pull up a chair and then the main event would
commence: Ivan Babichev's sermon.

What would he talk about?

"We," he would say, stomping his mug against the
marble tabletop as though it were a hoof, "are humanity
raised to its ultimate limit. Strong personalities, men who
have resolved to live their own lives, egoists, stubborn
men—it is to you that I address myself, to you, the most
intelligent of all—my avant-garde! Listen to me, you in
the forefront! An epoch is ending. A wave is crashing
against the stony shore, a wave is boiling, its foam is
flashing. And what is it that you want? What? To vanish
like the drops into nothingness, like the fine watery spray?
No, my friends, you must not perish thus! No! Come to
me—I will teach you."

The audience listened to him with a certain amount of
deference, though with scant attention. They did, however, support him with shouts of "Amen!" and sometimes

with applause. He would disappear suddenly, each time reciting the same four lines of verse as his farewell. Here they are:

> I am not here to gull the proles!
> No German swindler I!
> My Soviet hand's at the controls
> And faster than the eye!

He also said something like the following:

"The gates are closing. Do you hear the panels hushing as they shut? Stay where you are! Don't try to fling yourself over the threshold! Stop! There is pride in your stillness. Be proud. I am your leader, I am the king of vulgarians. You who sing and weep and wipe the table with your nose when all the beer's been drunk and they won't serve any more—your place is here, beside me. Come all ye who are burdened by sorrow, yet sustained by song. You who commit murder in a jealous rage, and you who are weaving the noose for your own neck—I call you all, you children of these perishing years, and you also, lowbrows and dreamers, you fathers who cherish your daughters, you honest bourgeois, you people loyal to the old traditions, subject to the norms of honor, duty, love, you who fear blood and disorder, my dear ones, my soldiers and generals, come join my crusade. Whither? I shall lead you."

He loved a meal of crayfish. His hands massacred crayfish. He was not a tidy eater. His shirt, looking something like the napkin one gets in a tavern, was always unbuttoned to the middle of his chest. On top of this he would sometimes turn up with starched French cuffs. Dirty starched French cuffs. If there exists the possibility of combining soiled linen with a tendency to foppishness, he did it. Item: the bowler hat. Item: the boutonniere (which remained there so long it almost bore fruit). Item: the fringe round the bottom of his trousers and the little tails that were the sole remnants of several jacket buttons.

"I devour crayfish. Watch this: I don't eat them, I sacrifice them like a priest. See? Splendid crayfish. They are wrapped round with seaweed. Oh, isn't that seaweed? Ordinary greens, you say? What difference does it make? Let us call it seaweed—that way we can compare the crayfish to a vessel raised from the ocean floor. Splendid crayfish. From the river Kama."

He licked his fist, peered into his cuff, and extracted therefrom a morsel of crayfish.

But was he ever really an engineer? Wasn't he lying? How impossible it was to imagine him with the soul of an engineer, close to machines, to metal and blueprints! One would sooner take him for an actor or an unfrocked priest. He himself understood that his audience didn't believe him and seldom spoke without a certain mirthful gleam in the corner of his eye.

This fat little preacher would turn up now in one beer hall, now in another. Once, he went so far as to permit himself to clamber up onto a table ... Awkward and wholly unprepared for acrobatics of this sort, he crawled about over people's heads, clutching at the palm fronds. Bottles were smashed, palms upset, before he finally established himself upon the table and, waving two empty steins about as though they were dumbbells, began shouting:

"Here I stand upon the heights viewing my sprawling army! Come to me! To me! Vast is my host! You bit players, dreaming of glory on the stage! You unhappy lovers! You old maids! Accountants! Ambitious men! Fools! Knights! Cowards! Come to me! Your king has arrived—Ivan Babichev! The moment has not yet come, but soon, soon we shall make our move ... Swarm, my army!"

He tossed away his stein and grabbed an accordion out of someone's hands and expanded it across his belly. The groan that he managed to extract from it sent a perfect storm of paper napkins upwards toward the ceiling.

Men in aprons and celluloid cuffs sprang out from behind the counter.

"Beer! Beer! Give us more beer! Bring us a keg of beer! We must drink to these great events!"

But no more beer was served, the entire company was

expelled into the outer dark, and preacher Ivan, a small, heavy little man, the least of the lot, who did not readily lend himself to being ejected, was chased out after them. His stubbornness and fury made him suddenly as ponderous and immovable as a steel oil drum.

To top off the shame, they crammed his bowler down on his head.

He went down the street staggering from side to side as though he were being passed from hand to hand, emitting the while a pitiable sound halfway between singing and wailing, which distressed the passersby.

"Ophelia!" he sang. "Ophelia!" Only that one word. It seemed to float above his route, to fly over the streets, weaving itself into brilliant figure eights.

That night he visited his celebrated brother. He found the two of them sitting at one table. One opposite the other. The lamp with the green shade was in the middle. His brother Andrei and Volodia. Volodia was asleep, his head resting on a book. Ivan, drunk, made for the sofa. With much difficulty he tried to position the sofa beneath him the way one moves a chair.

"You're drunk, Ivan," said his brother.

"I hate you," Ivan replied. "You're an idol."

"You ought to be ashamed of yourself, Ivan. Lie down and go to sleep. I'll get you a pillow. Take off that bowler."

"You don't believe a word I say. You're stupid, Andrei. Don't interrupt me, or I'll smash that lampshade over Volodia's head. Shut up. Why won't you believe that Ophelia exists? Why won't you believe that I've invented a wonderful machine?"

"You haven't invented anything, Ivan. It's an obsession of yours. It's a bad joke. Have you no sense of shame, none at all? You really do think I'm a fool. All right, what sort of machine is it? Can there really be such a machine? And why Ophelia? And why must you wear a bowler? What are you—a chimney sweep or an ambassador?"

Ivan was silent for a moment. Then, with every appearance of having sobered up instantly, he stood up and advanced on his brother with clenched fists:

"You don't believe it? You don't believe it? Stand up, Andrei, stand up when you're addressed by the leader of an army of many millions. How dare you disbelieve me? You say there is no such machine? Andrei, you have my word on it: That machine will be the death of you."

"Don't make such a fuss," his brother answered. "You'll wake Volodia."

"I spit on your Volodia. I know you, I know what you've got planned. You want to marry my daughter to Volodia. You want to develop a new breed. My daughter is no incubator. You won't get her. I won't give her to Volodia. I'd sooner strangle her with these hands."

He paused and then, his eyes bright with merriment and his hands plunged into his pockets as though to support his protruding belly, said, in a voice exuding malice:

"You are wrong, brother mine. You're pulling the wool over your own eyes. Ho-ho, what a sweetheart. You think you love Volodia because Volodia is the New Man? Purest banana oil, my dear Andryusha! That's not it at all—it's something altogether different . . ."

"What then?" Andrei asked angrily.

"Why, you're simply getting old, Andryusha. You simply need a son, that's all. You're simply experiencing the emotions of a father. The family, Andrei—the family is eternal. But to select as the symbol of the new world an unremarkable young man whose one skill involves a soccer ball—that is preposterous . . ."

Volodia raised his head.

"Greetings to the Edison of the new age!" exclaimed Ivan. "Hooray!" And he made an extravagant bow.

Volodia stared at him in silence. Ivan dissolved in laughter.

"What's the matter, Edison? You also can't believe there's such a thing as Ophelia?"

"You, Ivan Petrovich," said Volodia sleepily, "ought to be committed to Kanatchikov's institute."

Andrei snorted.

At this, the preacher threw his bowler onto the floor. "Scoundrels!" he shouted. And after a pause: "Andrei! You permit this? Why do you allow this hanger-on to insult your own brother?"

At this point Ivan could not see his brother's eyes—he could see only the glinting of the lenses.

"Ivan," said Andrei, "I shall have to ask you never to come to my house again. You are not a madman. You are a pig."

III

Everyone was talking about the new preacher.

From the beer parlors the rumor bounced around the apartments, thence up the back stairs to the communal kitchens, where, at the hour of the morning toilet, the hour of the lighting of the Primus stoves, some people were watching the milk about to boil over while others were dancing about washing themselves under the spigot and they were all swapping the gossip.

The rumor penetrated into offices, into rest homes, into markets.

A story was concocted about how an unknown citizen came to a wedding in the house of a tax collector on the Yakimanka (a bowler-hatted, shabby, suspicious-looking man: They got the details right, so it could only have been Ivan Babichev) and how he stood up before everyone at the very height of the solemnities, demanded to be heard, and addressed himself to the newlyweds, saying:

"Forget this love you have for each other. Forget your desire to be conjoined. Bridegroom, forsake your bride. What will be the issue of this union? You will bring into the world your own enemy. He will devour you."

The groom was ready for a fight. The bride collapsed on the floor in a faint. The guest departed in a towering rage, and it was immediately discovered, so the story went, that the port in all the bottles on the wedding table had turned to water.

Yet another remarkable story was invented.

According to this story, an automobile containing a solid citizen, a fat, red-cheeked man with a briefcase on his lap, was driving through some bustling intersection (some said it was Neglinnaya at the Kuznetsky Bridge, others Tverskaya at Strastny Monastery).

And then this man's brother Ivan, that same notorious little person, is supposed to have dashed out of the crowd on the sidewalk. He had caught sight of his brother's car rolling along and now stood directly in its path, his arms flung wide like a scarecrow or like a man trying to stop a runaway horse. The driver managed to brake in time. He beeped the horn, still inching forward, but the scarecrow wouldn't get out of the way.

"Stop!" shouted the little man at the top of his voice. "Stop, Commissar! Stop, kidnapper!"

And there was nothing the driver could do but step on the brake. The flow of traffic came to a sudden halt. Many cars all but reared on their heels as they slammed into the ones ahead of them, and a bus, blaring like an elephant, stopped abruptly, trembling all over, eager to obey, to lift its pachydermous tires and back away ... The man standing in the roadway with his arms outstretched demanded silence.

And the silence was total.

"Brother," said the little man, "why is it that you ride in a car and I go on foot? Open the door, move over, and let me in. I also find it unsuitable to walk. You are a leader, but I am also a leader."

And when they heard these words people did indeed come running up to him from all sides; some leapt out of the bus, others emerged from the nearby beer parlors, still others rushed over from the boulevard, and the one who had been sitting in the open limousine, his brother, now stood up, a huge man, his size magnified by his standing in a car, and found himself confronted by a living barricade.

The sight of him was so terrifying that it seemed as though he might at any moment take one step across the car, over the driver's back, toward them, the barricade, and fall down the whole length of the street upon them like a tower . . .

As for Ivan, he was quite literally lifted up on a platform of hands. He was raised above the heads of his adherents. He would rock about, drop out of sight, and reappear bolt upright. His bowler had ridden back on his head, revealing the large, bright forehead of a tired man.

And his brother Andrei, grabbing him by the trousers where his belt should have been, pulled him down from these heights and flung him into the arms of a policeman. "To the GPU!" he said.

No sooner had these magical initials been uttered than everything suddenly shot upwards out of its lethargy: Spokes gleamed, wheel bushings whirred into action, car doors slammed, and all of those actions that had been in progress before the onset of lethargy pursued their further development.

Ivan was held under arrest for ten days.

When he was set free his drinking companions asked him whether it was true that he had been arrested on the street by his own brother under such extraordinary circumstances. He laughed.

"That is all lies. A legend. I was simply picked up in a beer parlor and detained. I imagine they'd had me under surveillance for a long time. Still, it's good that legends are already being made up. The end of an era, the transitional period, these demand their own legends and fairy tales. Goodness—I'm glad to know that I shall be the hero of one of those tales. And there is to be still another legend, the legend of the machine called Ophelia . . . The age will die with my name on its lips. That is the aim of all my striving . . ."

They let him go with threats that next time he would be deported.

What might the GPU have charged him with?

"You called yourself a king?" his investigator asked.

"Yes. King of vulgarians."

"What's that supposed to mean?"

"Don't you see . . . I'm opening the eyes of a large category of people . . ."

"Opening their eyes to what?"

"To a realization of the fact that they're doomed."

"You said 'a large category of people.' Just whom do you have in mind?"

"Everyone whom you call decadent. The carriers of decadent tendencies. With your permission, I can explain this in greater detail."

"I should be much obliged."

". . . and a whole range of human feelings, it seems to me, ought to be eradicated."

"For instance? Feelings of . . . ?"

". . . of pity, of tenderness, of pride, of jealousy, of love—in a word, practically all the feelings that constituted the human soul in the era which is now coming to an end. The era of socialism will replace these earlier feelings with a new series of human soul-states."

"I see."

"I see you understand me. The communist who has been bitten by the serpent of jealousy is subject to persecution. And the communist with a heart touched by pity is also persecuted. The buttercup of pity, the lizard of vanity, the serpent of jealousy—all this flora and fauna must be driven out of the heart of the new man.

"Please forgive me, I tend to speak in a highly colored manner, in a manner that may even seem to you rather flowery, no? You follow me? I do thank you. Water? No thanks, I don't require any water . . . I like speaking beautifully . . .

"We know that the grave of a Komsomol youth who has taken his own life is bedecked in turn by wreaths and by the curses of his fellow Komsomol members. The man of the new world says that suicide is a decadent act. But a man of the old world used to say: He was obliged to take his own life in order to preserve his honor. Thus we see that the new man schools himself to despise the ancient sentiments glorified by poets and by the very muse of history. So there you have it. It is my wish to organize the last parade of these sentiments."

"And that is what you call the conspiracy of sentiments?"

"Yes. That is the conspiracy of sentiments, of which I am the head."

"Go on."

"Yes. I should like to gather round me a sort of troupe—you understand what I mean?

"For it is entirely possible, don't you see, that the old sentiments were splendid. There are for instance examples of a great love for a woman or for one's native land. For God knows what! You must admit that even today men are stirred by such memories. They *are*, you know! And so I should like . . .

". . . it sometimes happens, you know, that a light bulb will suddenly go out. Burnt out, you say. But you take this burnt-out bulb and shake it and it will flare up and burn for a while longer. There's a disaster inside the bulb. The tungsten filaments have parted. But the bulb comes alive again when the pieces are reunited. A short, unnatural, obviously doomed life—a fever, an excessive brilliance, a burst of light. Then—darkness, life will return no more, and now if you shake the dead, burnt-out filaments they will only tinkle in the darkness. Do you understand what I'm saying? But how splendid was that brief shining . . . !

"I want to shake . . . I want to shake the heart of a burnt-out epoch. The heart bulb, so that the fragments of filament will come into contact again . . .

". . . and call forth that momentary bright splendor . . .

". . . I want to find representatives from back there, from what you call the old world. Those are the feelings I have in mind: jealousy, love for a woman, ambition. I want to find a sort of fool so that I can demonstrate him to you and say: Here, comrades, is a specimen of that human condition that is called 'foolishness.'

". . . Many characters played parts in the comedy of the

old world. The curtain is coming down. The players must now come stage front and speak the final couplets. I want to be the intermediary between them and the audience. I shall direct the chorus and be the last to leave the stage.

"... The honor has fallen to me of conducting the ancient human feelings on their last parade ...

"... History has her brilliant eye trained upon us through the eye slits of her mask. And I want to show her: Here is one in love, here is an ambitious man, here is a traitor, here a man of reckless bravery, here a faithful friend, here a prodigal son—here they are, carriers of those great emotions that are now deemed to be worthless and vulgar. For one last time before they disappear, before they become objects of ridicule, let them appear with maximum intensity.

"... I hear someone else's conversation. They are talking about a razor. About a madman who cut his own throat. A woman's name flits through their talk. He didn't die, the madman, they sewed up his wound and he slit his throat again in the same place. Who is he? Show him to me, I need him, I'm looking for him. And for her, too. I'm looking for the demon woman and the tragic lover. But where am I to look for him? In Sklifossovsky Hospital? And for her? Who is she? A clerk? A woman in business for herself?

"... It's hard for me to find heroes.

"... There are no heroes.

"... I peer in through other people's windows, climb up other people's stairs. I sometimes pursue someone's smile, leaping about the way a naturalist chases a butterfly. I feel like shouting: 'Stop! What are the blossoms on that shrub from which the fleeting and hasty butterfly of your smile just emerged? What emotion is that the shrub of? Is it the pink sweetbrier of grief or the black currant of petty vanity? Stop! I need you ... '

"... I want to gather round me a multitude. So as to have a choice, to be able to select from among them the best, the most brilliant, a sort of elite, if you will, an elite group of the emotions.

"... Yes, it is a conspiracy, a peaceful revolution. A peaceful demonstration of the emotions.

"... Let's say that I locate somewhere a full-blooded, one hundred percent ambitious man. I'll say to him: Flaunt it! Show them, those people who are forever getting in your way, show them what *real* ambition is. Do something so outrageous that they will say: Oh! What vulgar ambition! Oh! Will ambition stop at nothing! Or suppose I have the good fortune to find a person of the most ideal frivolity. I'll say the same to him: Flaunt it, show the world how powerful frivolity can be, make the crowd wring their hands in dismay.

"... Human souls are in the power of these emotions. One soul is ruled by the spirit of pride, another by the spirit of pity. I want to extract them, these devils, and then turn them loose in the public arena."

Investigator: Right. And have you managed to find any such persons yet?

Ivan: I've been searching for a long time, a very long time. It is very hard. I may have been misunderstood. But I did find *one*.

Investigator: Who was that?

Ivan: You want the emotion he was carrying, or his name?

Investigator: Both.

Ivan: Nikolai Kavalerov. Envy.

IV

They walked away from the mirror.

Now the two comedians were walking along together. One, the shorter and fatter one, always kept one pace ahead of the other. This was a habit of Ivan Babichev's. In order to talk to his companion he was forever obliged to look backwards. Whenever he had to utter a long sentence—and his sentences were never short—he not infrequently collided, his head turned round toward his companion, with people coming from the opposite direction. He would then instantly whip the bowler hat off his head and burst into a flood of grandiloquent apologies. He was a courteous man. His face was never without its affable smile.

The day was closing up its shop. A rosy-cheeked, bearded gypsy in a blue vest was carrying on his shoulder a clean brass basin. The day was withdrawing on the shoulder of a gypsy. The disk of the basin was bright and blind. The gypsy walked slowly, the basin rocked gently, and the day turned round in the disk.

The travelers watched it go.

And the disk set, like the sun. The day was done.

The travelers immediately went into a beer parlor.

Kavalerov told Ivan the story of how an important personage had thrown him out of the house. He didn't mention the name. Ivan told him the identical story of how an important personage had thrown him out, too.

"And you probably know him. Everyone knows him. He's my brother, Andrei Petrovich Babichev. Have you heard of him?"

Kavalerov turned red and looked down. He didn't answer.

"So our fates are similar, and we have to be friends," said Ivan, beaming. "And I like the name Kavalerov: It's pompous *and* third-rate."

Kavalerov thought: That's me, all right—pompous and third-rate.

"Splendid beer," Ivan exclaimed. "The Poles say 'she has eyes the color of beer.' Good, no?"

". . . but the main thing is that that important personage, my brother, has stolen my daughter from me.

". . . I'll pay my brother back for that.

". . . He stole my daughter. Well, not literally 'stole,' of course. And don't pop your eyes, Kavalerov. And it wouldn't be a bad idea, either, to get a smaller nose. With a nose that thick you've got to be as famous as a hero in order to have a little everyday happiness. He used psychological pressure on her. And you can sue for that, can't you? I ought to take him to court, right? She left me. I

don't even blame Andrei as much as I do that bastard that
lives with him."

He told him about Volodia.

Kavalerov twiddled his big toes in embarrassment.

" . . . That brat has spoiled my life. Oh, if only he'd bust
a kidney on that soccer field! Andrei takes his every word
as gospel. This brat is the 'New Man,' don't you see! The
brat said that Valia was unhappy because I, her father,
was crazy and I was systematically (that bastard!) driving
her crazy. The bastard! They talked her into it together.
And Valia ran away. One of her girl friends gave her a
place to stay. I've put a curse on that girl friend. My curse
was that the two ends of her alimentary canal should swap
places. But you do see the pattern in all this? This bunch
of idiots . . .

" . . . the best, purest, most splendid light of all our culture was Woman. I was looking for a creature of the female sex. I was looking for a creature who would combine
all feminine qualities. I was looking for the very ovary of
femininity.The Feminine was the glory of the past age. I
wanted to make a brilliant display of this Feminine. We're
dying, Kavalerov. I wanted to carry Woman aloft like a
torch. I thought that Woman might be extinguished along
with our era. The millennia are like some garbage pit. The
pit is littered with machines, bits of scrap iron, tin, screws,
springs. It's a dark gloomy hole. But there's a glow from
the rotting wood, the phosphorescent fungi, the mold.
Those are our feelings! That's all there is left of our feelings, the flowering of our souls. The New Man comes up
to the pit, scrounges around, crawls into it, picks out what
he needs—some machine part that's still got some good in
it, a wrench maybe—but he crushes the rotting wood
under his foot and stamps out its glow. I dreamed of finding a woman who would blossom in this pit with the
flower of an unheard-of feeling. Like the miraculous flowering of a fern. So that the New Man who came to steal
our iron would be terrified, would snatch back his hand,
close his eyes against the blinding light of what had
seemed to him nothing but rotting wood.

". . . I found such a creature. Right beside me. Valia. I thought that Valia would shine forth above the dying age, light its path toward the great burial ground. But I was mistaken. She fluttered away. She left the bedside of the dying age. I thought that Woman was on our side, that tenderness and love were ours alone—but there I was mistaken. So here am I, the last dreamer on earth, wandering about the edge of the pit like a wounded bat."

Kavalerov thought: "I'll tear Valia away from them." He felt like telling about what he had witnessed in the side street with the flowering hedge. But something held him back.

"Our fates are similar," Ivan went on. "Give me your hand. So. I salute you. Very happy to see you, young man. Let us clink glasses. So you were thrown out, eh, Kavalerov? Go on, tell me about it. Oh, but you've already told me. It was a very important personage who kicked you out? You don't want to mention his name? Well, all right. You hate this man intensely."

Kavalerov nods.

"Oh, my dear fellow, how clearly I see it all! If I have correctly understood you, you have played a dirty trick on a powerful man. Don't interrupt me. You have conceived a hatred for a man who is universally esteemed. In your opinion, of course, it was he who insulted you. Don't interrupt me. Drink your beer.

". . . You are certain that he is the one who stands in the way of your getting on in the world, that he had taken away your rights, that he is running things in the very spot where, in your opinion, *you* ought to be running things. And you are furious . . ."

Somewhere in the smoke floats an orchestra. The pale face of the violinist is lying upon his violin.

"The violin looks like the violinist himself," says Ivan. "It is a little violinist in a wooden tailcoat. Do you hear? The wood is singing. Do you hear the voice of the wood? Wood sings with different voices in an orchestra. But how awful their playing is! God, how awful!"

He turned to the musicians.

"You think that's a drum you have? You think that's a drum playing its part? No—that is the god of music beating on you with his fist!

". . . My friend, envy is eating away at us. We envy the coming age. It is the envy of old age, if you like. The envy of a human generation that is undergoing its first experience of aging. Let us talk about envy. Give us some more beer . . ."

They were sitting near a wide window.

It had rained again. It was evening. The city glistened as though it had been carved out of Cardiff coal. The people outside on Samoteka Street looked in at the window, flattening their noses on the glass.

". . . yes, envy. A drama is to be played out here, one of those grandiose dramas in the theater of history that evoke long fits of weeping, ecstasy, pity, and anger from humanity. However little you yourself realize it, you are the bearer of a historical mission. You are, so to speak, a clot. An age is dying and you are its clot of envy. A dying age envies the one that is coming to replace it."

"What should I do?" asked Kavalerov.

"My dear fellow, you must make your peace with things as they are—either that or . . . raise hell. Or you have to go out with a bang. Slam the door, as they say. That's the main thing: Go out with a bang. Leave history with a scar on her face, explode in her face and to hell with it. Because she's not going to let you in, no matter what. Don't give up without a fight . . . I want to tell you about something that happened when I was a child.

"Someone gave a ball. The children put on a play and danced a ballet on a stage that had been specially built in a large reception room. And there was a little girl—do you know the sort I mean?—a perfectly typical little girl, twelve years old, with thin little legs, in a short dress, all rosy, satiny, all dressed up, and her whole figure made the impression, you know, with all the flounces and ribbons, of what they call a 'snapdragon,' a sort of flower—a beauty, stuck up, spoiled, tossing her curls—well, that little girl was the belle of the ball. She was the queen. She did whatever she pleased and everyone was in raptures over her, everything originated with her and everything gravitated toward her. She was better than anyone else at dancing, singing, jumping, thinking up games. She received the best presents, the best candy, flowers, oranges, and compliments ... I was thirteen, a Gymnasium student. She completely overshadowed me, although I was also accustomed to people going into raptures over me, I was also spoiled by admirers. I was top boy in my own class, I took all the prizes. I couldn't stand it. I caught the little girl in a hallway and beat her up, tore off her ribbons, pulled her curls in all directions, and covered her charming little face with scratches. I grabbed her by the back of the neck and banged her forehead against a column several times. At that moment I loved that little girl more than life itself, I adored her, and hated her with every fiber of my being. I thought that by tearing apart her beautiful curls I would cover her with shame, blow away her rosiness, her glamour, I thought I was correcting a mistake that everyone else had made. But nothing turned out that way. The shame fell on me. I was thrown out. *But,* my dear fellow, I was talked about the rest of the evening, *and* I ruined the ball for them, *and* my name was on everyone's lips wherever the little beauty appeared ... That was my first experience of envy. It's a terrible heartburn, envy. It's an awful burden! Envy crushes your throat like a spasm, it knocks your eyes out of their sockets. While I was beating her up there in the hallway, my victim, my captive, tears were pouring out of my eyes, I was choking—and still I kept on tearing her charming clothes, wincing at having to touch satin. It almost set my teeth on edge. You know what satin is like, the surface of satin, you know how one touch of it goes through your whole spine, your entire nervous system, and makes you wince! So every force of nature rose up against me to defend that nasty little brat. Revulsion, like a poison lurking in bushes and baskets, flowed out of what had seemed so captivatingly innocent in the ballroom, from her dress, tne pink satin that was such a feast for the eyes. I don't remember whether I shouted anything while I was having my revenge. I probably whispered: You had this coming! Keep out of my way! Don't touch what belongs to me ...

"Are you taking in everything I say? I want to draw a sort of analogy. I have in mind the struggle between epochs. Of course, at first glance the comparison might seem frivolous. But you understand what I'm talking about? I'm talking about envy."

The musicians had finished their piece.

"Oh, thank God," said Ivan, "they've shut up. Look at that—the cello. It didn't shine anything like that before they got hold of it. They put it through a long torture. Now it glistens as though it were wet—it's a completely refreshed cello. You ought to write down these sayings of mine, Kavalerov. I don't talk, I incise my words on marble. Isn't that so?

"My dear fellow, we used to win all the prizes, we were also spoiled by admirers, we were also accustomed to run things back home—back home? where?—why, back home in the age that is now growing dim. Oh, how splendid is the age now rising up, how brilliant is the celebration to which we shall never be admitted! Everything originates with it, this new age, everything gravitates to it, it will get all the presents and the praise. I love it, this world that is moving in on me, more than life itself, I adore it and I hate it with every fiber of my being! I'm choking, tears are pouring out of my eyes like hailstones, but I want to get my fingers into its clothes and tear it apart. Keep out of my way! Don't touch what belongs to me!

". . . we must have our revenge. You and I—there are many thousands of us—we must have our revenge. Kavalerov! Enemies don't always turn out to be windmills. It occasionally happens that what you would very much like to take for a windmill is in fact an enemy, an aggressor, a bearer of ruin and death. Your enemy, Kavalerov, is a real enemy. Take your revenge on him. Believe me, we're going out with a bang. We'll take the young world down a notch or two. We aren't exactly made of cotton candy ourselves. We've also been the darlings of history.

"... get yourself talked about, Kavalerov! It's clear enough that everything's going to hell, everything's on schedule, there's no way out—you're going to perish, big nose! The humiliations are going to multiply by the minute; with every new day your enemy, like that coddled youth, is going to flourish all the more. You're done for—that's clear. So decorate your ruin a bit, embellish it with fireworks, tear the clothes off the one who's in your way, take your leave in such a way that your 'good-bye' will thunder down the ages."

Kavalerov thought: "He's reading my mind."

"They insulted you? They kicked you out?"

"They insulted me terribly," Kavalerov said heatedly. "They humiliated me for a long time."

"Who insulted you? One of the chosen people of this age?"

Kavalerov wanted to shout, "Your brother! The same one who insulted you, too!" But he said nothing.

"You were lucky. You know the aggressor by sight. You have a concrete enemy. So have I."

"What should I do?"

"You're lucky. You can avenge yourself and at the same time avenge the epoch that gave you birth."

"But what should I do?"

"Kill him. Leave behind you the honorable memory of having been the hired assassin of an age. Crush your enemy on the threshold of two epochs. He's putting on airs, he thinks he's already arrived, he's already the genius, the cupid twining with his scroll about the gate of the new world—his nose is so high in the air he can't even see us—give him a good clout in farewell. I give you my blessing. And I (here Ivan lifted up his beer mug), I too am going to destroy my enemy. Let us drink, Kavalerov, to Ophelia. That is the weapon of my vengeance."

Kavalerov opened his mouth to say what was uppermost in his mind: We have the same enemy, you've given me your blessing to kill your brother. But he said not a word, for at that moment a man walked up to their table and invited Ivan to follow him instantly without asking any questions. He was arrested, as we have already mentioned in the previous chapter.

"Good-bye, my dear fellow," said Ivan, "they're taking me to Golgotha. Go to my daughter (he named the street that had long since been radiant in Kavalerov's memory), go and have a look at her. You'll see that if a creature like that could betray us, then there's nothing left but revenge."

He drank up his beer and walked off one pace ahead of the mysterious man.

On his way he winked at the other customers, wasted smiles in the most prodigal fashion, squinted into the mouth of the clarinet, and, when he'd reached the door, turned round, held his bowler in his outstretched hand, and declaimed the following:

> I am not here to gull the proles!
> No German swindler I!
> My Soviet hand's at the controls
> And faster than the eye!

V

"What are you laughing at? You think I'm sleepy?" asked Volodia.

"I wasn't laughing. I was coughing."

And Volodia began to drop off again, practically before he'd reached the chair.

The younger man got tired sooner. The other, the older, Andrei Babichev, was a giant. He worked all day and then worked half the night. Andrei struck the table with his fist. The lampshade jumped like the lid of a teakettle, but the young man slept on. The lampshade jumped. Andrei recalled James Watt looking at the lid of a teakettle jumping about over the steam.

Well-known legend. Well-known picture.

James Watt inventing the steam engine.

"What will you invent, my James Watt? What sort of

machine will you invent, Volodia? What new secret of nature will you discover, New Man?"

And now Andrei Babichev's conversation with himself was beginning. For the merest moment he would put aside his work and look at the sleeping youth and think as follows:

"But suppose Ivan is right? Maybe I am nothing more than a plain ordinary man with a yearning to have a family? Maybe that is the reason I love him, that he's lived with me since he was a boy—I simply got used to him and loved him as though he was my son. Is that all it is? That simple? But suppose he'd turned out to be a dunce? Everything I live for is concentrated in him. I had a stroke of luck. It's a long way off, the life of new humanity. I believe in it. And I had a stroke of luck. Here it is, sleeping so close to me, my splendid new world. The new world is living in my house. I dote on him. As a son? A support? Someone to close my eyelids on my deathbed? No! That's not what I need! I don't want to die in some four-poster, propped up on pillows. I know it will be the masses and not some family that will witness my last breath. Nonsense! I cherish him just as we cherish that new world. And I love him as a hope made flesh. I'll kick him out if I'm wrong about him, if he isn't new, if he isn't completely different from me, because I'm still mired up to my waist in the old world and there's no longer any chance that I'll crawl out of it. I'll kick him out then, I don't need a son, I'm not a father and he isn't my son, we aren't a family. I'm the one who had faith in him and he's the one who justified that faith.

"We aren't a family—we are humanity.

"Which means—what? Which means that one must eliminate the human feeling of paternal love? But why does he love me, he, the new man? So there, in the new world, the love between father and son will also flourish. Then I have a right to rejoice; I have the right to love him both as a son and as the new man. Ivan, Ivan, your conspiracy is pointless. Not *all* the emotions are going to perish. You're frantic over nothing, Ivan! There'll be *something* left."

One dark night a very long time ago two figures were running, falling into gullies, splashing up to their knees in reflected stars, flushing more stars from bushes—a Commissar and a boy. The boy had saved the Commissar's life. The Commissar was enormous, the boy very small. Anyone seeing them would have thought that only one figure was running, the giant, forever stumbling to the ground, and the boy might have seemed merely the palm of the giant's hand.

They had joined together for good.

The boy lived with the giant, grew, developed, became a member of the Komsomol, and finally a student. He had been born in a railroad workers' settlement, the son of a repairman.

His friends loved him, grown-ups loved him. He worried occasionally over being liked by everyone—it seemed to him at times that it was wrong, undeserved. His feeling of comradeship was his strongest trait. As though striving for some sort of equilibrium, for the correction of some error that nature had made in the allotment of her gifts, he even resorted at times to certain devious means of moderating the esteem in which he was held, of lowering it, of dimming his own brilliance.

He felt like recompensing his less successful companions by his devotion to them, his readiness for self-sacrifice, the ardent testimony of his friendship, and by searching in each of them for whatever remarkable traits and abilities they might possess.

Associating with him, his comrades were spurred on to compete.

"I was thinking," he once said, "why it is that people get angry and offended. Such people have no concept of time. They are ignorant of technology. For surely time is also a technical concept. If everyone was a technician, spite and vanity and all the other petty feelings would vanish. That makes you smile? But you see, one must understand time in order to free oneself from petty feelings. Resentment, let's say, can last for an hour or a year. People have enough imagination for a year. But a thousand years—that's beyond their range. They see only three or four of the calibrations on a clock face, they crawl, they bustle about ... It's too much for them! They can't encompass the whole dial. In fact, just try telling them what a dial is—they won't believe you!"

"But why should it be only the petty feelings? Because lofty feelings are also short-lived. How about ... magnanimity?"

"Well, you see. Let me explain. In magnanimity there is a certain rightness—a technical rightness. Don't smile. *Yes.* No, really ... I seem to have lost track of what I was going to say. You've mixed me up. No, wait! The Revolution was ... what? Very cruel, of course. God, was it cruel! But cruel for the sake of what? It was magnanimous, right? It was kind—kind enough for the whole dial! Right? You've got to be angry not just between 10:30 and 10:32 but right around the whole clock face ... Then there's no difference between cruelty and magnanimity. Then there's only one thing: time. The ironclad logic of history, as they say. And history and time are one and the same—doubles. Don't laugh, Andrei Petrovich. I say that a man's principal feeling must be the understanding of time."

He also said:

"The bourgeois world won't be so high and mighty when I'm through with it. They make fun of us. Their old men keep snuffling: Where are your engineers, your surgeons, your professors, your inventors? I'll collect a big group of my comrades, around a hundred of them, and we'll organize a union, a union for taking the bourgeois world down a peg or two. You think I'm boasting? You don't understand a thing. I'm not the least bit carried away. We'll work like dogs. You'll see. They'll beat a path to our door. And Valia will be in our group."

He woke up.

"I had a dream," said he, laughing. "I was sitting on a roof with Valia and looking at the moon through a telescope."

"What? You said what? A telescope?"

"And I told her, 'Look over there in the lower part—that's the Sea of Crises,' and she said, 'the Sea of Mices?' "

In the spring of that year Volodia went away for a short visit to his father in Murom. His father worked in a plant in Murom building locomotives. Early in the morning of the third day of this separation Andrei was in the back seat of his car, headed for home. The chauffeur slowed down at a corner, and there was enough daylight for Andrei to see a man slumped against a wall.

The sight of the man lying on the grating suddenly recalled to his mind the absent Volodia. It prompted him to sit bolt upright and lean toward the driver. "But they have of course absolutely nothing in common," Andrei all but shouted. And in actual fact, there was not the slightest resemblance between the man lying on the street and the absent Volodia. The simple fact was that he aroused in Andrei a vivid presentiment of Volodia. The thought crossed his mind: And what if something or other had put Volodia in the same position? So he simply acted foolishly and gave free rein to his sentimentality. The car stopped.

Nikolai Kavalerov was picked up and attention was paid to his hallucinated babble.

Andrei took him home, dragged him up to the fourth floor, and laid him on Volodia's sofa, making it into a bed for him and covering him up to the neck with a blanket. The newcomer lay flat on his back, the waffle imprint of the grating on his cheeks. The host went off to sleep the sleep of the just: His sofa was no longer vacant.

That same night he dreamt that the young man had hanged himself on a telescope.

VI

There was a remarkable bed in Anichka Prokopovich's room. It was made of an expensive wood, covered with a dark cherry lacquer, and on the inner face of the head-board and the footboard there were inset mirrors in the shape of arcs.

Once, at a fair that took place during a profoundly tran-quil year, to the sound of fanfares and littered with con-fetti, Anichka's husband had mounted a wooden platform, showed his lottery ticket, and received from the master of ceremonies a document conferring upon him the right to own the remarkable bed. It was carried off in a cart. Small boys whistled. The blue sky was reflected in the moving arcs of the mirrors so that they looked exactly like beauti-ful eyes opening and slowly closing.

The family lived on, then fell to pieces, and the bed passed intact through all its vicissitudes.

Kavalerov is now living in the corner behind the bed.

He had come to Anichka and said: "I can pay you thirty rubles a month for the corner."

And Anichka, with a long-drawn-out smile, had agreed. He had nowhere to go. A new tenant had settled solidly into his old room. The frightful bed upon which he had formerly slept Kavalerov had sold for four rubles, and it had groaned as it left him.

Anichka's bed resembled an organ.

It occupied half the room, and its upper parts were lost in the murk of the ceiling.

"If I were a child," thought Kavalerov, "Anichka's little son, how many poetical, magical fabrications would flow out of my childish imagination, gripped by the powerful aspect of such an extraordinary object! I'm a grown-up now, and now I grasp only the general outline and one or two of the details, but as a child I might have . . .

". . . But as a child, completely independent of distance, scale, time, weight, and gravity, I might have crawled along the corridors formed by the empty space between the springs and the side of the bed; I might have hidden behind those columns that now seem to me no larger than graduated cyclinders; I might have set up imaginary cata-pults on its barricades and fired at my enemies, who were exhausting their strength by fleeing across the soft spongy

earth of the blanket; I might have received foreign emis-
saries under the arc of a mirror, like the king in the novel
I'd just read; I might have set out on fantastic journeys
over the carvings, higher and higher, over the legs and
backsides of the cupids, crawling over them the way one
crawls over a statue of the Buddha, too large to be seen all
at once; and from the topmost arch, from that dizzying
height, I might have leapt down into the terrifying abyss,
the icy abyss of the pillows ..."

Ivan Babichev is leading Kavalerov along a green
bank ... The fluff of dandelions flies out from under their
feet—and its floating is a dynamic representation of the
heat. Babichev is pale from the heat. His round face glistens as though the heat were sculpting a mask out of his
face.

"This way!" he commands.

The environs of the city are in bloom.

They cut across some waste ground and walk along
fences behind which Alsatian dogs bark frantically, rattling their chains. Kavalerov whistles at the Alsatians to
tease them—but anything could happen: Suppose one of
them broke loose from his chain and leapt over the fence?
This is why a capsule of terror is dissolving somewhere in
the pit of the teaser's stomach.

The travelers descend a flourishing slope, practically on
the roofs of little red houses, along the tops of their gardens, a locale unfamiliar to Kavalerov, and, although he
can see the towers of the Krestovsky Prison ahead of him,
he has no notion of where he is. Locomotive whistles can
be heard, and the metallic clashing of trains.

"I shall show you my machine," says Ivan, looking back
at Kavalerov. "Go ahead and pinch yourself ... like that
... and again ... and again. It's not a dream, right? Remember that—you weren't asleep. Remember that it was
all quite simple. You and I crossed some waste ground, we
saw a gleaming puddle that never dries up, we saw some
pots hanging on the top of a fence. Remember, my friend,
there were some remarkable things to be seen in the trash

along our path, against the fences, in the ditches. Look at that for instance—a page from a book—lean down and have a look at it before the wind carries it away—you see: an illustration to *Taras Bulba*—recognize it?—it must have been thrown out of that window there when it had finished its function as the wrapping of some victuals. What is that, farther along? The eternal, traditional cast-off boot in a ditch. It's not worth our attention—as an image of desolation it is far too academic! Farther on is a bottle. Wait, it's still in one piece, but tomorrow a cart wheel will smash it, and if some other dreamer wastes no time in retracing our steps he will have the full satisfaction of contemplating the celebrated bottle glass, those celebrated fragments, hymned by writers for their ability suddenly to emerge from the garbage and desolation and provide lonely travelers with all sorts of mirages. Observe, my friend, observe: Here are buttons and hoops, there are shreds of bandage, there are the Babylonian towers of petrified human egesta. In a word, my friend, it is the ordinary landscape of waste ground. Remember it. It was all quite simple. And I was taking you to show you my machine. Pinch yourself. Like that. So it's not a dream? Fine. Because later on I know what will happen—later on you'll say that you weren't well, that it was too hot, that you might have imagined many things simply on account of the heat, your tiredness, and so on . . . No, my friend, I demand that you solemnly affirm that you are in the most normal state of mind. What you are about to see might prove to be excessively shocking to you."

Kavalerov solemnly affirmed: "I am in the most normal state of mind."

And there was a fence, a low board fence.

"It's there," said Ivan. "Wait a moment. Let's sit down—over here, above the little gully. I was telling you that what I had dreamt of was the machine of machines, the universal machine. I had in mind the perfect instrument. My hope was to concentrate in one small apparatus hundreds of different functions. Yes, my friend. It was a splendid, a noble problem. For something like this it was worth becoming a fanatic. My thought was to tame the mastodon of technology, to make him docile and domesticated, to give man a lever, so simple and familiar that he would not be afraid of it, that he would be as accustomed to it as to the bolt on the door ..."

"I have no understanding of mechanics," said Kavalerov. "I'm afraid of machines."

"And I succeeded. Listen to me, Kavalerov. I invented such a machine."

(The fence beckoned, and, yet, the likeliest of all hypotheses was that the ordinary gray boards concealed no secret of any kind.)

"It can blow up mountains. It can fly. It lifts heavy weights. It crushes ore. It can replace the kitchen stove, the perambulator, long-range artillery ... It is the quintessential genius of mechanism."

"What are you smiling at, Ivan Petrovich?"

(Ivan had a twinkle in the corner of his eye.)

"I am in bloom. I cannot speak about it without my heart bouncing about like an egg in boiling water. Listen to me. I endowed it with hundreds of abilities. I've invented a machine that is capable of doing everything. Do you understand? You'll see in a moment, but ..."

He stood up and, laying his hand on Kavalerov's shoulder, said in solemn tones:

"But I forbade it to do everything. One fine day I understood that I had been given the supernatural power to avenge my age. I ruined the machine. Deliberately. Out of spite."

He burst into a happy laugh.

"No, just try to understand, Kavalerov, what an enormous satisfaction it was. I endowed the supreme accomplishment of technology with the basest of human feelings! I disgraced the machine. I avenged my era, the era that provided me with that brain inside my skull, the brain that conceived the astonishing machine ... To whom was I to leave it? The new world? They're eating us alive—they're swallowing the nineteenth century the way a boa constrictor swallows a rabbit. They chew us up and digest us. What they find useful they absorb, what they find harmful they throw out. Our feelings they throw away, but they absorb our technology! I'll have revenge on behalf of our feelings. They won't get my machine, they aren't going to utilize me, absorb my brain . . . My machine might have made the new era happy right away, from the very first days of its existence, by introducing technology at the summit of its development. But now they aren't going to get it! My machine is the blinding insult offered by the dying age to the one being born. Their mouths will water the moment they glimpse it. Just think—a machine! Their idol, a machine! And suddenly this best of all machines is going to turn out to be a liar and a slut, a sentimental good-for-nothing! Let's go—I'll show you. It's capable of doing anything—and what it does is sing our love songs, the stupid love songs of the last century, and it gathers the flowers of the last century. It falls in love, it's jealous, it weeps, it dreams . . . I did this. I ridiculed this divinity of the new men, the machine. And I gave it the name of the girl who lost her mind from love and despair—the name of Ophelia. The most human, the most touching . . ."

Ivan dragged Kavalerov behind him.

Ivan pressed his eye to a chink, presenting to Kavalerov, meanwhile, his shiny bronze bottom, which looked for all the world like two dumbbells. Perhaps he really was affected by the heat, and the unaccustomed emptiness of this desolate region, and the novelty of a landscape that no one would expect to find in Moscow, or perhaps his fatigue really was making itself felt, but at any rate Kavalerov, finding himself alone in this unpopulated place, far from all the standard urban noises, had experienced some sort of mirage, some sort of auditory hallucination. It was as though he had heard the voice of Ivan talking with someone through the chink. Then Ivan jumped back. And so did Kavalerov, even though he was standing a goodish way off from Ivan. It was as though terror had concealed itself somewhere in the trees opposite and held them both by one string, which it had just jerked.

"Who is whistling?" shouted Kavalerov in a voice shrill with fright.

A piercing whistle flew by above them. Kavalerov turned away for an instant, covering his face with his hands, the way people turn away from a cold draft. Ivan ran away from the fence toward Kavalerov with his usual mincing little steps, and the whistle flew behind him, as though Ivan were not running but sliding, as though he had been threaded onto the dazzling beam of the whistle.

"I'm afraid of it! I'm afraid of it!" Kavalerov heard Ivan saying in a choking whisper.

Holding each other by the hand they raced downhill, followed by the curses of an excited tramp, whom they had mistaken for a bit of cast-off harness.

The tramp, woken from his sleep with a jolt, was sitting on a hummock and rummaging about in the grass looking for a rock. They took cover in a side street.

"I'm afraid of it," Ivan kept saying rapidly. "It hates me. It has betrayed me. It will kill me."

When Kavalerov had regained his composure, he was ashamed of his cowardice. He recalled that at the instant when Ivan had leapt back and started running he had also had something else in his field of vision but in his fright had not been able to focus upon it.

"Listen," he said, "what nonsense! It was nothing but a boy whistling with his two fingers in his mouth. I saw it. A boy turned up on the fence and whistled. Yes, yes . . . it was a boy."

"What did I tell you?" Ivan smiled. "Didn't I tell you you'd start looking for all sorts of explanations? Didn't I tell you to pinch yourself harder?"

A quarrel ensued. Ivan turned into a beer parlor that he'd had some trouble finding. He did not invite Kavalerov. The latter staggered on, not knowing the way and trying to follow the sound of a streetcar. But at the next corner he stamped his foot, turned about, and went back to the beer parlor. Ivan met him with a smile and waved with his hand in the direction of a chair.

"Okay now, just tell me," said Kavalerov, "just answer

me one thing, Why are you playing these games with me? Why are you trying to fool us? There *isn't* any such machine! There *can't* be any such machine! It's just crazy lying! What's the point of lying to us?"

At the end of his strength, Kavalerov dropped onto the chair.

"Listen, Kavalerov. Order yourself a beer, and I'll tell you a tale. Listen."

The Tale of the Meeting of Two Brothers

... The tender, always growing framework of The Quarter was surrounded by scaffolding.

Nothing special, this scaffolding: beams, tiers of planks, ladders, gangplanks, crosswalks, awnings. But at the base of the structure, where a crowd had gathered, there were various personalities and points of view. There were different sorts of smiles, though they all resembled one another. Some were inclined to simplicity and said: The structure is crosshatched.

Someone remarked: "Wooden structures were never intended to grow too tall. The eye has no respect for boards that have risen too high. Scaffolding detracts from the grandeur of a structure. The highest mast seems easily destroyed. There's something tender about such a mass of wood, no matter what. You can't help thinking right away of a fire."

Another exclaimed: "And over there—look!—the rafters are stretched out like catgut! It's a guitar, I tell you, a regular guitar!"

To which the preceding speaker replied: "Well, what was I just saying about the tenderness of wood? Its destiny is to serve the cause of music."

Whereupon a third sardonic voice intervened: "And how about brass? I, for one, acknowledge only wind instruments."

A schoolboy recognized in the arrangement of the boards a sort of arithmetic that no one else had noticed. But he never managed to determine what the signs of multiplication and division referred to, since the resemblance was very shaky and vanished at once.

"The siege of Troy," thought a poet, "the siege machines."

A comparison that was strengthened by the appearance of some musicians. Shielding themselves with their horns, they crept into a sort of wooden trench at the base of the structure.

The evening was black, the lanterns white and globular, the festive drapings extraordinarily crimson, the empty spaces beneath the steps lethally black. The lanterns swung about on their buzzing wires. The darkness seemed to be gesturing with its eyebrows. Midges swarmed and perished around the lanterns. Far into the distance the lanterns reached to rip away the shapes of neighboring buildings, which then, reflected in the blinking windows along the way, rushed upon the new structure. Then, until the wind finally left the lanterns in peace, the scaffolding came to stormy life: Everything surged into motion and the structure, like a tall ship, sailed into the throng.

From wooden piece to wooden piece along the base of the structure strode Andrei Babichev. All on its own a rostrum erected itself. The orator also received a flight of steps, and a stand, and a banister, and, behind him, a blindingly black backdrop and, directly on him, the limelight. There was so much light that even the most distant spectators could determine the level of the water in the carafe on the speaker's table.

Babichev moved above the crowd, very colorful and brilliant, something like a little tin figure propelled by electricity. He was to give a speech. Down below, behind a screen that had naturally formed itself, some actors were getting ready for their performance. An oboe, invisible to the crowd and therefore incomprehensible, began moaning sweetly. Incomprehensible also was the disk of the drum, silvered by the glare of the light and turned point-blank upon the crowd. The actors were making up in their wooden retreat. Everyone walking past above them moved the boards over their heads and showered them with a fog of sawdust.

Babichev's appearance on the platform tickled the crowd. They took him for the master of ceremonies. His person was far too fresh, too premeditated, too theatrical.

"Fat! Oh look at that fat!" One in the crowd was carried away.

"Bravo!" was shouted in various places.

But the moment it was announced from the rostrum that Comrade Babichev had the floor every trace of laughter vanished. Many stood on tiptoe. People strained to see and hear. Everyone was happy. It was very pleasant to see Babichev, and that for two reasons: one, he was a famous man, and two, he was fat. His fatness made them feel that the famous man was one of them. They gave Babichev an ovation. Half the applause was for his fatness. He gave his speech.

He spoke about what The Quarter would accomplish—so and so many dinners, such and such an output capacity, such and such a percent of overall nutrition, and how great would be the advantages of communal feeding.

He spoke about the feeding of children, saying that The Quarter would include a children's department, about the scientific preparation of porridge with milk, about children's growth, about the spine, about anemia. Like every orator, he looked into the distance, above the heads of the audience immediately in front of him, and for that reason remained oblivious to the very end of his speech of what was taking place directly beneath the rostrum. Meanwhile, a certain little man in a bowler hat had long since disrupted the attention of those in the front rows, who no longer listened to the speaker and were wholly occupied by the little man's doings—which, by the way, were entirely peaceful. In separating himself from the crowd he had, it is true, taken the risk of transgressing the roped-off area in front of the rostrum; and it is true that he had taken up an isolated position, which clearly indicated that he had certain privileges, either his by right or simply assumed. His back to the public, he stood leaning on the rope, or, rather, half sat on the rope, draping his backside across it, and, quite indifferent to the pandemonium that would ensue should the rope break, rocked himself back and forth on the rope in the utmost tranquillity and, apparently, with complete satisfaction.

He might have been listening to the speaker or perhaps observing the actors. The ballerina's dress flared up behind the crossbeams, and various funny faces peeped out of a little opening.

Yes, but what was the main thing? The main thing was that this odd little man had brought a pillow with him. He had with him a large old pillow in a yellow pillowcase, one that had been thoroughly slept upon by numerous heads. And when he had taken up his position on the rope he set the pillow down beside him on the ground, and the pillow sat there like his pig.

And when the speaker had ended his speech and, wiping his lips with a handkerchief, was pouring some water out of the carafe, while the applause was subsiding and the audience was rearranging its attention in order to hear and see the actors, the man with the pillow lifted his rear end from the rope, arose to his full, if rather small, height, and, raising one hand with the pillow in it, began to shout in a loud voice:

"Comrades! I wish to address the meeting!"

At that point the speaker saw his brother Ivan. His fists clenched. Brother Ivan began to mount the steps to the rostrum. He was climbing slowly. A man from among the dignitaries ran up to the barrier. His mission was to halt this stranger by manual and vocal means. But his raised hand hung there in the air and then, as though he were counting the stranger's progress up the steps, it dropped in rhythmic motions: Hup! Two! Three! Four! . . .

"He's hypnotized!" someone screamed in the crowd.

But the stranger walked on, carrying the pillow by a corner. And there he was on the rostrum. An extraordi-

nary little electrical figurine had appeared against the
black background. The background was black as a slate-
board. So black was the background that chalk lines even
seemed to stand out against it. The little figure halted.

A whisper went through the crowd: "The pillow!"

And the stranger began his speech as follows:

"Comrades! What they want to take away from you is
the greatest thing you've ever had—your own home. The
steeds of the Revolution, thundering up the back stairs,
crushing your children and your cats, smashing your beloved tiles and bricks, will burst into your kitchens.
Women! Your pride and glory, your very hearth, is in
danger. Mothers and wives! The elephants of the Revolution mean to smash your kitchen!

"What was he saying just now? He was jeering at your
saucepans, at your pots, at your quiet life, at your right to
stick a pacifier into your own children's mouths. What is it
he is teaching you to forget? What does he want to drive
out of your hearts? Your own home! Your dear, sweet
home! Tramps wandering about the wild fields of history—that's what he wants to make of you. Wives! He is
spitting into your soup. Mothers! He is dreaming of wiping away from the little faces of your babies their resemblance to you—that holy, beautiful, family resemblance.
He breaks into your most secluded little nooks, he darts
like a rat along your shelves, crawls under your beds, into
your blouses, into the very hair of your armpits. Chase
him the hell out!

"Here is a pillow. I am the king of pillows. Tell him:
We want to sleep each on his own pillow. Don't you touch
our pillows! When our little heads were still bald except
for some ruddy chicken down, they lay on these pillows,
during our nights of love these pillows knew our kisses,
we're used to dying on them—and those we killed also
died on them—don't you touch our pillows! Don't call us!
Don't lead us on, trying to trap us! What have you got to
offer us in exchange for what we can do already: love,
hate, hope, weep, pity, and forgive? Here is this pillow—
our coat of arms, our banner—this pillow. A pillow swal-

lows up bullets. A pillow is what we'll smother you with . . ."

His speech ended abruptly. He had said too much in any case. They grabbed him as it were by his last sentence, the way they grab one by the arm; they twisted his last sentence behind his back. He stopped short, suddenly frightened, and the reason for his fright was none other than the very one whom he had been lambasting and who was now standing silently and listening. The whole scene could have been taken for a performance. Which is how many did in fact take it. After all, actors do frequently come up out of the audience. This seemed all the more likely when the real actors came spilling out of their wooden hut. And the ballerina fluttered out from behind the boards like nothing so much as a butterfly. A clown in a monkey costume climbed onto the rostrum, holding onto the crossbeams with one hand and carrying in the other a strange sort of musical instrument, a long trumpet ending in three horns; and since there's no telling what a man in a monkey costume and a red wig mightn't do, it was easy to imagine that he was climbing by some magic or other on his own trumpet. Someone in a frock coat rushed about underneath the rostrum trying to restrain the actors, who were running off in various directions to catch a glimpse of the unusual speaker. For the actors also assumed that some vaudeville artist who had been invited to perform had dreamed up a stunt in which he arrived with a pillow and entered into a debate with the main speaker and that he would now do his usual number. But no. No. If the clown crawled down his absurd trumpet now it was because he was afraid! And a general sense of alarm began to spread. Nor was it the words that the stranger had so luxuriantly flung at the crowd that occasioned this agitation. On the contrary, the little man's speech had been taken as a premeditated, vaudevillian stunt; but now the ensuing silence had caused the hair on more than one neck to stand on end.

"Why are you looking at me like that?" asked the little man, dropping his pillow.

The giant's voice (no one knew that it was brother speaking to brother), the brief bellow of the giant was heard by the entire square, by the windows, by the entranceways, and by the old men who sat bolt upright in their beds.

"Who do you think you're fighting, you bastard?" the giant asked.

His face was about to explode. It seemed as though some sort of dark liquid was on the point of bursting out of that face as out of a wineskin—out of the nostrils, the mouth, the ears, the eyes—and everyone would clench his eyes shut in horror. It was not the giant who had said that. It was the boards around him, the concrete, the clamps, all the lines and formulas that had been realized in the building—it was they who said it. It was their wrath that was bursting him open.

But brother Ivan did not back away (everyone had expected him to back away farther and farther until he finally sat down on his pillow); on the contrary, he suddenly grew stronger, straightened up, walked over to the railing and, with his hand shielding his eyes, shouted:

"Where are you? I'm waiting for you, Ophelia!"

There was a blast of wind. There had been gusts of wind on and off the whole time, rocking the lanterns . . . The merging and sundering of the figures of the shadows (squares, Pythagorean trousers, little Hippocratic moons) were long since familiar to the audience—the tall ship of the structure kept ripping loose from its anchor and sailing into the throng—so that the new burst of wind, grabbing many by the shoulder and bending many a head, would have been met with no more than ordinary grumbling and immediately forgotten, had it not been for . . . What was said later on was that it flew up from behind and flew over the heads of the audience.

The giant sailing ship advanced on the crowd, its wooden hull creaking, the wind howling, and something black, a flying body, like a bird, smashed into the rigging, against a high crossbeam, and flew on, smashing a lantern . . .

"Did that scare you, brother?" asked Ivan. "Here's what I'm going to do. I'm going to send her against the scaffolding. She'll demolish your building. The screws are going to unscrew themselves, the nuts are going to fall off, the reinforced concrete is going to disintegrate like the body of a leper. How about that? She will teach each crossbeam how to disobey you. How's that? The whole thing is going to collapse. She will turn every one of your figures into a useless flower. There, brother Andrei, is what I can do . . ."

"Ivan, you are seriously ill. You are delirious, Ivan." These soft and cordial words came suddenly from the man whom everyone expected to utter threats. "Who are you talking about? Who is this 'she'? I don't see a thing! Who is going to turn my figures into flowers? It was only the wind that knocked a lantern against a beam and the lantern simply broke. Ivan, Ivan . . ."

And his brother walked toward Ivan, his arms outstretched. But Ivan pushed him aside.

"Look!" he exclaimed, raising his hand. "No, not there! There! There! To the left. Do you see it? What is that sitting there on the beam? You see it? Have some water. Give Comrade Babichev some water! What has lit on that perch there? You see it? Do you believe it?! Are you afraid?!!"

"It's a shadow!" said Andrei. "It's only a shadow, brother. Let's get away from here. I'll give you a lift. Let the concert begin. The actors don't know what to do with themselves. The audience is tired of waiting. Come on, Valia, let's go."

"A shadow, is it? That isn't a shadow, Andryusha. That is the machine that you jeered at . . . That's me sitting on the perch, Andryusha—me, the old world, that's my age sitting there. The brain of my age, Andryusha, a brain that knew how to make up not only songs but also formulas. A brain full of the dreams that you want to annihilate."

Ivan raised his arm and shouted:

"Go, Ophelia! I command you!"

And the thing that had alit on the beam turned, flashing as it turned, made a rapping and stamping sound like that of a big bird, and then vanished into the dark space between some crisscrossed boards.

Panic. Crush. People ran off screaming. But the thing clanked as it made its way along the boards. It suddenly reappeared, emitting an orange-colored ray, whistled— you couldn't make out its shape—and then like an airy shadow, like a spider, leapt up a sheer face of the building, higher, into a chaos of planks, lit again on some sort of rib, looked over its shoulder . . .

"Do your job, Ophelia! Get started!" yelled Ivan as he raced about the rostrum. "Did you hear what he said about the home? I order you to destroy this structure . . ."

People were running away, and their flight was accompanied by racing storm clouds, by a violent fugue of the sky.

The Quarter collapsed . . .

The narrator fell silent . . .

A drum was lying flat among the debris, and I, Ivan Babichev, climbed up on the drum. Ophelia hastened over to me, dragging the crushed, dying Andrei.

"Let me lie on the pillow, brother," he whispered. "I want to die on the pillow. I give up, Ivan . . . "

I put the pillow on my knees and he laid his head upon it.

"We've won, Ophelia," I said.

VII

On Sunday morning, Ivan Babichev dropped in to see Kavalerov.

"Today I want to show you Valia," he declared in a solemn voice.

They set out. Their walk was what might be called enchanting. It proceeded through an empty, idle city. They took a turn round Theater Square. There was practically no traffic. Tverskaya sloped upwards in the blue distance.

Sunday morning affords one of the best views of the Moscow summer. Undisturbed by traffic, the light remained seamless, as though the sun had just risen. Thus they walked across geometrical grids of light and shadow, or rather through three-dimensional bodies, for the light and shadow intersected each other not only on level planes but in the air as well. Before reaching the Moscow Soviet building they found themselves in total shadow. But in the passageway between two of its wings there was a great waterfall of light. It was dense, almost solid—one could no longer doubt that light was a material substance: The dust flying about in it could easily be taken for fluctuations of the ether.

Then came the side street linking Tverskaya and Nikitskaya. They stood for a while enjoying the flowering hedge.

They went in at the gate and ascended the wooden stairs leading to a glass-enclosed gallery, which, though it showed signs of neglect, was still gay with its abundance of glass and the view of the sky through the lattice of the panes.

The sky was broken up into plates of differing degrees of blue, some of them nearer the viewer, others farther away. A quarter of the panes had been broken out. Climbing along the lower row of windows were the green little tendrils of some plant that had crept alongside and boarded the gallery. Everything here was calculated to provide a happy childhood. It is on such galleries that bunny rabbits abound.

Ivan hastened toward a door. There were three of them giving onto the gallery. He was headed for the last one.

On the way, Kavalerov tried to pluck one of the green tendrils. He had no more than given it a tug when the entire invisible system hanging overboard reached out to rescue the tendril and from somewhere or other some sort of wire that had got tangled in the life of this ivy, or whatever the hell it was, gave a groan (as though this were Italy, not Moscow). With an effort, Kavalerov pressed his temple against the window and glimpsed a courtyard en-

closed by a stone wall. The gallery was located high up
between the third and fourth stories. At this height he had
a view beyond the wall of a terribly green plot of ground
(it was still Italy).

Already when they were entering the building he had
heard voices and laughter. They were coming from that
green yard. He had not managed to make anything out
before Ivan distracted him. He was knocking on the door.
Once, twice, three times.

"Nobody home," he grumbled. "She's already over
there . . ."

Kavalerov's attention had never left the broken window
above the green lawn. Why? His eye had not, after all,
seen anything astonishing. Just before he had turned at
Ivan's knocking, he had caught one measure of some gay
movement, one beat of a gymnastic rhythm. His vision
simply found the green of the lawn, so unexpected after
the ordinary courtyard, pleasant, sweet, and cold. Later on
he no doubt persuaded himself that what had gripped him
so instantly and strongly was the charm of the lawn.

"She's already left!" Babichev repeated. "Let's see . . ."

And he peered through one of the windows. Kavalerov
immediately did the same.

What had struck him as a lawn turned out to be a small-
ish courtyard overgrown with grass. The main impression
of greenery came from the tall, thickly crowned trees that
lined its sides. All this foliage was flourishing beneath the
high blind wall of the building. Kavalerov was looking
down from above. From where he stood the little courtyard seemed cramped within its walls. The neighboring
tall buildings that rose above his point of vantage seemed
to crush the little court. It lay like a doormat in a room full
of furniture. The roofs of other buildings disclosed their
secrets to Kavalerov. He saw a weather vane in its actual
dimensions, little dormer windows whose very existence
was unsuspected by those down below, and a child's ball,
now forever unreturnable, which had once flown too high
and rolled into a gutter. Buildings bristling with antennas
dropped away in stages from the little courtyard. The

onion dome of a church, freshly painted with red lead, dropped into an empty space on the skyline and seemed to have been flying until Kavalerov caught it with his gaze. At the other end of nowhere he saw the yoke of a streetcar mast and another observer who had leaned out of a distant window, either eating or sniffing something, and who had so far submitted to the laws of perspective as to be practically propping his elbows on the streetcar.

The main thing was still the little courtyard.

They went downstairs. It turned out that in the stone wall which separated the large courtyard from the small, the boring, empty courtyard from the little mysterious lawn, there was a breach. Several stones, like loaves of bread from an oven, had been removed. Through this aperture they could see everything. The sun was hot on the crown of Kavalerov's head. They were watching someone practicing the high jump. A cord had been stretched between two posts. A youth ran up and projected his body sideways over the cord, almost sliding, stretching his body out straight, parallel to the obstacle, as though he were not leaping but rolling over the obstacle as one rolls over a mound. And as he rolled over he threw up his legs and kicked like a swimmer propelling himself through the water. The next second his distorted, upturned face could be seen flying downwards, and then Kavalerov saw him hit the ground feet first, at which point he made a sound like "uff!"—either a grunt or the collision of his heels with the grass.

Ivan pinched Kavalerov's elbow.

"There she is . . . look . . ." (said in a whisper).

Everyone shouted and applauded.. The jumper, who was practically naked, walked off to the side, limping slightly—no doubt from the usual athlete's desire to seem fetching.

This was Volodia Makarov.

Kavalerov felt embarrassed. He was seized by feelings of shame and fear. An entire glistening mechanism of teeth appeared on Volodia's face when he smiled.

Back up on the gallery there was more knocking on the

door. Kavalerov turned round. It would be very stupid to get caught here at the wall spying on people. Someone was walking along the gallery. The little windows divide the walker up so that different parts of his body move independently of one another. A sort of optical illusion. The head precedes the trunk. Kavalerov recognizes the head. It is Andrei Babichev floating across the gallery.

On the lawn Valia shouts, "Andrei Petrovich! Over here! Here, Andrei Petrovich!"

The terrible visitor has dropped from sight. He is now looking for some way to get to the lawn. Various obstacles conceal him from Kavalerov. It is time to run.

"Over here! Here!" Valia's voice rings out.

Kavalerov looks. Valia is standing firmly planted on the grass with her legs wide apart. She is wearing black shorts, extremely brief, which reveal the whole length of her very naked legs. She has on white tennis shoes without socks, and the flat soles of the shoes lend her stance even more strength and solidity: It isn't a woman's posture, but that of a man or a child. Her legs are dirty, suntanned, and shining. They are little girl's legs, which are so often affected by the air, the sun, the stumblings onto the ground, the grass, into objects, that they become rough and covered with the waxy scars left by prematurely lifting off the scabs on scratches, and their knees become as rough as the skin of an orange. Her age and her subconscious confidence in her physical endowment confer upon the possessor of these legs the right to treat them so nonchalantly, so pitilessly, and so neglectfully. But higher up, under the black shorts, the purity and tenderness of her body show how beautiful she will be when she has matured and become a woman, when she herself will pay some attention to herself and will care about her grooming, when all the scratches will get well, the scabs will fall off, the suntan will even out and become her natural tint.

He leapt back and ran along the blind wall away from the opening, dirtying his shoulder on the stone in the process.

"Where are you going?" Ivan called to him. "Hey! Wait up!"

"He's yelling! They'll hear him!"—Kavalerov was horrified—"They'll see me!"

And on the other side of the wall, as a matter of fact, everything suddenly became deathly still. They were listening. Ivan caught up with Kavalerov.

"Did you hear that, my dear fellow? Did you see? That's my brother! You saw? Volodia, Valia, all of them, the whole camp! Just wait, I'll climb up on the wall and let them have the weight of my tongue ... You're covered with powder, Kavalerov, like a miller!"

In a quiet voice, Kavalerov replied:

"I am perfectly acquainted with your brother. It was he who kicked me out. He is the important personage that I told you about ... We have the same kind of luck. You said I was to kill your brother ... what am I to do?"

Valia was sitting on the stone wall.

"Oh! Papa!" she screamed.

Ivan threw his arms around her legs, which were dangling over the wall.

"Valia, put out my eyes. I want to be blind," said he, choking on his own words. "I don't want to see anything, no lawns, no boughs, no flowers, no cavaliers, no cowards ... I've got to go blind, Valia. Valia, I made a mistake—I thought all the emotions had died—love and devotion and tenderness—but they're all still alive, Valia, only not for us. All we have left is envy, envy, envy ... Put my eyes out, Valia. I want to be blind ..."

He slid down the girl's perspiring legs with his hands, his face, his chest, and fell heavily at the foot of the wall.

"Let us drink a toast, Kavalerov," said he. "Let us drink to youth that is gone forever, to the conspiracy of feelings that came to nothing, and to the machine that does not and never will exist ... "

"You are a son of a bitch, Ivan Petrovich!" Kavalerov had caught Ivan by his collar. "Youth is not gone! No! You hear me? It's a lie! I'll show you ... tomorrow ...

you hear me? . . . tomorrow at the soccer match I'm going to kill your brother . . ."

VIII

Nikolai Kavalerov was sitting in his seat in the grandstand. High up on his right Valia was sitting in a wooden box amidst banners, posters with enormous letters, short flights of stairs, and a latticework of boards. The box was filled with young people.

The wind was blowing and the day was very bright and gusty, with the wind whistling from all sides. The huge green field of flattened grass glistened as though it had been lacquered.

Kavalerov kept his gaze fixed on the box, straining to see, and when he got tired, allowed his imagination to work in the effort to perceive what he could neither see nor hear at that distance. He was not the only one. Many of those sitting near the box, though they were excited by a foretaste of the marvelous spectacle that was coming, kept their attention on the charming girl in the pink dress, almost a child, with a childish negligence about her movements and attitudes, but still so striking that everyone wished to be noticed by her, as though she were some celebrity, or the daughter of a celebrity.

Twenty thousand spectators overflowed the stadium. An unprecedented treat was in store—the long-awaited match between the teams of Moscow and Germany.

In the stands people were arguing, screaming, and kicking up a fuss over absolutely nothing. The stadium was about to burst with this enormous number of people. Somewhere a handrail gave way with the sound of a duck quacking. Kavalerov, who had got tangled in people's knees while looking for his seat, saw a dignified old man in a cream-colored vest lying flat across the track at the base of the stands, his arms flung wide and his breathing labored. People were trudging over him without giving him a second thought. The wind heightened the general excitement. At the top of the stadium flags snapped like lightning.

Kavalerov's whole being pressed toward the box. Valia was sitting above and behind him about twenty meters to the right. His vision was playing tricks. It would seem to him that their eyes had met, and then he would stand up. It would seem to him that the medallion round her neck had caught fire, that the wind was having its way with her. Every now and again she would grab her hat—a sort of hood of shining red straw. The wind blew the sleeve of her dress all the way back to her shoulder, revealing an arm as slender as a flute. Her program flew out of her hands and fell into the thick of the crowd, fluttering its wings.

For as much as a month before the match there had been speculation that the Germans would include in their team the famous Getzke, the center forward, the star of the five-man offensive line. The moment the German team emerged onto the field, to the tune of a military march, and even before the players had begun to take their places, the public, as always happens, recognized the celebrity, even though the celebrity was marching along in the crowd of others in the visiting team.

"Getzke! Getzke!" shouted the spectators, who derived enormous satisfaction from seeing the famous player and from applauding him.

Getzke, who turned out to be a short, swarthy, round-shouldered man, walked a bit to one side, stopped, and waved his clasped hands about over his head. This novel foreign gesture of greeting filled the crowd with still greater enthusiasm.

The German group—eleven men in all—stood out brilliantly on the green field and in the pure air with the bright oily colors of their uniforms. They were wearing black shorts and orange, almost golden, jerseys with greenish-purple stripes on the right side of the chest. The shorts fluttered in the wind.

Volodia Makarov, shivering from the coolness of the soccer shirt that he had just put on, was looking out the window of the players' quarters. The Germans had reached the middle of the field.

"Shouldn't we get going?" he asked.

"Let's go!" the team captain ordered.

The Soviet team ran out in their red shirts and white shorts. The spectators hung over the railings and stamped their feet on the boards. Their roar drowned out the music.

The toss of the coin decided that the Germans were to play the first half with the wind behind them.

Our side not only played and tried to do everything they were supposed to do to play as well as they could, but they also never ceased observing the German game, as spectators, and evaluating it, as professionals. A game lasts ninety minutes, with a short break after forty-five minutes. After the break the teams switch sides on the field. So, when the weather is windy, it's an advantage to play against the wind while you've got all your strength.

Since the Germans had the wind in their favor, and it was very strong, all the action was forever being blown in the direction of our goal. The ball practically never left the Soviet half of the field. Our backs would kick the ball in a high parabolic arc down the field, but it would then slide along the wall of the wind, turn, its yellow markings gleaming, and wander back where it had come from. The Germans attacked furiously. The famous Getzke, it turned out, was in actual fact a very dangerous opponent. Everyone's attention was fixed on him.

Whenever he got the ball, Valia, from her high vantage point, would shriek as though she were just on the point of seeing some hideous crime. Getzke would explode down the field, the speed of his onslaught leaving our backs sitting on their heels behind him, and kick for a goal. At such moments Valia would sway against her neighbor, grabbing his arm by both hands, pressing her cheek against his sleeve, and thinking of one thing only: to hide her face so as not to see some terrible event; but she kept on looking through clenched eyes at the horrifying actions of Getzke, who was black from the effort of running in such heat.

But Volodia Makarov, the Soviet goalkeeper, would catch the ball. Getzke, almost before having completed the kick for the goal, would gracefully transform that motion into the one required for turning and running, and would turn and run, the jersey stretched tightly across his back and almost black with sweat. Valia would immediately assume a more natural posture and begin to laugh—first, because no goal had been scored against our side, and, second, because she recalled having just screamed and grabbed her neighbor's arm.

"Makarov! Makarov! Bravo, Makarov!" she shouted along with everyone else.

The ball was forever flying toward Volodia's goal. It would hit against the uprights, which would then groan and shed a shower of whitewash ... Volodia was intercepting the ball at angles that made his feat seem mathematically impossible. The whole crowd, the whole living declivity of the grandstands, became as it were even steeper as each spectator rose to his feet, impelled by the terrible, unbearable craving to see the most interesting thing of all: the ball kicked in for a goal. The referee kept sticking his whistle in his mouth as he ran, ready to signal a goal. But Volodia would not so much catch the ball as rip it out of its line of flight, and, as one who had violated the laws of physics, he then endured the stunning reaction of outraged natural forces. He would fly up with the ball in its former trajectory, twirling and twisting himself upon it, embracing it with his whole body, his knees, his belly, his chin, throwing his weight against the speed of the ball the way you throw a rag on a sudden outburst of flame. The speed of the ball would knock Volodia two meters to one side, and he would fall to the ground like a party popper of colored paper. The German forwards would rush at him, but when it was all over there would be the ball above the fray.

Volodia would stay at his goal. He was unable to stand still. He would pace along the goal line from one post to the other, trying to contain the burst of energy that had been released in his struggle with the ball. Everything inside him was buzzing. He would swing his arms, shake himself all over, kick clods of earth with the toe of his boot. Neatly outfitted before the game, he now consisted of rags, a body black with dirt, and the leather of his huge goalie's mitts. The breathing spell did not last long. The German attack rolled toward the Moscow goal once again. Volodia passionately wanted his side to win and trembled for each of his teammates. He thought that he alone knew how to play against Getzke, what his weak points were, how to counter his onslaughts. He was also eager to learn what the famous German thought of the Soviet game. All the while he was applauding and shouting "Go! Go!" to his own mates he felt like shouting to Getzke: "Look how we play! Good, don't you think?"

As a soccer player, Volodia was the complete opposite of Getzke. Both were professionals, but Volodia was a sportsman, Getzke a star. What Volodia thought important was the overall progress of the game, the overall victory, the outcome; Getzke strove for one thing only—to exhibit his own skill. He was an old, experienced player who cared nothing for the reputation of his team; his own success was the one thing he held dear; he was not a regular member of any team, for he was forever compromising himself by switching from one club to another for the sake of the money. He had been barred from the national championship games, and was asked to play only among friends or in exhibition games or games played abroad. He had not only great skill but great good luck. Any team on which he played was dangerous. He despised the other players—both his own and those of the other side. He knew that he would score against any team. The rest meant nothing to him. He was a mercenary.

No more than halfway into the game it was clear to the spectators that the Soviet team was not going to be bested by the Germans, whose offense was all wrong, thanks to Getzke. He ruined, he demolished their strategy. He played for himself alone, at his own risk, without help and without giving any help to anyone. The moment he got the ball he would pull all the action on the field around himself, roll it up into a ball, then take it apart and lead it from one side of the field to the other, always following his own private plans, unknown to his teammates, relying only on himself, his running, and his ability to get round any opponent.

The spectators concluded from all this that the second half of the game, when Getzke would have played himself out and our side would have the wind in their favor, would end with the Germans being routed. If only our fellows could hold out for the moment and not let a single shot get past their goal line.

But the virtuoso Getzke had his way again. Ten minutes before halftime he broke out to the right side of the field, carrying the ball ahead of him with his whole body, then stopped abruptly, throwing off his pursuers, who hadn't foreseen this stop and plunged on ahead and to the right, turned with the ball into the open space of center field where there was only one Soviet back to get around, drove the ball straight toward the goal, glancing down at his feet then back at the goal as though measuring and calculating the speed, direction, and timing of his shot.

One long shout of "O o o o o" rolled down from the stands.

Volodia, his feet wide apart and his arms spread as though he were holding an invisible barrel, got ready to grab the ball. Getzke was running toward the goal, still not shooting, Volodia made a dive for his feet. The ball got jammed between them as though stuck in a barrel. Then the end of the scene was blotted out by the whistling and stamping of the crowd. One of them hit the ball so that it flew crazily up into the air, whereupon Getzke butted it into the net with a head shot that looked like a polite bow.

That is how the Soviet team had the first goal scored against them.

The whole stadium groaned. All the binoculars were turned toward the Soviet goal. Getzke, looking down at his shining boots, was running elegantly toward the center of the field.

His teammates were helping Volodia up.

IX

Valia turned to look along with everyone else. Kavalerov saw her face turned in his direction. He had no doubt that she saw him. He became suddenly nervous, and a weird notion drove him into a fury: He imagined that everyone around him was laughing at him, that they had noticed his excitement.

He looked round at those sitting near him. And what a surprise: In the same row of seats, not far away, was Andrei Babichev. Kavalerov was shocked all over again at the two white hands adjusting the binoculars, at the massive body enclosed in the gray jacket, at the trimmed mustache . . .

The binoculars hung over Kavalerov's head like black bombshells. The straps of the binoculars dangled from the cheeks of Babichev like the reins of a harness . . .

The Germans were already on the attack again.

Suddenly the ball, driven upwards by someone's powerful though clumsy kick, flew high into the air and to one side, out of bounds, in the direction of Kavalerov, whistled above the crouching spectators in the lower rows, paused for a moment, and, twirling all of its facets, fell onto the boards at Kavalerov's feet. The game came to a halt. The players froze, immobilized by this unexpected event. The spectacle on the field, with its green background and many colors, with its constant motion, was now instantly petrified. It stopped as instantly as the image on the screen when the film breaks, when the house lights have already come up and the projectionist has not yet managed to switch off his machine, and the public sees a strangely pale frame with the outlines of the hero absolutely immobile in a pose suggesting the swiftest action. Kavalerov's anger mounted. Everyone around him was laughing. Whenever the ball falls into the stands it makes people laugh: It is an instant when the spectators seem to realize the true silliness of men running about after a ball for an hour and a half while obliging them—the spectators, total strangers—to follow with such seriousness and passion their utterly frivolous pastime.

At that moment all of the thousands of spectators who were able to do so conferred upon Kavalerov their uninvited attention, and their attention was combined with laughter.

It was possible that Valia, too, was laughing at him—the man hit by the ball! It was possible that she was twice as tickled as everyone else, since she could make fun of an enemy caught in a ridiculous position. He grinned as he moved his foot away from the ball, but the ball, its support gone, rubbed itself against his heel with a truly feline affection.

"Well!" the surprised Babichev shouted angrily. Kavalerov remained impassive. Two large white hands stretched out for the ball. Someone picked up the ball and handed it to Babichev. He rose to his full height and stuck out his stomach as he raised the ball behind his head and swung it back and forth several times so as to throw it as far as possible. He could not be dignified at such a moment, but, knowing that he must be dignified, he exaggerated all the outward signs of his seriousness, scowling and puffing out his fresh red lips.

With a great lurch forward Babichev launched the ball onto the field, which became magically animated.

"He doesn't recognize me," thought Kavalerov, his fury surging.

At the end of the first half the score stood 1–0 in favor of the Germans. The players, their faces streaked with dark traces of sweat and covered all over with green blades of grass, walked toward the passageway, moving their bare legs with a strong, broad stride, as though they were walking through water. The Germans—who were red in an un-Russian way, the blush starting at their temples—made up a multicolored deck when shuffled together with the Moscow team. The players walked along, seeing everyone at once, the entire crowd at the boards that lined the passageway, but seeing no one individually. They smeared over the crowd their smiles and their lifeless eyes, which were too luminous for their blackened faces. The people to whom they had appeared only a moment ago as little figures of many colors, running and falling on the field, now encountered them close up. The uproar of the game had not died down; it moved along with them. Getzke, looking like a gypsy, walked along licking a slight wound that he'd just got above his elbow.

The gaping fans had the thrill of noting the details of this or that player's size and build, the extent of his injuries, his gasping for breath, the total dishevelment of his uniform. From a distance everything had made a lighter, more festive impression.

Kavalerov fought his way out among the backs and sides of others until he passed through some gate and felt with relief that he was once more on grass. He was rushing along with the crowd on a path that circled the back of the grandstand. The refreshment stand that had been set up on a lawn under some trees was instantly jammed. The little old man in the wrinkled cream-colored vest, still unhappily and cautiously glancing at the general public, was eating an ice cream. There was a crowd swarming around the players' quarters.

Ecstatic cries of "Hooray, Makarov!" could be heard from over there. Fans were clambering onto the fence, beating away the barbed wire as if it were a swarm of bees, and even higher: into the trees, into the dark foliage, swaying with the wind and their exertions like little arboreal creatures.

Then a gleaming body was lifted up above the crowd, its nakedness splashing light. They were carrying Volodia Makarov in triumph.

Kavalerov lacked the courage to try to break into this triumphant ring. He squinted through what openings he could find, jumping up and down behind the throng.

Volodia was already standing on the ground. The sock

on one leg had fallen down and lay rolled up like a green doughnut around his pear-shaped, downy calf. His torn shirt barely clung to his torso. He crossed his arms modestly over his chest.

And there was Valia standing next to him. And next to her Andrei Babichev.

The onlookers were applauding all three of them.

Babichev was gazing lovingly at Volodia.

At this point the wind intruded. A striped tent peg was pulled up, and all the foliage rolled to the right. The ring of onlookers broke up, the whole picture came apart, and people ran to escape the dust. More than anyone, Valia caught the brunt of it. Her pink dress, light as dry husks, blew up around her legs, and Kavalerov could see how transparent it was. The wind blew her dress round her face, and Kavalerov saw her profile in the shining translucency of the cloth, which had spread out like a fan. Kavalerov saw all this through a cloud of dust, and he saw also how in her attempt to control her dress she twirled round, wound herself into it, and nearly fell to one side. She was trying to gather the hem about her knees and hold it there, but couldn't manage it, and then for the sake of decency resorted to half-measures: She clasped her exposed legs with her arms, hid her knees, and doubled up like a woman taken unawares in her bath.

From somewhere came the sound of the referee's whistle. The band struck up the march. Thus ended the period of happy confusion. The second half was about to start. Volodia dashed away.

"Two goals against the Germans this time!" a little boy was yelling as he raced past Kavalerov.

Valia was still struggling with her dress. She changed positions ten times in the effort to trap the hem of it and wound up near Kavalerov, close enough to whisper.

She stood there with her legs wide apart. She held her hat, which she had caught in the air as it blew from her head, in her hand. Not yet recovered from all her exertions, she looked at Kavalerov without seeing him; her head, with its closely cropped chestnut hair making a sharp line at the cheek, tilted slightly to one side.

A ray of sunlight slipped along her shoulder, she rocked slightly, and her collarbones gleamed like daggers. His gazing at her lasted but the tenth part of a minute, yet he instantly understood, with a sudden chill, what an incurable longing had been lodged forever in his soul by his having seen her, this otherworldly creature, alien and extraordinary, and he felt how helplessly sweet she looked, how crushingly unattainable her purity, and—because she was a little girl and because she loved Volodia—how pointless was his fascination with her.

Babichev was waiting for her, his hand outstretched.

"Valia," said Kavalerov, "I've been waiting for you all my life ... Have pity on me ... "

But she did not hear him. She ran off, still struggling against the wind.

X

That night Kavalerov arrived home drunk.

He went along the hallway to the washbasin to gulp some water. He turned the faucet on full and got thoroughly wet. He left the water on roaring into the sink. When he went into Anichka's room he stopped. The light was still on. Wrapped in the yellow wadding of the light, the widow was sitting in her huge bed, her bare legs dangling over the side. She was ready for bed.

Kavalerov took a step. She said nothing, as though spellbound. It seemed to Kavalerov that she was smiling and coaxing him on.

He went toward her.

She offered no resistance and even welcomed him with open arms.

"Ah," she whispered, "you little demon, you ... "

Later, he kept waking up. He was tortured by thirst, a drunken, frenzied craving for water. When he woke up it would be utterly quiet. A second before waking he would remember the water gushing into the sink, and this vivid recollection would snap him awake, but there was no water. He would collapse again. While he was sleeping the widow was tidying up. She had shut off the faucet, undressed him, and mended his suspenders. The dawn arrived. At first Kavalerov was totally confused. Like the penniless drunk in the comedy who is picked up by a rich man and taken to his castle, he lay there, completely out of his mind, surrounded by unfamiliar luxury. In the mirror he saw an extraordinary reflection of himself, beginning with the soles of his feet. He lay in a magnificent pose, one arm behind his head. The sunlight illuminated him from one side. He seemed to be floating beneath the dome of a temple through broad, hazy layers of light. Over his head hung clusters of grapes, cupids danced, apples came rolling out of horns of plenty, and he could practically hear emerging from all this the solemn rumbling of an organ. He was lying in Anichka's bed.

"You remind me of him," said Anichka in an ardent whisper as she bent over him.

A glass-enclosed portrait hung on the wall over the bed. It was a man, someone's youthful-looking grandfather, dressed to the nines in one of the last frock coats of that age. You sensed that his neck must look like a massive, multibarreled piece of ordnance. A man of about fifty-seven.

The memory of his father changing his shirt flashed before Kavalerov's mind.

"You remind me very much of my husband," Anichka repeated, putting her arms around Kavalerov. And Kavalerov's head disappeared into her armpit as into a tent. The widow had opened the pavilions of her armpits. Ecstasy and shame stormed in her heart.

"He also took me . . . the same way . . . by a trick . . . softly, quietly, quietly, never saying a word . . . and *then!* Ah! You demon, you . . ."

Kavalerov hit her.

She was flabbergasted. Kavalerov leapt out of bed, sending the blankets and counterpane in all directions. A sheet fluttered out behind him. She threw herself at the door, her outstretched arms silently howling for help. She was fleeing before her own household goods, like a woman of Pompeii. A basket crashed down. A chair tilted crazily.

He hit her several times, across her back and across the spare tire of flab that encircled her waist.

The chair was standing on one foot.

"He used to beat me, too," said she, smiling through her tears.

Kavalerov returned to the bed. He collapsed on it, beginning to feel sick. He lay there unconscious the whole day. That night the widow lay down next to him. She snored. Kavalerov pictured her palate as a sort of archway leading into darkness. He hid under the vault of the arch. Everything was shivering and shaking, the very earth trembled. Kavalerov slipped and fell before the blast of air that was blowing out of the bottomless pit. She groaned. Then, with an immense smacking of her lips, she would suddenly stop groaning. The whole architecture of her palate was distorted. Her snore became powdery, then fizzed like seltzer water.

Kavalerov was tossing and turning and weeping. She got up and put a damp towel on his forehead. He reached out for the moisture, propped himself on his elbows, searching for the towel with his hands, then wadded it into a ball and put it under his cheek and kissed it, whispering, "They've stolen her . . . It's hard for me to live in this world . . . hard . . . "

But the widow hardly managed to lie back down before she was fast asleep, pressed against one of the inset mirrors. Sleep smeared sweetness all over her. She slept with her mouth open, gurgling, the way old women sleep.

The bedbugs were going about their lives with a slight rustling noise, as though someone were ripping off the wallpaper. Bedbug hiding places, unknown to the light of day, were revealed. The wooden bed grew and swelled.

A rosy glow fell upon the windowsill.

A murky darkness roiled around the bed. Nighttime secrets descended from the corners along the walls, flowed over the sleeping pair, and disappeared beneath the bed.

Kavalerov suddenly sat up, his eyes wide open.

Ivan was standing over the bed.

XI

And Kavalerov immediately began to pull himself together.

Anichka was sleeping next to the arched mirror, with her legs tucked up and her arms around her stomach. Carefully, so as not to wake her, he pulled the blanket off and, throwing it round his shoulders like a cape, presented himself to Ivan.

"Excellent," said Ivan. "You glisten like a lizard. This is the outfit in which you will appear before the people. Come on, let's go. We've got to hurry."

"I'm very sick," Kavalerov sighed. He gave a weak smile as though apologizing for having no desire to look for his trousers, jacket, and shoes. "Is it all right if I'm barefoot?"

Ivan was already in the hallway. Kavalerov rushed after him.

"I've suffered a long time, and for nothing," thought Kavalerov. "The day of my redemption is finally at hand."

They were swallowed up in a stream of people. Around the next corner they found a resplendent road before them.

"There it is!" said Ivan, squeezing Kavalerov's hand. "There is The Quarter!"

Kavalerov looked and saw gardens, spherical clumps of foliage, an arch of light, translucent stone, galleries, and the flight of a ball above the verdure . . .

"This way!" Ivan ordered.

They set off running along a wall entwined with ivy, and then they had to jump. The sky-blue blanket made it easy for Kavalerov to jump; he floated through the air above the crowd and alit at the foot of an immensely wide flight of stone steps. He immediately took fright and began to crawl away beneath his blanket like an insect folding up its wings. He went unnoticed, and sat down behind the base of a column.

At the summit of the stone steps, surrounded by a crowd of people, stood Andrei Babichev. He was holding Volodia close to his side, his arm round his shoulder.

"They'll bring her right away," said Andrei, smiling to his friends.

At that moment Kavalerov saw the following: An orchestra was marching along the asphalt road leading to the flight of steps, and Valia was floating above the orchestra. The playing of the instruments supported her in the air. Sound was carrying her. She rose and fell above the trumpets in accordance with the pitch and volume of the sound they emitted. Her ribbons were flying higher than her head, her dress was ballooning, her hair standing straight up.

The final few bars of the music deposited her at the top of the steps, and she fell into the arms of Volodia. Everyone stepped back. The two of them stood there in the circle all alone.

Kavalerov saw no more. A sudden terror seized him. A strange shadow abruptly rose up before him. Frozen with horror, he slowly turned round. There on the grass, one step behind him, sat Ophelia.

"A-a-a-a-a-a-h!" he screamed in terror. He made a run for it. With a clashing sound, Ophelia seized him by the blanket. He slipped out of it. In this indecent condition, stumbling, falling, smashing his jaw against the stone steps, he clambered up them. Those at the top watched his progress from above. The beautiful Valia stood there, leaning slightly forward.

"Back, Ophelia!" shouted the voice of Ivan. "She won't listen to me . . . Ophelia, stop!"

"Grab her!"

"She'll kill him!"

"Oh!"

"Look! Look! Look!"

From the center of the flight of steps Kavalerov turned

and looked round. Ivan was making an effort to climb up on the wall. The ivy was tearing loose. The crowd surged backwards. Ivan was hanging on the wall, his two arms spread wide. The terrifying iron thing was moving slowly across the grass in his direction. Out of what might be called the head of the thing a gleaming needle was slowly emerging. Ivan howled. He couldn't hold on. He fell, and his bowler hat rolled off among the dandelions. He sat pressing his back against the wall with his hands over his face. The machine kept coming, ripping up dandelions as it approached.

Kavalerov stood up and shouted in a desperate voice: "Save him! Are you going to let a machine kill a man?"

There was no answer.

"My place is with him!" said Kavalerov. "Teacher! I'll die with you!"

But it was already too late. Ivan squealed like a stuck rabbit and Kavalerov collapsed. As he fell, he saw Ivan pinned to the wall by the needle.

Ivan bent forward slowly and began to rotate on the ghastly axis.

Kavalerov hid his head in his arms so as not to see or hear anything more. But he could still hear a metallic sound. The machine was coming up the steps.

"Oh, no!" he screamed at the top of his lungs. "She'll kill me! Forgive me! Forgive me! Have mercy! I wasn't the one who derided the machines! I'm innocent. Valia! Valia! Help me!"

XII

Kavalerov lay ill for three days. As soon as he recovered, he resolved to escape.

He got up looking fixedly at one spot, the corner near the bed. He was putting on his clothes like a robot when he suddenly felt the new leather loop on his suspenders. The widow had replaced the safety pin. Where had she got the loop? Cut it off her husband's old suspenders? Kavalerov felt the full squalor of his position. He ran out into the hallway without his jacket. He undid and threw away the red suspenders as he ran.

At the entrance to the landing he paused. No voices could be heard in the courtyard. Then he stepped out onto the landing and all his thoughts became confused. The sweetest feelings of languor and joy suddenly welled up inside him. It was a lovely morning. There was a light breeze (as if someone were leafing through the pages of a book) and the sky was blue. Kavalerov was standing above a foul corner of the courtyard. A cat, alarmed at his suddenly bursting upon the scene, leapt out of a crate of garbage, trailing some sort of filth behind it. Could there be anything poetic in this accursed pigsty? And yet he stood there with his head thrown back and his arms outstretched.

At that instant he suddenly felt that the moment had come, the boundary reached between two existences, the moment of some huge convulsion! The moment to break away, to break with all the past, now, at once, in the space of two heartbeats, no more—it was time to cross that boundary, and the life, the revolting, ugly life, which was not even his own and had been forced upon him against his will, would fall away behind him . . .

He stood there with his eyes open wide, and the whole field of his vision—on account of his running and his excitement and the fact that he was still weak—was pulsating and glowing with a pink light.

He understood how low he had fallen. It had to happen. He had been living too easy, too presumptuous a life, with far too high an opinion of himself—and he was in fact a lazy, dirty, lewd man . . .

From his place above the pigsty Kavalerov understood everything.

He went back, picked up his suspenders, and got dressed. A spoon clinked—the widow reached out toward him—but he left the house without looking back. He spent the night once more on the street. And once more he came back. But this time he had firmly resolved:

"I'll show the widow her place. I won't let her so much

as mention what happened. What *doesn't* happen when you're drunk? But I can't live on the street."

The widow lit a taper over the cookstove. She gave him a sidelong glance and smiled in a self-satisfied way. He went into the room. Ivan's bowler hat was perched on a corner of the cupboard.

Ivan was sitting on the bed, looking like his brother, only smaller. The blanket surrounded him like a cloud. A wine bottle stood on the table. Ivan was gulping red wine from a glass. He had evidently just woken up: His face was still wrinkled from sleep, and he was drowsily scratching himself somewhere underneath the blanket.

Kavalerov was ready with the classic question: "What is the meaning of this?"

Ivan smiled brightly.

"The meaning of this, my friend, is that you must have a drink. Anichka, a glass!"

Anichka came in and went to the cupboard.

"Don't you be jealous, Kolia," said she, as she gave Kavalerov a hug. "He's terribly lonely, just like you. I feel sorry for you both."

"What is the meaning of this?" Kavalerov asked weakly.

"Oh, will you stop asking that!" said Ivan angrily. "It doesn't mean anything."

He got out of bed and, holding on to his underwear with one hand, poured Kavalerov some wine.

"Let us drink a toast, Kavalerov . . . We've done a lot of talking about feelings. And my friend, we forgot the main one. We forgot . . . indifference. Isn't that right? It is. I think that indifference is the best of all possible attitudes of the human mind. Let us be indifferent, Kavalerov. Open your eyes: We have found peace, my dear fellow. Drink! To indifference! Hooray! To Anichka! And, oh yes, today—listen, I've got lovely news for you—today, Kavalerov, it's your turn to sleep with Anichka. Hooray!"

———

(1927)

Vladimir Nabokov

(1899–1977)

Nabokov was born into a wealthy family of landed gentry in Saint Petersburg, and left a record of his blissfully happy childhood in one of the greatest autobiographies of this century, *Speak, Memory* (1967). He left Russia after the Revolution and was educated at Cambridge. Using the pseudonym V. Sirin, he became well known as a novelist and poet in the lively though constricted Russian émigré world that flourished in Berlin. Fearing for the safety of his wife, who was Jewish, Nabokov fled Europe for the United States in 1940, where he supported himself by teaching and where he accomplished the most astonishing metamorphosis known to the history of modern literature: He transformed himself from a Russian into an American writer. Not only did he lay aside the painstakingly formed instrument of his Russian style, but he also created in his new language one of the most idiosyncratic and powerful voices of the twentieth century. He even became an exemplary master of English prose, whose influence can be detected in the work of many a native-born writer.

Why, then, is he in an anthology of Russian writing? Because Nabokov would be a formidable presence in the history of contemporary Russian literature if he had never written a word in any other language. The four books of poetry, numerous short stories, and nine novels that he published in his native language before coming to America constitute a distinguished *oeuvre*. The novels include at least three masterpieces (the second date is that of the English translation): *The Defense* (1930, 1964); *The Gift* (1937, 1963); and *Invitation to a Beheading* (1938, 1959). What is more, the novels that he wrote in English, including his most "American" book, *Lolita*, contain a pervasive Russian subtext, which readers acquainted with that language delight in detecting.

Besides being a writer of genius, Nabokov was also a scientist—he made significant contributions to the field of lepidopterology—and an internationally known theorist of chess and composer of chess problems. Awesomely erudite in the history of Russian, English, and French *belles lettres*, he appears in his published lectures on literature (originally delivered to his classes at Cornell) not only as learned and monumentally nonconformist in his opinions, but also as one possessed by an uncommon zeal for teaching.

The worldwide success of the novel *Lolita* in 1958 (first published in France in 1955) enabled Nabokov to retire from teaching and spend the balance of his days in the alpine fastness of Montreux, Switzerland, whence poured, with meticulously calculated timing, a flood of new novels, translations of many of the novels first written in Russian, works of scholarship, and numerous interviews. It is a testimony to the preternatural shrewdness with which Nabokov managed his career that the interviews belong to the *oeuvre* proper, and not to journalistic dust: Nabokov's interviews consist of written questions to which he supplied carefully written answers.

The inextinguishable Russianness of Nabokov's character manifested itself in what can only be called the national piety with which he devoted himself to bringing Pushkin's *Eugene Onegin* across the barriers of time and language into English. If there is a single masterpiece of Russian literature, it is the *Onegin*, at once the greatest poem and the greatest novel of the language. Nabokov's voluminous edition contains an eccentrically provocative translation, a sort of bookish novella on Pushkin's African ancestry, a treatise on Russian as compared with English versification, and one of the most exhaustive and entertaining commentaries ever written. It provoked a furious debate on the topic of poetic translation, the intrusion of personality into the *apparatus criticus*, and so on. A merciless polemicist, Nabokov followed the great Russian tradition of literary dispute, which is rather like the great Russian tradition of military dispute: He advanced massively, taking no prisoners.

For the Russian reader, one of the happiest consequences of the collapse of the USSR was the publication of Nabokov in his native land.

THE RETURN OF
CHORB

The Kellers left the opera house at a late hour. In that pacific German city, where the very air seemed a little lusterless and where a transverse row of ripples had kept shading gently the reflected cathedral for well over seven centuries, Wagner was a leisurely affair presented with relish so as to overgorge one with music. After the opera Keller took his wife to a smart nightclub renowned for its white wine. It was past one in the morning when their car, flippantly lit on the inside, sped through lifeless streets to deposit them at the iron wicket of their small but dignified private house. Keller, a thickset old German, closely resembling Oom Paul Kruger, was the first to step down on the sidewalk, across which the loopy shadows of leaves stirred in the streetlamp's gray glimmer. For an instant his starched shirt front and the droplets of bugles trimming his wife's dress caught the light as she disengaged a stout leg and climbed out of the car in her turn. The maid met them in the vestibule and, still carried by the momentum of the news, told them in a frightened whisper about Chorb's having called. Frau Keller's chubby face, whose everlasting freshness somehow agreed with her Russian merchant-class parentage, quivered and reddened with agitation.

"He said she was ill?"

The maid whispered still faster. Keller stroked his gray brush of hair with his fat palm, and an old man's frown overcast his large, somewhat simian face, with its long upper lip and deep furrows.

"I simply refuse to wait till tomorrow," muttered Frau Keller, shaking her head as she gyrated heavily on one spot, trying to catch the end of the veil that covered her auburn wig. "We'll go there at once. Oh dear, oh dear! No wonder there's been no letters for quite a month."

Keller punched his gibus open and said in his precise, slightly guttural Russian:

"The man is insane. How dare he, if she's ill, take her a second time to that vile hotel?"

But they were wrong, of course, in thinking that their daughter was ill. Chorb said so to the maid only because it was easier to utter. In point of fact he had returned alone from abroad and only now realized that, like it or not, he would have to explain how his wife had perished, and why he had written nothing about it to his in-laws. It was all very difficult. How was he to explain that he wished to possess his grief all by himself, without tainting it by any foreign substance and without sharing it with any other soul? Her death appeared to him as a most rare, almost unheard-of occurrence; nothing, it seemed to him, could be purer than such a death, caused by the impact of an electric stream, the same stream which, when poured into glass receptacles, yields the purest and brightest light.

Ever since that spring day when, on the white highway a dozen kilometers from Nice, she had touched, laughing, the live wire of a storm-felled pole, Chorb's entire world ceased to sound like a world: it retreated at once, and even the dead body that he carried in his arms to the nearest village struck him as something alien and needless.

In Nice, where she had to be buried, the disagreeable consumptive clergyman kept in vain pressing him for details: Chorb responded only with a languid smile. He sat daylong on the shingly beach, cupping colored pebbles and letting them flow from hand to hand; and then, suddenly, without waiting for the funeral, he traveled back to Germany.

He passed in reverse through all the spots they had visited together during their honeymoon journey. In Switzerland where they had wintered and where the apple trees were now in their last bloom, he recognized nothing except the hotels. As to the Black Forest, through which they had hiked in the preceding autumn, the chill of the spring did not impede memory. And just as he had tried, on the southern beach, to find again that unique rounded black pebble with the regular little white belt, which she had happened to show him on the eve of their last ramble, so now he did his best to look up all the roadside items that retained her exclamation mark: the special profile of a cliff, a hut roofed with a layer of silvery-gray scales, a black fir tree and a footbridge over a white torrent, and something which one might be inclined to regard as a kind of fatidic prefiguration: the radial span of a spider's web between two telegraph wires that were beaded with droplets of mist. She accompanied him: her little boots stepped rapidly, and her hands never stopped moving, moving—to pluck a leaf from a bush or stroke a rock wall in passing—light, laughing hands that knew no repose. He saw her small face with its dense dark freckles, and her wide eyes, whose pale greenish hue was that of the shards of glass licked smooth by the sea waves. He thought that if he managed to gather all the little things they had noticed together—if he re-created thus the near past—her image would grow immortal and replace her for ever. Nighttime, though, was unendurable. Night imbued with sudden terror her irrational presence. He hardly slept at all during the three weeks of his trek—and now he got off, quite drugged with fatigue, at the railway station, which had been last autumn their point of departure from the quiet town where he had met and married her.

It was around eight o'clock of the evening. Beyond the houses the cathedral tower was sharply set off in black against a golden-red stripe of sunset. In the station square stood in file the selfsame decrepit fiacres. The identical newspaper seller uttered his hollow crepuscular cry. The same black poodle with apathetic eyes was in the act of raising a thin hindleg near a Morris pillar, straight at the scarlet lettering of a playbill announcing *Parsifal*.

Chorb's luggage consisted of a suitcase and a big tawny trunk. A fiacre took him through the town. The cabby kept indolently flapping his reins, while steadying the trunk with one hand. Chorb remembered that she whom he never named liked to take rides in cabs.

In a lane at the corner of the municipal opera house there was an old three-storied hotel of a disreputable type with rooms that were let by the week, or by the hour. Its black paint had peeled off in geographical patterns; ragged lace curtained its bleary windows; its inconspicuous front door was never locked. A pale but jaunty lackey led Chorb down a crooked corridor reeking of dampness and boiled cabbage into a room which Chorb recognized—by the picture of a pink *baigneuse* in a gilt frame over the bed—as the very one in which he and his wife had spent their first night together. Everything amused her then—the fat man in his shirt sleeves who was vomiting right in the passage, and the fact of their having chosen by chance such a beastly hotel, and the presence of a lovely blond hair in the wash basin; but what tickled her most was the way they had escaped from her house. Immediately upon coming home from church she ran up to her room to change, while downstairs the guests were gathering for supper. Her father, in a dress coat of sturdy cloth, with a flabby grin on his apish face, clapped this or that man on the shoulder and served ponies of brandy himself. Her mother, in the meantime, led her closest friends, two by two, to inspect the bedroom meant for the young couple: with tender emotion, whispering under her breath, she pointed out the colossal eiderdown, the orange blossoms, the two pairs of brand-new bedroom slippers—large checkered ones, and tiny red ones with pompons—that she had aligned on the bedside rug, across which a Gothic inscription ran: "*We are together unto the tomb.*" Presently, everybody moved toward the *hors d'oeuvres*—and Chorb and his wife, after the briefest of consultations, fled through the back door, and only on the following morning, half an hour before the express train was to leave, reappeared to collect their luggage. Frau Keller had sobbed all night; her husband, who had always regarded Chorb (destitute Russian émigré and *littérateur*) with suspicion, now cursed his daughter's choice, the cost of the liquor, the local police that could do nothing. And several times, after the Chorbs had gone, the old man went to look at the hotel in the lane behind the opera house, and henceforward that black, purblind house became an object of disgust and attraction to him like the recollection of a crime.

While the trunk was being brought in, Chorb kept staring at the rosy chromo. When the door closed, he bent over the trunk and unlocked it. In a corner of the room, behind a loose strip of wallpaper, a mouse made a scuffing noise and then raced like a toy on rollers. Chorb turned on his heel with a start. The light bulb hanging from the ceiling on a cord swayed ever so gently, and the shadow of the cord glided across the green couch and broke at its edge. It was on that couch that he had slept on his nuptial night. She, on the regular bed, could be heard breathing with the even rhythm of a child. That night he had kissed her once—on the hollow of the throat—that had been all in the way of love-making.

The mouse was busy again. There exist small sounds that are more frightening than gunfire. Chorb left the trunk alone and paced the room a couple of times. A moth struck the lamp with a ping. Chorb wrenched the door open and went out.

On the way downstairs he realized how weary he was, and when he found himself in the alley the blurry blue of the May night made him dizzy. Upon turning into the boulevard he walked faster. A square. A stone *Herzog*. The black masses of the City Park. Chestnut trees now were in flower. *Then*, it had been autumn. He had gone for a long stroll with her on the eve of the wedding. How good was the earthy, damp, somewhat violety smell of the dead leaves strewing the sidewalk! On those enchanting overcast days the sky would be of a dull white, and the small twig-reflecting puddle in the middle of the black pavement resembled an insufficiently developed photograph. The gray-stone villas were separated by the mellow and motionless foliage of yellowing trees, and in front of the Kellers' house the leaves of a withering poplar had acquired the tone of transparent grapes. One glimpsed, too, a few birches behind the bars of the gate; ivy solidly muffed some of their boles, and Chorb made a point of telling her that ivy never grew on birches in Russia, and she remarked that the foxy tints of their minute leaves reminded her of spots of tender rust upon ironed linen. Oaks and chestnuts lined the sidewalk; their black bark was velveted with green rot; every now and then a leaf broke away to fly athwart the street like a scrap of wrapping paper. She attempted to catch it on the wing by means of a child's spade found near a heap of pink bricks at a spot where the street was under repair. A little way off the funnel of a workers' van emitted gray-blue smoke which drifted aslant and dissolved between the branches—and a resting workman, one hand on his hip, contemplated the young lady, as light as a dead leaf, dancing about with that little spade in her raised hand. She skipped, she laughed. Chorb, hunching his back a bit, walked behind her—and it seemed to him that happiness itself had that smell, the smell of dead leaves.

At present he hardly recognized the street, encumbered as it was with the nocturnal opulence of chestnut trees. A streetlamp glinted in front; over the glass a branch drooped, and several leaves at its end, saturated with light, were quite translucent. He came nearer. The shadow of the wicket, its checkerwork all distorted, swept up toward him from the sidewalk to entangle his feet. Beyond the gate, and beyond a dim gravel walk, loomed the front of the familiar house, dark except for the light in one open window. Within that amber chasm the housemaid was in the act of spreading with an ample sweep of her arms a snow-bright sheet on a bed. Loudly and curtly Chorb called out to her. With one hand he still gripped the wicket and the dewy touch of iron against his palm was the keenest of all memories.

The maid was already hurrying toward him. As she was to tell Frau Keller later, what struck her first was the fact that Chorb remained standing silently on the sidewalk although she had unlocked the little gate at once. "He had no hat," she related, "and the light of the streetlamp fell on his forehead, and his forehead was all sweaty, and the hair was glued to it by the sweat. I told him master and mistress were at the theater. I asked him why he was alone. His eyes were blazing, their look terrified me, and he seemed not to have shaved for quite a time. He said softly: 'Tell them that she is ill.' I asked: 'Where are you staying?' He said: 'Same old place,' and then added: 'That does not matter. I'll call again in the morning.' I suggested he wait—but he didn't reply and went away."

Thus Chorb traveled back to the very source of his recollections, an agonizing and yet blissful test now drawing to a close. All there remained was but a single night to be spent in that first chamber of their marriage, and by tomorrow the test would be passed and her image made perfect.

But as he trudged back to the hotel, up the boulevard, where on all the benches in the blue darkness sat hazy figures, Chorb suddenly understood that, despite exhaustion, he would not be able to sleep alone in that room with its naked bulb and whispery crannies. He reached the square and plodded along the city's main avenue—and now he knew what must be done. His quest, however, lasted a long while: This was a quiet and chaste town, and the secret by-street where one could buy love was unknown to Chorb. Only after an hour of helpless wandering, which caused his ears to sing and his feet to burn, did he enter that little lane—whereupon he accosted at once the first girl who hailed him.

"The night," said Chorb, scarcely unclenching his teeth.

The girl cocked her head, swung her handbag, and replied: "Twenty-five."

He nodded. Only much later, having glanced at her casually, Chorb noted with indifference that she was pretty enough, though considerably jaded, and that her bobbed hair was blond.

She had been in that hotel several times before, with other customers, and the wan, sharp-nosed lackey, who was tripping down as they were going upstairs, gave her an amiable wink. While Chorb and she walked along the corridor, they could hear, from behind one of the doors, a bed creaking, rhythmically and weightily, as if a log was being sawed in two. A few doors further the same monotonous creak came from another room and as they passed by the girl looked back at Chorb with an expression of cold playfulness.

In silence he ushered her into his room—and immediately, with a profound anticipation of sleep, started to tear off his collar from its stud. The girl came up very close to him:

"And what about a small present?" she suggested, smiling.

Dreamily, absentmindedly, Chorb considered her, as he slowly grasped what she meant.

Upon receiving the banknotes, she carefully arranged them in her bag, uttered a light little sigh, and again rubbed herself against him.

"Shall I undress?" she asked with a shake of her bob.

"Yes, go to bed," muttered Chorb. "I'll give you some more in the morning."

The girl began to undo hastily the buttons of her blouse, and kept glancing at him askance, being slightly taken aback by his abstraction and gloom. He shed his clothes quickly and carelessly, got into the bed and turned to the wall.

"This fellow likes kinky stuff," vaguely conjectured the girl. With slow hands she folded her chemise, placed it upon a chair. Chorb was already fast asleep.

The girl wandered around the room. She noticed that

the lid of the trunk standing by the window was slightly ajar; by squatting on her heels, she managed to peep under the lid's edge. Blinking and cautiously stretching out her bare arm, she palpated a woman's dress, a stocking, scraps of silk—all this stuffed in anyhow and smelling so nice that it made her feel sad.

Presently she straightened up, yawned, scratched her thigh, and just as she was, naked, but in her stockings, drew aside the window curtain. Behind the curtain the casement was open and one could make out, in the velvety depths, a corner of the opera house, the black shoulder of a stone Orpheus outlined against the blue of the night and a row of light along the dim façade which slanted off into darkness. Down there, far away, diminutive dark silhouettes swarmed as they emerged from bright doorways onto the semicircular layers of illumined porch steps, to which glided up cars with shimmering headlights and smooth glistening tops. Only when the breakup was over and the brightness gone, the girl closed the curtain again. She switched off the light and stretched on the bed beside Chorb. Just before falling asleep she caught herself thinking that once or twice she had already been in that room: she remembered the pink picture on its wall.

Her sleep lasted not more than an hour: a ghastly deep-drawn howl roused her. It was Chorb screaming. He had woken up some time after midnight, had turned on his side and had seen his wife lying beside him. He screamed horribly, with visceral force. The white specter of a woman sprang off the bed. When, trembling, she turned on the light, Chorb was sitting among the tumbled bed-clothes, his back to the wall, and through his spread fingers one eye could be seen burning with a mad flame. Then he slowly uncovered his face, slowly recognized the girl. With a frightened mutter she was hastily putting on her chemise.

And Chorb heaved a sigh of relief for he realized that the ordeal was over. He moved onto the green couch, and sat there, clasping his hairy shins and with a meaningless smile contemplating the harlot. That smile increased her terror; she turned away, did up one last hook, laced her boots, busied herself with the putting on of her hat.

At this moment the sound of voices and footsteps came from the corridor.

One could hear the voice of the lackey repeating mournfully: "But look here, there's a lady with him." And an irate guttural voice kept insisting: "But I'm telling you she's my daughter."

The footsteps stopped at the door. A knock followed.

The girl snatched her bag from the table and resolutely flung the door open. In front of her stood an amazed old gentleman in a lusterless top hat, a pearl stud gleaming in his starched shirt. From over his shoulder peered the tear-stained face of a stout lady with a veil on her hair. Behind them the puny pale lackey strained up on tiptoe, making big eyes and gesturing invitingly. The girl understood his signs and shot out into the corridor, past the old man, who turned his head in her wake with the same puzzled look and then crossed the threshold with his companion. The door closed. The girl and the lackey remained in the corridor. They exchanged a frightened glance and bent their heads to listen. But in the room all was silence. It seemed incredible that inside there should be three people. Not a single sound came from there.

"They don't speak," whispered the lackey and put his finger to his lips.

(1925)

THE VISIT TO
THE MUSEUM

Several years ago a friend of mine in Paris—a person with
oddities, to put it mildly—learning that I was going to
spend two or three days at Montisert, asked me to drop in
at the local museum where there hung, he was told, a portrait of his grandfather by Leroy. Smiling and spreading
out his hands, he related a rather vague story to which
I confess I paid little attention, partly because I do not
like other people's obtrusive affairs, but chiefly because I
had always had doubts about my friend's capacity to remain this side of fantasy. It went more or less as follows:
after the grandfather died in their St. Petersburg house
back at the time of the Russo-Japanese War, the contents
of his apartment in Paris were sold at auction. The portrait, after some obscure peregrinations, was acquired by
the museum of Leroy's native town. My friend wished to
know if the portrait was really there; if there, if it could be
ransomed: and if it could, for what price. When I asked
why he did not get in touch with the museum, he replied
that he had written several times, but had never received
an answer.

I made an inward resolution not to carry out the request—I could always tell him I had fallen ill or changed
my itinerary. The very notion of seeing sights, whether
they be museums or ancient buildings, is loathsome to me;
besides, the good freak's commission seemed absolute
nonsense. It so happened, however, that, while wandering
about Montisert's empty streets in search of a stationery
store, and cursing the spire of a long-necked cathedral, always the same one, that kept popping up at the end of
every street, I was caught in a violent downpour which

immediately went about accelerating the fall of the maple leaves, for the fair weather of a southern October was holding on by a mere thread. I dashed for cover and found myself on the steps of the museum.

It was a building of modest proportions, constructed of many-colored stones, with columns, a gilt inscription over the frescoes of the pediment, and a lion-legged stone bench on either side of the bronze door. One of its leaves stood open, and the interior seemed dark against the shimmer of the shower. I stood for a while on the steps, but, despite the overhanging roof, they were gradually growing speckled. I saw that the rain had set in for good, and so, having nothing better to do, I decided to go inside. No sooner had I trod on the smooth, resonant flagstones of the vestibule than the clatter of a moved stool came from a distant corner, and the custodian—a banal pensioner with an empty sleeve—rose to meet me, laying aside his newspaper and peering at me over his spectacles. I paid my franc and, trying not to look at some statues at the entrance (which were as traditional and as insignificant as the first number in a circus program), I entered the main hall.

Everything was as it should be: gray tints, the sleep of substance, matter dematerialized. There was the usual case of old, worn coins resting in the inclined velvet of their compartments. There was, on top of the case, a pair of owls, Eagle Owl and Long-eared, with their French names reading "Grand Duke" and "Middle Duke" if translated. Venerable minerals lay in their open graves of dusty papier-mâché; a photograph of an astonished gentleman with a pointed beard dominated an assortment of strange black lumps of various sizes. They bore a great resemblance to frozen frass, and I paused involuntarily over them, for I was quite at a loss to guess their nature, composition and function. The custodian had been following me with felted steps, always keeping a respectful distance; now, however, he came up, with one hand behind his back and the ghost of the other in his pocket, and gulping, if one judged by his Adam's apple.

"What are they?" I asked.

"Science has not yet determined," he replied, undoubtedly having learned the phrase by rote. "They were found," he continued in the same phony tone, "in 1895, by Louis Pradier, Municipal Councillor and Knight of the Legion of Honor," and his trembling finger indicated the photograph.

"Well and good," I said, "but who decided, and why, that they merited a place in the museum?"

"And now I call your attention to this skull!" the old man cried energetically, obviously changing the subject.

"Still, I would be interested to know what they are made of," I interrupted.

"Science. . . ." he began anew, but stopped short and looked crossly at his fingers, which were soiled with dust from the glass.

I proceeded to examine a Chinese vase, probably brought back by a naval officer; a group of porous fossils; a pale worm in clouded alcohol; a red-and-green map of Montisert in the seventeenth century; and a trio of rusted tools bound by a funereal ribbon—a spade, a mattock and a pick. "To dig in the past," I thought absentmindedly, but this time did not seek clarification from the custodian, who was following me noiselessly and meekly, weaving in and out among the display cases. Beyond the first hall there was another, apparently the last, and in its center a large sarcophagus stood like a dirty bathtub, while the walls were hung with paintings.

At once my eye was caught by the portrait of a man between two abominable landscapes (with cattle and "atmosphere"). I moved closer and, to my considerable amazement, found the very object whose existence had hitherto seemed to me but the figment of an unstable mind. The man, depicted in wretched oils, wore a frock coat, whiskers and a large pince-nez on a cord; he bore a likeness to Offenbach, but, in spite of the work's vile conventionality, I had the feeling one could make out in his features the horizon of a resemblance, as it were, to my friend. In one corner, meticulously traced in carmine against a black background, was the signature *Leroy* in a hand as commonplace as the work itself.

I felt a vinegarish breath near my shoulder, and turned to meet the custodian's kindly gaze. "Tell me," I asked, "supposing someone wished to buy one of these paintings, whom should he see?"

"The treasures of the museum are the pride of the city," replied the old man, "and pride is not for sale."

Fearing his eloquence, I hastily concurred, but nevertheless asked for the name of the museum's director. He tried to distract me with the story of the sarcophagus, but I insisted. Finally he gave me the name of one M. Godard and explained where I could find him.

Frankly, I enjoyed the thought that the portrait existed. It is fun to be present at the coming true of a dream, even if it is not one's own. I decided to settle the matter without delay. When I get in the spirit, no one can hold me back. I left the museum with a brisk, resonant step, and found that the rain had stopped, blueness had spread across the sky, a woman in besplattered stockings was spinning along on a silver-shining bicycle, and only over the surrounding hills did clouds still hang. Once again the cathedral began playing hide-and-seek with me, but I outwitted it. Barely escaping the onrushing tires of a furious red bus packed with singing youths, I crossed the asphalt thoroughfare and a minute later was ringing at the garden gate of M. Godard. He turned out to be a thin, middle-aged gentleman in high collar and dickey, with a pearl in the knot of his tie, and a face very much resembling a Russian wolfhound; as if that were not enough, he was licking his chops in a most doglike manner, while sticking a stamp on an envelope, when I entered his small but lavishly furnished room with its malachite inkstand on the desk and a strangely familiar Chinese vase on the mantel. A pair of fencing foils hung crossed over the mirror, which reflected the narrow gray back of his head. Here and there photographs of a warship pleasantly broke up the blue flora of the wallpaper.

"What can I do for you?" he asked, throwing the letter

he had just sealed into the wastebasket. This act seemed unusual to me; however, I did not see fit to interfere. I explained in brief my reason for coming, even naming the substantial sum with which my friend was willing to part, though he had asked me not to mention it, but wait instead for the museum's terms.

"All this is delightful," said M. Godard. "The only thing is, you are mistaken—there is no such picture in our museum."

"What do you mean there is no such picture? I have just seen it! Portrait of a Russian Nobleman, by Gustave Leroy."

"We do have one Leroy," said M. Godard when he had leafed through an oilcloth notebook and his black fingernail had stopped at the entry in question. "However, it is not a portrait but a rural landscape: The Return of the Herd."

I repeated that I had seen the picture with my own eyes five minutes before and that no power on earth could make me doubt its existence.

"Agreed," said M. Godard, "but I am not crazy either. I have been curator of our museum for almost twenty years now and know this catalogue as well as I know the Lord's Prayer. It says here Return of the Herd and that means the herd is returning, and, unless perhaps your friend's grandfather is depicted as a shepherd, I cannot conceive of his portrait's existence in our museum."

"He is wearing a frock coat," I cried. "I swear he is wearing a frock coat!"

"And how did you like our museum in general?" M. Godard asked suspiciously. "Did you appreciate the sarcophagus?"

"Listen," I said (and I think there was already a tremor in my voice), "do me a favor—let's go there this minute, and let's make an agreement that if the portrait is there, you will sell it."

"And if not?" inquired M. Godard.

"I shall pay you the sum anyway."

"All right," he said. "Here, take this red-and-blue pen-

cil and using the red—the red, please—put it in writing
for me."

In my excitement I carried out his demand. Upon
glancing at my signature, he deplored the difficult pronun-
ciation of Russian names. Then he appended his own signature and, quickly folding the sheet, thrust it into his
waistcoat pocket.

"Let's go," he said, freeing a cuff.

On the way he stepped into a shop and bought a bag of
sticky-looking caramels which he began offering me insistently; when I flatly refused, he tried to shake out a couple
of them into my hand. I pulled my hand away. Several
caramels fell on the sidewalk; he stopped to pick them up
and then overtook me at a trot. When we drew near the
museum we saw the red tourist bus (now empty) parked
outside.

"Aha," said M. Godard, pleased. "I see we have many
visitors today."

He doffed his hat and, holding it in front of him, walked
decorously up the steps.

All was not well at the museum. From within issued
rowdy cries, lewd laughter, and even what seemed like the
sound of a scuffle. We entered the first hall; there the elderly custodian was restraining two sacrilegists who wore
some kind of festive emblems in their lapels and were altogether very purple-faced and full of pep as they tried to
extract the municipal councillor's merds from beneath the
glass. The rest of the youths, members of some rural athletic organization, were making noisy fun, some of the
worm in alcohol, others of the skull. One joker was in
rapture over the pipes of the steam radiator, which he
pretended was an exhibit; another was taking aim at an
owl with his fist and forefinger. There were about thirty
of them in all, and their motion and voices created a condition of crush and thick noise.

M. Godard clapped his hands and pointed at a sign
reading "Visitors to the Museum must be decently at-
tired." Then he pushed his way, with me following,
into the second hall. The whole company immediately

swarmed after us. I steered Godard to the portrait; he froze before it, chest inflated, and then stepped back a bit, as if admiring it, and his feminine heel trod on somebody's foot.

"Splendid picture," he exclaimed with genuine sincerity. "Well, let's not be petty about this. You were right, and there must be an error in the catalogue."

As he spoke, his fingers, moving as it were on their own, tore up our agreement into little bits which fell like snowflakes into a massive spittoon.

"Who's the old ape?" asked an individual in a striped jersey, and, as my friend's grandfather was depicted holding a glowing cigar, another funster took out a cigarette and prepared to borrow a light from the portrait.

"All right, let us settle on the price," I said, "and, in any case, let's get out of here."

"Make way, please!" shouted M. Godard, pushing aside the curious.

There was an exit, which I had not noticed previously, at the end of the hall and we thrust our way through to it.

"I can make no decision," M. Godard was shouting above the din. "Decisiveness is a good thing only when supported by law. I must first discuss the matter with the mayor, who has just died and has not yet been elected. I doubt that you will be able to purchase the portrait but nonetheless I would like to show you still other treasures of ours."

We found ourselves in a hall of considerable dimensions. Brown books, with a half-baked look and coarse, foxed pages, lay open under glass on a long table. Along the walls stood dummy soldiers in jack boots with flared tops.

"Come, let's talk it over," I cried out in desperation, trying to direct M. Godard's evolutions to a plush-covered sofa in a corner. But in this I was prevented by the custodian. Flailing his one arm, he came running after us, pursued by a merry crowd of youths, one of whom had put on his head a copper helmet with a Rembrandtesque gleam.

"Take it off, take it off!" shouted M. Godard, and some-one's shove made the helmet fly off the hooligan's head with a clatter.

"Let us move on," said M. Godard, tugging at my sleeve, and we passed into the section of Ancient Sculpture.

I lost my way for a moment among some enormous marble legs, and twice ran around a giant knee before I again caught sight of M. Godard, who was looking for me behind the white ankle of a neighboring giantess. Here a person in a bowler, who must have clambered up her, suddenly fell from a great height to the stone floor. One of his companions began helping him up, but they were both drunk, and, dismissing them with a wave of the hand, M. Godard rushed on to the next room, radiant with Oriental fabrics; there hounds raced across azure carpets, and a bow and quiver lay on a tiger skin.

Strangely, though, the expanse and motley only gave me a feeling of oppressiveness and imprecision, and, per-haps because new visitors kept dashing by or perhaps be-cause I was impatient to leave the unnecessarily spreading museum and amid calm and freedom conclude my busi-ness negotiations with M. Godard, I began to experience a vague sense of alarm. Meanwhile we had transported our-selves into yet another hall, which must have been really enormous, judging by the fact that it housed the entire skeleton of a whale, resembling a frigate's frame; beyond were visible still other halls, with the oblique sheen of large paintings, full of storm clouds, among which floated the delicate idols of religious art in blue and pink vest-ments; and all this resolved itself in an abrupt turbulence of misty draperies, and chandeliers came aglitter and fish with translucent frills meandered through illuminated aquariums. Racing up a staircase, we saw, from the gallery above, a crowd of gray-haired people with umbrellas ex-amining a gigantic mock-up of the universe.

At last, in a somber but magnificent room dedicated to the history of steam machines, I managed to halt my care-free guide for an instant.

"Enough!" I shouted. "I'm leaving. We'll talk tomorrow."

He had already vanished. I turned and saw, scarcely an inch from me, the lofty wheels of a sweaty locomotive. For a long time I tried to find the way back among models of railroad stations. How strangely glowed the violet signals in the gloom beyond the fan of wet tracks, and what spasms shook my poor heart! Suddenly everything changed again: in front of me stretched an infinitely long passage, containing numerous office cabinets and elusive, scurrying people. Taking a sharp turn, I found myself amid a thousand musical instruments; the walls, all mirror, reflected an enfilade of grand pianos, while in the center there was a pool with a bronze Orpheus atop a green rock. The aquatic theme did not end here as, racing back, I ended up in the Section of Fountains and Brooks, and it was difficult to walk along the winding, slimy edges of those waters.

Now and then, on one side or the other, stone stairs, with puddles on the steps, which gave me a strange sensation of fear, would descend into misty abysses, whence issued whistles, the rattle of dishes, the clatter of typewriters, the ring of hammers and many other sounds, as if, down there, were exposition halls of some kind or other, already closing or not yet completed. Then I found myself in darkness and kept bumping into unknown furniture until I finally saw a red light and walked out onto a platform that changed under me—and suddenly, beyond it, there was a bright parlor, tastefully furnished in Empire style, but not a living soul, not a living soul. . . . By now I was indescribably terrified, but every time I turned and tried to retrace my steps along the passages, I found myself in hitherto unseen places—a greenhouse with hydrangeas and broken windowpanes with the darkness of artificial night showing through beyond; or a deserted laboratory with dusty alembics on its tables. Finally I ran into a room of some sort with coatracks monstrously loaded down with black coats and astrakhan furs; from beyond a door came a burst of applause, but when I flung the door open, there was a theater, but only a soft opacity and splendidly counterfeited fog with the perfectly convincing blotches of indistinct streetlights. More than convincing! I advanced, and immediately a joyous and unmistakable sensation of reality at last replaced all the unreal trash amid which I had just been dashing to and fro. The stone beneath my feet was real sidewalk, powered with wonderfully fragrant, newly fallen snow, in which the infrequent pedestrians had already left fresh black tracks. At first the quiet and the snowy coolness of the night, somehow strikingly familiar, gave me a pleasant feeling after my feverish wanderings. Trustfully, I started to conjecture just where I had come out, and why the snow, and what were those lights exaggeratedly but indistinctly beaming here and there in the brown darkness. I examined and, stooping, even touched a round spur stone on the curb, then glanced at the palm of my hand, full of wet granular cold, as if hoping to read an explanation there. I felt how lightly, how naively I was clothed, but the distinct realization that I had escaped from the museum's maze was still so strong that, for the first two or three minutes, I experienced neither surprise nor fear. Continuing my leisurely examination, I looked up at the house beside which I was standing and was immediately struck by the sight of iron steps and railings that descended into the snow on their way to the cellar. There was a twinge in my heart, and it was with a new, alarmed curiosity that I glanced at the pavement, at its white cover along which stretched black lines, at the brown sky across which there kept sweeping a mysterious light, and at the massive parapet some distance away. I sensed that there was a drop beyond it; something was creaking and gurgling down there. Further on, beyond the murky cavity, stretched a chain of fuzzy lights. Scuffling along the snow in my soaked shoes, I walked a few paces, all the time glancing at the dark house on my right; only in a single window did a lamp glow softly under its green-glass shade. Here, a locked wooden gate. . . . There, what must be the shutters of a sleeping shop.... And by the light of a streetlamp whose shape had long been shouting to me its impossible message, I made out the ending of a sign— "... *inka Sapog*" ("... *oe Repair*")—but no, it was not the snow that had obliterated the "hard sign" at the end. "No, no, in a minute I shall wake up," I said aloud, and, trembling, my heart pounding, I turned, walked on, stopped again. From somewhere came the receding sound of hooves, the snow sat like a skullcap on a slightly leaning spur stone and indistinctly showed white on the woodpile on the other side of the fence, and already I knew, irrevocably, where I was. Alas, it was not the Russia I remembered, but the factual Russia of today, forbidden to me, hopelessly slavish, and hopelessly my own native land. A semiphantom in a light foreign suit, I stood on the impassive snow of an October night, somewhere on the Moyka or the Fontanka Canal, or perhaps on the Obvodny, and I had to do something, go somewhere, run: desperately protect my fragile, illegal life. Oh, how many times in my sleep I had experienced a similar sensation! Now, though, it was reality. Everything was real—the air that seemed to mingle with scattered snowflakes, the still unfrozen canal, the floating fish house, and that peculiar squareness of the darkened and the yellow windows. A man in a fur cap, with a briefcase under his arm, came toward me out of the fog, gave me a startled glance, and turned to look again when he had passed me. I waited for him to disappear and then, with a tremendous haste, began pulling out everything I had in my pockets, ripping up papers, throwing them into the snow and stamping them down. There were some documents, a letter from my sister in Paris, five hundred francs, a handkerchief, cigarettes; however, in order to shed all the integument of exile, I would have to tear off and destroy my clothes, my linen, my shoes, everything, and remain ideally naked; and, even though I was already shivering from my anguish and from the cold, I did what I could.

But enough. I shall not recount how I was arrested, nor

tell of my subsequent ordeals. Suffice it to say that it cost me incredible patience and effort to get back abroad, and that, ever since, I have foresworn carrying out commissions entrusted one by the insanity of others.

(*1939*)

Nadezhda Mandelstam

(1899–1980)

Nadezhda Yakovlevna Mandelstam (née Khazina) was born in Saratov but always regarded Kiev as her hometown, for all her early memories derived from there. Her parents were Jewish, though her father, Yakov Khazin, had converted to Christianity and had been baptized in the Russian Orthodox Church. Her mother was a doctor—it being as extraordinary in Czarist Russia for a woman to be a doctor as it is now, in the Soviet Union, common. Her childhood was spent in comfortable and cultivated surroundings. She traveled with her family in Europe and was at home in the principal languages of the Continent. Her earliest ambition was to be a painter.

She met her future husband, the poet Osip Mandelstam (see p. 169), on May Day 1919 in a Kiev restaurant catering to the avant-garde of that city. On a later May Day, in 1938, she watched as the secret police arrested him for the second time and took him away in a truck, never to be seen again. The nineteen years enclosed by these dates, rendered fatidic by sheer coincidence, were spent by two people who appear to have been enlarged and ennobled by their association, becoming somehow greater than the sum of their parts—a third spiritual entity. We are the richer for this happy union; it has provided us, one partner magnifying the other, with infinitely more than we should otherwise have known about Russian life and letters in this century. Certainly we owe to these two something of what we have learned about the power of uncorruptible character and courage.

If Nadezhda Mandelstam had not lived through the balance of the Stalinist nightmare and into the relatively mild reigns of Khrushchev and Brezhnev, we should no doubt be ignorant today of an immensely important fund of Osip Mandelstam's writing. She preserved it in her memory. She hid from the authorities whatever unpublished works had been committed to paper, of course, but she memorized even them, just in case. She carried not only the poetry but even the prose in her head, rehearsing it in a cycle of daily routines—a feat of literary devotion not unknown to the history of sacred letters but surely unequaled in our secular times.

She did not waste the forty-two years of left-over life that remained to her after that second May Day. The first task was to preserve her husband's legacy. The second was to keep herself out of the way of the genocidal fury—this she did by teaching English in a series of remote teachers' training establishments in the Russian outback. She was qualified to teach English not only by having learned it as a child (with "parsons' daughters" for governesses) but also by having earned the equivalent of an American doctoral degree with a dissertation on Old English grammar. The third task was to write the true story of Osip Mandelstam's life, of her own, and of their time, and, when she was old enough to be past caring, to publish it.

This task was accomplished in two volumes, *Hope against Hope* and *Hope Abandoned*, which have revised our notion of how biography and autobiography might be written. They combine the narrative of two lives—principally his in the first book and hers in the second—with memoirs of other persons and events, with essays, with sharp political invective and speculation, with literary criticism, and with a sort of dry lamentation, alternately witty and anguished. It hardly needs to be said that they were published first in the West; but in the West they have been published in every major language. Nearly everything she wrote has now been printed in Russia.

Something of Nadezhda's method can be surmised from the first sentence of *Hope against Hope*—one of the great openings of modern writing: "After slapping Alexei Tolstoi in the face, M. immediately returned to Moscow." The sentence is more than abrupt, more than the technically easy trick of beginning *in medias res*—it is also, under the circumstances, conspiratorial; it is illicitly intimate. From the outset we are in the author's dangerous confidence, and the balance of the book has an air of being not so much written as urgently whispered. From this beginning—at a point in the latter part of the account of Osip Mandelstam's life— the story weaves backward and forward in its various narrative and meditative modes, threatening at times to lose us but never actually doing so.

Her covenant with Osip Mandelstam discharged and her two books written, Nadezhda Mandelstam lived out the rest of her days smoking ruinous cigarettes and admitting haphazardly to her presence friends, journalists, and utter strangers who had absolutely to see her. The more her government practiced against her such petty atrocities as the denial of all postal service, the greater was her personal ascendancy. When she finally died, her corpse figured in a macabre farce staged by the KGB, whose agents confiscated the eighty pounds or so of used-up body to prevent the Christian burial requested by Nadezhda that was in the process of being carried out by her friends. Then they eventually returned it. Then Nadezhda Mandelstam was put decently underground beneath a wooden structure in the shape of the Cross.

A MAY NIGHT

(from *Hope against Hope*)

After slapping Alexei Tolstoi in the face, M. immediately returned to Moscow. From here he rang Akhmatova every day, begging her to come. She was hesitant and he was angry. When she had packed and bought her ticket, her brilliant, irritable husband Punin asked her, as she stood in thought by a window: "Are you praying that this cup should pass from you?" It was he who had once said to her when they were walking through the Tretiakov Gallery: "Now let's go and see how they'll take you to your execution." This is the origin of her lines:

"And later as the hearse sinks in the snow at dusk ...
What mad Surikov will describe my last journey?"

But she was not fated to make her last journey like this. Punin used to say, his face twitching in a nervous tic: "They're keeping you for the very end." But in the end they overlooked her and didn't arrest her. Instead, she was always seeing others off on their last journey—including Punin himself.

Akhmatova's son, Lev Gumilev, went to meet her at the station—he was staying with us at that time. It was a mistake to entrust him with this simple task—he of course managed to miss her, and she was very upset. It wasn't what she was used to. That year she had come to see us a great deal and she was always greeted at the station by M. himself, who at once started to amuse her with his jokes. She remembered why he had once said angrily, when the train was late: "You travel at the same speed as Anna Karenina." And another time: "Why are you dressed like a deep-sea diver?"—it had been raining in Leningrad and she had put on boots and a rubber mac with a hood, but in Moscow the sun was shining and it was very hot. Whenever they met they were cheerful and carefree like children, as in the old days at the Poets' Guild. "Stop it," I used to shout, "I can't live with such chatterboxes!" But this time, in May 1934, they had nothing to be cheerful about.

The day dragged on with excruciating slowness. In the evening the translator David Brodski turned up and then just wouldn't leave. There wasn't a bite to eat in the house and M. went around to the neighbors to try and get something for Akhmatova's supper. We hoped that Brodski might now get bored and leave, but no, he shot after M. and was still with him when he returned with the solitary egg he had managed to scrounge. Sitting down again in his chair, Brodski continued to recite the lines he liked best from his favorite poets, Sluchevski and Polonski (there was nothing he didn't know about both Russian and French poetry). He just went on and on, quoting and reminiscing, and it was only after midnight that we realized why he was being such a nuisance.

Whenever she came to see us, Akhmatova stayed in our small kitchen. The gas had not yet been installed and I cooked our semblance of a dinner on a kerosene stove in the corridor. In honor of our guest we covered the gas cooker with oilcloth to disguise it as a table. We called the kitchen "the sanctuary" after Narbut had once looked in there to see Akhmatova and said: "What are you doing here, like a pagan idol in a sanctuary? Why don't you go to some meeting or other where you can sit down properly?" Akhmatova and I had now taken refuge there, leaving M. to the mercy of the poetry-loving Brodski. Suddenly, at about one o'clock in the morning, there was a sharp, unbearably explicit knock on the door. "They've come for Osip," I said, and went to open the door.

Some men in civilian overcoats were standing outside—there seemed to be a lot of them. For a split second I had a tiny flicker of hope that this still wasn't it—my eye had not made out the uniforms under the covert-cloth topcoats. In fact, topcoats of this kind were also a sort of uniform—though they were intended as a diguise, like the old pea-green coats of the Czarist okhrana. But this I did not know then. All hope vanished as the uninvited guests stepped inside.

I had expected them to say "How do you do?" or "Is this Mandelstam's apartment?" or something else of the kind that any visitor says in order to be let in by the person who opens the door. But the night visitors of our times do not stand on such ceremony—like secret-police agents the world over, I suppose.

Without a word or a moment's hesitation, but with consummate skill and speed, they came in past me (not pushing, however) and the apartment was suddenly full of people already checking our identity papers, running their hands over our hips with a precise, well-practiced movement, and feeling our pockets to make sure we had no concealed weapons.

M. came out of the large room. "Have you come for me?" he asked. One of the agents, a short man, looked at him with what could have been a faint smile and said: "Your papers." M. took them out of his pocket, and after checking them, the agent handed him a warrant. M. read it and nodded.

In the language of the secret police this was what was known as a "night operation." As I learned later, they all firmly believed that they were always liable to meet with opposition on such occasions, and to keep their spirits up they regaled each other with romantic tales about the dangers involved in these night raids. I myself once heard the daughter of an important Chekist,* who had come to prominence in 1937, telling a story about how Isaac Babel had "seriously wounded one of our men" while resisting arrest. She told such stories as an expression of concern for her kindly, loving father whenever he went out on "night operations." He was fond of children and animals—at home he always had the cat on his knees—and he told his daughter never to admit that she had done anything wrong, and always to say "no." This homely man with the cat could never forgive the people he interrogated for admitting everything they were accused of. "Why did they do it?" the daughter asked, echoing her father. "Think of the trouble they made for themselves and for us as well!" By "us," she meant all those who had come at night with warrants, interrogated and passed sentence on the accused, and whiled away their spare time telling stories of the risks they ran. Whenever I hear such tales I think of the tiny hole in the skull of Isaac Babel, a cautious, clever man with a high forehead, who probably never once in his life held a pistol in his hands.

* Member of the Cheka, the secret police. At later periods the Cheka was known successively as the OGPU, GPU, NKVD, MVD, MGB. It is now called the KGB.

And so they burst into our poor, hushed apartments as though raiding bandits' lairs or secret laboratories in which masked carbonari were making dynamite and preparing armed resistance. They visited us on the night of May 13, 1934. After checking our papers, presenting their warrants and making sure there would be no resistance, they began to search the apartment. Brodski slumped into his chair and sat there motionless, like a huge wooden sculpture of some savage tribe. He puffed and wheezed with an angry, hurt expression on his face. When I chanced at one point to speak to him—asking him, I think, to get some books from the shelves for M. to take with him—he answered rudely: "Let M. get them himself," and again began to wheeze. Toward morning, when we were at last permitted to walk freely around the apartment and the tired Chekists no longer even looked searchingly at us as we did so, Brodski suddenly roused himself, held up his hand like a schoolboy and asked permission to go to the toilet. The agent directing the search looked at him with contempt. "You can go home," he said. "What?" Brodski said in astonishment. "Home," the man repeated and turned his back. The secret police despised their civilian helpers. Brodski had no doubt been ordered to sit with us that evening in case we tried to destroy any manuscripts when we heard the knock on the door.

(1970)

LAST LETTER

(from *Hope Abandoned*)

This letter was never read by the person it is addressed to. It is written on two sheets of very poor paper. Millions of women wrote such letters—to their husbands, sons, brothers, fathers, or simply to sweethearts. But next to none of them have been preserved. If such things ever survived here, it could only be owing to chance, or a miracle. My letter still exists by chance. I wrote it in October 1938, and in January I learned that M. was dead. It was thrown into a trunk with other papers and lay there for nearly thirty years. I came across it the last time I went through all my papers, gladdened by every scrap of something that had survived, and lamenting all the huge, irreparable losses. I read it not at once, but only several years later. When I did, I thought of all the other women who shared my fate. The vast majority of them thought as I, but many dared not admit it even to themselves. Nobody has yet told the story of what was done to us by other people—by those selfsame compatriots whom I do not wish to see destroyed, lest I thereby come to resemble them. Their present-day successors, the spiritual brothers of those who murdered M. and millions of others, will curse on reading this letter—why didn't they destroy the bitch (that is, me), they will ask, while they were about it? And they will also curse those who have so "relaxed vigilance" that forbidden thoughts and feelings have been allowed to break to the surface. Now again we are not supposed to remember the past and think—let alone speak—about it. Since the sole survivors of all the myriad shattered families are now only the grandchildren, there is in fact nobody left to remember and speak of it. Life goes on, and few indeed are those who wish to stir up the past. Not many years ago it was admitted that some "mistakes" had been made, but now it is denied again—nothing wrong is seen with the past. But neither can I speak of the past as a "mistake." How can one thus describe actions that were part of a system and flowed inexorably from its basic principles?

Instead of an epilogue, then, I end my book with this letter. I shall do what I can to see that both book and letter survive. There is not much hope, even though our present times are like honey and sugar compared with the past. Come what may, here is the letter:

22/10(38)

Osia, my beloved, faraway sweetheart!

I have no words, my darling, to write this letter that you may never read, perhaps. I am writing it into empty space. Perhaps you will come back and not find me here. Then this will be all you have left to remember me by.

Osia, what a joy it was living together like children—all our squabbles and arguments, the games we played, and our love. Now I do not even look at the sky. If I see a cloud, who can I show it to?

Remember the way we brought back provisions to make our poor feasts in all the places where we pitched our tent like nomads? Remember the good taste of bread when we got it by a miracle and ate it together? And our last winter in Voronezh. Our happy poverty, and the poetry you wrote. I remember the time we were coming back once from the baths, when we bought some eggs or sausage, and a cart went by loaded with hay. It was still cold and I was freezing in my short jacket (but nothing like what we must suffer now: I know how cold you are). That day comes back to me now. I understand so clearly, and ache from the pain of it, that those winter days with all their troubles were the greatest and last happiness to be granted us in life.

My every thought is about you. My every tear and every smile is for you. I bless every day and every hour of our bitter life together, my sweetheart, my companion, my blind guide in life.

Like two blind puppies, we were, nuzzling each other and feeling so good together. And how fevered your poor head was, and how madly we frittered away the days of our life. What joy it was, and how we always knew what joy it was.

Life can last so long. How hard and long for each of us to die alone. Can this fate be for us who are inseparable? Puppies and children, did we deserve this? Did you deserve this, my angel? Everything goes on as before. I know nothing. Yet I know everything—each day and hour of your life are plain and clear to me as in a delirium.

You came to me every night in my sleep, and I kept asking what had happened, but you did not reply.

In my last dream I was buying food for you in a filthy hotel restaurant. The people with me were total strangers. When I had bought it, I realized I did not know where to take it, because I do not know where you are.

When I woke up, I said to Shura: "Osia is dead." I do not know whether you are still alive, but from the time of that dream, I have lost track of you. I do not know where you are. Will you hear me? Do you know how much I love you? I could never tell you how much I love you. I cannot tell you even now. I speak only to you, only to you. You are with me always, and I who was such a wild and angry one and never learned to weep simple tears—now I weep and weep and weep.

It's me: Nadia. Where are you?

Farewell.

Nadia.

(1974)

Daniil Kharms

(1905–1942)

Tyrants would appear to be more comfortable with outright sedition, which they can at least understand, than with deliberate silliness. Autocrats of whatever tendency have one thing in common—the conviction that Truth exists, and that they have it firmly in hand. Their favorite opponents are those who share this conviction, differing only with details of the second part. But the true philosophical anarchists, those who see the world as devoid of reason and order, and who celebrate this vacancy by filling it with gleeful nonsense, violate all the rules of the great game. They strike at the very roots of legitimacy and—ultimate outrage to the sensibilities of puritanical ideologues—they seem to enjoy themselves immensely. What exactly is their little game? The latest refinements in torture cannot elicit an answer (there being none), and thus the practitioners of Terror, itself founded upon unpredictable illogic, are themselves terrified.

Kharms (the name is one of the numerous pseudonyms of Daniil Ivanovich Yuvachev) belonged to a fugitive group that flourished, if that is the word, for about three years at the end of the 1920s and called itself the Oberiu. The first five letters of this name derive from the Russian words meaning "Association for Real Art." Nothing is more typical of the Oberiuty than the sixth letter, the *u*, which they tacked on for the sheer hell of it. "Real Art" for Kharms and his friends meant the Absurd, and it comes as something of a shock to learn that Stalin's Russia harbored writers whose aesthetic ideals resembled those of Alfred Jarry, Tristan Tzara, Eugène Ionesco, and, in the contemporary United States, the *New Yorker* writer Donald Barthelme.

Like many another clown (see the note on Zoshchenko, p. 215), Kharms had to struggle against periodic bouts of depression, which he did in part by making his everyday life a sequence of absurdist happenings. One of the few furnishings in his room was a contraption made of bits of metal, bicycle wheels, springs, and other scrap, which must have resembled the constructions of Francis Picabia and which was, like them, ideally functionless. At a time when the real aristocrats of Saint Petersburg were being systematically eradicated, Kharms publicly and dangerously flaunted his own imaginary nobility, refusing in bars to drink from anything but the family silver, which he carried about with him. Very little of what the Oberiuty wrote reached an audience except in the form of public readings. Kharms supported himself by writing for children. He was arrested in August 1941, and early in 1942 his wife was informed that he had died in prison.

ANECDOTES ABOUT PUSHKIN'S LIFE

1

Pushkin was a poet, and all the time he was writing something. Once Zhukovsky found him writing and shouted at him, "You really are a scribbler!"

From that time on, Pushkin loved Zhukovsky and in friendly fashion called him simply Zhukov.

2

As is known, Pushkin could never grow a beard. This bothered him a lot, and he always envied Zakharyn, who on the contrary really had a properly growing beard. "His grows and mine doesn't grow," Pushkin often complained, pointing at Zakharyn with his fingernails. And each time he was right.

3

Once Petrushevsky broke his watch and sent for Pushkin. Pushkin came, looked at Petrushevsky's watch, and put it back on the chair. "What do you say, Brother Pushkin?" Petrushevsky asked. "The wheels stopped going round," Pushkin said.

4

When Pushkin broke his legs, he got about on wheels. His friends liked to tease Pushkin and caught the wheels. Pushkin became angry and wrote poems in which he swore at his friends. He called these poems "erpigarms."

5

Pushkin spent the summer of 1829 in the country. He would get up early in the morning, drink a pitcher of milk, and run to the river to bathe. After bathing in the river, Pushkin would lie down on the grass and sleep till lunch. After lunch Pushkin would sleep in his hammock. When he met smelly peasants, Pushkin would nod to them and hold his nose with his fingers. The smelly peasants would take off their caps and say, "It's nothing."

6

Pushkin loved to throw rocks. As soon as he saw a rock, he would throw it. Sometimes he became so excited that he stood, all red in the face, waving his arms, throwing rocks, simply something awful.

7

Pushkin had four sons, all idiots. One didn't even know how to sit on a chair and fell off all the time. Pushkin himself also sat on a chair rather badly. It was simply killing: they sat at the table; at one end, Pushkin kept falling off his chair continually, and at the other end, his son. Simply enough to make one split one's sides with laughter.

THE CONNECTION

Philosopher!

1. I am writing to you in answer to your letter which you are about to write to me in answer to my letter which I wrote to you.

2. A violinist bought a magnet and was carrying it home. Along the way, hoods jumped him and knocked his cap off his head. The wind picked up the cap and carried it down the street.

3. The violinist put the magnet down and ran after the cap. The cap fell into a puddle of nitric acid and dissolved.

4. In the meantime, the hoods picked up the magnet and hid.

5. The violinist returned home without a coat and without a cap, because the cap had dissolved in the nitric acid, and the violinist, upset by losing his cap, had left his coat in the streetcar.

6. The conductor of the streetcar took the coat to a secondhand shop and exchanged it there for sour cream, groats, and tomatoes.

7. The conductor's father-in-law ate too many tomatoes, became sick, and died. The corpse of the conductor's father-in-law was put in the morgue, but it got mixed up, and in place of the conductor's father-in-law, they buried some old woman.

8. On the grave of the old woman, they put a white post with the inscription "Anton Sergeevich Kondratev."

9. Eleven years later, the worms had eaten through the post, and it fell down. The cemetery watchman sawed the post into four pieces and burned it in his stove. The wife

of the cemetery watchman cooked cauliflower soup over that fire.

10. But when the soup was ready, a fly fell from the wall, directly into the pot with this soup. They gave the soup to the beggar Timofey.

11. The beggar Timofey ate the soup and told the beggar Nikolay that the cemetery watchman was a good-natured man.

12. The next day the beggar Nikolay went to the cemetery watchman and asked for money. But the cemetery watchman gave nothing to the beggar Nikolay and chased him away.

13. The beggar Nikolay became very angry and set fire to the cemetery watchman's house.

14. The fire spread from the house to the church, and the church burned down.

15. A long investigation was carried on but did not succeed in determining the cause of the fire.

16. In the place where the church had stood a club was built, and on the day the club opened a concert was organized, at which the violinist who fourteen years earlier had lost his coat performed.

17. In the audience sat the son of one of those hoods who fourteen years before had knocked the cap off that violinist.

18. After the concert was over, they rode home in the same streetcar. In the streetcar behind theirs, the driver was the same conductor who once upon a time had sold the violinist's coat in a secondhand shop.

19. And so here they are, riding late at night through the city: in front, the violinist and the hood's son; and in back, the driver, the former conductor.

20. They ride along and don't know what connection there is between them, and they won't know till the day they die.

(1937)

Varlam Shalamov

(1907-1982)

In the mid-1960s the editor of these pages met Varlam Shalamov several times a week at the kitchen table of Nadezhda Mandelstam (see p. 387). There, too, he read some of the most remarkable Russian prose of this century—Shalamov's *Kolyma Tales*, which existed then only in typed copies, clandestinely circulated. They have now been published in the United States in two volumes, skillfully translated by John Glad: *Kolyma Tales* (1980) and *Graphite* (1981).

These volumes have only recently appeared in what was the Soviet Union, for even Solzhenitsyn (see p. 419) agrees that Shalamov is the most powerful witness to the extermination by Stalin of many millions of human lives. Kolyma is a region in northeastern Siberia that is over five times the size of France; it registers the lowest temperatures of any inhabited area in the Northern Hemisphere. It has abundant mineral deposits, the most valuable being gold. Under the oddest, most schizoid, and most self-defeating management policy ever conceived, the work force had the dual assignment to mine much-needed gold and die miserably in the process. When millions of men whose replacements are assured are thrown at a simple physical task, only a small percentage need survive and function for a reasonable time. The Soviet government always had an urgent need for the wealth buried in its remote eastern regions, and an equally urgent need to rid itself of those deemed to be a threat to its existence. Kolyma was the answer, and Shalamov was its poet.

In 1937 Shalamov was informed on by someone who overheard him express the opinion that Ivan Bunin (see p. 58) was a classical Russian author. For this crime he spent seventeen years in Kolyma. Hitler acknowledged the Bolsheviks as his teachers in certain techniques of population control, but his preferred instrument was fire. Stalin used ice.

In his person, Shalamov rather resembled a prehistoric creature discovered intact in a glacier and revived, though his terrifying exhumed appearance was no guide at all to his remarkably courteous and good-humored nature. Gorky's marvelous description of Tolstoy's hands (see p. 31) could be applied word for word to the immense, restless hands of Shalamov.

His prose has what can only be described as a rough-hewn finish, and the stories themselves—which are by no means all "stories" in the traditional sense—seem to have been put together out of whatever materials and primitive tools came to hand. Shalamov makes no distinction between what he witnessed and what he imagined (the account of the death of Osip Mandelstam, for instance, is sheer invention, as Shalamov himself told me, to comment obliquely on our ignorance of what actually became of him).

This description of his work would hardly seem to promise the reader the experience of a work of art, and it is true that some of the prose pieces, taken individually, have an unfinished and haphazard air. The cumulative effect, however, is that of a masterfully planned and executed replica of life so near the edge of madness, exhaustion, and death that it seems at times hallucinated, with gaps in consciousness. Shalamov is the least rhetorical and most impersonal of modern Russian writers. He *presents* without comment.

PROSTHETIC APPLIANCES

(from *Kolyma Tales*)

The camp's solitary confinement block was old, old. It seemed that all you had to do was to kick one of the wooden walls and its logs would collapse, disintegrate. But the block did not collapse and all seven cells did faithful service. Of course, any loudly spoken word could be heard by one's neighbors, but the inmates of the block were afraid of punishment. If the guard on duty marked the cell with a chalk X, the cell was deprived of hot food. Two Xs meant no bread as well. The block was used for camp offenses; anyone suspected of something more dangerous was taken away to Central Control.

For the first time all the prisoners entrusted with administrative work had suddenly been arrested. Some major affair, some camp trial was being put together. By someone's command.

Now all six of us were standing in the narrow corridor, surrounded by guards, feeling and understanding only one thing: that we had been caught by the teeth of that same machine as several years before and that we would learn the reason only tomorrow, no earlier.

We were all made to undress to our underwear and were led into a separate cell. The storekeeper recorded things taken for storage, stuffed them into sacks, attached tags, wrote. I knew the name of the investigator supervising the "operation"—Pesniakevich.

The first man was on crutches. He sat down on a bench next to the lamp, put the crutches on the floor, and began to undress. He was wearing a steel corset.

"Should I take it off?"

"Of course."

The man began to unlace the cords of the corset and the investigator Pesniakevich bent down to help him.

"Do you recognize me, old friend?" The question was asked in thieves' slang, in a confidential manner.

"I recognize you, Pleve."

The man in the corset was Pleve, supervisor of the camp tailor shop. It was an important job involving twenty tailors who, with the permission of the administration, filled individual orders even from outside the camp.

The naked man turned over on the bench. On the floor lay the steel corset as the report of the confiscated items was composed.

"What's this thing called?" asked the block storekeeper, touching the corset with the toe of his boot.

"A steel prosthetic corset," answered the naked man.

Pesniakevich went off to the side and I asked Pleve how he knew him.

"His mother kept a whorehouse in Minsk before the Revolution. I used to go there," Pleve answered coldly.

Pesniakevich emerged from the depths of the corridor with four guards. They picked Pleve up by his arms and legs and carried him into the cell. The lock snapped shut.

Next was Karavaev, manager of the stable. A former soldier of the famous Budyony Brigade, he had lost an arm in the Civil War.

Karavaev banged on the officer of the guards' table with the steel of his artificial limb.

"You bastards."

"Drop the metal. Let's have the arm."

Karavaev raised the untied limb, but the guards jumped the cavalryman and shoved him into the cell. There ensued a flood of elaborate obscenities.

"Listen, Karavaev," said the chief guard of the block. "We'll take away your hot food if you make noise."

"To hell with your hot food."

The head guard took a piece of chalk out of his pocket and made an X on Karavaev's cell.

"Who's going to sign for the arm?"

"No one. Put a check mark," commanded Pesniakevich.

Now it was the turn of our doctor, Zhitkov. A deaf old man, he wore a hearing aid. After him was Colonel Panin, manager of the carpentry shop. A shell had taken off the colonel's leg somewhere in East Prussia during the First World War. He was an excellent carpenter, and he explained to me that before the Revolution children of the nobility were often taught some hand trade. The old man unsnapped his prosthetic leg and hopped into his cell on one leg.

There were only two of us left—Shor, Grisha Shor the senior brigade leader, and myself.

"Look how cleverly things are going," Grisha said; the nervous mirth of the arrest was overtaking him. "One turns in a leg; another an arm; I'll give an eye." Adroitly he plucked out his porcelain right eye and showed it to me in his palm.

"You have an artificial eye?" I said in amazement. "I never noticed."

"You are not very observant. But then the eye is a good match."

While Grisha's eye was being recorded, the chief guard couldn't control himself and started giggling.

"That one gives us his arm; this one turns in his leg; another gives his back, and this one gives his eye. We'll have all the parts of the body at this rate. How about you?" He looked over my naked body carefully.

"What will you give up? Your soul?"

"No," I said. "You can't have my soul."

(*1980*)

A CHILD'S DRAWINGS

(from *Kolyma Tales*)

They didn't have any lists when they took us out for work assignments—just stood us in groups of five, since not all the guards knew their multiplication table. Any arithmetical computation is tricky when it has to be done with live objects in the cold. The cup of convict patience can suddenly overflow, and the administration knew it.

Today we had easy work, the kind they normally reserve for criminals—cutting firewood on a circular saw. The saw spun, knocking lightly as we dumped an enormous log onto the stand and slowly shoved it toward the blade. The saw shrieked and growled furiously. Like us, it detested working in the north, but we kept pushing the log forward until it split into two, unexpectedly light pieces.

Our third companion was chopping wood, using a heavy blue splitting ax with a long yellow handle. He worked on the thicker pieces from the ends, chopped the smaller ones in half with one blow. He was just as hungry as we were and the ax struck the wood in a feeble fashion, but the frozen larch split easily. Nature in the north is not impersonal or indifferent; it is in conspiracy with those who sent us here.

We finished the work, stacked the wood, and waited for the guards. Our guard was keeping warm in the building for which we'd been chopping wood, but we were supposed to march back in formation, breaking up in town into smaller groups.

We didn't go to warm up, though, since we had long since noticed, next to a fence, a large heap of garbage—something we could not afford to ignore. Both my companions were soon removing one frozen layer after another with the adroitness that comes from practice. Their booty consisted of lumps of frozen bread, an icy piece of hamburger, and a torn pair of men's socks. The socks were the most valuable item, of course, and I regretted that I hadn't found them first. "Civvies"—socks, scarfs, gloves, shirts, pants—were prized by people who for decades had nothing to wear but convict garb. The socks could be darned and exchanged for tobacco or bread.

I couldn't reconcile myself with my companions' success, and I too began to use my hands and legs to break off brightly colored pieces of the garbage pile. Beneath a twisted rag that looked like human intestines, I saw—for the first time in many years—a blue school notebook.

It was an ordinary child's drawing book.

Its pages were all carefully and diligently colored, and I began turning the bright cold naive pages, grown brittle in the frost. I also used to draw once upon a time, sitting next to the kerosene lamp on the dinner table. A dead hero of a fairy tale would come alive at the touch of the magic brush, as if it contained the water of life.

Looking like women's buttons, the water colors lay in their white tin box, and Prince Ivan galloped through the pine forest on a gray wolf. The pines were smaller than the wolf and Prince Ivan rode him like an Eskimo on a reindeer, his heels almost touching the moss. Smoke spiraled into the blue sky, and the neat Vs of birds could be seen among the stars.

The more I strained to recall my childhood, the more clearly I realized that it would not repeat itself and I would not encounter even a shade of it in the drawing book of another child.

It was a frightening notebook.

The northern city was wooden, its fences and walls painted in a bright ochre, and the brush of the young artist faithfully duplicated the yellow color wherever he wanted to show buildings and creations of man.

In the notebook there were many, very many fences. The people and the houses in almost every drawing were surrounded by even, yellow fences or circumscribed with the black lines of barbed wire. Iron threads of the official type topped all the fences in the child's notebook.

Near the fences stood people. The people in the notebook were not peasants or hunters; they were soldiers, guards, and sentries with rifles. Like mushrooms after the rain, the sentry booths stood at the feet of enormous guard towers. On the towers soldiers walked, their rifle barrels gleaming.

It was a small notebook, but the boy had managed to paint into it all the seasons of his native town.

The ground was bright and uniformly green, as in paintings by the young Matisse, and the blue, blue sky was fresh, pure, and clear. Sunrises and sunsets were conscientiously crimson, and this was no childish inability to capture halftones, color shifts, or shading. Nor was it a Gauguin-type prescription for art where everything that gave an impression of green was painted in the best green color.

The color combinations in the schoolbook were a realistic depiction of the sky in the far north where colors are unusually pure and clear and do not possess halftones.

I remember the old northern legend of how God created the taiga while he was still a child. There were few colors, but they were childishly fresh and vivid, and their subjects were simple.

Later, when God grew up and became an adult, he learned to cut out complicated patterns from his pages and created many bright birds. God grew bored with his former child's world and he threw snow on his forest creation and went south forever. Thus went the legend.

The child remained faithful in his winter drawings as well. The trees were black and naked. They were the enormous deciduous trees of the Daurian Mountains, and not the firs and pines of my childhood.

The northern hunt was on, and a toothy German shepherd strained at a leash held by Prince Ivan. . . . Prince Ivan wore a military hat that covered his ears, a white sheepskin coat, felt boots, and deep mittens. Prince Ivan had a submachine gun slung over his shoulder. Naked, triangular trees were poked into the snow.

The child saw nothing, remembered nothing but the yellow houses, barbed wire, guard towers, German shepherds, guards with submachine guns, and a blue, blue sky.

My companion glanced at the notebook and rubbed a sheet between his fingers.

"Find some newspaper if you want to smoke." He tore the notebook from my hands, crumpled it, and threw it onto the garbage pile. Frost began to form on the notebook. . . .

(*1980*)

LEND-LEASE

(from *Kolyma Tales*)

The fresh tractor prints in the marsh were tracks of some prehistoric beast that bore little resemblance to an article of American technology delivered under the terms of Lend-Lease.

We convicts had heard of these gifts from beyond the sea and the emotional confusion they had introduced into the minds of the camp bigwigs. Worn knit suits and secondhand pullovers collected for the convicts of Kolyma were snapped up in near fistfights by the wives of the Magadan generals.

As for the magical jars of sausage sent by Lend-Lease, we saw them only at a distance. What we knew and knew well were the chubby tins of Spam. Counted, measured by a very complex table of replacement, stolen by the greedy hands of the camp authorities, counted again and measured a second time before introduction to the kettle, boiled there till transformed into mysterious fibers that smelled like anything in the world except meat—this Spam excited the eye, but not the taste buds. Once tossed in the pot, Spam from Lend-Lease had no taste at all. Convict stomachs preferred something domestic such as old, rotten venison that couldn't be boiled down even in seven camp kettles. Venison doesn't disappear, doesn't become ephemeral like Spam.

Oatmeal from Lend-Lease we relished, but we never got more than two tablespoons per portion.

But the fruits of technology also came from Lend-Lease—fruits that could not be eaten: clumsy tomahawk-like hatchets, handy shovels with un-Russian work-saving handles. The shovel blades were instantaneously affixed to long Russian handles and flattened to make them more capacious.

Barrels of glycerin! Glycerin! The guard dipped out a bucketful with a kitchen pot on the very first night and got rich selling it to the convicts as "American honey."

From Lend-Lease also came enormous black fifty-ton Diamond trucks with trailers and iron sides and five-ton Studebakers that could easily manage any hill. There were no better trucks in all of Kolyma. Day and night, Studebakers and Diamonds hauled American wheat along the thousand-mile road. The wheat was in pretty white linen sacks stamped with the American eagle, and chubby, tasteless bread "rations" were baked from this flour. Bread from Lend-Lease flour possessed an amazing quality: anyone who ate it stopped visiting the toilet; once in five days a bowel movement would be produced that wasn't even worth the name. The stomach and intestines of the convict absorbed without remainder this magnificent white bread with its mixture of corn, bone meal, and something else in addition—perhaps hope. And the time has not yet come to count the lives saved by this wheat from beyond the sea.

The Studebakers and Diamonds ate a lot of gas, but the gas also came from Lend-Lease, a light aviation gas. Russian trucks were adapted to be heated with wood: two stoves set near the motor were heated with split logs. There arose several wood supply centers headed by party members working on contract. Technical leadership at these wood supply centers was provided by a chief engineer, a plain engineer, a rate setter, a planner, and bookkeepers. I don't remember whether two or three laborers ran the circular saw at the wood-processing plant. There may have been as many as three. The equipment was from Lend-Lease, and when a tractor came to the camp, a new word appeared in our language: "bulldozer."

The prehistoric beast was freed from its chain: an American bulldozer with caterpillar tracks and a wide blade. The vertical metal shield gleamed like a mirror reflecting the sky, the trees, the stars, and the dirty faces of the convicts. Even the guard walked up to the foreign monster and said a man could shave himself before such a mirror. But there was no shaving for us; even the thought couldn't have entered our heads.

The sighs and groans of the new American beast could be heard for a long time in the frosty air. The bulldozer coughed angrily in the frost, puffed and then suddenly roared and moved boldly forward, crushing the shrubbery and passing easily over the stumps; this then was the help from beyond the sea.

Everywhere on the slope of the mountain were scattered construction-quality logs and firewood. Now we would not have the unbearable task of hauling and stacking the iron logs of Daurian larch by hand. To drag the logs over the shubbery, down the narrow paths of the mountain slope, was an impossible job. Before 1938 they used to send horses for the job, but horses could not tolerate the north as well as people, were weaker than people, died under the strain of the hauling. Now the vertical knife of the foreign bulldozer had come to help us (us?).

None of us ever imagined that we would be given some light work instead of the unendurable log hauling that was hated by all. They would simply increase our norms and we would be forced to do something else—just as degrading and contemptible as any camp labor. Our frostbitten toes and fingers would not be cured by the American bulldozer. But there was the American machine grease! Ah yes, the machine grease! The barrel was immediately attacked by a crowd of starving men who knocked out the bottom right on the spot with a stone.

In their hunger, they claimed the machine grease was butter sent by Lend-Lease and there remained less than half a barrel by the time a sentry was sent to guard it and the camp administration drove off the crowd of starving, exhausted men with rifle shots. The fortunate ones gulped down this Lend-Lease butter, not believing it was simply machine grease. After all, the healing American bread was also tasteless and also had that same metallic flavor. And everyone who had been lucky enough to touch the grease licked his fingers hours later, gulping down the minutest amounts of the foreign joy that tasted like young stone. After all, a stone is not born a stone, but a soft oily creature. A creature, and not a thing. A stone becomes a thing in old age. Young wet limestone tuffs in the mountains enchanted the eyes of escaped convicts and workers from the geological surveys. A man had to exert his will to tear himself away from these honeyed shores, these milky rivers of flowing young stone. But that was a mountain, a valley, stone; and this was a delivery from Lend-Lease, the creation of human hands. . . .

Nothing terrible happened to those who had dipped their hands into the barrel. Trained in Kolyma, stomach and bowels proved themselves capable of coping with machine grease. A sentry was placed to guard the remainder, for this was food for machines—creatures infinitely more important to the state than people.

And thus from beyond the ocean there had arrived one of those creatures as a symbol of victory, friendship, and something else.

Three hundred men felt boundless envy toward the prisoner sitting at the wheel of the American tractor—Grinka Lebedev. There were better tractor operators than Lebedev among the convicts, but they had all been convicted according to Article 58 of the Criminal Code (political prisoners). Grinka Lebedev was a common criminal, a parricide to be precise. Each of the three hundred witnessed his earthly joy: to roar over to the logging area sitting at the wheel of a well-lubricated tractor.

The logging area kept moving back. Felling the taller trees suitable for building materials in Kolyma takes place along the stream banks where deep ravines force the trees to reach upward from their wind-protected havens toward the sun. In windy spots, in bright light, on marshy mountain slopes stand dwarfs—broken, twisted, tormented from eternally turning after the sun, from their constant struggle for a piece of thawed ground. The trees on the mountain slopes don't look like trees, but like monsters fit for a sideshow. Felling trees is similar to mining gold in those same streams in that it is just as rushed: the stream, the pan, the launder, the temporary barracks, the hurried predatory leap that leaves the stream and area without forest for three hundred years and without gold—forever.

Somewhere there exists the science of forestry, but what kind of forestry can there be in a three-hundred-year-old larch forest in Kolyma during the war when the response to Lend-Lease is a hurried plunge into gold fever, harnessed, to be sure, by the guard towers of the "zones."

Many tall trees and even prepared, sectioned firelogs were abandoned. Many thick-ended logs disappeared into the snow, falling to the ground as soon as they had been hoisted onto the sharp, brittle shoulders of the prisoners. Weak prisoner hands, tens of hands cannot lift onto a shoulder (there exists no such shoulder!) a two-meter log, drag its iron weight for tens of meters over shrubs, potholes, and pits. Many logs had been abandoned because of the impossibility of the job, and the bulldozer was supposed to help us.

But for its first trip in the land of Kolyma, on Russian land, it had been assigned a totally different job.

We watched the chugging bulldozer turn to the left and begin to climb the terrace to where there was a projection of rock and where we had been taken to work hundreds of times along the old road that led past the camp cemetery.

I hadn't given any thought to why we were led to work for the last few weeks along a new road instead of the familiar path indented from the boot heels of the guards and the thick rubber galoshes of the prisoners. The new road was twice as long as the old one. Everywhere there were hills and dropoffs, and we exhausted ourselves just getting to the job. But no one asked why we were being taken by a new path.

That was the way it had to be; that was the order; and we crawled on all fours, grabbing at stones that ripped open the skin of the fingers till the blood ran.

Only now did I see and understand the reason for all of this, and I thank God that He gave me the time and strength to witness it.

The logging area was just ahead, the slope of the mountain had been laid bare, and the shallow snow had been blown away by the wind. The stumps had all been rooted out; a charge of ammonal was placed under the larger ones, and the stump would fly into the air. Smaller stumps were uprooted with long bars. The smallest were simply pulled out by hand like the shrubs of dwarf cedar. . . .

The mountain had been laid bare and transformed into a gigantic stage for a camp mystery play.

A grave, a mass prisoner grave, a stone pit stuffed full with undecaying corpses of 1938 was sliding down the side of the hill, revealing the secret of Kolyma.

In Kolyma, bodies are not given over to earth, but to stone. Stone keeps secrets and reveals them. The permafrost keeps and reveals secrets. All of our loved ones who died in Kolyma, all those who were shot, beaten to death, sucked dry by starvation, can still be recognized even after tens of years. There were no gas furnaces in Kolyma. The corpses wait in stone, in the permafrost.

In 1938 entire work gangs dug such graves, constantly drilling, exploding, deepening the enormous gray, hard, cold stone pits. Digging graves in 1938 was easy work; there was no "assignment," no "norm" calculated to kill a man with a fourteen-hour working day. It was easier to dig graves than to stand in rubber galoshes over bare feet in the icy waters where they mined gold—the "basic unit of production," the "first of all metals."

These graves, enormous stone pits, were filled to the brim with corpses. The bodies had not decayed; they were just bare skeletons over which stretched dirty, scratched skin bitten all over by lice.

The north resisted with all its strength this work of man, not accepting the corpses into its bowels. Defeated, humbled, retreating, stone promised to forget nothing, to wait and preserve its secret. The severe winters, the hot summers, the winds, the six years of rain had not wrenched the dead men from the stone. The earth opened, baring its subterranean storerooms, for they contained not only gold and lead, tungsten and uranium, but also unde-caying human bodies.

These human bodies slid down the slope, perhaps at-tempting to arise. From a distance, from the other side of the creek, I had previously seen these moving objects that caught up against branches and stones; I had seen them through the few trees still left standing and I thought that they were logs that had not yet been hauled away.

Now the mountain was laid bare, and its secret was re-vealed. The grave "opened," and the dead men slid down the stony slope. Near the tractor road an enormous new common grave was dug. Who had dug it? No one was taken from the barracks for this work. It was enormous, and I and my companions knew that if we were to freeze and die, a place would be found for us in this new grave, this housewarming for dead men.

The bulldozer scraped up the frozen bodies, thousands of bodies of thousands of skeleton-like corpses. Nothing had decayed: the twisted fingers, the pus-filled toes which were reduced to mere stumps after frostbite, the dry skin scratched bloody and eyes burning with a hungry gleam.

With my exhausted, tormented mind I tried to under-stand: How did there come to be such an enormous grave in this area? I am an old resident of Kolyma, and there hadn't been any gold mine here as far as I knew. But then I realized that I knew only a fragment of that world sur-rounded by a barbed-wire zone and guard towers that re-minded one of the pages of tent-like Moscow architecture. Moscow's taller buildings are guard towers keeping watch over the city's prisoners. That's what those buildings look like. And what served as models for Moscow architec-ture—the watchful towers of the Moscow Kremlin or the guard towers of the camps? The guard towers of the camp "zone" represent the main concept advanced by their time and brilliantly expressed in the symbolism of architecture.

I realized that I knew only a small bit of that world, a pitifully small part, that twenty kilometers away there might be a shack for geological explorers looking for uranium or a gold mine with thirty thousand prisoners. Much can be hidden in the folds of the mountain.

And then I remembered the greedy blaze of the fireweed, the furious blossoming of the taiga in summer when it tried to hide in the grass and foliage any deed of man—good or bad. And if I forget, the grass will forget. But the permafrost and stone will not forget.

Grinka Lebedev, parricide, was a good tractor driver, and he controlled the well-oiled foreign tractor with ease. Grinka Lebedev carefully carried out his job, scooping the corpses toward the grave with the gleaming bulldozer knife-shield, pushing them into the pit and returning to drag up more.

The camp administration had decided that the first job for the bulldozer received from Lend-Lease should not be work in the forest, but something far more important.

The work was finished. The bulldozer heaped a mound of stones and gravel on the new grave, and the corpses were hidden under stone. But they did not disappear.

The bulldozer approached us. Grinka Lebedev, common criminal and parricide, did not look at us, prisoners of Article 58. Grinka had been entrusted with a task by the government, and he had fulfilled that task. On the stone face of Grinka Lebedev were hewn pride and a sense of having accomplished his duty.

The bulldozer roared past us; on the mirror-like blade there was no scratch, not a single spot.

(1980)

Alexander Solzhenitsyn

(1918–   )

That the most celebrated inhabitant of the state of Vermont since Calvin Coolidge should be Alexander Isayevich Solzhenitsyn appeals to those who relish the wry incongruities of history. As voluble as the thirtieth president was taciturn, Solzhenitsyn nevertheless allows suitably impressive intervals to separate his oracular pronouncements and denunciations. His passion for sharing his truth with the world predated his expulsion from the USSR in 1974: He said exactly the same madly courageous and outrageous things when he was vulnerably there as he now does from the relative safety of his estate in Cavendish. Nor do these things offend political leaders of the West noticeably less than they used to offend the Politburo. Solzhenitsyn's middle name (which, like all Russian patronymics, indicates the Christian name of his father) means "son of Isaiah," and he does indeed share much of the wrathful intensity of the Old Testament prophets. Like them, he appears at times to be a man divinely inspired to carry out some mission in the world, outraged by the general miscreancy here below, and gifted with an avenging angel's tongue, from which roll imprecations and bitterly minatory witticisms worthy of Tolstoy himself. The perverted use to which the West puts its freedom is no less an abomination to Solzhenitsyn than was the denial of freedom in his homeland. What is the difference, after all, between being forbidden the fruits of culture and religion and simply ignoring them in favor of the blandishments of a mindless materialism? The result is the same.

This intimidating moralist belongs to the first generation of Russians who never knew, even in infancy, the world before the Revolution: They are "Soviet" to the core of their being. Like most such Russians, Solzhenitsyn grew to manhood with an unquestioning devotion to an idealized Lenin and to the Communist plan for the perfection of human life. When Hitler invaded Russia in 1941, Solzhenitsyn enlisted in the army and served as an artillery officer. In 1945 he was arrested for having written something mildly critical of Stalin in private correspondence with a friend, and he spent eight years in the "Gulag," the vast system of forced labor camps that he was later to describe to an incredulous world. These years thoroughly disabused Solzhenitsyn of whatever illusions his preceding twenty-seven years had instilled in him. They gave him at the same time, much as Dostoevsky's experience of a Siberian prison had done, an unshakable belief in the moral ascendancy of the suffering people of Russia. Released from the camps, he was still forced to live in rural exile far from the metropolitan centers of Russia. He earned his living as a teacher of physics and mathematics during the day. At night he wrote—but only "for the desk drawer," as the Russian phrase has it.

Finally, in November 1962, through the combined efforts of Nikita Khrushchev and the courageous editor Alexander Tvardovsky, Solzhenitsyn's story *One Day in the Life of Ivan Denisovich* appeared in the leading literary journal *Novy Mir*. This first literary treatment of the forbidden theme of Stalin's death camps altered Solzhenitsyn's life and that of contemporary Russian letters forever. But with the exception of "Matryona's Home" (which appeared in the same journal the following year) and one or two other pieces, that was effectively the end of Solzhenitsyn's domestic career in print. His work had encouraged such a flood of prison camp writings that the alarmed authorities felt they had gone too far. His long novels, *The First Circle* and *Cancer Ward*, were considered for publication in the Soviet Union but saw the light of day only in the West. Awarded the Nobel Prize in 1970, Solzhenitsyn became an intolerable scourge of the regime, which finally exiled him and stripped him of his citizenship. When the collapse of Soviet power made possible the full publication of all his works, their bulk so dominated the available media that other writers found themselves temporarily crowded aside.

The novel in Russia has traditionally been regarded as the appropriate narrative vehicle for social commentary and for religious and philosophical exhortation—for changing the world, in short—whereas the shorter forms of fiction have been reserved for "mere art." Allowing for the monumental exceptions that need hardly be named, the ironic result is that a vast expenditure of literary effort more often than not results in a work of temporary interest, while an almost offhand sketch can prove more lasting than bronze. Turgenev's excruciatingly boring *On the Eve* is still read, of course, but only at the insistence of pedagogues. Meanwhile, his "King Lear of the Steppes," to say nothing of the small masterpieces collected under the title *Notes of a Hunter*, are permanent works of Apollonian mastery, and alone guarantee his claim as an artist.

Though I am certainly in a minority, I believe that these observations apply also to the art of Solzhenitsyn. His first published works will probably outlive in every sense the vast productions that succeeded them (the one exception being the encyclopedia of the Gulag, which is fictional only in its procedures). Ivan Denisovich and Matryona do not require footnotes, nor do they plead with us, exhort us, or excoriate us: They simply *are*. Their significance is that of emblematic witnesses not to some transient episode in the tragic history of humanity but to that history as a whole, which they encapsulate in the simplicity of their mute being. For all the local detail that convinces us of their reality, they finally exist in a realm above circumstance, and belong to that reserved segment of our memory where we keep Falstaff, Huck Finn, Werther, Augie March, and others whom you will add to this list at your leisure.

MATRYONA'S HOME

A hundred and eighty-four kilometres from Moscow trains were still slowing down to a crawl a good six months after it happened. Passengers stood glued to the windows or went out to stand by the doors. Was the line under repair, or what? Would the train be late?

It was all right. Past the crossing the train picked up speed again and the passengers went back to their seats.

Only the engine-drivers knew what it was all about.

The engine-drivers and I.

In the summer of 1953 I was coming back from the hot and dusty desert, just following my nose—so long as it led me back to Russia. Nobody waited or wanted me at any particular place, because I was a little matter of ten years overdue. I just wanted to get to the central belt, away from the great heats, close to the leafy muttering of forests. I wanted to efface myself, to lose myself in deepest Russia . . . if it was still anywhere to be found.

A year earlier I should have been lucky to get a job carrying a hod this side of the Urals. They wouldn't have taken me as an electrician on a decent construction job. And I had an itch to teach. Those who knew told me that it was a waste of money buying a ticket, that I should have a journey for nothing.

But things were beginning to move. When I went up the stairs of the N—— Oblast Education Department and asked for the Personnel Section, I was surprised to find Personnel sitting behind a glass partition, like in a chemist's shop, instead of the usual black leather-padded door.

I went timidly up to the window, bowed, and asked, "Please, do you need any mathematicians somewhere where the trains don't run? I should like to settle there for good."

They passed every dot and comma in my documents through a fine comb, went from one room to another, made telephone calls. It was something out of the ordinary for them too—people always wanted the towns, the bigger the better. And lo and behold, they found just the place for me—Vysokoe Polye. The very sound of it gladdened my heart.

Vysokoe* Polye did not belie its name. It stood on rising ground, with gentle hollows and other little hills around it. It was enclosed by an unbroken ring of forest. There was a pool behind a weir. Just the place where I wouldn't mind living and dying. I spent a long time sitting on a stump in a coppice and wishing with all my heart that I didn't need breakfast and dinner every day but could just stay here and listen to the branches brushing against the roof in the night, with not a wireless anywhere to be heard and the whole world silent.

Alas, nobody baked bread in Vysokoe Polye. There was nothing edible on sale. The whole village lugged its victuals in sacks from the big town.

I went back to Personnel Section and raised my voice in prayer at the little window. At first they wouldn't even talk to me. But then they started going from one room to another, made a telephone call, scratched with their pens, and stamped on my orders the word *"Torfoprodukt."*

Torfoprodukt? Turgenev never knew that you can put words like that together in Russian.

On the station building at Torfoprodukt, an antiquated temporary hut of grey wood, hung a stern notice, BOARD TRAINS ONLY FROM THE PASSENGERS' HALL. A further message had been scratched on the boards with a nail, *And Without Tickets*. And by the booking-office, with the

* Literally "high field."

same melancholy wit, somebody had carved for all time the words, *No Tickets*. It was only later that I fully appreciated the meaning of these addenda. Getting to Torfoprodukt was easy. But not getting away.

Here too, deep and trackless forests had once stood, and were still standing after the Revolution. Then they were chopped down by the peat-cutters and the neighbouring kolkhoz. Its chairman, Shashkov, had razed quite a few hectares of timber and sold it at a good profit down in Odessa oblast.

The workers' settlement sprawled untidily among the peat bogs—monotonous shacks from the 'thirties, and little houses with carved façades and glass verandahs, put up in the 'fifties. But inside these houses I could see no partitions reaching up to the ceilings, so there was no hope of renting a room with four real walls.

Over the settlement hung smoke from the factory chimney. Little locomotives ran this way and that along narrow-gauge railway lines, giving out more thick smoke and piercing whistles, pulling loads of dirty brown peat in slabs and briquettes. I could safely assume that in the evening a loudspeaker would be crying its heart out over the door of the club and there would be drunks roaming the streets and, sooner or later, sticking knives in each other.

This was what my dream about a quiet corner of Russia had brought me to . . . when I could have stayed where I was and lived in an adobe hut looking out on the desert, with a fresh breeze at night and only the starry dome of the sky overhead.

I couldn't sleep on the station bench, and as soon as it started getting light I went for another stroll around the settlement. This time I saw a tiny market-place. Only one woman stood there at that early hour, selling milk, and I took a bottle and started drinking it on the spot.

I was struck by the way she talked. Instead of a normal speaking voice she used an ingratiating sing-song, and her words were the ones I was longing to hear when I left Asia for this place.

"Drink, and God bless you. You must be a stranger round here?"

"And where are you from?" I asked, feeling more cheerful.

I learnt that the peat workings weren't the only thing, that over the railway lines there was a hill, and over the hill a village, that this village was Talnovo, and it had been there years ago, when the "gypsy woman" lived in the big house and the wild woods stood all round. And further on there was a whole countryside full of villages—Chaslitsy, Ovintsy, Spudni, Shevertni, Shestimirovo, deeper and deeper into the woods, farther and farther from the railway, up towards the lakes.

The names were like a soothing breeze to me. They held a promise of backwoods Russia. I asked my new acquaintance to take me to Talnovo after the market was over, and find a house for me to lodge in.

It appeared that I was a lodger worth having: in addition to my rent, the school offered a lorry-load of peat for the winter to whoever took me. The woman's ingratiating smile gave way to a thoughtful frown. She had no room herself, because she and her husband were "keeping" her aged mother, so she took me first to one lot of relatives then to another. But there wasn't a separate room to be had and both places were crowded and noisy.

We had come to a dammed-up stream that was short of water and had a little bridge over it. No other place in all the village took my fancy as this did: there were two or three willows, a lop-sided house, ducks swimming on the pond, geese shaking themselves as they stepped out of the water.

"Well, perhaps we might just call on Matryona," said my guide, who was getting tired of me by now. "Only it isn't so neat and cosy-like in her house, neglects things she does. She's unwell."

Matryona's house stood quite nearby. Its row of four windows looked out on the cold backs, the two slopes of the roof were covered with shingles and a little attic window was decorated in the old Russian style. But the shingles were rotting, the beam-ends of the house and the once mighty gates had turned grey with age, and there were gaps in the little shelter over the gate.

The small door let into the gate was fastened, but instead of knocking my companion just put her hand under and turned the catch, a simple device to prevent animals from straying. The yard was not covered, but there was a lot under the roof of the house. As you went through the outer door a short flight of steps rose to a roomy landing, which was open to the roof high overhead. To the left, other steps led up to the top room, which was a separate structure with no stove, and yet another flight down to the basement. To the right lay the house proper, with its attic and its cellar.

It had been built a long time ago, built sturdily, to house a big family, and now one lonely woman of nearly sixty lived in it.

When I went into the cottage she was lying on the Russian stove under a heap of those indeterminate dingy rags which are so precious to a working man or woman.

The spacious room, and especially the best part near the windows, was full of rubber-plants in pots and tubs standing on stools and benches. They peopled the householder's loneliness like a speechless but living crowd. They had been allowed to run wild, and they took up all the scanty light on the north side. In what was left of the light, and half-hidden by the stove-pipe, the mistress of the house looked yellow and weak. You could see from her clouded eyes that illness had drained all the strength out of her.

While we talked she lay on the stove face downwards, without a pillow, her head towards the door, and I stood looking up at her. She showed no pleasure at getting a lodger, just complained about the wicked disease she had. She was just getting over an attack; it didn't come upon her every month, but when it did, "It hangs on two or three days so as I shan't manage to get up and wait on you. I've room and to spare, you can live here if you like."

Then she went over the list of other housewives with whom I should be quieter and cosier, and wanted me to make the round of them. But I had already seen that I was destined to settle in this dimly lit house with the tarnished mirror in which you couldn't see yourself, and the two garish posters (one advertising books, the other about the harvest), bought for a rouble each to brighten up the walls.

Matryona Vasilyevna made me go off round the village again, and when I called on her the second time she kept trying to put me off, "We're not clever, we can't cook, I don't know how we shall suit. . . ." But this time she was on her feet when I got there, and I thought I saw a glimmer of pleasure in her eyes to see me back. We reached agreement about the rent and the load of peat which the school would deliver.

Later on I found out that, year in year out, it was a long time since Matryona Vasilyevna had earned a single rouble. She didn't get a pension. Her relatives gave her very little help. In the kolkhoz she had worked not for money but for credits; the marks recording her labour-days in her well-thumbed work-book.

So I moved in with Matryona Vasilyevna. We didn't divide the room. Her bed was in the corner between the door and the stove, and I unfolded my camp-bed by one window and pushed Matryona's beloved rubber-plants out of the light to make room for a little table by another. The village had electric light, laid on back in the 'twenties, from Shatury. The newspapers were writing about "Ilyich's little lamps," but the peasants talked wide-eyed about "Tsar Fire."

Some of the better-off people in the village might not have thought Matryona's house much of a home, but it kept us snug enough that autumn and winter. The roof still held the rain out, and the freezing winds could not blow the warmth of the stove away all at once, though it was cold by morning, especially when the wind blew on the shabby side.

In addition to Matryona and myself, a cat, some mice, and some cockroaches lived in the house.

The cat was no longer young, and gammy-legged as well. Matryona had taken her in out of pity, and she had stayed. She walked on all four feet but with a heavy limp: one of her feet was sore and she favoured it. When she jumped from the stove she didn't land with the soft sound a cat usually makes, but with a heavy thud as three of her feet struck the floor at once—such a heavy thud that until I got used to it, it gave me a start. This was because she stuck three feet out together to save the fourth.

It wasn't because the cat couldn't deal with them that there were mice in the cottage: she would pounce into the corner like lightning, and come back with a mouse between her teeth. But the mice were usually out of reach because somebody, back in the good old days, had stuck embossed wallpaper of a greenish colour on Matryona's walls, and not just one layer of it but five. The layers held together all right, but in many places the whole lot had come away from the wall, giving the room a sort of inner skin. Between the timber of the walls and the skin of wallpaper the mice had made themselves runs where they impudently scampered about, running at times right up to the ceiling. The cat followed their scamperings with angry eyes, but couldn't get at them.

Sometimes the cat ate cockroaches as well, but they made her sick. The only thing the cockroaches respected was the partition which screened the mouth of the Russian stove and the kitchen from the best part of the room.

They did not creep into the best room. But the kitchen at night swarmed with them, and if I went in late in the evening for a drink of water and switched on the light the whole floor, the big bench, and even the wall would be one rustling brown mass. From time to time I brought home some borax from the school laboratory and we mixed it with dough to poison them. There would be fewer cockroaches for a while, but Matryona was afraid we might poison the cat as well. We stopped putting down the poison and the cockroaches multiplied anew.

At night, when Matryona was already asleep and I was working at my table, the occasional rapid scamper of mice behind the wallpaper would be drowned in the sustained and ceaseless rustling of cockroaches behind the screen, like the sound of the sea in the distance. But I got used to it because there was nothing evil in it, nothing dishonest. Rustling was life to them.

I even got used to the crude beauty on the poster, forever reaching out from the wall to offer me Belinsky, Panferov, and a pile of other books—but never saying a word. I got used to everything in Matryona's cottage.

Matryona got up at four or five in the morning. Her wall-clock was twenty-seven years old, and had been bought in the village shop. It was always fast, but Matryona didn't worry about that—just so long as it didn't lose and make her late in the morning. She switched on the light behind the kitchen screen and moving quietly, considerately, doing her best not to make a noise, she lit the stove, went to milk the goat (all the livestock she had was this one dirty-white goat with twisted horns), fetched water and boiled it in three iron pots: one for me, one for herself, and one for the goat. She fetched potatoes from the cellar, picking out the littlest for the goat, little ones for herself and egg-sized ones for me. There were no big ones, because her garden was sandy, had not been manured since the war and was always planted with potatoes, potatoes, and potatoes again, so that it wouldn't grow big ones.

I scarcely heard her about her morning tasks. I slept late, woke up in the wintry daylight, stretched a bit and stuck my head out from under my blanket and my sheepskin. These, together with the prisoner's jerkin round my legs and a sack stuffed with straw underneath me, kept me warm in bed even on nights when the cold wind rattled our wobbly windows from the north. When I heard the discreet noises on the other side of the screen I spoke to her, slowly and deliberately.

"Good morning, Matryona Vasilyevna!"

And every time the same good-natured words came to me from behind the screen. They began with a warm, throaty gurgle, the sort of sound grandmothers make in fairy tales.

"M-m-m . . . same to you too!"

And after a little while, "Your breakfast's ready for you now."

She didn't announce what was for breakfast, but it was easy to guess: taters in their jackets or tatty soup (as everybody in the village called it), or barley gruel (no other grain could be bought in Torfoprodukt that year, and even the barley you had to fight for, because it was the cheapest and people bought it up by the sack to fatten their pigs on it). It wasn't always salted as it should be, it was often slightly burnt, it furred the palate and the gums, and it gave me heartburn.

But Matryona wasn't to blame: there was no butter in Torfoprodukt either, margarine was desperately short, and only mixed cooking fat was plentiful, and when I got to know it I saw that the Russian stove was not convenient for cooking: the cook cannot see the pots and they are not heated evenly all round. I suppose the stove came down to our ancestors from the Stone Age because you can stoke it up once before daylight, and food and water, mash and swill, will keep warm in it all day long. And it keeps you warm while you sleep.

I ate everything that was cooked for me without demur, patiently putting aside anything uncalled-for that I came across: a hair, a bit of peat, a cockroach's leg. I hadn't the heart to find fault with Matryona. After all, she had warned me herself.

"We aren't clever, we can't cook—I don't know how we shall suit. . . ."

"Thank you," I said quite sincerely.

"What for? For what is your own?" she answered, disarming me with a radiant smile. And, with a guileless look of her faded blue eyes, she would ask, "And what shall I cook you for just now?"

For just now meant for supper. I ate twice a day, like at the front. What could I order for just now? It would have to be one of the same old things, taters or tatty soup.

I resigned myself to it, because I had learnt by now not to look for the meaning of life in food. More important to me was the smile on her roundish face, which I tried in vain to catch when at last I had earned enough to buy a camera. As soon as she saw the cold eye of the lens upon her Matryona assumed a strained or else an exaggeratedly severe expression.

Just once I did manage to get a snap of her looking through the window into the street and smiling at something.

Matryona had a lot of worries that winter. Her neighbours put it into her head to try and get a pension. She was all alone in the world, and when she began to be seriously ill she had been dismissed from the kolkhoz as well. Injustices had piled up, one on top of another. She was ill, but not regarded as a disabled person. She had worked for a quarter of a century in the kolkhoz, but it was a kolkhoz and not a factory, so she was not entitled to a pension for herself. She could only try and get one for her husband, for the loss of her bread-winner. But she had had no husband for twelve years now, not since the beginning of the war, and it wasn't easy to obtain all the particulars from different places about his length of service and how much he had earned. What a bother it was getting those forms through! Getting somebody to certify that he'd earned, say, 300 roubles a month; that she lived alone and nobody helped her; what year she was born in. Then all this had to be taken to the pensions office. And taken somewhere else to get all the mistakes corrected. And taken back again. Then you had to find out whether they would give you a pension.

To make it all more difficult the Pensions Office was

twenty kilometres east of Talnovo, the Rural Council Offices ten kilometres to the west, the Factory District Council an hour's walk to the north. They made her run around from office to office for two months on end, to get an *i* dotted or a *t* crossed. Every trip took a day. She goes down to the rural district council—and the secretary isn't there to-day. Secretaries of rural councils often aren't here to-day. So come again to-morrow. To-morrow the secretary is in, but he hasn't got his rubber stamp. So come again the next day. And the day after that back she goes yet again, because all her papers are pinned together and some cock-eyed clerk has signed the wrong one.

"They shove me around, Ignatich," she used to complain to me after these fruitless excursions. "Worn out with it I am."

But she soon brightened up. I found that she had a sure means of putting herself in a good humour. She worked. She would grab a shovel and go off to lift potatoes. Or she would tuck a sack under her arm and go after peat. Or take a wicker basket and look for berries deep in the woods. When she'd been bending her back to bushes instead of office desks for a while, and her shoulders were aching from a heavy load, Matryona would come back cheerful, at peace with the world and smiling her nice smile.

"I'm on to a good thing now, Ignatich. I know where to go for it (peat she meant), a lovely place it is."

"But surely my peat is enough, Matryona Vasilyevna? There's a whole lorry-load of it."

"Pooh! Your peat! As much again, and then as much again, that might be enough. When the winter gets really stiff and the wind's battling at the windows, it blows the heat out of the house faster than you can make the stove up. Last year we got heaps and heaps of it. I'd have had three loads in by now. But they're out to catch us. They've summoned one woman from our village already."

That's how it was. The frightening breath of winter was already in the air. There were forests all round, and no fuel to be had anywhere. Excavators roared away in the bogs, but there was no peat on sale to the villagers. It was delivered, free, to the bosses and to the people round the bosses, and teachers, doctors, and workers got a load each. The people of Talnovo were not supposed to get any peat, and they weren't supposed to ask about it. The chairman of the kolkhoz walked about the village looking people in the eye while he gave his orders or stood chatting, and talked about anything you liked except fuel. He was stocked-up. Who said anything about winter coming?

So just as in the old days they used to steal the squire's wood, now they pinched peat from the trust. The women went in parties of five or ten so that they would be less frightened. They went in the day-time. The peat cut during the summer had been stacked up all over the place to dry. That's the good thing about peat, it can't be carted off as soon as it's cut. It lies around drying till autumn, or, if the roads are bad, till the snow starts falling. This was when the women used to come and take it. They could get six peats in a sack if it was damp, or ten if it was dry. A sackful weighed about two poods and it sometimes had to be carried over three kilometres. This was enough to make the stove up once. There were two hundred days in the winter. The Russian stove had to be lit in the mornings, and the "Dutch" stove in the evenings.

"Why beat about the bush?" said Matryona angrily to someone invisible. "Since there've been no more horses, what you can't heave around yourself you haven't got. My back never heals up. Winter you're pulling sledges, summer it's bundles on your back, it's God's truth I'm telling you."

The women went more than once in a day. On good days Matryona brought six sacks home. She piled my peat up where it could be seen, and hid her own under the passage way, boarding up the hole every night.

"If they don't just happen to think of it, the devils will never find it in their born days," said Matryona smiling and wiping the sweat from her brow.

What could the peat trust do? Its establishment didn't run to a watchman for every bog. I suppose they had to show a rich haul in their returns, and then write off so much for crumbling, so much washed away by the rain. . . . Sometimes they would take it into their heads to put out patrols and try to catch the women as they came into the village. The women would drop their sacks and scatter. Or somebody would inform and there would be a house-to-house search. They would draw up a report on the stolen peat, and threaten a court action. The women would stop fetching it for a while, but the approach of winter drove them out with sledges in the middle of the night.

When I had seen a little more of Matryona I noticed that apart from cooking and looking after the house, she had quite a lot of other jobs to do every day. She kept all her jobs, and the proper times for them, in her head and always knew when she woke up in the morning how her day would be occupied. Apart from fetching peat, and stumps which the tractors unearthed in the bogs, apart from the cranberries which she put to soak in big jars for the winter ("Give your teeth an edge, Ignatich," she used to say when she offered me some), apart from digging potatoes and all the coming and going to do with her pension, she had to get hay from somewhere for her one and only dirty-white goat.

"Why don't you keep a cow, Matryona?"

Matryona stood there in her grubby apron, by the opening in the kitchen screen, facing my table, and explained to me.

"Oh, Ignatich, there's enough milk from the goat for me. And if I started keeping a cow she'd eat me out of house and home in no time. You can't cut the grass by the railway track, because it belongs to the railway, and you can't cut any in the woods, because it belongs to the foresters, and they won't let me have any at the kolkhoz because I'm not a member any more, they reckon. And those who are members have to work there every day till the white flies swarm, and make their own hay when there's snow on the ground—what's the good of grass like that?

In the old days they used to be sweating to get the hay in at midsummer, between the end of June and the end of July, while the grass was sweet and juicy. . . ."

So it meant a lot of work for Matryona to gather enough hay for one skinny little goat. She took her sickle and a sack and went off early in the morning to places where she knew there was grass growing—round the edges of fields, on the roadside, on hummocks in the bog. When she had stuffed her sack with heavy fresh grass she dragged it home and spread it out in her yard to dry. From a sackful of grass she got one forkload of dry hay.

The farm had a new chairman, sent down from the town not long ago, and the first thing he did was to cut down on the garden-plots for those who were not fit to work. He left Matryona fifteen hundredths of sand—when there were ten hundredths just lying idle on the other side of the fence. Yet when they were short of working hands, when the women dug in their heels and wouldn't budge, the chairman's wife would come to see Matryona. She was from the town as well, a determined woman whose short grey overcoat and intimidating glare gave her a somewhat military appearance. She walked into the house without so much as a good morning and looked sternly at Matryona. Matryona was uneasy.

"Well now, Comrade Vasilyevna, " said the chairman's wife, drawing out her words. "You will have to help the kolkhoz! You will have to go and help cart muck out tomorrow!"

A little smile of forgiveness wrinkled Matryona's face—as though she understood the embarrassment which the chairman's wife must feel not being able to pay her for her work.

"Well—er," she droned, "I'm not well, of course, and I'm not attached to you any more . . . ," then she hurried to correct herself, "what time should I come then?"

"And bring your own fork!" the chairman's wife instructed her. Her stiff skirt crackled as she walked away.

"Think of that!" grumbled Matryona as the door closed. "Bring your own fork! They've got neither forks nor shovels on the kolkhoz. And I don't have a man who'll put a handle on for me!"

She went on thinking about it out loud all evening.

"What's the good of talking, Ignatich. I must help, of course. Only the way they work it's all a waste of time—don't know whether they're coming or going. The women stand propped up on their shovels and waiting for the factory hooter to blow twelve o'clock. Or else they get on to adding up who's earned what and who's turned up for work and who hasn't. Now what I call work, there isn't a sound out of anybody, only ... oh dear, dear—dinner time's soon rolled round—what, getting dark already...."

In the morning she went off with her fork.

But it wasn't just the kolkhoz—any distant relative, or just a neighbour, could come to Matryona of an evening and say, "Come and give me a hand to-morrow, Matryona. We'll finish lifting the potatoes."

Matryona couldn't say no. She gave up what she should be doing next and went to help her neighbour, and when she came back she would say without a trace of envy, "Ah, you should see the size of her potatoes, Ignatich! It was a joy to dig them up. I didn't want to leave the allotment, God's truth I didn't."

Needless to say, not a garden could be ploughed without Matryona's help. The women of Talnovo had got it neatly worked out that it was a longer and harder job for one woman to dig her garden with a spade than for six of them to put themselves in harness and plough six gardens. So they sent for Matryona to help them.

"Well—did you pay her?" I asked sometimes.

"She won't take money. You have to try and hide it on her when she's not looking."

Matryona had yet another troublesome chore when her turn came to feed the herdsmen. One of them was a hefty deaf mute, the other a boy who was never without a cigarette in his drooling mouth. Matryona's turn only came around every six weeks, but it put her to great expense.

She went to the shop to buy tinned fish, and was lavish with sugar and butter, things she never ate herself. It seems that the housewives showed off in this way, trying to outdo each other in feeding the herdsmen.

"You've got to be careful with tailors and herdsmen," Matryona explained. "They'll spread your name all round the village if something doesn't suit them."

And every now and then attacks of serious illness broke in on this life that was already crammed with troubles. Matryona would be off her feet for a day or two, lying flat out on the stove. She didn't complain, and didn't groan, but she hardly stirred either. On these days, Masha, Matryona's closest friend from her earliest years, would come to look after the goat and light the stove. Matryona herself ate nothing, drank nothing, asked for nothing. To call in the doctor from the clinic at the settlement would have seemed strange in Talnovo, and would have given the neighbours something to talk about—what does she think she is, a lady? They did call her in once, and she arrived in a real temper and told Matryona to come down to the clinic when she was on her feet again. Matryona went, although she didn't really want to; they took specimens and sent them off to the district hospital—and that's the last anybody heard about it. Matryona was partly to blame herself.

But there was work waiting to be done, and Matryona soon started getting up again, moving slowly at first and then as briskly as ever.

"You never saw me in the old days, Ignatich. I'd lift any sack you liked, I didn't think five poods was too heavy. My father-in-law used to say, 'Matryona, you'll break your back.' And my brother-in-law didn't have to come and help me lift on the cart. Our horse was a war-horse, a big strong one. . . ."

"What do you mean, a war-horse?"

"They took ours for the war and gave us this one instead—he'd been wounded. But he turned out a bit spirited. Once he bolted with the sledge right into the lake, the men-folk hopped out of the way, but I grabbed the bridle, as true as I'm here, and stopped him. . . . Full of oats that horse was. They liked to feed their horses well in our village. If a horse feels his oats he doesn't know what heavy means."

But Matryona was a long way from being fearless. She was afraid of fire, afraid of "the lightning," and most of all she was for some reason afraid of trains.

"When I had to go to Cherusti the train came up from Nechaevka way with its great big eyes popping out and the rails humming away—put me in a proper fever. My knees started knocking. God's truth I'm telling you!" Matryona raised her shoulders as though she surprised herself.

"Maybe it's because they won't give people tickets, Matryona Vasilyevna?"

"At the window? They try to shove first-class tickets on to you. And the train was starting to move. We dashed about all over the place, 'Give us tickets for pity's sake.'

"The men-folk had climbed on top of the carriages. Then we found a door that wasn't locked and shoved straight in without tickets . . . and all the carriages were empty, they were all empty, you could stretch out on the seat if you wanted to. Why they wouldn't give us tickets, the hard-hearted parasites, I don't know. . . ."

Still, before winter came Matryona's affairs were in a better state than ever before. They started paying her at last a pension of eighty roubles. Besides she got just over a hundred from the school and me.

Some of her neighbours began to be envious.

"Hm! Matryona can live for ever now! If she had any more money she wouldn't know what to do with it at her age."

Matryona had herself some new felt boots made. She bought a new jerkin. And she had an overcoat made out of the worn-out railwayman's greatcoat given to her by the engine-driver from Cherusti who had married Kira, her foster-daughter. The hump-backed village tailor put a padded lining under the cloth and it made a marvellous coat, such as Matryona had never worn before in all her sixty years.

In the middle of winter Matryona sewed two hundred roubles into the lining of this coat for her funeral. This made her quite cheerful.

"Now my mind's a bit easier, Ignatich."

December went by, January went by—and in those two months Matryona's illness held off. She started going over to Masha's house more often in the evening, to sit chewing sunflower seeds with her. She didn't invite guests herself in the evening out of consideration for my work. Once, on the feast of the Epiphany, I came back from school and found a party going on and was introduced to Matryona's three sisters who called her "nan-nan" or "nanny" because she was the oldest. Until then not much had been heard of the sisters in our cottage—perhaps they were afraid that Matryona might ask them for help.

But one ominous event cast a shadow on the holiday for Matryona. She went to the church five versts away for the blessing of the water, and put her pot down among the others. When the blessing was over the women went rushing and jostling to get their pots back again. There were a lot of women in front of Matryona and when she got there her pot was missing, and no other vessel had been left behind. The pot had vanished as though the devil had run off with it.

Matryona went around the worshippers asking them, "Has any of you girls accidentally mistook somebody else's holy water? In a pot?"

Nobody owned up. There had been some boys there, and boys got up to mischief sometimes. Matryona came home sad.

No one could say that Matryona was a devout believer. If anything, she was a heathen, and her strongest beliefs were superstitious. You mustn't go into the garden on the fast of St. John or there would be no harvest next year. A blizzard meant that somebody had hanged himself. If you pinched your foot in the door you could expect a guest. All the time I lived with her I didn't once see her say her prayers or even cross herself. But, whatever job she was doing, she began with a "God bless us," and she never failed to say "God bless you," when I set out for school. Perhaps she did say her prayers, but on the quiet, either because she was shy or because she didn't want to embarrass me. There were ikons on the walls. Ordinary days they were left in darkness, but for the vigil of a great feast, or on the morning of a holiday, Matryona would light the little lamp.

She had fewer sins on her conscience than her gammy-legged cat. That cat did kill mice. . . .

Now that her life was running more smoothly, Matryona started listening more carefully to my radio. (I had, of course, installed a speaker, or as Matryona called it, a peeker.)

When they announced on the radio that some new machine had been invented, I heard Matryona grumbling out in the kitchen, "New ones all the time, nothing but new ones. People don't want to work with the old ones any more, where are we going to store them all?"

There was a programme about the seeding of clouds from aeroplanes. Matryona, listening up on the stove, shook her head, "Oh dear, dear, dear, they'll do away with one of the two—summer or winter."

Once Chaliapin was singing Russian folk-songs. Matryona stood listening for a long time before she gave her emphatic verdict, "Queer singing, not our sort of singing."

"You can't mean that, Matryona Vasilyevna . . . just listen to him."

She listened a bit longer, and pursed her lips, "No, it's wrong. It isn't our sort of tune, and he's tricky with his voice."

She made up for this another time. They were broadcasting some of Glinka's songs. After half a dozen of these drawing-room ballads, Matryona suddenly came from behind the screen clutching her apron, with a flush on her face and a film of tears over her dim eyes.

"That's our sort of singing," she said in a whisper.

So Matryona and I got used to each other and took each other for granted. She never pestered me with questions about myself. I don't know whether she was lacking in normal female curiosity or just tactful, but she never once asked if I had been married. All the Talnovo women kept at her to find out about me. Her answer was, "You want to know—you ask him. All I know is he's from distant parts."

And when I got round to telling her that I had spent a lot of time in prison she said nothing but just nodded, as though she had already suspected it.

And I thought of Matryona only as the helpless old woman she was now, and didn't try to rake up her past, didn't even suspect that there was anything to be found there.

I knew that Matryona had got married before the Revolution and come to live in the house I now shared with her, that she had gone "to the stove" immediately. (She had no mother-in-law and no older sister-in-law, so it was her job to put the pots in the oven on the very first morning of her married life.) I knew that she had had six children and that they had all died very young, so that there were never two of them alive at once. Then there was a sort of foster-daugher, Kira. Matryona's husband had not come back from the last war. She received no notification of his death. Men from the village who had served in the same company said that he might have been taken prisoner, or he might have been killed and his body not found. In the eight years that had gone by since the war Matryona had decided that he was not alive. It was a good thing that she thought so. If he was still alive he was probably in Brazil or Australia, and married again. The village of Talnovo, and the Russian language, would be fading from his memory.

* * *

One day, when I got back from school, I found a guest in the house. A tall, dark man, with his hat on his lap, was sitting on a chair which Matryona had moved up to the Dutch stove in the middle of the room. His face was completely surrounded by bushy black hair with hardly a trace of grey in it. His thick black moustaches ran into his full black beard, so that his mouth could hardly be seen. Black side-whiskers merged with the black locks which hung down from his crown, leaving only the tips of his ears visible; and broad black eyebrows met in a wide double span. But the front of his head as far as the crown was a spacious bald dome. His whole appearance made an impression of wisdom and dignity. He sat squarely on his chair, with his hands folded on his stick, and his stick resting vertically on the floor, in an attitude of patient expectation, and he obviously hadn't much to say to Matryona who was busy behind the screen.

When I came in he eased his majestic head round towards me and suddenly addressed me, "Master, I can't see you very well. My son goes to your school. Grigoriev, Antoshka. . . ."

There was no need for him to say any more. . . . However strongly inclined I felt to help this worthy old man I knew and dismissed in advance all the pointless things he was going to say. Antoshka Grigoriev was a plump, red-faced lad in 8-D who looked like a cat that's swallowed the cream. He seemed to think that he came to school for a rest and sat at his desk with a lazy smile on his face. Needless to say, he never did his home-work. But the worst of it was that he had never been put into the next class from year to year because our district, and indeed the whole oblast and the neighbouring oblasts, were famous for the high percentage of passes they obtained, and the school had to make an effort to keep its record up. So Antoshka had got it clear in his mind that however much the teachers threatened him they would put him up in the end, and there was no need for him to learn anything. He just laughed at us. There he sat in the eighth class, and he hadn't even mastered his decimals and didn't know one triangle from another. In the first two terms of the school year I had kept him firmly below the pass line and the same treatment awaited him in the third.

But now this half-blind old man, who should have been Antoshka's grandfather rather than his father, had come to humble himself before me—how could I tell him that the school had been deceiving him for years, and that I couldn't go on deceiving him, because I didn't want to ruin the whole class, to become a liar and a fake, to start despising my work and my profession.

For the time being I patiently explained that his son had been very slack, that he told lies at school and at home, that his mark-book must be checked frequently, and that we must both take him severely in hand.

"Severe as you like, master," he assured me, "I beat him every week now. And I've got a heavy hand."

While we were talking I remembered that Matryona had once interceded for Antoshka Grigoriev, but I hadn't asked what relation of hers he was and I had refused to do what she wanted. Matryona was standing in the kitchen doorway like a mute suppliant on this occasion too. When Faddei Mironovich left saying that he would call on me to see how things were going, I asked her, "I can't make out what relation this Antoshka is to you, Matryona Vasilyevna."

"My brother-in-law's son," said Matryona shortly, and went out to milk the goat.

When I'd worked it out I realised that this determined old man with the black hair was the brother of the missing husband.

The long evening went by, and Matryona didn't bring up the subject again. But late at night, when I had stopped thinking about the old man and was working in a silence broken only by the rustling of the cockroaches and the heavy tick of the wall-clock, Matryona suddenly spoke from her dark corner, "You know, Ignatich, I nearly married him once."

I had forgotten that Matryona was in the room. I hadn't heard a sound from her—and suddenly her voice came out of the darkness, as agitated as if the old man were still trying to win her.

I could see that Matryona had been thinking about nothing else all evening.

She got up from her wretched rag bed and walked slowly towards me, as though she were following her own words. I sat back in my chair and caught my first glimpse of a quite different Matryona.

There was no overhead light in our big room with its forest of rubber-plants. The table lamp cast a ring of light round my exercise books, and when I tore my eyes away from it the rest of the room seemed to be half-dark and faintly tinged with pink. I thought I could see the same pinkish glow in her usually sallow cheeks.

"He was the first one who came courting me, before Yefim did . . . he was his brother . . . the older one. . . . I was nineteen and Faddei was twenty-three. . . . They lived in this very same house. Their house it was. Their father built it."

I looked round the room automatically. Instead of the old grey house rotting under the faded green skin of wall-paper where the mice had their playground, I suddenly saw new timbers, freshly trimmed, and not yet discoloured, and caught the cheerful smell of pine-tar.

"Well, and what happened then?"

"That summer we went to sit in the coppice together," she whispered. "There used to be a coppice where the stable-yard is now. They chopped it down. . . . I was just going to marry him, Ignatich. Then the German war started. They took Faddei in the army."

She let fall these few words—and suddenly the blue and white and yellow July of the year 1914 burst into flower before my eyes: the sky still peaceful, the floating clouds, the people sweating to get the ripe corn in. I imagined them side by side, the black-haired Hercules with a scythe over his shoulder, and the red-faced girl clasping a sheaf. And there was singing out under the open sky, such songs as nobody can sing nowadays, with all the machines in the fields.

"He went to the war—and vanished. For three years I kept to myself and waited. Never a sign of life did he give. . . ."

Matryona's round face looked out at me from an elderly threadbare head-scarf. As she stood there in the gentle reflected light from my lamp her face seemed to lose its slovenly workaday covering of wrinkles, and she was a scared young girl again with a frightening decision to make.

Yes. . . . I could see it. . . . The trees shed their leaves, the snow fell and melted. They ploughed and sowed and reaped again. Again the trees shed their leaves, and snow fell. There was a revolution. Then another revolution. And the whole world was turned upside down.

"Their mother died and Yefim came to court me. You wanted to come to our house, he says, so come. He was a year younger than me, Yefim was. It's a saying with us—sensible girls get married after Michaelmas, and silly ones at midsummer. They were short-handed. I got married. . . . The wedding was on St. Peter's day, and then about St. Nicholas' day in the winter he came back. . . . Faddei, I mean, from being a prisoner in Hungary."

Matryona covered her eyes.

I said nothing.

She turned towards the door as though somebody were standing there. "He stood there at the door. What a scream I let out! I wanted to throw myself at his feet! . . . but I couldn't. If it wasn't my own brother, he says, I'd take my axe to the both of you."

I shuddered. Matryona's despair or her terror, conjured up a vivid picture of him standing in the dark doorway and raising his axe to her.

But she quietened down and went on with her story in a sing-song voice, leaning on a chair-back, "Oh dear, dear me, the poor dear man! There were so many girls in the village—but he wouldn't marry. I'll look for one with the same name as you, a second Matryona, he said. And that's what he did—fetched himself a Matryona from Lipovka. They built themselves a house of their own and they're still living in it. You pass their place every day on your way to school."

So that was it. I realised that I had seen the other Matryona quite often. I didn't like her. She was always coming to my Matryona to complain about her husband—he beat her, he was stingy, he was working her to death. She would weep and weep, and her voice always had a tearful note in it. As it turned out, my Matryona had nothing to regret, with Faddei beating his Matryona every day of his life and being so tight-fisted.

"Mine never beat me once," said Matryona of Yefim. "He'd pitch into another man in the street, but me he never hit once.... Well, there was one time ... I quarrelled with my sister-in-law and he cracked me on the forehead with a spoon. I jumped up from the table and shouted at them, 'Hope it sticks in your gullets, you idle lot of beggars, hope you choke!' I said. And off I went into the woods. He never touched me any more."

Faddei didn't seem to have any cause for regret either. The other Matryona had borne him six children (my Antoshka was one of them, the littlest, the runt) and they had all lived, whereas the children of Matryona and Yefim had died, every one of them, before they reached the age of three months, without any illness.

"One daughter, Elena, was born and was alive when they washed her, and then she died right after.... My wedding was on St. Peter's day, and it was St. Peter's day I buried my sixth, Alexander."

The whole village decided that there was a curse on Matryona.

Matryona still nodded emphatic belief when she talked about it. "There was a *course* on me. They took me to a woman as used to be a nun to get cured, she set me off coughing and waited for the *course* to jump out of me like a frog. Only nothing jumped out ..."

* * *

And the years had run by like running water.... In 1941 they didn't take Faddei into the army because of his poor sight, but they took Yefim. And what had happened to the elder brother in the first war happened to the younger in the second ... he vanished without trace. Only he never came back at all. The once noisy cottage was deserted, it became old and rotten, and Matryona, all alone in the world, grew old in it.

So she begged from the other Matryona, the cruelly beaten Matryona, a child of her womb (or was it a spot of Faddei's blood?), the youngest daughter, Kira.

For ten years she brought the girl up in her own house, in place of the children who had not lived. Then, not long before I arrived, she had married her off to a young engine-driver from Cherusti. The only help she got from anywhere came in dribs and drabs from Cherusti: a bit of sugar from time to time, or some of the fat when they killed a pig.

Sick and suffering, and feeling that death was not far off, Matryona had made known her will: the top room, which was a separate frame joined by tie-beams to the rest of the house, should go to Kira when she died. She said nothing about the house itself. Her three sisters had their eyes on it too.

That evening Matryona opened her heart to me. And, as often happens, no sooner were the hidden springs of her life revealed to me than I saw them in motion.

Kira arrived from Cherusti. Old Faddei was very worried. To get and keep a plot of land in Cherusti the young couple had to put up some sort of building. Matryona's top-room would do very well. There was nothing else they could put up, because there was no timber to be had anywhere. It wasn't Kira herself so much, and it wasn't her husband, but old Faddei who was consumed with eagerness for them to get their hands on the plot at Cherusti.

He became a frequent visitor, laying down the law to Matryona and insisting that she should hand over the top room right away, before she died. On these occasions I saw a different Faddei. He was no longer an old man propped up by a stick, whom a push or a harsh word would bowl over. Although he was slightly bent by backache, he was still a fine figure; he had kept the vigorous black hair of a young man in his sixties; he was hot and urgent.

Matryona had not slept for two nights. It wasn't easy for her to make up her mind. She didn't grudge them the top room, which was standing there idle, any more than she ever grudged her labour or her belongings. And the top room was willed to Kira in any case. But the thought of breaking up the roof she had lived under for forty years was torture to her. Even I, a mere lodger, found it painful to think of them stripping away boards and wrenching out beams. For Matryona it was the end of everything.

But the people who were so insistent knew that she would let them break up her house before she died.

So Faddei and his sons and sons-in-laws came along one February morning, the blows of five axes were heard and boards creaked and cracked as they were wrenched out. Faddei's eyes twinkled busily. Although his back wasn't quite straight yet he scrambled nimbly up under the rafters and bustled about down below, shouting at his assistants. He and his father had built this house when he was a lad, a long time ago. The top room had been put up for him, the oldest son, to move in with his bride. And now he was furiously taking it apart, board by board, to carry it out of somebody else's yard.

After numbering the beam-ends and the ceiling boards they dismantled the top room and the store-room underneath it. The living-room, and what was left of the landing, they boarded up with a thin wall of deal. They did nothing about the cracks in the wall. It was plain to see that they were wreckers, not builders, and that they did not expect Matryona to be living there very long.

While the men were busy wrecking, the women were

getting the drink ready for moving day—vodka would cost a lot too much. Kira brought a pood of sugar from Moscow oblast, and Matryona carried the sugar and some bottles to the distiller under cover of night.

The timbers were carried out and stacked in front of the gates, and the engine-driver son-in-law went off to Cherusti for the tractor.

But the very same day a blizzard, or "a blower" as Matryona called it, began. It howled and whirled for two days and nights and buried the road under enormous drifts. Then, no sooner had they made the road passable and a couple of lorries gone by, than it got suddenly warmer. Within a day everything was thawing out, damp mist hung in the air and rivulets gurgled as they burrowed into the snow, and you could get stuck up to the top of your knee-boots.

Two weeks passed before the tractor could get at the dismantled top room. All this time Matryona went around like someone lost. What particularly upset her was that her three sisters came and with one voice called her a fool for giving the top room away, said they didn't want to see her any more, and went off. At about the same time the lame cat strayed and was seen no more. It was just one thing after another. This was another blow to Matryona.

At last the frost got a grip on the slushy road. A sunny day came along and everybody felt more cheerful. Matryona had had a lucky dream the night before. In the morning she heard that I wanted to take a photograph of somebody at an old-fashioned hand-loom. (There were looms still standing in two cottages in the village; they wove coarse rugs on them.) She smiled shyly and said, "You just wait a day or two, Ignatich, I'll just send the top room there off and I'll put my loom up, I've still got it, you know, and then you can snap me. Honest to God!"

She was obviously attracted by the idea of posing in an old-fashioned setting. The red, frosty sun tinged the window of the curtailed passageway with a faint pink, and this reflected light warmed Matryona's face. People who are at ease with their consciences always have nice faces.

Coming back from school before dusk I saw some movement near our house. A big new tractor-drawn sledge was already fully loaded, and there was no room for a lot of the timbers, so old Faddei's family and the helpers they had called in had nearly finished knocking together another home-made sledge. They were all working like madmen, in the frenzy that comes upon people when there is a smell of good money in the air or when they are looking forward to some treat. They were shouting at one another and arguing.

They could not agree whether the sledges should be hauled separately or both together. One of Faddei's sons (the lame one) and the engine-driver son-in-law reasoned that the sledges couldn't both be taken at once because the tractor wouldn't be able to pull them. The man in charge of the tractor, a hefty fat-faced fellow who was very sure of himself, said hoarsely that he knew best, he was the driver, and he would take both at once. His motives were obvious: according to the agreement the engine-driver was paying him for the removal of the upper room, not for the number of trips he had to make. He could never have made two trips in a night—twenty-five kilometres each way, and one return journey. And by morning he had to get the tractor back in the garage from which he had sneaked it out for this job on the side.

Old Faddei was impatient to get the top room moved that day, and at a nod from his lads gave in. To the stout sledge in front they hitched the one which they had knocked together in such a hurry.

Matryona was running about amongst the men, fussing and helping them to heave the beams on to the sledge. Suddenly I noticed that she was wearing my jerkin and had dirtied the sleeves on the frozen mud round the beams. I was annoyed, and told her so. That jerkin held memories for me: it had kept me warm in the bad years.

This was the first time that I was ever angry with Matryona Vasilyevna.

Matryona was taken aback. "Oh dear, dear me," she said. "My poor head. I picked it up in a rush, you see, and never thought about it being yours. I'm sorry, Ignatich."

And she took it off and hung it up to dry.

The loading was finished, and all the men who had been working, about ten of them, clattered past my table and dived under the curtain into the kitchen. I could hear the muffled rattle of glasses and, from time to time, the clink of a bottle, the voices got louder and louder, the boasting more reckless. The biggest braggart was the tractor-driver. The stench of hooch floated in to me. But they didn't go on drinking long. It was getting dark and they had to hurry. They began to leave. The tractor-driver came out first, looking pleased with himself and fierce. The engine-driver son-in-law, Faddei's lame son and one of his nephews were going to Cherusti. The others went off home. Faddei was flourishing his stick, trying to overtake somebody and put him right about something. The lame son paused at my table to light up and suddenly started telling me how he loved Aunt Matryona, and that he had got married not long ago, and his wife had just had a son. Then they shouted for him and he went out. The tractor set up a roar outside.

After all the others had gone Matryona dashed out from behind the screen. She looked after them, anxiously shaking her head. She had put on her jerkin and her head-scarf. As she was going through the door she said to me, "Why ever couldn't they hire two? If one tractor had cracked up the other would have pulled them. What'll happen now, God only knows!"

She ran out after the others.

After the booze-up and the arguments and all the coming and going it was quieter than ever in the deserted cottage, and very chilly because the door had been opened so many times. I got into my jerkin and sat down to mark exercise books. The noise of the tractor died away in the distance.

An hour went by. And another. And a third. Matryona still hadn't come back, but I wasn't surprised. When she had seen the sledge off she must have gone round to her friend Masha.

Another hour went by. And yet another. Darkness and with it a deep silence had descended on the village. I couldn't understand at the time why it was so quiet. Later I found out that it was because all evening not a single train had gone along the line half a verst from the house. No sound was coming from my radio and I noticed that the mice were wilder than ever. Their scampering and scratching and squeaking behind the wallpaper was getting noisier and more defiant all the time.

I woke up. It was one o'clock in the morning and Matryona still hadn't come home.

Suddenly I heard several people talking loudly. They were still a long way off, but something told me that they were coming to our house. And sure enough I heard soon afterwards a heavy knock at the gate. A commanding voice, strange to me, yelled out an order to open up. I went out into the thick darkness with a torch. The whole village was asleep, there was no light in the windows, and the snow had started melting in the last week so that it gave no reflected light. I turned the catch and let them in. Four men in great-coats went on towards the house. It's a very unpleasant thing to be visited at night by noisy people in great-coats.

When we got into the light though, I saw that two of them were wearing railway uniforms. The older of the two, a fat man with the same sort of face as the tractor-driver, asked, "Where's the woman of the house?"

"I don't know."

"This is the place the tractor with a sledge came from?"

"This is it."

"Had they been drinking before they left?"

All four of them were looking around them, screwing up their eyes in the dim light from the table-lamp. I realised that they had either made an arrest or wanted to make one.

"What's happened then?"

"Answer the question!"

"But ..."

"Were they drunk when they went?"

"Were they drinking here?"

Had there been a murder? Or hadn't they been able to move the top room? The men in great-coats had me off balance. But one thing was certain: Matryona could do time for making hooch.

I stepped back to stand between them and the kitchen door. "I honestly didn't notice. I didn't see anything." (I really hadn't seen anything—only heard.) I made what was supposed to be a helpless gesture, drawing attention to the state of the cottage: a table-lamp shining peacefully on books and exercises, a crowd of frightened rubber-plants, the austere couch of a recluse, not a sign of debauchery.

They had already seen for themselves, to their annoyance, that there had been no drinking in that room. They turned to leave, telling each other this wasn't where the drinking had been then, but it would be a good thing to put in that it was. I saw them out and tried to discover what had happened. It was only at the gate that one of them growled, "They've all been cut to bits. Can't find all the pieces."

"That's a detail. The express at 21.00 hours nearly went off the rails. That would have been something." And they walked briskly away.

I went back to the hut in a daze. Who were "they"? What did "all of them" mean? And where was Matryona?

I moved the curtain aside and went into the kitchen. The stink of hooch rose and hit me. It was a deserted battlefield: a huddle of stools and benches, empty bottles lying around, one bottle half-full, glasses, the remains of pickled herring, onion, and sliced fat pork.

Everything was deathly still. Just cockroaches creeping unperturbed about the field of battle.

They had said something about the express at 21.00. Why? Perhaps I should have shown them all this? I began to wonder whether I had done right. But what a damnable way to behave—keeping their explanation for official persons only.

Suddenly the small gate creaked. I hurried out on to the landing, "Matryona Vasilyevna?"

The yard door opened, and Matryona's friend Masha came in, swaying and wringing her hands. "Matryona . . . our Matryona, Ignatich. . . ."

I sat her down and through her tears she told me the story.

The approach to the crossing was a steep rise. There was no barrier. The tractor and the first sledge went over, but the tow-rope broke and the second sledge, the homemade one, got stuck on the crossing and started falling apart—the wood Faddei had given them to make the second sledge was no good. They towed the first sledge out of the way and went back for the second. They were fixing the tow-rope—the tractor-driver and Faddei's lame son, and Matryona, heaven knows what brought her there, was with them, between the tractor and the sledge. What help did she think she could be to the men? She was forever meddling in men's work. Hadn't a bolting horse nearly tipped her into the lake once, through a hole in the ice?

Why did she have to go to the damned crossing? She had handed over the top room, and owed nothing to anybody. . . . The engine-driver kept a look-out in case the train from Cherusti rushed up on them. Its headlamps would be visible a long way off. But two engines coupled together came from the other direction, from our station, backing without lights. Why they were without lights nobody knows. When an engine is backing, coal-dust blows into the driver's eyes from the tender and he can't see very well. The two engines flew into them and crushed the three people between the tractor and the sledge to pulp. The tractor was wrecked, the sledge was matchwood, the rails were buckled, and both engines turned over.

"But how was it they didn't hear the engines coming?"

"The tractor engine was making such a din."

"What about the bodies?"

"They won't let anybody in. They've roped them off."

"What was that somebody was telling me about the express?"

The nine o'clock express goes through our station at a good speed and on to the crossing. But the two drivers weren't hurt when their engines crashed, they jumped out and ran back along the line waving their hands and they managed to stop the train. . . . The nephew was hurt by a beam as well. He's hiding at Klavka's now so that they won't know he was at the crossing. If they find out they'll drag him in as a witness. . . . "Don't know lies up, and do know gets tied up. Kira's husband didn't get a scratch. He tried to hang himself, they had to cut him down. It's all because of me, he says, my aunty's killed and my brother. Now he's gone and given himself up. But the mad-house is where he'll be going, not prison. Oh, Matryona, my dearest Matryona. . . ."

Matryona was gone. Someone close to me had been killed. And on her last day I had scolded her for wearing my jerkin.

The lovingly-drawn red and yellow woman in the book advertisement smiled happily on.

Old Masha sat there weeping a little longer. Then she got up to go. And suddenly she asked me, "Ignatich, you remember, Matryona had a grey shawl. She meant it to go to my Tanya when she died, didn't she?"

She looked at me hopefully in the half-darkness . . . surely I hadn't forgotten?

No, I remembered. "She said so, yes."

"Well, listen, maybe you could let me take it with me now. The family will be swarming in to-morrow and I'll never get it then." And she gave me another hopeful, imploring look. She had been Matryona's friend for half a century, the only one in the village who truly loved her.

No doubt she was right.

"Of course . . . take it."

She opened the chest, took out the shawl, tucked it under her coat and went out.

The mice had gone mad. They were running furiously up and down the walls, and you could almost see the green wallpaper rippling and rolling over their backs.

In the morning I had to go to school. The time was three o'clock. The only thing to do was to lock up and go to bed.

Lock up, because Matryona would not be coming.

I lay down, leaving the light on. The mice were squeaking, almost moaning, racing and running. My mind was weary and wandering, and I couldn't rid myself of an uneasy feeling that an invisible Matryona was flitting about and saying good-bye to her home.

And suddenly I imagined Faddei standing there, young and black-haired, in the dark patch by the door, with his axe uplifted. "If it wasn't my own brother I'd chop the both of you to bits."

The threat had lain around for forty years, like an old broad-sword in a corner, and in the end it had struck its blow.

When it was light the women went to the crossing and brought back all that was left of Matryona on a hand-sledge with a dirty sack over it. They threw off the sack to wash her. There was just a mess ... no feet, only half a body, no left hand. One woman said, "The Lord has left her her right hand. She'll be able to say her prayers where she's going...."

Then the whole crowd of rubber-plants was carried out of the cottage ... these plants that Matryona had loved so much that once when smoke woke her up in the night she didn't rush to save her house but to tip the plants on to the floor in case they were suffocated. The women swept the floor clean. They hung a wide towel of old home-spun over Matryona's dim mirror. They took down the jolly posters. They moved my table out of the way. Under the icons, near the windows, they stood a rough unadorned coffin on a row of stools.

In the coffin lay Matryona. Her body, mangled and lifeless, was covered with a clean sheet. Her head was swathed in a white kerchief. Her face was almost undamaged, peaceful, more alive than dead.

The villagers came to pay their last respects. The women even brought their small children to take a look at the dead. And if anyone raised a lament, all the women, even those who had looked in out of idle curiosity, always joined in, wailing where they stood by the door or the wall, as though they were providing a choral accompaniment. The men stood stiff and silent with their caps off.

The formal lamentation had to be performed by the women of Matryona's family. I observed that the lament followed a coldly calculated age-old ritual. The more distant relatives went up to the coffin for a short while and made low wailing noises over it. Those who considered themselves closer kin to the dead woman began their lament in the doorway and when they got as far as the coffin, bowed down and roared out their grief right in the face of the departed. Every lamenter made up her own melody. And expressed her own thoughts and feelings.

I realised that a lament for the dead is not just a lament, but a kind of politics. Matryona's three sisters swooped took possession of the cottage, the goat, and the stove locked up the chest, ripped the two hundred roubles f the funeral out of the coat lining, and drummed it in everybody who came that only they were near relativ Their lament over the coffin went like this, "*Oh nan nanny! Oh nan-nan!* All we had in the world was y You could have lived in peace and quiet, you could. A we should always have been kind and loving to you. No your top room's been the death of you. Finished you off has, the cursed thing! Oh why did you have to take i down? Why didn't you listen to us?"

Thus the sisters' laments were indictments of Matryona's husband's family: they shouldn't have made her take the top room down. (There was an underlying meaning too: you've taken the top room all right but we won't let you have the house itself!)

Matryona's husband's family, her sisters-in-law, Yefim and Faddei's sisters, and various nieces lamented like this, *"Oh poor auntie, poor auntie!* Why didn't you take better care of yourself! Now they're angry with us for sure. Our own dear Matryona you were, and it's your own fault! The top room is nothing to do with it. Oh why did you go where death was waiting for you? Nobody asked you to go there. And what a way to die! Oh why didn't you listen to us?" (Their answer to the others showed through these laments: we are not to blame for her death, and the house we'll talk about later.)

But the "second" Matryona, a coarse, broad-faced woman, the substitute Matryona whom Faddei had married so long ago for the sake of her name, got out of step with family policy, wailing and sobbing over the coffin in her simplicity, *"Oh my poor dear sister!* You won't be angry with me, will you now? Oh-oh-oh! How we used to talk and talk, you and me! Forgive a poor miserable woman! You've gone to be with your dear mother, and you'll come for me some day for sure! Oh-oh-oh-oh! . . ."

At every "oh-oh-oh" it was as though she were giving up the ghost. She writhed and gasped, with her breast against the side of the coffin. When her lament went beyond the ritual prescription the women, as though acknowledging its success, all started saying, "come away now, come away."

Matryona came away, but back she went again, sobbing with even greater abandon. Then an ancient woman came out of a corner, put her hand on Matryona's shoulder, and said, "There are two riddles in this world: how I was born I don't remember, how I shall die I don't know."

And Matryona fell silent at once, and all the others were silent, so there was an unbroken hush.

But the old woman herself, who was much older than

all the other old women there and didn't seem to belong to Matryona at all, after a while started wailing, "Oh my poor sick Matryona! Oh my poor Vasilyevna! Oh what a weary thing it is to be seeing you into your grave!"

There was one who didn't follow the ritual, but wept straightforwardly, in the fashion of our age, which has had plenty of practice at it. This was Matryona's unfortunate foster-daughter, Kira, from Cherusti, for whom the top room had been taken down and moved. Her ringlets were pitifully out of curl. Her eyes looked red and bloodshot. She didn't notice that her head-scarf was slipping off out in the frosty air and that her arm hadn't found the sleeve of her coat. She walked in a stupor from her foster-mother's coffin in one house to her brother's in another. They were afraid she would lose her mind, because her husband had to go for trial as well.

It looked as if her husband was doubly at fault: not only was he moving the top room, but as an engine-driver he knew the regulations about unprotected crossings, and should have gone down to the station to warn them about the tractor. There were a thousand people on the Urals express that night, peacefully sleeping in the upper and lower berths of their dimly-lit carriages, and all those lives were nearly cut short. All because of a few greedy people, wanting to get their hands on a plot of land, or not wanting to make a second trip with a tractor.

All because of the top room, which had been under a curse ever since Faddei's hands had started itching to take it down.

The tractor-driver was already beyond human justice. And the railway authorities were also at fault, both because a busy crossing was unguarded and because the coupled engines were travelling without lights. That was why they had tried at first to blame it all on the drink, and then to keep the case out of court.

The rails and the track were so twisted and torn that for three days, while the coffins were still in the house, no trains ran—they were diverted on to another line. All Friday, Saturday, and Sunday, from the end of the investigation until the funeral, the work of repairing the line went on day and night. The repair gang was frozen, and they made fires to warm themselves and to light their work at night, using the boards and beams from the second sledge which were there for the taking, scattered around the crossing.

The first sledge just stood there, undamaged and still loaded, a little way beyond the crossing.

One sledge, tantalisingly ready to be towed away, and the other perhaps still to be plucked from the flames—that was what harrowed the soul of black-bearded Faddei all day Friday and all day Saturday. His daughter was going out of her mind, his son-in-law had a criminal charge hanging over him, in his own house lay the son he had killed, and along the street the woman he had killed and whom he had once loved. But Faddei stood by the coffins clutching his beard only for a short time, and went away again. His tall brow was clouded by painful thoughts, but what he was thinking about was how to save the timbers of the top room from the flames and from Matryona's scheming sisters.

Going over the people of Talnovo in my mind I realised that Faddei was not the only one like that.

Property, the people's property, or my property, is strangely called our "goods." If you lose your goods, people think you disgrace yourself and make yourself look foolish.

Faddei dashed about, never stopping for a sitdown, from the settlement to the station, from one official to another, stood there with his bent back, leaning heavily on his stick, and begged them all to take pity on an old man and give him permission to recover the top room.

Somebody gave permission. And Faddei gathered together his surviving sons, sons-in-law and nephews, got horses from the kolkhoz and from the other side of the wrecked crossing, by a roundabout way that led through three villages, brought the remnants of the top room home to his yard. He finished the job in the early hours of Sunday morning.

On Sunday afternoon they were buried. The two coffins met in the middle of the village, and the relatives argued about which of them should go first. Then they put them side by side on an open sledge, the aunt and the nephew, and carried the dead over the damp snow, with a gloomy February sky above, to the churchyard two villages away. There was an unkind wind, so the priest and the deacon waited inside the church and didn't come out to Talnovo to meet them.

A crowd of people walked slowly behind the coffins, singing in chorus. Outside the village they fell back.

When Sunday came the women were still fussing around the house. An old woman mumbled psalms by the coffin, Matryona's sisters flitted about, popping things into the oven, and the air round the mouth of the stove trembled with the heat of red-hot peats, those which Matryona had carried in a sack from a distant bog. They were making unappetizing pies with poor flour.

When the funeral was over and it was already getting on towards evening, they gathered for the wake. Tables were put together to make a long one, which hid the place where the coffin had stood in the morning. To start with they all stood round the table, and an old man, the husband of a sister-in-law, said the Lord's prayer. Then they poured everybody a little honey and warm water, just enough to cover the bottom of the bowl. We spooned it up without bread or anything, in memory of the dead. Then we ate something and drank vodka and the conversation became more animated. Before the jelly they all stood up and sang *"Eternal remembrance"* (they explained to me that it had to be sung before the jelly). There was more drinking. By now they were talking louder than ever, and not about Matryona at all. The sister-in-law's husband started boasting, "Did you notice, brother Christians, that they took the funeral service slowly to-day? That's because Father Mikhail noticed me. He knows I know the service. Other times it's saints defend us, homeward wend us, and that's all."

At last the supper was over. They all rose again. They sang *"Worthy is she."* Then again, with a triple repetition of *"Eternal remembrance."* But the voices were hoarse and out of tune, their faces drunken, and nobody put any feeling into this "eternal memory."

Then the main guests went away, and only the near relatives were left. They pulled out their cigarettes and lit up, there were jokes and laughter. There was some mention of Matryona's husband and his disappearance. The sister-in-law's husband, striking himself on the chest, assured me and the cobbler who was married to one of Matryona's sisters, "He was dead, Yefim was dead! What could stop him coming back if he wasn't? If I knew they were going to hang me when I got to the old country I'd come back just the same!"

The cobbler nodded in agreement. He was a deserter and had never left the old country. All through the war he was hiding in his mother's cellar.

The stern and silent old woman who was more ancient than all the ancients was staying the night and sat high up on the stove. She looked down in mute disapproval on the indecently animated youngsters of fifty and sixty.

But the unhappy foster-daughter, who had grown up within these walls, went away behind the kitchen screen to cry.

Faddei didn't come to Matryona's wake—perhaps because he was holding a wake for his son. But twice in the next few days he walked angrily into the house for discussions with Matryona's sisters and the deserting cobbler.

The argument was about the house. Should it go to one of the sisters or to the foster-daughter? They were on the verge of taking it to court, but they made peace because they realised that the court would hand over the house to neither side, but to the rural district council. A bargain was struck. One sister took the goat, the cobbler and his wife got the house, and to make up Faddei's share, since he had "nursed every bit of timber here in his arms," in addition to the top room which had already been carried away, they let him have the shed which had housed the goat, and the whole of the inner fence between the yard and the garden.

Once again the insatiable old man got the better of sickness and pain and became young and active. Once again he gathered together his surviving sons and sons-in-law, and they dismantled the shed and the fence, and he hauled the timbers himself, sledge by sledge, and only towards the end did he have Antoshka of 8-D, who didn't slack this time, to help him.

They boarded Matryona's house up till the spring, and I moved in with one of her sisters-in-law, not far away. This sister-in-law on several occasions came out with some recollection of Matryona, and made me see the dead woman in a new light. "Yefim didn't love her. He used to say, 'I like to dress in an educated way, but she dresses any old way, like they do in the country.' Well then, he thinks, if she doesn't want anything, he might as well drink whatever's to spare. One time I went with him to the town to work, and he got himself a madam there and never wanted to come back to Matryona."

Everything she said about Matryona was disapproving. She was slovenly, she made no effort to get a few things about her. She wasn't the saving kind. She didn't even keep a pig, because she didn't like fattening them up for some reason. And the silly woman helped other people without payment. (What brought Matryona to mind this time was that the garden needed ploughing and she couldn't find enough helpers to pull the plough.)

Matryona's sister-in-law admitted that she was warm-hearted and straightforward, but pitied and despised her for it.

It was only then, after these disapproving comments from her sister-in-law, that a true likeness of Matryona formed itself before my eyes, and I understood her as I never had when I lived side by side with her.

Of course! Every house in the village kept a pig. But she didn't. What can be easier than fattening a greedy piglet that cares for nothing in the world but food! You warm his swill three times a day, you live for him—then you cut his throat and you have some fat.

But she had none. . . .

She made no effort to get things round her. . . . She didn't struggle and strain to buy things and then care for them more than life itself.

She didn't go all out after fine clothes. Clothes, that beautify what is ugly and evil.

She was misunderstood and abandoned even by her husband. She had lost six children, but not her sociable ways. She was a stranger to her sisters and sisters-in-law, a ridiculous creature who stupidly worked for others without pay. She didn't accumulate property against the day she died. A dirty-white goat, a gammy-legged cat, some rubber-plants. . . .

We had all lived side by side with her and never understood that she was that righteous one without whom, as the proverb says, no village can stand.

Nor any city.

Nor our whole land.

(*1963*)

Andrei Sinyavsky

(1925-   )

In 1966 the Soviet government determined that Andrei Sinyavsky, writing illegally under the name Abram Tertz, had
composed a pamphlet and a handful of fictional pieces that
tended, in the language of the Soviet Criminal Code, "to sub-
vert or weaken the Soviet regime." For this he was condemned to suffer seven years of the mindless brutality that the
entire world now knows to have been the rule in the Soviet
prison system.

What did he do while carting sawdust, sawing wood, loading timber, and enduring at night the stink, cold, noise, and
loneliness of the crowded barracks? He wrote three books,
mailing them out—ostensibly as letters to his wife—in bi-
monthly installments that, of course, duly passed through the
paws of the censor. *Three books*. It is like flinging a man in
jail for counterfeiting a dollar bill and allowing him while
there to engrave, print, and send out through the ordinary
post a couple of million.

Two of the books deal, respectively, with Pushkin and
Gogol, the two complementary geniuses who inspired all
subsequent Russian literature. These have provoked scandal-
ized outcries in the Russian émigré press. It is a pretty fair
rule that any Russian anathematized by *both* the Soviet regime *and* the émigré establishment—witness the case of Vladimir Nabokov (see p. 363)—requires no further credential
as an original genius. These are literary studies, and for all
their heterodox shape and outlook they are still classifiable as

such (the censor inspecting these "letters to his wife" must have thought the Sinyavskys the most cerebral couple since the invention of marriage).

But the third book, *A Voice from the Chorus*, is as resistant to classification as Burton's *Anatomy of Melancholy*, the Sudelbücher of Georg Christoph Lichtenberg, or Cyril Connolly's *The Unquiet Grave*, those great masterpieces of disjunction. The unforewarned reader who bypasses the blurb and the excellent introduction by Max Hayward would be hard put to make out what precisely is going on behind this jumble of voices and styles.

The structure of the book and its basic device are actually quite straightforward. The seven parts correspond chronologically to the years, from March 1966, to June 1971, which Sinyavsky spent in three successive Soviet concentration camps. The device is that of a solo Voice (Sinyavsky-Tertz), which stands out vividly against a background babble of many voices—the chorus of other prisoners. These are distinguished not only by being printed in italics but also by their relative brevity, lack of coherence, and, as compared with the stylistic elegance of the foreground Voice, by their often vulgar, dialectal, or illiterate Russian.

To describe this background would be to inventory the entire rabble of human types whose constant buzzing presence accompanies the placidly invulnerable sanity of the consciousness closest to us. It is alternately picturesque, absurd, ribald, pointlessly flat, obscene, hilarious, stupid, touching, cruel, or simply ethnographically and linguistically interesting. There are little squibs of truncated conversation, single phrases, a résumé of tattoos on various parts of the anatomy, swatches of the protean Russian vernacular—for example: "Moscow is a capital city: people from all over the world arrive there in hats." "Would I have enough strength of will and courage to burn a cat in a furnace?" "In the dark smells are stronger, I've noticed." "Shut your great porridge-eating gob!" "What is Western culture? It's carrying snot around in your pocket: you blow it into a handkerchief and carry it about with you." "Oh, I did laugh in '59: a man fell down a hole, and then his wife fell in after him!"

But everything depends upon the Voice in roman type, for which the italic babble in the background is little more than foil. This voice bodies forth the endlessly attractive personality of Andrei Sinyavsky, a lion in the path of anyone who thinks he has understood the character of *homo sovieticus*. Sinyavsky is wholly a product of the Soviet state, of which he was for the greater part of his life a son of exemplary loyalty, having passed through the Komsomol and the University into the comfortable job of literary researcher and teacher, with an apartment in the capital. By some miracle, this normally stultifying experience produced in his case a mind of flabbergasting originality, fortitude, and a sort of insouciantly gay independence. In his ability to swing from sublime nonsense and even silliness to the profoundest meditations on literature and religion (Sinyavsky is devoutly Russian Orthodox, with a profound knowledge of Church history and philosophy), he reminds one of the most influential modern Russian philosopher, Vladimir Soloviev.

Some of the Voice's nonsense looks as if it ought to be in italics with the rest of the chorus ("I simply can't imagine why mice should have tails"), but Sinyavsky, whose isolation needs no underlining, is sometimes at pains to emphasize his solidarity with his fellow inmates, even with the proud class of professional thieves, which leads him to muse in a way reminiscent of Osip Mandelstam (see p. 169) upon the essential illegality of all genuine literary creation.

Sinyavsky's comments on literature are profoundly original and amount sometimes to polished essays of several pages. He evidently managed to lay his hands on a few books, borrowed or sent from home. Not that he absolutely required them: In 1974 at the Sorbonne I attended Sinyavsky's lectures on modern Russian poetry, delivered without so much as a *fiche* in his hands and filled with long poems recited entirely from memory.

Comparisons with Sinyavsky's much better known fellow exile Alexander Solzhenitsyn (see p. 419) almost insist upon being made. Solzhenitsyn differs from all the other great Russians recently expelled by their government in many ways, including the dimensions of his ambition. At times one has the impression that his unexpressed aim was to dismantle the Soviet regime and then, having combined in his single person Patriarch and Czar, to oversee the millennial era in which an abjectly penitent world would lay aside the delusions of materialism and unbridled individual liberty and submit to the universal spiritual dominion of the Russian Soul.

Sinyavsky has no such ambition. Compared with Solzhenitsyn, he is a stay-at-home, practically a recluse. It was he, after all, who concealed his identity behind a *nom de plume* that he still uses (while Solzhenitsyn insisted upon the recognition he felt was due him). The primary motive behind Sinyavsky's duplicity is too obvious to mention, but in addition to his merely prudent concealment from the police, he evidently required (and requires) a quite different kind of concealment—that of the artist, the private man, the idiot, for whom solitude is a condition of existence. Sinyavsky is a Russian writer and nothing else. He does not know foreign languages, and if he is at home in the greatest books of the world it is because he has read them in Russian.

I asked him once whether he had ever studied English. He replied that a Lithuanian had in fact proposed to teach him English in one of the camps. "But," he said, "suppose that by the age of forty-seven I knew enough English to read good books. How many would I have time to read? Some six or seven. And so I decided to write."

Exactly this sort of practical cogitation has gone into most of the decisions of his life, but the result of them all has been roughly: "I decided to write." If nearly all the writings of Solzhenitsyn have a megaphonic and public tone, those of Sinyavsky come to us from the quiet center of one intensely private being. Osip Mandelstam once wrote that at a certain time the pensive citizens of Saint Petersburg would have to go off to a Finnish village to think to the end thoughts that could not be thought to the end in the capital. Sinyavsky's aids to reflection consist of nothing more than a sheet of paper and the tranquil inner space where he confronts himself. "A sheet of paper is to me," he writes, "what the forest is to a man on the run." Day after day, unbeknownst to the guards and their dogs and his fellow prisoners, Sinyavsky escaped into the paper forest of his erudition and imagination, there to inhale, in the undying phrase of Pushkin, "secret freedom," beyond the reach of all authority.

PKHENTZ

I met him at the laundry again today. He pretended to be completely taken up with his dirty washing and unaware of me.

First came the sheets which people here use for reasons of hygiene. Along one edge of every sheet they stitch in tiny letters the word "FEET." This is by way of precaution against one's lips touching any part which the soles of one's feet may have rubbed and contaminated the night before.

Similarly a kick is considered more insulting than a blow with the hand, and not just because the foot hurts more. The distinction is probably a sign that Christianity still lives on: the foot must be wickeder than the rest of the body for the simple reason that it is farther from heaven. Only the sexual organs are treated with less respect, and here there is some mystery.

Next came pillow-cases with dark impressions in the middle. Then towels, which unlike pillow-cases get dirtier round the edges, and, last of all, a colourful bundle of crumpled personal linen.

At this point he started tossing his stuff in at such a rate that I couldn't take a good look. Either he was afraid of giving away a secret, or else he was ashamed, as people always are, to exhibit objects directly pertaining to his legs.

But it was suspicious, I thought, that he had worn his clothes so long without getting them laundered. Ordinarily hunchbacks are clean. They are afraid that their clothes may make them still more repulsive. But this one, surprisingly, was such a sloven that he wasn't like a hunchback at all.

The woman who checked the laundry had seen everything. The marks left by the rarest of juices were old acquaintances to her. But even she couldn't help saying quite loudly: "What are you shoving it under my nose for, citizen? If you can't sleep properly, do your own laundry!"

He paid his money without a word and rushed out. I didn't follow him, because I didn't want to attract attention.

At home things were as usual. The minute I got into my room Veronica appeared. She bashfully suggested that we should have supper together. It was a bit awkward for me to say no to the girl. She's the only one in the apartment who treats me decently. It's a pity that her sympathy is grounded in sexual attraction. I'm absolutely convinced of this after what happened today.

"How's Kostritskaya?" I asked, steering the conversation on to common enemies.

"Oh, Andrei Kazimirovich, she's been making threats again."

"What's wrong?"

"The same as before. Light on in the bathroom and the floor all splashed. Kostritskaya informed me that she's going to complain to the superintendent."

The news infuriated me. I make less use of the plumbing than any of the others. I hardly ever go into the kitchen. Can't I make up for it by using the bathroom?

"Well, let her get on with it," I answered sharply. "She burns light by the kilowatt herself. And her children broke my bottle. Let the superintendent come."

But I knew very well that an appeal to the authorities would be a very risky business for me. Why draw attention to myself unnecessarily?

"Don't upset yourself, Andrei Kazimirovich," said Veronica. "I'll look after any trouble with the neighbours. Please don't upset yourself."

She put out her hand to touch my forehead, but I managed to dodge. "No, no, I'm quite well, I haven't got a temperature. Let's have supper."

Food stood on the table, steaming and stinking. The sadism of cookery has always amazed me. Would-be chickens are eaten in liquid form. The innards of pigs are stuffed with their own flesh. A gut that's swallowed itself garnished with stillborn chickens—what else, when you think of it, is scrambled egg with sausage?

Wheat is treated more unmercifully still: they cut it, beat it, crush it to dust.

"Eat up now, Andrei Kazimirovich," said Veronica coaxingly. "Please don't let it worry you. I'll take the blame for everything."

What about preparing a man to the same recipe? Take an engineer or writer, stuff him with his own brains, place a violet in one braised nostril, and dish him up to his colleagues for dinner. Yes, the torments of Christ, Jan Hus, and Stenka Razin are a bagatelle compared with the agonies of a fish jerked out of water on a hook. They at least knew what it was all for.

"Tell me, Andrei Kazimirovich, are you very lonely," asked Veronica, coming back with the tea-pot. When she had gone to fetch it I had emptied my plate into a sheet of newspaper.

"Did you ever have any friends"—she put in sugar—"or children"—another spoonful—"or a woman you loved?" . . . stir, stir, stir.

It was easy to see that Veronica was agitated.

"You are all the friends I need," I answered cautiously. "And as for women, you can see for yourself: I'm old and hump-backed. Old and hump-backed," I repeated with ruthless insistence.

I honestly wanted to forestall a declaration of love: things were difficult enough without it. It wasn't worth spoiling our alliance against the spiteful neighbours by rousing this unattached girl to a keener interest in myself.

To avoid trouble I thought of pretending to be an alcoholic. Or a criminal. Or perhaps better still a madman, or even a pederast? But I was afraid that any one of these roles would lend my person a dangerous fascination.

All I could do was to dwell on my hump, my age, my wretched salary, my humble job as a book-keeper, and all the time it took up, to insist that only a woman with a hump to match would be right for me, whereas a normal, beautiful woman needed a symmetrical man.

"No, you are too noble," Veronica decided. "You think of yourself as a cripple, and you're afraid of being a burden. Don't think it's pity on my part. It's just that I like cactus, and you are like a cactus. What a lot of them you've got growing there on your window-sill!"

Her hot fingers touched my hand. I jumped as if I'd been scalded.

"You're freezing—are you ill?" asked Veronica anxiously. She was puzzled by my body temperature.

This was too much. I pleaded a migraine and asked her to leave me.

"Till tomorrow," said Veronica, waving her hand like a little girl. "And you can give me a cactus for a present tomorrow. I know you will."

This gentle girl talked to me like a head book-keeper. She declared her love for me and demanded a reward.

Didn't I read somewhere that people in love are like humble slaves? Nothing of the kind. A man only has to fall in love to feel himself lord and master, with the right to boss anyone who doesn't love him enough. How I wish that nobody loved me!

When I was alone I set about watering my cacti from an enamel mug. I fed them slowly, my little hump-backed children, and relaxed.

It was two o'clock in the morning, when, faint from hunger, I crept on tiptoe along the dark corridor to the bathroom. But what a splendid supper I had then!

It isn't at all easy, eating only once a day.

That was two weeks ago. Since then Veronica has informed me that she has two beaus: a lieutenant and an actor at the Stanislavsky Theatre. But it hasn't stopped her showing her predilection for me. She has threatened to shave her head so that I can't keep saying how stupid it would be to sacrifice her beauty to an old freak. Now she has got around to spying on me, lying in wait for me on the way to the bathroom.

"Cleanliness makes hunchbacks handsome"—that's my stock answer when she keeps asking why I take so many baths.

Just in case, I have started blocking up the frosted window between the bathroom and the lavatory with a piece of ply-wood. I always try the bolts before undressing. I couldn't stand the thought of somebody watching me.

Yesterday morning I wanted to fill my fountain-pen, to continue my irregular diary, so I knocked at her door. Veronica wasn't up yet. She was reading *The Three Musketeers* in bed.

"Good morning," I said politely. "You'll be late for your lecture."

She closed her book. "Do you know," she said, "that the whole house thinks I'm your mistress?"

I said nothing, and then something horrible happened. Veronica, her eyes flashing, threw back the counterpane, and her whole body, completely uncovered, stared up at me angrily. "Look what you've turned down, Andrei Kazimirovich!"

Fifteen years ago I came across a textbook on anatomy. I wanted to know what was what, so I studied carefully all the pictures and diagrams. Later on, I had an opportunity of watching little boys bathing in the river at the Gorky Park of Culture and Rest. But, as it happened, I had never seen a naked woman in the flesh and at such close quarters.

It was—I repeat—horrible. I found that her whole body was of the same unnatural whiteness as her neck, face, and hands. A pair of white breasts dangled in front. At first I took them for secondary arms, amputated above the elbow. But each of them terminated in a round nipple like a push-button.

Farther on, and right down to her legs, the whole available space was occupied by a spherical belly. That is where the food swallowed in the course of a day collects in a heap. Its lower half was over-grown with curly hair like a little head.

The problem of sex, which plays such a major role in their intellectual and moral life, had long troubled me. For safety's sake, I suppose, it has been wrapped from ancient times in a veil of impenetrable secrecy. Even the textbook on anatomy has nothing to say on the subject, or says it so vaguely and cursorily that no one can guess what it truly means.

So now, overcoming my confusion, I decided to take advantage of the opportunity, to take a look at the place mentioned in the anatomy textbook as the site of that genital apparatus which shoots out ready-made infants like a catapult.

I caught a glimpse of something resembling human features. Only it didn't look female to me, but more like an old man's face, unshaven and baring its teeth.

A hungry, angry man dwelt there between her legs. He probably snored at night, and relieved his boredom with foul language. This must explain woman's dual nature, of which the poet Lermontov has aptly said:

> Fair as an angel of heaven,
> As a fiend cruel and false.

There was no time to work the thing out, because Veronica suddenly shuddered and said:

"Come on!"

She shut her eyes and opened her mouth, like a fish pulled out of water. She thrashed about on the bed like a great white fish, helplessly, vainly, and bluish goose-pimples covered her body.

"Forgive me, Veronica Grigorievna," I said timidly. "Forgive me," I said, "it's time for me to go to the office."

And I tried to tread lightly and not to look back as I went away.

* * *

It was raining outside, but I was in no hurry. It was cleaning day in the department. I had escaped from Veronica, pleading official business (the estimates, the nicotine, Head Book-keeper Zykov, those crazy typists— all for 650 roubles a month), and now I could afford the great luxury of a walk in the open in wet weather.

I found a leaky drain-pipe and stationed myself under the stream. It ran right down my neck, cool and delicious, and in about three minutes I was damp enough.

The people hurrying past, all of them with umbrellas and rubber soles, looked at me sideways, intrigued by my behaviour. I had to change my position, so I took a stroll through the puddles. My shoes were letting water in nicely. Down below, at least, I was enjoying myself.

"Oh Veronica, Veronica," I repeated indignantly. "Why were you so cruel as to fall in love with me? Why weren't you just the least bit ashamed of your appearance, why did you behave with such ruthless candour?"

Shame, after all, is man's fundamental virtue. It is a dim realisation that he is irredeemably ugly, an instinctive dread of what he hides under cloth. Only shame, shame, shame can lend him a certain nobility, make him not of course more beautiful but at least more modest.

Needless to say, when I got here I followed the general fashion. You must observe the laws of the country you're compelled to live in. And anyway the constant danger of being caught, of being found out, made me force my body into this fancy-dress.

But in their place I wouldn't shed my fur coat, let alone my suit, not even at night. I would find a plastic surgeon to shorten my legs and at least put a hump on my back. Hunchbacks are certainly a bit better-looking than the rest of them here, though they are monsters too.

Dejectedly I made my way to Herzen Street. My hunchback lodged there in a semi-basement opposite the Conservatoire. For six weeks now I had had my eye on this gracefully vaulted person who was so unlike a human being, and reminded me somehow of my lost youth.

I had seen him three times at the laundry and once in a flower-shop, buying a cactus. I had been lucky enough to find out his address from a receipt which he had tendered to the laundress.

The time had come to dot the *i*'s.

I told myself that it was impossible, that they had all perished and that I was the sole survivor, like Robinson Crusoe. Why, I had liquidated, with my own hands, all that was left after the crash. There were no others here but me.

But what if they'd sent him to look for me? Pretending to be a hunchback, in disguise.... They hadn't forgotten me! They'd realised what had happened and mounted a search!

But how could they know? After thirty-two years. By local time, but still. Alive and well. That was quite something.

But why here precisely? That was the question. Nobody had meant to come here. Quite a different direction. It couldn't happen. We missed our way. Back of beyond. Seven and a half months. Then it happened.

Perhaps it was accidental. Exactly the same mistake. A deviation from course and the winter time-table. Any port in a storm. Do coincidences happen? Alike as two peas. Where none had set foot. It can happen, can't it? Disguised as a hunchback. Exactly like me. Even if there were only one, exactly like me!

The door was opened by a lady like Kostritskaya. Only this Kostritskaya was bigger and older. She exuded a smell of lilac, ten times normal strength. Perfume, that was.

"Leopold will be back soon. Come in, please."

An unseen dog was barking at the other end of the corridor. It couldn't make up its mind to spring at me. But I had had nasty experiences with animals of this kind.

"What's wrong? She won't bite. Down, Niksa, quiet!"

We wrangled politely while the animal raged, and three heads emerged from side doors. They looked me up and down with interest and cursed the dog. The din was awful.

I got through to the room, at great risk, and found there a small child armed with a sabre. When he saw us he asked for berries and sugar and set up a yell, wriggling and pulling faces.

"He's a sweet-tooth. Just like me," Kostritskaya explained. "Stop whining, or this man will eat you."

To please my hostess, I said jokingly that for soup I drank children's blood, warmed-up. The child was quiet at once. He dropped his sabre and cowered in the far corner. He didn't take his eyes off me. They were full of animal terror.

"Is he like Leopold?" the Kostritskaya asked, as though casually, but with a hoarse tenderness in her voice.

I pretended to believe the innuendo. The stale air, laced with the exhalations of lilac, made me feel sick. The smell irritated my skin, and a rash broke out in several places. I was afraid that my face might come out in green spots.

I could hear the savage Niksa scratching the corridor floor with her claws, and sniffing my tracks with a noisy snuffle. The excited lady lodgers, unaware of my heightened aural sensitivity, were conversing in half-whispers.

"Anybody can see he's Leopold Sergeevich's brother. . . ."

"No, you're wrong, our hunchy is Pushkin's twin compared to this one."

"Hope to God I never dream of anything like that. . . ."

"Makes you feel funny just to look at him. . . ."

All this was interrupted by Leopold's arrival. I remember that I liked the way he plunged straight into his part—the classic part of the hunchback who meets a monster like himself in the presence of third parties.

"Aha, a companion in misfortune! With whom have I the honour. . . . To what am I indebted. . . ."

He was copying a psychological pattern as fine-spun as a spider's web, pride protected by self-mockery, shame hiding itself in buffoonery. He mounted his chair like a horseman, gripping the seat between his legs, jumping up and sitting down again back to front, resting his head on the chair-back, pulling weird faces, and continually shrugging his shoulders as though feeling the hump that loomed over him like a ruck-sack.

"Yes, yes. So you're Andrei Kazimirovich. And my name, funnily enough, is Leopold Sergeevich. As you can see I'm a bit of a hunchback too."

I was delighted with this skilful caricature of humanity, this art which was all the more natural because it was so absurd, and I realised rather sadly that he was my superior at the game of living, that I lacked his ability to enter into the only form of being possible for us on earth ... that of hunchbacked monsters and injured egotists.

But business is business, and I gave him to understand that I wished to talk to him—*confidentially*.

"I don't mind going," said Kostritskaya huffily, and gave me a farewell gust of her caustic aroma as she left the room.

I revenged myself with the thought that she was saturated through and through in this smell. Even her excrement must smell of perfume, instead of boiled potatoes and home comforts, as is usually the case. She must piss pure eau-de-Cologne. In this atmosphere poor Leopold would soon wither away.

When we were alone, except for the petrified child sitting in the far corner with a dazed look of horror and mystification on his face, I asked him straight out:

"How long since you left?"

"Left where?" he answered evasively.

Our hostess' departure had wiped the assumed merriment from his face. Not a trace of that clownish exhibitionism found in most hunchbacks, who are clever enough to hide their spines and proud enough not to suffer because of it. I thought that he hadn't pulled himself together yet, and that from inertia he was wearily keeping up the pretence of being something other than his true self.

"Cut it out," I said quietly. "I recognised you at first sight. You and I come from the same place. We're rela-

tives, so to speak. PKHENTZ! PKHENTZ!" I whispered, to
remind him of a name sacred to us both.

"What did you say? . . . You know, I thought there was
something rather familiar about you. Where could I have
seen you before?"

He rubbed his brow, frowned, twisted his lips. The mo-
bility of his face was almost human, and again I envied his
extraordinarily well rehearsed technique, although these
cautious habits were beginning to irritate me.

"Of course!" he exclaimed. "Didn't you work once in
the Stationery Supplies set-up? The director there in
'forty-four was Yakov Solomonovich Zak—such a nice
little Jew. . . ."

"I don't know any Zak," I answered curtly. "But I
know very well that you, Leopold Sergeevich, are not
Leopold Sergeevich at all, and no hunchback, although
you keep flourishing your hump all over the place. We've
had enough of pretences now. After all, I'm taking just as
big a risk as you are."

It was as though the devil had got into him:

"How dare you tell me who I am? Spoiling my relations
with the landlady, and then insulting me as well! Go and
find yourself a gorgeous woman like that," he said, "and
then you can discuss my physical defects. You're more of
a hunchback than I am! You're more disgusting. Monster!
Hunchback! Wretched cripple!"

Suddenly he burst out laughing and clapped his hand to
his head: "Now I remember! I've seen you at the laundry.
The only resemblance between us is that we got our
clothes washed in the same place."

This time I didn't doubt his sincerity. He really did
think that he was Leopold Sergeevich. He had entered
too fully into his part, gone native, become human, over-
adjusted to his surroundings, surrendered to alien influ-
ences. He had forgotten his former name, betrayed his
distant homeland, and unless somebody helped him he
was as good as lost.

I grabbed him by his shoulders and shook him carefully. I shook him, and implored him in a gentle, friendly

way to remember, to make an effort and remember, to return to his true self. What did he want with that Kostritskaya, who oozed such a poisonous odour? Even among humans bestiality was not respectable. And besides, betrayal of the homeland, even without malice aforethought, even out of ordinary forgetfulness. . . .

"PKHENTZ! PKHENTZ!" I said over and over again, and repeated other words which I still remembered.

Suddenly an inexplicable warmth reached me through his Boston jacket. His shoulders were getting hotter and hotter, as hot as Veronica's hand, and thousands of other hot hands which I have preferred not to shake in greeting.

"Forgive me," I said, relaxing my hold. "I think there's some mistake. A regrettable misunderstanding. You see, I—how can I explain to you?—I'm subject to nervous attacks. . . ."

Just then I heard a terrible row and turned round. The child was dancing about behind me, at a respectful distance, and threatening me with his sabre.

"Let Leopold alone!" he shouted. "Nasty man! Let Leopold alone! My mommy loves him. He's my daddy, he's my Leopold, not yours!"

There could be no doubt about it. I had mistaken my man. He was a normal human, the most normal of humans, hunchback or not.

I feel worse every day. Winter has arrived—the coldest season in this part of the world. I never put my nose out of the house.

Still, it's a sin to grumble. I retired on pension after the November holiday.* I don't get much, but it's less worrying this way. How should I have managed otherwise during my last illness? I shouldn't have had the strength to dash to the office, and getting a doctor's note would have been awkward and dangerous. I wasn't going to submit to medical examination in my old age. It would have been the end of me.

*The annual celebration of the 1917 Revolution.

Sometimes I ask myself a tricky question: why shouldn't I, after all, legalize my position? Why have I spent thirty years pretending to be somebody else, like a criminal? *Andrei Kazimirovich Sushinski. Half-Polish, half-Russian. Aged 61. Disabled. Not a Party member. Bachelor. No relatives, no children. Never been abroad. Born at Irkutsk. Father: clerk. Mother: housewife. Both died of cholera in 1901.* And that's it!

But what about going to the police, apologizing, and telling the whole story simply, explaining it all just as it happened?

Well then, I'd say, it's like this. You can see for yourselves—I'm a creature from another world. Not from Africa or India, not even from Mars or one of your Venuses, but from somewhere still more remote and inaccessible. You don't even have names for such places, and if you spread out all the star maps and charts in existence before me, I honestly couldn't show you where that splendid point of light, my birthplace, has got to.

In the first place, I'm not an expert on astronomical matters. I went where I was taken. And in the second place, the picture's quite different, I can't recognise my native skies from your books and maps and things. Even now, I go out into the street at night, look up and there it is again—all wrong. I don't even know in which direction to yearn. It may be that not even my sun, let alone my earth, can be seen from here. It may be one of those on the other side of the galaxy. I can't work it out.

Please don't think that I came here with some ulterior motive. Migration of peoples, war of the worlds, and all that rot. Anyway, I'm not a military man, nor a scientist, nor an explorer. Book-keeping is my profession—my profession here, that is. What I did before is best not mentioned. You wouldn't understand if I did.

In fact we had no intention of flying into space. To put it crudely we were going to a holiday resort. Then, on the way, something occurred—let's say it was a meteorite to make it easier for you—well then, we lost buoyancy and down we fell, into the unknown, for seven and a half months we went on falling—our months, though, not yours—and by pure chance we landed up here.

When I came to and looked around—all my fellow-travellers were dead. I buried them in the prescribed way, and started trying to adapt myself.

Everything around was exotic and unfathomable. A moon was burning in the sky, huge and yellow—but only one moon. The air was wrong, the light was wrong, and all the gravities and pressures were strange. What can I say? The most elementary pine-tree affected my other-worldly senses as a porcupine affects you.

Where could I go? I had to eat and drink. Of course, I'm not a man and not an animal; I incline more to the vegetable kingdom than to anything else you have here; but I too have my basic needs. The first thing I need is water, for want of a better form of moisture, and preferably at a certain temperature, and now and then I want the missing salts added to my water. And besides I felt a growing chill in the surrounding atmosphere. I don't have to tell you what Siberian frosts are like.

There was nothing for it, I had to leave the forest. For some days past I'd been looking at people from behind the bushes, sizing them up. I realised at once that they were rational creatures; but I was afraid to begin with that they might eat me. I draped myself in a bunch of rags (this was my first theft, and it was pardonable in the circumstances) and came out of the bushes with a look of friendship written all over me.

The Yakuts are a trusting and hospitable people. It was from them that I acquired the simplest human habits. Then I made my way to more civilised regions. I learnt the language, obtained an education, and taught arithmetic in a secondary school in the town of Irkutsk. I resided in the Crimea for a time, but soon left because of the climate: it's oppressively hot in summer, and not warm enough in winter, so that you still need a room with radiators, and conveniences of that sort weren't too common there in the 'twenties and cost a lot of money, more than I could manage. So I made my home in Moscow, and I've been here ever since.

If I were to tell this sad tale, no matter to whom, no matter how skilfully edited for the general reader, nobody would believe me, not at any price. If I could only cry as my story requires. But though I've learnt to laugh after a fashion I don't know how to weep. They'd think I was a madman, a phantasist, and what's more they might put me on trial for having a false passport, forging signatures and stamps, and other illegal activities.

And if, against all reason, they did believe me it would be worse still.

Academics from all the academies everywhere would flock in—astronomers, agronomists, physicists, economists, geologists, philologists, psychologists, biologists, microbiologists, chemists, and biochemists, to study me down to the last spot on my body, omitting nothing. They would be for ever questioning, interrogating, examining, extracting.

Theses, films, and poems about me would circulate in millions of copies. Ladies would start wearing green lipstick and having their hats made to look like cactus, or failing that like rubber-plants. For years to come all hunchbacks would enjoy enormous success with women.

Motor-cars would be called after my homeland, and after me hundreds of new-born infants, as well as streets and dogs. I should become as famous as Leo Tolstoy, or Gulliver, or Hercules. Or Galileo Galilei.

But in spite of this universal interest in my humble person nobody would understand a thing. How could they understand me, when I myself am quite unable to express my inhuman nature in their language. I beat about the bush and try to make some headway with metaphors, but when it comes to the point I can find nothing to say. I can only see a short, solid GOGRY, hear a rapid VZGLYAGU, and an indescribably beautiful PKHENTZ beams down upon my trunk. Fewer and fewer such words remain in my memory. I can convey their structure only approximately in human speech. If I were surrounded by linguists asking "what do you call this" I could only shrug my shoulders and say: GOGRY TUZHEROSKIP.

No, I'd better put up with living lonely and incognito. If anything as special as me turns up it should exist unnoticed. And die unnoticed.

But then, when I die they may put me in a glass jar, pickle me in alcohol, and exhibit me in a Natural History Museum. And the people filing past will shiver with horror and laugh insultingly to cheer themselves up, and say with a grimace of disgust: "Heavens, how abnormal, what an ugly freak!"

I'm not a freak, I tell you! Just because I'm different do you have to be rude? It's no good measuring my beauty against your own hideousness. I'm handsomer than you, and more normal. Every time I look at myself I have the evidence of my own eyes for it.

Just before I fell ill the bath was cracked. I found out about it late one evening and realised that Kostritskaya had done it to vex me. I couldn't expect any help from poor Veronica. Veronica had been offended with me ever since the occasion when she offered me what was, humanly speaking, her most valuable possession, and I'd gone for a walk instead.

She has married the actor from the Stanislavsky, and sometimes the sound of their ethereal kisses wings to my ears through the thin wall. I was genuinely glad, for her sake, and on their wedding day I went so far as to send them an anonymous cake, with her initials and some arabesques executed in chocolate.

But I was incredibly hungry, and Kostritskaya had damaged the bath to destroy me, and, pending repairs, the hole where the water ran out had been stopped up with a wooden bung, and the water turned off. So when everybody had gone to bed and I could hear snores from the floor above and the floor below and all the rooms either side, I took Veronica's wash-tub off its nail in the lavatory, where it hangs with all the neighbours' tubs. It banged like thunder as I dragged it along the corridor, and some-body downstairs stopped snoring. But I finished the job, boiled a kettle in the kitchen, drew a bucketful of cold water, carried the lot into my room, bolted the door and stuck the key in the key-hole.

What pleasure it gave me to throw off my clothes, re-move my wig, tear off my genuine India-rubber ears, and unbuckle the straps which constrict my back and chest. My body opened out like a potted palm brought home from the shop in wrapping paper. All the limbs which had grown numb in the course of the day came to tingling life.

I installed myself in the tub, seized a sponge in one hand to squeeze water over all the dry places, and held the kettle in my second hand. With my third hand I grasped a mug of cold water, added some hot to it, and tried it with my fourth and last remaining hand to see that it wasn't too hot. What comfort!

My skin freely absorbed the precious fluid pouring down on me from the enamel mug, and when the first pangs of hunger were allayed I decided to inspect myself closely, and wash off the unhealthy slime which had seeped out of my pores and congealed in some places in dry mauve clots. True, the eyes in my hands and feet, on the crown of my head and the nape of my neck were get-ting appreciably dimmer, from being covered up in the day time by rough clothes and false hair. The friction of my right shoe had cost me the sight of one eye back in 1934. It wasn't easy to carry out a really thorough inspec-tion.

But I swivelled my head, not limiting myself to a half-circle—the miserable 180 degrees allotted to the human neck—I blinked simultaneously all the eyes which were still intact, driving away fatigue and darkness, and I suc-ceeded in viewing myself on all sides and from several dif-ferent angles at once. What a fascinating sight it is, and what a pity that it is only accessible to me in the all-too-short hours of night. I only have to raise my hand and I can see myself from the ceiling, soaring and hovering over myself as it were. And at the same time I keep in view my lower parts, my back, my front, all the spreading branches of my body. If I hadn't been living in exile for thirty-two years I should probably never dream of admiring my exterior. But here I am the only example of that lost harmony and beauty which I call my homeland. What is there for me to do on this earth except delight in my person?

Yes, my rear hand is twisted by its permanent duty of representing a human hump. Yes, my fore hand is so maimed by the straps that two fingers have withered, and my old body has lost its former suppleness. I'm still beautiful for all that! Proportionate! Elegant! Whatever envious carpers may say.

These were my thoughts as I watered myself from the enamel mug, on the night when Kostritskaya took it into her head to murder me by means of a cracked bath. But by morning I was ill. I must have caught cold in the tub. The worst time in my life had begun.

For a week and a half I lay on my hard couch and felt myself drying up. I hadn't the strength to go along to the kitchen for water. My body, a tightly swaddled anthropoid sack, grew numb and inert. My desiccated skin cracked. I couldn't raise myself to slacken my wire-sharp bonds.

A week and a half went by and nobody came in.

I could imagine my neighbours joyfully ringing up the health center when I was dead. The district medical officer would come to certify the fatal outcome, would bend over my couch, cut open my clothing, my bandages and my straps with his surgical scissors, recoil in horror and give orders for my corpse to be delivered to the biggest and best of dissecting theaters as soon as possible.

Here it came—the jar of spirit, caustic as Kostritskaya's perfume! Into the toxic jar, into a glassy dungeon, into history—for the edification of posterity to the end of time they would plunge me, the monster, the greatest monster on earth.

I started groaning, quietly at first, then louder and louder, in hateful and indispensable human language.

"Mama, mama, mama," I groaned, imitating the intonation of a tearful child and hoping to awaken the pity of anybody who heard me. And in those two hours, while I was calling for help, I vowed that if I lived I would keep my secret to the end, and not let this last vestige of my homeland, this beautiful body, fall into the hands of my enemies for them to rend and mock.

Veronica came in. She had obviously lost weight, and her eyes, purged of love and resentment, were serene and indifferent.

"Water!" I croaked.

"If you're ill," said Veronica, "you ought to get undressed and take your temperature. I'll call the doctor. They'll bleed you."

The doctor! Bleed me! Get undressed! Next she'd be touching my forehead, which was as cool as the air in the room, and feeling for my non-existent pulse with her red-hot fingers. But Veronica only straightened the pillow, and snatched her hand away in disgust when it came into contact with my wig. Evidently my body only revolted her, like all other humans.

"Water! Water for Christ's sake!"

"Do you want it out of the tap or boiled?"

In the end she went out and came back with a decanter. She polished a dusty tumbler with such a pensive and leisurely air that I should have thought she was taking her revenge on me if I hadn't known that she knew nothing.

"You know, Andrei Kazimirovich, I really did love you. I realise that I loved you—how shall I put it—out of pity. . . . Pity for a lonely, crippled human being, if you will forgive my frankness. But I loved you so much . . . didn't notice . . . physical blemishes. . . . To me you were the handsomest man on earth, Andrei Kazimirovich . . . the most . . . man. And when you laughed at me so cruelly . . . make an end of myself . . . loved . . . won't conceal from you . . . worthy man. . . . Fell in love . . . man . . . human . . . humanity . . . man to man. . . ."

"Veronica Grigorievna," I interrupted, unable to bear it any longer, "please hurry. Water. . . ."

"Human ... manhu ... hanumanu.... Human ... manhu ... umanu ... hanumanu ... human...."

"Water! Water!"

Veronica filled the tumbler and suddenly raised it right to my mouth. My false teeth rattled on the glass, but I couldn't bring myself to take the liquid internally. I need watering from above, like a flower or an apple-tree, not through my mouth.

"Drink, drink!" Veronica urged me. "I thought you wanted water...."

I pushed her off and struggled up into a sitting position, feeling like death. Water ran out of my mouth on to the couch. I managed to put out my hand and catch a few drops.

"Give me the flask and go away," I ordered with all the firmness I could muster. "Leave me in peace! I'll drink it myself."

Slow tears trickled from Veronica's eyes.

"Why do you hate me?" she asked. "What have I done to you? You were the one who didn't want my love, who rejected my pity.... You're just vicious and nasty, Andrei Kazimirovich, you're a very bad man."

"Veronica, if you have so much as a grain of pity left in you, go away, I beg you, I implore you, go away, leave me alone."

She went out dejectedly. Then I unbuttoned my shirt and stuck the flask inside it, neck downwards.

Nature is all scurry and bustle. Everything is in a fever of excitement. Leaves come out hurriedly. Sparrows sing in broken snatches. Children hurry off to their exams. Outside the voices of nannies are shrill and hysterical. The air has a tang in it. The Kostritskaya smell—in a low concentration—is all pervading. Even the cacti on my window-sill have a lemony aroma in the mornings. I mustn't forget to make Veronica a present of them before I leave.

I'm afraid my last illness has done for me. It hasn't just wrecked my body, it's crippled me spiritually as well.

Strange desires come upon me at times. I feel an urge to go to the pictures. Or else I think I should like a game of draughts with Veronica Grigorievna's husband. He's said to be a first-class chess player.

I have re-read my notes, and am not happy about them. The influence of an alien *milieu* is felt in every sentence. What good to anybody is this idle chatter in a local dialect? Another thing I mustn't forget before I leave—to burn them. I've no intention of showing them to people. And my own kind will never read them or hear anything about me. They'll never fly such an unearthly distance to this outlandish place.

It's getting harder and harder for me to recall the past. Only a few words of my native tongue have survived. I've even forgotten how to think as I used to, let alone read or write. I remember something beautiful, but what exactly it was I don't know.

Sometimes I fancy that I left children behind at home. Ever such bonny little cacti. Mustn't forget to give them to Veronica. They must be quite big now. Vasya's going to school. What am I saying, school! He must be a sturdy adult. He's gone in for engineering. And Masha is married.

Lord, oh Lord! I seem to be turning into a man!

No, it wasn't for this that I stood thirty-two years of suffering, and lay on a hard couch without water last winter. The only reason I got better was so that I could go and hide in some quiet spot and die without causing a sensation. That's the only way I can preserve what is left.

Everything is ready for my departure: my ticket and seat-reservation to Irkutsk, my can for water, a decent sum of money. I've got practically my whole pension for the winter on my savings book. I didn't spend anything on a fur coat, nor on trams or trolley-buses. I didn't go to the pictures once in all that time. And I gave up paying rent three months ago now. I've got 1,657 roubles altogether.

The day after tomorrow, when everybody's gone to bed, I shall leave the house unnoticed and take a taxi to the station. A hoot of the whistle—and that's the last you'll see of me. Forests, forests as green as my mother's body, will take me in and hide me.

I'll make it somehow or other. For part of the way I'll hire a boat. It's about 350 kilometres. And all by river. Water right beside me. Drench myself three times a day if I want to.

There was a hole. I'll search till I find it. The hole we made when we fell. Put wood all round it. Juniper blazes up like gunpowder. I'll sit down in the hole, untie myself and wait. Not a single human thought will I think, not a single word of alien speech will I utter.

When the first frosts begin and I see that the time is ripe—just one match will be enough. There will be nothing left of me.

But that's a long time off. There will be many warm and pleasant nights. And many stars in the summer sky. Which one of them? . . . Who knows? I will gaze at them all, together and individually, gaze with all my eyes. One of them is mine.

Oh native land! PKHENTS! GOGRY TUZHEROSKIP! I am coming back to you. GOGRY! GOGRY! GOGRY! TUZHEROS-KIP! TUZHEROSKIP! BONJOUR! GUTENABEND! TUZHEROS-KIP! BU-BU-BU! MIAOW, MIAOW! PKHENTS!

(*1966*)

Yuri Kazakov

(1927–1982)

Critics who demand of a writer that he declare himself ideologically will find Kazakov irritating. He was not conspicuously "dissident": His fiction reflects little dissatisfaction with the arrangements of the Soviet state, and he gave every sign of living contentedly within its boundaries. Praised by some as a leading continuator of the greatest traditions of classical Russian realism, he was seen by the guardians of loyalty as anything other than "loyal." His characters, when sad, seem unpatriotically so; and when they are happy, their happiness is mysterious in origin and derives from sources irksomely private and unexaminable. He was, in short, like Turgenev, to whom he is rather too often compared, the man in the middle, mistrusted and resented by every extreme.

Kazakov was not a prolific writer—certainly not by Russian standards—but such is his range of human sympathy that one recalls his work as an imposing oeuvre. Kazakov resembles Tolstoy (see p. 1) in his ability to make us enter into the very soul of a tremendous variety of characters—a blind hunting dog, very old men, children, drunken outcasts, lonely artists, young girls. His ability to compress vivid descriptions of landscape and weather and to convey the "tone" of a place in a minimum of words also contributes to our surprise that a story which lives in the memory as a major narrative actually occupies only a few pages.

"We live in the mind," wrote Wallace Stevens, and this adagium might serve as the motto for Kazakov's characters, who pursue their destinies against a background of recognizable present-day reality—the collective farm, the factory, fisheries on the White Sea—but always within a unique interior space, their inviolable individual psyches. The blind dog Arcturus is mauled by furious cattle and then beaten by their owner, and we suffer with him the terrible physical pain in an inner blackness that Kazakov renders almost tangible. All his principal characters are in some sense blind hunters.

This obsession with interiority does not, however, prevent the reader from sensing the interaction of characters. An engineer on his three-day fishing holiday at his special place on the river is too pent within himself to realize in time that an equally lonely girl seated beside him on the bus had yearned to spend the days with him. It is Kazakov's special skill to keep the reader always inside the engineer's mind yet aware, as the man is not, of the girl's feelings.

To persist in living private lives in a relentlessly public and prying world does not, of course, often result in conventional happiness for the people whom Kazakov imagines; but to call him flatly a pessimist is greatly to oversimplify the psychological complexity of his world, where the simultaneous experience of contradictory emotions is no less frequent than in the real world. Also, as in the case of Beckett, Kazakov's masterful prose is forever there to remind the reader that very sad matters can be conveyed in a medium brimming with vivifying and creative joy. Kazakov was a professional musician (a cellist) who played in both symphony orchestras and jazz ensembles before deciding to become a writer, and his ear for the phonic and rhythmic effects of language enabled him to convey messages that go beyond the ordinary import of the words.

ADAM AND EVE

The painter Ageyev was staying at a hotel in a northern town where he had come to paint the fishermen. The town was spaciously laid out; it had broad squares, streets, and avenues, and because of this it looked empty.

It was autumn. Low, ragged clouds came scudding from the west over the grey-brown woods misted with hoarfrost, it rained a dozen times a day, and the lake loomed over the town like a leaden wall. Ageyev stayed late in bed, smoked on an empty stomach, and stared at the window lined and streaming with rain. Below it the roofs of the houses gleamed sullenly, reflecting the sky; the room reeked of tobacco smoke and of something else peculiar to hotel rooms. His head ached, he had a ceaseless buzzing in his ears and an occasional twinge of pain in his heart.

Ageyev had been talented from his childhood up, and now, at twenty-five, his expression was scornful: there was a disdain, a weariness about the drooping brown eyelids and the lower lip, and his dark eyes were languid and arrogant. He wore a velvet jacket and a beret, and walked with a slouch, his hands in his pockets, hardly seeming to give an inattentive glance to people in the street or indeed to anything he came across in general, but retaining of everything a memory so indestructibly sharp that his breast actually ached with it.

There was nothing for him to do in the town itself and he spent the morning sitting at the table in his room holding his head, or lying down, waiting for 12 o'clock when the bar would open downstairs. When at last it came he walked down unsteadily, and each time looked with hatred at the picture in the hall. The picture showed the near-by lake with its inlets, and an unnaturally orange growth of stunted birches on the ledges of unnaturally purple rocks. It was autumn in the picture as well.

In the bar he ordered a brandy and squinting inwards with the effort of not spilling it slowly drank it down. Having drunk, he lit a cigarette, and looked round at whoever might be there as he waited impatiently for the first jolting warmth which he knew would at once make him feel well, and lovingly disposed to everything—life, people, the town, and even the rain.

After that he would go out and walk about the streets, wondering where to go with Vika, and what to do in general and how to go on living. A couple of hours later he was back in the hotel; by then he was sleepy and he went to bed and slept.

And when he woke up he went down again, to the restaurant. Now the day was nearly over, it was dusk outside the windows, and when evening came the jazz band in the restaurant struck up. Girls with made-up faces came in, sat in pairs at little tables, chewed wax-like chops, drank vermouth, danced with anyone who asked them, and wore an expression of happiness and of intoxication with high life. Ageyev gazed in misery around the large, familiar, smoke-filled hall. He hated the girls, and their boyfriends, and the wretched band with its piercing pipes and thumping drums, and the awful food, and the local vodka which the waitress invariably served short.

At midnight the restaurant closed. Ageyev staggered back to his third floor, wheezed as he fumbled at the keyhole, undressed, made mooing noises, ground his teeth, and pitched headlong into blackness until morning.

That day was like all the others, but on the next at 2 o'clock he went to meet Vika's train. He arrived early and, with only a brief glance at the platform and the passengers with their luggage, went straight into the refreshment room. Yet there had been a time when the mere sight of a railway platform excited him and filled him with wander-lust.

A tall waitress with red hair brought him his vodka.

"What a girl," Ageyev muttered, his eyes following her with greedy pleasure, and when she came up to him again he said: "Hello, baby. You're just what I've been looking for all my life."

The waitress smiled unmoved. She was used to hearing this sort of thing from almost everyone. People would drop in for half an hour and sit muttering—usually vul-garities—never to come back and see the station or the red-haired waitress again.

"I must paint you," said Ageyev, getting tipsy. "I'm an artist."

She shifted the glasses on his table and smiled: she liked hearing it all the same.

"You listen to me, I'm a genius, I'm known in the West! What about it?"

"It is not us the artists come to paint." She spoke with a slightly un-Russian accent.

"How do you know?" He looked at her breast.

"Oh! They always want fishermen. And workmen—signalmen. Or else there's a little island with a wooden church—they all go there, they come ... from Moscow, from Leningrad. And they're all like you—with berets—that what you call them?"

"They're all idiots. Well, we'll meet again, eh?" he added hurriedly as he heard the sound of the approaching train. "What's your name?"

"Zhanna, if you must know."

"You're not Russian, are you?"

"No, I'm a Finn. Yuonaleinen."

"Hell of a name," Ageyev mumbled, finishing his vodka and coughing.

He paid, gave Zhanna's shoulder a squeeze, and walked out on to the platform in high spirits. "What a waste of a woman!" he thought, screwing up his eyes at the light-blue express as its coaches flashed past him. The eyestrain made him feel giddy and he turned away. "Shouldn't have had that drink," he thought absentmindedly and, in a sudden fright at the thought of Vika's arrival, lit a cigarette.

The passengers were already moving from the train to the exit. He sighed, threw the cigarette away, and went to look for Vika. She saw him first and shouted at him. He turned and watched her as she came towards him in her fleecy black coat. The coat swung unfastened and her knees pushing at the hem of her skirt made it billow out.

She shyly gave him her net-gloved hand. Her hair, bleached by the sun, short and ruffled, fell over her forehead. From under it her slanted Tartar eyes looked up at him alarmed, while her mouth was crimson and taut, with dry cracked lips half open like a child's.

"Hello," she said a little breathlessly, and wanted to go on, perhaps to say something gay and clever, prepared in advance, but faltered into silence.

Ageyev unaccountably fixed his eyes on the transparent scarf round her neck, then with a scared schoolboy expression snatched her shiny suitcase from her, and together they walked down the wide street from the station.

"Your face is a bit puffy somehow . . ." she said. "How are you getting on?" She looked around her. "I like it here."

"Ugh!" He made the unpleasant guttural sound he always used to express contempt.

"Have you been drinking?" She pushed her hands into her pockets and bent her head. Her hair fell forward.

"Ugh!" he said again, with a side-glance at Vika.

Vika was very pretty and about her clothes, her ruffled hair, her way of speaking, there was something elusively Muscovite to which he had become unused in the north. In Moscow they had only met a couple of times, they didn't know each other properly, and her arrival, the leave he knew she had wangled with difficulty, and the fact—which he also sensed—that she was ready for anything, all struck him as somehow unexpected and strange.

"I'm lucky with women," he thought with pleased surprise, and deliberately stopped as if to put on his gloves, but really to look at Vika from the back. She slowed down, half-turning and looking at him questioningly, then glanced round absentmindedly at the shops and the passers-by.

She was pretty from the back as well, and the fact that she had not walked on but slowed down with that interrogative glance which seemed in itself to express her dependence on him—all this pleased him enormously, even though a moment ago he had felt embarrassed and confused by her arrival. He vaguely realized that he had only had that drink to get rid of his embarrassment.

"I've brought you your press cuttings," said Vika when he had caught up with her. "You know they're giving you hell? There was a terrific row going on at the exhibition the day I went."

"Ugh!" he said again, though with profound satisfaction, adding in immediate alarm: "They haven't taken down the 'Kolkhoz Girl'?"

"No, it's still up," Vika laughed. "Nobody can make head or tail of it, they're all shouting and arguing—the boys with the beards and the jeans, they don't know where they are, they're going round in circles."

"And you, do you like it?"

Vika smiled vaguely, and Ageyev, suddenly furious, frowned and snorted, pouting his lower lip, his dark eyes listless and sullen. "I'll get drunk," he decided.

And all that day he walked about the town with Vika like a stranger, yawned, mumbled indistinguishable answers to her questions, waited at the pier while she found out the times of the steamers, and in the evening got drunk, hard as she begged him not to, locked himself in his room, and, while knowing with deep, acute pain that she was alone in hers, upset and bewildered, only smoked and sniggered to himself. And thought about red-haired Zhanna.

The telephone rang a couple of times. He knew it was Vika, but let it ring. "Go chase yourself, you silly goose," he thought furiously.

* * *

The next day Vika woke Ageyev early and made him wash and dress while she packed his rucksack herself, dragged his paintbox, easel, and fishing tackle from under the bed, looked in the desk drawers, clinked empty bottles, and was generally aloof and businesslike, paying him no attention whatsoever.

"Just like a wife," thought Ageyev, watching her in amazement. He scowled and thought how quickly a woman could get used to a man and become as cold and masterful as if they had been living together for ages.

He had a headache and wanted to go down to the bar but, remembering it wouldn't yet be open, coughed, grunted, lit a cigarette on an empty stomach, and felt still worse. Meanwhile Vika had been down and paid the bill and called a taxi. "Oh hell, let her," he thought dully, going out and getting into it. He sat back and closed his eyes. The early morning rain meant that it would rain all day. It even began to snow, the heavy, wet flakes falling fast and turning black almost before the first touch of the wet roofs and pavements.

At the pier Ageyev felt worse than ever. Overcome with misery, half asleep and without an idea of why or where he was going, he listened drowsily to the wind hooting and whistling, water smacking the landing steps, motor-boats starting up on a high note, spluttering and dying down. Vika too had quite lost her spirits and was sad and cold as she sat beside him looking round helplessly, wilting in her short tight trousers and still bareheaded. The wind ruffled her hair and blew it over her forehead, and she looked as if she had just received a telegram and was going to a funeral.

"She would wear trousers," Ageyev thought spitefully, closing his eyes and trying to make himself comfortable against the wooden partition. "Where the devil am I off to? God, I feel awful!"

They could hardly wait for their boat and watched impatiently as it pulled alongside, hissing, steaming, pounding, creaking against the pier and scraping white shavings off its timber stanchions.

Even when they went aboard Ageyev felt no better. Somewhere down below, where everything blissfully seethed and rumbled, and yellow pistons went up and down in hot oil, it was warm, but the forward cabin was gloomy, cold, and had a musty smell. The wind howled, the waves splashed against the sides of the ship, and glasses tinkled nervously as it gently lurched. Brown, thinned-out woods, villages darkened by the rain, buoys and battered markers drifted slowly past the bleary portholes. Ageyev shivered feverishly and went out.

After wandering about on the ribbed metal flooring of the lower deck, he found shelter next to the engine room and close to the restaurant. The restaurant was not yet open, although an evil smell came from the salt cod cooking in the galley. Ageyev climbed on to the warm top of a metal bunker, leaned against a stack of birch logs glossy in their satin bark, and listened to the measured sighing of the engine, the splashing of the paddles and the discordant voices of the passengers. As usual those who were still excited by their send-off were gabbling noisily and cracking jokes, while from the stern came the sounds of a concertina, shouts, and the loud tapping of heels on the iron deck.

Near the hot water tap tea was being brewed in mugs and teapots, and people sat on bundles and suitcases, drinking it and breaking pieces off French rolls, glancing out, warm and cosy, at the dark dishevelled waves which the wind chased across the lake. Women were taking off their kerchiefs and doing their hair, children had already settled down to play and were running and bustling about.

The lights went on, yellow through frosted glass, and at once it became still more dark and cold outside. Ageyev idly shifted his gaze. The gangways were cluttered up with sacks of potatoes, hampers, barrels of gherkins and bales of other stuff. The passengers were all people from the neighbourhood, making their way to some place or other up the coast, and their talk was all of local things:

cattle, new regulations, mothers-in-law, fishing, the lumber camps, and the weather.

"It doesn't matter!" thought Ageyev. "It's only one day—then the island, a cottage, silence and solitude . . . It doesn't matter!"

The restaurant opened at last, and immediately Vika pushed her way towards him through the crowd. She gave him a sad look and a smile.

"Want a drink, you poor dear?" she said. "Well, go along and get it!"

Ageyev went and came back with a small bottle and some bread and gherkins. Vika, who had climbed on to the bunker, met him with a look of attentive concern. He sat down next to her, worked the cork out of the bottle, took a pull at it and munched a gherkin. Feeling better, he turned to her with a certain animation.

"Eat!" he mumbled, and Vika too began to eat.

"Tell me, what's the matter with you?" she asked after a while.

Ageyev had another drink and thought a while. Then he lit a cigarette and looked down at the suede shoe dangling from Vika's foot.

"Just fed up, old girl," he said quietly. "I expect I'm just no good as an artist and a fool as well. Here I am painting on and on with everybody telling me it's no good, it's all wrong . . .

"What do they say? 'Ideological immaturity!' 'On a slippery slope!' 'A spirit alien to our people!' . . . As if the whole nation were behind them nodding in agreement. You know?"

"You're silly!" Vika said gently. She suddenly laughed and put her head on his shoulder. Her hair had a strange, bitter smell. Ageyev rubbed his cheek against it and shut his eyes.

Suddenly she was close and dear to him. He remembered the first time he kissed her in Moscow, in the passage at the flat of an artist friend. He had arrived a little drunk and gay, Vika was quiet and looked bewildered;

they had had a long talk in the kitchen, or rather he had talked to her, telling her he was a genius and no one else was any good. Then they went to join the others and in the passage he kissed her and told her he was terribly in love with her.

She didn't believe him but she caught her breath and blushed, her eyes dark and her lips dry, and began to chatter and laugh with some other girls who were there without looking at him again. He too stuck to the men, arguing about some drawings or other, and he and Vika sat in different rooms.

Vika talked and giggled with her girl-friends and with someone who kept coming in and going out, feeling happy because he was in the next room sitting in an arm-chair and, like her, making conversation with someone. She told him so afterwards.

It was good now, in this out-of-the-way place in the north, suddenly to remember that recent yet for ever vanished evening. It meant that they had a past. They did not yet really love each other, nothing bound them together, they were still seeing other people who had been in their lives before, they had never spent a night together, they still didn't know one another. But they already had a past, and this was good.

"Seriously," said Ageyev, "out here I've kept on thinking about my life. You know it was horrid here without you, pouring rain and nowhere to go. I sat in my room or downstairs, drunk, and kept brooding ... I've just about had enough. When I was at art school I used to imagine I'd turn everything upside down, I'd knock them all sideways with my painting. I'd travel, I'd live in a cave—like a sort of Rockwell Kent, you know. Then I got my diploma and at once they started on me—'You bastard, you so-and-so!'—preaching at me. They haven't stopped hounding me ever since, the swine. And the longer it goes on the worse it gets. 'You abstractionist, you neo-realist, you formalist, you've got this and that deviation—just you wait, we'll get you!' ..."

He moved a little aside from her and had another drink.

His headache had stopped, and he felt like sitting and talking and thinking on and on, because Vika was sitting next to him and listening. He looked at her out of the corner of his eyes—her face was alive and grave, the eyes under their shadow of lashes long and black. He looked closer—they really were black, and her lips were rough, and Ageyev's heart began to thump. As for Vika, she had tucked up her feet on the bunker, unfastened her coat, propped her chin on her knees and was gazing into his face.

"You're not looking well," she said, touching his chin. "You haven't shaved, you're so rough."

"I'm kind of stale," he grinned and looked away at the lake. "I keep on thinking about myself and Van Gogh . . . Do I really have to kick the bucket too before they take me seriously? As if my colours, my drawings, my figures weren't as good as theirs. All those opportunists—I'm sick of the whole business!"

"You don't expect time-servers to admit you're any good," she said quickly, as though by the way.

"Why not?"

"I just know . . . For them to recognize you they'd have to recognize they've been wrong all their lives."

"Oh!" Ageyev lit a cigarette and smoked it in silence, looking at his feet and rubbing his face; the stubble on his shallow cheeks scraped against his fingers. "Three years!" he said. "And I'm still doing illustrations to earn my keep. Three years since I finished art school, and there are good-for-nothings who envy me: 'Ah, he's famous! Ah, he's known in the West . . .' Idiots. If they only knew. Every picture I do . . . And I still haven't a studio. You paint a spring landscape—it's the wrong spring! It isn't nature, it's biology! they say. What do you think of that? You can't get into a show, the selection committees make your life a misery, and if you do get in with something unimportant it's still worse. And the reviewers! They rave about being modern, but what they understand by it is beneath contempt. And the lies they tell, and if they do say a word of truth it's only for a demagogic end!"

"And has there never been a word of truth said about you?" She broke off a sliver of birch and nibbled it thoughtfully.

"Oh you!" Ageyev went pale. "You little college girl! You're still on the sidelines, you haven't run foul of them, you've got your books, your dialectical materialism, your field-work . . . If they say 'man,' it has to be with a capital M. Their enlightened gaze sees nothing but Man as a Whole—the country, whole millennia, the cosmos! One individual is no good to them. They don't think about him. You have to give them millions. They hide behind the millions, and we, those of us who are something, we're beatniks . . . Spiritual teddy boys, that's what we are! We haven't a heroic style!" He laughed unpleasantly. "We don't portray the masses! There they are, the masses," Ageyev nodded at the passengers. "And I love them, and it makes me sick to drool over them in ecstasy. I love them in the flesh—their eyes, their hands—see? Because it's they who hold up the earth. That's the whole point. If everyone is good, then society is good as well, that's what I'm telling you! I think about it day and night. I'm in a bad way, I've no commissions, no money. To hell with it, I don't mind. What matters is that I'm right all the same, and let nobody try to teach me. It's life that teaches me— and as for being optimistic and believing in the future and in those masses they go on about—I can give 100 yards' start to any one of those critics."

He snorted, his nostrils flared, and his eyes clouded.

"It's bad for you to drink . . ." Vika said softly, looking up at him with pity.

"Wait a second!" Ageyev said hoarsely. "I've got something the matter with me . . . asthma or something. Can't breathe properly."

His cigarette had gone out, he lit it and inhaled but had a fit of coughing and threw it down, putting one foot on the floor to stamp it out. He looked at Vika and made a face.

"Get out of the way, I'm going to bed!" He blinked angrily, got off the bunker and went below.

* * *

While they were talking the heating had been turned on, the cabin was warm and the porthole had steamed over. Sitting beside it, Ageyev rubbed the glass with his sleeve; his left eyelid was twitching. He knew that Vika was now his salvation. But there was something about her that infuriated him. She had come to him . . . fresh, pretty, in love—oh hell! Why, why did he always have to be arguing and proving something or other? And to her of all people! To Vika, who had come all that way, her heart turning over and her knees weak at the thought of their first night together, of him, of holding him close to her, and he the drunken devil . . . Oh God! And it would all have been all right, perfect—if only she had agreed with him at once, if she had said, "Yes, you're right!" He would have gone out of his mind with joy, he would have carried her off to the lake, to a cottage, he would have sat her by the window and rushed to his canvas. Her tiny face, her slanted eyes and sun-bleached hair, her chin propped on her fist . . . He might never paint anything better in his life! Oh God!

He began to take off his clothes, feeling lonely and sorry for himself to the point of tears. "What the hell," he thought, "it doesn't matter! It isn't the first time!" He shuddered at the things he had said to her. He must work, not talk.

When he was undressed he climbed on to the upper bunk and turned to the wall, but even then went on moving his head about restlessly on the shiny pillow-case, unable to settle down.

It was evening by the time the steamer neared the island. A brief sunset, dim and remote, burnt itself out, and dusk was falling as the boat nosed its way through countless reefs. They could now see the church with its many domes; as they drew closer to the island it shifted on the horizon, now right, now left, and at one moment was behind them.

Vika had a stubborn, hurt face. Ageyev whistled between his teeth, glancing indifferently from side to side at the flat islands and the villages, and inspecting with some interest the splendid boats which looked like Viking sailing ships.

When they came right up to the island, they saw a windmill and a beautiful ancient farmhouse with its outbuildings and barns—all empty and without a sign of life, like pieces in a museum. Ageyev grinned.

"Just the right thing for me," he muttered, looking at Vika with rage. "Right in the forefront of the seven-year plan as you might say—no?"

Vika said nothing. Her expression was now withdrawn as if she had planned it all in advance and come on her own and found everything as expected.

No one except the two of them landed on the island. And there was no one on the open wooden landing-stage except an old woman with a lantern shining, although it was still daylight.

"Well, here we are, you and I, like Adam and Eve." Ageyev grinned again, stepping down on the damp planks of the jetty.

Vika again made no reply.

A woman in a wadded coat and boots appeared on the bank, smiling in welcome while she was still far off.

"Only the two of you?" she shouted gaily as she hurried towards them, shifting her eyes from one to the other. When she came up to them she took Vika's suitcase from her and talked to them as if they were long-expected guests.

"Well, thank goodness," she rattled on in her friendly voice, climbing up the bank. "I was beginning to think no one else would come this year, the season was over, time to dig in for the winter, and now you've come. I'll take you to our hotel."

"Hotel?" Ageyev asked in his disagreeable voice.

The woman laughed.

"They all say that, they're all surprised, though it's more than a year since I came. Had my old man with me but he died. Now I'm alone. Certainly there's a hotel! For tourists and artists and people like that. There's a lot of them come in the summer and stay on and paint."

Thinking of his misery at the hotel, Ageyev sighed and screwed up his face. He had been looking forward to a cottage, a small farmhouse with a smell of cows and a porch and an attic.

But the hotel turned out to be attractive. There was a big stove in the kitchen, and three bedrooms—all empty, and another very odd room with slender pillars down the middle, carved and painted in old-Russian style, supporting the ceiling, and big modern windows reaching to the floor on three sides, as in a glassed-in hall.

In every bedroom there were bare beds showing their webbing and bare bedside tables of rough wood.

Ageyev and Vika chose a room with a stove and a window to the south. Framed water-colours hung on the walls. Ageyev glanced at them and twitched his lip. They were painstaking student sketches of either the church or the windmill.

The landlady kept going in and out carrying sheets, pillows, and pillow-cases, and with them came a good smell of clean linen.

"Well, now you can settle down," she said, pleased. "That's nice. I get bored all by myself. It's nice in summer with all those jolly painters, but now there's hardly another soul on the island."

"How do we manage about food?" asked Vika.

"Oh, you won't starve," she shouted cheerfully from somewhere down the passage. "There's a village at the other end of the island, you can get milk and things, or there's a shop on Pog Island, you can go by boat. Are you from Leningrad?"

"No, Moscow," said Vika.

"Well, that's nice, we always get Leningraders. I've plenty of logs and kindling—they were restoring the church last summer, a lot of stuff was left over. And I've got the keys of the church. When you want to go just tell me and I'll open it up."

The landlady went away and Vika, happy and tired, flopped on her bed.

"It's too good to be true!" she said. "It really is! It's brilliant of you, my darling Adam. Do you like baked potatoes?"

Ageyev smirked, twitched his lip and went out. He walked quietly past the graveyard round the church. It had grown dark and, as he walked towards it from the east, the church towered above him with its magnificent silhouette, luminous in spaces between its onion domes and in the open arches of its belfry. Two birds were calling to each other from different places in measured, monotonous voices, and there was a strong smell of grass and of autumn cold.

"It's the end of the world," thought Ageyev as he passed the church and came to the lake. He went down to the landing-stage and sat on a bollard, looking at the west. A couple of hundred yards away there was another island, flat and bare except for willow bushes. Beyond it lay still another, and there seemed to be a village: a lone light shone far off through the trees. Soon a motor-boat started up on a high thin note somewhere over there, and went on and on, then suddenly spluttered out.

Ageyev felt lonely, but he sat on smoking, getting used to the silence and the clean smell of the autumn freshness and the water, thinking about himself, about his pictures, thinking that he was a messiah, a great artist, and that here he was, all alone at the end of the world, while various critics who lived in Gorky Street in Moscow were at this moment sitting with girls in restaurants, drinking brandy, eating roast chicken, wiping their greasy lips with their napkins and uttering various fine and lofty words, and that everything they said was a lie, because they weren't thinking about lofty things but only about getting the girls into bed. And in the mornings they would take coffee for their hangover and drops for their heart condition, and write articles about him, and again tell lies, because not one of them believed in what he wrote but only thought of how much he would get for it, and not one of them had ever sat in solitude on a damp pier, looking at a dark, un-inhabited island and preparing for creative achievement.

These thoughts were both sad and comforting: there was a bitter sweetness in them. He enjoyed thinking such thoughts and he often did.

At one moment he found himself mentally humming the tune, remembered out of the blue, of the old Count-ess's solo in *The Queen of Spades*. And this ghostly music—which he heard somewhere deep inside him with all its orchestral accompaniment including the sinister note of the clarinets and the bassoons and the painful sus-pense of the pauses—began to terrify him because it was death.

Then, as suddenly and sharply, to the point of pain, like the longing for air, he felt a longing for the smell of tea— not brewed tea, not tea in a glass, but dry tea leaves. At once there came to him straight out of his childhood, the memory of a milky glass teapot with a touching landscape painted on it, and his dream of living in the little house with the red roof, and the dry rustling sound as his mother took the lid off the teapot and poured the tea leaves in, and the smell as the cloudy-opal teapot filled with darkness.

This immediately made him remember his mother, her love for him, her life lived in him and for him. And him-self, so quick and lively, with moments of such unac-countable joy and vitality that he could hardly believe that this could ever have been himself.

With belated pain he thought of how often he had been rude, inconsiderate, and unfeeling towards his mother, how rarely, while he had the chance, he had been willing to listen to her childhood stories of a remote, long-van-ished past. Of how little, in his childish selfishness, he had appreciated the constancy of her love, a love such as he had never since experienced from anyone in all his life.

And remembering all this, he at once began to doubt himself and to think that perhaps his critics were right and he was wrong and was doing nothing as it should be done. He thought that all his life some basic idea—an idea in the highest sense—must have been lacking in him. That he had all too often, talented as he was, looked down with lazy indifference on everything except his talent and his life—and this at such a time!

With helpless rage he remembered all the arguments he had had, ever since his student days, with painters, with art experts, with whoever would not accept his view of painting, colour, design. He thought now that the reason he could not convince them, rout them, prove to them his messianic role, was that he lacked the inspiration of an idea. How indeed could you have a prophet without an idea?

So he sat for a long time. Vika came out of the house, walked a little way along the wooden boards towards the shore, stood looking around her and called him in a low voice. He heard her but neither moved nor spoke. And yet he loved her, his heart quickened at the thought of her. And the two of them were like Adam and Eve, alone with the stars and the water on this dark uninhabited island—and it was not for nothing that she had come to him, and how miserable she must have been in that hotel room when he had drunk himself into a stupor and gone away, deserting her!

A bitter alienation, an estrangement from the world came over him and he wanted nothing and no one. He remembered that wild animals when they are sick go off and hide in some far-away place in the forest, there to cure themselves by means of some mysterious herb or else to die. He regretted that it was the fall and the weather was so chilly, that he was in boots and a sweater—how nice, if it were summer, to find a corner of this or some other island, with rocks, sand, and clear water, and to lie all day in the sun and to think of nothing. And to walk barefoot. And fish. And watch sunsets. He realized that he was boundlessly weary—of himself, his thoughts, his corroding doubts, of getting drunk—and that altogether he was ill.

"Nice to go to the south, somewhere by the sea . . ." he

thought nostalgically as he got up. Leaving the pier and turning his back on the lake, he again came face to face with the enormous ancient church and the small hotel sheltering beside it. The windows of the hotel shone brightly while the church was dark, locked up, and strange to him. Yet there was something masterful and commanding about the church, something which aroused thoughts of history and of the greatness of the people— and also of quietness and solitude.

"*Seg Pogost,*"* he recalled the name of the island and the church. "*Seg Pogost.*"

He walked up to the house and stood on the steps, peering into the darkness, trying to guess at what for so many centuries without him had lived its own life—the genuine life of the earth, the water, and the people. But he could make out nothing except the dim radiance of the surrounding waters and the few cosmically gleaming tatters of sky in the rifts between the clouds, and so he went inside.

The room was brightly lit by a paraffin lamp. The stove roared and crackled and there was a smell of baked potatoes. Vika was flushed and busy, the whole place had acquired a friendly, lived-in air, and everything in it—the blouses and dresses hanging up or flung on the bed, the black gloves on the bedside table, the powder compact with a zip—told of the presence of a young woman and gave off a smell of scent.

"Where were you?" Vika asked with a quiver of her eyebrows. "I looked for you."

Ageyev said nothing and went into the kitchen to wash. There he spent some time inspecting his stubble in the mirror but decided not to shave and only washed, cheerfully clattering the things on the washstand and drying himself on the warm rough towel; then he came back, lay down, put his boots on the headboard, stretched, and lit a cigarette.

"Come and eat," said Vika.

* *Seg:* a Finnish corruption of St. Serge; *Pogost:* churchyard.

They ate in silence. Clearly Vika was delighted with her surroundings and her only trouble was Ageyev. The kettle purred and whistled on the stove.

"How long is your leave?" Ageyev asked abruptly.

"Ten days," Vika sighed. "Why?"

"Nothing . . ."

"Three days gone," thought Ageyev.

Again there was a long silence. When they had their tea it was time for bed. Vika blushed hotly and looked in desperation at Ageyev. He looked away and frowned, then got up, lit a cigarette, and walked over to the window. He too was blushing and glad that Vika could not see it. There were rustling sounds behind him; finally Vika couldn't stand it and begged him:

"Do put out the light!"

Without looking at her, Ageyev blew out the flame of the oil lamp, quickly undressed, got into his bed and turned to the wall. "Just try and come to me," he thought. But Vika didn't come. She lay so still that he couldn't even hear her breathing.

Some twenty minutes went by; neither of them was asleep and they both knew it. It was dark in the room and the sky outside the window was black. The wind rose and buffeted the walls. Suddenly the window curtain was lit up for a brief moment. Ageyev thought at first that someone had walked past and shone a torch on the wall and the window, but a few seconds later there came a low rumble of thunder.

"There's a storm," Vika said softly, sitting up in bed and looking at the dark window. "An autumn storm."

After another flash and rumble, the wind died down and it began at once to pelt with rain, water gurgled in the rain-pipe.

"It's raining," said Vika. "I like it when it rains. I like thinking when it rains."

"You couldn't keep quiet, could you?" Ageyev lit a cigarette and blinked: his eyes were smarting.

"You know what? I'm leaving," said Vika, and Ageyev felt her hating him. "I'm going by the first boat. You're nothing but an egoist. I've been thinking and thinking these past two days—what are you? What's the matter with you? Well, I know now—you're just selfish. You talk about the people, about art, but all you can think about is yourself and absolutely no one else ... You don't need anyone. It's revolting! Why on earth did you ask me to come, why? I know why—to pat you on the back and say, 'yes, darling,' isn't that it? Well, my lad, you can look for another victim. I'm ashamed to think how I pestered the Dean of the Faculty and told lies about my father being ill ..."

She burst into loud sobs.

"Shut up, you fool!" Ageyev said miserably, realizing it was all over. "And get out of here, go away, the sooner the better!"

He got up and sat in front of the window, leaning his elbows on the bedside table. It was still raining and there was something large, dark and quivering on the ground-outside—he looked at it for a long time before he realized it was a puddle. He wanted to cry, to blink his eyes and rub them with his sleeve as he did when he was a child, but it was many years since he'd been able to cry.

Vika had buried her head in her pillow and lay sobbing and catching her breath, while Ageyev sat still, breaking matchsticks and crumbling cigarette ends in the ash-tray. At first he had felt sick and cold with misery and disgust. Now this had passed, he had somehow risen above it, aloof, detached from pettiness, and feeling sorry for everyone, quiet and saddened by the insurmountable resistance of the human mass. And yet everything deep inside him was boiling, seething, hurt, and he could not be silent, he could no longer smile his condescending smile or get out of things with his loathsome "Ugh!" He had to say something.

But he said nothing, he only thought, though he wasn't really thinking about anything, only keeping quiet and glancing through the window at the dark, quivering puddle outside. There was a singing, a jangling in his head as if he was ill and had a temperature, and he saw before him an endless procession of people walking silently through the halls of a gallery, their expressions enigmatic, elusive, and sorrowful. "Why sorrowful?" he was held up by the thought; "I've got it wrong somehow." But he was at once distracted and began to think of higher things, of the highest, the loftiest of all, as it seemed to him.

He was thinking that whatever happened he would do what he must. And that no one would stop him. And that in the end this would be to his credit.

He stood up, and without dressing, with swollen veins in his temples, went out on to the porch. There he stood and spat—for some reason his mouth was full of sweetish saliva, it kept filling with it and he kept spitting it out, and there was a lump in his throat, choking him.

"It's all over!" he muttered softly. "To hell with it. It's all over."

All next day Ageyev slumped on his bed with his face to the wall. He would go to sleep and wake up and hear Vika walk about the room and round the house. She called him to lunch and to dinner but he lay with his teeth angrily clenched and not opening his eyes, in a kind of stupor, until he fell asleep again.

By the evening his muscles were aching and he was forced to get up. Vika was out; Ageyev went to find the landlady.

"Would you give me the key of the boat," he begged her. "I have to go to the shop for some cigarettes."

The landlady gave him the key of the padlock, told him where to find the oars, and showed him the direction in which to row.

There was a headwind, the oars were heavy and awkward, the boat was heavy too, though so fine to look at, and Ageyev had blisters on his hands by the time he reached the other island.

He bought cigarettes, a bottle of vodka, and some snacks, and walked back to the mooring-stage.

On the way he was overtaken by a stocky, bow-legged fisherman in a winter hat and with a red face.

"Hello, there," said the fisherman, drawing level with him and looking him over. "You an artist? From Seg Pogost?"

He had parcels wrapped in newspaper which he held carefully in both hands and two bottles of vodka stuffed in the pockets of his jacket.

"We've got a party on today! After our steam bath," he gave the news joyfully as to an old friend. "Shall we have one for the road?"

The fisherman clumped across into his boat which had an outboard-motor with a bright-green casing, produced four bottles (two out of his trouser pockets), and carefully put three of them down on the tarpaulin in the prow; the fourth he opened at once and after fumbling for an empty jam jar and rinsing it in the lake poured Ageyev a drink. Ageyev drank it down and chewed a biscuit. The fisherman poured one out for himself and climbed ashore.

"Glad to know you," he said cheerfully. "Been here long?"

"Only since yesterday," said Ageyev, inspecting him deliberately.

"Painting the church?" he winked.

"Whatever I find."

"You should come over and visit our work-gang," the fisherman offered, the vodka rushing to his head. "Got a woman with you? We've got women," he spread his hands, "like that! See? You'll want to paint the lot, see?"

He went back to the boat for the bottle they had started and poured Ageyev another drink.

"Let's finish it up, shall we?"

"Actually, I've got my own," said Ageyev, also getting out a bottle.

"We'll drink yours when you come to us," said the fisherman. "It's not far; you just say when you want to come and we'll fetch you by motor-boat. We like artists, they're all right. We had a professor from Leningrad staying a while back. He said, never in my life, he said, have I seen people like you!" The fisherman roared with laughter. "We'll give you fish soup. You'll have a good time, when the girls start making a row it goes on all night. It's a fine life."

"Where do you fish?" asked Ageyev smiling.

"Off Kizhm Island, but don't worry, we'll fetch you. Or if you think of coming over by yourself just ask for Stepan's gang—that's me, Stepan, get it? Soon as you're out of the reefs, turn left, past the lighthouse, and you'll see the island. You can't miss it. There they'll tell you."

"I'll certainly come!" Ageyev said happily.

"That's right! You come along! You respect me, right? You treat me like a human being, right? Well, that's all there is to it! That's the lot ... That's settled then. Right? Well, that's all. Good-bye for now, I've got to run, the boys are waiting ..."

He climbed over into his boat, unmoored it, pushed off, and started the engine. It set up a thin buzzing. He threw himself into the bows but they reared up all the same; using the tiller the fisherman steered the boat into deep water and skimmed away, leaving a white frothing arc on the water behind him.

Smiling to himself, Ageyev got into his boat and started back. He now sat facing the sunset and he couldn't help stopping and resting on his oars from time to time, to watch the colours of the sky and the lake. Half-way to Seg Pogost there was a small island, and when he rounded it the wind died down and the water lay still and heavy like molten gold.

In the perfect silence and the calm Ageyev shipped his oars and turned round to look at the church. A rain-cloud, almost like a black wall, rose in the east, while from the west the sun was shedding its last rays, and everything they lit—the island, the church, the windmill, the old farm—seemed, against the cloud, to glow with a particularly ominous red. Far away on the side of the horizon from which the cloud was moving, hung tattered drapes of rain and a huge rainbow shone funereally.

Ageyev settled himself more comfortably in the boat, had another drink, and nibbling a biscuit sat looking at the church. The sun was setting, the cloud was drawing nearer, it already overshadowed almost everything in sight, the rain had by now reached Seg Pogost. The boat was drifting slightly with the current.

But around Ageyev all was as yet calm and still, while in the west the sky burned with a wide band of misty red flung around the setting sun.

Ageyev sat examining the church and felt like painting it. He was thinking that it was not, of course, only three centuries old, but immeasurably older; it was as old as the earth and the stones. The other thing he couldn't get out of his mind was the image of the jolly fisherman, and he felt like painting him as well.

When he turned to the west the sun had set. The rain had come at last. He pulled his hood over his head and picked up the oars. The heavy rain was for some reason warm and gay, and fish jumped all around him as he rowed.

Coming up to the landing-stage at full tilt, Ageyev saw Vika. She stood motionless in the rain, a plastic raincoat thrown over her shoulders, and watched him as he moored and padlocked the boat, took out the oars and the rucksack with his purchases and stuffed the half-empty bottle into his pocket.

"You can look!" Ageyev thought cheerfully as he walked in silence to the house.

Vika stayed at the pier. Without turning to look at him she continued to watch the lake in the afterglow and the rain.

Coming into the warm room Ageyev saw that her things were no longer around and her suitcase stood by the door. "Ah!" he said, and lay down. The rain drummed on the roof. Calm and comfortable after his vodka, he shut his eyes and dozed off. He soon woke up; it was not yet dark but the rain had stopped and the sky had cleared and had a cold, high radiance.

Ageyev yawned and went to find the landlady. Taking

from her the keys of the church, he went inside the fence which surrounded the churchyard, crossed it, stepping between old tombs, unlocked the door of the bell tower, and started up the dark, narrow, creaking stairs.

There was a smell of jackdaw droppings and of dry wood, and it was dark, but the higher he climbed the more light there was and the cleaner the air. At last he reached the platform of the belfry, his heart wobbly and his legs weak from the sensation of height.

At first, as he climbed on to the platform through the trap-door, he saw only the sky through the arches—high up, with a few fleecy clouds in it and the first large stars, and with light in its depth from the blue rays of the long extinguished sun.

Then as he looked down he saw another sky, as enormous and as light as the one above. Stretching to the horizon on all sides, the whole immeasurable mass of the surrounding water was luminous with reflected light, and the small islands on it were like clouds.

From the moment Ageyev sat down on the balustrade, his arm hooked round a pillar, he never moved again until it was quite dark and Cassiopeia stood out in all its pearly brilliance, and later, after he came down, he walked round and round the church along the path, peering at it this way and that and sighing.

When he came home, the stove was crackling once again. Vika was cooking supper, but she was quiet and already far away.

"Is the boat coming soon? Did you find out?" asked Ageyev.

"At 11 o'clock, I think," Vika said, after a silence.

Ageyev's heart lurched, he wanted to say something, to ask her some question, but he said nothing and only dragged his paintbox from under the bed, set out paint tubes and small bottles of turpentine on the window-sill and the bed, sorted his brushes, and began to knock at a set of stretchers. Vika kept glancing at him in amazement.

They sat down to supper in silence like the first time,

and looked each other in the eyes. Ageyev saw Vika's dry lips, her face suddenly so dear to him. His heart gave another lurch and he realized that the time to say good-bye had come.

He got a bottle of vodka from under the bed and poured out for Vika and himself.

"Well ..." he said huskily, and cleared his throat. "Here's to our parting!"

Vika put down her glass without drinking, leaned back in her chair and thus, with her head thrown back, looked at him from under lowered eyelids. Her face was quivering, a vein was throbbing in her neck, her lips moved, it was more than Ageyev could bear to see. He felt hot. Getting up, he opened the window and leaned out for a breath of the strong night air.

"It's stopped raining," he said, coming back to the table and taking another drink. "It isn't raining any more."

"You don't need any money?" asked Vika. "I've got too much. I brought a lot, you know thinking ..." She bit her lip and smiled pitifully.

"No, I don't," said Ageyev. "I'll stop drinking now."

"I still think you're wrong," Vika said sadly. "You're just ill. If you gave up drinking everything would go right."

"Oh, would it," he grinned. "I'd have a one-man show at once, would I? Cheers!" He drank again. "And the opportunists would realize they're no artists, right?"

"Where were you this evening?" Vika asked, after a silence.

"Over there," he gestured vaguely. "Upstairs. Calling on God."

"You won't be coming to Moscow soon?" she asked again, looking at the paints, brushes, and easels scattered round the room.

"Not yet, no," he said, seeing in his imagination the fisherwomen he would get to know, their legs, their breasts. Their eyes. Seeing them at their work, with clenched teeth and red arms as they hauled the nets. "In about a month, I should think. Or later still. I'll have a go at painting the fisherfolk. And the water." He paused. "And the sky. That's how it is, old girl."

Vika went outside to listen for the boat.

"It's too early," she said, coming back. After looking at herself thoughtfully in the mirror she got her scarf out of her suitcase, put it on her head and tied the ends under her chin. Then she sat down and clenched her hands between her knees. She sat in silence, her head bowed low, as if she were sitting at a station, as if Ageyev were unknown to her; her thoughts were far away. Her hair had golden lights under the chiffon scarf. Ageyev lay on the bed, squinting, examining her with curiosity and smoking nervously.

"I can't stand it," said Vika with a sigh. "I'll go to the pier."

She got up, sighing again, stared for a few seconds fixedly, unblinking, at the lamp, and put on her coat. Ageyev swung his legs to the floor and sat up.

"Well, all right," he said. "*Good-bye,* * old girl! Like me to see you off? . . ."

Vika went to get her identity card from the landlady. Ageyev took a quick drink, snorted, pulled a face and began to dress, looking attentively at his shaking hands and hearing Vika's and the landlady's voices behind the partition. He picked up the suitcase and went out on to the porch. The steps, the handrail, the plankway to the pier, were still damp from the recent rain. He waited for Vika to come out and walked down. She followed him, her heels tapping on the planks.

When they came to the pier Ageyev put the suitcase on the ground and Vika immediately sat down on it, shrank into herself, and froze into stillness. Ageyev shivered with cold and turned up his collar. Suddenly, out of the dead, unnatural silence of the night there came the high, robust

* *Good-bye* in English in the text.

sound of a plane. As it approached, it grew louder, stronger, but at the same time lower in tone, more velvety, muffled, as if someone were ceaselessly drawing a bow over the strings of a cello, gradually lowering the peg, until at last it receded, dying down to a low belly rumble.

Once again there was dead silence. After stamping about next to Vika, Ageyev moved away and climbed the bank. He paused at the top, then walked a few steps towards the southern tip of the island and looked round.

The stars were burning steadily overhead, while all over the reefs on the water below were small red and white lights gleaming and blinking on buoys and markers. Suddenly it was as if a breath rushed through the sky; the stars blinked and shuddered. The sky grew black, shuddered again and rose, filling with blue trembling light. Ageyev turned to look at the north and immediately saw its origin. From behind the church—from behind its silent blackness—there came, spreading its beams and swaying, billowing, folding in and swelling out, the faint, pale-blue-golden radiance of the Northern Lights. Whenever they flared out everything—the lake, the shore, the stones, and the wet grass—shone, and the church stood out in firm silhouette; when it faded everything became diminished, and obscure, and vanished.

The earth was turning. Ageyev suddenly felt it with his legs and his heart as it turned and flew, together with its lakes, cities, people and their hopes—turned and flew, ringed with light, into frightening infinity. And here he stood upon this earth, this island, in the silent light of the night, and Vika was leaving him. Adam was being left by Eve—and not at some uncertain future time but now, at once. And it was like death, which you can laugh at from a distance but cannot ever bear to think about when it is close beside you.

He couldn't bear it and walked quickly back to the landing-stage, feeling his boots getting soaked through in the wet grass, seeing nothing in the darkness but knowing that now they were black and shiny.

* * *

When he came back to the pier the lantern was already shining on a post, the old woman stood yawning on the steps below, while from beyond a low hill in the north came a new beam, trembling like the Aurora but warmer in tone. The beam shifted, there came the quick noises of paddles, and suddenly, high and resonant, the ship's siren, echoing on and on from island to island.

"Did you see the Northern Lights? It was that, wasn't it?" Vika asked in a quick and low voice. She was excited and no longer sitting on her suitcase but standing by the railings.

"Yes, I saw," Ageyev cleared his throat.

The ship wheeled into sight around a bend and could now be heard more clearly. The small star of its searchlight shone brightly in the bow. Now the light reached the landing-stage and the lamp glistened on the planks. The engines stopped and the ship drifted on of its own momentum towards the pier. The old woman shielded her eyes with her hand from the brilliant light, peering at something on board. Turning his back on the searchlight Ageyev saw its beam tremble smokily on the beautiful old farm as if spotlighting an antique.

As the steamer pulled alongside the searchlight turned and flooded the pier with a dazzling milky brightness. Vika and Ageyev watched silently as the ship was moored. A sailor on deck flung the end of the cable to the old woman. The old woman unhurriedly slipped the loop over a bollard. The sailor bent down and wound the cable in. The cable tautened and creaked and the pier shuddered. The steamer softly bumped against it. The sailor let down the gangway and stood under the lamp, checking the ticket of some passenger who was getting off. At last he let him through and turned to Vika and Ageyev.

"Coming aboard?" he asked uncertainly.

"Well, off with you," said Ageyev, giving Vika's shoulder a careless pat. "All the best!"

Her lips trembled.

"Good-bye," she said, and climbed on deck, her shoes tapping on the gangway.

* * *

The boat was almost empty, the lower deck dimly lit and the cabin portholes dark. Either there was no one in the cabins or the passengers were asleep. Steam hissed between the ship's side and the pier and floated up in transparent puffs.

Vika went below without looking back and vanished in the ship's bowels. The siren shrieked hurriedly—one long and three short blasts, the old woman slipped the noose off the bollard, the gangway was pulled up, the ventilators clanged shut on deck—and the boat, a warm, familiar, breathing creature, the only thing alive in the cold night, was pulling out, gurgling with its paddles and whirling sharply right.

The old woman yawned again, muttered that the Northern Lights were early this year and this meant a hard winter, picked up her lantern and walked up the bank, throwing a patch of light in front of her, smearing yellow light over her boots and carrying on her left side a big unsteady shadow which, as she swung the lantern, leapt from the bank over the pier into the lake.

Ageyev stood still smoking a cigarette, and walked back to the warm hotel. The Northern Lights were still flashing but were now faint and all of the same colour—white.

(*1962*)

Georgi Vladimov

(1931-   )

Vladimov, whose real name is Volosevich, was born in Kharkov. His father died in the war, and his mother was arrested and sent to the camps in 1952. After studying law at Leningrad University he worked as a critic, writer, and, at *Novy Mir*, the leading Soviet literary journal, as editor. Readers knew him for his novel *The Great Ore* (1961) and the story "Three Minutes of Silence" (1969). His masterpiece *Faithful Ruslan* (1974) was unpublishable in the Soviet Union at the time it was written.

A man of extraordinary moral courage, he soon came to be known as a sort of dissident's dissident. In 1977 he took the unheard-of step of resigning from the Writers' Union, the equivalent of professional suicide, and at the same time organized the Moscow unit of Amnesty International, then a completely illegal organization, thus ensuring for himself a lifetime of harassment by the KGB. In the spring of 1983 Vladimov fell victim to the fate that most Russian writers dread as a form of creative death: He and his family reluctantly left the Soviet Union. In Germany, he was for a time editor of the influential Russian-language journal *Grani*, which had been the first to publish his forbidden novel. In August, 1990, Vladimov was one of several prominent exiles to whom Gorbachev restored Soviet citizenship.

When *Faithful Ruslan* appeared in the West, the date at

the end was given, at Vladimov's request, as "1963–1965." Though meant to conceal the author's part in its foreign publication, it is not entirely wrong, for *Ruslan* derives from "The Dogs," a story written and secretly circulated in the early 1960s. As bad luck would have it, "The Dogs" just missed the period of relative freedom after Khrushchev's denunciation of Stalin. Or it might have been good luck, for after Vladimov spent a decade mulling over the straightforward anecdote of former prison dogs attacking peaceful citizens marching in a May Day parade, he transformed and ennobled it, creating a novel that, for the breadth and depth of its implications as well as its masterful execution, is one of the most significant works of modern Russian literature.

Ruslan, the hero, is a dog of the breed especially developed in Russia to guard the millions of prisoners of the Gulag. Called "Caucasian Sheepdog," it resembles the German shepherd except for its longer coat, needed to survive the Siberian winter. It is a large, immensely strong, and, properly trained, a terrifying, ferocious, and quite lethal animal. Ex-prisoners still find it all but impossible to maintain their composure in the presence of even the most amiable member of this breed. We are to assume that Ruslan, through whose perceptions we learn of almost every event in the novel, has been a faithful instrument of Stalin's bloody tyranny and has no doubt terrified if he has not actually maimed or killed many an innocent inmate of the camps. He is nevertheless a true hero, a compendium of all the canine virtues—absolute loyalty, devotion to duty, total selflessness, and resplendent courage—to whose character no blame could be attached by any contortion of moral reasoning. The reader has occasionally to remind himself that his sympathies are invested in a beast who would unhesitatingly chew a famished old woman to pieces if ordered to do so—he has to remind himself of this and to sort out the ethical perplexities it entails. This is not easy, but then no great novel is easy.

Ruslan's world collapses as his prison camp is disbanded around 1957, when Khrushchev issued massive rehabilitations and amnesties in an effort to de-Stalinize a hopelessly Stalinized Russia. The animal's god—the handsome young prison guard whose every word he obeyed, whose approval was life's supreme good, and from whose hands alone he would accept food—abandons Ruslan without a qualm, though not before having nearly poisoned him by forcing him, as a merry KGB prank, to swallow a pot of searingly hot mustard.

Foraging for his own food, Ruslan more or less lives in a touchingly equivocal cohabitation with a former prisoner, whom he considers himself to be guarding in the crazy world where he alone seems to remember how things are supposed to be. The "Shabby Man" (not otherwise identified) is probably one of those hapless soldiers or civilians captured by Hitler's troops and, repatriated at the end of the war, instantly imprisoned by Stalin's troops. Such people were not "rehabilitated" (entitled to their former social and professional status) but merely "amnestied." Sick, confused, and alone, they were at liberty to fend for themselves in the workers' paradise. Some "amnestied" persons must have longed for the camps.

Ruslan reasonably supposes that his guardianship of the Shabby Man will end with the return of his master and the world's reversion to its former sensible routine. When a trainload of workers arrives to begin work at the new factory on the site of the old concentration camp (these are the May Day marchers of the germ story), Ruslan logically takes them to be a consignment of prisoners, and, though puzzled by the absence of the masters and their submachine guns, throws himself into his old duties, relieved that the incomprehensible and shameful disorder known as "freedom" has come to an end.

From FAITHFUL RUSLAN

V

He had waited—and was rewarded. Anyone who waits with such single-minded devotion is always rewarded in the end. Nor was the good news brought to him by someone else who by a lucky chance happened to be there: that morning Ruslan himself was on the platform when the red light began to glow and a dirty, wheezy little switching engine, tender first, pushed the train of gray-green passenger cars into the siding.

The wheels were still clicking over the rail joints, a hissing sound could still be heard beneath the cars when an astonishing, incredible horde of people started pouring and tumbling out of the doors with a great deal of shouting, hubbub and laughter, with much clattering of boots, shuffling of shoes, banging of suitcases, trunks and backpacks. Ruslan was almost stunned, blinded and overwhelmed by a wave of stupefying smells; he jumped up and ran, barking furiously, to the other end of the train—something that he had never done before, but then never before had he been called upon to meet such a huge party nor one that was so strange, noisy and slovenly, half of it, for some reason, made up of women.

The Service had come back, though—and Ruslan was ready for it. In a moment he was transformed: flexible, alert, his yellow eyes sharp and keen; the hairs on his ruff stood on end like a collar, while ears, stomach and the tip of his extended tail quivered with a low metallic growl. If he allowed himself to misbehave slightly, it was out of joyous excitement: he grabbed and tugged at a backpack, whose owner, roaring with laughter, pulled it away from him by the straps, and although he almost yanked Ruslan's teeth out with it, this did not annoy him. He jumped up with his forepaws on the men's chests and licked their salty faces until someone stuffed the corner of a prickly army blanket into his mouth—and this did not upset him either, although it took him a long time to spit the wool out of his mouth. They had all come back! And what's more, they had come back voluntarily! They had realized after all that there was no better life beyond the forests, far away from the camp—which, of course, the masters and the dogs had known all the time—and they were obviously delighted at their discovery.

Ruslan, however, did not forget his duties, which were

to check that everyone except the uniformed conductors had left the cars, and to make sure that the passengers lined up two paces back from the edge of the platform, where they must wait until the masters arrived.

The masters were disgracefully late, especially since in the old days they had always been standing there long before the train pulled in, each one with his dog, opposite the door assigned to him. There, on the concrete platform, the train escort had handed over the incoming batch of prisoners to the camp escort; the new arrivals were then made to sit down in line, hands clasped behind their necks, while the masters walked up and down between the rows calling the roll, counting and recounting them, and examining their luggage. Anything that could not be carried was removed and loaded onto a truck, and if any of them objected to this, the dogs would intervene without orders.

On this occasion, however, nothing seemed to be done according to the rules: they did not sit down or pile their baggage alongside them, but simply picked up their belongings and surged off in a disorderly crowd. This upset Ruslan very much, but he was reassured when he saw that they obviously had no intention of trying to escape, that they were not jumping down from the platform, but were taking the familiar route—down the steps and into the square. His only concern was to see that the party did not get too strung out, for which purpose he had to prod a few people with his paws or his muzzle. Who had been the first to think of this method of urging on the stragglers? No doubt it was Ingus. Who else could have dreamed up anything so stupid? The men he prodded did not like it at all; he was, after all, urging them on so that they would get into the warmth all the sooner, but they shied away and shrieked in terror—as if the dogs' only pleasure was to bite, whereas they were in just as much of a hurry to get back indoors. Later, Djulbars had adopted this method, and of course the swine had ruined everything as he always did—but then he was Djulbars!

Out on the square, around the railing of the little central

plot of grass, they all gathered into a crowd again, put down their luggage and turned to face the station. There on the steps stood two short men wearing identical gray suits, with something red at their throats; one was fat, the other, thin. The fat one only smiled, his hands clasped behind his back, but the thin one put a pair of spectacles on his nose, unfolded a piece of paper and talked to it for a very long time, occasionally flinging his hand into the air as though throwing a stick to be retrieved. Two or three times, after a pause, he repeated the words: "And so you, young builders of the cellulose fiber factory . . ." As soon as he had finished and was folding up his piece of paper, the fat man unclasped his hands from behind his back and started to smack his palms together. Everybody else started to slap their own hands, too, and to shout "Hurrah!" while some at the very back shouted "Boo!" and seemed very pleased with themselves for this. Then one of the newcomers mounted the steps, put his suitcase at his feet and also took out a piece of paper. He did not talk to his paper for quite so long, and repeated a slightly different phrase: "And so we, young builders of the cellulose fiber factory . . ." All these strange words tickled Ruslan's ears—rather like the words that the Shabby Man liked to shout after he had been at his bottle for a while: "sandalwood," "palisander," "White Finns . . ." By the way, thought Ruslan, he might like to be here. Shall I go and fetch him?

There was, however, no time for him to go—the people had finished talking, waving their arms and smoking; they picked up their luggage from the ground—luggage which no one had examined!—and began to form up into a column. This was a surprise—and a pleasant one: they were forming a column on their own initiative! Although they had so far broken almost every rule, they had at least remembered the most important one of all—not to move in a disorderly crowd but in a proper column. Feeling very satisfied and immeasurably proud that he alone was escorting such a large party and knew where to lead it, Ruslan took up his position on the right-hand side near the head of the column, and set out on the road—a road whose end he was not to see.

The column headed out onto the main street. Moving at a leisurely pace, it flowed over the permanent ruts in the street, while its thousand boot-soles trampled the wayside plantains and raised a cloud of pale, clay-colored dust which settled on the sparse poplar trees and sharp-pointed tops of fences. Somewhere amid the ranks a guitar tinkled and accordions began to wheeze, at which a girl wearing men's pants and with short-cropped hair like a boy eagerly ran out ahead, turned to face the front rank and started to dance backward, neatly and deftly, singing in a raucous, cracked voice:

> "I stepped out on the road so smooth,
>   Along the road so wide-oh!
> My lover wants to have his due,
>   But I won't be his bride-oh!"

This was an unheard-of breach of regulations, but since it was being committed by a woman, Ruslan was not sure what to do. In the columns he had escorted in the past, women had been an exceptional rarity. They had never given any trouble, except that they were more prone to lag behind and had to be made to catch up; on the other hand they never tried to escape, so on balance he felt indifferent toward them. He decided to leave this girl alone, especially as her performance was not causing the others to break ranks. The accordions were bellowing away at full blast, the girl twirled around on her own axis so that she ended up again facing the front rank and dancing backward, smiling all over her high-cheekboned, sunburned face. She was still singing but now quite inaudibly, because the men's voices were roaring out their own nonsensical song:

> "Ruble for the hay, the cart costs two,
> Ruble for the ride for me and you—
> Beans and peas, peas and beans,
> Load it to the top with peas and beans ..."

Farther down the column they were singing about the soldier and his girl who had to part because:

> "He's been ordered to march westward
> But eastward she must turn her steps . . ."

While from the back came the strains of a song about the old tomcat who ". . . sat on the mat, eating bread and mutton fat . . ."

Windows were opened along the street and people looked out—some as though stunned, others with a mirthless grin of amazement. In some front yards, women with their long skirts hitched up for gardening straightened their backs and stared, shading their eyes from the sun. A white-haired old man wearing a patched army tunic walked over to his low fence and watched silently and impassively with his faded blue eyes. His hands, grasping the handle of a spade, were covered in large veins as dark in color as the spade handle, as dark as his lined, weather-beaten face, while his elbows and open neck were thin and white, the skin underlain by a network of little blue veins. The old man moved his lips for a long time before stroking the top of his head and asking:

"Where are you boys from? You from Moscow? Or from someplace else, maybe?"

"We're from all over, granddad," they replied. "Moscow, Bryansk, Smolensk. Guess you never saw people from so many places before."

"Sure, I've seen 'em," said the old man. "All sorts used to go down this street. Some from Bryansk, some from Smolensk, too. Only they didn't sing."

He gave a gap-toothed smile and hobbled back to his flower beds.

And so the column marched on, yelling, laughing, exchanging shouts with the bystanders—which made Ruslan less than happy. He did not like these new rules, which upset the grave solemnity of the Service. He knew, however, that he must be patient; the newcomers' loud, nervous and silly behavior would very soon cease, just as they would soon stop looking so cheerful and fat-faced. Before long they would all be looking subdued, foreheads and eyes appearing disproportionately large in thin, pale faces which would seem to glow with an inner light. He only regretted that he could not tell them the good news: they clearly did not know what a spacious camp had been prepared for their benefit, what big, wonderful, new huts awaited them, huts in which they could all fit easily— well, maybe a few would have to be packed in a bit tightly—and that there was no barbed wire yet, although this did not matter because they themselves would soon be put to work stringing it between the posts. Once the wire was in position they would never again dare to cross it, nor even approach it, but it would be their very own wire, because it was always the prisoners' job to put it up.

Suddenly he noticed that the other dogs had all started to converge on the column from every direction. They came running out of alleyways and yards, jumping over fences, all similar in looks—with smooth, black backs and fluffy yellow fur on their stomachs, and all with identical grins of joyous anticipation; even their tongues, it seemed, were all hanging out on the same side. All were erstwhile comrades: Djulbars, Yenisei, Baikal, the inseparable Era and Cartridge, Trigger and Breechblock, Dick and Caesar, Whitey, Daring, Graycoat, Alma and her boyfriend with the white-ringed eyes—hey, what was that civilian doing here? He was not the only civilian to turn up; with him came a whole horde of mongrels—all those nondescript Treasures, Spots, Patches, Busters and Fidos, along with several who had no names at all. Last to appear was Lux (whose masters never called him anything but Luxy)—a creature Ruslan found repellent, who looked like a bitch and was rotten to the core. In fights, Lux immediately rolled over onto his back or whined to Djulbars, who treated him as his protégé. He had earned this status by pretending to bite Djulbars's fleas for him, of which he had none, but Lux put on such a convincing act that everyone thought they could really see them. That was how he had kept his place in the pack—by playing the toady and the fool. Just now he had been rolling in the dust, then jumping up and snapping his teeth as though catching a flea in midair. This performance was the cause of his being late, yet because of it the other dogs greeted him with smiles and wagging tails, whereas they seemed not to notice Ruslan at all. He was not the first to encounter this perverse instinct of the mob: it adores a clown yet spurns a hero.

As he ran forward to take up his leading position as the senior dog, Djulbars gave Ruslan a friendly nip on the shoulder. Ruslan turned away with a growl; he had not forgotten the woodpile and Djulbars's revolting display of servility to that puny little man with the motorcycle. He was not envious by nature, but now he bitterly envied Djulbars—the swine always took first place in the column and Ruslan only second place, and now once again he was obliged to drop back. He ended up trotting alongside a young man wearing new shoes with thick rubber soles—how that rubber stank! Yet he could not help feeling a warm wetness in his eyes, could not help admitting that for all their backsliding his comrades had come at once as soon as they heard the call of the Service. Even the blind Asa came trotting along and unerringly took up her correct position—fourth on the left. Everything was done in the proper manner, silently and without fuss. None but the mongrels barked, and they only at a distance; once on the main street they, too, fell silent, for although they had almost forgotten it, they had seen this sight often enough in the past and knew the procedure.

Just because it all happened so easily and calmly, none of the newcomers was scared, no one shied away from the dogs which had suddenly appeared from nowhere to flank the column at regular intervals. Some even dared to reach out and stroke them, and although this did not exactly please the dogs, they tolerated it and did no more than utter a slight growl; they had either grown slacker or more easygoing during the prisoners' absence.

"Hey, Misha!" shouted the young man in rubber-soled

shoes, a thin boy with a blubbery, childish mouth. "Look—what service! Have you seen our escort?"

"They must have been provided by the town council," answered Misha. "Or by the factory management."

"Well, whoever sent them, it shows that somebody cares. It would make a good movie shot. Hey, maybe they'd carry our stuff for us?"

"That's an idea!"

And the boy actually laid his pack on Ruslan's back. Perplexed by this novel behavior, Ruslan good-naturedly carried the pack, to the marchers' general amusement, until the boy grew bored with the trick.

"Thank you," he said, raising his cap. "We'll all take it in turns."

The girl alongside him stretched out her hand to tickle Ruslan's ruff. He sidled away, suppressing a growl, and thought how little sense these dimwits had acquired during their long absence. If they really wanted to please the dogs by doing something with their hands, then they could best hold them behind their backs in the manner prescribed by prison regulations.

The people standing on the sidewalks, leaning out of windows or over fences to watch this strange procession of people and dogs, for some reason did not smile, but looked on in gloomy silence. Gradually, too, the people in the column stopped laughing, stopped irritating the dogs by patting them and shouting at them, until finally there was quiet, in which the only sounds to be heard were the regular tramp of feet and the dogs' loud, hot breathing. Right away this silence struck Ruslan as ominous and gave him an uncomfortable feeling that maybe the prisoners suspected something. But what could this be, since they knew all about everything in advance? Perhaps they were regretting their return, perhaps they had changed their minds about going back to the camp and might at any moment break out in an attempt to escape. He glanced around and saw Dick, with his usual sly look on a muzzle that bore the still unhealed scar of his beating; behind him, keeping the regulation interval, trotted the hefty, imperturbable Baikal; farther back, her shoulder blades twitching faintly but rhythmically, Era was jogging along in her place; all of them were busy doing the job for which they were born and trained, and none seemed troubled by any forebodings, which Ruslan found reassuring. He turned and looked ahead to where the street ended at the edge of the town, and the open road started to curve uphill toward the camp. At last he could truly appreciate the meaning of what was happening: they had come back! They had really come back! It was the greatest moment of Ruslan's life, the moment when his star reached its zenith. For the sake of this moment he had endured hunger and homelessness, had warmed himself on heaps of cinders and been soaked to the skin by the spring rains, had eaten mice and taken nothing from strangers; for this moment he had guarded the Shabby Man, and rejected his master when he had shown himself to be a traitor. At this moment he was happy, and full of love for the people he was escorting. He was taking them to the bright abode of peace and virtue, in which an orderly regime would cure them of all ills—just as a medical orderly takes to the hospital a patient whose reason has been unbalanced by the importunate attentions of his family. And that love, compassion and pride were vividly expressed in the dazzling smile that was spread across Ruslan's features from ear to ear.

He was still smiling when he turned around, surprised by a momentary disturbance—a muffled growl and a fearful, almost deathly human scream. The smile was still on his face when he suddenly knew he was the most miserable of all dogs, having instantly grasped the import of what he saw. The inevitable had happened. Here, along the town's main street, were all its stores, shops, kiosks and bars—and no one had reminded the returning inmates that they were forbidden to step out of line. There had been no masters present to read out the customary simple instructions; instead of mumbling to a piece of paper about "cellulose fiber factory . . . ," the thin man should have announced briefly and intelligibly: "If you move out of line one pace to the right or one pace to the left ... the escort will open fire without warning ..." In the past, the regulations had been read out daily to these dimwits—in fact, every time they were mustered into columns, because by the next time they might forget.

Clearing his throat, Djulbars trotted unhurriedly past Ruslan, accompanied by Dick, leaving Ruslan to watch over the still undisturbed ranks. At the back of the column everything was in confusion: angry barking, the shrieks of people bitten or just frightened, the sound of the thumps and wheezing gasps as dogs were kicked in the stomach. Numbly he watched the scuffle in the dust, the glint of bare teeth, the falling bodies, the flailing legs and fists, the suitcases with which the people tried to beat off the infuriated dogs. For a moment he felt a thrilling surge of excitement that made everything around him turn yellow, but immediately the feeling ebbed away again, leaving nothing but sickening despair at the way everything had gone so absurdly wrong. The growls that he could hear told him how it had begun: it was the hot-tempered Cartridge, who always went to extremes. She invariably lunged straight for the throat and brought the man down. Era, of course, immediately joined in; neither of them had the sense to give a warning push to bring the offender back into line with a nudge of the shoulder or forehead, nor would they be content with a simple nip on the leg. . . . Oh, there were any number of ways of making a man obey without going for the throat!

He watched the affray almost apathetically, concerned only that someone might break ranks. For a while no one did step out of line until suddenly the girl next to the boy in rubber-soled shoes stopped and ran back before Ruslan could prevent her. When she returned and seized her neighbor by the elbow, he seemed utterly stupefied. Ruslan rushed between them and nipped her on the knee. She leaped away with a squeal, which surprised Ruslan; he could not have hurt her, because even in an emergency he had the knack of closing his jaws on a human limb without even breaking the skin. The young man alongside her, who had moved half a pace out of line, had no need of such a reprimand: Ruslan only had to curl back his quivering lips and the boy was already standing in his proper place, furiously offended but also frightened to an equal degree. Ruslan immediately felt he could trust him—he seemed a good boy, who had quickly grasped what he was supposed to do.

Now Ruslan saw an amazing sight: Djulbars running away from the fight. He had a bloody mouth, his piglike eyes were bloodshot, but it was still Djulbars, deserting his post when the situation was not yet under control. Near him was Lux, whimpering as he limped away—exaggerating as usual, since he had no visible injuries. Djulbars on the other hand was not only covered in wounds, but was panting with enthusiasm!

With a nod of his head he beckoned Ruslan to follow him. Together they ran to the corner of a side street, but there Ruslan stopped. And Djulbars stopped, too. It was clear that he was not panting with the thrill of the fight but with exhaustion, that his trembling legs could hardly support his body and he was longing to lie down. Now, with no masters present, he could admit this. Ruslan understood him, but even so he insisted that Djulbars return to the fray. He knew that the dogs would go on fighting as long as Djulbars was there; old, tired and lazy though he might be, provided that they could hear his commanding growl, none of them would dare to retreat. Djulbars could scarcely meet Ruslan's accusing look, while Lux could not tolerate it: forgetting to limp, he bounded up to Ruslan and bit him savagely in the neck. Infuriated by this, Djulbars made a move to punish Lux, but the mongrel jumped back, whining that he had suffered enough already.

Once again the two dogs stared at each other. There was a certain pity in Djulbars's eyes, even though he had never liked Ruslan, who, in his opinion, carried devotion to the point of fanaticism. Now their mutual incomprehension was complete. As Djulbars saw it, they had all had a good scrap and it was time to go home; from now on it was none of the dogs' business, since the masters had long since abandoned their responsibilities. Finally exercising his right of seniority, Djulbars relieved Ruslan from his post—but in vain: the fanatic was already on his way back to the column. Djulbars watching him go shook his head sadly. Then, growling at Lux to get lost, he trotted off up the side street and retreated into old age with his regal, leonine gait, scattering drops of his own and others' blood, glad yet regretful that this was his last fight.

Another shock awaited Ruslan: he found the front ranks exactly as he had left them. Surprising though it may seem, a deep-rooted human habit had ensured that the lines at the head of the column remained virtually unbroken: no one had told them to disperse. He ran up and down the ranks, straightening them out and keeping the marchers in line with a warning growl.

The trouble had started outside a bar, but the brawl had already moved across to the other side of the street: there almost all the dogs were fighting as a pack, attacking, dodging and maneuvering, occasionally jumping up onto the sidewalk to catch their breath, while the tail end of the column continued to march on, treading on those who had fallen down in the scuffle. Three men leaned calmly on the railings of the porch outside the bar, each holding a mug of yellow liquid in one hand and in the other a small skinned fish. They were local people, and of no interest to Ruslan; what was more, they politely moved aside to let them pass.

Strangely enough, he saw neither Era nor Cartridge, who should have been in the thick of it. The rule was simple—while some attacked, the others kept the rest of the flock in order. But although he could not hear the inseparable pair among the dogs in the melee, he did notice a gap in a nearby fence, through which the trail of their scent disappeared. Obviously the marchers had wrenched out several fence posts with which to beat Era and Cartridge, and this had only helped them to make their escape; it was, of course, useless to imagine that Era and Cartridge could be beaten into submission with mere fence posts—nothing less than beams or cart shafts would suffice. Yet the fact remained that the two most hotheaded dogs, who had started it all, had also been the first to run away. A little beyond the gap in the fence, Ruslan could see more of their handiwork: a man who had either crawled there, crossing the ditch unaided, or had been carried there by his friends who had then sat him down against the fence. He had been well and truly savaged. He was clutching hs throat with both hands, blood was seeping through his fingers onto his torn white shirt, his eyes were glazed and a deathly pallor was creeping over his face, visible even through his suntan. Era and Cartridge had clearly been beaten off very quickly; otherwise the man would not even be sitting up.

Man and beast stared into each other's eyes. At first the man struggled to decide whether he was delirious or whether this white-fanged monster really was no farther away from him than the width of the ditch, then his eyes filled with despair and entreaty, and large drops of sweat began running down his face. The animal merely gave him a look of sullen reproach: have you forgotten, he was saying, that no guard dog ever attacks a man on the ground without being ordered to? He waggled his ears, as a signal of peace, and turned away. At that moment a woman flew past him, wearing a flowered dress and holding something white. She was hastening to the wounded man and did not notice Ruslan, but something that she had seen out of the corner of her eye made her look around. Ruslan's calm and silent approach frightened her more than if he had growled and lunged at her. Slowly teetering backward, eyes wide with fear, whispering to herself, she leaned her back against the side wall of the bar, while her hands continued mechanically to twist her strip of white cloth into a tourniquet. Was she really hoping to beat Ruslan off with that piece of plaited material?

He was about to walk past her when a savage blow winded him and threw him off his feet, hurling him up against the same wall. Only because he fell against the woman's legs was he able to stay upright. With a wild scream she started lashing him with her tourniquet; this only served to reassure him that he had nothing to fear from her.

Which of these three men, converging on him with furious looks and grasping heavy pieces of luggage, had kicked him in the stomach? Anyway, it didn't matter. The time had clearly come for Ruslan to intervene. He weighed up the three men in a swift glance. One had been bitten in the hand and had only just staggered to his feet again after being knocked down by Baikal. Still only able to shuffle forward, he had not yet fully recovered his senses. The second man—short, stocky and tough with a blank round face and one swollen eye—was really dangerous; men of his build were hard to bring down, and because they thought slowly they were not usually in a hurry to retreat. The third was the boy in rubber-soled shoes, the same boy with the sulky, blubbery mouth who had made Ruslan carry his pack. Ruslan had excused him for one violation of the rules—why was he trying to make trouble again? Why were the three of them advancing on him, when only one of them was any good in a fight?

Ah, that was why! They were talking to the woman in the flowered dress to encourage her and were going to her rescue. This was ridiculous, because Ruslan had no intention of harming her; she had merely been standing between him and the ditch, which she had not dared to jump over because that would have meant turning her back on him. How stupid the whole thing was!

He advanced toward the men, teeth bared, his weight shifted slightly backward onto his hind legs. Not expecting this attack, two of them backed away. The squat man stood his ground. Ruslan had calculated on this, and crouched in preparation for a leap.

He did succeed in flooring his stocky opponent, but the man had time to swivel and meet Ruslan's onslaught with a shoulder that was as hard as mahogany. It was a mistake to try biting that shoulder, but he had already started to get mad—if only the man would at least shout! Silently and deliberately the squat man freed both hands and gripped Ruslan by the neck. Everything around him became blurred and a chill began spreading through his body. Helplessly scrabbling with his claws at the squat man's chest, he fought and strained to tauten the muscles in his neck, as oblivious to the blows on his back as if it had turned to wood. He felt nothing until a heavy, solid object with a sharp edge struck him on the forehead between the eyes. As it hit him, though, the backpack frame must also have hit his adversary's fingers, because the man's grip relaxed, enabling Ruslan to wrench himself free, gulp down some air and leap back toward the wall of the bar. The woman in the flowered dress was no longer there.

The column had disintegrated and turned into sheer chaos, into a nightmarish shrieking mob gathered on the far side of the street, from whence Ruslan could still hear the voices of three or four dogs. Yes, there were now only three or four, headed by Baikal. He was a good fighter, Baikal, levelheaded, brave and strong, who never panicked, took a long time to tire and was able to infect others with his calmness—but if only Djulbars had been there! They might all have fallen in the struggle, but they would have tamed the flock.

The three men, who were far from beaten yet, were advancing again. The squat man was on his feet once more, calm and silent, not even holding his shoulder—and Ruslan realized that the situation was serious.

A fourth man had appeared from somewhere and was now moving forward ahead of the others. He was wearing an army tunic, army breeches and boots, and he had a short, straw-blond forelock. From the way he walked, his hands spread wide to grasp Ruslan's collar, and from the way he talked—with a sibilant whistle in his voice as he called out in an affectionate but authoritative tone: "Here, good dog, come to me, good dog"—Ruslan guessed that the man had been trained to handle dogs. The old Ruslan would probably have obeyed this soldier, but not the Ruslan who had taken poison from the hand of his treacherous master. A master who was in league with the prisoners was an enemy many times more dangerous than the prisoners themselves.

Out of the corner of his eye Ruslan saw Dick, sneaking away behind a man's back, between another person's legs, limping across the street toward a gateway. He was holding one bloodstained forepaw off the ground. Infuriated, he would turn and lunge at his tormentors, but each time he forgot about his paw and fell whimpering to the ground. Several people were beating the blind Asa as she cowered helplessly against a fence—surely she had not been fighting, too? The soldier could see all this—and yet he could still say, "Come here, good dog!"

Only at the very last instant did the soldier give up his attempt to cajole Ruslan. As he flung up his elbow in defense, Ruslan sank his teeth into it and brought the man crashing down into the dust. The soldier squirmed and groaned, feebly attempting to push the dog away with his other hand; he would probably have given in had he not been surrounded by his companions, who were kicking Ruslan in the ribs, pulling at his tail and ears. Ruslan hung on and would not let go of the man's elbow, although he now realized that it was useless. He was unlikely to intimidate them even if he bit through the soldier's bone: the only effective move was to get one of them by the throat. Seizing a moment when the other men seemed to hesitate, Ruslan suddenly leaped away from the soldier in order to catch his breath and size up the situation.

His despair at seeing Alma escape through the gap in the fence was only slightly relieved by the fact that her mongrel companion managed to make a worthier exit, taking a hefty bite at the leg of a prisoner who was whacking him with a fence post. If only that white-eyed mutt had been properly trained, he would have known it was useless to go for a man's leg when he had a stick in his hand.

Where the crowd was thinner, Ruslan caught sight of Baikal, trying to counterattack against two men who had chased him up a side street and were roaring with laughter as each tried to jab a fence post into Baikal's mouth. That was it: Ruslan was alone. He alone must now reassemble this whole maddened, yelling, disobedient herd of lunatics, and even though he had lost all hope of escorting them all the way to the camp, at least he must hold them here until the masters arrived—surely they must be coming soon!

His rear was protected by the wall of the bar. No need to worry about the three men leaning on the railing; they had not changed their pose the whole time, and were simply watching the affray with drunken amazement. Nor was there anything to fear from the woman leaning on her spade behind the fence and frowning sorrowfully all over her brown, sunburned face. Most dangerous of all was the soldier, who was now sitting up in the dust, pressing his bitten elbow to his stomach. That man obviously knew something about the Service and might, filthy traitor that he was, encourage the others and instruct them in the proper tactics, but fortunately he seemed too concerned with his wound. There remained the low fence, which he could jump over in case of need, elude pursuit and return to the attack from another direction. That was his only hope. Meanwhile the crowd had formed into a semicircle and was closing in on the lone Ruslan—a crowd of angry faces, each person clutching either a stick or a heavy piece of luggage.

He growled—angrily, menacingly, savagely, to show that he was in no mood to joke but ready to kill or to die himself—and advanced on them, baring his quivering fangs. They stopped, but did not retreat. No, he had not managed to intimidate them. Again and again he made rushes, first at one, then at another, and they dodged him, held up their packs like a wall, then lunged at him from the side and jabbed him in the flanks with fence posts, or purposely exposed themselves to his attack, taunting him with their proximity, in order to smother him with a canvas jacket or a raincoat. He knew that they were purposely wearing him out while the others, behind their backs, could run away in all directions.

He must get to grips with at least one of them and give

him a proper trouncing. This was what he had been taught by the masters, by the Instructor and by the men in gray overalls: better to go for one man properly than to make halfhearted attacks on four or five. By now, though, he was seeing the world through a yellow film: the grass and the dust were yellow, the blue afternoon sky was yellow, as were the men's faces and his own blood trickling from the cut on his forehead—and in this state he had no more dangerous enemy than himself. He picked out the boy in rubber-soled shoes, who for some reason angered him more than any of them, although he was standing well out of the way and only watching. Perhaps, in fact, he chose him for the very reason that an attack on this boy would act as more of a shock to the others and restrain them for longer. When two men made a grab at him, Ruslan outwitted them, slipped between their legs and hurled himself at his victim.

Ruslan leaped, his long body fully stretched, his bare-fanged, bloodstained muzzle thrusting ahead with ears flattened. But even while he was in the air he sensed that he was going to miss his target. Because he could now only see with one eye, the other being covered with blood, he had misjudged the distance and jumped too soon. The boy gave a wild, inhuman shriek, and an instantaneous, purely animal instinct made him double up his body. Ruslan brushed him with his stomach, somersaulted over his head and crashed to the ground. Immediately, before he had time to get up, he was thumped on the head by two fence posts, and another man, running up unseen, took a swing with all his strength and brought down a heavy trunk with metal-reinforced corners onto Ruslan's back.

After a blow like that, what power could lift a stricken animal to his feet? Fear of being hit again? But they had stopped hitting him, and he sensed that if he stayed lying down they would not touch him again. The urge to protect his young would have made him get up, but Ruslan had no offspring and he had never known that feeling. He did, however, know another feeling, one that had been taught to him by man: duty—which we, who hardly know the meaning of the word ourselves, had imprinted on his consciousness—and it was duty which obliged Ruslan to raise himself up.

His mouth was full of dust. Nearly choking, he spat it out, then with an incredible effort straightened out his forelegs and sat up. He could do no more, and it was not this fact in itself that horrified him, but the thought that the Enemy might guess that he was helpless. They had moved in quite close now, near enough for him to get at them, but he did not move and only shook his head, growling hoarsely.

"Leave the poor devil alone, boys; don't tease him anymore," said the soldier. He was still sitting on the ground, tearing at his sleeve and binding up his elbow. "He's only doing his duty."

"Who's teasing him?" said the boy indignantly. "You call *that* doing his duty? Filthy beast!"

"He is nothing of the sort," said the soldier. "That's what he was trained to do, so he does it. If only everyone did their duty half as well. You and I can learn a lesson from him." He grinned though wincing with pain. "And I wouldn't mind having a dog like that myself."

"But he's just attacked you . . ."

"That's exactly why I'd like to have him. Don't go near him! You're not his master."

The soldier began tying his torn sleeve into a knot with the aid of his teeth. The boy came up to him.

"Can I help you? They've called for a truck. There are about twenty people wounded."

"Well, if a truck's on the way someone will help me anyway, so you needn't bother. As for the number of people wounded, my friend, you don't go around broadcasting it to all and sundry. You just say: 'Casualties were sustained.'"

His head drooping, Ruslan kept himself in a sitting position by exerting all his strength on his forepaws. Now and again he gave a growl to remind people that he had not capitulated, but he could not understand what was holding them back—didn't they realize that he could not get up?

This was how the Shabby Man found Ruslan: sitting in the dust, bloodstained, wretched yet terrible. His flanks rose and fell, steaming. His hind legs were splayed out on either side in such an absurd, unnatural attitude, and his spine was bent in such an odd curve that it convinced the Shabby Man that the dog's backbone must be broken. In this the Shabby Man was wrong, and the mistake was to prove fatal for Ruslan.

"What did you have to break his back for?" asked the Shabby Man. "You didn't need to do that. Ah, you young people—love a fight, don't you? And it has to be to the death."

"Yes, they did get a bit excited," said the soldier.

"You can't talk!" said the boy to the Shabby Man, his indignation flaring up again. "You didn't see what happened!"

"No matter what happened," said the Shabby Man, "I know for sure that you didn't have to smash the dog's spine."

"We both know that," said the soldier.

As the Shabby Man approached Ruslan, wanting to stroke him, that terrible head was raised, the lips were curled back and the teeth bared. Usually this was sufficient warning to induce a human to understand and retreat; besides, the Shabby Man needed reminding that never for one moment had he ever been Ruslan's master.

The Shabby Man needed no such reminder. He stepped back into the ranks as quickly as he could—or rather, into the place where the ranks had once been.

"I see you haven't forgotten," said the soldier with a grin. "You remember the rules, don't you? Only one other thing—hands behind your back!"

The Shabby Man did not answer him.

The boy, looking sad and thoughtful, also seemed to understand the situation.

"Well, what's to be done with him?" he asked, glancing

around in perplexity. "We can't just leave him like this. He must be taken to a vet."

"You're joking," said the Shabby Man. "What vet can mend a broken spine?"

"This is a job for the weight lifter," said the soldier. "Hey, weight lifter!" he called out to the squat man. "You still feeling mad at this dog? Get a spade and finish him off. It's got to be done, see? Orders are orders."

The squat man gave Ruslan a swift glance from his puffy little eyes and walked over to the fence. At once the woman obediently handed him her spade and turned away, but through the big holes that had been torn in her fence she could still see everything that was happening.

The squat man turned the spade this way and that. It looked like a toy in his huge, muscular hands, but he had no doubt never had to kill before; he was clearly unwilling, and not sure how to do it.

"Why must it be done like that?" asked the boy. "Doesn't anyone here have a gun?"

"No," said the Shabby Man. "No one in this town ever had a gun. It was forbidden."

The crowd made way for the squat man. Ruslan was no longer growling and had hung his head again. He saw the legs in their dusty boots planted wide, the shadow of the spade flickered past him as it was raised, and suddenly Ruslan was seized with fury—this time, though, the fury was his own, and not a response bred by human conditioning. He knew that there was no one to restrain him now, and he knew that he was beaten. But an animal will always fight for its life to the bitter end; no animal ever licks the boots of his executioner. Thrusting out his head, Ruslan lunged toward the spade and caught the iron in his teeth.

Although the pain was terrible, he had the satisfaction of seeing the squat man's face turn pale, his eyes fill with terror and confusion.

"Hey, he's a tough one!" said the squat man, wrenching the spade free and smiling guiltily—no doubt in the same way that he smiled when one of his weight-lifting exercises failed at the first attempt. "What the hell am I to do with him?"

"Well, whatever you're going to do—do it," said the Shabby Man. "You've got to finish him off. He can't live—he's a goner."

Flushing red in the face, the squat man raised the spade again. He approached Ruslan's blind side, and let out a hoarse grunt as he brought the spade down in a slantwise blow. Turning his head at the sound of the grunt, Ruslan just caught sight of the flashing metal—dull and cold, like the bottom of an aluminum feeding bowl that has been licked clean. . . .

Then the two of them, the squat man and the boy, picked him up by the forelegs and dragged him to the ditch, leaving an intermittent trail of red, caked dustballs. But the owners of the nearby houses protested vigorously at having a carcass left to rot outside their windows, so they had to drag the body a long way beyond the last house and fling it down the embankment made by the bulldozer.

With it, they also threw the spade, stained with saliva and blood.

VI

When blind Asa had licked clean the wounds on Ruslan's flanks and his back and the terrible deep wound behind his ear, she howled a lament for him, instinctively lifting her sightless head toward the sun. Then she went away, certain that Ruslan would never regain his senses.

But regain them he did. It may seem improbable that with a horribly bruised back, with all his weight on his forelegs, his hind legs only scraping along the ground, he should have climbed up the stony-sided embankment and dragged himself all the way to the station. It seems improbable, unless one knows how obstinately, purposefully and unerringly any stricken animal will find its way to the same place where in the past it has endured suffering and recovered. No doubt if Ruslan had been fully conscious he

would not have done this, but his mind was clouded now
and in his inward eye he could see only one thing—that
secluded corner beside a stone wall, between the public
lavatory and the garbage cans, where he had recovered
from being poisoned.

The sultry afternoon had driven all the people indoors,
into cool shuttered rooms where the wooden floors were
sprinkled with water. There was not a living soul to be
seen. Stupefied by the heat, the yard dogs were dozing in
their kennels or under porches, and none of them raised a
bark when Ruslan crawled along the wooden sidewalks
past their homes. As twilight approached, however, the
dogs awoke and began to show an interest in him. It was
they, in fact, who forced him into full consciousness. On
top of all his misfortunes, he was fated to undergo one
more ordeal, and the most humiliating of all: to be tormented by the mongrels of the town, those Buttons,
Blackies, Busters and Fidos that he had once so despised.
Unaware of what he had done to wound their pride, he
had forgotten that peculiarly nasty streak in the canine
nature (perhaps explicable in these wretched little creatures by their defenselessness and their frequent maltreat-
ment by humans) which makes them gang up and attack
another animal when he is weak and defeated—and the
bigger he is the more gusto they put into their persecution. Strangely enough, however, many of their attacks
petered out ineffectually or seemed much weaker than he
had been led to fear by the fury that seethed in their
voices. Somehow they failed in their cowardly attempts to
settle accounts with Ruslan. Some strong, resolute companion, keeping pace with him on his blind side—perhaps
it was Alma or Baikal, but he could no longer recognize
them by their voices—was beating off all their attacks or
taking the brunt of them on himself, and the rest of the
little dogs' aggression was diverted into snapping and biting each other. Eventually the whole pack was driven off
by some kindhearted passerby. The mongrels took to their
heels willingly and in a high state of self-satisfaction; all
they had wanted, in any case, was to get one bite at him

apiece, and afterward the tales of their valor would grow large enough in the telling.

A little later, as he was hauling himself painfully across the station square, Ruslan saw his defender, and his immediate thought was to wish that he had stayed and died at the bottom of the embankment. The dog who had defended him against that vicious rabble was Treasure—that same squat, potbellied little mutt, whose help only yesterday he would have disdained as beneath his dignity.

Treasure stayed with him to the end of his journey. When Ruslan's hind legs proved too infirm to move unaided into the narrow space of his chosen refuge, it was Treasure who now performed that service for him. Ruslan was now protected on three sides, and he hoped to be able to defend himself from the fourth side. Treasure could go now. But he still sat there, resting, occasionally giving a violent shiver and whimpering with persistent fright and the pain of his many bites. He wanted an answer to the final question which he was asking Ruslan with the sad, reproachful look in his eyes—something on the lines of, "Why did you do it, brother?"

Ruslan dismissed him with a shake of the head—the head that so terrified Treasure, with its blood-caked eye—and Treasure understood that it was no use putting the question: Ruslan himself did not know the answer. He also knew that he must leave at once, because what was about to happen to Ruslan was more terrible and more important than anything else he might want to know, and that no one must be present to see it. He backed away, his hairs standing on end with fear, and as soon as he had turned the corner around the trash cans, he ran off with a howl that nothing could stop.

Sometimes you may have seen a little dog running down the middle of the street in the gathering darkness, uttering now and again a muffled whine as if through clenched teeth, and apparently running away from something, even though no one is chasing him. It is almost as though he is running away from himself—or from the edge of an abyss over which he has peeped from curiosity or lack of caution, a gulf into which no living creature should look, and from whence he has brought back a secret to make him shiver with cold even in the warmest, safest place of refuge. Treasure had discovered the merest inkling of that secret, yet he was condemned to shiver as with cold, to spurn his food, to ignore his mistress's call, and to crawl into the dimmest, darkest hole, to thrust his nose into the corner and screw up his eyes. Yet even there the thread linking him to Ruslan would not be broken; even there he could not hide himself, and he would go numb with terror as he listened to his swelling, thumping heart, not knowing that it was beating in time to another heart—and that so it would be until that other heart stopped beating. Only then would the link be snapped, allowing him at last, exhausted and in pain, to sink into the oblivion of sleep.

The sound of Treasure's howl fading into the distance was not the last noise to disturb Ruslan. For a long time he could hear footsteps and voices as they approached and died away again, the banging of trash-can lids right above his ear, and the clank followed by a gurgle of water each time the lavatory cistern was emptied. Each sound made him freeze and hold his breath, but by the mercy of fate no one noticed him. Even if anyone had seen him, they would have taken him for a heap of gray rags or some other garbage.

He was waiting for night, when the place would be quiet and deserted, for there was something that he longed to recall, some fleeting memory that he must catch. He did not know what would happen to him by morning, yet he had nevertheless prepared himself for some event; he felt that he was due to return to a certain place: was it perhaps to that black oblivion from which he had once come? And gradually time began to turn backward for Ruslan.

His days in the Service flickered past—most of them as identical as the barbed-wire fence posts or the rows of huts—his turns of sentry duty, his escort duty, his chases and fights. He recalled them all as colored with the yellow of anger and aggression, and everywhere he was a captive—whether on the leash or not—for at no time had he ever been free or on the loose. He wanted now to return to an animal's first joy—to freedom, which he never forgot and to the loss of which he was never reconciled; he hurried on and on until finally he reached it, and saw himself in the spacious enclosure at the breeding kennels, saw the pink and brown-spotted teats of his mother, a famous prizewinning bitch, and his five brothers and sisters fighting and tumbling over one another on the soft bedding. Through the wire-mesh fence which formed the outer wall could be seen bright greenery, yellow sand and a dazzling blue sky, but they never noticed the fence itself and it never occurred to them what it was for. Two men approached from the other side of the fence, opened the wire-mesh gate, and in walked his master. He entered with another man, already familiar to them, who often came in with food for their mother and swept out the kennel with his harmless broom. This was the first time that Ruslan saw his master: young, strong, well-built, wearing the beautiful dress of the masters, with his handsome, godlike face, his terrible flashing eyes filled, like saucers, with cloudy blue water, and for the first time he felt an unaccountable fear that not even the closeness of his mother could assuage.

"Choose one," said the man with the broom.

Squatting down on his haunches, the Master looked them over for a long time and then stretched out his hand. Immediately Ruslan's five brothers and sisters crawled toward that outstretched hand—submissive, whining pathetically, shivering with fear and impatience. Their mother, delighted and proud of them, prodded them forward with her nose. Only Ruslan, his hackles rising, crawled away growling into a dark corner. It was the first time in his life that he had growled, in fear of the Master's hand, whose short fingers were dotted with a sparse growth of red hairs. The hand passed over all the other puppies and stretched itself out to him alone, picked him up by the scruff of his neck and carried him out into the light. The dread face came nearer—the face which he was to love, and then to hate—and grinned, at which he growled and struggled, wriggling all his paws and his little tail, full of anger and terror.

It was in this position that he came to know his name, which was not the name that his mother had given him to distinguish him from her other children—to her he was known as something like "Yrrm."

"What's his name in the register?" asked his master.

The man with the broom came closer and stared.

"Ruslan."

"Why 'Ruslan'? That's usually a name for retrievers. I thought of calling him Jerry, but we already have a Jerry. What the hell, Ruslan will do. . . . Do you hear what your name is? Why are you squirming so much? Don't you trust your new master?"

With two fingers he opened the puppy's mouth and inspected his palate.

"Seems like he's a bit of a coward," observed the man with the broom.

"Much you know!" said Master. "He's mistrustful, the little brute. Just the sort to make a good guard dog. . . . Ah, temper, temper! Bite my finger, would you?" Laughing, he gave Ruslan a painful slap on his little bare belly and put him down separately in a corner. "Feed up this little fellow for a bit longer. And you can drown all the rest. They're just ass-lickers—not worth shit."

Without even looking at her other puppies, the mother gathered Ruslan alone to her side. The five that had been rejected were put into a bucket and carried away, to be replaced by five greedy foster children, whose teeth had already started to come through and who hurt her teats; she accepted them uncomplainingly and licked them all over, gazing devotedly into Master's face.

Why hadn't she attacked him and bitten him? Seeing himself again as a helpless little puppy, he was still puzzled by her serenity, her untroubled brow. Horrified, Ruslan had tried to make a dash to save his brothers and sisters, only to be struck down by a blow from her heavy paw. What kind of pact existed between her and the Master? There must have been some grim truth that she knew which made her obediently submit to the murder of her children—for when a mother animal's young are taken from her, it can only be to destruction.

That grim truth had been revealed to him today—when he had been knocked down and saw the three men advancing on him with faces twisted with hate; when the backpack had struck him on the head; when the spade flew up; when the Shabby Man had said, "Finish him off." Never, never was the hatred stilled in the hearts of those dimwits; they were only ever awaiting their hour when they could vent it on you—and all because you were doing your duty. The masters were right: in every human who was not of their number there lurked an enemy. But were even the masters his friends? Only the Instructor, who had eventually turned into a dog, had been a real friend—and what had he been barking on that frosty night, to the howling of a snowstorm? He had said: "Let us leave them. They are no brothers of ours. They are our enemies. Every last one of them is an enemy!" So everything that had happened today had, after all, been foreseen by that wise she-dog, his mother, doomed as she was in exchange for her food to bear and suckle aggressive, mistrustful creatures for the Service. Was that why she had shown no distress when her puppies had been removed from her—because she knew that the five who were carried away in a tin bucket were going to the better fate?

. . . Every animal, when stricken by misfortune, crawls away to a place where in the past he has found refuge in which to endure suffering and recover. This was not the reason, however, that had made Ruslan crawl to this place; he knew that this time he could be cured neither by Asa's healing saliva nor by the bitter herbs and plants whose scent he always smelled whenever he was unwell or injured. A wounded animal lives for as long as he wants to live; but now he had sensed that there, in the place where he had been before, there would be no murky cellar, no beating with the leash, no jabs with a needle, no mustard, nothing, no sound, no smells, no alarms, only darkness and calm—and for the first time he longed for that. He had nowhere to go back to. His humble, imperfect love for man had died completely; he knew no other kind of love, he was unfitted for any other form of existence. Lying in his stinking hideaway and sobbing with pain, he heard the distant hooting of locomotives and the clicking wheels of approaching trains, but he had no more expectations from them. Even his erstwhile visions, which had once brought him such delight, now only gave him pain, like a bad dream that leaves a sense of shame and unease on awakening. He had learned enough in his waking life about the world of humans, and it stank of cruelty and treachery.

It is time for us to leave Ruslan, and that indeed is now his only wish—that all of us, who share the guilt of what was done to him, should finally leave him and never come back. Any other thoughts that may arise in his brain (which is beginning to suffer from inflammation) will be beyond our comprehension—and it is useless for us to expect enlightenment.

It was, however, Ruslan's fate that even in his last hour the Service did not leave him. It summoned him at the very moment of his crossing to the other shore—calling upon him to make some last response. At that hour, when the Service was being betrayed by the truest of the true, who had sworn without reserve to give their lives for it; when it was being renounced and forsaken by ministers and generals, judges and hangmen, by hired spies and voluntary informers alike; when the very standard-bearers were trampling upon its despised banners—at that hour the Service sought for a prop and stay, called for at least one whose loyalty had not faltered—and the dying soldier heard the call of the war trumpets.

He thought that his master had returned—no, not his previous master, the Corporal; it was someone else, who had no scent and was wearing new boots, to whose smell he still had to grow accustomed. But the hand which he laid on Ruslan's forehead was firm and masterful.

... The buckle clicked, releasing his collar. Stretching

his arm toward the distance, his master pointed to where the Enemy was. And Ruslan, breaking loose, raced away in that direction—in long, springy strides, without touching the ground—powerful, free of pain, free of fear and free of love for man or beast. Behind him rang out Ruslan's favorite word, the one and only reward for all his pain and for all his faithfulness:

"Get him, Ruslan! . . . Get!"

(*1975*)

Vladimir Voinovich

(1932–   )

Had nature not saddled him with a most unbiddable sense of the absurd, Voinovich might have enjoyed all the usual perquisites of successful authorship in the Soviet Union: the top scale of royalties, the nice apartment, the country house, the paid vacations in resorts guaranteed to be proletarian-free, and so on. Gregory Svirsky, in his *History of Post-War Soviet Writing*, remembers a state occasion honoring Soviet cosmonauts when the irrepressible Khrushchev, from the reviewing stand atop Lenin's tomb, suddenly burst into song: "On the dusty paths of far planets/Our tracks will remain . . ." The lyrics were by Voinovich. And his first novel, *We Live Here* (1961), duly set on a collective farm, displayed a mild satire safely inside the tolerated type that aims ultimately at encouraging civic morality.

In addition to this short novel, between 1961 and 1972 Voinovich published some five stories and a historical novel. With the exception of the latter (*Degree of Trust*, published in 1972 and seen as an attempt to buy official favor for his increasingly daring and rejected work), these works reveal a satirical and "disloyal" talent edging ever closer to the limits of the permissible.

But Voinovich's masterpiece, *The Life and Extraordinary Adventures of Private Ivan Chonkin*, went beyond all bounds of official patience. It was rejected at home, and was eventually published in Paris in 1975. He had been expelled from the Writers' Union in 1974 as a sort of general prophylaxis against his expected success abroad and apparently resigned himself thenceforth to *tamizdat* (publication *there*— i.e., in the West).

Chonkin, one of the most delightful characters in Russian literature since Pushkin's aborted Belkin, is the embodiment of *sancta simplicitas*—a blissfully simpleminded citizen who stands out as a moral and intellectual genius against the inspissated stupidity of the official culture. He has the mental clarity of the child who has yet to unlearn (to use a formula dear to the heart of nineteenth-century Russian realism) that two times two makes four. Naive questioning of everything is the disease of which Chonkin is the carrier, and he thus becomes a sort of ideological accident going somewhere to happen. He is an alien, like Gogol's Mr. Chichikov in *Dead Souls*, going from one earthling to another and offering them the opportunity to be themselves. Chichikov, the Evil One incarnate, offers the landowners of the nineteenth century the chance to be their worst selves, and most of them accept. Chonkin, who has been compared to every conceivable predecessor except Christ, offers the bureaucrats of the new regime a chance to be their best selves; after weighing the practical results, most of them decline.

Voinovich was expelled from the Soviet Union in 1980. By that time he had published several works of nonfiction in the West. In one, "An Incident in the Metropole" (published in the émigré magazine *Kontinent* in 1975), he described with his characteristic amusement an attempt by the KGB to assassinate him with a poisoned cigarette. In the novelistic memoir *The Ivankiad* (published in Russian in the United States in 1976, and in English translation in 1977) he detailed in hilariously mock-heroic terms and with the same equable temper his colossal struggle against the literary bureaucracy to affirm his right to a newly available two-room apartment (rather than the one room in which he and his wife had always lived). Along with a number of other prominent exiled writers, Voinovich was reinvested with his Soviet citizenship by Gorbachev in August 1990.

The epic of Chonkin has been continued in *Pretender to the Throne** and in translations of his stories (including

* Translated by Richard Lourie from the Russian (New York: Farrar, Straus and Giroux, 1981).

some hitherto unpublished), gathered in the collection *In Plain Russian*, from which I have drawn the most gleefully macabre picture of Stalin and his henchmen that I have ever seen, "A Circle of Friends." "Comrade Koba" is, of course, Stalin, and the names on p. 562 thinly disguise his chief lieutenants, Beria, Khrushchev, Voroshilov, Kaganovich, Malenkov, Mikoyan, and Molotov. Some are not so subtly satirical, Molotov's first name, for example, deriving from the Russian for *urine*.

Postscript: When I undertook the compilation of this anthology, Vladimir Voinovich was an embattled "dissident" thrashing about in the usual difficulties associated with being such a writer in Moscow. By the time I came to write this note he had completed a year as my colleague on the faculty at Princeton. He is blameless, of course, for the above note on his life and work, but he approves the selection of "A Circle of Friends."

A CIRCLE OF
FRIENDS

(A Not Particularly Reliable Tale
concerning a Certain Historic Get-together)

The building stands behind the high red-brick wall known to the entire world. There are many windows in that building, but one was distinguished from all the others because it was lit twenty-four hours a day. Those who gathered in the evening on the broad square in front of the red-brick wall would crane their necks, strain their eyes to the point of tears, and say excitedly to one another: "Look, over there, the window's lit. He's not sleeping. He's working. He's thinking about us."

If someone came from the provinces to this city or had

to stop over while in transit, he'd be informed that it was obligatory to visit that famous square and look and see whether that window was lit. Upon returning home, the fortunate provincial would deliver authoritative reports, both at closed meetings and at those open to the public, that yes, the window was lit, and judging by all appearances, he truly never slept and was continually thinking about them.

Naturally, even back then, there were certain people who abused the trust of their collectives. Instead of going to look at that window, they'd race around to all the stores, wherever there was anything for sale. But, upon their return, they, too, would report that the window was lit, and just try and tell them otherwise.

The window, of course, was lit. But the person who was said never to sleep was never at that window. A dummy made of gutta-percha, built by the finest craftsmen, stood in for him. That dummy had been so skillfully constructed that unless you actually touched it there was nothing to indicate that it wasn't alive. The dummy duplicated all the basic features of the original. Its hand held a curved pipe of English manufacture, which had a special mechanism that puffed out tobacco smoke at pre-determined intervals. As far as the original himself was concerned, he only smoked his pipe when there were people around, and his moustache was of the paste-on variety. He lived in another room, in which there were not only no windows but not even any doors. That room could only be reached through a crawl-hole in his safe, which had doors both in the front and in the rear and which stood in the room that was officially his.

He loved this secret room where he could be himself and not smoke a pipe or wear that moustache; where he could live simply and modestly, in keeping with the room's furnishings—an iron bed, a striped mattress stuffed with straw, a washbasin containing warm water, and an old gramophone, together with a collection of records which he personally had marked—good, average, remarkable, trash.

There in that room he spent the finest hours of his life in peace and quiet; there, hidden from everyone, he would sometimes sleep with the old cleaning woman who crawled in every morning through the safe with her bucket and broom. He would call her over to him, she would set her broom in the corner in business-like fashion, give herself to him, and then return to her cleaning. In all the years, he had not exchanged a single word with her and was not even absolutely certain whether it was the same old woman or a different one every time.

One time a strange incident occurred. The old woman began rolling her eyes and moving her lips soundlessly.

"What's the matter with you?"

"I was just thinking," the old woman said with a serene smile. "My niece is coming to visit, my brother's daughter. I've got to fix some eats for her, but all I've got is three roubles. So it's either spend two roubles on millet and one on butter, or two on butter and one on millet."

This peasant sagacity touched him deeply. He wrote a note to the storehouse ordering that the old woman be issued as much millet and butter as she needed. The old woman, no fool, did not take the note to the storehouse but to the Museum of the Revolution, where she sold it for enough money to buy herself a little house near Moscow and a cow; she quit her job, and rumor has it that to this day she's still bringing in milk to sell at Tishinsky market.

Recalling this incident, he would often tell his comrades that genuine dialectical thinking had to be learned directly from the people.

One day, having parted with the cleaning woman and finding himself alone, he wound up the gramophone and began thinking great thoughts to the music. It recalled for him the far-off days of his childhood in a small town in the Caucasus: his mother, a simple woman with a wrinkled, sorrowful face; his father, a stubborn man who, through daily toil, had achieved considerable success in the art of shoemaking.

"Soso, you'll never make a real shoemaker. You're too

crafty, you try to save on nails," his father would say, hitting him over the head with the last.

All this did not pass without its effect, and now, in later life, he suffered from fierce and frequent headaches. If only he could resurrect his father and ask him how was it possible to beat a child over the head with a last. How much, how passionately he wanted to resurrect his father and ask him . . .

But at that moment something else had him excited. Ominous rumors had reached his ears: Dolph, with whom he had recently become fast friends, was planning to betray their friendship and march across the border. He considered himself the most treacherous man in the world and could not bring himself to believe that there existed someone even more treacherous than he. When the others urged him to prepare to defend himself against Dolph, he treated their words as provocation and did nothing, so as not to offend Dolph with their groundless suspicions. The most suspicious man in the world was as gullible as a child in his relations with Dolph.

The closer the shortest night of the year drew, the more his soul was filled with foreboding. It would be frightening to spend that night alone.

On the eve of the shortest night of the year, he put on his faded, semi-military suit, pasted on his moustache, lit up his pipe, and became the person known to all, Comrade Koba. But before going out among people he turned to the large mirror which hung on the wall across from his bed. Pipe in hand, he ambled past the mirror a few times, gazing at his reflection out of the corner of his eye. He found his reflection satisfactory; it returned some of the grandeur the original possessed, if you didn't examine it too closely. (And who would ever allow himself the luxury of examining Comrade Koba that closely?) He grinned, nodded to his reflection, and then crawled into his office by the usual route, through his safe. He sat down at his desk and struck a pose which indicated that he'd been working days on end without a moment's rest. Without changing his position, he pressed the button on his bell. His private secretary Pokhlebyshev entered.

"Listen, my good man," said Comrade Koba to him. "Why are you always walking around with an armful of papers like some kind of bureaucrat? My word. Better you get the boys together, they can come by after work, a person has to relax somehow, get away from it all, talk, have some fun in the company of close friends."

Pokhlebyshev left and returned a short while later.

"They're all here and waiting for you, Comrade Koba."

"Very good. Let them wait a little."

For in the meantime Koba had found himself a most interesting diversion—cutting the pictures of various industrial leaders from the latest issue of *Ogonyok* and pasting the men's heads on the women's bodies and vice versa. It made for the most curious combinations, though it did use up quite a bit of his precious time.

Finally he appeared in the room where they were waiting for him. There was three rows of bottles on the table: Moskovskaya vodka, and Borzhomi, and Tsinandali dry wine. There were appetizers galore. To avoid confusion, the boys had seated themselves in alphabetical order: Leonty Aria, Nikola Borshchev, Efim Vershilov, Lazar Kazanovich, Zhorzh Merenkov, Opanas Mirzoyan, and Mocheslav Molokov. They all rose from their chairs when Koba appeared, and greeted his entrance with stormy applause and cries: "Long live Comrade Koba!" "Glory to Comrade Koba!" "Hurrah for Comrade Koba!"

Comrade Koba ran his eyes down the boys' faces noting with no little surprise the empty chair between Vershilov and Kazanovich.

"And where is our trusty Comrade Zhbanov tonight?" he asked.

Pokhlebyshev stepped out from behind Koba and reported: "Comrade Zhbanov requested permission to be late. His wife is in the hospital dying and she wanted him there in her final moments."

Comrade Koba frowned. A faint shadow flashed across his face.

"Interesting situation we have here," he said, making no attempt to conceal his bitter irony. "We're all here waiting, and as you see, some woman's whim means more to him than being with his friends. It's all right, though. We'll wait a little longer."

Shaking his head in distress, Koba left the room and returned to his office. There wasn't much he could do there. He'd already cut out all the pictures from *Ogonyok;* only the crossword puzzle was left. He pushed it over to Pokhlebyshev.

"You read them off to me, I'll try and figure them out. What's 1 across?"

"The first illegal newspaper in Georgia," read Pokhlebyshev, and shouted out the answer to himself: "*Brdzola! Brdzola!*"

"What are you giving me the answer for?" said Koba angrily. "I could have guessed it myself if I'd had time to think. All right, what's 1 down?"

"The largest prehistoric animal," read Pokhlebyshev.

"That's too easy," said Comrade Koba. "The largest animal was the elephant. Why aren't you writing 'elephant'?"

"Doesn't fit, Comrade Koba," said the secretary timidly.

"Doesn't fit? Of course, prehistoric. So write—'mammoth.'"

Pokhlebyshev bent over the crossword puzzle with his pencil, tapping the squares with the point, and then raised desperate eyes to Koba.

"Doesn't fit either?" asked Koba, amazed. "What's going on here? Was there really some animal bigger than a mammoth? Give it here." Sucking on his pipe, he examined the puzzle, counting the squares and thinking out loud: "Twelve letters. First letter—B. Could it be 'badger'? No. 'Beaver,' 'bulldog,' but they're all pretty small animals if I'm not mistaken. Why don't we call up one of our eminent biologists? Why should we rack our brains when they can give us a scientific answer if there was an animal beginning with B bigger than a mammoth. And if there wasn't, I don't envy the author of that crossword puzzle."

The telephone rang shrilly in the apartment of Academician Pleshivenko. A hoarse, imperious voice demanded that Pleshivenko come immediately to the phone. His sleepy wife answered angrily that Comrade Pleshivenko could not come to the phone, he was ill and sleeping.

"Wake him up!" An abrupt order was her reply.

"How dare you!" she said indignantly. "Do you know who you're speaking to?"

"I know," the voice answered impatiently. "Wake him up!"

"This is outrageous! I'll lodge a complaint! I'll phone the police!"

"Wake him up!" the voice insisted.

But by that time the academician was already awake.

"Trosha," said his wife, running to him, "Trosha, here, you take it."

Trosha took the phone irritably.

"Comrade Pleshivenko? Comrade Koba will speak personally with you in one moment."

"Comrade Koba?" Pleshivenko leaped out of bed as if lifted by the wind. Barefoot and naked except for his underpants, he stood on the cold floor, his wife beside him, immobile, her expression a mixture of joy and terror.

"Comrade Pleshivenko," a familiar voice with a Georgian accent boomed through the receiver. "Forgive me for calling so late . . ."

"Don't mention it, Comrade Koba," sputtered Pleshivenko. "It's my pleasure . . . mine and my wife's . . ."

"Comrade Pleshivenko," interrupted Koba, "to get right to the point, I'm calling on business. Certain of our comrades here have come up with a rather odd and unusual idea—with the aim of increasing the production of meat and milk, what if we were to somehow reintroduce to our fauna the largest prehistoric animal, what the hell is the name of it again, it's a twelve-letter word, I remember, beginning with B."

"Brontosaurus?" asked Pleshivenko uncertainly after a moment's thought.

Koba made quick use of his fingers: "B, r, o, n . . ." He covered the phone with the palm of his hand and, winking slyly, whispered to Pokhlebyshev: "Fill in 'brontosaurus.'" And then he said loudly into the phone: "Yes, exactly right, brontosaurus. And what's your reaction to this idea?"

"Comrade Koba," said Pleshivenko, all composure lost, "it's a very bold and original idea . . . That is, I mean to say it's simply an idea of . . ."

"Genius!" said the academician's wife with a little punch in his side as she awoke from her stupor. She did not know exactly what they were talking about, but she did know that the word "genius" was never out of place in such situations.

"Simply an idea of genius!" said the academician decisively, squinting off into space.

"For me it's only a working hypothesis," said Comrade Koba modestly. "We sit around, we work, we think."

"But it's a hypothesis of genius," objected the academician boldly. "It's a magnificent plan for the transformation of the animal world. If only you would permit our institute to get to work on elaborating some of the individual aspects of the problem . . ."

"I think some more hard thinking is still required. Once again I apologize for calling so late."

Pleshivenko stood for a long time with the receiver pressed to his ear and, listening intently to the distant, rapid, whistling sounds, whispered reverently but loud enough to be heard: "A genius! A genius! How fortunate I am to have the chance to live in the same era with him!"

The academician was not sure that anyone had heard him but still hoped that his words had not gone amiss.

Everything was in order when Comrade Koba returned. Anton Zhbanov had been found and installed in his usual seat. Leonty Aria had filled their tall glasses with vodka. Comrade Koba proposed the first toast.

"Dear friends," he said, "I invited you here to celebrate, among friends, the shortest night of the year, which is now beginning and which shall be followed by the longest day of the year . . ."

"Hurrah!" cried Vershilov.

"Not so fast," said Comrade Koba, knitting his brows. "You're always jumping the gun. I want to propose a toast—that all our nights be short, and that all our days be long . . ."

"Hurrah!" said Vershilov.

"You son of a bitch!" Enraged, Comrade Koba spat in his face.

Vershilov wiped the spit off with his sleeve and grinned.

"I also want to propose a toast to our wisest statesman, the staunchest revolutionary, the most brilliant . . ." began Koba.

Vershilov was about to shout "Hurrah!" just to be on the safe side, realizing that butter never spoils the porridge, but this time Comrade Koba managed to spit directly into Vershilov's open mouth.

". . . to a man great in both theory and practice, to Comrade . . ." Koba prolonged his significant pause, which he then terminated sharply: "Molokov."

The room fell silent. Merenkov and Mirzoyan exchanged glances. Borshchev unbuttoned the collar of his Ukrainian shirt. Aria clapped, then grabbed at his back pocket, which some angular object was bulging out of shape.

Two silent figures appeared in the doorway and froze.

Turning pale, Molokov set his glass aside and rose to his feet, holding on to the back of his chair so as not to fall.

"Comrade Koba," Molokov said in tongue-tied reproach, "what's this about? You're hurting my feelings without any reason to. You know I'm unworthy of all that praise, that nothing of the sort ever enters my mind. All my modest achievements are only a reflection of your great ideas. I am, if I may so express myself, merely a rank-and-file advocate of Kobaism, the greatest doctrine of our age. At your command, I am ready to give my all for you, even my life. It is you who are the staunchest revolutionary, you who are the greatest practitioner and theoretician . . ."

"A genius!" proclaimed Aria, raising his glass with his left hand since his right hand was still on his pocket.

"A marvelous architect!" acclaimed Merenkov.

"Best friend of the Armenian people!" interjected Mirzoyan.

"And the Ukrainian!" added Borshchev.

"Antosha, why aren't you saying anything?" Koba turned to Zhbanov, who had a sorrowful look about him.

"What is there left for me to say, Comrade Koba?" objected Zhbanov. "The comrades have done a first-rate job of illuminating your comprehensive role in history and contemporary life. Perhaps we say too little about it, perhaps we shy away from high-flown talk, but it's the truth all the same, that's the way it all really is. Everyday life furnishes us with dozens of striking examples which demonstrate how Kobaism is constantly penetrating deeper and deeper into the consciousness of the masses and truly becoming a guiding star for all mankind. But, Comrade Koba, here, in the free and open company of friends, I would like to point out yet another enormous talent you possess which your innate modesty prevents you from ever mentioning. It is your literary talent I have in mind. Yes, comrades," he said, elevating his tone and now addressing the entire company, "not long ago I had occasion to read once again Comrade Koba's early poetry, which he wrote under the pen name of Sosello. And in all candor I must say that this poetry, like precious pearls, could adorn the treasure house of any nation's literature, of all world literature, and if Pushkin were alive today . . ."

At that point Zhbanov burst into tears.

"Hurrah!" said Vershilov, but quietly this time and without retaliation from Koba.

The tension left the room. Leonty clapped his hands and the two silent figures by the door vanished into the air. Comrade Koba wiped away the tear running down his cheek. Perhaps he did not enjoy such things being said to him, but he enjoyed it even less when they were not.

"Thank you, dear friends," he said, though his tears interfered with his speaking. "Thank you for putting so high a value on the modest services I have rendered for the people. I personally think my doctrine, which you have so aptly named Kobaism, is truly good, not because it's mine, but because it's a progressive doctrine. And you, my dear friends, have put no little effort into making it that progressive. So, without any false modesty, let's drink to Kobaism."

"To Kobaism! To Kobaism!" They all joined in.

They drank down their vodka, knocked their glasses against the table, then drank again. After the fourth glass, Comrade Koba decided he needed a little entertainment and requested Borshchev to dance the *gopak*.

"You're Ukrainian, you'll do fine," he said encouragingly.

Borshchev hopped from his chair into a squat, Zhbanov accompanied him on the piano, and the rest of them clapped their hands in time to the music.

At that moment a messenger appeared without making a sound and handed Zhbanov a telegram informing him that his wife had just died in the hospital.

"Don't bother me," said Zhbanov. "Can't you see I'm busy."

The messenger withdrew. Then Comrade Koba personally strode over to Zhbanov. He stroked his trusty comrade's head with his rough and manly hand.

"You're a true Bolshevik, Antosha," said Koba with feeling.

Zhbanov raised his eyes, full of tears and devotion, to his teacher.

"Keep playing, keep playing," said Comrade Koba. "You could have made a name for yourself as a musician, but you chose to devote all your strength and talent to our party, our people."

Koba walked back to the table and sat down across from Molokov, Mirzoyan, and Merenkov, who were involved in a discussion.

"And what are we talking about here?" asked Comrade Koba.

"We were just saying," Molokov, who was sitting in the middle, answered readily, "that the agreement with Dolph, concluded on your initiative, of course, was both wise and timely."

Koba glowered. Because of the reports that had recently come to his attention, there was nothng he wanted to hear about less than that blasted agreement.

"I'm curious," he said, staring at Molokov, "I'm curious to know why you wear glasses, Mocha?"

Another whiff of danger. Zhbanov began playing more softly. Borshchev, still squatting and dancing, looked from Molokov to Koba. Just to be on the safe side, Merenkov and Mirzoyan moved away, each to one end of the table, Molokov, pale as a ghost, rose on legs out of his control and, not knowing what to say, looked in silence at Comrade Koba.

"So, you cannot tell me why you wear glasses?"

Molokov remained silent.

"But I know already. I'm well aware why you wear glasses. But I won't tell you. I want you to use your head and then tell me the real reason you wear glasses."

Shaking a threatening finger at Molokov, Koba suddenly let his head drop into a plate full of green peas and immediately fell asleep.

"I've got to stretch my legs a bit," said Mirzoyan cheerfully and slipped away from the table with an independent air. Then Merenkov, too, slipped away. Taking advantage of the absence of authority, Vershilov and Kazanovich found a corner and started playing cards. Borshchev, who had not received permission to rest, continued dancing to Zhbanov's accompaniment, but he, too, had already begun to slacken off—he was no longer squatting fully, just bending his knees a little.

Aria was sitting by himself, playing mumbletypeg with his knife.

Suddenly this peaceful picture was shattered. Vershilov's hand shot out and slapped Kazanovich resoundingly across the face. This was more than Kazanovich could bear, and screeching, he dug his fingernails into Vershilov's face. They rolled on the floor.

Awakened by the commotion. Comrade Koba raised his head. Catching sight of this, Borshchev sank back into a deep squat with renewed vigor, Zhbanov began playing at a livelier tempo, and Merenkov and Mirzoyan began clapping their hands in time to the music.

"Enough." Koba waved angrily at Borshchev. "Take a break."

Borshchev staggered to the table and polished off a glass of Borzhomi. Vershilov and Kazanovich continued rolling on the floor, which was strewn with their cards. Kazanovich succeeded in grabbing hold of his opponent's right ear; Vershilov kept on trying to knee Kazanovich below the belt. Koba summoned Aria over.

"Listen, Leonty, what kind of people are these, anyway? Leaders or gladiators?"

Aria brushed off his knee and stood up in front of Koba, holding his curved Caucasian dagger, with which, a moment before, he'd been playing mumbletypeg.

"Shall I pry them apart?" he asked darkly, testing the blade with his thumbnail.

"Please. Except do me one favor and put that dagger away. God forbid something terrible might happen."

Leonty slipped the dagger into his belt, walked over to the combatants, and gave them each individually a good kick. They both hopped to their feet and made quite an unsavory sight as they presented themselves to Comrade Koba. Vershilov was smearing blood across his face, Kazanovich gently feeling the dark bruise swelling under his left eye.

"So, so," said Koba, shaking his head. "Our people have entrusted their fate to men like you. What game were you playing?"

Embarrassed, the two enemies looked at their feet.

"Come on, I'm asking you a question."

Kazanovich glowered up sullenly at Koba.

"Blackjack, Comrade Koba."

"Blackjack?"

"Nothing to it, Comrade Koba, just a little game."

"I don't understand," said Comrade Koba, spreading out his hands. "What do we have here? Bosses? Leaders? Or just a bunch of crooks. What was the fight about?"

"That kike was cheating," answered Vershilov.

"What kind of word is that, 'kike'?" asked Koba angrily.

"I'm sorry, the Jew," Vershilov corrected himself.

"You're a stupid person." Koba sighed. "An anti-Semite. How many times have I told you to get rid of those great-power ways of yours. I'm giving you one week to study all my works on the question of nationalities, you understand me?"

"I do."

"All right, go. And you, Kazanovich, you didn't behave right either. You Jews do nothing but furnish anti-Semitism with ammunition by your appearance and provocative behavior. I'm getting tired of struggling with anti-Semitism; at some point I'll get fed up."

Koba was about to develop this thought further when Pokhlebyshev appeared. "Comrade Koba, we've just received a dispatch. Dolph's troops have moved right up to the border."

These words made Comrade Koba uneasy. "Come over here," he said to his secretary. "Bend close to me."

Koba took his pipe from the table and began knocking out the ashes on Pokhlebyshev's balding head.

"Dolph's my friend," he said as if hammering his words into his secretary's head. "It's our custom in the Caucasus to stand up for our friends with everything we've got. We can forgive someone insulting our sister or our brother, we can forgive someone insulting our father or our mother, but we cannot forgive someone insulting a friend. To insult my friend is to insult me."

He threw his pipe to the floor and raised Pokhlebyshev's head, using the one-finger-under-the-chin method. Fat tears were running down Pokhlebyshev's face.

"Oh, you're crying!" said Comrade Koba in surprise. "Tell me why you're crying."

"I'm crying because you spoke so touchingly about friendship," said Pokhlebyshev, sobbing and tugging at his nose.

Comrade Koba softened. "So, all right then," he said with a little more warmth in his voice, "I know you're a good man at heart, you're just severe on the outside. Go rest up a bit and tell the doctor to put some iodine on your head, God forbid you should get an infection."

Comrade Koba then reassembled all the boys at the table and proposed a toast to friendship.

"Comrade Koba," asked Molokov, "may I drink with you, too?"

Comrade Koba did not answer, letting the question slip in one ear and out the other. Molokov continued to hold his glass of vodka, and, unable to make up his mind one way or the other, stayed just as he was.

Next, Comrade Koba expressed a desire to play a little music. He walked over to the piano and, playing with one finger, sang the following well-known ditty:

> I was up on the hill,
> I gave Egor all I had,
> Now don't you think I was bad,
> It was just my rolling tobacco ...

Everyone broke into amiable laughter and applauded. In a short speech Comrade Zhbanov remarked on the high artistic merits of the piece. Vershilov took out a pad of paper and a stubby indelible-ink pen from his pocket and requested permission to take down the words of the ditty on the spot.

"I'll copy them down, too," said Borshchev. "I'll sing it to Zinka tomorrow. She'll get a laugh out of it."

"Sure, let her have a laugh," said Koba, returning to his place at the table. He laid his head on his arms and again fell immediately asleep.

The earliest dawn of that summer began, the night growing gradually lighter like ink being diluted with water. Everything stood out with increasing clarity against the background of the brightening sky, the golden cupolas sharpened in relief.

No little vodka had been drunk that night, and now the group was beginning to fade. Comrade Koba was sleeping at the table. Aria, his hand still on his back pocket, had reclined on the sofa and dozed off. Mirzoyan was snoring noisily under the table, using Merenkov's cheek for a pillow. Still not daring to budge, his face like stone, Molokov was sitting in front of Comrade Koba. Kazanovich and Vershilov had made their peace and were playing cards again. Zhbanov was standing in the corner, his forehead against the cold wall, trying to vomit. Only Borshchev was still wandering quietly about the room with a look of great concentration on his face, as if he had lost something and was trying to find it. He had apparently sobered up and now a hangover was torturing his brain, which was filled with vague and gloomy thoughts. Crinkling his face in sympathy, Borshchev stood near Zhbanov and recommended the old folk remedy—two fingers down the throat. Zhbanov mooed something resembling words and shook his head. Borshchev then walked over to the card players. He started following their game out of simple curiosity, but Vershilov soon drove him away. Borshchev looked over at Leonty and, convinced that he was sleeping, sat down by Molokov, keeping, however, a certain distance. He sighed loudly in an attempt to attract Molokov's attention. Without turning his head, Molokov looked out of the corner of his eye at Borshchev, who winked back and said in a whisper: "You should take off your glasses for the time being. Comrade Koba's been a little nervous lately, you shouldn't get him riled up. Later on he'll forget all about it and you can put them back on."

Borshchev grabbed a cucumber from the table, took a bite of it, and spat it right back out. Bitter! He gave Koba a sidelong look and then sighed once again. "Of course it's tough working with him. He's not a regular person, he's a genius. But what am I doing here? I used to work in the mines, drilling coal. Not what you might call the cleanest work, but it was a living. Now look at me, I've ended up as one of the leaders, they carry portraits of me when the people parade through the streets. But what kind of leader can I be when all I've got is a third-grade education and Advanced Party School? The rest of you are all prominent people. Theoreticians. I've heard that you know twelve languages. Now take me, for example; I consider myself a Ukrainian, I lived in the Ukraine, but I couldn't speak their language if you put a gun to my head. It's a funny language they've got. We say 'staircase' and they say 'stairladder.' " Borshchev burst out laughing as if the strangeness of Ukrainian had just struck him for the first time.

Even Molokov smiled. The rumors about his knowledge of foreign languages were greatly exaggerated. The fact of the matter was that at one point, to increase the authority of the ruling body, Comrade Koba had endowed them with merits that none of them had previously even suspected themselves of possessing. Thus, Merenkov became a major philosopher and the theoretician of Kobaism; Mirzoyan became a man of business; Kazanovich a technician; Aria a psychologist; Vershilov an outstanding general; Zhbanov a specialist in all the arts; Borshchev a Ukrainian; and he, Molokov, who knew a few foreign words and expressions, a linguist.

Naturally, Molokov said nothing of this to Borshchev, remarking only that his life was no bowl of cherries either.

"There's something I don't get," sighed Borshchev. "Where's your conscience if you can pick on someone because of his glasses. He asked you why you wear glasses. Maybe you just like to. If he talked about me like that," said Borshchev, growing heated, "I'd spit right in his face and not be shy about it either."

At that moment Comrade Koba stirred in his sleep. Borshchev froze in horror, but his fears were groundless; Koba remained asleep. "What a fool I am," thought Borshchev with a sigh of relief. "Like they say, the tongue's loose, it's got no bones in it. But with a tongue like mine, oi, what trouble you could get in!" He decided not to talk any more with his colleague who was out of favor, but he couldn't restrain himself and once again he bent close to Molokov's ear.

"Listen, Mocheslav," he whispered, "what about asking him to let us go? Look, if he's a genius, let him decide everything himself. What the hell does he need us for?"

"All right," said Molokov, "but what would we live on?"

"We'll go to the mines. I'll teach you how to mine coal, it's simple. First you dig down into the bed, then you pull out the coal from the top. The money's not like the money we're making here, but the work's less risky. Of course you might get buried in a cave-in but that's a one-time thing; here you die from terror every single day."

Borshchev shuddered, then straightened up, having heard someone breathing behind him. It was Aria. Rubbing his ear with the handle of his dagger, Aria cast a curious glance from Borshchev to Molokov. "What could you be talking about that has you so absorbed, I wonder," he said, imitating Koba's intonation.

Did he hear or not? flashed through both minds.

He heard, decided Molokov, and immediately found the surest way out of the predicament.

"Comrade Borshchev here," he said with a touch of sarcasm, "was just suggesting that he and I abandon our political activities and join the inner emigration."

But you couldn't put anything over on Borshchev either. "You fool!" he said, rising and smoothing his chest. "I only wanted to feel you out and see what makes you tick. Doesn't matter anyway, nobody's going to believe you. Everybody knows I don't wear glasses. My eyes are clear when I look into Comrade Koba's eyes and into the distance shining with our beautiful future."

"Here's the future for you," mimicked Molokov. "First learn Russian properly, and then . . ."

He never finished his sentence. Fortunately for both of them, Pokhlebyshev came flying into the room, his head swathed in bandages.

"Comrade Koba! Comrade Koba!" he shouted as he entered the room, for which he immediately received a box on the ear from Leonty.

"Can't you see that Comrade Koba's busy with his predawn sleep?" said Leonty. "What's happened now?"

Shaking with extraordinary excitement, Pokhlebyshev kept repeating one word: Dolph. It required tremendous effort to squeeze out of him the fact that Dolph's troops had poured across the border.

An urgent, special, and extraordinary meeting then took place, chaired by Leonty Aria. Comrade Koba, still sleeping in his chair, was elected honorary chairman. The group began deliberations on which course to take. Vershilov said that it was imperative to announce a general mobilization. Kazanovich proposed that all bridges and train stations should be blown up at once. Mirzoyan, taking the floor to reply, noted that although their meeting was both timely and business-like, they should not lose sight of the presence and at the same time the absence of Comrade Koba.

"We can of course make one decision or another," he said, "but after all it's no secret that none of us has any guarantees against making some serious mistakes."

"But we'll be acting as a collective," said Kazanovich.

"A collective, Comrade Kazanovich, consists of individuals, as everyone knows. If a single individual can commit a single error, several individuals can commit several errors. Only one man can reach an infallibly wise and correct decision. And that one man is Comrade Koba. He, however, unfortunately, at the moment is busy with his pre-dawn sleep."

"Why do you say 'unfortunately'?" interrupted Leonty Aria. "I'm obliged to correct Comrade Mirzoyan here. It is truly fortunate that at a time so difficult for us all Comrade Koba is busy with his pre-dawn sleep, building up his strength for the wise decisions he will soon be making."

Merenkov requested a point of order and said: "I totally and completely support Comrade Aria for rebuffing Comrade Mirzoyan for his ill-considered words. It would appear that Comrade Mirzoyan had no criminal intentions and his statement should be considered a simple slip of the tongue, though of course at times it is quite difficult to draw a sufficiently clear boundary between a simple slip of the tongue and a premeditated offense. At the same time I think it would be advisable to acknowledge that Comrade Mirzoyan is correct in thinking that only Comrade Koba can make a correct, wise, and principled decision concerning Dolph's treacherous invasion. However, in this connection, yet another question arises, one that requires immediate resolution, one which I now propose be discussed, namely, shall we wake Comrade Koba or wait until he wakes up himself?"

The comrades' opinion was divided on the subject. Some thought he should be awakened; others proposed waiting, since Comrade Koba himself knew best when he needed to sleep and when he should wake up.

In spite of having just learned of his wife's death and in spite of being ill from alcohol poisoning, Comrade Zhbanov took an active part in the debate and said that, before deciding the question of whether or not to wake Koba, it was necessary to decide a question which preceded that one, a sub-question so to speak, concerning the seriousness of Dolph's intentions and whether this might simply be a provocation designed to interrupt Comrade Koba's sleep. But to decide whether this was a serious invasion or a mere provocation was again something that could only be determined by Comrade Koba personally.

Finally two issues were put to vote:

1. To wake Comrade Koba.

2. Not to wake Comrade Koba.

The results of the voting on both propositions were as follows: For—no one. Against—no one. Abstaining—no one.

It was noted in the minutes of the meeting that both questions had been decided unanimously and that certain of Comrade Mirzoyan's ill-considered statements had been pointed out to him. After the minutes had been drawn up, Comrade Molokov unexpectedly asked for the floor to make some supplementary remarks. He realized that now his only salvation lay in taking an active role. Molokov said that in view of the developing situation he intended to wake up Comrade Koba at once and take full responsibility for the consequences of his act.

That said, he walked decisively over to Comrade Koba and began shaking his shoulder. "Comrade Koba, wake up!"

Comrade Koba shook his head without yet waking up. His legs twitched.

"Comrade Koba, it's war!" In desperation Molokov shouted right in his ear, this time shaking him so hard that Koba woke up.

"War?" repeated Koba, looking at his comrades' faces with uncomprehending eyes. He poured a bottle of vodka over his head and halted his gaze at Molokov. "War with who?"

"With Dolph," said Molokov, who had nothing left to lose.

"So, it's war?" Comrade Koba was gradually coming around. "And when was it declared?"

"That's just it, Comrade Koba, that's the treachery of it all, war hasn't been declared."

"Hasn't been declared?" said Koba in surprise, filling his pipe with the tobacco from a pack of Kazbek cigarettes. "Interesting. And how do you know it's war if war hasn't been declared?"

"We received a dispatch," said Molokov desperately.

"But if war hasn't been declared, it means there's no war. For that reason we Kobaists do not accept or acknowledge it, for to accept something which doesn't exist is to slip into the swamp of idealism. Isn't that so, comrades?"

Everyone was staggered. A thought of such brilliance could never have entered any of their minds. Only a genius could have resolved such a complex problem with such ease.

"Hurrah!" cried Vershilov boldly.

"Hurrah!" seconded all the remaining comrades.

"And now I want to sleep," Comrade Koba announced decisively. "Who'll give me a hand?"

Molokov and Kazanovich took their teacher under the arm. Vershilov, too, rushed forward but wasn't quick enough.

"You shout louder than anybody else," Koba remarked disapprovingly, "but when it comes to action, you're not quick enough. Next time be a little faster on your feet. And you, Mocha," said Koba, giving Molokov a little slap on the cheek, "you're a true staunch warrior and Kobaist and I'll tell you straight off why you wear glasses. You wear glasses because you don't have such good eyesight. And every person who doesn't have good eyesight should wear glasses so he can see clearly what's in front of him. All right, let's get going!"

He dismissed his two helpers at the door to his office and locked himself in. He listened for a while until he was sure that Kazanovich and Molokov had walked away, and only then did he crawl into his room, taking the usual route through the safe. Upon arrival, he threw his pipe in the corner, then ripped off his moustache and flung it to the corner as well. He was perfectly sober. He had realized what was happening. He had not been sleeping when Pokhlebyshev reported Dolph's attack and he had not been sleeping during the meeting of his comrades. He had been playing the role of a drunken man asleep and he had played it very well because, of all the talents ascribed to him, he did possess one—he was an actor.

Now, with no spectators, there was no reason to play a part. Comrade Koba sat down on his bed, pulled off his boots, unbuttoned his pants, and sank into thought. Somehow things weren't turning out right. He had never trusted anybody except this once and look what had happened. How could he have any faith in people after this? Still, he had to find some way out. In this country, he thought to himself, it's you alone who does the thinking for everyone and nobody is going to do any thinking for you. What to do? Address an appeal to the people? And say what? Forgive me, my dear people, it seems I've just about fuc ... Oh, he had almost said a dirty word. Request military assistance from the Americans? Or political asylum for himself? Then what? Settle somewhere in Florida and write his memoirs: *My Life as a Tyrant*. Or maybe go into hiding in Georgia and live there disguised as a simple shoemaker?

"Soso," his father used to tell him, "you'll never make a real cobbler."

Comrade Koba lifted his eyes and noticed a pitiable, moustacheless old man on the opposite wall. Mechanically rubbing his scrawny knees, the old man was sitting on an iron bed, his pants at his ankles. Comrade Koba smiled bitterly.

"So there it is," he said to the old man. "Now you see. You thought you were the most cunning, the craftiest. You wouldn't listen to anyone's advice or warning. You ripped out every tongue that tried to tell you the truth. And the one man in the world you trusted turned out to be more cunning and crafty than you. Who's going to help you now? Who's going to support you now? The people? They hate you. Your so-called comrades? Comrades, that's a laugh. A bunch of court flatterers and flunkies. They'd be the first to sell you out as soon as they got the chance. In the old days, at least jesters and saints were allowed to tell the truth. But who'll tell the truth now? You demanded lies; now you can choke on them. Everybody lies now—your newspapers, your public speakers, your spies, your informers. But there still is one man with the courage to tell you the truth to your face. And he's sitting right in front of you now. He sees right through you like you were his own self. Look at yourself, you who considered yourself a superman. What kind of superman are you, anyway? You're small, pockmarked, you've got aches and pains everywhere. Your head aches, your liver aches, your intestines do a lousy job of digesting what you gobble down, the meat you steal from your hungry people. Why then, if you're such a superman, are your teeth and hair falling out? Superparasite, why did you kill so many people? Mensheviks, Bolsheviks, priests, peasants, intellectuals, children, mothers . . . Why did you ruin agriculture and decapitate the army? For the sake of a brighter future? No, for your own personal power. You like it when everyone fears you like the plague. But you, the creator of an empire of fear, aren't you the most frightened person in it? What is there you don't fear? A shot from behind, poison in your wine, a bomb under your bed. You're afraid of your own comrades, guards, cooks, barbers, your own shadow and reflection. Driven by your own fear, you ferret out enemies of the people and counter-Kobaists everywhere. There's no need to. Just look at yourself—you are the number-one enemy of the people, the number-one counter-Kobaist."

While Koba was speaking, the old man's face glowered and grew increasingly malicious. It was obvious that, as usual, the truth was not to his liking. He fended off the reproaches hurled at him by flailing his arms, grimacing, and crinkling up his face. As he spoke his final words, Koba's hand began moving of its own toward the pillow. He noticed the old man doing the same thing. He had to beat him to it. Koba darted and grabbed the pistol from under the pillow. At that same instant an identical pistol flashed in the old man's hand. But Koba had already pulled the trigger.

Gunfire in an enclosed area always produces a great deal of noise. One shot followed by another and the old man's pockmarked face cracked into a web of crooked lines. The room smelled of hot gun oil. Koba's eardrums vibrated; the old man's nasty face burst apart, flew into falling pieces, creating the illusion of a living man writhing in the throes of death.

Suddenly everything was silent. The pistol was empty, Koba looked up—now there was no one there.

"That's it," said Koba sadly, and with significance, though to exactly whom was unclear. "I have saved the people from the hangman." And with those words he tossed away the pistol, which was of no further use to him.

It later appeared that no one had heard the shots. This should cause no surprise—the walls of Koba's room were so thick that even sounds of a much greater magnitude would not have escaped them.

The old woman who came the next morning to clean the room saw the slivers of glass strewn everywhere. She found the master lying on his back in bed. His left leg was on the bed, his right leg, with his pants caught around the ankle, was on the floor. His right hand hung lifelessly, almost touchng the floor. At first deciding that Comrade Koba had shot himself, the old woman was about to sound the alarm, but then, convinced that the body on the bed had suffered no harm, she decided against it, not wishing to be called in as a witness. She put his arm and leg up on the bed, finished pulling off his pants, and covered Comrade Koba with a camel's hair blanket, carefully tucking it in around him. That done, she set about cleaning up the glass, hoping that Comrade Koba would certainly sleep off his drunkenness by the next day. But he did not wake up the next day, or the day after; reliable sources indicate he spent the next ten days in a lethargic sleep. They say that it was sometime during those ten days that the old woman retired and brought the note concerning the millet to the Museum of the Revolution. I, however, do not believe that. I believe the note's value would have fallen somewhat during those ten days, then risen back in value afterward. Clearly, the old woman was clever enough to bring that note to the best possible place to sell and therefore would also have waited for the best possible price. Besides, there now exist many contradictory opinions concerning the old woman. Supporters of the pro-Kobaist line in our historical scholarship, while not denying the existence of the old woman, doubt that she actually removed Comrade Koba's pants, which they consider unremovable. These scholars point out that just as Comrade Koba was born in a generalissimo's uniform, he lived his life in it as well, without ever having once removed it. The adherents of the anti-Kobaist line, on the other hand, maintain that Comrade Koba was born naked but that his body was covered with thick fur. From a distance his contemporaries mistook this fur for a common soldier's overcoat or a generalissimo's uniform. Not adhering myself to either of these versions, I admit finding each of them interesting in their own way.

(1967)

P.S. *This story is solely the product of the author's fantasy. Any resemblance of any of the characters to actual people is purely coincidental.*

Sasha Sokolov

(1943–   )

This anthology began with Tolstoy's "Alyosha the Pot" and now concludes with another saintly idiot, the emotionally disturbed and retarded boy at the center of Sokolov's *A School for Fools*. He is nameless, except for the flower name that he himself adopts—*Nymphea alba* (Latin for "white water lily"). He lives for the most part outside of time and space and within the private world of his own mind, which is, on the whole, a delightful place. He perceives in his surroundings what it pleases him to perceive, and both remembers the past and prospectively experiences the future in the same selective fashion. He has an alter ego with whom he discusses the plot and with whom he frequently argues, and they both chat with the author from time to time.

The school of the title is a special training institution for the mentally handicapped. Some teachers are callous and sadistic, others kindly and supportive. His therapist, the dreaded Dr. Zauze, whom Nymphea mistrusts absolutely, has a plan for reintegrating the two halves of his patient: He suggests that one self might sedulously keep track of the other, recording his every movement, and thus eventually become one with him. No reader familiar with Soviet history could fail to see in this an oblique comment on the relationship of the informer with his victim. The special school itself is not unlike the psychiatric institutions where citizens with inconvenient political ideas were chemically induced to abandon them.

But to read this brilliant novel only for its almost diffident satire on Soviet life would be as misconceived as to read *Dr. Zhivago* for its commentary on the Revolution and its aftermath. Sokolov's real concern is to write the Russian language truthfully, with unembarrassed freedom and gaiety, and to create one of the most memorable characters in modern Russian literature. His imagination is endlessly inventive—he reminds one at times of Olesha (see p. 230)—and though he makes us see the world through the eyes of a gentle idiot, that world is a kaleidoscope of melding images, beautifully achieved verbal vistas, and irrepressible wordplay. "A charming, tragic and infinitely touching book," Vladimir Nabokov (see p. 363) called *A School for Fools*.

It is a measure of the book's strength that it is, like Bely's *Petersburg* (see p. 81), almost unexcerptible. The reader should approach the following passage as a sample of Sokolov's manner, but without expecting fully to understand it. An adequate annotation would be almost as long as the piece itself. The dreamed orchestra is dispersed by mowers, yet the music goes on without the players: The image can be savored simply as an image, without knowing that it is a complex metaphor for the "disappearance" of the ego of the narrator, who continues to exist in the temporal vacuum of his mental space. The voice that asks "why did you pluck it [the lily]?" is that of the other self. Trachtenberg (also called Tinbergen; many characters have vaguely two names), an old widow, is one of the detested administrators at the school.

Sokolov was variously educated in the USSR and held jobs including lab assistant in a morgue, lathe operator, and boilerman. He studied for a while in a military language school, but dropped out and finally received a degree in journalism (as an external student) from Moscow State University. He worked as a newspaperman in numerous regions of the Soviet Union and, in October 1975, was granted a visa to emigrate. He lived for a while in Austria (in the Wienerwald) before coming to the U.S.A. and then to Canada, where he became a citizen. His residence now appears to alternate between Canada and the United States. Sokolov has published two novels, both with Ardis: *A School for Fools* (Russian, 1976; English, translated by Carl R. Proffer, 1977) and *Mezhdu sobakoi i volkom* (Between Dog and Wolf, 1980; not yet translated).

From A SCHOOL FOR FOOLS

Somewhere in a glade a wind orchestra assumed position. The musicians sat down on the fresh stumps of pine trees, and put their sheet music in front of them not on music-stands but on the grass. The grass is tall and thick and strong, like lake rushes, and it supports the music without difficulty, and the musicians can make out all of the symbols without difficulty. You probably don't know this, but it's possible there is no orchestra in the glade, but you can hear music from beyond the forest and you feel good. You feel like taking off your shoes, socks, standing on tiptoe and dancing to this distant music, staring at the sky, you hope it will never end. Veta, my dear, do you dance? Of course, my sweet, I do so love to dance. Then allow me to ask you for a turn. With pleasure, with pleasure, with pleasure! But then mowers appear in the glade. Their instruments, their twelve-handled scythes, glitter in the sun too, not gold like the musicians', but silver, and the mowers begin to mow. The first mower approaches a trumpeter, and lifting his scythe in time to the playing music, with a quick swish he severs the grassy stems upon which the trumpeter's music rests. The book falls and closes. The trumpeter chokes off in mid-bar and quietly goes away into a bower where there are many cool springs and all kinds of birds singing. The second mower ad-

vances to the French horn player and does the same
thing—the music is still playing—that the first did: cuts.
The French horn player's book falls. He gets up and goes
off after the trumpeter. The third mower strides expan-
sively up to the bassoon: and his book—the music is still
playing but it is getting softer—falls too. And then all
three musicians, noiselessly, single-file, go to listen to the
birds and drink the spring water. Soon—the music is
playing *piano*—they are succeeded by the cornet, the per-
cussion section, the second and third trumpets, and also
the flutists, and they are all carrying their instruments—
each carries his own, the entire orchestra disappears into
the bower, and although no one touches his lips to the
mouthpieces, the music continues playing. Now *pianis-
simo*, it lingers in the glade, and the mowers, shamed by
this miracle, weep and wipe their wet faces with the
sleeves of their red Russian shirts. The mowers cannot
work—their hands tremble, and their hearts are like the
mournful swamp frogs—but the music continues to play.
It lives independently, it is a waltz which only yesterday
was one of us: a man disappeared, transposed into sounds,
and we will never find out about it. Dear Leonardo, as for
the incident with me and the boat, the river, the oars, and
the cuckoo, obviously I too disappeared. I turned into a
nymphea then, into a white river lily with a long golden-
brown stem, or to be more precise put it this way: *I par-
tially* disappeared into a white river lily. That way's better, more precise. I remember well, I was sitting in the
boat, the oars at rest. On one of the shores a cuckoo was
counting the years of my life. I asked myself several questions and was all ready to answer, but I couldn't and I was
amazed. And then something happened to me, there, inside, in my heart and in my head, as if I were turned off.
And then I felt that I had disappeared, but at first I decided not to believe it, I didn't want to. And I said to myself: it's not true, this is just an illusion, you are a bit tired,
it's very hot today, take the oars and row, row home. And
I tried to take the oars, I stretched out my hands toward
them, but nothing happened: I saw the grips, but my

palms did not feel them, the wood of the oars flowed through my fingers, past the phalanges, like sand, like air. No, on the contrary, I, my former and now no longer existing palms, let the wood flow through like water. This was worse than if I had become a ghost, because a ghost can at least pass through a wall, but I couldn't have, there would have been nothing to pass through, and there was nothing left of me. But that's not right either: something was left. A desire for my former self was left, and even if I was incapable of remembering who I was before the disappearance, I felt that then, that is, *before*, my life had been fuller and more interesting, and I wanted to become the same unknown, forgotten what's-his-name again. The waves beat the boat to shore in a deserted spot. After taking several steps along the beach I looked back: there was nothing resembling my tracks on the sand behind. And in spite of this I still did not want to believe. It could be a lot of things, one, it could turn out that all this was a dream, two, it's possible that the sand here is extraordinarily firm and I, weighing a total of only so many kilograms, did not leave tracks in it because of my lightness, and, three, it is quite probable that I hadn't even gotten out of the boat onto shore yet, but was still sitting in it and, naturally, I could not leave tracks where I had not yet been. But next, when I looked around and saw what a beautiful river we have, what wonderful old willows and flowers grow on this shore and the other, I said to myself: you are a miserable coward, and becoming an inveterate liar, you were afraid that you had disappeared and decided to fool yourself, you're inventing absurdities and so on, it's high time you became honest, like Pavel, who is also Savl. What happened to you is certainly no dream, that's clear. Further: even if you didn't weigh as much as you do, but a hundred times less, your tracks would still have been left in the sand. But from this day forth you do not weigh even a gram, for you no longer are, you simply disappeared, and if you want to be convinced of that turn around and look at the boat again: you will see that you are not in the boat either. But no, I replied to my *other* self (although Doctor Zauze tried to prove to me that supposedly no *other* me exists, I am not inclined to trust his totally unfounded assertions), true, I am not in the boat, but then there is a white river lily with golden-brown stem and yellow, faintly aromatic stamens lying in the boat. I picked it an hour ago at the western shores of the island in the backwater where such lilies, and also yellow water-lilies, are so numerous that one doesn't want to touch them, it is better to just sit in the boat and look at them, at each individually or all at once. One can also see there the blue dragonflies called in Latin *simpetrum*, quick and nervous water-striding beetles resembling daddy-longlegs, and in the sedge swim ducks, honest-to-goodness wild ducks. Some mottled species with nacreous shadings. There are gulls there too: they have concealed their nests on the islands, amid the so-called weeping willows, weeping and silvery, and not once did we manage to find a single nest, we cannot even imagine what one of them looks like—the nest of a river gull. But then, we do know how a gull fishes. The bird flies rather high over the water and peers into the depths, where the fish are. The bird sees the fish well, but the fish does not see the bird, the fish sees only gnats and mosquitoes which like to fly right over the water (they drink the sweet sap of the water-lilies), the fish feed on them. From time to time a fish leaps from the water, swallowing one or two mosquitoes, and at that instant the bird, wings folded, falls from on high and catches the fish and bears it in its beak to its nest, the gull's nest. True, the bird occasionally fails to catch the fish, and then the bird again achieves the necessary altitude and continues flying, peering into the water. There it sees the fish and its own reflection. That's another bird, thinks the gull, very similar to me, but different, it lives on the other side of the river and always flies out hunting along with me, it goes fishing too, but that bird's nest is somewhere on the reverse side of the island, right under our nest. It's a good bird, muses the gull. Yes, gulls, dragonflies, water striders and the like—that's what there is on the western shores of the island, in the backwater, where I picked the nymphea which is now lying in the bottom of the boat, withering.

But why did you pluck it, was there some necessity for that, you don't even like to pick flowers—I know—you don't even like to, you only like to stare at them or cautiously touch them with your hand. Of course, I shouldn't have, I didn't want to, believe me, at first I didn't want to, I never wanted to, it seemed to me that if I ever picked it something unpleasant would happen—to me or to you, or to other people, or to our river, for example, it might evaporate. You just uttered a strange word, what did you say, what was that word—*eshakurate?* No, you're imagining things, hearing things, there was no such word, something like that, but not that, I can't remember now. But what was I just talking about in general, could you help me to recapture the thread of my discussion, it's been broken. We were chatting about how one day Trachtenberg unscrewed a handle in the bathroom and hid it somewhere, and when the custodian came he stood in the bathroom for a long time just staring. He was silent for a long time, because none of it made sense. The water was running, making noise, and the bathtub was gradually filling, and then the custodian asked Trachtenberg: where's the faucet handle? And the old woman answered him: I have a record player (that's not true, I'm the only one who has a record player), but no faucet handle. But there's no faucet handle in the bathtub, said the custodian. That's your problem, citizen, I don't answer to you—and she went into her room. And the custodian went up to the door and started knocking, but neither Trachtenberg nor Tinbergen opened to him. I was standing in the entrance hall and thinking, and when the custodian turned to me and asked what to do, I said: knock, and it shall be opened unto you. He started knocking again, and Trachtenberg soon opened to him, and he again expressed his curiosity: where's the handle? I don't know, objected old Tinbergen, ask the young man. And with her bony finger she pointed in my direction. The custodian observed: maybe that kid doesn't have everything upstairs, but it strikes me that he's not so stupid as to unscrew the faucet handle, you're the one who did that, and I'll complain to Building Superintendent Sorokin. Tinbergen burst out laughing in the custodian's face. Ominously. And the custodian went off to lodge his complaint. I just stood there in the entrance hall meditating. Here, on the hat-rack, hung an overcoat and head-gear, here stood two containers used for moving furniture. These things belonged to the neighbors, i.e., Trachtenberg-Tinbergen and her excavator. At least, the greasy, eight-pointed cap was his definitely, because the old woman wore only hats. I often stand in the entrance hall examining all of the objects on the hat-rack. It seems to me they are benevolent and I feel at home with them, I'm not a bit afraid of them when no one is dressed in them. I also think about the containers, wondering what wood they are made of, how much they cost, and what train, on what branch, brought them to our town.

Dear student so-and-so, I, the author of this book, have a pretty clear picture of that train—a long freight. Its cars, for the most part brown, were covered with scrawls in chalk—letters, ciphers, words, whole sentences. Apparently workers wearing special railway uniforms and caps with tin cockades made their computations, notes, and estimates on some of the cars. Let's suppose the train has been standing on a stub for several days and no one knows when it will start up again or where it will go. And then a commission comes to the stub, examines the seals, bangs hammers on wheels, peeps into the axle-boxes, checking for cracks in the metal and to see if anyone has mixed sand in the oil. The commission squabbles and swears, its monotonous work has long been a bore, and it would take pleasure in going on pension. But how many years is it to pension?—penses the commission. It takes a piece of chalk and writes on anything at hand, usually on one of the boxcars: year of birth—such-and-such, work seniority—such-and-such, therefore such-and-such a number of years to pension. Then the next commission comes to work, it is deep in debt to its colleagues on the first commission, which is why the second commission doesn't squabble and swear, but tries to do everything quietly, without even using hammers. This commission is sad, it too takes chalk from its pocket (here I should note in parentheses that the station where this action takes place could never, even during two world wars, complain about a lack of chalk. It had been known to have shortages of: sleepers, handcars, matches, molybdenum ore, semaphores, wrenches, hoses, crossing barriers, flowers for decorating the embankments, red banners with the requisite slogans commemorating events of varying qualities, spare brakes, siphons and ashpits, steel and slag, bookkeeping records, warehouse logs, ashes and diamonds, smokestacks, speed, cartridges and marijuana, levers and alarm-clocks, amusements and firewood, record players and porters, experienced scriveners, surrounding forests, rhythmical timetables, drowsy flies, cabbage soup, oatmeal, bread, and water. But there was always so much chalk at this station that, as indicated in the telegraph agency's announcement, it would require such-and-such number of trains each with such-and-such payload capacity, to carry away from the station all of the potential chalk. More accurately, not from the station, but from the chalk quarries in the area around the station. The station itself was called *Chalk*, and the river—the misty white river with chalky banks—could have no other name than the *Chalk*. In short, everything here at the station and around was made out of this soft white stone: people worked in chalk quarries and mines, they received chalky rubles dusted with chalk, they made the houses and streets out of chalk, they whitewashed with chalk, in school the children were taught to write with chalk, chalk was used for washing hands, cooking pots and teeth were cleaned and scrubbed with chalk, and, finally, when dying, people willed that they be buried in the local cemetery where instead of earth there was chalk and every grave was decorated with a chalk headstone. One would have to think that the settlement of Chalk was singularly clean, all white and neat, and cirrus or cumulus clouds pregnant with chalky rains constantly hung over it, and when the rains fell the settlement got even whiter and cleaner, that is, absolutely white, like a fresh sheet in a good hospital. As for the hospital, it was here too, a good one and big. In it the miners suffered their illnesses and died, sick with a special disease which in conversations among themselves they called "the chalky." Chalk dust settled in the workers' lungs, penetrated their blood, their blood became weak and anemic. The people paled, their pellucid white faces glowed in the murk of the night-shift hours, they glowed against a background of astonishingly clean curtains in the windows of the hospital, they glowed in farewell against the background of pillows on which they would die, and after that the faces glowed only in the photographs of family albums. The snapshot would be pasted on a separate page and someone from the household would carefully draw a box around it with a black pencil. The frame came out solemn, if uneven. However, let us return to the second railroad commission which is getting chalk out of its pocket, and—let us close the parentheses) and writes on the car: so much for Petrov, so much for Ivanov, so much for Sidorov, total—so many chalk rubles. The commission moves along, writing on some of the boxcars and flatcars the word *checked*, but on others—*to be checked*, for it is impossible to check them all at once, and there is after all a third commission: let it check the remaining cars. But besides the commissions there is *noncommission* at the station too, or to put it another way, people who are not members of commissions, they stand outside them, employed at other jobs, or they don't work here at all. Nevertheless, they are among those who cannot resist the desire to take a piece of chalk and write something on the side of a boxcar—wooden and warm from the sun. Here comes a soldier wearing a forage cap, he heads for a boxcar: *two months to demob*. A miner appears, his white hand produces a laconic: *scum*. A D-student from fifth grade, whose life is perhaps harder than all of ours put together:

Maria Stepanna's a bitch. A woman station laborer in an orange sleeveless jacket, whose duty is to tighten the nuts and clean out the viaducts, throwing the waste onto the rails below, knows how to draw a sea. She draws a wavy line on the car, and truly, a sea is the result, and an old beggar who doesn't know how to sing or play the accordion, and hasn't yet managed to buy a hurdy-gurdy, writes two words: *thank you*. Some drunk and scraggly guy who has accidentally discovered that his girlfriend is being unfaithful, in despair: *Three loved Valya*. Finally the train leaves the stub and rolls along the railways of Russia. It is made up of cars checked by the commissions, of clean words and curse words, fragments of someone's heartaches, memorial inscriptions, business notes, idle graphical exercises, of laughter and curses, howls and tears, blood and chalk, of white on black and brown, of fear of death, of pity for friends and strangers, of wracked nerves, of good impulses and rose-colored glasses, of boorishness, tenderness, dullness and servility. The train rolls along, Sheina Solomonovna Trachtenberg's containers on it, and all Russia comes out onto windswept platforms to look it in the eye and read what has been written—the passing book of their own life, a senseless book, obtuse, boring, created by the hands of incompetent commissions and pitiful, misled people. After a certain number of days the train arrives in our town, at the freight station. The people who work at the railroad post office are worried: they have to inform Sheina Trachtenberg that the containers with her furniture have finally been received. It's raining outside, the sky is full of storm clouds. In the special postal office at the so-called border of the station a one-hundred-watt bulb burns, dispelling the semidarkness and creating comfort. In the post office there are several worried office workers wearing blue uniforms. They worriedly make tea on a hotplate, and worriedly they drink it. It smells of sealing wax, wrapping paper, and twine. The window opens onto the rusty reserve lines, where grass is sprouting up among the sleepers and some kind of small but beautiful flowers are growing. It is quite nice to look at them from the window. The vent in the window is open, therefore certain sounds which are characteristic of a junction station are quite audible: a lineman's horn, the clank of air hoses and buffers, a hissing of pneumatic brakes, the dispatcher's commands, and also various types of whistles. It is nice to hear all this too, especially if you are a professional and can explain the nature of each sound, its meaning and its symbolism. And of course the office workers of the railroad post office are professionals, they have many railway kilometers behind them, in their time they have all served as heads of postal cars or worked as conductors of those same cars, a few of them on international runs even, and as they are wont to say, they've seen the world and know what's what. And if one were to show up and ask their supervisor, is it so . . .

(1977)

Acknowledgments

Grateful acknowledgment is made to the following for permission to reprint copyrighted material:

Associated Book Publishers Ltd: "A Girl Was Singing" and "The Stranger," from *The Twelve and Other Poems,* by Alexander Blok. Translated by Jon Stallworthy and Peter France. Used by permission of Methuen London.

Atheneum Publishers: Chapter 1 from *Hope against Hope,* by Nadezhda Mandelstam, translated from the Russian by Max Hayward, with an Introduction by Clarence Brown. Copyright © 1970 by Atheneum Publishers. English translation copyright © 1970 by Atheneum Publishers. Chapter 42 from *Hope Abandoned,* by Nadezhda Mandelstam, translated from the Russian by Max Hayward. Copyright © 1972 by Atheneum Publishers. English translation copyright © 1973, 1974 by Atheneum Publishers.

Atheneum Publishers and *Oxford University Press:* "Theodosia," "The Admiralty," "The thread of gold cordial flowed," "Leningrad," "O Lord, help me to live through this night," and "The Last Supper," from *Osip Mandelstam Selected Poems* (*1974*). English translation copyright © 1973 by Clarence Brown and W. S. Merwin.

The Bodley Head and *Farrar, Straus and Giroux, Inc.:* "Matryona's Home," from *Stories and Prose Poems,* by Alexander Solzhenitsyn, translated by H. T. Willetts. Farrar, Straus and Giroux, Inc.'s American edition of *Stories and Prose Poems* is translated by Michael Glenny.

Cornell University Press: "Anecdotes about Pushkin's Life" and "The Connection," by Daniil Kharms, from *Russia's Lost Literature of the Absurd, A Literary Discovery: Selected Works of Daniil Kharms and Alexander Vvedensky,* edited and translated by George Gibian. Copyright © 1971 by Cornell University Press.

E. P. Dutton Publishers and *Hodder and Stoughton Limited:* "The Potudan River," from *The Fierce and Beautiful World,* by Andrei Platonov, translated by Joseph Barnes. English translation copyright © 1970, 1969 by E. P. Dutton & Co., Inc.

Encounter Limited: "Pkhentz," by Andrei Sinyavski. Translated by Manya Harari. Copyright © 1963 by Encounter Limited.

FOR THE BEST IN CLASSIC LITERATURE LOOK FOR THE

Collected Stories
Isaac Babel
Edited and Translated with an Introduction and Notes by David McDuff
These stories, including Babel's masterpiece, "Red Cavalry," illuminate the author's lifelong struggle both to remain faithful to his Russian Jewish roots and to be free of them, a duality of vision that infuses his work with a powerful energy. *ISBN 0-14-018462-7*

The Master and Margarita
Mikhail Bulgakov
Translated by Richard Pevear and Larissa Volokhonsky
with an Introduction by Richard Pevear
An artful collage of grotesqueries, dark comedy, and timeless ethical questions, Bulgakov's devastating satire of Soviet life was written during the darkest period of Stalin's regime and remained unpublished for more than twenty-five years after its completion. This brilliant translation was made from the complete and unabridged Russian text. *ISBN 0-14-118014-5*

The Gentleman from San Francisco and Other Stories
Ivan A. Bunin
Translated with an Introduction by David Richards and Sophie Lund
This collection of seventeen stories hails from one of Russia's great realist writers, a modern heir to Chekhov and Turgenev. *ISBN 0-14-018552-6*

My Childhood
Maxim Gorky
Translated with an Introduction by Ronald Wilks
The first part of Gorky's celebrated autobiography, this volume records with charm and poignancy the childhood of extreme poverty and brutality that deepened Gorky's understanding of the "ordinary Russian," an experience that would influence some of his greatest works.
ISBN 0-14-018285-3

Selected Poems
Osip Mandelstam
Selected and Translated by James Greene with an Introduction by
Donald Rayfield Forewords by Nadezhda Mandelstam and Donald Davie
James Greene's acclaimed translations of the poetry of Osip Mandelstam are now in an extensively revised and augmented edition.
ISBN 0-14-018474-0

We
Yevgeny Zamyatin
Translated with an Introduction and Notes by Clarence Brown
Yevgeny Zamyatin's masterpiece describes life under the regimented totalitarian society of OneState, ruled over by the all-powerful "Benefactor."
ISBN 0-14-018585-2